フランク・ロイド・ライト——世界を結ぶ建築

The Wright Imperial Hotel at 100: **Frank Lloyd Wright and the World**

この展覧会は、フランク・ロイド・ライト財団(アリゾナ州スコッツデール)の協力のもと開催されます。
1940年にライト自身によって設立された当財団は、
自然と芸術の融合を通じた、
より良い暮らしを実現する建築の普及のため活動しています。
詳細は、当財団のHPをご覧ください。
www.franklloydwright.org.

This exhibition is supported through generous donations
from the Frank Lloyd Wright Foundation, Scottsdale, Arizona.
The Frank Lloyd Wright Foundation,
founded by Frank Lloyd Wright in 1940,
inspires people to discover and embrace an architecture
for better living through meaningful connections
to nature, the arts, and each other.
Learn more at www.franklloydwright.org.

ADVANCING THE WAY WE BUILD AND LIVE

フランク・ロイド・ライト——世界を結ぶ建築 The Wright Imperial Hotel at 100: **Frank Lloyd Wright and the World**

監修・著――ケン・タダシ・オオシマ、ジェニファー・グレイ
著――水上優＋田中厚子＋田根剛＋マシュー・スコンスバーグ
編――豊田市美術館＋パナソニック汐留美術館＋青森県立美術館

Supervised by Ken Tadashi Oshima, Jennifer Gray
with essays by Yutaka Mizukami, Atsuko Tanaka, Tsuyoshi Tane, Matthew Skjonsberg
Edited by Toyota Municipal Museum of Art, Panasonic Shiodome Museum of Art, Aomori Museum of Art

鹿島出版会

［帝国ホテル二代目本館100周年］**フランク・ロイド・ライト——世界を結ぶ建築**｜**開催要項**

［会期・会場］

2023年10月21日［土］——12月24日［日］｜豊田市美術館
主催：豊田市美術館、フランク・ロイド・ライト財団｜共催：中日新聞社

2024年1月11日［木］——3月10日［日］｜パナソニック汐留美術館
主催：パナソニック汐留美術館、フランク・ロイド・ライト財団、東京新聞

2024年3月20日［水・祝］——5月12日［日］｜青森県立美術館
主催：フランク・ロイド・ライト展青森実行委員会（青森県立美術館、青森放送、青森県観光国際交流機構）、フランク・ロイド・ライト財団

［展覧会名称］

［帝国ホテル二代目本館100周年］**フランク・ロイド・ライト——世界を結ぶ建築**
The Wright Imperial Hotel at 100: **Frank Lloyd Wright and the World**
• 東京展は冠に「20th Anniversary Exhibition／開館20周年記念展」

［特別協力］ **コロンビア大学エイヴリー建築美術図書館、株式会社 帝国ホテル**
［助成］ **公益財団法人ユニオン造形文化財団**
［展示協力］ **有限責任事業組合 森の製材リソラ**
［後援］ **アメリカ大使館、一般社団法人日本建築学会、公益社団法人日本建築家協会、一般社団法人 DOCOMOMO Japan、有機的建築アーカイブ**

The Wright Imperial Hotel at 100: **Frank Lloyd Wright and the World**｜**Overview**

Date/Venue:

October 21 — December 24, 2023｜Toyota Municipal Museum of Art
Organizers: Toyota Municipal Museum of Art, Frank Lloyd Wright Foundation
Co-organizer: The Chunichi Shimbun

January 11 — March 10, 2024｜Panasonic Shiodome Museum of Art
Organizers: Panasonic Shiodome Museum of Art, Frank Lloyd Wright Foundation, The Tokyo Shimbun

March 20 — May 12, 2024｜Aomori Museum of Art
Organizers: Frank Lloyd Wright Exhibition Aomori Executive Committee (Aomori Museum of Art, Aomori Broadcasting Corporation, Aomori Prefectural Organization for Tourism and Globalization), Frank Lloyd Wright Foundation

Title: The Wright Imperial Hotel at 100: **Frank Lloyd Wright and the World**

+

With the special cooperation of:
Avery Architectural & Fine Arts Library, Columbia University, Imperial Hotel, Ltd.
With the grant given from: Union Foundation For Ergodesign Culture
With the exhibit cooperation of: Forest Sawmill Risola Limited Liability Partnership
With the support of: Embassy of the United States of America, Architectural Institute of Japan, The Japan Institute of Architects, DOCOMOMO Japan, Archives of Organic Architecture Japan

近代建築の巨匠、フランク・ロイド・ライト(1867–1959)の、日本では四半世紀ぶりとなる回顧展を開催致します。自然と人間が共生する「有機的建築」を提唱し、落水荘やグッゲンハイム美術館といった数々の美しい建築を遺したライトは、アメリカ史上最も偉大な建築家と称されてやみません。文化と科学技術が大きな変化を遂げた時代に生み出された数多くの作品の特徴である華麗な装飾、独自の存在感を放つ造形、素材と構法の革新的な扱い、未来的なヴィジョンにはまさに天才の所業が感じられます。そしてここ日本には、本国・アメリカ以外で唯一ライトの建築が現存しています。熱心な浮世絵コレクター・ディーラーとしての顔を持つ彼は、実は日本と意外なほどゆかりの深い建築家でもありました。

このたびの展覧会はケン・タダシ・オオシマ氏(ワシントン大学教授)とジェニファー・グレイ氏(フランク・ロイド・ライト財団副代表、タリアセン・インスティテュート・ディレクター)を迎えて日米共同でキュレーションを行ない、ライトが日本で実現した大作、帝国ホテル二代目本館が1923年の竣工から100年を迎えるのを機に、グローバル・アーキテクトの先駆としてライトを紹介します。両氏が参画した2017年のニューヨーク近代美術館における展覧会「フランク・ロイド・ライト生誕150周年：紐解かれるアーカイヴ」に続いて、本展はコロンビア大学エイヴリー建築美術図書館で近年大きな成果を上げつつあるアーカイヴの調査研究が基となっております。そこから浮かび上がってきたライトの幅広い視野と活動は、彼が提唱した、人間の主体性と自由のための建築を裏付けるものに他なりません。世界を横断して活躍したライトのグローバルな視点は、21世紀の今日的な課題と共鳴し、来るべき未来への提言にもなるでしょう。

最後になりますが、本展はフランク・ロイド・ライト財団、およびライトの貴重な図面の数々をお貸し出しいただいた、コロンビア大学エイヴリー建築美術図書館の全面的な協力のもとで実現しました。両機関のご尽力に、深く感謝いたします。加えて、本展に貴重な作品・資料をご出品くださいました国内外の所蔵者および美術館の皆様、ならびにご協力、ご後援を賜りました関係各機関の皆様に、心よりお礼申し上げます。

主催者

Foreword

We are pleased to present this retrospective of the architectural work by Frank Lloyd Wright (1867–1959), known as one of the great masters of modern architecture. This is the first such exhibition to be held in Japan in twenty-six years. Wright, an advocate of "organic architecture" in which nature and humans coexisted, left a magnificent legacy including Fallingwater and the Solomon R. Guggenheim Museum as one of the greatest American architects. The tremendous structures he created during a time of ongoing cultural and technological change feature vibrant ornament and distinctive forms, and demonstrate the innovative use of materials and construction methods. Wright's true acumen is evident in his futuristic vision expressed through architecture. Japan is the only country outside of the United States fortunate to have surviving buildings designed by Wright. It was also the country he had extraordinarily close ties with, not only as an architect but also as an avid ukiyo-e collector and dealer.

This exhibition was jointly curated by Japanese and US teams with Ken Tadashi Oshima (Professor at the University of Washington) and Jennifer Gray (Vice-President and Director of the Taliesin Institute, Frank Lloyd Wright Foundation) invited from the United States. In celebration of the 100th anniversary of the completion of Wright's Imperial Hotel in 1923, we are proud to introduce the pioneering practice by the global architect. Following the exhibition *Frank Lloyd Wright at 150: Unpacking the Archive* held at the Museum of Modern Art in New York, in which both curators participated in 2017, this exhibition highlights fresh insight into Wright's achievements based on recent groundbreaking research within the vast scope of his archives maintained by Columbia University's Avery Architectural & Fine Arts Library. Wright's broad vision and practice that became apparent through the examination is nothing but a confirmation of his advocacy of architecture for human individuality and freedom. The global perspective of this international architect resonates with present-day challenges and assists us in navigating the future.

Lastly, we would like to thank the Frank Lloyd Wright Foundation and the Avery Architectural & Fine Arts Library at Columbia University, for kindly loaning a rare collection of Wright's drawings and their undivided cooperation. We also would like to express our deepest gratitude to the collectors and museums in Japan and abroad who allowed us to exhibit their valuable artwork and materials, and all other contributors for their support and sponsorship.

フランク・ロイド・ライトと日本との関係については、これまで数多くの書物が主題としてとりあげてきました――インスピレーションの源として、彼の作品が建てられ評価される場所として、あるいは設計の受注や美術品の売買を通じての収入源として。そしてライトが日本文化に対していだいた敬意についても、彼自身の著作や20世紀の美術史家、建築史家の著作を通じてよく知られてきました。一方で、ライトが世界の多様な文化を探求し、しばしば作品に取り入れたことは十分には知られていないでしょう。ライトの「有機的建築」の核にはつねに、さまざまな色合いと形であらわれる人間の文化があり、それらの建築がいつ、どこに、誰によって、どのように建てられ、どのように使われたかという固有性への尊重がありました。

この展覧会「フランク・ロイド・ライト――世界を結ぶ建築」は、ライトの建築に核心的な特徴を探求するものです。1923年に竣工した帝国ホテル二代目本館の100周年を記念して開催される展覧会と本書は、日本やその他のアジアの国々、メソアメリカや北米の先住民族、ヨーロッパからの影響を、（アメリカ的ではあるが、まだユーソニアンではない）彼自身の建築言語を用いることによって、交差する世界の時空のなかでひとつのデザインとしてまとめようとした彼の努力を明らかにしています。帝国ホテルの設計においてライトは、多様な文化の構成要素が、日本の古き良き文化と近代化の両方と手をたずさえながら超越的でありつつもじつに人間的な何かを達成しうることを示したといえましょう。

　文化の幅広い交流に基づくライトの建築は、新しい建築技術や近代的な生活様式を実現したこともあいまって、近代建築の発展に重要な影響を与えたとしてユネスコの世界遺産に登録されています。

フランク・ロイド・ライト財団は、この活動を支援することを誇りに思うと同時に、ライトのレガシーに新たな視点を提供してくださった主催者とご所蔵者皆様に感謝を申し上げます。特に、パナソニック汐留美術館の大村理恵子氏、本展監修者のケン・タダシ・オオシマ氏、スペシャルアドヴァイザーのジェニファー・グレイ氏、寄稿くださったマシュー・スコンスバーグ氏をはじめ、開催館の学芸員および水上優氏ほか日本側アドヴァイザリーボードの皆様には、ライトによる作品資料を一堂に展覧し、その調査、研究と新たな解釈にご尽力いただいたことに厚く御礼申し上げます。また展覧会の実現を支えてくださった東京新聞にも感謝を申し上げます。

フランク・ロイド・ライト財団｜代表取締役・最高経営責任者｜スチュワート・グラフ

Frank Lloyd Wright's relationship with Japan—as a source of inspiration, as a place where his work would be built and appreciated, and as a source of income through both architectural commissions and art dealing—has been the subject of myriad publications. Wright's respect for Japanese culture is well-documented, through his own writings and those of art and architectural historians over the last century. Less commonly known is Wright's approach to the many cultures of the world that he explored and often incorporated into his work. Human culture, in its many hues and forms, was central to Wright's "organic architecture," respecting as it did the unique circumstance of when and where a building was constructed, who would inhabit it, and how it would be used.

Wright's Imperial Hotel at 100: Frank Lloyd Wright and the World explores this central attribute of Wright's work. Celebrating the centennial of the 1923 Imperial Hotel, the exhibition and the essays in this volume reveal Wright's efforts to bring together unique elements of culture from Japan and other Asian countries; from Meso-America and indigenous groups of North America; European influences; and his own architectural vocabulary (American, but not yet Usonian) at a moment, and in a place, that was designed to be a crossroads of culture. In the Imperial Hotel, Wright demonstrated how the components of global culture could work alongside both ancient and modern elements of Japanese culture to achieve something both transcendent and profoundly human.

Because of his broad embrace of culture, as well as new building technologies and modes of living, the UNESCO World Heritage organization calls Wright's architecture "pivotal in the development of modern architectural design" across the world.

The Frank Lloyd Wright Foundation is proud to support this work, and grateful to the organizers and exhibitors for sharing new perspectives on Wright's legacy. In particular, we acknowledge Rieko Omura, Dr. Ken Tadashi Oshima, Dr. Jennifer Gray, and Dr. Matthew Skjonsberg for their expertise in assembling and interpreting Wright's work; Dr. Yutaka Mizukami and the other Japanese advisory committee members and curators of each hosting museum; and the Tokyo Shimbun for its support of this exhibition.

Stuart Graff | President and CEO | Frank Lloyd Wright Foundation

本展の開催にあたり、ご協力いただきました皆様に厚く御礼申し上げます。
ことに多大なる尽力を賜りました方々のお名前をここに記します［敬称略、50音順］

We would like to express our sincere thanks to all those who have generously assisted in the realization of the exhibition. In particular we gratefully acknowledge the invaluable support of the following individuals and institutions:

- Jennifer Gray
- Ken Tadashi Oshima
- Stuart Graff
- フランク・ロイド・ライト財団｜The Frank Lloyd Wright Foundation

所蔵家・機関｜Lenders

- コロンビア大学エイブリー建築美術図書館｜Avery Architectural & Fine Arts Library, Colombia University
- ニューヨーク近代美術館｜MoMA, The Museum of Modern Art
- 米国議会図書館｜Library of Congress
- 株式会社 帝国ホテル｜Imperial Hotel, Ltd.

- 大阪中之島美術館
- 神奈川県立歴史博物館
- 京都大学
- 自由学園資料室
- 自由学園明日館
- 成城大学図書館
- 土浦亀城アーカイブズ
- 東京大学工学・情報理工学図書館工1号館図書館A
- 東京大学駒場図書館
- 東京大学駒場博物館
- 東京都市大学図書館
- 一般社団法人日本建築学会
- 博物館明治村
- 公益財団法人吉野石膏美術振興財団

協力 | Special thanks to

- 太田記念美術館
- 京都工芸繊維大学 KYOTO Design Lab
- A.D.A.EDITA Tokyo
- Alvar Aalto Museum
- Amsterdam School Museum het Schip, Amsterdam.
- The Art Institute of Chicago
- Chicago History Museum
- The City of Los Angeles Department of Cultural Affairs and Hollyhock House
- The Avery Coonley School
- Getty Images
- The Estate of Pedro E. Guerrero
- Solomon R. Guggenheim Museum
- SC Johnson
- Frank Lloyd Wright's Martin House
- Fondazione Angelo Masieri, Heritage Asset Management, Galerie Negropontes
- Massachusetts Institute of Technology, Cambridge, MA. Walter Burley and Marion Mahony Griffin Collection
- MAXXI Museo nazionale delle arti del XXI secolo
- The Morton Arboretum
- Museum of Fine Arts Boston
- National Broadcasting Company
- National Library of Sweden
- Neuwe instituut, Rotterdam
- Price Tower Art Center
- Stanford University
- University of Michigan Bentley Historical Library
- Architectural Archives of the University of Pennsylvania Weitzman School of Design
- Richard Guy Wilson Architecture Archive, University of Virginia
- The Western Pennsylvania Conservancy
- Wisconsin Historical Society
- Frank Lloyd Wright Trust

- 朝香智有
- 浅野良介
- 磯矢亮介
- 井上智博
- 植木啓子
- 内野 聡
- 遠藤 現
- 岡田泰史
- 岡山理香
- 折茂克哉
- 北澤興一
- 北野裕太
- 北廣麻貴
- 草野千智
- 桑山童奈
- 斎藤日登美
- 定保英弥
- 佐藤熊弥
- 佐藤菜々子
- 渋沢雅道
- 鈴木一生
- 鈴木敏彦
- 高橋麻帆
- 田路貴浩
- 立野純三
- 田中厚子
- 谷川ヒロシ
- 田根 剛
- 津田和俊
- 冨島義幸
- 中野裕子
- 長沼 徹
- 西村祐子
- 服部真吏
- 花田雅久
- 濱田伊織
- 樋澤 明
- 日野原健司
- 平井直子
- 福田 竜
- 藤川加奈代
- 藤本貴子
- 前田尚武
- 水上 優
- 村尾真由子
- 村上 民
- 森 優美子
- 八嶋有司
- 安田幸一
- 山口 希
- 山崎鯛介
- 山田純平
- 山田新治郎
- 湯本志朗
- 渡邊謙一郎
- 渡辺秀樹
- 渡邊真理子

- Elvira Allocati
- Deshane Atkins
- Barna Gergely Pétér
- Jeanine F. Beharka
- Jennifer Belt
- Hannah Bennett
- Barry Bergdoll
- Terri Boesel
- Abbey Chamberlain Brach
- Maristella Casciato
- Pamela Casey
- James Caulfield
- Christopher Cronin
- Carolyn Cruthirds
- Matthew Digati
- Sara W. Duke
- Kelly Dyson
- Paul Galloway
- Dixie Guerrero
- Teresa Harris
- Rita Hassert
- Henry Hendrix
- Michelle Jackson-Beckett
- Giulio Mangano
- Lisa Marine
- Mari Nakahara
- Tim Noake
- Angela Parente
- Andrew Pielage
- Charlotte Raymond
- Timo Riekko
- Alice Roegholt
- David Romero
- Matthew Skjonsberg
- Michael Slade
- Kathryn Smith
- Margaret Smithglass
- Martino Stierli
- Kristen Teague
- Susana Tejada
- Henrik Thunberg
- Elena Tinacci
- JT de la Torre
- Christine Trevino
- Andrew van Leeuwen
- Rachel Waldron
- William Whitaker

012 フランク・ロイド・ライト——世界を結ぶ建築 ケン・タダシ・オオシマ
Frank Lloyd Wright and the World Ken Tadashi Oshima

026 フランク・ロイド・ライトとランドスケープ ジェニファー・グレイ
Frank Lloyd Wright and Landscape Jennifer Gray

037 SECTION 1 | モダン誕生 シカゴ–東京、浮世絵的世界観
Modern Beginnings: Chicago – Tokyo and the Culture of Ukiyo-e

057 SECTION 2 | 「輝ける眉」からの眺望
Views from the Shining Brow

077 日本におけるライト建築 水上 優
Frank Lloyd Wright's Architecture in Japan Yutaka Mizukami

085 SECTION 3 | 進歩主義教育の環境をつくる
Designing Progressive Educational Environments

109 SECTION 4 | 交差する世界に建つ帝国ホテル
Imperial Hotel at the Global Crossroads

137 ライトの日本の弟子たち 田中厚子
Frank Lloyd Wright and his Japanese Apprentices Atsuko Tanaka

145 SECTION 5 | ミクロ/マクロのダイナミックな振幅
Micro/Macro Dynamics of Wright's Building Blocks

162 ユーソニアン・オートマチック・システム——個人の主権から公共デザインまで マシュー・スコンスバーグ
Usonian Automatic System – From Individual Sovereignty to Civic Design Matthew Skjonsberg

169 SECTION 6 | 上昇する建築と環境の向上
Elevating Environments

183 SECTION 7 | 多様な文化との邂逅
Wright and Global Cultures

202 帝国ホテル・ライト館から新本館へ 田根 剛
From the Imperial Hotel Wright Building to the New Main Building Tsuyoshi Tane

208 **フランク・ロイド・ライト年表** | **Chronology**
216 **一般公開作品リスト** | **Public Wright Site**
218 **参考文献** | **Bibliography**
222 **出品作品リスト** | **List of Works**

［凡例］

- 本書は「帝国ホテル二代目本館100周年：フランク・ロイド・ライト――世界を結ぶ建築」展に際して出版される図録である。
- 図版ページには、出品作品および展示写真の図版を掲載しているが、一部、掲載されていないものがある。
  全図版は巻末の「出品資料リスト」に掲載した。
- セクション名に続く⬢ストーリーボードの番号と名称は会場構成に対応している。
- ● 建築作品のデータは「建築作品名｜所在地｜建築期間｜用途」を記した。
- 作品データは、所蔵先から提供されたデータに基づき、作品番号、作品資料名、作者名、製作・出版先、制作年の順に記載し、
  英文のみ、所蔵先、クレジット、所蔵先の目録番号を加えた。
- 年号は建築の場合は建築期間を、作品資料の場合は制作年・出版年・撮影年を表す。
- 解説は、ケン・タダシ・オオシマ［SECTION 1、4、6、7］、ジェニファー・グレイ［SECTION 2、3］、
  ケン・タダシ・オオシマおよびジェニファー・グレイ［SECTION 5］が担当した。
- 英文翻訳はフレーズ・クレーズ（論考）および各館学芸員（各セクション解説）が担当した。
  千葉真智子［SECTION 1、4］、板倉容子［SECTION 2、3］、西崎紀衣［SECTION 5、6］、大村理恵子［SECTION 7］。
- 書簡の翻訳は、3-15と7-33は板倉容子、4-7は遠藤現による。

［**Remarks**］

- This publication has been issued in conjunction with the exhibition "The Wright Imperial Hotel at 100: Frank Lloyd Wright and the World."
- The illustrations of the exhibited works and photographs are shown on the catalogue pages, however some of the images are not included.
- The number and name of the ⬢ storyboard following the section name corresponds to those at the exhibition.
- The data of the catalogue entry is based on the information provided by the owner and is written as follows:
  catalogue entry number, title, artist's name, production company or the publishers' name, date of production,
  collection, credit and the inventory number.
- The year indicates the project years in case of architecture, and the year of production, publication,
  or photography in case of artwork and materials.
- The description of each section are written by Ken Tadashi Oshima [section 1, 3, 4, 6, and 7], Jennifer Gray [section 2],
  Ken Tadashi Oshima with Jennifer Gray [section 5].
- Translation was conducted by Fraze Craze Inc. and by the curators at each venue.

フランク・ロイド・ライト——世界を結ぶ建築

ケン・タダシ・オオシマ

この素晴らしい作品は、自由な精神をもち、発想の巨匠として世界的名声を確立した、フランク・ロイド・ライトの傑作である[1]。

ルイス・サリヴァン、1923年

この賛辞は、フランク・ロイド・ライトの設計による帝国ホテル(1913–23)が竣工した際に、シカゴ派を代表するアメリカの建築家ルイス・サリヴァン(1856–1924)が贈ったものである。「摩天楼の父」とも「モダニズムの父」とも呼ばれたサリヴァンは、ライトにとって生涯の師であった。帝国ホテルについてのサリヴァンの寄稿は、サリヴァンの死の翌年となった1925年に、オランダの前衛建築雑誌である『ヴェンディンゲン』に掲載された。この号を含む7回にわたったライト特集は、オランダのみならず全世界にライトの名声と影響力を広めることとなった。ライトは70年に及ぶ設計活動の中で、さまざまな規模と用途にわたる1,114件もの作品を設計し、実現に至った作品は532件を数える[2]。最終的に、アメリカ建築家協会により「アメリカ史上最も偉大な建築家」と認定された。ライトに関する書籍は1,200冊を超え、ライトを取り上げた記事は20の言語で3,300本以上に達する。ライトは、世界で最も多く出版物に登場する建築家のひとりといえる[3]。

帝国ホテルは、外交官、政府職員、政治家といった世界中からの来訪者を想定した、ライトにとって初の国際的なプロジェクトであり、ライトの設計活動における重要なテーマが凝縮されている。帝国ホテルは東京の歴史的中心地に位置し、周囲にも影響を及ぼす都市的な規模であった。客室数270室、回り舞台を有する850人収容の演芸場、ダンス場と宴会場、300人収容のキャバレー・レストラン、大食堂、さらに椅子を配した90メートルもの長いプロムナードを備えていた。このように、1万6,000m^{2}の敷地いっぱいに、あまたの用途をちりばめた帝国ホテルは、東京の中にもうひとつ街をつくるようなものであり、ライトにとってもこれまでで最大の仕事であった。一方で、オリジナルの家具、絨毯、食器、壁画、石のレリーフ、建築装飾、テキスタイル・ブロック(すだれレンガ)などの小さなスケールにまでライトの細やかなこだわりは及んでおり、統合的なデザインのアプローチによって広大な複合施設をまとめ上げるライトの手法が感じられる[図1]。ライトは、この一生に一度の大プロジェクトを、長年温めてきたアイデアを試す機会としても捉えており、その主題のいくつかは、ホテルの完成後の仕事に再び登場している。例えば、ともに近代化を推し進める大都市であるシカゴと東京の都市的対話。アメリカ中西部のプレイリーから、日本、イタリア、さらにそれを超えた、景観への関わり方の有機的進化(ジェニファー・グレイ氏の寄稿を参照)。生涯を通じた進歩主義教育への取り組み。直線や円形の幾何学システムと同様に、極大と極小のスケールを橋渡しするコンクリート製テキスタイル・ブロックのダイナミクス(マシュー・スコンスバーグ氏の寄稿を参照)。「生きている都市/リヴィング・シティをつくり出すための、景観とダイナミックに釣り合う高層建築の採用。そして、日本文化に加えて、メソアメリカ、アメリカ先住民文化などのグローバル文化への生涯にわたる関心など。21世紀において、ライトの作品は現代的諸問題と共鳴している。ブロードエーカー・シティ構想(1929–35)は都市と農村の間の生態学的バランスを探求するものであったし、超高層建築マイル・ハイ・イリノイ計画案(1956)[cat. no. 6–28]は高さにおいても野心においてもこれまでの高層建築を遥かに凌駕し、都市の限界を突き抜けるものであった。ライトの作品は来るべき世界にインスピレーションを与えるものであった。

19世紀と20世紀、そして21世紀をつなぐ

帝国ホテルが正式に開業した1923年9月1日は、ホテルにとっても、ライトにとっても、そして世界にとっても極めて重要な転換点となった。開業当日に関東大震災に襲われたが、この震災を「生き延びた」ことで、ホテルにもライト自身にも伝説的な名声がもたらされた。ライトが生ま

れたのは、アメリカ南北戦争(1861-65)終結の数年後、日本では明治改元の前年の、急速に近代化が進行しつつある時代であった。帝国ホテル開業は56歳という彼のキャリアの中間点であり、その後の30年間に、彼はアメリカ西海岸における作品のほかに、イタリア、インド、イラクでの国際プロジェクト、そして落水荘(1934-37)やグッゲンハイム美術館(1943-59)といった傑作を生み出すことになる。帝国ホテルは10年がかりのプロジェクトであり、ライトは3年を超えて、東京に滞在した。彼はホテル竣工と震災に先立つ1922年7月27日に日本を離れ、その後再び来日することはなかったが、この貴重な設計の経験は生涯を通して彼の心に残り続けた。彼は著書『テスタメント』(1957)の中で、「浮世絵、桃山時代、日本建築や庭園といった日本の文化は生き生きとしており、完全に国土から生み出された有機的なものであった。それは仕事に対する私独自の感覚を立証するものであり、私に喜びを与えてくれた」と記している[4]。

浮遊する世界

ライトの設計活動全般にインスピレーションを与えた浮世絵の描く世界は、直訳すれば「浮遊する世界」である。1893年のシカゴ万博で初めて日本のデザイン文化に触れたライトは、以来、生涯にわたって日本美術や建築と対話し続けた。万博のパビリオンである鳳凰殿は、左右対称のデザインと渡り廊下の伸びやかな構成で知られる11

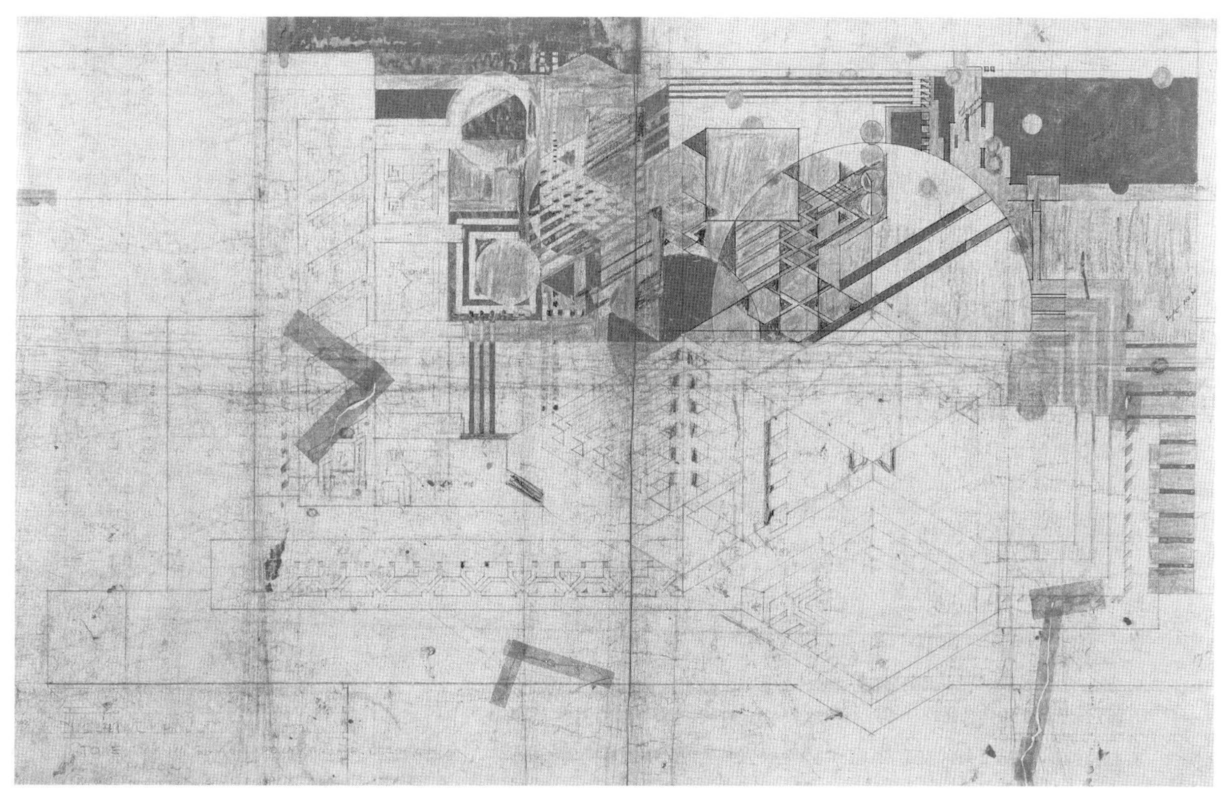

図1　帝国ホテル二代目本館(東京、日比谷) プロムナード中央パーラー(宝の間)南側暖炉の上の着彩レリーフ | フランク・ロイド・ライト | 1921年　4-52

Fig. 1　Imperial Hotel, Tokyo, Japan. Project, 1913-23. Carved stone and polychrome mural for the parlor southern fireplace.
Frank Lloyd Wright. 1921. Prints and Photographs Division, Library of Congress, Washington, D.C. LC-DIG-ppmsca-85261

世紀の平等院鳳凰堂を模したものであり、ライトの帝国ホテルのデザインにも呼応している[5]。また、ジャポニズムの時代には、師であるジョゼフ・シルスビー(1848–1913)やルイス・サリヴァンをはじめとするアジア美術愛好家の輪にも加わり、海の向こうから日本への想像を膨らませていた[6]。1896–97年の書籍『ハウス・ビューティフル』[cat. no. 2–12]では、ライトのコレクションにもある歌川広重(1797–1858)の《撫子に蝶》(1836–40)[cat. no. 2–13]と非常に似た構図で、自ら撮影した草花の写真を和紙にフォトグラヴュールで印刷し、日本の版画についての自分なりの解釈を表現している[7]。さらに1893–1900年頃に撮影した、ウィスコンシン州スプリンググリーン周辺の雪に覆われた風景写真[cat. nos. 2–1,2]は、日本の巻物に描かれた墨絵を思い起こさせるミニマルな構図から、芸術的な情景へのライトの熱意が強くうかがえる。

ライトはまた、コレクターとして、教師として、さらに日本から帰国後はディーラーとして、本人いわく日本美術への「執念」に駆られていた[8]。彼は数百点の広重の作品をシカゴに持ち帰り、1906年3月にはシカゴ美術館において展覧会を行うとともに、日本の版画に関する自身初の解説を収録した書籍を出版した[9]。この高い関心が、ライトを熱心な浮世絵コレクターであるフレデリック・ウィリアム・グーキン(1853–1936)と出会わせ、帝国ホテルの設計の推薦に導いたと考えられている[10]。また、ライトは施主に対しても、家の壁に浮世絵を飾るよう勧めていた[11]。1908年3月には、シカゴ美術館でさらに大規模な浮世絵展が開催され、展覧会をグーキンが企画し、ライトは会場の設計を行った。ライトは、会場に適切に配置したベンチの上に、レールから浮世絵を吊るす展示システムを考案した。展示に用いた専用のスタンドは、イリノイ州オークパークの自邸にあるハイバック・チェアに似たものであり、浮世絵を垂直に飾るフレームとなるように空間に合わせて設計されていた[cat. no. 1–77]。ライトはこうしたアイデアをさらに発展させ、その後もウィリアム・スポールディングのための浮世絵ギャラリー(計画、ボストン、1914)や、シカゴのファイン・アーツ・ビル内部の改装であるモリ東洋美術ギャラリー(1914)で繰り返し用いている。いずれの例においても、ライトは浮世絵を的確に見せることに注力して空間全体を設計しており、キャビネット、ピクチャーレール、布地、漆喰の壁、絨毯、そしてヘリット・リートフェルト(1888–1964)によるデ・ステイルの椅子デザインを先取りしたような驚くほどミニマルな四角い椅子によって構成されていた[cat. no. 1–76]。展示のためのライトの設計は総合芸術(*Gesamtkunstwerk*)であり、自然の風物をフレームに収める手法は、自身の住宅設計に近いものであった。帝国ホテルの設計では、このようなアイデアをさらに発展させている。

ライトの初期のデザインは、ドイツの出版社エルンスト・ヴァスムートによる『フランク・ロイド・ライトの建築と設計(ヴァスムート・ポートフォリオ)』[cat. no. 7–11 | 巻末リスト参照]の出版によって世界的な注目を集めた[12]。自費出版したこの書籍は、ライトにとっての浮世絵と例えられる大型の図版(40×64 cm)100枚で構成され、ライトによる長文の解説が添えられていた。この豪華本は、ヨーロッパでは100部が限定販売され、アメリカのライトの元には1,000部が送られている。1911年には、英国のアーツ・アンド・クラフツのデザイナーであるC.R.アシュビー(1863–1942)による序文を掲載した、より小型で安価な写真集が出版され、ライトの設計を広く一般に知らしめることとなった[13][cat. no. 6–1]。

ヴァスムート・ポートフォリオの図版作成はイタリアのフィエーゾレにて、同地にライトが滞在していた1910年の春から夏にかけて、彼の息子ロイド・ライト(1890-1978)と助手のテイラー・ウーレイ(1884–1965)の手を借りて行われた。そこには日本とイタリアの美術的理念が組み合わされている[14]。リトグラフは、彼が後に著書『日本の浮世絵:或る解釈』(*The Japanese Print: An Interpretation*)(1912)[cat. no. 1–76]で称賛する浮世絵の簡略化した線に倣ってライトのデザインを表現しており、ライト事務所の初代所員であったマリオン・マホニー(1871–1961)の感性が生かされていた。1906年のデローズ邸の透視図[cat. no. 1–56]には、「FLW(訳注:フランク・ロイド・ライトの頭文字)と広重に倣って、マホニー画」と記されていることから、マホニーは透視図作者の一人であったと思われる。ヴァスムート・ポートフォリオの図版は、ライトがイタリアでトスカーナの風景からインスピレーションを得て作成されたことが、彼の写真からだけでなく、次のような言葉からも読み取れる。「人生の喜びの証しは、どの地よりもイタリアにある。建築、絵画、彫刻が路傍の花のように生まれ、存在を高らかに歌う。それらの芸術に共感して近づけば、彼らが歌う生命の歌で私たちを奮い立たせてくれるのだ」[15]。また、これらの図版は、オーストリアの建築家ヨーゼフ・マリア・オルブリッヒ(1867–1908)の画法とも通じるものがあった。その後、ライトはブルーノ・メーリング(1863–1929)やオットー・ワーグナー(1841–1918)らに注目され、「ヨーロッパにおける尊崇と模倣」をもたらした[16]。

ライトの建築は、とりわけオランダの建築家たちを魅了した。その中には、アムステルダム派の父と称される建築家ヘンドリク・ペトルス・ベルラーヘ(1856–1934)や、オランダのモダニズム建築家ウィレム・マリヌス・デュドック(1884–1974)、表現主義の建築誌『ヴェンディンゲン』の編集長であったヘンドリクス・ヴェイデフェルト(1885–1987)が含まれていた[17]。ライトに興味を持ったヴェイデフェルトは、『ヴェンディンゲン』で7回にわたりライトの作品や著作を特集している[18][cat. nos. 7–14, 17]。そこには、ヤーコプス・J. P. アウト(1890–1963)による「ヨーロッパの建築におけるフランク・ロイド・ライトの影響」、ロベール・マレ=ステヴァンス(1886–1945)による「フランク・ロイド・ライトと新しい建築」(フランス語からの翻訳)、エーリヒ・メンデルゾーン(1887–1953)による文章(ドイツ語からの翻訳)が掲載された。メンデルゾーンは1924年にタリアセンを訪れており、そこでリチャード・ノイトラ(1892–1970)、土浦亀城(1897–1996)・信子(1900–98)夫妻と共にライトを囲んでいる。『ヴェンディンゲン』は、大量の写真と図面に、ルイス・サリヴァンによる熱烈な賛辞を添えて帝国ホテルを特集し、日本の読者のみならず世界中にこのホテルの存在を知らしめた[cat. no. 7–20|巻末リスト参照]。

その後の数十年間で、ライトをめぐる出版物は急増した。『ライト自伝』は1932年に初版が、1943年と1977年には自身による加筆と修正を施した改訂版が発行された[cat. no. 7–12|巻末リスト参照]。これにより英国でも称賛の声が高まり、ニコラス・ペヴスナー(1902–83)は1936年の著書『モダン・デザインの展開 モリスからグロピウスまで』でライトを取り上げ、大きな反響を得た[19]。ヘンリー=ラッセル・ヒッチコック(1903–87)による『素材の本性:フランク・ロイド・ライトの建築1887–1941』は、ライトの半世紀にわたる作品を白黒写真、図面や分析を通して振り返り、帝国ホテルを中心に環太平洋地域での業績を紹介している[20]。この本は世界中に影響を与え、特に戦後のラテンアメリカにおいては「爆弾ほどの威力」と言わしめた[21]。

日本でのライトに関する出版物も、やはり長く豊富な歴史を持っている。建築家の武田五一(1872–1938)は、ライトが訪日した1905年に出会い、日本で最初となるライトの作品集を1916年に出版した[22]。1923年に洪洋社より出版された『帝国ホテル』[cat. no. 4–40|巻末リスト参照]は、関東大震災前に完成していた帝国ホテルの姿を捉えている[23]。その後には、渡辺義雄(1907–2000)、村井修(1928–2016)、二川幸夫(1932–2013)らによって、1967年に取り壊される前の戦後1960年代のホテルの姿が写真に収められている[24]。土浦亀城は1931年の『国際建築』においてニューヨークのセント・マークス教区における高層ビルの近代的な開発計画[cat. no. 6–21]を特集し、帝国ホテル以後のライト作品を紹介した[25]。さらに、1971年3月号の『建築』誌でもライトの作品が掲載された。その後、日本におけるライト研究の第一人者である谷川正己(1930–2019)がライト解釈に大きな影響を与え、代表作である『ライトと日

本』(1977)をはじめとする多くの著作を残した。二川幸夫は、ブルース・ブルックス・ファイファー(1930–2017)ならびにフランク・ロイド・ライト財団の協力により、ライトの全作品集を12巻の大型本で出版(1984–87)し、ライトの業績を体系的にまとめている[26]。

展示にみるライトの世界

19世紀から現在に至るまで進化し続けるライトの小宇宙は、展覧会によっても紹介されてきた。1893年のシカゴ万博では、クリストファー・コロンブスの「新世界」到達400年を記念して46か国からの展示が一堂に会した。当時26歳だったライトは、そこで目にした展示を、その後の数十年間にわたる設計に発展させていくことになる。存命中だけでも、ライトの作品は100の展覧会で展示され、その大半は時代の先端を行く前衛芸術家兼建築家として彼自身が企画したものである[27]。ライト研究者のキャサリン・スミスは、「彼の芸術理念の背景には、1890年代にシカゴで過ごした青年期と、シカゴ建築クラブとのつながりがある」と繰り返し主張している[28]。1914年の「フランク・ロイド・ライト作品展」は、1911年の春以降の特に優れた建築として帝国ホテルを取り上げ、ライトがデザインした浮世絵スタンドも展示された[29]。

展覧会開催への想いが最も極まったのが、1951年にイタリアのフィレンツェで開催された「生ける建築の60年」展である[30]。15世紀に建てられたストロッツィ宮殿内にあるギャラリー、ラ・ストロッツィーナが会場となった。単独の建築家の展覧会としては史上最大の規模となり、ブロードエーカー・シティ構想の巨大な模型が出展され、1951–54年の間でヨーロッパと北米のいくつかの会場を巡回した。これ以降、ライトはイタリア建築の未来をめぐる議論の中心的存在として、カルロ・スカルパ(1906-78)やブルーノ・ゼヴィ(1918-2000)といった著名なイタリア人建築家や建築史家との関係を築いていった。これがきっかけとなり、ライトはヴェネツィアの大運河に面する建築家アンジェロ・マシエリを記念する学生会館(1951/1952–55)の設計依頼を受けることとなる[cat.no.7-36]。スカルパは、ヴェネチア・ビエンナーレにおいてカステッロ公園内の「芸術の書」館やベネズエラ館(1954–56)といった作品を通して、イタリアにおけるライト解釈に最も大きな影響を与えた。さらにスカルパは、1960年の第12回ミラノ・トリエンナーレでのフランク・ロイド・ライト展の展示設計も手がけている[31] [cat.nos.7-41~43]。

ライトのデザインは、ニューヨーク近代美術館(MoMA)においても多様な方向から展示が行われた。フィリップ・ジョンソン(1906–2005)とヘンリー=ラッセル・ヒッチコックによる「モダン・アーキテクチャー:インターナショナル・スタイル展」(1932)は、ライトの住宅デザインを、プレファブリケーションや標準化といった手法に光を当てて、モダニズムの先駆けとして取り上げた。一方で帝国ホテルなどの作品は、機能主義に反する装飾的な特徴のある作品とみなされ、展示されなかった[32]。多数の作品を集めた回顧的な展覧会とは対照的に、落水荘だけを扱った1938年の写真展「フランク・ロイド・ライトによるペンシルベニア州ベア・ランの新築住宅」や、1952年の展示「フランク・ロイド・ライト:ジョンソン・ワックス社のための建築」といったひとつの作品にスポットを当てた展覧会も行われ、再び注目を集めるきっかけとなった[33]。それ以後のライト単独展は、その業績をもって「アメリカン・アーキテクト」(1940)と題したものから、図面、透視図、施工、ランドスケープなどに焦点を当てた「建築家フランク・ロイド・ライト」(1994)まで、さまざまな形で開催された[34]。21世紀に入り、フランク・ロイド・ライト財団が所有する図面などの資料がコロンビア大学エイヴリー建築美術図書館とニューヨーク近代美術館(MoMA)に移管されたことにより、ライトの展覧会や研究は新たな展開をみせる[35]。膨大な資料の再調査に基づく展示として、MoMAにおいて「フランク・ロイド・ライトと都市:密集と分散」(2014)が開催され、「高層ビルの新しい形態と、アメリカの田園風景の都市化に対する包括的計画である「ブロードエーカー・シティ構想」の双方に取り組んでいたライトが、1920年代から30年代にかけて拡大し続けるアメリカの都市に対してどのような懸念を抱いていたか」に着目した[36]。同じくMoMAにおける「フランク・ロイド・ライト生誕150周年：紐解かれるアーカイヴ」展(2017)は、生誕150年を記念して、ライトの多岐にわたる業績を12の主要な観点にまとめ解説した。

ライトと日本に関する展覧会も、生前から没後まで発展を続けてきた。ライトは1905年の日本訪問の後、シカゴ美術館で「広重 フランク・ロイド・ライト所蔵多色版画展」(1906)を開催し、浮世絵コレクターとしての意欲を表した。その1世紀後、ニューヨークのジャパン・ソサエティー・ギャラリーで開催された「フランク・ロイド・ライトと日本美術」(2001)では、学芸員のジュリア・ミーチ(1940-)が詳細な研究成果を発表した。ライトは復刻版浮世絵をめぐるスキャンダルに直面しながらも、死去の時点でなお6,000点ものコレクションを所有していたという。日本では、バブル期にセゾン美術館で「フランク・ロイド・ライト回顧展」(1991)が開催され、その後の「フランク・ロイド・ライトと日本展」(1997)ではライトの建築を通して彼の日本美術コレクションに光が当てられた。

本書および展覧会「フランク・ロイド・ライト——世界を結ぶ建築」においては、これまでの主要なテーマを一望のもとにし、それらが1923年から2023年までの時間と空間の重要な節目において、どのように交わってきたかを俯瞰する。各テーマはそれぞれ単独の展覧会に値するものだが、それらを並置することでフランク・ロイド・ライトの作品のダイナミズムを明らかにし、今後の建築界に示唆を与えるものである。

ミクロとマクロの世界

フランク・ロイド・ライトの世界は、ユニット・システムで結ばれたミクロレベルとマクロレベルの両面から理解することができる。ライト自身も、「私がこれまでに設計した建物は、大小を問わずユニット・システムに基づいて組み立てられている」と書いている[37]。帝国ホテルのテラコッタの装飾ブロック[cat. no. 4-63]は、実寸のままでも存在感があるが、そのデザインはホテル全体のスケールモデルとしても機能している。多重反復の特徴は、ルイス・サリヴァンの下で設計を始めたころの作品であるチャーンリー邸(1891-92)の階段まわりの直線的な花台や手すりにも見られ、晩年に設計したマイル・ハイ・イリノイを予見している。帝国ホテルの食器に見られる軽快な円形模様は、以降のライトの設計に見られる円形のデザイン、例えばゴードン・ストロング自動車体験娯楽施設とプラネタリウム計画案(1924-25)[cat. no. 5-42]やグッゲンハイム美術館(1943-59)[cat. nos. 5-44~47]、そして大バグダッド計画案(1957)[cat. no. 7-52]にも通じる。1912-13年に行われたシカゴ・シティ・クラブ・コン

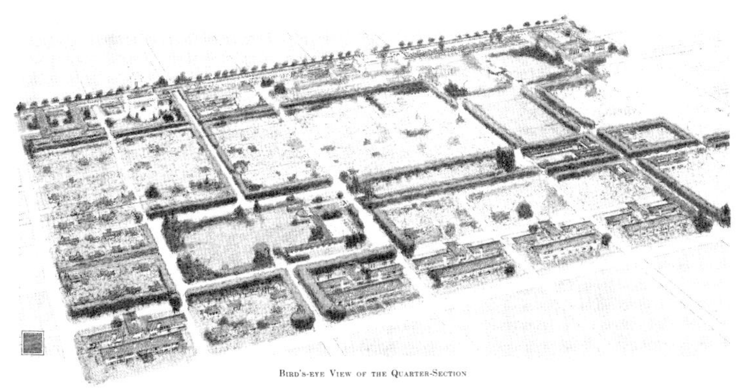

図2　シカゴ・シティ・クラブ・コンペティションのための4分割ブロックプラン鳥瞰透視図

Fig. 2　Scheme of Development for a Quarter Section. Aerial Perspective. From Alfred B.Yeomans, ed., *City Residential Land Development: Studies in Planning. Competitive Plans for Subdividing a Typical Quarter Section of Land in the Outskirts of Chicago.* Publications of the City Club of Chicago. Chicago: University of Chicago Press, December 1916.

ペティションのために、ライトは4分割ブロックプラン[図2]の中に公共および住宅要素を配する設計を行ったが、その全体的な都市計画パターンはルイス・サリヴァンの装飾的で有機的なデザインと観念的に通じるものであった[38]。ライトはこのパターンを帝国ホテルの構成に発展させ、後にブロードエーカー・シティでも展開している。

ライトは1932年、アメリカの田園地域における居住と労働を根本的に再構築するために、ブロードエーカー・シティ構想のコンセプトを初めて発表した。コロナ禍を経験した現代の世界でも共感を呼び、距離を取り分散して暮らすという課題に応えるものとなっている。1930年代に登場した遠隔通信や自動車、飛行機といった技術は、空間と時間の関係をつくり変えた。さらに、インターネットやドローンが普及した今日も、「生きている都市」を成り立たせているのは何であるのかという根源的な問いを投げかけ続けている。デイヴィッド・ロメロのレンダリング[cat.no.7-56]に表現されたブロードエーカー・シティの現代性は、鮮やかな色彩とディテールで、ライトの理想に息を吹き込んだ。マイル・ハイ・イリノイなどのランドマーク的なプロジェクトと、小規模のユーソニアン・ハウスが一体となることで、あらゆるスケールのユートピア社会が実現された。ライト自身も「永遠の変化の法則」を受け入れ、次のように述べている。「私たちが望んでやまない成長とは、人類の過去の文明が築いて私たちに残してくれた叡智を、最終的に理解することにある。その間に、真理に沿ったとしても逆らったとしても、等しく真理に貢献することに慰められるのだ[39]。現在、ライトの理想はさらなる発展を遂げようとしている。田根剛(1979-)による高層ビルとしての新しい帝国ホテルの設計(2021-36)[cat.no.4-18n]、ミラノからドバイまで世界各地に建設予定の建築における生物多様性のプロトタイプであるステファノ・ボエリ(1956-)による垂直の森(2007-)、ブロードエーカー・シティ構想における食料生産に関する研究内容を活用した重松象平/OMAのウエスト・ルイスヴィル・フード・ポート計画は中国で実現している[40][図3]。ライトは、「生きている都市」への絶ゆまぬ洞察こそが、創造的な精神を有する社会を根本的に支えるものと考えており、1957年の著書『テスタメント』において次のように述べている。

> 我々の生活を久しく味わい深いものとするために、人間の崇高な宇宙的精神が久しく生きながらえることを望んでやまない。我々の文明がこの世界を、単に素晴らしい文明としてではなく、文化として示してくれるほどに。単なる好奇心と、文化がまさにそこに成立する美。この両者の間の基本的な区別が、創造的精神を有する社会とそうでない社会との違いをもたらすのである[41]。

図3　ウエスト・ルイスヴィル・フード・ポート計画｜OMA｜2015年
Fig. 3　West Louisville Food Port | OMA | 2015

1 Louis H Sullivan, 1994. “Concerning the Imperial Hotel Tokyo, Japan,” 1923. In *The Early Work of the Great Architect Frank Lloyd Wright* (New York: Gramercy Books, 1994), pp. 101–123.

2 Frank Lloyd Wright Foundation, “About Frank Lloyd Wright,” accessed March 5, 2023, https://franklloydwright.org/frank-lloyd-wright/.

3 Carole Ann Fabian, “About Wright at Avery,” accessed March 5, 2023, https://library.columbia.edu/libraries/avery/franklloydwright/about.html.

4 フランク・ロイド・ライト著、樋口清訳『テスタメント』（中央公論美術出版、2010）Frank Lloyd Wright, “A Testament” in *Frank Lloyd Wright: Writings and Buildings: Selected* by Edgar Kaufmann and Ben Raeburn (New York, 1960), p. 303.

5 ライトの1893年の万博との出会いに関するより詳細な議論は以下を参照。Julia Meech, *Frank Lloyd Wright and the Art of Japan: The Architect's Other Passion* (New York: Japan Society/Harry N. Abrams, 2001), pp. 30–33.

6 同書、pp. 28–47; および Kevin Nute, *Frank Lloyd Wright and Japan* (New York: Van Nostrand, 1993), pp. 9–34.
（ケヴィン・ニュート著、大木順子訳『フランク・ロイド・ライトと日本文化』鹿島出版会、1997）

7 前掲書 註5、pp. 35–37; および W. C. Gannett et al., *The House Beautiful* (River Forest, Ill.: Auvergne Press, 1896).

8 前掲書 註5、pp. 35–37.

9 Frank Lloyd Wright, *Hiroshige: An Exhibition of Colour Prints from the Collection of Frank Lloyd Wright* (Chicago: Art Institute of Chicago, 1906).

10 グーキンが帝国ホテル新築の提案募集について耳にしたのは1911年の前半である。Kathryn Smith, “Frank Lloyd Wright and the Imperial Hotel: A Postscript,” in *Art Bulletin* (June 1, 1985), p. 297.

11 前掲書 註5、p. 55.

12 Frank Lloyd Wright, *Ausgeführte Bauten und Entwürfe von Frank Lloyd Wright [Completed Buildings and Designs by Frank Lloyd Wright]* (Berlin: Ernst Wasmuth A.G., 1910–11).

13 David Van Zanten, “Ausgeführte Bauten und Entwürfe von Frank Lloyd Wright [Completed Buildings and Designs by Frank Lloyd Wright]” in *Chicago by the book: 1010 publications that shaped the city and its image* (Chicago: University of Chicago Press, 2018), pp. 76–77.

14 ヴァスムート版の制作および1910年のライトのイタリア滞在の全容については以下参照。Filippo Fici, “Frank Lloyd Wright in Florence and Fiesole, 1909–10, in ” *Frank Lloyd Wright Quarterly*, vol. 22, no. 4 (Fall 2011): 4–17 および H. Allen Brooks, *The Art Bulletin*, vol. 48, no. 2 (Jun 1966): pp. 193–202.

15 Frank Lloyd Wright, "Ausgeführte Bauten und Entwürfe von Frank Lloyd Wright," reprinted in *The Essential Frank Lloyd Wright: Critical Writings on Architecture*, ed. By Bruce Brooks Pfeiffer (Princeton: Princeton University Press, 2008), p. 52.

16 Van Zanten, *Chicago by the book: 1010 publications that shaped the city and its image*, p. 76.

17 Mariette van Stralen, “Kindred Spirits: Holland, Wright, and Wijdeveld,” in *Frank Lloyd Wright: Europe and Beyond*, ed. Anthony Alofsin (Berkeley: University of California Press, 1999), pp. 45–65.

18 これらの特集号は以下で再刊された。*Frank Lloyd Wright: The Early Work of the Great Architect* (New York: Gramercy Books, 1994).

19 Andrew Saint, “Wright and Great Britain,” in *Frank Lloyd Wright: Europe and Beyond*, 133; Nicholas Pevsner, *Pioneers of Modern Design* (London: Faber & Faber, 1936).

20 Henry-Russell Hitchcock, *In the Nature of Materials: The Buildings of Frank Lloyd Wright* (New York: Hawthorne Books, 1942).

21 Alberto Sartoris, “Wright and South America,” in *Frank Lloyd Wright: Europe and Beyond* (Berkeley: University of California Press, 1999) p. 152.

22 武田五一『フランクロイドライト氏建築図案集』（積善館本店、1916）2007年、ふくやま美術館にて武田とライトの関係に注目した展覧会が開かれた。https://www.museum.or.jp/event/36081.

23 高梨由太郎編『帝国ホテル』（洪洋社、1923）

24 渡辺義雄写真、内藤多仲、明石信道、山本学治文『帝国ホテル1921–67』（鹿島研究所出版会、1968）、明石信道『旧帝国ホテルの実證的研究』（東光堂書店、1972）

25 土浦亀城「フランク・ロイド・ライト作品展」（『国際建築』1931.8）、pp. 270–271

26 二川幸夫企画・撮影『フランク・ロイド・ライト全集』（全12巻）（東京：A.D.A. EDITA、1984–1986）

27 Kathryn Smith, *Wright on Exhibit* (Princeton: Princeton University Press, 2017).

28 同書、p. 222.

29 前掲書 註27、pp. 31–39.

30 イタリア語の展覧会名は“Mostra dell'Opera di Frank Lloyd Wright”だったが、ライト自身は「イタリアの展覧会」と呼んでおり、その後の2年間でヨーロッパと北米を巡回するにあたり『フランク・ロイド・ライト：生きている建築60年の軌跡』として知られるようになった。Smith, *Wright on Exhibit*, pp. 236–238.

31 Maristella Casciato, “Wright and Italy: The Promise of Organic Architecture,” in *Frank Lloyd Wright: Europe and Beyond*, pp. 93–95.

32 Smith, *Wright on Exhibit*, pp. 74–77.

33 https://www.moma.org/calendar/exhibitions/2962

34 Terence Riley, “Frank Lloyd Wright: Architect, Visions and Revisions since 1910,” *MoMA, Winter-Spring*, no. 16 (Winter–Spring, 1994): pp. 1–5.

35 https://library.columbia.edu/libraries/avery/franklloydwright.html

36 https://www.moma.org/calendar/exhibitions/1410

37 “In the Cause of Architecture by Frank Lloyd Wright: The Third Dimension, 1925,” in *The Life-Work of the American Architect Frank Lloyd Wright, Wendingen* (1925; repr., New York: Horizon Press, 1965), p. 57.

38 この4分割ブロックプランは約5,000人の居住者を想定し、商業、行政、教育、レクリエーションなどの施設も組み込まれていた。*City Residential Land Development Studies in Planning Competition Plans for Subdividing a Typical Quarter Section of Land in the Outskirts of Chicago*, ed. Alfred B. Yeomans (Chicago: University of Chicago Press, 1916).

39 前掲書 註37、p. 439.

40 https://www.stefanoboeriarchitetti.net/en/project/dubai-vertical-forest/
https://hypebeast.com/2020/2/shohei-shigematsu-oma-architecture-interview

41 Wright, “A Testament” (1957) reprinted in *Essential Frank Lloyd Wright* (Princeton: Princeton University Press, 2010), p. 438.

Frank Lloyd Wright and the World

Ken Tadashi Oshima

> *This great work is the masterpiece of Frank Lloyd Wright, a great free spirit, whose fame as a master of ideas is an accomplished worldwide fact.*[1]
>
> Louis Sullivan, 1923

These laudatory words published upon the 1923 completion of the Imperial Hotel (1913–1923) by Frank Lloyd Wright (1867–1959) came from leading Chicago School American architect Louis Sullivan (1856–1924). A life-long mentor to Wright, Sullivan has been called a "father of skyscrapers" and "father of modernism." Sullivan's essay on the Imperial Hotel was published in 1925, the year after his own passing, in the Dutch avant-garde architectural journal *Wendingen* as part of seven special issues that helped propagate Wright's fame and impact in Holland and the world at large. Wright eventually designed 1,114 structures of all types and scales, realizing 532 through the course of his seven-decade career.[2] He would become recognized as "the greatest American architect of all time" by the American Institute of Architects. Over 1,200 books by and about Wright have been published, and the architect appears in more than 3,300 periodical entries in twenty languages. Wright is one of the most published architects in the world.[3]

The Imperial Hotel, Wright's first international project intended for a global audience of visiting diplomats, government officials, and politicians, is a palimpsest of salient themes of Wright's career. Its scale was unapologetically urban, engaging the surrounding historic center of Tokyo. It incorporated within its own walls 270 hotel rooms, 850-person theater with a revolving stage, a ballroom and banquet hall, a 300-person cabaret, extensive dining rooms, and a grand 90-meter promenade with seating. With these myriad programs stretching across a 16,000 square-meter (four-acre) site, the Imperial Hotel was Wright's largest commission to date, a veritable city within the city of Tokyo. At the same time, Wright's meticulous attention to detail—original furniture, textiles, tableware, murals, stone reliefs, architectural ornament, and textile blocks—operated at a small scale to unify the vast complex and showcased Wright's integrated approach to design [Fig. 1]. It was the commission of a lifetime, and Wright used the opportunity to experiment with ideas that had been in gestation for years, which later resurfaced in other commissions after the hotel's completion. The themes of Wright's career that intersect with the Imperial Hotel design are as follows: a dialogue between the modernizing metropolises of Chicago and Tokyo; the organic evolution of Wright's engagement of landscapes from the American midwestern prairie to Japan, Italy and beyond (as discussed in Jennifer Gray's essay); his lifelong engagement with progressive education; the micro/macro dynamics of Wright's concrete textile blocks, which were capable of bridging scales, as well as rectilinear and circular geometric systems (as discussed in Matthew Skjonsberg's essay); an embrace of the tall building in dynamic balance with landscapes to create the living city; and a lifelong interest in global cultures, such as Japanese culture but also Mesoamerican, Native American, and beyond. In the twenty-first century, Wright's work resonates with contemporary issues such as seeking an ecological balance between town and country in Broadacre City (1929-35) and pushing urban limits in his Mile-High Illinois skyscraper (1956), still well beyond any tower in height and ambition realized thus far. Wright's work provided inspiration for the world yet to come.

Connecting the 19th, 20th, and 21st Centuries

The Imperial's official completion on September 1, 1923, was a pivotal moment for the hotel, Wright, and the world at large. The coincidence of the Great Kanto Earthquake with the hotel's official opening and subsequent "survival" led to its legendary status for both the hotel and Wright's career. Wright was born into a rapidly modernizing world a few years after the end of the American Civil War (1861–1865) and a year before the start of the Meiji Period. He was 56 years old when the Imperial opened at a midpoint of his career, to be followed by three decades of practice that included work in the American West; international commissions in Italy, India, and Iraq; and masterworks such as Fallingwater (1934–37) and the Guggenheim Museum (1943–59). The hotel commission was a decade-long project that required

Wright to spend for more than three years living in Tokyo. Wright departed from Japan on July 27, 1922, shortly before the hotel's completion and the 1923 earthquake, never to physically return; however, the epic design experience lived on in Wright's mind throughout his life. He wrote in *A Testament* (1957): "The *ukiyo-e* and the Momoyama, Japanese architecture and gardening, confirmed my own feeling for my work and delighted me, as did Japanese civilization which seemed so freshly and completely of the soil, organic." [4]

Floating Worlds

The printed world of *ukiyo-e*, which literally translates as "floating world," inspired Wright's entire professional career. Wright's own encounter with Japanese design culture on American soil at the 1893 Chicago World's Fair was followed by a lifelong dialogue with the country's art and architecture. The presentation at the fair of the Ho-o-den pavilion, a translation of the eleventh-century Byodo-in Phoenix Hall, noted for its symmetrical design and extended composition of corridors, would resonate with Wright's own Imperial Hotel design [cat. no. 1-11].[5] Wright also had been exposed to a circle of Asian art enthusiasts, including his mentors Joseph Silsbee (1848–1913) and Louis Sullivan, in the age of Japonisme and the imagination of Japan from outside the country.[6] Wright expressed his own interpretation of Japanese prints in his 1896–97 book *The House Beautiful* [cat. no. 2-12]. Accompanied by his own photography of weeds and wildflowers, photogravures on Japanese paper, the compositions are strongly resonant with Utagawa Hiroshige's *Nadeshiko (Pink) Butterfly and Poem* (c. 1840), from Wright's private collection.[7] Around 1893–1900, Wright took photographs of snow-covered landscapes around Spring Green, Wisconsin [cat. nos. 2-1, 2], that recall the minimal composition of Japanese ink paintings on hand scrolls, underscoring his passion for this artistic view.

Wright also pursued his self-described "obsession" with Japanese art as a collector, teacher, and dealer from Japan back to America.[8] He returned to Chicago with several hundred Hiroshige prints, which he exhibited in March 1906 at the Art Institute of Chicago, along with the publication of his first essay on Japanese prints.[9] Wright's intense interest led him to meet avid Japanese print collector Frederick William Gookin (1853–1936), who is believed to have suggested Wright for the Imperial Hotel commission.[10] Wright also encouraged his clients to hang Japanese prints on the walls of their homes.[11] For a second, even larger exhibition of *ukiyo-e* prints at the Art Institute, in March 1908, Wright designed special stands—akin to his high-backed dining chairs from his home in Oak Park, Illinois—that vertically framed Japanese prints tailored to fit the space. Gookin organized this exhibition, and Wright designed the exhibition space with its system of hanging prints from the rail above precisely placed benches [cat. no. 1-77]. Wright developed further iterations of these ideas in designs such as the Japanese Print Gallery for William Spaulding (project, Boston, 1914) and the S. Mori Japanese Print Shop (1914), a remodeled interior in the Fine Arts Building in Chicago. In both instances, he designed the entire space around the precise viewing of prints, composing the cabinets, picture rails, fabrics, and plaster for the walls, carpets, and the remarkably minimal square chair design that predates the *de Stijl* furniture designs of Gerrit Rietveld (1888–1964) [cat. no. 1-76]. Wright's exhibition design was a total work of art (*Gesamtkunstwerk*), with their framed artistic views of natural subjects akin to Wright's residential designs. Wright would further develop such ideas in his design for the Imperial Hotel.

Wright's early designs attracted international attention through the publication of *Ausgeführte Bauten und Entwürfe von Frank Lloyd Wright* [*Completed Buildings and Designs by Frank Lloyd Wright*] [cat. no. 7-11. see list] by the German publisher Ernst Wasmuth.[12] This monograph consisted of 100 oversized loose plates (40 x 64 cm), arguably Wright's own ukiyo-e, with a lengthy text by Wright and production costs funded by the architect. This lavish edition was limited to 100 copies to be sold in Europe and 1,000 copies were sent to Wright in the United States. A smaller, less expensive publication of photographs of Wright's work [cat. no. 6-1], which included an introduction by British Arts and Crafts designer C.R. Ashbee (1863–1942), came out in

1911 to further disseminate Wright's designs far and wide.[13]

The plates, prepared in Fiesole, Italy, during Wright's sojourn in the spring and summer of 1910 with the help of his son Lloyd (1890–1978) and assistant Taylor Woolley (1884-1965), combined Japanese and Italian artistic ideals.[14] The lithographs articulated Wright's designs using the simplified line that he subsequently praised in *The Japanese Print* (1912) [cat. no. 1-76] and the sensitivity of Marion Mahony (1871–1961). Mahony was Wright's first employee and one of his most acclaimed delineators, as evidenced by her 1906 rendering of the DeRhodes House [cat. no. 1-56] with the inscription "drawn by Mahony after FLW and Hiroshige." The *Wasmuth* folio sheets were prepared as Wright took inspiration from Italian Tuscan landscapes as captured in his photographs and own words: "Of this joy in living, there is greater proof in Italy than elsewhere. Buildings, pictures, and sculptures seem to be born, like the flowers by the roadside, to sing themselves into being. Approached in the spirit of their conception, they inspire us with the very music of life."[15] The sheets further resonated with the touch of the Austrian designer Joseph Maria Olbrich (1867–1908) and subsequently garnered Wright "admiration and imitation in Europe," including Bruno Mohring (1863–1929) and Otto Wagner (1841–1912).[16]

Wright's work was especially attractive to architects in the Netherlands. This included architect Hendrik Petrus Berlage (1856-1934), father of the Amsterdam School, Dutch modernist Willem Marinus Dudok (1884-1974), and Hendricus Wijdeveld (1885–1987), editor-in-chief of the expressionist architectural journal, *Wendingen*.[17] Wijdeveld's interest led him to feature the work and writings of Wright in seven issues of *Wendingen* [cat. nos. 7-14, 17].[18] They featured essays including J.J.P. Oud's "The Influence of Frank Lloyd Wright on the Architecture of Europe," R. Mallet-Stevens' "Frank Lloyd Wright and the New Architecture" (translated from French), as well as a text by Erich Mendelsohn (translated from German). The latter had visited Taliesin in 1924, where he gathered with Richard Neutra (1892–1970), Kameki (1897–1996) and Nobuko Tsuchiura (1900–98), and Wright. *Wendingen* also featured the Imperial Hotel through extensive photographs, drawings, and an effusive essay by Louis Sullivan, providing a global audience for the Imperial Hotel, including the journal's subscribers in Japan [cat. no. 7-20. see list].

Wright's world in print continued to proliferate in the ensuing decades. *Frank Lloyd Wright: An Autobiography* was first published in 1932, with his additions and revisions shaping the 1943 and 1977 editions [cat. no. 7-12]. Its impact resulted in the rise of British admirers and Wright's inclusion in Nicholas Pevsner's seminal book, *Pioneers of Modern Design*, in 1936.[19] Henry-Russell Hitchcock's *In the Nature of Materials: The Buildings of Frank Lloyd Wright, 1887-1941* featured a half-century of Wright's work through black and white photographs, drawings, and analysis, with a central chapter featuring the Imperial Hotel along with his work on the Pacific Rim.[20] This book had a global impact, especially in postwar Latin America, where it is said to have "had the force of a bomb."[21]

The publication of Wright in Japan has had an equally long and wide-ranging history. Wright met architect Takeda Goichi during his 1905 trip to Japan and published his first monograph in Japan in 1916.[22] The fully illustrated book published in 1923, *Teikoku hoteru* [cat. no. 4-4. see list], captured the Imperial Hotel upon completion before the Great Kanto Earthquake.[23] By contrast, later publications featuring photographs of Yoshio Watanabe (1907–2000), Osamu Murai (1928–2016), and Yukio Futagawa (1932–2013) spotlighted the hotel in postwar Japan in the 1960s prior to its demolition in 1967.[24] Kameki Tsuchiura published Wright's post-Imperial work in 1931 in *Kokusai kenchiku*, which featured Wright's modern development of the high-rise building Saint Mark's Tower in New York [cat. no. 6-21].[25] Wright would later be included in the March 1971 issue of *Kenchiku*. Subsequent interpretations of Wright were profoundly shaped by the lifework of Masami Tanigawa (1930–2019), whose extensive publications are highlighted by *Wright and Japan* (1977). Yukio Futagawa, in collaboration with Bruce Brooks Pfeiffer (1930–2017) and the Frank Lloyd Wright Foundation, published the architect's complete works in 12 oversized volumes (1984-1987) that summarized the encyclopedic scope of Wright in the world of publishing.[26]

Wright's World on Display

From the nineteenth century to the present, exhibitions have displayed Wright's constantly evolving microcosmic world. The 1893 Chicago World's Fair brought together the display of 46 countries upon the 400th anniversary of Christopher Columbus's arrival in the "New World," the expression of which would be expanded by the 26-year-old Wright through the subsequent decades. More than 100 exhibitions of Wright's work were mounted during his lifetime, a majority of which were organized by himself as an avant-garde artist/architect engaging in a continually evolving world.[27] As Wright scholar Kathryn Smith has argued extensively, "His intentions can be directly traced to his formative years in Chicago in the 1890s and to his association with the Chicago Architectural Club, specifically."[28] In 1914, "The Work of Frank Lloyd Wright" exhibition featured the Imperial Hotel among his most impressive public buildings "realized since Spring of 1911," along with Wright-designed Japanese print stands [cat. no. 1-79].[29]

The apex of Wright's curatorial pursuits could be seen in his "Sixty Years of Living Architecture" exhibition held in Florence, Italy, in 1951 at La Strozzina, a gallery housed in the fifteenth-century Palazzo Strozzi.[30] As the largest one-person show ever realized for an architect, it featured the massive model of Broadacre City and traveled to venues throughout Europe and North America for the next five years. Wright was subsequently at the center of discussions about the future of Italian architecture and concretized relationships with important Italian architects and historians, such as Bruno Zevi (1918–2000) and Carlo Scarpa (1906–78). This led to a commission for Wright to design a memorial to the architect Angelo Masieri on the Grand Canal in Venice (1951/1952–55) [cat. no. 7-36]. Scarpa exercised the greatest influence on Wright's interpretation in Italy through his Pavilion of the Book of Art (1950) and the Venezuelan Pavilion (1954–56) at the Giardini di Castello at the Venice Biennale. Scarpa also designed the 1960 Frank Lloyd Wright exhibition at the 12th Triennale di Milano [cat. nos. 7-41~43].[31]

The curation of Wright's design took on equally diverse directions at the Museum of Modern Art (MoMA) in New York. Philip Johnson (1906–2005) and Henry-Russell Hitchcock's "Modern Architecture: International Exhibition" featured Wright's residential designs as a precursor to modernism, highlighting techniques of prefabrication and standardization. However, they avoided works such as the Imperial Hotel due to its perceived anti-functionalist ornamental character.[32] In contrast to extensive monographic exhibitions, Wright regained prominence in 1938 with the one-building exhibition featuring photographs of Fallingwater as "A New House on Bear Run, Pennsylvania by Frank Lloyd Wright" and also in the 1952 installation "Frank Lloyd Wright: Building for Johnson's Wax Company."[33] Subsequent monographic exhibitions of Wright varied from framing his work as an "American Architect" (1940) to highlighting the architectural drawings, delineators, tectonic construction, and landscape in "Frank Lloyd Wright: Architect" (1994).[34] In the twenty-first century, Wright exhibitions and scholarship entered a new phase with the co-acquisition of the Frank Lloyd Wright Foundation Archives by Avery Architectural & Fine Arts Library at Columbia University and the Museum of Modern Art (MoMA).[35] Exhibitions based on reevaluation of the extensive archive include "Frank Lloyd Wright and the City: Density vs. Dispersal" (2014) at MoMA, which highlighted "the tension in Wright's thinking about the growing American city in the 1920s and 1930s when he worked simultaneously on radical new forms for the skyscraper and on a comprehensive plan for the urbanization of the American landscape titled Broadacre City.[36] "Frank Lloyd Wright at 150: Unpacking the Archive", also at MoMA, marked the 150th anniversary of the architect's birth through an anthology of 12 critical interpretations of Wright's multifaceted practice.

Exhibitions about Wright and Japan similarly have a long evolution throughout Wright's life and beyond.

Wright illustrated his passion and role as a collector of *ukiyo-e* through *HIROSHIGE: An Exhibition of Colour Prints from the collection of Frank Lloyd Wright* at the Art Institute of Chicago (1906) following his 1905 trip to Japan. A century later, *Frank Lloyd Wright and the Art of Japan* (2001), held at the Japan Society Gallery, New York, featured curator Julia Meech's rigorous scholarship. She revealed Wright's career as a dealer and collector of Japanese prints, who faced a scandal over revamped prints but nonetheless possessed six thousand prints at the time of his death. In Japan, "Frank Lloyd Wright Retrospective" (1991) opened at the Sezon Museum of Art during the Bubble Period, and "Frank Lloyd Wright and Japan" (1997) highlighted Wright's collection of Japanese art in connection with his architecture.

The exhibition and book, *The Wright Imperial Hotel at 100: Frank Lloyd Wright and the World*, thus charts the respective critical themes that together form a broader constellation intersecting at critical junctures of time and space between 1923 and 2023. While each theme is worthy of an entire exhibition, their juxtaposition demonstrates the dynamics of Wright's work for further consideration in the future.

Micro/Macro Worlds

The world of Frank Lloyd Wright can be powerfully understood on micro and macro levels, linked by a unit system. As Wright himself wrote, "All the buildings I have built—large and small—are fabricated upon a unit system." [37] The ornamental terra cotta blocks [cat. no. 4-63] of the Imperial Hotel have a presence at their actual scale, while the design of each block also operates as a scale model of the overall hotel itself. The multi-scalar quality could be seen in the vertical vases and vertical rails around the Charnley Residence (1891–92) stairs that Wright designed under Louis Sullivan at the start of his career, foreshadowing his Mile-High Illinois design at the end of his career. The play of circular forms in the Imperial Hotel dinnerware would resonate with subsequent circular designs by Wright, from the Gordon Strong Automotive (1924–25) to the Guggenheim Museum (1943–59) and the plan for Greater Baghdad (1957). When Wright composed civic and residential elements in his Quadruple Block Plan [Fig. 2] for the Chicago City Club Competition of 1912-13, the overall urban pattern had an abstract resonance with the ornamental organic designs of Louis Sullivan. [38] Wright further developed this pattern in the Imperial Hotel composition and later in Broadacre City.

Wright first presented the concept of Broadacre City in 1932 as a radical restructuring of living and working across the American countryside. It continues to have resonance in the contemporary world, addressing challenges of distancing and dispersal in the age of the COVID-19 pandemic and beyond. Modern technologies of telecommunications, automobiles, and airplanes reshaped relationships of space and time in the 1930s, and today the world of the internet and drones continue to pose fundamental questions about what constitutes a "Living City." The contemporaneity of Broadacre City expressed in David Romero's renderings [cat. no. 7-56] brings Wright's ideal to life in vivid color and detail. Wright's landmark projects, including the Mile-High Illinois, are brought together with the smaller-scale Usonian homes to create a utopian society on all scales. Wright himself embraced an "eternal law of change," noting, "Growth, our best hope, consists in understanding at last what other civilizations have only known about and left to us—ourselves comforted meantime by the realization that all one does either for or against Truth serves it equally well." [39] Today, a further evolution of Wright's vision can be seen in the design of the new high-rise Imperial Hotel (2021-2036) by Tsuyoshi Tane (1979-) [cat. no. 4-18n. and pp. 198-199] and projects such as Stefano Boeri's Vertical Forest (2007-), a prototypical building for architectural biodiversity for sites around the world, from Milan to Dubai, and Shohei Shigematsu/OMA's research into food production in Broadacre City for their West Louisville Food Port project (2015–16) that is actually happening in China [Fig. 3]. [40] Wright fundamentally looked to his continuing vision of the Living City to advocate a society with a creative soul in his 1957 *Testament*:

> *...we continue to hope that the Cosmic Spirit in which we as a people do excel may survive long enough to*

salt and savor life among us long enough for our civilization to present us to the world as a culture, not merely as an amazing civilization. The basic distinction between the curious and the beautiful, in which culture really consists, will make all the difference between a society with a creative soul and a society with none.[41]

Louis H Sullivan, 1994. "Concerning the Imperial Hotel Tokyo, Japan," 1923. In *The Early Work of the Great Architect Frank Lloyd Wright* (New York: Gramercy Books, 1994), pp. 101–123.

Frank Lloyd Wright Foundation, "About Frank Lloyd Wright," accessed March 5, 2023, https://franklloydwright.org/frank-lloyd-wright/.

Carole Ann Fabian, "About Wright at Avery," accessed March 5, 2023, https://library.columbia.edu/libraries/avery/franklloydwright/about.html.

4 Frank Lloyd Wright, "A Testament" in *Frank Lloyd Wright: Writings and Buildings: Selected by Edgar Kaufmann and Ben Raeburn* (New York: Meridian Books, 1960), p. 303.

5 For a further discussion of Wright's encounter with the 1893 World's Fair, see Julia Meech, *Frank Lloyd Wright and the Art of Japan: The Architect's Other Passion* (New York: Japan Society/Harry N. Abrams, 2001), pp. 30–33.

6 See ibid., 28–47; and Kevin Nute, *Frank Lloyd Wright and Japan* (New York: Van Nostrand, 1993), pp. 9–34.

7 See Meech, *Frank Lloyd Wright and the Art of Japan*, pp. 35–37; and W. C. Gannett, et al., *The House Beautiful* (River Forest, Ill.: Auvergne Press, 1896).

8 Meech, *Frank Lloyd Wright and the Art of Japan*, pp. 35-37.

9 Frank Lloyd Wright, *Hiroshige: An Exhibition of Colour Prints from the Collection of Frank Lloyd Wright* (Chicago: Art Institute of Chicago, 1906).

10 Gookin heard about the proposal to build a new Imperial Hotel by the first half of 1911. Kathryn Smith, "Frank Lloyd Wright and the Imperial Hotel: A Postscript," in *Art Bulletin* (June 1, 1985), p. 297.

11 See Meech, *Frank Lloyd Wright and the Art of Japan*, p. 55.

12 Frank Lloyd Wright, *Ausgeführte Bauten und Entwürfe von Frank Lloyd Wright [Completed Buildings and Designs by Frank Lloyd Wright]* (Berlin: Ernst Wasmuth A.G., 1910-11).

13 David Van Zanten, "Ausgeführte Bauten und Entwürfe von Frank Lloyd Wright [Completed Buildings and Designs by Frank Lloyd Wright]" in *Chicago by the Book: 1010 publications that shaped the city and its image* (Chicago: University of Chicago Press, 2018), pp. 76–77.

14 For a full account of the production of the Wasmuth volume and Wright's 1910 stay in Italy, see Filippo Fici, "Frank Lloyd Wright in Florence and Fiesole, 1909–10," *Frank Lloyd Wright Quarterly*, vol. 22, no. 4 (Fall 2011): 4–17 and H. Allen Brooks, *The Art Bulletin*, vol. 48, no. 2 (June 1966): pp. 193–202.

15 Frank Lloyd Wright, "Ausgeführte Bauten und Entwürfe von Frank Lloyd Wright," reprinted in*The Essential Frank Lloyd Wright: Critical Writings on Architecture*, ed. Bruce Brooks Pfeiffer (Princeton: Princeton University Press, 2008), p. 52.

16 Van Zanten, *Chicago by the Book: 1010 publications that shaped the city and its image*, p. 76.

17 Mariette van Stralen, "Kindred Spirits: Holland, Wright, and Wijdeveld," in *Frank Lloyd Wright: Europe and Beyond*, ed. Anthony Alofsin (Berkeley: University of California Press, 1999), pp. 45–65.

18 These issues were republished as *Frank Lloyd Wright: The Early Work of the Great Architect*(New York: Gramercy Books, 1994).

19 Andrew Saint, "Wright and Great Britain," in *Frank Lloyd Wright: Europe and Beyond,* 133; and Nicholas Pevsner, *Pioneers of Modern Design* (London: Faber & Faber, 1936).

20 Henry-Russell Hitchcock, *In the Nature of Materials: The Buildings of Frank Lloyd Wright* (New York: Hawthorne Books, 1942).

21 Alberto Sartoris, "Wright and South America," in *Frank Lloyd Wright: Europe and Beyond,* p. 152.

22 Takeda Goichi, *Frank Lloyd Wright Kenchiku Zuan-shu* (Osaka: Sekizenhonkan, 1916). An exhibition on Takeda's connection with Wright was held in 2007 at the Fukuyama Museum: https://www.museum.or.jp/event/36081.

23 Takanashi Yutaro, ed., *Teikoku hoteru (Imperial Hotel)* (Tokyo: Koyosha, August 1923).

24 *Imperial Hotel* (Kajima Institute Publishing Co., Ltd, 1968); and Akashi Shindo, *Kyu Teikoku hoteru no jisshoteki kenkyu* (Chiba: Tokodo Bookstore, 1972).

25 Tsuchiura Kameki, "Frank Lloyd Wright Exhibition of Works," *Kokusai kenchiku*, 8.1931: pp. 270–271.

26 Futagawa Yukio, ed. *Frank Lloyd Wright Complete Works* (12 volumes) (Tokyo: A.D.A. Edita, 1984–1986).

27 Kathryn Smith, *Wright on Exhibit* (Princeton: Princeton University Press, 2017).

28 Smith, *Wright on Exhibit*, p. 222.

29 Smith, *Wright on Exhibit*, pp. 31–39.

30 While the Italian title was "Mostra dell'Opera di Frank Lloyd Wright," Wright himself referred to it as "The Italian Exhibition" and it subsequently became known as "Frank Lloyd Wright: 60 Years of Living Architecture" as it traveled in the following two years around Europe and North America. Smith, *Wright on Exhibit*, pp. 236–238.

31 Maristella Casciato, "Wright and Italy: The Promise of Organic Architecture," *Frank Lloyd Wright: Europe and Beyond*, pp. 93–95.

32 Smith, *Wright on Exhibit*, pp. 74–77.

33 https://www.moma.org/calendar/exhibitions/2962

34 Terence Riley, "Frank Lloyd Wright: Architect, Visions and Revisions since 1910," M*oMA, Winter-Spring*, no. 16 (Winter-Spring, 1994): 1–5.

35 https://library.columbia.edu/libraries/avery/franklloydwright.html

36 https://www.moma.org/calendar/exhibitions/1410

37 "In the Cause of Architecture by Frank Lloyd Wright: The Third Dimension, 1925," in *The Life-Work of the American Architect Frank Lloyd Wright, Wendingen* (1925; repr., New York: Horizon Press, 1965), p. 57.

38 The Quadruple Block Plan was for approximately five thousand people and included commercial, government, educational, and recreational facilities. Published in *City Residential Land Development Studies in Planning Competition Plans for Subdividing a Typical Quarter Section of Land in the Outskirts of Chicago*, ed. Alfred B. Yeomans (Chicago: University of Chicago Press, 1916).

39 Ibid., p. 439.

40 https://www.stefanoboeriarchitetti.net/en/project/dubai-vertical-forest/ https://hypebeast.com/2020/2/shohei-shigematsu-oma-architecture-interview

41 Wright, "A Testament" (1957) reprinted in *Essential Frank Lloyd Wright* (Princeton: Princeton University Press, 2010), p.438.

大地こそ建築の最も簡素な形態

フランク・ロイド・ライトとランドスケープ

ジェニファー・グレイ

フランク・ロイド・ライトは、度々「大地こそ建築の最も簡素な形態である」と述べ、生涯にわたって自然やランドスケープへの情熱を抱き続けた[1]。このテーマに関する著述を、生涯を通して多く残し、自然、抽象、リアリズムといった概念の違いに加え、構築された環境と既存の環境との違いを慎重に区別して論じ、ランドスケープ・アーキテクトとしての経験を重ねた。ライトは、自然をインスピレーション源とした独自の有機的建築の理論を打ち立て、建築と周辺環境との深いつながりを明確に表現しようと試みた。建築史家はライトと風景の関わりを、初期にはアメリカ中西部のプレイリー、後には南西部の荒涼たるソノラ砂漠といった特定の風景としばしば関係づけてきた。しかし、ライトの風景への関わりは、建築作品と同様にグローバルな広がりを有するものである。彼は日本やイタリアを広く旅し、そこで出合った風景、なかでも建築とインフラと自然が統合された様子に魅了された。そうした知見を、シカゴ、カリフォルニア、アリゾナにおける自らの作品、とりわけ彼の自宅兼スタジオであるタリアセンならびにタリアセン・ウエストに反映したのである。本稿では、ライトの自然との関わりを、世界に広がる彼の建築作品と照らし合わせながらたどることで、ライトにとってランドスケープと建築がいかに表裏一体であったかを解説していく。

大地の自然

> われわれ中西部の人間はプレイリーに暮らしている。プレイリーには、それ自体に美しさがあり、その静かな自然美を認識し、引き立てねばならない[2]。

ライトの名を大きく知らしめたのは、1900年代初頭に設計した「プレイリー・スタイル」の住宅群である。ダーウィン・D.マーティン邸（ニューヨーク州バッファロー、1903–05）[cat. nos.2-22~27]、クーンリー邸（イリノイ州リバーサイド、1906–09）[cat. nos.2-28~39]、ブース邸計画案（イリノイ州グレンコー、1911）[cat. nos.2-46~48]、ロビー邸（シカゴ、1908–10）[cat.nos.2-41~45]といった住宅群は、低い寄棟屋根、深い庇、連続窓を用いて中西部の風景の水平性を強調した。こうした作品における装飾は、抽象的かつ幾何学的であり、自然に由来したものであっても形状そのものを模倣することはなかった。自然の中に秩序だった形状や潜在的な構造、すなわちある種の建築性を見いだし、芸術家として「様式化」することで自然に近づくことができると述べている[3]。こうした考えは、アメリカで超絶主義哲学を学び、フリードリヒ・フレーベル（1782–1852）の教えに接したことも影響しているだろう[4]。しかし、デザインと自然との関係にまつわるライトの哲学にとって、もうひとつ重要な源となったのは日本美術、とりわけ浮世絵であった。浮世絵の熱心なコレクターにして研究者でもあったライトは、自然の形態を抽象的な文様やデザインへと様式化する日本の浮世絵師たちの手法を以下のように称賛している。「日本美術は一貫して構造的な芸術といえるだろう。日本の美意識は、重要でないものを排除した厳格な単純化にあるのだ」[5]。

ライトは、自然を建築的なパターンや形態へと抽象化した一方で、植物、花、樹木といった実際の自然にも手を加え、多くのプレイリー・ハウスで庭園やランドスケープを緻密に設計した。より意欲的なランドスケープを実現するにあたっては、環境活動家の先駆けでありネイティブ・ランドスケープを提唱したジェンス・ジェンセン（1860–1951）や、当時ライトのオークパーク・スタジオの所員であったウォルター・バーリー・グリフィン（1876–1937）といった第一線のランドスケープ・アーキテクトたちとも手を組んだ。彼らの多くは、土地固有の植生と自然な配置を重んじる、ランドスケープ・デザインにおけるいわゆる「プレイリースクール」ともいえる手法を用いていた。しかし、実際にはそれほど厳格なものではなく、土地固有の品種にヨーロッパやアフリカの植物を混植したり、東アジアの植物を多く用いたりもしていた。その中には、タチアオイ、シャクヤク、アヤメ、モクレン、ガマズミ、スイカズラなど、日本の浮世絵に描かれたアジア原産の植物も取り入れていた。1890年代に入ってからではあるが、日米間の苗木の輸出入が盛んになり、植物の安定供給が可能になるといった世界的な園芸市場の高まりも相まって、ライトの日本美術への傾倒は、実際の植物や庭園に至るまで徹底されていったのである[6]。

日本の風景を切り取る

> 日本の家屋は、すぐに私を魅了した。どこからどこまでが庭なのかわからないが、答えを探そうともしなかった。その問いは、解決を試みるにはあまりに心地よかったのだ[7]。

1905年から7度にわたって訪れた日本で、ライトはそれまでコレクションの浮世絵を通してしか知ることのできなかった風景を、目の当たりにしたのである。日本の伝統文化に魅了された彼は、東京から、名古屋、京都、大阪、奈良、神戸を周り、さらに瀬戸内の城下町である岡山を経て高松へと西へ向かった。道中では、日本の名だたる寺院、集落、そしてとりわけ庭園を巡っている[8]。ライトは、日本建築が周辺環境と密接に関係していることに感銘を受け、建物と風景、人工物と自然が一体となって継ぎ目のない全体像となっていることを指摘し、日本の建物は「あるべき場所にある岩や木のようだ」と述べた[9]。静謐な水鏡や力強い滝がある水景、曲がりくねる小径に次々と眺望が現れる回遊式庭園は、ライトにとって特に忘れがたいものとなった。1905年5月にアメリカへ戻ると、こうした特徴を自らの住宅設計に取り入れるようになる。例えばクーンリー邸では、起伏を設けた庭園、テラス、バルコニーなどが水盤を囲むように配置されている。この水盤は、日本の伝統の中から「生け捕りにして」リビングルームの眺望に取り入れたものである[10]。

日本からイタリアへ

> 真のイタリアの建築物は、イタリアの地で違和感を覚えることはない。いずれの建築物も、ごく自然に備わった装飾と色彩で十分に満ち足りているからだ。土地にある木々や石、庭園の斜面も建築物と一体になっている[11]。

日本から帰国した5年後に、ライトはイタリアを旅している。まず、フィレンツェに滞在した後、丘の中腹にある絵のように美しい中世の町フィエーゾレで、『フランク・ロイド・ライト建築と設計』(1910–11)、通称ヴァスムート・ポートフォリオの作成にとりかかった。日本での体験と同様に、イタリアの田園は、建築と周辺環境を統合するという考えを確信させるものだった。ライトが幼少期の夏を過ごし、やがてタリアセンを建設することになるウィスコンシン州南部と似て、トスカーナの風景を特徴づけていたのは農業と採石であった。フィエーゾレ周辺には、小さな採石場が点在し、ピエトラ・セレーナという灰色の砂岩が無尽蔵に産出されていた。仕上げ用の薄板、舗装用の厚板、玉石用の小さなブロックから、そのまま基礎に用いるための大きなブロックに切り分けられてさまざまな用途で建築に用いられ、フィレンツェの一体感のある景色を形成していた。街はずれの素朴な建物には、その土地の砂を混ぜた漆喰仕上げが施され、大地の粒子が建物に染み込んで、まるで集落全体が周囲の野原から生えてきたかのように見えるのだ[12]。ライトが滞在中に撮影した写真からは、建物と建物の間にある人間的なスケールの空間に惹かれていたことがわかる。中庭、広場、庭園、あずまやなどによって、内部と外部、建築と自然との境界が、さらに曖昧となっていたのである。

こうした日本とイタリア両国における経験は、ライトが1911年にウィスコンシン州のスプリンググリーンに戻り、自邸兼事務所であるタリアセンの建設を始めた際に明確に表れることとなる。丘の中腹斜面にはめ込まれたようなタリアセンは、ロッジア、擁壁、サンクンガーデン、囲われた中庭、テラス、水景、階段などによって、建物と風景が一体となっており、イタリアの邸宅の庭園や日本の住宅建築を彷彿とさせる。半円形に囲まれた「ティー・サークル（茶亭）」は、日本の待合に触発されて、屋外の諸空間をつなぐ中心となっていた［cat. nos. 2-7, 8, 53, 54］。加えて、堰、池、小川、滝といった水景が、タリアセンのランドスケープにおいて極めて重要な役割を担っていた。ライトは、この水辺のランドスケープを継続的に再設計している。池の底をさらい、岸の形状を整え、水力発電のために堰を改築した。また、初期の堰の曲線的な縁から水面が滑らかに流れ出る水流や、後期の階段状の岩に水しぶきが跳ねる小滝など、さまざまな滝を生み出していった[13]［cat. no. 2-5］。ペンシルベニア州ミル・ランに、代表作となるカウフマン邸「落水荘」（1934–37）［cat. nos. 2-67, 68］を設計するずっと前から、ライトは滝の魅力を追求していた。おそらく、そのきっかけとなったのは、日本での自然の滝との出合いかもしれない。

生産する風景

> イタリアの農地を見れば、開墾や農耕がいかに建築的な行為であり、模様を生み出すものであるかがわかる[14]。

タリアセンに隣接する耕作地の先には、草と樹木の生い茂る野生の風景と、果樹園やブドウ畑、農耕地といった生産的な風景があった[15]。こうした農地は、イタリア・トスカーナ地方の小さな町フィエーゾレの格子状耕地や日本の段々畑などの伝統に基づいて植付けされており、色彩と質感の織り成す抽象的なパターンは、人々が車で見物に訪れるほどだったという[16]。実際にライトが外国の風景の印象について語るときには、イタリアや日本の庭園、集落、自然地形にはほとんど触れず、土地の耕作について多くを語っている[17]。日本については、「段々に上る棚田が、さらに上の畑にまで広がり、緑が点在している」[18]、イタリアについては「この国の農地を見れば、開墾や農耕作がいかに建築的な行為であり、模様を生み出すものであるかがわかる」[19] と語っていた。

ライトにとって、農業は非常に重要であった。農家に生まれたライトは、幼少期を農村で過ごしている。当時は農業が美徳とみなされていた。農民であり高名なユニテリアン派の牧師でもあったライトの叔父のジェンキン・ロイド・ジョーンズ（1843–1918）は、鋤き込み、播種、除草、収穫、植樹、植林、納屋づくりなどの説法を『農園の福音書』と題してまとめていた[20]。タリアセンでの暮らしは田園生活と知的探究を結び付け、アメリカの「紳士農場主」であったトーマス・ジェファーソン（1743–1826）や、超越論哲学者であるラルフ・ワルド・エマーソン（1803–1882）などの豊かな伝統を取り入れていた。確かに、「開化（cultivated）」という言葉は、文化（culture）と農業（agriculture）の架け橋であり、タリアセンにも、その所有者のライトにも当てはまるものである[21]。刈取機、種蒔き機、耕うん機、脱穀機、鋸、乾草架など、19世紀に農業に革命をもたらした新たな農工具によって、タリアセンの周囲の風景にはトウモロコシや穀類などさまざまな作物の縞模様が描き出された。ライトが風景から切り取った4×4フィートのグリッドは、耕運機の刃の間隔や、馬をつないで畑を耕す農具の間隔と密接に関わるものである。「鮮やかに塗装された刈取機が3頭の白馬に引かれて次々に刈り進んでいくと、畑地全体が手の入った縞模様になっていく」[22] とライトが述べたように、農地のグリッドは作業の手順の現れであって、抽象化された形ではない。もちろん、グリッドは建築の設計を構成するものでもあるため、ライトが農業と建物、風景と建築の双方を理解する有効な手段になり得たのだ。

環太平洋域での建築

> この偉大なる山を生んだ恐るべき力は、常に犠牲をもたらすのである。山は沈み、谷は隆起して、海岸線は移り変わる[23]。

ライトの風景に対する思想は、日本とイタリアからアメリカ中西部に取り入れられ、1913年に帝国ホテルの設計を始めると、再び東京に持ち込まれた。テラス、柱廊、ポーチ、プロムナードをはじめとする半屋外空間がホテル内のさまざまなエリアをつなぐために機能し、所々で建物内の中庭に設けられた日本庭園を眺めることができた。加えて、庭園を流れるせせらぎや正面玄関の水盤など、敷地の至る所に水の演出が施されていた。ライトはホテル全体に大谷石という一般的な材料を用いている。大谷石は孔質の火山岩で、日本では車道や歩道、建物までのさまざまな用途に用いられていた。ライトがトスカーナで見いだしたピエトラ・セレーナと同様である。

一方で、環太平洋域の反対側にあたるカリフォルニアでは、1920年代にミラード夫人邸「ミニアトゥーラ」(1923–24)[cat. nos. 5-20~22]やエニス邸(1924–25)といったコンクリートのテキスタイル・ブロックを用いた邸宅を設計している。ライトは、これまでの工夫を、乾燥して日差しの強いロサンゼルスの気候に適合させていった。コンクリートを使った背景には、ピエトラ・セレーナや大谷石という安価でそれぞれの地域で豊富に産出する材料との出合いが影響したのは間違いないだろう。ライトはコンクリートについて「建築の世界では、最も安く最も醜いものだが、そんなねずみ色の物体で何ができるか試してみようではないか。もしかしたら永続的で、高貴で、美しいものができるかもしれない」[24]と語っている。ライトはカリフォルニアにおけるテキスタイル・ブロックを用いたプロジェクトで、コンクリートの工法は普遍的であるが、ブロックの材料に建設地の土を骨材として混ぜて地域特有の材料にしようとした。フィエーゾレ地域の漆喰の建物のように、建物の材料を環境と融合させたのである。ドヘニー・ランチ宅地開発計画案(1923)[cat. nos. 5-27~31]と呼ばれる未完のプロジェクトでは、ランドスケープとインフラと建築の融合が非常に顕著にみられる。住宅や中庭、緑化された屋上テラスが、橋や道路でつながれて段状の大きな構造物となり、尾根と峡谷が入り組むロサンゼルス盆地の地形に溶け込んでいた。そしてそれら全てが同じコンクリート・ブロックでできている。コンクリートはブロック1個の単位からインフラに至るまでのスケールを全て扱えるため、ドヘニー・ランチは、構成要素と全体との関係を表現した作品であった。

タリアセン・ウエストでの結実

> 砂漠は太陽に屈服し岩に覆われた大地である。岩の上に住まうすべての生命は頑強な太陽の生命であり、すべての生命は太陽により死するのだ[25]。

ウィスコンシン州スプリンググリーンのタリアセンをライトの出発点とするならば、アリゾナ州のソノラ砂漠の自邸兼事務所であるタリアセン・ウエストは終着点である[cat. nos. 2-76~82]。ライトは砂漠の地層を「巨人たちの広大なる戦場」と呼び、地形自体が建築的であることに魅了された。砂漠の構造は、柱サボテン〈ベンケイチュウ〉、チョーヤ・カクタス、スタグホーン・カクタスといった植物の形態にも反映されている。それらの細胞構造は「完璧な格子構造」と「溶接された管状構造」といった経済的な建築構造の手本となるからである[26]。

ライトは、タリアセン・ウエストの設計に斜めに角度を振った平面計画を採用し、デザート・メーソンリー(砂漠の石造術)と呼ばれる建築技術によって厳しい自然条件に応えた。タリアセン・ウエストは、建物、中庭、庭園が一体となった複合建築物であり、岩だらけの大地にはめ込まれ、動線はジグザグに蛇行している。そのランドスケープは、日本の回遊式庭園のように歩くことを前提としているため、遠方の山々や噴石丘などのランドマークを捉えながら、曲がるたびにさまざまな眺めや空間が見え隠れした。建物の壁のコンクリートには砂漠の岩石を使用し、丸石、角石、川床で採れた丸い「ガチョウの卵」のような石が埋め込まれている。いずれも長年の湿気と蒸発にさらされて黒や赤の色調に覆われ、周囲の砂漠の「巨大なメサ（台地）の底から立ち上がる大自然の石組み」を再現していた[27]。トスカーナのピエトラ・セレーナと同様に、タリアセン・ウエストで用いた材料は風景と呼応しており、その建築は「建てたというよりも掘り出したかのように見える」とライトに言わしめるほどであった[28]。屋根はキャンバス地のパネルで、通風や日除けのために昇降が可能である。建物全体に点在する巨大な暖炉が唯一の暖房源であり、多種多様な水景が、焼け付く日差しの中に涼やかな冷却要素をもたらしていた。タリアセン・ウエストは、永続性のある砂漠の石造の壁に対して過度的なキャンバス地の屋根、暖を採る火に対して涼をもたらす水、古代遺跡に対して現代的なデザインというように、相反する傾向を均衡関係に保った「両義性の建築」と評されている[29]。

結び

ライトの作品全体には、時代や地域を超えたグローバルな影響や引用が繰り返し現れている。ロサンゼルスのアリーン・バーンズドール（1882–1946）のために建てられた「立葵の家」［cat.no.3-29］と文化施設の計画案は、コロンブス以前のアメリカ大陸の寺院や聖域に見られるピラミッド状の祭壇を想起させる。その防御的な姿は、環太平洋域の地震に対する回答にも見える[30]。ウィスコンシン州マディソンのナコマ・カントリー・クラブ計画案［cat.no.7-47］のデザインは、アメリカ先住民のモチーフが用いられている。タリアセン・ウエストでは、かつてソルト・ヒラ峡谷に住んでいた先史時代のホホカム族が遺したペトログリフ（彫刻入りの岩石）を使用することで、風景の中にある民族的側面に目を向けた[31]。晩年には、イラクのバグダッドとイタリアのヴェネツィアのプロジェクトを設計しており、それぞれが地域特有の文化や自然環境に呼応するものとなっている［cat.no.7-36, 52］。またブロードエーカー・シティ構想と呼ばれる理想郷の計画では、ライトが活動の初期に日本やイタリアにおいて称賛した耕地によってランドスケープのほぼ全体が構成されていた。ライトのアーカイヴにある旅行写真のコレクションからは、こうした世界各地の環境のつながりがそのままにうかがわれる。この写真コレクションは、ライトと共に帝国ホテルの建設にアルバイトで設計に参画した際にライトに出会った土浦亀城・信子の2人が、ライトのロサンゼルスのスタジオで働き、タリアセンにも行った年月のなかでアメリカ南西部の国立公園やランドスケープを旅した記録である［cat.no.5-23］。2人は、その後ライトの下でカリフォルニアのミラード夫人邸などのテキスタイル・ブロック・システムによる住宅の設計に携わった。これらの場所や人々が重なり合う足跡をたどると、ライトがアメリカ建築の理想を前進させると同時に、グローバル化しつつある世界にも深くかかわっていたことが読み取れる。

Baker Brownell and Frank Lloyd Wright, "Architecture and Modern Life" (New York: Harper and Brothers, 1937), p. 17; quoted in Anne Whiston Spirn, "Frank Lloyd Wright: Architect of Landscape" in *Frank Lloyd Wright: Designs for an American Landscape, 1922–1932*, ed. David G. De Long (New York: Harry N. Abrams, Inc., 1996), p. 135.

Frank Lloyd Wright, "In the Cause of Architecture" (1908), repr. In *Frank Lloyd Wright Collected Writings*, vol. 1, ed. Bruce Brooks Pfeiffer (New York: Rizzoli, 1992), p. 87.

Frank Lloyd Wright, "A Philosophy of Fine Art," speech delivered to the Architectural League of the Art Institute of Chicago in 1909; repr. in *Frank Lloyd Wright Collected Writings*, vol. 1, p. 42.

William Cronon, "Inconstant Unity: The Passion of Frank Lloyd Wright," in *Frank Lloyd Wright: Architect*, ed. Terence Riley (New York: The Museum of Modern Art, 1994), pp. 13–16.

Frank Lloyd Wright, "The Japanese Print" (1912), repr. in *Frank Lloyd Wright Collected Writings*, vol. 1, p. 117, 119.

6 Therese O'Malley, "The Floricycle: Designing with Native and Exotic Plants," in *Frank Lloyd Wright: Unpacking the Archive* (New York: The Museum of Modern Art, 2017), pp. 17–19.

7 Frank Lloyd Wright, *An Autobiography* (New York: Barnes & Noble, Inc., 1943), p. 197.

8 Margo Stipe, "Wright's First Trip to Japan," in *Frank Lloyd Wright Quarterly*, v. 6, n. 2 (Spring 1995): pp. 21–22. Also see *Frank Lloyd Wright's Fifty Views of Japan: The 1905 Photo Album*, ed. Melanie Birk, Frank Lloyd Wright Home and Studio Foundation (San Francisco: Pomegranate Artbooks, 1996).

9 Kevin Nute, *Frank Lloyd Wright and Japan: The Role of Traditional Japanese Art and Architecture in the Work of Frank Lloyd Wright* (New York: Van Nostrand Reinhold, 1993), p. 159; Frank Lloyd Wright, "The Print and the Renaissance," 15 November, 1917, Taliesin.

10 Charles E. Aguar and Berdeana Aguar, *Wrightscapes: Frank Lloyd Wright's Landscape Designs* (New York: McGraw-Hill, 2002), pp. 115–117.

11 Frank Lloyd Wright, "Sovereignty of the Individual," preface to the *Ausgeführte Bauten und Entwürfe von Frank Lloyd Wright* (Berlin: Ernst Wasmuth, 1910–11), p. 2.

12 Terence Riley, "The Landscapes of Frank Lloyd Wright: A Pattern of Work," in *Frank Lloyd Wright: Architect*, pp. 99–100.

13 Spirn, "Frank Lloyd Wright: Architect of Landscape" in *Frank Lloyd Wright: Designs for an American Landscape, 1922–1932*, pp. 148–149.

14 Bruce Brooks Pfeiffer, *Letters to Architects* (Fresno: The Press at California State University, 1984) pp. 148–152; quoted in Aguar, *Wrightscapes: Frank Lloyd Wright's Landscape Designs*, p. 139.

15 Aguar, *Wrightscapes: Frank Lloyd Wright's Landscape Designs*, pp. 151–160; 前掲書 註13 論考 pp. 140–145.

16 Aguar, *Wrightscapes: Frank Lloyd Wright's Landscape Designs*, p. 151; Spirn, "Frank Lloyd Wright: Architect of Landscape" in *Frank Lloyd Wright: Designs for an American Landscape, 1922–1932*, p. 145.

17 Aguar, *Wrightscapes: Frank Lloyd Wright's Landscape Designs*, p. 139.

18 Wright, *An Autobiography*, p. 194.

19 Pfeiffer, *Letters to Architects* (1984); quoted in Aguar, *Wrightscapes: Frank Lloyd Wright's Landscape Designs*, p. 139.

20 前掲書 註13 論考 p. 148; Riley, "The Landscape of Frank Lloyd Wright: A Pattern of work" in *Frank Lloyd Wright: Architect*, pp. 96–97.

21 前掲書 註20 論考 p.96.

22 前掲書 註20 論考 pp.97–98; Wright, *An Autobiography*, p. 121.

23 前掲書 註7 p. 213.

24 前掲書 註7 pp. 234–35.

25 前掲書 註7 p. 310.

26 前掲書 註7 pp. 308–314.

27 Wright, *An Autobiography*, p. 309; Spirn, "Frank Lloyd Wright: Architect of Landscape" in *Frank Lloyd Wright: Designs for an American Landscape, 1922–1932*, p. 152.

28 Wright, *An Autobiography*, p. 454.

29 Quentin Béran, "Taliesin West, or the Hymn to Ambivalence," unpublished manuscript, 2023.

30 Neil Levine, *The Architecture of Frank Lloyd Wright* (Princeton, New Jersey: Princeton University Press, 1996), p. 114.

31 Levine, *The Architecture of Frank Lloyd Wright*, p. 263.

The Land is the Simplest Form of Architecture: **Frank Lloyd Wright and Landscape**

Jennifer Gray

Frank Lloyd Wright had a lifelong passion for nature and landscape, often remarking that "Land is the simplest form of architecture."[1] He wrote prolifically on the subject throughout his career—carefully distinguishing between metaphysical concepts of nature and terrestrial landscapes, between abstraction and realism, and between constructed and found environments—and was an experienced architect of landscape. He developed his own theory of organic architecture that looked to nature for design inspiration and attempted to articulate the deep connections between architecture and its environment. Historians have often situated Wright within specific landscapes, primarily that of the Midwestern prairies and later the arid Sonoran Desert of the American southwest, but his engagement with landscape was as global as his architecture. He traveled extensively in Japan and Italy, where he was taken with the landscapes he encountered, especially their integration of architecture, infrastructure, and nature. He brought these lessons back to his work in Chicago, California, Arizona, and specifically to Taliesin and Taliesin West. This essay traces Wright's engagement with nature against the global arc of his architectural practice, demonstrating that for Wright, landscape and architecture were inextricably connected.

Terrestrial Nature

We of the Middle West are living on the prairie. The prairie has a beauty of its own, and we should recognize and accentuate this natural beauty, its quiet level.[2]

Wright is perhaps best known for the "prairie style" houses he built in the early 1900s, such as the Darwin D. Martin House (Buffalo, New York, 1903–05) [cat. nos. 2-22~27], the Coonley House (Riverside, Ill., 1906–09) [cat. nos. 2-28~39], the Booth House (Glencoe, Ill. [project], 1911) [cat. nos. 2-46~48], and the Robie House (Chicago, 1908–10) [cat. nos. 2-41~45], which emphasized the horizontality of the Midwestern landscape through the use of low, hipped roofs, overhanging eaves, and ribbon windows. Ornament in these projects was abstract and geometric, often derived from nature but not mimicking its outward appearance. Wright saw in nature ordering geometries and underlying structure—a kind of architecture—and argued that the artist approximated nature through a process of "conventionalization."[3] These ideas stemmed in part from Wright's study of American transcendentalism and his exposure to the pedagogy of Friedrich Froebel (1782–1852);[4] however, Japanese art, particularly the woodblock print, was another significant source of Wright's philosophy about the relationship between design and nature. Wright was an avid collector and student of Japanese prints, admiring how Japanese artists conventionalized natural forms to create abstract patterns and designs: "Japanese art is a thoroughly structural art...Japanese aesthetics consists in stringent simplification by elimination of the insignificant..."[5]

Yet even as Wright abstracted nature into architectural patterns and geometries, he also engaged with terrestrial nature—living plants, flowers, and trees—to design elaborate gardens and landscapes for many of his prairie houses. To realize the more ambitious landscapes, Wright collaborated with leading landscape architects—such as Jens Jensen (1860–1951), an early environmentalist and advocate of native landscapes, and Walter Burley Griffin (1876–1937), an employee in Wright's Oak Park Studio during these years—most of whom were associated with a "prairie school" of landscape design that emphasized the use of indigenous plants and natural arrangements. In practice, however, they were less orthodox and used native varieties mixed with European and African plants, as well as large numbers of plants from East Asia. Many of the Asian plants were the same species that appear in Japanese woodblock prints: hollyhock, peony, iris, magnolia, viburnum, and honeysuckle. Thus, Wright's passion for Japanese art seems to have carried through to the level of living plants and gardens, aided in part by an emerging global horticultural exchange. It was only in the 1890s that American and Japanese nurseries were sufficiently established in the import-export business to ensure a stable supply of plants.[6]

Capturing Japanese Landscapes

The Japanese house naturally fascinated me...you

couldn't tell where the garden leaves off and the garden begins. I soon ceased to try, too delighted with the problem to attempt to solve it. [7]

In 1905 Wright made his first of seven trips to Japan, where he encountered physical landscapes that he had only known through the woodblock prints he collected. Fascinated with traditional Japanese culture, Wright traveled first to Tokyo and then west through Nagoya, Kyoto, Osaka, Nara, and Kobe to the castle towns of Okayama and Takamatsu on the Seto Inland Sea. During his journey, he explored the country's renowned temples, villages, and especially gardens.[8] He was particularly impressed with the intimate relationship between Japanese architecture and its surroundings—structure and landscape, man-made and natural integrated into seamless wholes—observing that Japanese buildings "like the rocks and trees grew in their places."[9] Water features, whether meditative reflecting pools or powerful waterfalls, and stroll gardens, with their twisting paths and successive views, were especially memorable for Wright. When he returned to the United States in May 1905, Wright began incorporating many of these features into his residential designs. For example, the Coonley House is organized around a series of sunken and raised gardens, terraces, and balconies that surround a reflecting pool, which is "captured alive" in the Japanese tradition and brought into the views of the living room.[10]

From Japan to Italy

No really Italian building seems ill at ease in Italy. All are happily content with what ornament and color they carry naturally. The native rocks and trees and garden slopes are at one with them.[11]

Five years after Wright returned from Japan, he traveled to Italy, first residing in Florence and then in Fiesole, a picturesque medieval town just up the hillside, to prepare the *Ausgeführte Bauten und Entwürfe von Frank Lloyd Wright* (1910–11), also known as the Wasmuth portfolio. As with his experience in Japan, the Italian countryside provided "confirmation" of his ideas about the integration of architecture with its surroundings. Like southern Wisconsin, where Wright spent his childhood summers and would soon build Taliesin, the Tuscan landscape was characterized by farming and stonecutting. The numerous small quarries around Fiesole provided a seemingly endless supply of *pietra serena*, a gray sandstone with many architectural applications—cut into thin slabs as a finish, thick slabs for paving, small blocks for cobbles, and large blocks as raw material for foundations—which gave much of Florence its consistent character. Rustic buildings outside of town relied primarily on stucco finishing mixed with local sand, which imparted earth pigments to the buildings that made entire villages appear to have grown out of the surrounding fields.[12] Photographs Wright took during his sojourn indicate his attraction to the humanely scaled spaces between buildings—courtyards, plazas, gardens, and pergolas—which further blurred the boundaries between inside and outside, architecture and nature.

These experiences, both in Japan and Italy, fully manifested when Wright returned to Spring Green, Wisconsin, to build Taliesin, his home and studio, in 1911. Notched into a hillside just below its crown, Taliesin recalls Italian secular gardens and Japanese domestic architecture in its integration of building and landscape through a series of loggias, retaining walls, sunken courts, enclosed gardens, terraces, water features, and stairways. An exedra-shaped "tea circle," inspired by Japanese precedents, was a focal point connecting these various outdoor rooms and spaces. Water features—dams, ponds, streams, and waterfalls—played a pivotal role in the landscape of Taliesin. Wright continuously redesigned this aquatic terrain: dredging lakebeds, reshaping shorelines, and reconfiguring the dam to produce hydroelectricity and also to create different waterfalls, a sheet of water smoothly flowing over the curved lip of an early dam or later, a cascade splashing over stepped rocks.[13] [cat. no. 2-5] Long before he designed his masterpiece, Edgar J. Kaufmann House (Fallingwater) [cat. nos. 2-67, 68], in Mill Run, Pennsylvania (1934–37), Wright explored the magic of waterfalls, perhaps due to his initial encounters with this natural phenomenon in Japan.

Productive Landscapes

When you see Italy, when you see the fields...you see how cultivation, tillage, is architecture...how it makes a pattern.[14]

Beyond the cultivated landscapes adjacent to Taliesin were wild landscapes of long grasses and trees, but also productive landscapes, such as an orchard, vineyard, and working farm.[15] The latter were planted following traditions of grid tillage in Fiesole and contour tillage in Japan, creating abstract patterns of color and texture that people reportedly drove by to view.[16] Indeed, when Wright discoursed on his impressions of foreign landscapes, he made little reference to the gardens, villages, or natural features of Italy or Japan, but to the tillage of the land.[17] In Japan, Wright observed that "the cultivated fields [rise] tier on tier to still higher terraced vegetable fields, green dotted"[18] and in Italy, "you see how cultivation, tillage, is architecture...how it makes a pattern."[19]

The importance of farming for Wright cannot be underestimated. Born into a farming family, Wright's childhood was spent in agricultural communities. Farming at this time was considered a virtuous activity, an association sanctioned by Wright's uncle, Jenkin Lloyd Jones (1843–1918), a farmer and well-regarded Unitarian minister, in a series of sermons he delivered on topics such as plowing, sowing, weeding, reaping, tree planting, reforestation, and barn building that he collected under the title *The Gospel of the Farm*.[20] Life at Taliesin combined rural living with intellectual pursuit, thus tapping into a rich tradition of American "gentleman farmers," such as Thomas Jefferson (1743–1826), and transcendentalist philosophers, such as Ralph Waldo Emerson (1803–1882). Indeed, the term *cultivated* applies to both Taliesin and its owner, Wright, as it bridges the distinction between culture and agriculture.[21] Rows of corn, grains, and other crops imparted a pattern to the landscape around Taliesin that was determined by new machinery—reapers, seeders, cultivators, threshing machines, saws, hayracks, and the like—that revolutionized farming in the nineteenth century. The four-by-four foot grid that Wright perceived in the landscape was directly related to the spacing of the tiller blades and how closely a team of horses could be hitched to pull machinery through the fields. The grid of the farm signified the process of work, not an abstraction: "The gaily painted reaper, pulled by three white horses, cuts its way around, round after round...the entire field is becoming a linear pattern of Work."[22] The grid, of course, also organizes architectural design, thus providing Wright a way to understand both the work of farming and building, the landscape and architecture.

Building on the Pacific Rim

The dreaded force that made the great mountain, continually takes its toll...shores are reversed as mountains are laid low and valleys lifted up.[23]

Wright's ideas about landscape, first imported to the Midwest from Japan and Italy, were soon repackaged and exported back to Tokyo when Wright began to design the Imperial Hotel in 1913. Terraces, loggias, porticos, promenades, and other indoor-outdoor spaces serve as the connective tissue between different zones of the hotel, often overlooking Japanese gardens installed in the interior courtyards of the building. Water features appear throughout the property, from the meandering streams in the gardens to the large reflection pool at the entrance. Wright used a common material called Oya stone throughout the hotel. The porous, volcanic stone unique to the Oya region was used for a variety of applications in Japan, such as roadways, sidewalks, and buildings, not unlike the *pietra serena* he encountered in Tuscany.

On the other side of the Pacific Rim, in California, Wright tailored these experiments for the arid, sun-drenched climate of Los Angeles when he designed the first of his concrete textile-block houses in the 1920s, such as the Millard House (*La Miniatura*) (1923–24) [cat. nos. 5-20~22] and the Ennis House (1924). The architect's embrace of concrete surely owed something to his encounters with *pietra serena* and Oya stone, both affordable, abundant materials in their respective regions. According to Wright,

"Concrete was the cheapest (and ugliest) thing in the building world. Why not see what could be done with that gutter-rat? It might be permanent, noble, beautiful."[24] Concrete, as a material, is arguably universal, but Wright attempted to localize it in the California textile-block projects by using soil from the building site in the aggregate when casting the blocks. In this way, the building materials were fused with their environment in a strategy not unlike the rustic stucco buildings around Fiesole. The integration of landscape, infrastructure, and architecture was especially remarkable in an unbuilt project called Doheny Ranch Development (1923) [cat. nos. 5-27~31], where a terraced megastructure incorporates housing, walled gardens, and landscaped roof terraces linked together by a stabilizing system of bridges and roadways—all made from the same concrete block—capable of negotiating the ridge-ravine topography of the Los Angeles Basin. Because the concrete blocks could scale from a single block to infrastructure, Doheny Ranch was a genuine expression of parts relating to the whole.

Culminating at Taliesin West

Desert is rock-bound-earth prostrate to the sun. All life there above the crystal is tenacious sun-life. All life there dies a sun-death.[25]

If Taliesin in Spring Green, Wisconsin, marks a beginning for Wright, its bookend and counterpoint is Taliesin West, his home and studio in the Sonoran Desert of Arizona [cat. nos. 2-76~82]. Wright was enamored with the stratified geological environment of the desert—calling it a "vast battleground of titanic forces"—because its very terrain appeared architectural. The tectonics of the desert extended to its plant forms, especially the saguaro, cholla, and staghorn cactuses, because their cellular structure offered lessons in economical construction, such as "the perfect lattice...and welded tubular construction."[26]

Wright responded to these conditions by introducing diagonal planning into the design of Taliesin West and through a construction technique called desert masonry. Taliesin West is an integrated complex of buildings, courtyards, and gardens notched into the rocky earth in which lines of movement zig and zag. As in a Japanese stroll garden, Taliesin West is a landscape meant to be walked through, with repeated turns revealing episodic views and spaces, all the while "capturing" views of the mountains, cinder cones, and other landmarks in the distance. The walls of the compound are concrete made from desert rocks—boulders, sharp-edged stones, and rounded "goose eggs" from the wash, all varnished in black and red tones from years of exposure to moisture and evaporation—that reproduce the appearance of "the great nature-masonry we see rising from the great mesa floors" of the surrounding desert.[27] Not unlike the *pietra serena* of Tuscany, the materials of Taliesin West resonate with its landscape, so much so that, according to Wright, its architecture "looked more like something we had been excavating, not building."[28] Roofs were canvas panels that could be raised and lowered to capture breezes or shade the sun; massive fireplaces scattered across the complex provided the only heat source; and various water features introduced a refreshing, cooling element to the otherwise sun-seared environment. Taliesin West has been described as an "architecture of ambiguity" for the way it holds contradictory tendencies in tension: the permanence of the desert masonry walls versus the ephemeral nature of the canvas roofs; fires for warmth and water for coolness; and ancient ruin or modern design.[29]

Conclusion

Global references and influences continued to reverberate throughout Wright's career, spanning time and geography. The cultural center and Hollyhock House for Aline Barnsdall (1882–1946) in Los Angeles (1923) recalls the pyramidal, hieratic shapes of Pre-Columbian temples and sanctuaries, its defensive posture interpreted as a reaction to the unstable, seismic conditions of the Pacific Rim.[30] American Indian motifs inform the design of the Nakoma Country Club (project, 1923–24) [cat. no. 7-47] in Madison, Wisconsin. At Taliesin West, Wright considered the ethnographic aspects of the landscape when he incorporated petroglyph boulders made by the prehistoric Hohokam tribes who had inhabited the Salt-Gila Valley long before.[31] Towards the end of his career, Wright designed projects in Baghdad, Iraq [cat. no. 7-52], and Venice, Italy [cat. no. 7-36], both of which responded to their unique cultural and natural environments, as well as a utopian vision called Broadacre City, the landscape of which is organized almost entirely by the tillage Wright had so admired in Japan and Italy at the beginning of his career. A collection of travel snapshots in Wright's archive captures the literal connections between these global environments. They document Kameki and Nobuko Tsuchiura, two designers who met Wright when Kameki worked part-time on the Imperial Hotel in Japan, traveling through the national parks and landscapes of the American Southwest while working for Wright on textile-block houses in Los Angeles and also visiting Taliesin in Wisconsin. As these places and people overlap, their paths show that Wright was simultaneously advancing an ideal about American architecture and deeply engaged with a globalizing world.

1 Baker Brownell and Frank Lloyd Wright, "Architecture and Modern Life" (New York: Harper and Brothers, 1937), p. 17; quoted in Anne Whiston Spirn, "Frank Lloyd Wright: Architect of Landscape," in *Frank Lloyd Wright: Designs for an American Landscape, 1922-1932*, ed. David G. De Long (New York: Harry N. Abrams, Inc., 1996), p. 135.
2 Frank Lloyd Wright, "In the Cause of Architecture" (1908), repr. in *Frank Lloyd Wright: Collected Writings*, vol. 1, ed. Bruce Brooks Pfeiffer (New York: Rizzoli, 1992), p. 87.
3 Frank Lloyd Wright, "A Philosophy of Fine Art," speech delivered to the Architectural League of the Art Institute of Chicago in 1909; repr. in *Frank Lloyd Wright: Collected Writings*, vol. 1, p. 42.
4 William Cronon, "Inconstant Unity: The Passion of Frank Lloyd Wright," in *Frank Lloyd Wright: Architect*, ed. Terence Riley (New York: The Museum of Modern Art, 1994), pp. 13–16.
5 Frank Lloyd Wright, "The Japanese Print" (1912), repr. in *Frank Lloyd Wright: Collected Writings*, vol. 1, p. 117, 119.
6 Therese O'Malley, "The Floricycle: Designing with Native and Exotic Plants," in *Frank Lloyd Wright: Unpacking the Archive* (New York: The Museum of Modern Art, 2017), pp. 17–19.
7 Frank Lloyd Wright, *An Autobiography* (New York: Barnes & Noble, Inc., 1943), p. 197.
8 Margo Stipe, "Wright's First Trip to Japan," in *Frank Lloyd Wright Quarterly*, v. 6, n. 2 (Spring 1995): pp. 21-22. Also see *Frank Lloyd Wright's Fifty Views of Japan: The 1905 Photo Album*, ed. Melanie Birk and Frank Lloyd Wright Home and Studio Foundation (San Francisco: Pomegranate Artbooks, 1996).
9 Kevin Nute, *Frank Lloyd Wright and Japan: The Role of Traditional Japanese Art and Architecture in the Work of Frank Lloyd Wright* (New York: Van Nostrand Reinhold, 1993), p. 159; Frank Lloyd Wright, "The Print and the Renaissance," 15 November, 1917, Taliesin.
10 Charles E. Aguar and Berdeana Aguar, *Wrightscapes: Frank Lloyd Wright's Landscape Designs* (New York: McGraw-Hill, 2002), pp. 115–117.
11 Frank Lloyd Wright, "Sovereignty of the Individual," preface to the *Ausgeführte Bauten und Entwürfe von Frank Lloyd Wright* (Berlin: Ernst Wasmuth, 1910–11), p. 2.
12 Terence Riley, "The Landscapes of Frank Lloyd Wright: A Pattern of Work," in *Frank Lloyd Wright: Architect*, pp. 99–100.
13 Spirn, "Frank Lloyd Wright: Architect of Landscape," in *Frank Lloyd Wright: Designs for an American Landscape, 1922-1932*, pp. 148–149.
14 Bruce Brooks Pfeiffer, *Letters to Architects* (Fresno: The Press at California State University, 1984), pp. 148–152; quoted in Aguar, *Wrightscapes*, p. 139.
15 Aguar, *Wrightscapes*, pp. 151–160; Spirn, "Frank Lloyd Wright: Architect of Landscape," in *Frank Lloyd Wright: Designs for an American Landscape, 1922-1932*, p. 145.
16 Aguar, *Wrightscapes*, p. 151; Spirn, "Frank Lloyd Wright: Architect of Landscape," in *Frank Lloyd Wright: Designs for an American Landscape, 1922-1932*, p. 145.
17 Aguar, *Wrightscapes*, p. 139.
18 Wright, *An Autobiography*, p. 194.
19 Pfeiffer, *Letters to Architects*, pp. 148–152; quoted in Aguar, *Wrightscapes*, p. 139.
20 Spirn, "Frank Lloyd Wright: Architect of Landscape," in *Frank Lloyd Wright: Designs for an American Landscape, 1922-1932*, p. 148; Riley, "The Landscapes of Frank Lloyd Wright: A Pattern of Work," in *Frank Lloyd Wright: Architect*, pp. 96–97.
21 Riley, "The Landscapes of Frank Lloyd Wright: A Pattern of Work," in *Frank Lloyd Wright: Architect*, p. 96.
22 Riley, "The Landscapes of Frank Lloyd Wright: A Pattern of Work," in *Frank Lloyd Wright: Architect*, pp. 97–98; Wright, *An Autobiography*, p. 121.
23 Wright, *An Autobiography*, p. 213.
24 Ibid., pp. 234–35.
25 Ibid., p. 310.
26 Ibid., pp. 308-314.
27 Wright, *An Autobiography*, p. 309; Spirn, "Frank Lloyd Wright: Architect of Landscape," in *Frank Lloyd Wright: Designs for an American Landscape, 1922-1932*, p. 152.
28 Wright, *An Autobiography*, p. 454.
29 Quentin Béran, "Taliesin West, or the Hymn to Ambivalence," unpublished manuscript, 2023.
30 Neil Levine, *The Architecture of Frank Lloyd Wright* (Princeton, New Jersey: Princeton University Press, 1996), p. 114.
31 Levine, *Architecture of Frank Lloyd Wright*, p. 263.

SECTION 1

モダン誕生
シカゴ–東京、浮世絵的世界観

Modern Beginnings:
Chicago – Tokyo and the Culture of Ukiyo-e

1

フランク・ロイド・ライトによる帝国ホテルのデザインは、19世紀末から20世紀初めにかけて近代都市として台頭したシカゴと東京との対話の中から生まれた。明治維新に伴い1868年に江戸が東京に改称され、近代的な首都へと変貌していったのと同じ頃、シカゴはアメリカ中西部最大の中心都市となった。それは、1871年のシカゴ大火からの復興事業を追い風に、進歩時代における都市美運動である1909年のシカゴの都市計画「バーナム・プラン」[cat. no. 1-4]に想を得ていた。ライトは、ウィスコンシン州立大学で1年間学んだ後、1887年にシカゴに移住すると、建築事務所での実務経験を求めて、住宅建築で著名なジョセフ・ライマン・シルスビーと、さらにダンクマール・アドラーとルイス・サリヴァンの事務所で建築家としての道を歩み始めた。ライトは、アドラー＆サリヴァンの代表作の一つであるオーディトリアム・ビルの内部空間[cat. no. 1-6]のデザインに携わった。彼はまた、石積みと鋼鉄と鋳鉄という異なる素材を組み合わせた、ダニエル・バーナム(1846-1900)とジョン・ルート(1850-91)のルッカリー・ビル(1888)や、巨大な板ガラス窓のある初の鉄骨フレーム高層ビル、リライアンス・ビル(1890-95)[cat. no. 1-7]が建ち上がるのも目撃した。そして1905年には、ルッカリー・ビルの天窓つき2層吹き抜けロビーの改修を手がけ[cat. no. 1-5]、シカゴに彼独自の足跡を残した。

その頃東京では、ドイツの建築家エンデ＆ベックマンが、1887年の都市計画のなかで東京の行政区域を再編成するための壮大な構想を提言した[cat. nos. 1-16, 17]。東京とシカゴはどちらもドイツの建築文化と深いつながりをもっていた。都市計画自体は実現しなかったものの、彼らが担当した新古典主義様式による庁舎は、かつての江戸の町並みを一変させた。イギリス人建築家ジョサイア・コンドル(1852-1920)が手がけた東京・日比谷の中心地にある2階建てのフランス系のルネサンス様式の迎賓館、鹿鳴館(1883)、続いてエンデ＆ベックマン由来のマンサード屋根を持つ初代帝国ホテル(1890)[cat. no. 1-27]、そして日本初の近代公園とされる日比谷公園(1903)。丸の内中心部の開発は、辰野金吾(1854-1919)設計によるネオ・バロック様式の鉄骨煉瓦造建築、東京駅の完成(1914)によって頂点に達した。

ライトと日本のデザイン文化との関わりは1893年のシカゴ万博を背景に生まれた。そこにはミシガン湖の浅瀬に浮かぶように建つパビリオン、鳳凰殿[cat. no. 1-11]があった。時はジャポニスムの時代であり、日本の「浮世絵」に魅了された時代であった。ライトはシルスビーやサリヴァンなど、東洋美術愛好者たちの輪に触れた。そして、1896年に出版した『ハウス・ビューティフル』[cat. no. 2-12]のなかで、草や野の花の写真を通して、浮世絵についての彼自身の解釈を披露した。和紙にコロタイプ印刷したそれらの写真は、彼がコレクションしていた歌川広重の《撫子に蝶》(1836-40)[cat. no. 2-13]と強く共鳴している[1]。さらに、1902年ごろに撮影した、ウィスコンシンのスプリンググリー

1 Julia Meech, *Frank Lloyd Wright and the Art of Japan*, (New York: Japan Society / Harry N. Abrams, 2001) pp. 35-37; and W. C. Gannett et al., *The House Beautiful* (River Forest, Ill.: Auvergne Press, 1896).

2 同書、pp. 37-40、および Melanie Birk, ed., *Frank Lloyd Wright's Fifty Views of Japan: The 1905 Photo Album* (San Francisco: Pomegranate, 1996).

3 1956年2月5日、タリアセン・ウエストの日曜の朝の浮世絵パーティーでの会話の記録。前掲書 註1, pp. 38より

ン近郊の雪景色[cat. nos. 2-1, 2]は、日本の巻物に描かれた墨絵のミニマルな構成を彷彿させ、こうした芸術観へのライトの熱い思いを強く示している。

日本の風景や伝統的な建築構造に対するライトの関心は、1905年の7週間に及ぶ日本旅行を通してさらに深まった[2]。この旅によって彼は、建物を周囲の山々や森と相まったダイナミックな空間として理解するようになり、「大いに勉強になる経験だった」と記している[3]。

ライトはまた、日本からアメリカへの帰国にあたり、コレクターとして、教師として、またディーラーとして、彼自身が言うところの日本美術への「執着」も発揮した[4]。ライトは数百枚に及ぶ広重の浮世絵をシカゴに持ち帰ると、1906年3月にシカゴ美術館で展示をし、日本の浮世絵についての最初のエッセイも出版した[5][cat. no. 1-74]。この熱烈な関心に導かれ、ライトは、浮世絵のコレクターであり、帝国ホテルの依頼にライトを推薦したとされるフレデリック・ウィリアム・グーキンと出会った[6]。ライトはまた、施主たちに自邸に浮世絵を飾るよう熱心に勧めた[7]。1908年3月にはシカゴ美術館でより大規模な二度目の浮世絵展を開き、空間に合うように縦長にフレーミングした、イリノイ州オークパークにある自邸のハイバック・チェアにも通じる特別な展示台もデザインした[cat. no. 1-77]。この展覧会はグーキンが企画し、展示空間はライトが手がけ、作品を見やすい位置に配置したベンチの上に、レールから浮世絵を吊るす展示システムを考案した。ライトはさらに、ウィリアム・スポールディングのための浮世絵ギャラリー(1914)[cat. no. 1-76]や、シカゴにあるファイン・アート・ビルの室内を改装して設けられたモリ東洋美術ギャラリー(1914)などのデザインでこれらのアイデアを発展させた。いずれの例においても、ライトは浮世絵を的確に見せることに注力して空間全体を設計しており、キャビネット、ピクチャーレール、布地、漆喰の壁、絨毯、そしてヘリット・リートフェルトによるデ・ステイルの椅子デザインを先取りしたような驚くほどミニマルな四角い椅子によって構成されていた。このシカゴにおけるライトの「総合芸術」は、住宅デザインにおける窓と同じように、自然の事物を切り取る芸術的な視点をもち、同時期に行った東京の帝国ホテルのデザインと対をなす。

ライトはキャリアの始まりから、有機的な幾何学装飾というサリヴァンの概念から想を得ていた。サリヴァンのウェインライト家の墓(1892)[cat. nos. 1-36, 37]で体現されたように、円/正方形/立方体といった基本形態は、葉やチューリップなどのモチーフを石で抽象化し、2次元や3次元で表現したものである。この考えは、オーウェン・ジョーンズ(1809-74)の『装飾の文法』(1856)とサリヴァンが彼独自の『建築装飾の体系』(1924)[cat. no. 1-39]で示した、19世紀の自然と装飾の考えに基づくものであった。

4 前掲書 註1 pp. 37–103.

5 Frank Lloyd Wright, *Hiroshige: An Exhibition of Colour Prints from the Collection of Frank Lloyd Wright* (Chicago: Art Institute of Chicago, 1906).

6 グーキンは、1911年の上半期に新しい帝国ホテルの建設計画について耳にしている。Kathryn Smith, "Frank Lloyd Wright and the Imperial Hotel: A Postscript," *Art Bulletin* (June 1, 1985), p. 297.

7 前掲書 註1 p. 55.

Modern Beginnings: Chicago–Tokyo and the Culture of Ukiyo-e

Frank Lloyd Wright's Imperial Hotel design emerged amidst a dialogue between Chicago and Tokyo, both developing as modern metropolises in the late nineteenth and early twentieth centuries. In the same years that Edo was renamed Tokyo in 1868 with the Meiji Restoration unleashing its transformation as a modern capital, Chicago became the largest urban center in the American Midwest. Transformed by reconstruction after the 1871 Great Chicago Fire, the city evolved again in response to the 1909 "Burnham" Plan of Chicago [cat. no. 1-4], that proposed to rationalize and beautify the city in the Progressive Era. Wright arrived in Chicago in 1887 after leaving his one-year of study at the University of Wisconsin. Seeking architectural office training, he apprenticed for an esteemed residential architect, Joseph Lyman Silsbee, and for the firm of Dankmar Adler and Louis Sullivan. Wright worked on some of the interior design of the Auditorium Building (1889) [cat. no. 1-6], one of the masterworks of Adler and Sullivan. He also witnessed the rise of Daniel Burnham (1846–1900) and John Root's hybrid masonry/steel/iron Rookery Building (1888) and Root's Reliance Building (1895) [cat. no. 1-7], the first steel-framed tall building with large plate glass windows. Wright subsequently made his own mark on Chicago, redesigning the Rookery's two-story, sky-lit lobby in 1905 [cat. no. 1-5].

Meanwhile, in Tokyo, the German architects Ende and Böckmann proposed their own visionary plan for reorganizing the governmental center of Tokyo in their 1887 plan [cat. nos. 1-16, 17]. Tokyo and Chicago were both closely tied to German design culture. While the urban plan itself was not realized, neoclassical government buildings transformed the former Edo urbanscape: Rokumeikan (1883), a two-story French Renaissance-style party palace in Tokyo's central Hibiya district designed by British architect Josiah Conder; Imperial Hotel (1890) [cat. no. 1-27], the first building with mansard roofs that can be traced back to Ende and Böckmann; and Hibiya Park as Japan's first modern park (1903). The central Marunouchi district reached an apex with the completion of Kingo Tatsuno's neo-baroque Tokyo Station (1914), employing steel frame to support its brick construction.

Wright's interchange with Japanese design culture emerged in the context of the 1893 Chicago World's Fair, which featured the Ho-o-den pavilion [cat. no. 1-11], located on a wooded isle in a lagoon nearby Lake Michigan. This was the age of *Japonisme* and fascination with Japanese *ukiyo-e* (floating world) prints. Wright was exposed to a circle of Asian art enthusiasts, including Silsbee and Sullivan. Wright expressed his own interpretation of Japanese prints in his 1896 book *The House Beautiful* [cat. no. 2-12] through his photographs of weeds and wildflowers—photogravures on Japanese paper strongly resonant with Utagawa Hiroshige's *Nadeshiko (Pink) Butterfly and Poem* (1836–40) [cat. no. 2-13] from his own collection.[1] Soon after, he created a series of collotypes, around 1902, of snow-covered landscapes around Spring Green, Wisconsin, that recall the

1 Julia Meech, *Frank Lloyd Wright and the Art of Japan*, (New York: Japan Society / Harry N. Abrams, 2001), 35–37; and W. C. Gannett et al., *The House Beautiful* (River Forest: Auvergne Press, 1896).

2 Meech, 37–40; and Melanie Birk, ed., *Frank Lloyd Wright's Fifty Views of Japan: The 1905 Photo Album* (San Francisco: Pomegranate, 1996).

3 Transcript of a Sunday morning ukiyo-e party talk, Taliesin West, Scottsdale, Arizona, February 5, 1956. FLWA, quoted in Meech, 38, 273n29.

4 Meech, pp. 37–103.

minimal composition of Japanese ink paintings on hand scrolls, underscoring his passion for this artistic view [cat. nos. 2-1, 2].

Wright's interest in Japanese landscapes and traditional structures deepened during the seven weeks he spent traveling throughout Japan in 1905.[2] This journey provided a dynamic spatial understanding of buildings in the context of surrounding mountains and forests, which he noted as "a great educational experience."[3]

Wright also pursued his self-described "obsession" with Japanese art as a collector, teacher, and dealer from Japan back to America.[4] He returned to Chicago with several hundred Hiroshige prints, which he exhibited in March 1906 at the Art Institute of Chicago, and also published his first essay on Japanese prints [cat. no. 1-74].[5] Wright's intense interest led him to meet an avid Japanese print collector, Frederick William Gookin, who is thought to have suggested Wright for the Imperial Hotel commission.[6] Wright also encouraged his clients to hang Japanese prints on the walls of their homes.[7] In March 1908, for the second and even larger exhibition of ukiyo-e prints at the Art Institute, Wright designed special stands—akin to his high-backed dining chairs from his home in Oak Park, Illinois—that vertically framed Japanese prints tailored to fit the space [cat. no. 1-77]. Gookin organized this later exhibition, and Wright designed the exhibition space using its system of hanging prints from the rail above the precisely placed benches. Wright developed further iterations of these ideas in designs such as the Japanese Print Gallery for William Spaulding (project, Boston, 1914) [cat. no. 1-76] and the Mori Oriental Art Studio (1914), a remodeled interior in the Fine Art Building in Chicago. In both instances, he designed the entire space around the precise viewing of prints by composing the cabinets, picture rails, fabrics, carpets, and plaster for the walls, as well as the remarkably minimal square chair design that predates the *de Stijl* furniture designs of Gerrit Rietveld. The window designs of Wright's residential projects, with their framed artistic views of natural subjects, reflected the spirit of *Gesamtkunstwerk*. Thus, Wright provided a counterpoint in Chicago to his concurrent design for the Imperial Hotel in Tokyo.

From the outset of his career, Wright found inspiration in Sullivan's conception of organic geometric ornament. As embodied in Sullivan's Wainwright tomb (1892) [cat. nos. 1-36, 37], the primary forms of the circle, square, and cube were expressed in two and three dimensions, such as in the abstraction of leaf and tulip motifs in stone. This conception was based on nineteenth-century ideas of nature and ornament that Owen Jones (1809–74) disseminated in *Grammar of Ornament* (1856) [cat. no. 1-40] and Sullivan in his book *A System of Architectural Ornament according with a Philosophy of Man's Powers* (1924).

[Ken Tadashi Oshima]

5 Frank Lloyd Wright, *Hiroshige: An Exhibition of Colour Prints from the Collection of Frank Lloyd Wright* (Chicago: Art Institute of Chicago, 1906).

6 Gookin heard about the proposal to build a new Imperial Hotel by the first half of 1911. Kathryn Smith, "Frank Lloyd Wright and the Imperial Hotel: A Postscript," *Art Bulletin* (June 1, 1985): p. 297.

7 Meech, p. 55.

1-1

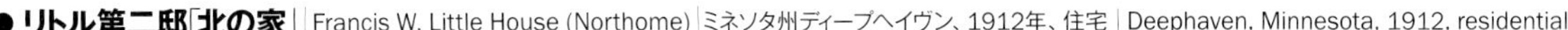

● リトル第二邸「北の家」| Francis W. Little House (Northome) | ミネソタ州ディープヘイヴン、1912年、住宅 | Deephaven, Minnesota, 1912, residential

1-2

1-1　フランク・ロイド・ライト、タリアセンにて | 撮影者不詳 | 撮影:1924年
1-2　リトル第二邸「北の家」窓ガラス | デザイン:フランク・ロイド・ライト、製作:テンプル・アート・グラス・カンパニー | 1912年

1-1　Portrait of Frank Lloyd Wright at Taliesin, Spring Green, Wisconsin. Photographer unidentified. Photo: 1924. Personal and Taliesin Fellowship photographs, 1870s-2004, The Frank Lloyd Wright Foundation Archives (The Museum of Modern Art | Avery Architectural & Fine Arts Library, Columbia University, New York)
1-2　Art Glass Windows from the Francis W. Little House (Northome). Frank Lloyd Wright, designer. Temple Art Glass Company, manufacturer. 1912. Toyota Municipal Museum of Art

1 モダン都市シカゴ

Chicago, the modern metropolis

1-3

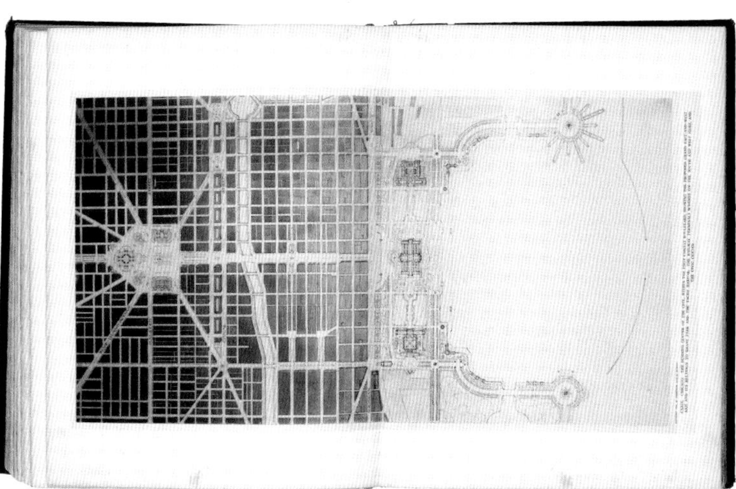

1-4

1-5

1-6

1-7

1-3　1871年のシカゴ大火後の空撮｜撮影：ショー｜1871年

1-4　『シカゴ計画』(バーナム・プラン)｜著：ダニエル・バーナム、エドワード・H. ベネット、図版：ジュール・ゲラン、出版：シカゴ商業クラブ｜1909年

1-5　ルッカリー・ビル(イリノイ州シカゴ)エントランスホール｜建築：バーナム＆ルート、改修：フランク・ロイド・ライト｜撮影：1893年

1-6　オーディトリアム・ビル(イリノイ州シカゴ)南西からの外観｜建築：アドラー＆サリヴァン、撮影：J.W. テイラー｜1897年

1-7　リライアンス・ビル(イリノイ州シカゴ)｜建築：チャールズ・アトウッド(バーナム設計事務所)、撮影：バーンズ・クロスビー社｜1897–1904年

1-3　Aerial view of ruins after the Chicago Fire of 1871. Shaw, photographer. Photo: 1871. Chicago History Museum, ICHi-059803

1-4　*Plan of Chicago* (Burnham Plan). Daniel Burnham and Edward H. Bennett, authors. Jules Guerin, lithographer. Commercial Club of Chicago, publisher. 1909. Engineering Bldg. 1 Library A (Civil Engineering), Libraries for Engineering and Information Science & Technology, The University of Tokyo

1-5　Interior view of the Rookery Building entrance hall, Chicago, Illinois. Burnham & Root, architects. Frank Lloyd Wright, renovator. Photographer unidentified. Photo: 1893. Chicago History Museum, ICHi-017281

1-6　Auditorium Building, Chicago, Illinois. Exterior view from the southwest. Adler & Sullivan, architects. J. W. Taylor, photographer. Photo: 1897. Chicago History Museum, ICHi-018768

1-7　Reliance Building, Chicago, Illinois. Charles Atwood of D. H. Burnham & Company, architect. Barnes-Crosby Company, photographer. Photo: 1897-1904. Chicago History Museum, ICHi-001066

1 モダン都市シカゴ

Chicago, the modern metropolis

シカゴ万国博覧会と鳳凰殿 | Chicago World's Fair and Ho-o-den

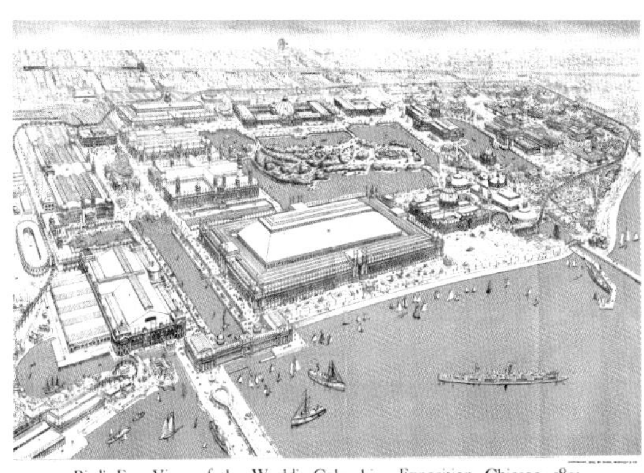

1-8

1-9
1-10

1-11
1-13

1-15

1-8 シカゴ万国博覧会 鳥瞰絵図 | 製作:ランド・マクナリー社 | 1893年
1-9 シカゴ万国博覧会 コート・オブ・オナーの大人工池の西端からの眺望 | 撮影者不詳 | 1893年
1-10 シカゴ万国博覧会 交通館 | 撮影:C.P. ラムフォード | 1893年
1-11 シカゴ万国博覧会日本館 鳳凰殿 | 撮影:1893年
1-13 『閣龍世界博覧会 美術品画譜 第弐集』 | 画・著:久保田米僊 | 1893-94年
1-15 『閣龍世界博覧会 美術品画譜 第四集』 | 画・著:久保田米僊 | 1893-94年

1-8 Map of a bird's-eye view of the 1893 Chicago World's Fair, Chicago, Illinois. Rand McNally & Co., creator. 1893. Chicago History Museum, ICHi-025161
1-9 1893 Chicago World's Fair, Chicago, Illinois. View across west end of Great Basin in the Court of Honor. Photographer unidentified. Photo: 1893. Chicago History Museum, ICHi-025057
1-10 1893 Chicago World's Fair, Chicago, Illinois. Transportation Building. C. P. Rumford, photographer. Photo: 1893. Chicago History Museum, ICHi-170223
1-11 1893 Chicago World's Fair, Chicago, Illinois. The Japanese Pavillion. Photo: 1893. Imperial Hotel
1-13 *Report on Chicago Columbian World Fair. Volume 2*. Beisen Kubota, artist. 1893-94. Yoshino Gypsum Art Foundation
1-15 *Report on Chicago Columbian World Fair. Volume 4*. Beisen Kubota, artist. 1893-94. Yoshino Gypsum Art Foundation

2 モダン都市東京

Tokyo, the modern metropolis

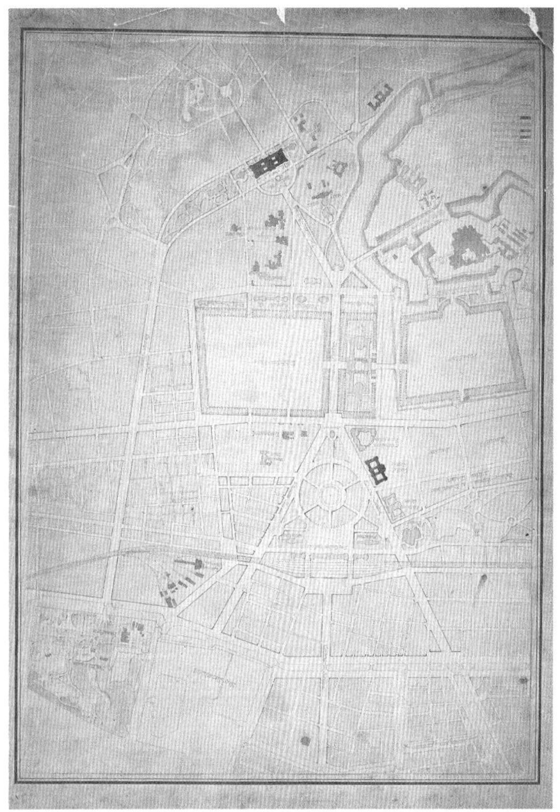

1-16

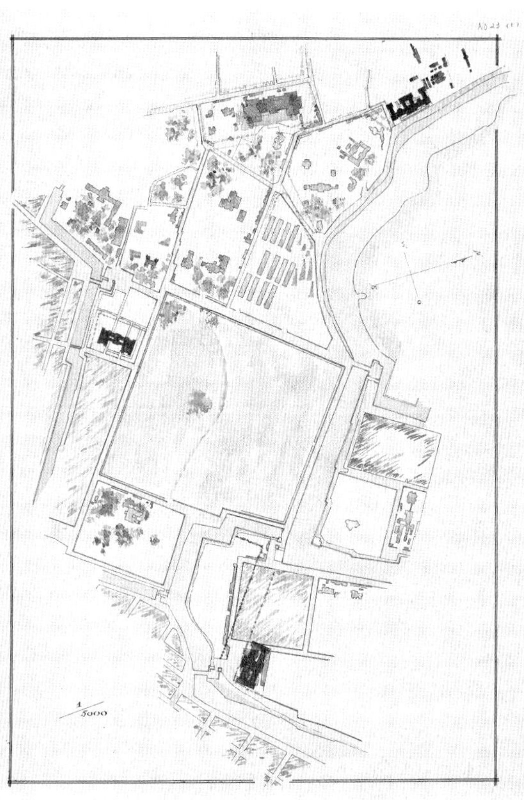

1-17

1-18

1-19
1-25
1-26

1-27
1-28
1-29

1-30
1-31
1-34

1-16　官庁集中計画エンデ&ベックマン 第一案｜計画：ヘルマン・エンデ&ヴィルヘルム・ベックマン｜1886年
1-17　官庁集中計画エンデ&ベックマン 第二案｜計画：ヘルマン・エンデ&ヴィルヘルム・ベックマン｜1887年
1-18　諸官庁新築眺望図『Arkitekten, Ende&Böckmann』｜ヘルマン・エンデ&ヴィルヘルム・ベックマン｜1886年
1-19　絵葉書 東京名所 東京駅（1914年）
1-25　絵葉書 東京名所 警視庁（1911年）
1-26　絵葉書 丸の内より俯瞰せる日比谷公園扞に霞が関諸官庁
1-27　絵葉書 東京名所 帝国ホテル（一代目、1890年）
1-28　絵葉書 東京名所 日比谷公園正門（1903年）
1-29　絵葉書 東京名所 日比谷公園音楽堂（1905年）
1-30　絵葉書 大東京高架鉄道より据然たる帝国ホテル（1923年）を望む
1-31　絵葉書 東京 桜田門
1-34　絵葉書 米国貴賓一行新橋停車場着之光景

1-16　Ende & Böckmann Plan. Proposal for a new monumental center in Tokyo. (1).
Hermann Ende and Wilhelm Böckmann, architects. 1886. Japan Architectural Institute
1-17　Ende & Böckmann Plan. Proposal for a new monumental center in Tokyo. (2).
Hermann Ende and Wilhelm Böckmann, architects. 1887. Japan Architectural Institute
1-18　Ende Böckmann Plan. Proposal for a new monumental center for Tokyo. Aerial view.
From the series *Arkitekten, Ende & Böckmann*. Hermann Ende and Wilhelm Böckmann. 1886. Japan Architectural Institute
1-19　Postcard. Tokyo Station, 1914. The Famous Views of Tokyo. Hideki Watanabe Collection
1-25　Postcard. The Metropolitan Police Office, 1911. The Famous Views of Tokyo. Hideki Watanabe Collection
1-26　Postcard. Kasumigaseki Governmental Buildings and Hibiya Park Seen from Marunouchi. Hideki Watanabe Collection
1-27　Postcard. Imperial Hotel (1st building), 1890. The Famous Views of Tokyo. Hideki Watanabe Collection
1-28　Postcard. Main Gate of the Hibiya Park, 1903. The Famous Views of Tokyo. Hideki Watanabe Collection
1-29　Postcard. Music Hall in Hibiya Park, 1905. The Famous Views of Tokyo. Hideki Watanabe Collection
1-30　Postcard. View of the Magnificient Teikoku (Imperial) Hotel Building, 1923. Looking from the Elevated Railway. Hideki Watanabe Collection
1-31　Postcard. The Sakurada Gate of the Imperial Palace. Hideki Watanabe Collection
1-34　Postcard. Arrival of a Group of US Distinguished Visitors at Shimbashi Station. Hideki Watanabe Collection

キャリアのはじまり

Early career

師サリヴァンと自然モチーフの装飾 | Louis Sullivan: A mentor, and his motifs of nature

1-35

1-37

1-36

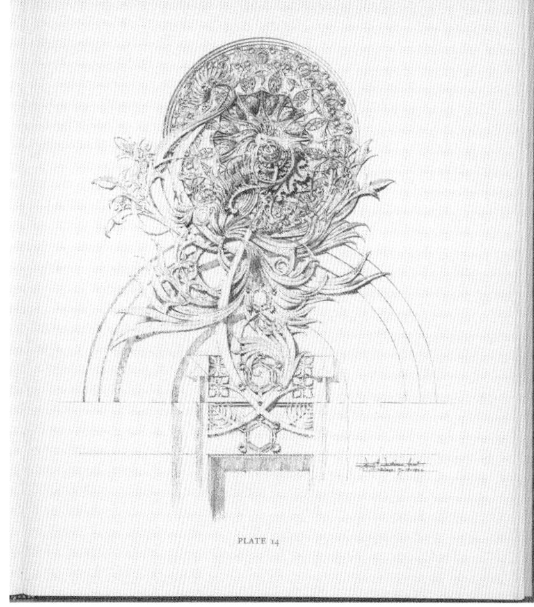

1-39

1-35 シカゴで働き始めた頃のフランク・ロイド・ライト | 撮影者不詳 | 1890年頃

1-36 ベルフォンテーヌ墓地のウェインライト家の墓(ミズーリ州セントルイス) 1892年 フランク・ロイド・ライトによる門の装飾 | 建築:ルイス・サリヴァン、レンダリング:フランク・ロイド・ライト

1-37 ベルフォンテーヌ墓地のウェインライト家の墓(ミズーリ州セントルイス) 1892年 装飾の詳細 | 建築:ルイス・サリヴァン | 撮影:1996年

1-39 『建築装飾の体系 人間の力の原理に基づく』| 著:ルイス・サリヴァン、出版:リツォーリ社(再版) | 1924/1990年

1-35 Portrait of Frank Lloyd Wright shortly after he arrived in Chicago. Photographer unidentified. c. 1890. Wisconsin Historical Society

1-36 Wainwright Tomb. Bellefontaine Cemetery, Saint Louis, Missouri. Project, 1892. Ornamental gate rendered by Frank Lloyd Wright. Louis Sullivan, architect. Frank Lloyd Wright, renderer. Louis Sullivan collection, 1873-1910, Avery Architectural & Fine Arts Library, Columbia University

1-37 Wainwright Tomb. Bellefontaine Cemetery, Saint Louis, Missouri. Project, 1892. Exterior detail view. Louis Sullivan, architect. Photo: 1996. Richard Guy Wilson Architecture Archive, University of Virginia

1-39 *A System of Architectural Ornament According with a Philosophy of Man's Powers*. Louis H. Sullivan, author. Rizzoli, publisher (facsimile ed.). 1924/1990. The Komaba Library, The University of Tokyo

3 キャリアのはじまり
Early career

初期の実践 | Early works

● **ウィンズロー邸** | Winslow House | イリノイ州リバーフォレスト、1893–94年、住宅 | River Forest, Illinois, 1893–94, residential

TAFEL I. VILLA FÜR HERRN WINSLOW IN RIVER FOREST, ILLINOIS. EINGANGSDETAIL.
GEDRUCKT UND VERLEGT VON ERNST WASMUTH A.-G., BERLIN

1-41

1-42

1-43

1-41 第1葉 ウィンズロー邸、透視図『フランク・ロイド・ライトの建築と設計』| フランク・ロイド・ライト、出版：エルンスト・ヴァスムート社 | 1910年
1-42 ウィンズロー邸（イリノイ州リバーフォレスト）1893–94年 | 建築：フランク・ロイド・ライト、撮影：ジェームズ・コールフィールド | 2005年
1-43 ウィンズロー邸（イリノイ州リバーフォレスト）1893–94年 | 応接ホール内観 | 建築：フランク・ロイド・ライト、撮影：ジェームズ・コールフィールド | 2014年

1-41 Plate I. Perspective of Winslow House. *Ausgeführte Bauten und Entwürfe von Frank Lloyd Wright*, 1910. Frank Lloyd Wright. Ernst Wasmuth, publisher. 1910. Toyota Municipal Museum of Art
1-42 Winslow House, River Forest, Illinois. Project, 1893-94. Exterior. Frank Lloyd Wright, architect. James Caulfield, photographer. Photo: 2005
1-43 Winslow House, River Forest, Illinois. Project, 1893-94. Interior view of the reception hall. Frank Lloyd Wright, architect. James Caulfield, photographer. Photo: 2014

● **ヒコックス邸** | Hickox House | イリノイ州カンカキー、1900年、住宅 | Kankakee, Illinois, 1900, residential

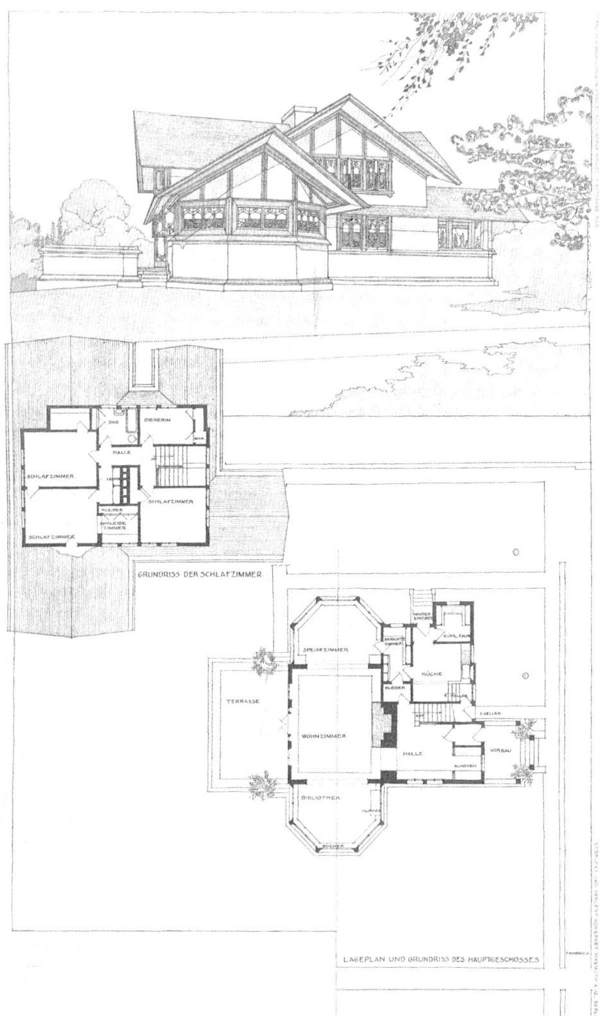

1-44

1-45

1-44 第24葉 ヒコックス邸、平面図および透視図『フランク・ロイド・ライトの建築と設計』| フランク・ロイド・ライト、出版：エルンスト・ヴァスムート社 | 1910年
1-45 ヒコックス邸 ハイバック・チェア | デザイン：フランク・ロイド・ライト | 1900年頃

1-44 Plate XXIV. Ground plan and perspective of the Hickox House. *Ausgeführte Bauten und Entwürfe von Frank Lloyd Wright*. Frank Lloyd Wright. Ernst Wasmuth, publisher. 1910. Toyota Municipal Museum of Art
1-45 Tall-back Spindle Chair from the Hickox House. Frank Lloyd Wright, designer. c. 1900. Toyota Municipal Museum of Art

4 ユニティ・テンプル：鉄筋コンクリート造の神殿
Unity Temple: A reinforced concrete sanctuary

● **ユニティ・テンプル** | Unity Temple | イリノイ州オークパーク、1905–08年、宗教施設 | Oak Park, Illinois, 1905–08, religious

1-47

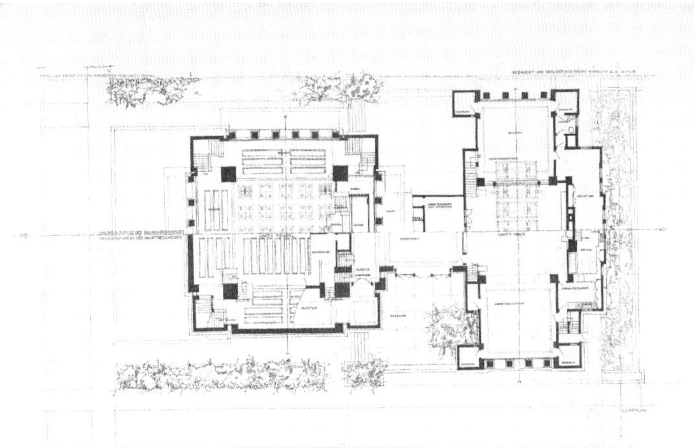

1-49

1-50

1-47　第63葉 ユニティ・テンプル、透視図『フランク・ロイド・ライトの建築と設計』| フランク・ロイド・ライト、出版：エルンスト・ヴァスムート社 | 1910年
1-49　第64葉 ユニティ・テンプル、平面図『フランク・ロイド・ライトの建築と設計』| フランク・ロイド・ライト、出版：エルンスト・ヴァスムート社 | 1910年
1-50　模型 ユニティ・テンプル（イリノイ州オークパーク）| フランク・ロイド・ライト | 1920年頃

1-47　Plate LXIII. Perspective of the House and Temple for Unity Temple. *Ausgeführte Bauten und Entwürfe von Frank Lloyd Wright*. Frank Lloyd Wright. Ernst Wasmuth, publisher. 1910. Toyota Municipal Museum of Art
1-49　Plate LXIV. Ground plan of Unity Temple Oak Park, Illinois. *Ausgeführte Bauten und Entwürfe von Frank Lloyd Wright, 1910*. Frank Lloyd Wright. Ernst Wasmuth, publisher. 1910. Toyota Municipal Museum of Art
1-50　Model. Unity Temple, Oak Park, Illinois. Project, 1905–08. Frank Lloyd Wright. c. 1920. Kyoto University

1-52

1-53

1-51

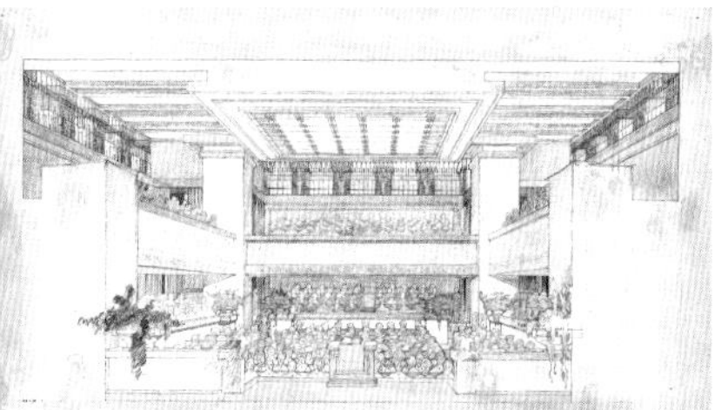

1-54

1-55

1-51 ユニティ・テンプル(イリノイ州オークパーク)1905–08年 外観、礼拝堂を左手に見る | 建築:フランク・ロイド・ライト、撮影:ジェームズ・コールフィールド | 2021年
1-52 ユニティ・テンプル(イリノイ州オークパーク)1905–08年 礼拝堂内観、説教壇から見る | 建築:フランク・ロイド・ライト、撮影:ジェームズ・コールフィールド | 2019年
1-53 ユニティ・テンプル(イリノイ州オークパーク)1905–08年 礼拝堂の照明器具 | 建築:フランク・ロイド・ライト、撮影:ジェームズ・コールフィールド | 2018年
1-54 ユニティ・テンプル(イリノイ州オークパーク)1905–08年 礼拝堂内観図 | フランク・ロイド・ライト
1-55 浮絵 歌舞妓芝居之図 | 歌川豊春 | 明和4(1767)年頃

1-51 Unity Temple, Oak Park, Illinois. Project, 1905-08. Exterior, sanctuary on the left side.
Frank Lloyd Wright, architect. James Caulfield, photographer. Photo: 2021
1-52 Unity Temple, Oak Park, Illinois. Project, 1905-08. Interior perspective, sanctuary, view from the pulpit.
Frank Lloyd Wright, architect. James Caulfield, photographer. Photo: 2019
1-53 Unity Temple, Oak Park, Illinois. Project, 1905-08. Lighting fixture in the sanctuary.
Frank Lloyd Wright, architect. James Caulfield, photographer. Photo: 2018
1-54 Unity Temple, Oak Park, Illinois. Project, 1905-08. Interior perspective, sanctuary. Frank Lloyd Wright. The Frank Lloyd Wright Foundation Archives (The Museum of Modern Art | Avery Architectural & Fine Arts Library, Columbia University, New York)
1-55 Kabuki Theater in Ukie Style. Utagawa Toyoharu, artist. c. 1767 (Meiwa 4). Ota Memorial Museum of Art

5 日本の発見

Discovery of Japan

浮世絵的視覚と建築ドローイング | Ukiyo-e through the lens of Wright and his architectural drawings

● **デローズ邸** | DeRhodes House | インディアナ州サウスベンド、1906年、住宅 | South Bend, Indiana, 1906, residential

● **ハーディ邸** | Hardy House | ウィスコンシン州ラシーン、1905年、住宅 | Racine, Wisconsin, 1905, residential

1-56

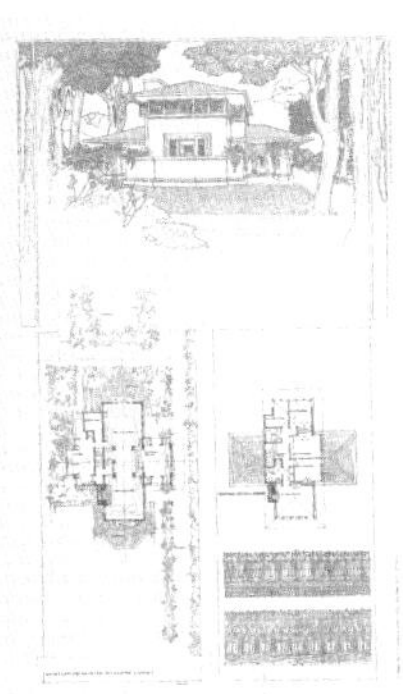

1-57

1-61

1-62

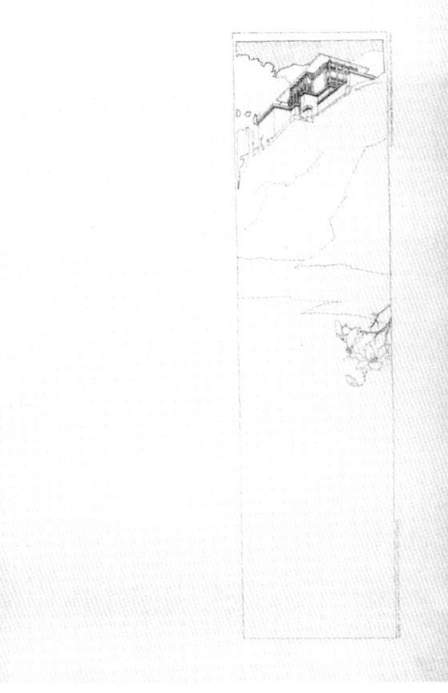

1-66

1-68

1-67

1-56　デローズ邸(インディアナ州サウスベンド)1906年 透視図 | 建築：フランク・ロイド・ライト、レンダリング：マリオン・マホニー

1-57　第29葉 デローズ邸、平面図および透視図『フランク・ロイド・ライトの建築と設計』| フランク・ロイド・ライト、出版：エルンスト・ヴァスムート社 | 1910年

1-61　名所江戸百景 八ツ見のはし | 歌川広重 | 安政3(1856)年

1-62　名所江戸百景 真間の紅葉 手古那の社 継はし | 歌川広重 | 安政4(1857)年

1-66　第15葉 ハーディ邸、透視図『フランク・ロイド・ライトの建築と設計』| フランク・ロイド・ライト、出版：エルンスト・ヴァスムート社 | 1910年

1-67　東海道五拾三次 亀山 雪晴 | 歌川広重 | 天保4(1834)年頃

1-68　フィエーゾレ、ヴィリーノ・ベルヴェデーレのライトの住まいを見上げる、前景に藪と塀 | 撮影：テイラー・A. ウーレイ | 1910年

1-56　DeRhodes House, South Bend, Indiana. Project, 1906. Exterior perspective. Frank Lloyd Wright, architect. Marion Mahony Griffin, renderer. The Frank Lloyd Wright Foundation Archives (The Museum of Modern Art | Avery Architectural & Fine Arts Library, Columbia University, New York)

1-57　Plate XXIX. Ground plan and perspective of the DeRhodes House. *Ausgeführte Bauten und Entwürfe von Frank Lloyd Wright*. Frank Lloyd Wright. Ernst Wasmuth, publisher. 1910. Toyota Municipal Museum of Art

1-61　Yatsumi Bridge. From the series "One Hundred Famous Views of Edo". Utagawa Hiroshige, artist. 1856 (Ansei 3). Kanagawa Prefectural Museum of Cultural History

1-62　Maple Leaves and the Tekona Shrine and Tsugi Brdge at Mama. From the series "One Hundred Famous Views of Edo". Utagawa Hiroshige, artist. 1857 (Ansei 4). Kanagawa Prefectural Museum of Cultural History

1-66　Plate XV. Perspective view of the Hardy House. *Ausgeführte Bauten und Entwürfe von Frank Lloyd Wright*. Frank Lloyd Wright. Ernst Wasmuth, publisher. 1910. Toyota Municipal Museum of Art

1-67　Clear Weather after Snow at Kameyama. From the series "Fifty-three Stations on the Tokaido". Utagawa Hiroshige, artist. c. 1834 (Tempo 4). Kanagawa Prefectural Museum of Cultural History

1-68　Villino Belvedere from below, garden and wall. Taylor A. Woolley, photographer. Photo: 1910. Personal and Taliesin Fellowship photographs, 1870s-2004, The Frank Lloyd Wright Foundation Archives (The Museum of Modern Art | Avery Architectural & Fine Arts Library, Columbia University, New York)

5 日本の発見
Discovery of Japan

日本初訪問 | The first trip to Japan

1-69

1-70

1-71

1-73

1-69 「ライトの来日旅行写真アルバム」| 1905年
1-70 東本願寺名古屋別院 本堂「ライトの来日旅行写真アルバム」| 撮影：フランク・ロイド・ライト | 1905年
1-71 岡山後楽園 延養亭と庭園「ライトの来日旅行写真アルバム」| 撮影：フランク・ロイド・ライト | 1905年
1-73 長崎丸山遊郭の通り | 撮影：アレキサンダー・ウールコット | 1932年頃
1-79 展示風景：シカゴ建築クラブの1914年の年次展、シカゴ美術館にて | 撮影：ファーマン・アンド・サンズ | 1914年

1-69 The Photo Album from the Wright's 1905 Trip to Japan. 1905. Collection of Frank Lloyd Wright Trust, Chicago
1-70 Higashi-Honganji Temple, Nagoya-Betsuin, Nagoya, The 1905 Photo Album. Frank Lloyd Wright, photographer. Photo: 1905. Collection of Frank Lloyd Wright Trust, Chicago
1-71 Koraku-en, Okayama. Exterior of the main hall with gardens. The 1905 Photo Album. Frank Lloyd Wright, photographer. Photo: 1905. Personal and Taliesin Fellowship photographs, 1870s-2004, The Frank Lloyd Wright Foundation Archives (The Museum of Modern Art | Avery Architectural & Fine Arts Library, Columbia University, New York)
1-73 Maruyama, Nagasaki, Japan. Street view. Alexander Woollcott, photographer. Photo: c. 1932. Personal and Taliesin Fellowship photographs, 1870s-2004, The Frank Lloyd Wright Foundation Archives (The Museum of Modern Art | Avery Architectural & Fine Arts Library, Columbia University, New York)
1-79 Chicago Architectural Club Annual Exhibition at the Art Institute of Chicago, Chicago, Illinois. 1914. Fuermann and Sons, photographer. Photo: 1914. Project photographs, circa 1887-2008, The Frank Lloyd Wright Foundation Archives (The Museum of Modern Art | Avery Architectural & Fine Arts Library, Columbia University)

5 日本の発見

Discovery of Japan

日本美術愛好家、アートディーラー、展覧会プロデューサーとして

Wright as a collector of Japanese art, art dealer, and exhibition curator

1-79

● ウィリアム・スポールディングのための浮世絵ギャラリー計画案 | Japanese Print Gallery for William Spaulding, unbuilt project

マサチューセッツ州ボストン、1914年、美術館 | Boston, Massachusetts, 1914, institutional civic

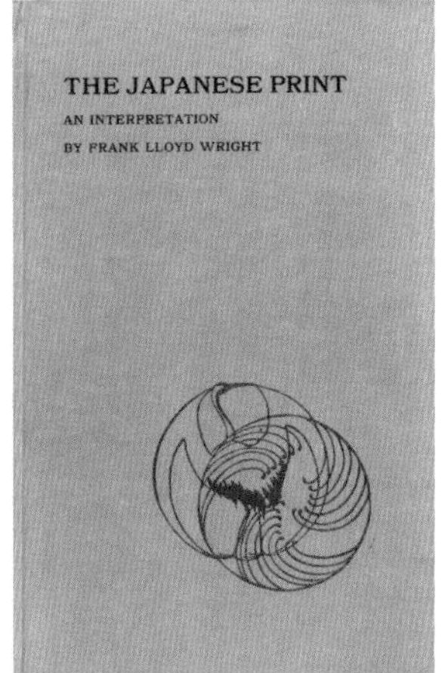

1-74

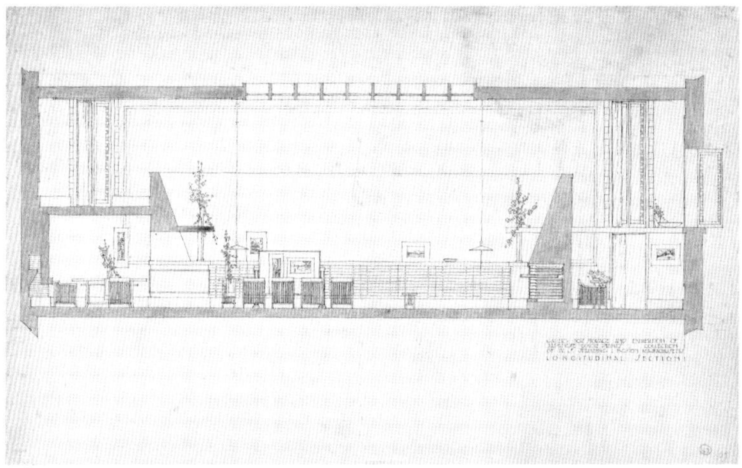

1-76

1-77

1-80

1-82

1-83

1-74 『日本の浮世絵：或る解釈』| 著：フランク・ロイド・ライト、出版：ラルフ・フレッチャー・シーモア | 1912年
1-76 ウィリアム・スポールディングのための浮世絵ギャラリー計画案（マサチューセッツ州ボストン）1914年 縦展開図 | フランク・ロイド・ライト
1-77 シカゴ美術館における1908年の浮世絵展 | 撮影：1908年
1-80 名所江戸百景 亀戸天神境内 | 歌川広重 | 安政3（1856）年
1-82 二代目市川門之助の清十郎 三代目瀬川菊之丞のおなつ | 勝川春常 | 安永10／天明元（1781）年
1-83 見立て浄瑠璃姫 | 礒田湖龍斎 | 江戸時代、1770年代初頭

cat.nos. 1-80～83は前頁のcat.no.1-79の中に見ることができる。

1-74 *The Japanese Print: An interpretation*. Frank Lloyd Wright, author. The Ralph Fletcher Seymour, Chicago, publisher. 1912. Seijo University Library
1-76 Japanese Prints Gallery for William Spaulding, Boston, Massachusetts. Unbuilt Project, 1914, Longitudinal section. Frank Lloyd Wright. The Frank Lloyd Wright Foundation Archives (The Museum of Modern Art | Avery Architectural & Fine Arts Library, Columbia University, New York)
1-77 Exhibition of Japanese Prints at the Art Institute of Chicago, 1908. Photo: 1908. The Art Institute of Chicago Photo © The Art Institute of Chicago / Art Resource, NY
1-80 Precincts of the Kameido Tenjin Shrine. From the series "One Hundred Famous Views of Edo". Utagawa Hiroshige, artist. 1856 (Ansei 3)
1-82 Actors Ichikawa Monnosuke II as Seijûrô (R) and Segawa Kikunojô III as Onatsu (L). Katsukawa Shunjô, artist. 1781 (An'ei 10/Tenmei 1). Museum of Fine Arts Boston. William Sturgis Bigelow Collection Photograph © 2023 Museum of Fine Arts, Boston
1-83 A Modern Version of the Story of Ushiwakamaru Serenading Jôruri-hime. Isoda Koryûsai, artist. Edo period, about early 1770s. Museum of Fine Arts Boston. William S. and John T. Spaulding Collection Photograph © 2023 Museum of Fine Arts, Boston

cat.nos. 1-80 to 83 can be seen exhibited in the photograph (cat. no. 1-79) on the previous page.

SECTION 2

「輝ける眉」からの眺望

Views from the Shining Brow

建築に対するライトの有機的アプローチは、さまざまな環境や気候と関わりあった。ウィスコンシン州のなだらかな地域やシカゴ周辺の中西部大草原から、地震の多い日本の環境、ロサンゼルスの乾燥した地中海性気候、アメリカ南西部のソノラ砂漠まで、地域特有の建築はそれぞれ独自の環境に呼応していた。

ニューヨーク州バッファローのダーウィン・D. マーティン邸(1903–05)では、ポーチと道路との間にプライバシー境界をつくり出すため、特別な植栽計画「フロリサイクル」がつくり出された[cat.no.2-26]。そのため、東側ポーチの周囲に何千もの球根、多年草、二年草、花が咲く低木や樹木が、きれいな半円形のデザインで植えられた。開花時期の異なるさまざまな種類の植物を植えたことで、フロリサイクルでは1年の大半にわたって花を咲かせることができた。ハナショウブ、タチアオイ、オオデマリもしくはバイカウツギ、オニユリ、ツタなど東アジア原産の植物を数多く使ったフロリサイクルをデザインしたのは、おそらく、この時期、ライトのオークパークのスタジオのスタッフであったウォルター・バーリー・グリフィン(1896–1937)であった。多くの外来植物も植えるということは、より許容度の高い庭園デザインにおけるある種の「生態学的コスモポリタニズム」を示唆しており、在来植物を重要視していたランドスケープ・デザインの「プレイリー・スタイル」に対する、ライトとグリフィンの考え方を広げることになった。

ライトは、イリノイ州リバーサイドのクーンリー邸(1906–09)[cat.no.2-28]とイリノイ州グレンコーのブース邸計画案(1911)[cat.no.2-46]の庭園設計において、気鋭の造園家ジェンス・ジェンセンと共同作業を行った。ジェンセンは在来植物と原生植物庭園の提唱者としてよく知られていたが、クーンリー邸の庭園のためのジェンセンによる手書き目録には、ボケやオニゲシなど、在来植物と外来植物が含まれていた。この家の施主であるクィーン・フェリー・クーンリー(1874–1920)は、後に世界最大となるデトロイトの高収益種苗会社の創設者、D.W.フェリー(1833–1907)の娘であった。このようなつながりは、風景さえも世界的な経済と政治の流れの一部であったことを如実に物語っている。

ライトとジェンセンは、ブース邸において、氷河渓谷とミシガン湖に流れ込む支流が作り出す険しくもドラマチックな敷地を巧みに処理しつつ、景観とインフラの複雑な介入をデザインした。その精巧な庭園は、在来植物や外来植物の群生、クリアリングと呼ばれる開けた草地、不規則な形のプール、成層岩が並んだ蛇行する「プレイリー・リバー」など、ジェンセン特有のランドスケープの目録であるかのようだ。ジェンセンはまた、ネイティブ・アメリカンの儀式に由来する、アメリカのアイデンティティの象徴としての「集

1 Therese O'Malley, "The Floricycle: Designing with Native and Exotic Plants," in *Frank Lloyd Wright: Unpacking the Archive*, eds. Barry Bergdoll and Jennifer Gray (New York: The Museum of Modern Art, 2017), pp. 18–19.

2 前掲書 註1 p. 18.

3 前掲書 註1 p. 20.

4 Robert Grese, *Jens Jensen: Maker of Natural Parks and Gardens* (Baltimore: John Hopkins University Press, 1998), pp. 136–37, pp. 172–73.

い の輪」[cat. no. 2-48]、あるいは円形のキャンプファイヤーも取り入れた。そこで見えてきたのは、ライトとジェンセンが自然やランドスケープへのアプローチにおいて、時間や空間をも越えて、グローバルにおいてもローカルにおいても多様な文化に関与していたということである。

日本の帝国ホテルの仕事の後、ライトはしばらくの間、環太平洋の反対側、カリフォルニア州ロサンゼルスの地中海性気候の地で活動し、エニス邸(1924–25)やミラード夫人邸「ミニアトゥーラ」(1923–24)[cat. no. 5-20]といったいくつかのテキスタイル・ブロックの住宅や、傑作バーンズドール邸「立葵の家」(1918–21)[cat. no. 3-29]などを手がけた。「立葵の家」は、ホリホック(タチアオイ)にインスパイアされたデザイン・モチーフが家の内外にいくつも用いられていたことから、その名がついた。クライアントのアリーン・バーンズドール[cat. no. 3-30]は、中西部で過ごした幼少期からこの「プレイリー」の花を好んでいた。タチアオイは、アメリカ原産ではなく、東アジアが原産地ではあるが。

ウィスコンシン州のタリアセンにおけるダム[cat. no. 2-5]や水力発電による初期の実験から、ライトがその後タリアセン・ウエストを建設する場所に程近いアリゾナ州チャンドラーに、計画はされたが実現されなかった高級リゾート、サン・マルコス砂漠リゾート・ホテル計画案(1928–29)[cat. no. 5-32]まで、水は、ライトの仕事を通して一つの重要なデザイン上の要件であった。

ライトの水との関わりにおいて最も注目すべき取り組みは、「落水荘」として知られるエドガー・カウフマン邸(1934–37)であろう[cat. nos. 2-67, 68]。ペンシルベニア州ミルランの人里離れた森林地帯に位置するこの邸宅は、敷地が持つユニークな特性を十全に生かした設計となっている。劇的なコンクリート製キャンチレバーが急勾配の滝の上に伸び、地元で切り出した石で建造された支柱によって支えられた空中テラスは、この家が岩だらけの川岸から直接湧き出てきたかのような印象を与える。ライトは実際にリビングルームのインテリアに自然岩盤を取り込み、自然岩盤の上に暖炉を据え、滝のすぐ上の浅瀬の水面へと降りていくオープン階段を取り入れている。「落水荘」は、ライトの最も有名な滝の建築物かもしれないが、最初の作品は、その数十年前に日本の、人里離れた森の中に設計された小田原ホテル計画案(1917)[cat. no. 2-66]であった。

日本からアメリカ、さらにその先の世界へと広がるこのような共鳴は、外来植物や多様な文化との関わりとともに、彼の活動のグローバルな視野を示しているのである。

5 Lester Pottenger, "The Council Ring as Jensen Sees It,"(「Vistas」[A student paper published by the Landscape Council Ring at the University of Wisconsin, Morton Arboretum, Chicago; Jens Jensen, "The Campfire or Council Fire," *Outdoors with the Prairie Club* (1941), reprinted in William H. Tischler, ed., *Jens Jensen: Writings Inspired by Nature* (Madison, Wisconsin: Wisconsin Historical Society Press, 2012), pp. 121–22.]より抜粋)

6 Charles E. Aguar and Berdeana Aguar, *Wrightscapes: Frank Lloyd Wright's Landscape Designs* (New York: McGraw-Hill, 2002), p. 176; O'Malley, p. 19.

7 Terence Riley, "The Landscapes of Frank Lloyd Wright: A Pattern of Work," in Terence Riley, ed., *Frank Lloyd Wright: Architect* (New York: The Museum of Modern Art, 1994), p. 104.

Wright's organic approach to architecture engaged a variety of landscapes and climates. From the Driftless Area of Wisconsin and Midwestern prairies around Chicago, to the seismic environment of Japan, the arid Mediterranean climate of Los Angeles, and the Sonoran Desert in the American Southwest, site-specific buildings responded to their unique surroundings.

At the Darwin D. Martin House in Buffalo, New York (1903–05), the planting plan calls for an extraordinary "Floricycle" containing thousands of bulbs, perennials, biennials, and flowering shrubs and trees to be planted in a formal, half-circle design around the east porch in order to create a privacy screen between the porch and adjacent streets [cat. no. 2-26]. The diversity of plant species meant that the Floricycle was in flower for much of the year, as the plants flowered at different times. Walter Burley Griffin (1896–1937), an employee in Wright's Oak Park Studio during these years, likely designed the Floricycle featuring large numbers of plants originating in East Asia such as Japanese iris, hollyhock, snowball or mock orange, tiger lily, and Boston Ivy. The incorporation of large numbers of exotic species suggests a certain "ecological cosmopolitanism" that embraced more inclusive practices in garden design and broadens Griffin and Wright's association with a "prairie style" landscape design previously seen to emphasize the use of indigenous plants.[1]

Wright collaborated with leading landscape architect Jens Jensen (1860–1951) on the garden designs for the Coonley House in Riverside, Illinois (1906–09) [cat. no. 2-28] and the Booth House in Glencoe, Illinois (project, 1911) [cat. no. 2-46]. Jensen was a well-known advocate for native plants and indigenous gardens, but his handwritten inventory for the Coonley gardens included native and exotic plant species, such as Japanese quince and Oriental poppies.[2] Wright's client, Queene Ferry Coonley (1874–1920), was the daughter of D. W. Ferry (1833–1907), the founder of a highly profitable Detroit seed company that would become the largest in the world. These connections underscore the degree to which even landscapes were part of global economic and political flows.[3]

At the Booth House, Wright and Jensen designed a complex interpolation of landscape and infrastructure capable of negotiating the rugged, dramatic site with glacial ravines and a tributary stream that emptied into Lake Michigan. The elaborate gardens read as a veritable inventory of Jensen's signature landscape features: dense groupings of native and imported plants, open meadows called clearings, irregular shaped swimming pools, and meandering "prairie rivers" lined with stratified rock.[4] Jensen also included "council rings" or circular campfires as symbols of American identity derived from Native American rituals [cat. no. 2-48].[5] The picture that emerges is one in which Wright and Jensen were

1 Therese O'Malley, "The Floricycle: Designing with Native and Exotic Plants," in *Frank Lloyd Wright: Unpacking the Archive*, eds. Barry Bergdoll and Jennifer Gray (New York: The Museum of Modern Art, 2017), pp. 18–19.

2 Ibid, p. 18.

3 Ibid, p. 20.

4 Robert Grese, *Jens Jensen: Maker of Natural Parks and Gardens* (Baltimore: John Hopkins University Press, 1998), pp. 136–37, pp. 172–73.

engaging with multiple cultures, both global and local, across time and space in their approaches to nature and landscape.

After Wright completed the Imperial Hotel in Japan, he practiced for a time on the other side of the Pacific Rim in the Mediterranean climate of Los Angeles, California, where he produced several textile-block houses, such as the Ennis House (1924–25) and Mrs. Millard House, La Miniatura (1923–24) [cat. no. 5-20], as well as the masterful Barnsdall House (Hollyhock House) (1918–21) [cat. no. 3-29]. The latter gained its name due to the prevalence of hollyhock-inspired design motifs inside and outside the house. The client, Aline Barnsdall [cat. no. 3-30], favored this "prairie" flower from her childhood in the Midwest, though hollyhocks are not native to the United States, but rather, originate in East Asia.[6]

Water was an important design consideration for Wright throughout his career, from early experiments with dams and hydroelectricity at Taliesin in Wisconsin [cat. no. 2-5] to large-scale environmental planning, as in his unrealized design for the San Marcos-in-the-Desert Hotel (1928–29), a luxury resort planned for Chandler, Arizona [cat. no. 5-32], not far from where Wright would soon build Taliesin West.

Wright's most notable engagement with water is arguably the Kaufmann House (1934–37), otherwise known as Fallingwater [cat. nos. 2-67, 68]. Located on a remote wooded site in Mill Run, Pennsylvania, the design fully exploits the unique characteristics of its site. Dramatic concrete cantilevers extend over a steep waterfall, the hovering terraces supported by piers constructed from locally quarried stone, giving the impression that the house sprung directly from the rocky river banks. Indeed, the fireplace was located above a natural rock formation that Wright allowed to penetrate into the interior of the living room, which also incorporated an open staircase that descends to the surface of the stream's shallows just above the falls.[7] Though Fallingwater might be Wright's most well-known waterfall building, his first was the Odawara Hotel (project, 1917) [cat. no. 2-66], designed decades earlier for another remote, wooded site in Japan.

Such resonances—from Japan to the United States and beyond—together with Wright's engagement with exotic plants and global cultures, demonstrates the international scope of his practice.

[Jennifer Gray]

5 Lester Pottenger, "The Council Ring as Jensen Sees It," typescript copied from *Vistas*, a student paper published by the Landscape Council Ring at the University of Wisconsin, Morton Arboretum, Chicago; Jens Jensen, "The Campfire or Council Fire," Outdoors with the Prairie Club (1941), reprinted in William H. Tischler, ed., *Jens Jensen: Writings Inspired by Nature* (Madison, Wisconsin: Wisconsin Historical Society Press, 2012), pp. 121–22.

6 Charles E. Aguar and Berdeana Aguar, *Wrightscapes: Frank Lloyd Wright's Landscape Designs* (New York: McGraw-Hill, 2002), p. 176; O'Malley, p. 19.

7 Terence Riley, "The Landscapes of Frank Lloyd Wright: A Pattern of Work," in Terence Riley, ed., *Frank Lloyd Wright: Architect* (New York: The Museum of Modern Art, 1994), p. 104.

6 アメリカ中西部プレイリーの風土と気候

Prairies of the American Midwest: Landscape and climate

2-1

2-2

2-5

2-7

2-8

2-1 谷を下りる | 撮影:フランク・ロイド・ライト | 1898-1900年頃
2-2 ヒルサイド・ホームスクール近くの風景 | 撮影:フランク・ロイド・ライト | 1893-1900年頃
2-5 タリアセンにつくられた水門 土浦亀城、信子夫妻のアルバム「Taliesin Life(2)」| 撮影:土浦亀城 | 1924-25年
2-7 タリアセンの丘の眺望、風車「ロメオとジュリエット」が見える。土浦亀城、信子夫妻のアルバム「Taliesin Life(2)」| 撮影:土浦亀城 | 1924-25年
2-8 タリアセン鳥瞰写真 | 撮影年不詳

2-1 Down the Valley. Frank Lloyd Wright, photographer. Photo: c. 1898-1900. Wisconsin Historical Society
2-2 Landscape Near Hillside Home School. Frank Lloyd Wright, photographer. Photo: c. 1893-1900. Wisconsin Historical Society
2-5 Watergate at Taliesin. Kameki and Nobuko Tsuchiura's photo album "Taliesin Life"(2). Kameki Tsuchiura, photographer. Photo: 1924-25. TSUCHIURA Kameki Archives
2-7 Landscape at Taliesin with a view of Romeo and Juliet Windmill. Kameki and Nobuko Tsuchiura's photo album "Taliesin Life"(2). Kameki Tsuchiura, photographer. Photo: 1924-25. TSUCHIURA Kameki Archives
2-8 Taliesin. Aerial view. undated. Edgar Tafel architectural records and papers, 1919-2005, Avery Architectural & Fine Arts Library, Columbia University

7 ルーツとしてのウェールズ
Welsh heritage

2-11

2-10

2-10 祖父リチャード・ロイド・ジョーンズとライトの一族 後列：左から9番目ライトの両親ウィリアム・キャリー・ライトとアンナ・ロイド・ライト。前列：左から6番目妹のマジネルを抱いた少年フランク・ロイド・ライト｜撮影者不詳｜1883年

2-11 フランク・ロイド・ライトと家族 左から：叔父ジェンキン、ジェンキンの妻、ジェーン・ライト、息子ロイドを抱いた妻キャサリン・ライト、母アンナ、妹マジネル、ライト本人、ジェンキンの娘｜撮影者不詳｜1890年頃

2-10 The Lloyd Jones Family. Back row from left: ninth is William Carey Wright and his wife Anna (Frank Lloyd Wright's parents). Front row from left: sixth is Frank Lloyd Wright holding his sister Maginel. Photographer unidentified. Photo: 1883. Wisconsin Historical Society

2-11 The Wright family on the front steps of the Oak Park Home, c. 1890. From left to right: Jenkin Lloyd-Jones, Jenkins' wife, Jane Wright, Catherine Wright (Frank Lloyd Wright Jr. in her arms), Anna Lloyd Wright, Maginel Wright, Frank Lloyd Wright, and Jenkin's daughter. Photographer unidentified. Photo: c. 1890. Courtesy of Frank Lloyd Wright Trust, Chicago

8 草原植物と『ハウス・ビューティフル』

Prairie plants and House Beautiful

● ウィンズロー邸 厩舎 | Winslow House, Stable | イリノイ州リバーフォレスト、1894年、厩舎 | River Forest, Illinois, 1894, agricultural

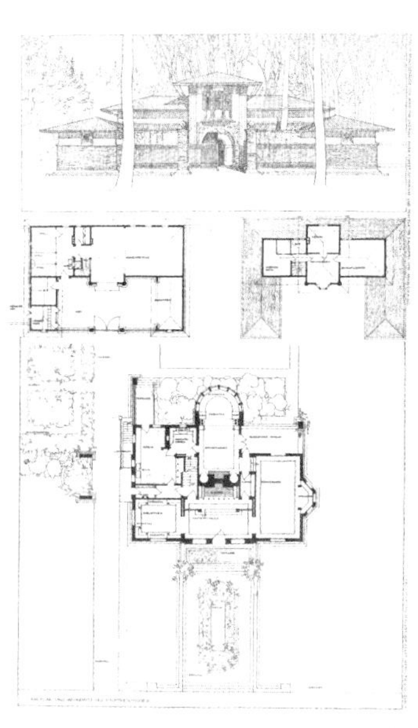

2-19

2-13 2-14 2-16 2-18

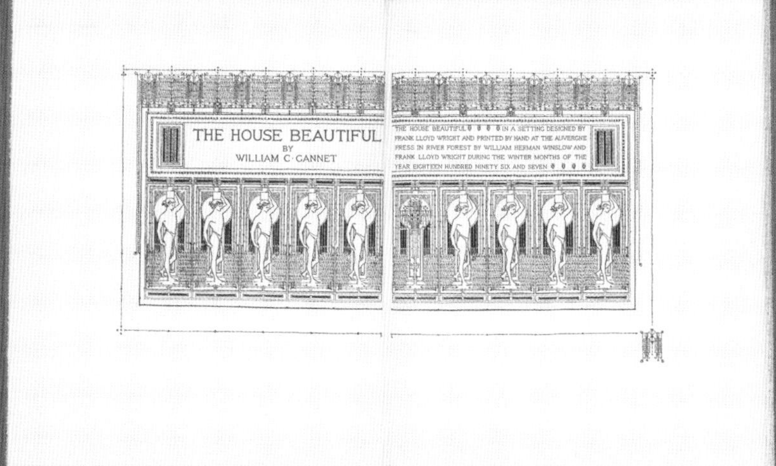

2-12

2-12 『ハウス・ビューティフル』| 著:ウィリアム・ガネット、デザイン:フランク・ロイド・ライト、出版:オーヴェルニュ・プレス、ハスブルック(ファクシミリ版)| 1896–97/1963年
2-13 撫子に蝶 | 歌川広重(初代) | 天保6–10(1836–40)年
2-14 山茶花に雀 | 歌川広重(初代) | 弘化年間(1845–48年)
2-16 雀に秋海棠 | 歌川広重(初代) | 弘化年間(1845–48年)
2-18 野菊に小鳥 | 歌川広重(初代) | 弘化年間(1845–48年)
2-19 第3葉 ウィンズロー邸の厩舎、平面図および透視図 『フランク・ロイド・ライトの建築と設計』| フランク・ロイド・ライト、出版:エルンスト・ヴァスムート社 | 1910年

2-12 *The House Beautiful*. William C. Gannett, author. Frank Lloyd Wright, designer. Auvergne Press, publisher. Hasbrouck, publisher for Facsimile edition. 1896–97/1963. The Komaba Library, University of Tokyo
2-13 Nadeshiko (Pink) Butterfly and Poem. Utagawa Hiroshige, artist. 1836–40 (Tempo 6–10). Kanagawa Prefectural Museum of Cultural History
2-14 Sparrow and Camellia sasanqua. Utagawa Hiroshige, artist. 1845–48 (Kōka). Kanagawa Prefectural Museum of Cultural History
2-16 Sparrow and Begonia grandis. Utagawa Hiroshige, artist. 1845–48 (Kōka). Kanagawa Prefectural Museum of Cultural History
2-18 Dickybird and wild crysanthemum. Utagawa Hiroshige, artist. 1845–48 (Kōka). Kanagawa Prefectural Museum of Cultural History
2-19 Plate III. Ground plan and perspective of the stable for the Winslow House. *Ausgeführte Bauten und Entwürfe von Frank Lloyd Wright*. Frank Lloyd Wright. Ernst Wasmuth, publisher. 1910. Toyota Municipal Museum of Art

9 住空間の革新

Innovation of dwelling space

A Home in a Prairie Town

By FRANK LLOYD WRIGHT

This is the Fifth Design in the Journal's New Series of Model Suburban Houses Which Can be Built at Moderate Cost

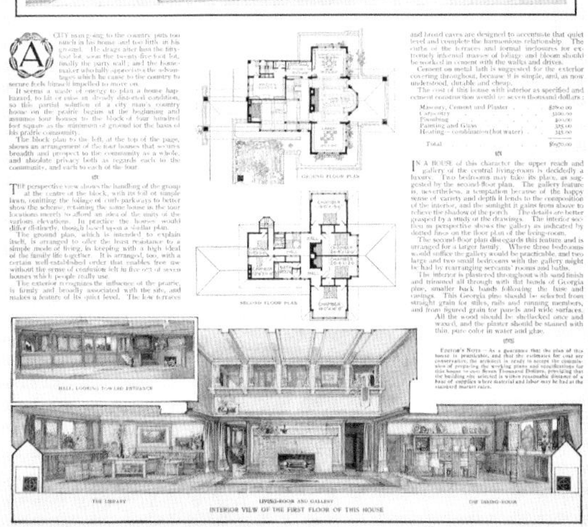

A Small House with "Lots of Room in It"

By Frank Lloyd Wright

NINTH DESIGN IN THE JOURNAL'S NEW SERIES OF MODEL SUBURBAN HOUSES AT MODERATE COST

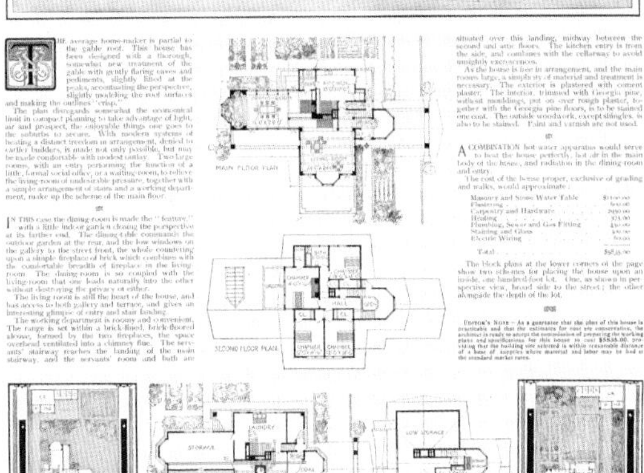

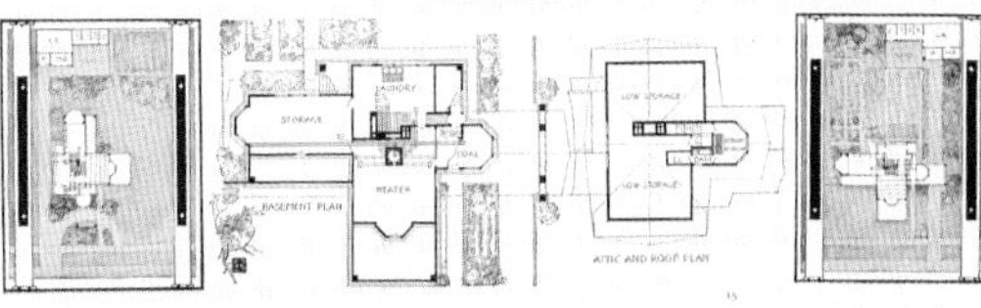

2-20

2-21

2-20　『レディース・ホーム・ジャーナル』1901年2月号 | 出版：カーチス社
2-21　『レディース・ホーム・ジャーナル』1901年7月号 | 出版：カーチス社

2-20　*Ladies Home Journal*, Feb 1901 issue. The Curtis Publishing Company, Philadelphia, publisher. Yutaka Mizukami Collection
2-21　*Ladies Home Journal*, Jul 1901 issue. The Curtis Publishing Company, Philadelphia, publisher. Yutaka Mizukami Collection

住空間の革新
Innovation of dwelling space

花の環で世界をめぐる | Traversing the World through the Floricycle

● **ダーウィン・D.マーティン邸** | Darwin D. Martin House | ニューヨーク州バッファロー、1903–05年、住宅 | Buffalo, New York, 1903–05, residential

2-22

2-24

2-25

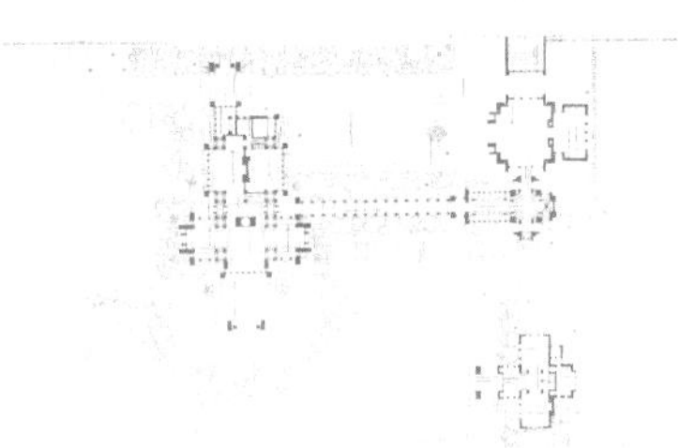

2-23

2-27

2-22 第32葉 ダーヴィン・D. マーティン邸、鳥瞰図『フランク・ロイド・ライトの建築と設計』| フランク・ロイド・ライト、出版:エルンスト・ヴァスムート社 | 1910年
2-23 第33葉 ダーヴィン・D. マーティン邸、平面図『フランク・ロイド・ライトの建築と設計』| フランク・ロイド・ライト、出版:エルンスト・ヴァスムート社 | 1910年
2-24 ダーウィン・D. マーティン邸(ニューヨーク州バッファロー)1903–05年 | 建築:フランク・ロイド・ライト、撮影:トーマス・ラッセル | 1904年頃
2-25 ダーウィン・D. マーティン邸(ニューヨーク州バッファロー)1903–05年 空撮 | 建築:フランク・ロイド・ライト、撮影:マシュー・ディガティ | 2022年
2-27 ダーウィン・D. マーティン邸(ニューヨーク州バッファロー)1903–05年 バレル・チェアが並べられた応接ホール | 建築:フランク・ロイド・ライト、撮影:マシュー・ディガティ | 2022年

2-22 Plate XXXII, Bird-eye view of the dwelling for Darwin D. Martin House. *Ausgeführte Bauten und Entwürfe von Frank Lloyd Wright.* Frank Lloyd Wright. Ernst Wasmuth, publisher. 1910. Toyota Municipal Museum of Art
2-23 Plate XXXII, Ground plan of the Darwin D. Martin House. *Ausgeführte Bauten und Entwürfe von Frank Lloyd Wright.* Frank Lloyd Wright. Ernst Wasmuth, publisher. 1910. Toyota Municipal Museum of Art
2-24 Darwin D. Martin House, Buffalo, New York. Project 1903–05. Exterior view. Frank Lloyd Wright, architect. Thomas Russell, photographer. Photo: c. 1904. Project photographs, circa 1887–2008, The Frank Lloyd Wright Foundation Archives (The Museum of Modern Art | Avery Architectural & Fine Arts Library, Columbia University, New York)
2-25 Darwin D. Martin House, Buffalo, New York. Project 1903–05. Aerial view. Frank Lloyd Wright, architect. Matthew Digati, photographer. Photo: 2022. Courtesy of Frank Lloyd Wright's Martin House
2-27 Darwin D. Martin House, Buffalo, New York. Project 1903–05. Interior of the reception room showing barrel chairs. Frank Lloyd Wright, architect. Matthew Digati, photographer. Photo: 2022. Courtesy of Frank Lloyd Wright's Martin House

9 住空間の革新
Innovation of dwelling space

外と内をつなぐ庭 | Connecting outside and inside via a garden

● **クーンリー邸** | Coonley House | イリノイ州リバーサイド、1906–09年、住宅 | Riverside, Illinois, 1906–09, residential

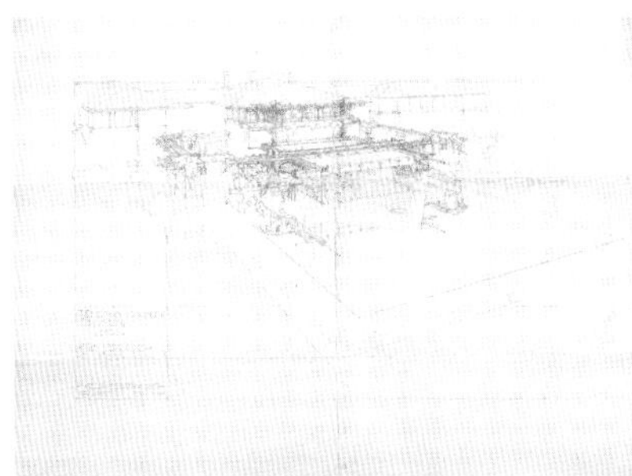

2-29

2-35

2-39

2-28

2-34

2-33

2-28　クーンリー邸（イリノイ州リバーサイド）1906–09年　初期案、外観とステンド・グラスが見える透視図 | フランク・ロイド・ライト | 1907年
2-29　クーンリー邸（イリノイ州リバーサイド）1906–09年　テラスのスタディ | フランク・ロイド・ライト、レンダリング：ウィリアム・ドラモンド | 1911年
2-33　クーンリー邸　椅子 | デザイン：フランク・ロイド・ライト、ジョージ・M. ニーデッケン（共同制作）、製作：ニーデッケン＝ウォルブリッジ社 | 製造：1908年頃
2-34　クーンリー邸　壁面照明器具 | デザイン：フランク・ロイド・ライト | 1908年頃
2-35　クーンリー邸（イリノイ州リバーサイド）1906–09年　池越しに見た正面外観 | 建築：フランク・ロイド・ライト | 撮影：1907年頃
2-39　クーンリー邸（イリノイ州リバーサイド）1906–09年　食堂内観、ニーデッケンによる壁画を正面に見る | 建築：フランク・ロイド・ライト、撮影：ジェームズ・コールフィールド | 2019年

2-28　Coonley House, Riverside, Illinois. Project 1906–09. Perspective. Preliminary drawing showing house and stained glass. Frank Lloyd Wright. 1907. Prints and Photographs Division, Library of Congress, Washington, D.C. LC-DIG-ppmsca-84876
2-29　Coonley House, Riverside, Illinois. Project 1906–09. Study for the Terrace. Frank Lloyd Wright. William Drummond, renderer. 1911. Toyota Municipal Museum of Art
2-33　Chair from the Coonley House. Frank Lloyd Wright in collaboration with George M. Niedecken, designers. Niedecken-Walbridge, manufacturer. c. 1908. Toyota Municipal Museum of Art
2-34　Lighting fixture from the Coonley House. Frank Lloyd Wright, designer. c. 1908. Toyota Art Museum of Art
2-35　Coonley House. Project 1906–09. Exterior view, from across reflecting pool. Frank Lloyd Wright, architect. Photo: c. 1907. Edgar Tafel architectural records and papers, 1919–2005, Avery Architectural & Fine Arts Library, Columbia University
2-39　Coonley House, Riverside, Illinois. Project, 1906–09. Dining room interior. View towards the mural by George M. Niedecken. Frank Lloyd Wright, architect. James Caulfield, photographer. Photo: 2019

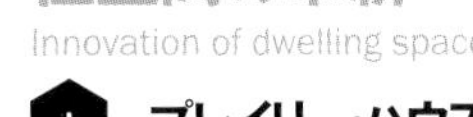

住空間の革新
Innovation of dwelling space

プレイリー・ハウスの到達点——有機的建築 | Organic Architecture: The achievement of prairie houses

● **ロビー邸** | Robie House | イリノイ州シカゴ、1908–10年、住宅 | Chicago, Illinois, 1908–10, residential

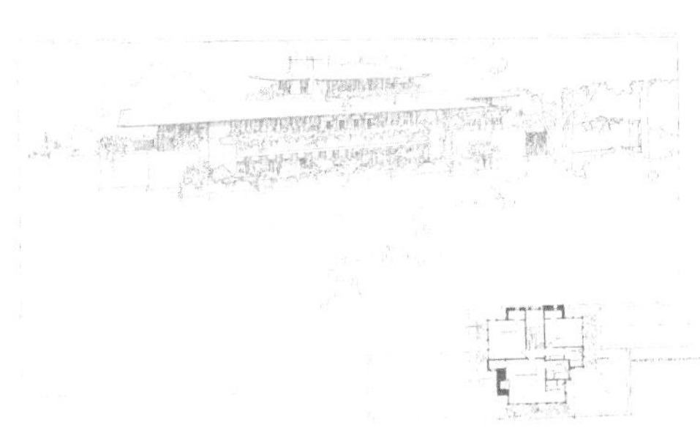

2-42

2-41

2-44

2-41 ロビー邸(イリノイ州シカゴ)1908–10年 | 建築:フランク・ロイド・ライト、撮影:ジェームズ・コールフィールド | 2013年
2-42 第37葉 ロビー邸、透視図『フランク・ロイド・ライトの建築と設計』| フランク・ロイド・ライト、出版:エルンスト・ヴァスムート社 | 1910年
2-44 ロビー邸(イリノイ州シカゴ)1908–10年 居間から暖炉を見る | 建築:フランク・ロイド・ライト、撮影:ジェームズ・コールフィールド | 2019年
2-45 ロビー邸(イリノイ州シカゴ)1908–10年 南側窓 | 建築:フランク・ロイド・ライト、撮影:ジェームズ・コールフィールド | 2014年

2-41 Robie House, Chicago, Illinois. Project 1908–10. Exterior view. Frank Lloyd Wright, architect. James Caulfield, photographer. Photo: 2013
2-42 Plate XXXVII, Perspective of the city dwelling for Frederick C. Robie. *Ausgeführte Bauten und Entwürfe von Frank Lloyd Wright*. Frank Lloyd Wright. Ernst Wasmuth, publisher. 1910. Toyota Municipal Museum of Art
2-44 Robie House, Chicago, Illinois. Project, 1908–10. Interior view of the living room. Frank Lloyd Wright, architect. James Caulfield, photographer. Photo: 2019
2-45 Robie House, Chicago, Illinois. Project, 1908–10. Interior view to the balcony. Frank Lloyd Wright, architect. James Caulfield, photographer. Photo: 2014

9 住空間の革新

Innovation of dwelling space

エコロジー住宅の発想 | Ideas for ecological dwelling

2-45

⑩ 在来と外来：ジェンス・ジェンセンの庭園思想

Native and exotic plants: Jens Jensen's concept of landscaping

● ブース邸計画案 | Booth House, unbuilt project | イリノイ州グレンコー、1911年、住宅 | Glencoe, Illinois, 1911, residential

2-46

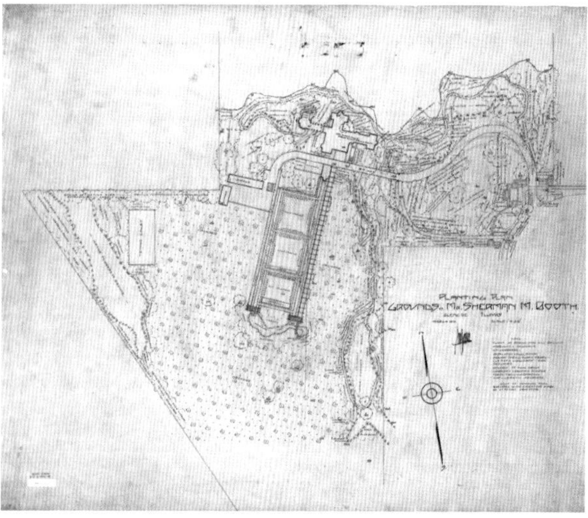

2-47

2 48

2-46　ブース邸計画案(イリノイ州グレンコー)1911年 第1案、透視図 | フランク・ロイド・ライト | 1911年
2-47　ジェンス・ジェンセンによるブース邸計画案 第1案、植栽計画 | デザイン：ジェンス・ジェンセン | 1911年
2-48　ジェンス・ジェンセンによる「集いの輪」| デザイン：ジェンス・ジェンセン | 撮影年不詳

2-46　Booth House. Glencoe, Illinois, Unbuilt Project, 1911. Perspective of scheme 1. Frank Lloyd Wright. 1911. The Museum of Modern Art, New York. Christopher H. Browne Purchase Fund, 2002 DIGITAL IMAGE©2023, The Museum of Modern Art/Scala, Florence
2-47　Booth House, Glencoe, Illinois, Unbuilt Project, 1911. Planting plan by Jens Jensen, scheme 1. Frank Lloyd Wright, architect. Jens Jensen, landscape designer. 1911. University of Michigan Library Digital Collections
2-48　Council Ring designed by Jens Jensen. Jens Jensen, landscape designer. undated. Courtesy of The Morton Arboretum, Lisle, Illinois, USA

11 タリアセン:最初の理想郷
Taliesin: The first utopia

● タリアセン第一・第二・第三(ライト自邸とスタジオ) | Taliesin I, II, III (Wright House and Studio)
ウィスコンシン州スプリンググリーン、1911、1914、1925年–、住宅、教育施設、事務所 | Spring Green, Wisconsin, 1911, 1914, 1925–, residential/educational/office

2-50

2-52

2-53

2-54

2-50 フィエーゾレ、ヴィリーノ・ベルヴェデーレのライトの住まい。壁面に図面が見える | 撮影:テイラー・A. ウーレイ | 1910年
2-52 ヴィリーノ・ベルヴェデーレからのフィエーゾレ眺望 | 撮影:テイラー・A. ウーレイ | 1910年
2-53 タリアセン第一(ウィスコンシン州スプリンググリーン) 中庭より西をのぞむ | 建築:フランク・ロイド・ライト、撮影:ファーマン・アンド・サンズ | 1912年頃
2-54 タリアセン第二(ウィスコンシン州スプリンググリーン) | 建築:フランク・ロイド・ライト、撮影:ヘンリー・ファーマン | 1915年
2-58 タリアセン(ウィスコンシン州スプリンググリーン) 居間 | 建築:フランク・ロイド・ライト、撮影:アンドリュー・ピラージ | 2011年

2-50 Interior with drawings at Villino Belvedere, Fiesole. Taylor A. Woolley, photographer. Photo: 1910. Personal and Taliesin Fellowship photographs, 1870s–2004, The Frank Lloyd Wright Foundation Archives (The Museum of Modern Art | Avery Architectural & Fine Arts Library, Columbia University, New York)
2-52 Fiesole, from Villino Belvedere. Taylor A. Woolley, photographer. Photo: 1910. Personal and Taliesin Fellowship photographs, 1870s–2004, The Frank Lloyd Wright Foundation Archives (The Museum of Modern Art | Avery Architectural & Fine Arts Library, Columbia University, New York)
2-53 Taliesin I, Spring Green, Wisconsin. Courtyard Looking West. Frank Lloyd Wright, architect. Henry Fuermann and Sons, photographer. Photo: c. 1912. Wisconsin Historical Society
2-54 Taliesin II, Spring Green, Wisconsin. Exterior view. Frank Lloyd Wright, architect. Henry Fuermann, photographer. Photo: 1915. Project photographs, circa 1887–2008, The Frank Lloyd Wright Foundation Archives (The Museum of Modern Art | Avery Architectural & Fine Arts Library, Columbia University, New York)
2-58 Taliesin, Spring Green, Wisconsin. Interior view of the living room. Frank Lloyd Wright, architect. © Andrew Pielage, photographer. Photo: 2011. Courtesy of the Frank Lloyd Wright Foundation

2-58

12 地形と建築
Terrain and architecture

● **山邑邸**（現・ヨドコウ迎賓館）｜Yamamura House (Yodoko Guest House)｜兵庫県芦屋市、1918–24年、住宅｜Ashiya, Japan, 1918–24, residential
● **小田原ホテル計画案**｜Odawara Hotel, unbuilt project｜神奈川県小田原市、1917年、宿泊施設｜Odawara, Japan, 1917, hospitality

2-60

2-63

2-62

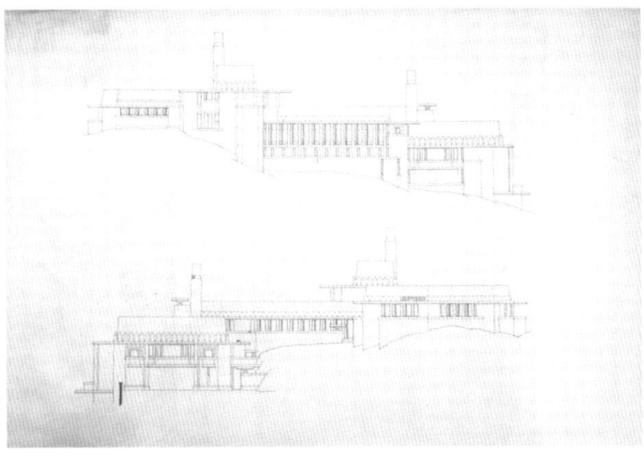
2-64

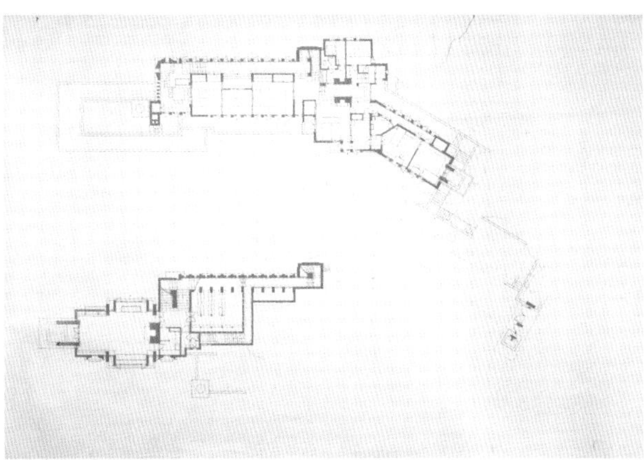
2-65

2-66

2-60　山邑邸（現・ヨドコウ迎賓館、兵庫県芦屋市）1918–24年 遠景｜建築：フランク・ロイド・ライト、撮影：山田新治郎｜2021年
2-62　山邑邸（現・ヨドコウ迎賓館）建築装飾｜デザイン：フランク・ロイド・ライト
2-63　山邑邸（現・ヨドコウ迎賓館、兵庫県芦屋市）1918–24年 窓の装飾から光が差し込んでいる｜建築：フランク・ロイド・ライト、撮影：山田新治郎｜2021年
2-64　山邑邸（現・ヨドコウ迎賓館、兵庫県芦屋市）1918–24年 実測立面図 西立面図、東立面図｜フランク・ロイド・ライト｜1985年
2-65　山邑邸（現・ヨドコウ迎賓館、兵庫県芦屋市）1918–24年 実測平面図 3、4階｜フランク・ロイド・ライト｜1985年
2-66　小田原ホテル計画案（神奈川県小田原市）1917年 透視図｜フランク・ロイド・ライト

2-60　Yamamura House (Yodoko Guest House), Ashiya, Japan. Project, 1918–24. Panoramic view. Frank Lloyd Wright, architect. Shinjiro Yamada, photographer. 2021
2-62　Ornament from Yamamura House, Frank Lloyd Wright, designer. 2021
2-63　Yamamura House (Yodoko Guest House), Ashiya, Japan. Project, 1918–24. Sunlight casting through the window ornament. Frank Lloyd Wright, architect. Shinjiro Yamada, photographer, 2021
2-64　Yamamura House (Yodoko Guest House), Ashiya, Japan. West and East measured elevation. Frank Lloyd Wright. 1985. Gen Endo Collection
2-65　Yamamura House (Yodoko Guest House), Ashiya, Japan. Third and forth floor, measured plan. Frank Lloyd Wright. 1985. Gen Endo Collection
2-66　Odawara Hotel, Odawara, Japan. Unbuilt Project, 1917. Perspective. The Frank Lloyd Wright Foundation Archives (The Museum of Modern Art | Avery Architectural & Fine Arts Library, Columbia University, New York)

● **エドガー・カウフマン邸「落水荘」** | Edgar J. Kaufmann House (Fallingwater)
ペンシルベニア州ミルラン、1934–37年、住宅 | Mill Run, Pennsylvania, 1934–37, residential

2–68

2–67

2–69

2–67 エドガー・カウフマン邸「落水荘」(ペンシルベニア州ミルラン) 1934–37年 | 建築:フランク・ロイド・ライト、撮影:アンドリュー・ピラージ | 2018年
2–68 エドガー・カウフマン邸「落水荘」(ペンシルベニア州ミルラン) 1934–37年 居間内観 | 建築:フランク・ロイド・ライト、撮影:二川幸夫 | 1980年代
2–69 映像「落水荘の建設現場」

2–67 Edgar J. Kaufmann House (Fallingwater), Mill Run, Pennsylvania. Project, 1934–37. Exterior. Frank Lloyd Wright, architect.
© Andrew Pielage, photographer. All Rights Reserved. Photo: 2018. Courtesy of the Western Pennsylvania Conservancy
2–68 Edgar J. Kaufmann House (Fallingwater), Mill Run, Pennsylvania. Project, 1934–37. Interior view of the living room.
© Yukio Futagawa, photographer. Photo: 1980s. Courtesy of GA / A.D.A. EDITA Tokyo Co., Ltd.
2–69 Film. Edgar J. Kaufmann House (Fallingwater), under construction.
The Frank Lloyd Wright Foundation Archives (The Museum of Modern Art | Avery Architectural & Fine Arts Library, Columbia University, New York)

13 タリアセン・ウェスト：砂漠のなかのもうひとつの理想郷

Taliesin West: Another utopia in the desert

● **タリアセン・ウェスト** | Taliesin West | アリゾナ州スコッツデール、1938年–、住宅、教育施設 | Scottsdale, Arizona, begun 1938, residential/educational

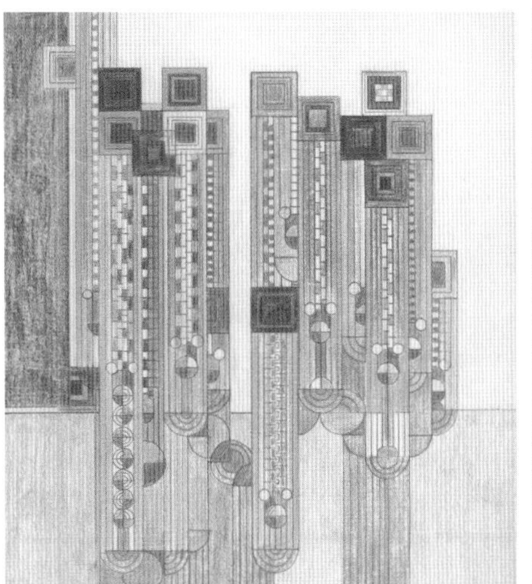

2-74

2-75

2-76

2-79

2-82

2-74 『リバティ』誌のための表紙デザイン案 柱サボテンとサボテンの花(部分) | デザイン：フランク・ロイド・ライト | 1927–28年
2-75 『リバティ』誌のための表紙デザイン案 4月の雨(部分) | デザイン：フランク・ロイド・ライト | 1926–27年
2-76 サボテンの横に立つジェンス・ジェンセン | 撮影：コーネリア・ブライアリー | 撮影年不詳
2-79 タリアセン・ウェスト(アリゾナ州スコッツデール)1938年– サボテンの見える外観 | 建築：フランク・ロイド・ライト | 撮影：1940年
2-82 映像「タリアセン・ウェストのフランク・ロイド・ライト」| 1953年

2-74 Cover design for *Liberty* Magazine. *Saguaro Forms and Cactus Flowers*. Frank Lloyd Wright, designer. 1927–28.
Prints and Photographs Division, Library of Congress, Washington, D.C. LC-DIG-ppmsca-84873
2-75 Cover design for *Liberty* Magazine. *April Showers*. Frank Lloyd Wright, designer. 1926–27.
Prints and Photographs Division, Library of Congress, Washington, D.C. LC-DIG-ppmsca-84874
2-76 Jens Jensen with cactus. Cornelia Brierly, photographer. undated. Personal and Taliesin Fellowship photographs, 1870s–2004,
The Frank Lloyd Wright Foundation Archives (The Museum of Modern Art | Avery Architectural & Fine Arts Library, Columbia University, New York)
2-79 Taliesin West, Scottsdale, Arizona. Project begun 1938. Exterior view, with cactuses. Frank Lloyd Wright, architect. Photo: 1940.
Project photographs, circa 1887–2008, The Frank Lloyd Wright Foundation Archives
(The Museum of Modern Art | Avery Architectural & Fine Arts Library, Columbia University, New York)
2-82 Film. Frank Lloyd Wright at Taliesin West, 1953. The Frank Lloyd Wright Foundation Archives
(The Museum of Modern Art | Avery Architectural & Fine Arts Library, Columbia University, New York)

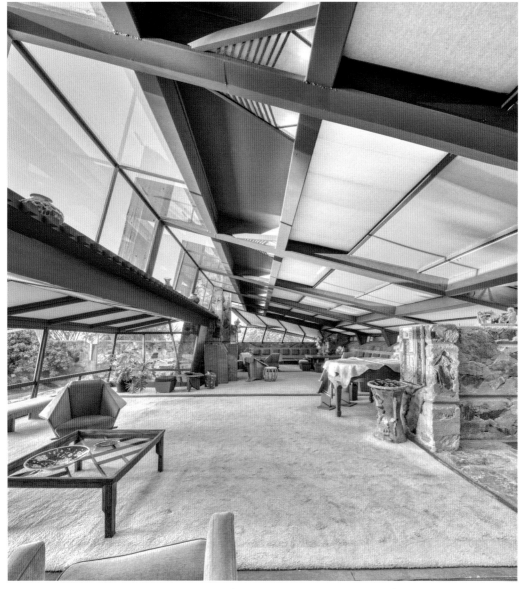

2-80 タリアセン・ウェスト(アリゾナ州スコッツデール)1938年– 全景 | 建築:フランク・ロイド・ライト、撮影:フォスケット | 2016年

2-81 タリアセン・ウェスト(アリゾナ州スコッツデール)1938年– ガーデンルーム内観 | 建築:フランク・ロイド・ライト、撮影:アンドリュー・ピラージ | 2020年

2-80 Taliesin West, Scottsdale, Arizona. Project begun 1938. Panoramic view. Frank Lloyd Wright, architect. © Foskett, photographer. Photo: 2016. Courtesy of the Frank Lloyd Wright Foundation

2-81 Taliesin West, Scottsdale, Arizona. Project begun 1938. Interior view of the Garden Room. Frank Lloyd Wright, architect. © Andrew Pielage, photographer. Photo: 2020. Courtesy of the Frank Lloyd Wright Foundation

日本におけるライト建築

水上 優

ライトの業績はそのほとんどが母国米国でのものである。2019年、在米8件の作品が「フランク・ロイド・ライトの20世紀建築」として世界文化遺産に登録されたが、その登録申請書によれば、ライトの生涯1,100件以上の設計において、建設されたものは約530件あり、そのうち約430件が現存する[1]。しかしこのうち米国外の業績は、設計されたもので日本に16件、カナダに13件、イラク8件、他11件[2]の計48件であり、実現したものは日本に8件、カナダに2件の計10件あるに過ぎない。そして現存となれば、わずかに日本に4件、カナダに1件、計5件あるばかりである[3]。その数少ない米国外地域の業績中突出しているのが日本での業績である。実施と計画を合わせた全プロジェクト数、実現数、現存数、そのいずれにおいても筆頭となる。海を渡ったアジアの東国日本はライトにとってもまさに異なる文化圏になるが、そこにこれだけの実績を残しているのである。

その背景には、ライトの日本文化への関心の高さ（ケン・タダシ・オオシマの巻頭エッセイ参照）と、帝国ホテル二代目本館建設のための来日があった。ライトの来日は7度を数えるが、当時の移動は片道約1か月の船旅であった。最初の来日は1905年、ウィリッツ邸（1902–03）の施主夫妻と共に妻キャサリン・トビン（1889–1922）と連れ立って、ライト初の海外旅行であった。2度目の来日は1913年である。それは新パートナーのチェイニー夫人（1869–1914）を伴ったプライベートな旅行であっただけでなく、浮世絵収集の機会であり、また何より帝国ホテル支配人林愛作（1873–1951）と会って新館設計に関する調整を行う重要な機会でもあった。当時ライトは、林が先に話を持ちかけた建築家、下田菊太郎（1866–1931）の案への対案を出す必要があった。帝国ホテル新本館第1案（東京、計画案、1913）のパースは1913年に描かれている[4]。それに加えライトには、一般的な公共建築や大規模建築の設計実績、あるいはそれらの設計能力のアピールも必要であっただろう。依頼なく設計されたアメリカ大使館（東京、計画案、1914）は、そのようなデモンストレーション的意図をもつものと捉えられている[5]。それは、1906年設計のショー邸第1案の平面をそのまま再採用し、かなり急いだ設計であったようだ[6]。

日本におけるライトの最初の実施作品は、帝国ホテル支配人でありライトの最大の理解者であった林愛作の自邸である。林邸（東京、1917）［図1］は東京駒沢に現存する[7]。当時、周囲は民家もまばらな開けた土地で、林自ら設立した日本初のゴルフクラブ、東京ゴルフ倶楽部の駒沢ゴルフ場がすでにあった。林邸はそのクラブハウスの役割も兼ね備え、テニスコートもあり、外国からの賓客をもてなすこともできる施設として、「朋来居」と名づけられた[8]。木造であるが、玄関車寄せ、居間の暖炉や四隅には帝国ホテル同様大谷石が用いられ、室内の石組みの目地には金泥が塗られている。玄関と居間ホール周辺を残して、住宅のインテリアは現在は大きく改変されている。北西部分には大谷石の蔵らしきものもあった。石と木の素材感を生かした構成や雁行しながら低く伸びやかに水平線を強調する庇など、この時期のライトのプレイリー・ハウスの手法が展開されており、敷地内に風車なども備えるところからはライトの本拠地タリアセンの構成をも想起させる。

1916年3月17日、林愛作がタリアセンを訪れ、晴れてライトは帝国ホテル二代目本館（東京、1914、取り壊して一部移築）の設計契約を結ぶ。これは日本での業績においてのみならず、ライトの全業績において最大規模の建築である。ライト・アーカイヴズは、新本館付随の建物をそれぞれ別の業績として捉えている。1918年、後に玄関前の池となる場所に現場事務所（東京、1918、現存せず）が建てられた。ありきたりの仮設事務所ではなく、ひと目でライトの設計とわかるものであった[9]。続いて1919年、新本館に先立って[10]動力棟（1919／東京／現存せず）[11]が建てられた。新本館は全館のエネルギー源を電力とした建築であり、大量の電力の供給源をまず必要としたのである[12]。

初代本館（渡辺譲設計／1890）の客室数を補うために1906年に建てられた旧別館が、1919年12月に焼失した。これを受け急遽ライトによって新別館（アネックス）（1920／東京／現存せず）が設計された[13]［cat. no. 4–34］。新本館は1923年9月1日の関東大震災でも大きな被害を受けず、復興の拠点となって名声を獲得したが、新別館は地震被害で復旧困難となり取り壊された[14]。大震災の被害を受けたライトの建物はもう1件あった。箱根強羅に建設された資生堂創業者福原有信（1848–1924）の別荘、福原邸（1920／神奈川／現存せず）［図2］は、震災で倒壊した[15]。

帝国ホテル二代目本館（ライト館）は長年日本のフラッグシップホテルとしての役割を果たし、惜しまれながら1968年に取り壊されたが[16]、正面玄関ホール部分はいったん解体され、現在は愛知県犬山市にある博物館明治村に移築保存されている。

ライトは日本にもう1件ホテルを設計していた。帝国ホテル支配人である林を迎えて日本初の郊外型リゾートホテルを志向した小田原ホテル計画案（神奈川、1917）である[17]。外観パースには林へ捧げる書き込みが見られる[cat. no. 2-66]。実際に着工され、建設が進んでいたことがわかっているが、開業されなかった[18]。アーカイヴズには外観パースと敷地測量図上に建物の配置計画をスケッチしたもの2点しか資料はなく、詳細は不明である。

1917年1月の3度目の来日から最後の離日となった1922年7月までの間、その半分以上の期間をライトは日本で過ごしている。帝国ホテルの仕事以外にもいくつかの業績が日本に残されている。その契機のひとつは愛弟子である遠藤新(1889-1951)であった。自由学園(東京、1921)[cat. no. 3-32]は生活に密着した理想教育実践の場として羽仁もと子(1873-1957)と吉一(1880-1955)夫妻によって1921年に設立された女学校の校舎であるが[19]、羽仁にライトを紹介したのは遠藤であった。図面クレジットには共同設計者として遠藤新が明記されている[20]。「生徒はいかにも、校舎に咲いた花にも見えます。木も花も本来一つ。そのように、校舎も生徒もまた一つに」[21]というライトにとって、自由学園の運営と建築のあり方もまた、自然の本性を「一からの多」と捉える彼の思想の実現であった。

灘の造り酒屋山邑酒造8代目当主山邑太左衛門(1873-1944)の別邸である山邑邸(1918-24/兵庫県芦屋市/現ヨドコウ迎賓館)の設計にも遠藤が関わっている[cat. no. 2-60, 63]。太左衛門の娘婿である代議士星島二郎(1887-1980)が遠藤の親友であった縁で、ライトに設計が依頼された。ライトは基本スケッチを残して1922年に帰国したため、以降は弟子の遠藤新と南信(1892-1951)が実施設計を担当した[22]。4層構成の建物であるが、背後の六甲山系へ連なる尾根伝いに階段状にセットバックしながら展開するため4階建てと感じさせない。

星島二郎は実業家でもあり、帝国ホテルの程近くに所有する三角形の敷地をライトに見せ、10階建ての集合住宅兼オフィスビルの設計を依頼した[23]。ライトは帰国直前に日比谷三角ビル(東京、計画案、1922)[図3]のスケッチを渡し、星島はそれを遠藤に図面化させた[24]。23年に着工予定であったが、大震災によって計画は頓挫した[25]。

建築家武田五一とのつながりも深い。ライトは初回(1905)、2度目(1913)いずれの来日時にも武田に会っている。2度目にはヴァスムート・ポートフォリオを贈り、武田はそこから図版32葉を抜粋し、日本で最

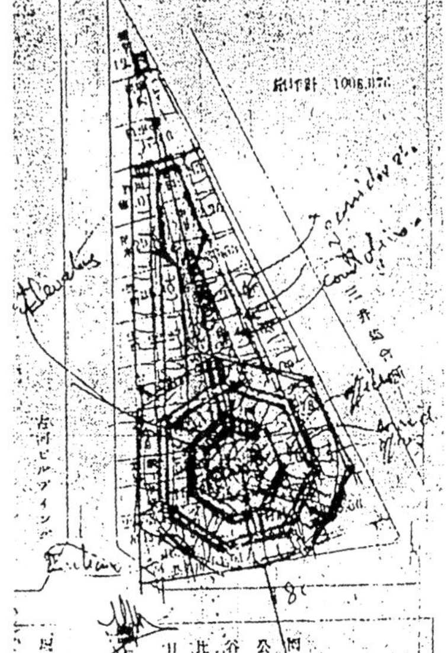

図3　日比谷三角ビル
(出典:『東京朝日新聞』1922年8月20日)

Fig.3　Hibiya Triangle Buildhing,
The Tokyo Asahi Shimbun, 20 September 1922

初のライト作品集を出版している[26]。ライト帰国時には3つの石膏模型、帝国ホテル、ユニティ・テンプル(1905-08)、劇場計画案(活動写真館/1918/東京)[cat. no. 3-28]を武田に寄贈している[cat. nos. 1-50, 3-28, 4-29]。劇場はこの模型以外の資料はないが、内部の舞台や客席は精巧につくられている。外観のみならず内部も含めて、1920年にロサンゼルスに計画されたバーンズドール邸劇場案に酷似しているが、敷地は銀座に想定されている。井上匡四郎子爵邸(計画案/1918/東京)[図4]の立面図には武田へ捧げる書き込みが見られる。広大な敷地に計画されたRC造2階建てで、大谷石、簾煉瓦、銅板屋根などが用いられ、帝国ホテルを彷彿とさせる重厚なデザインで、実現していれば日本国内の住宅では最大規模となるはずであった。施主より基本設計に対する設計料も支払われたが、実施には至らなかった[27]。

図1　林邸(撮影:水上優)

Fig.1　Hayashi House (photo: Yutaka Mizukami)

図2　福原邸(出典:『建築之日本』1巻2号、建築之日本社、1924年)

Fig.2　Fukuhara House, *Kenchiku no Nihon*, vol.1, No.2, Kenchiku no Nihon-sha, 1924

三原繁吉邸(計画案/1918/東京)の資料はアーカイヴズにある1枚の図面だけで、長く詳細不明の扱いであったが、谷川正己の調査によって浮世絵つながりの施主像が明らかになった[28]。三原繁吉(1862-1945)は日本浮世絵協会初代理事長であり、ライトは同協会の浮世絵展のポスターを作成している。城門のような建物と住居によって構成されるが、前者のみ立面図2面が併記され、そのレイアウトも併せ1913年にミルウォーキーに計画されたアーサー・リチャーズ中華レストラン案に酷似している。

施主とのつながりが不明であるものに後藤邸(計画案/1921/東京)[図5]がある。当時東京市長であった施主の後藤新平男爵(1857-1929)の自邸に付属する迎賓館的性格をもつ。アーカイヴズには「首相公邸」と誤記された別案もある[29]。帝国ホテル建設中にライトの下を離れたアントニン・レーモンド(1888-1976)が知人の紹介で後藤邸の設計を依頼されている[30]が、ライトへの依頼の有無は不明である[31]。

ライトが日本に残したもの、とりわけ帝国ホテル・ライト館は当時の日本の建築に影響を与え、「ライト式」なる流行語も生み出された。一方、日本はライトに何をもたらしたのであろうか。この問いは大きなテーマであり、本稿では一端を指摘するにとどめざるを得ないが、山邑邸3階に見られる「平面図における30度屈折」[cat.no.2-65]は、ライトの作品における初出であると思われる。この屈折は尾根という敷地に沿うかたちで生じている。ライトは『自伝』の中で、日本人が使う「仕方がない」という言葉を数回引用し、驚いている[32]。地震や火事といった人為を超えた出来事に対する日本人の諦観に驚いているのである。自然の地形に逆らわないかたちで山邑邸に初めて現れた30度屈折は、以後ライトの建築設計に頻出することになる。自然に倣う日本人の自然観は、ライトに新たな造形表現の突破口を与えたのである。

図4　井上匡四郎子爵邸

Fig.4　Viscount Tadashiro Inoue House, The Frank Lloyd Wright Foundation Archives (The Museum of Modern Art | Avery Architectural & Fine Arts Library, Columbia University, New York), FLWDR1804.006

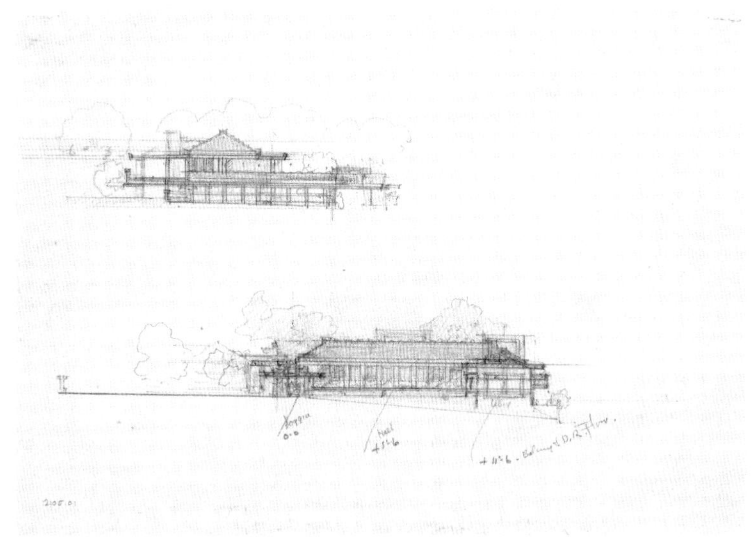

図5　後藤新平男爵邸

Fig.5　Baron Shimpei Goto House, The Frank Lloyd Wright Foundation Archives (The Museum of Modern Art | Avery Architectural & Fine Arts Library, Columbia University, New York), FLWDR2105.001

1 “The 20-th Century Architecture of Frank Lloyd Wright, Nomination to the World Heritage List by the United States of America (2016) Revised 2019,” p.248. 申請書作成後、2018年1月にロックリッジ診療所が解体され、同年11月、南カリフォルニアのウールジー火災によりアーチ・オボラー・ゲストハウス群(1940)が焼失した(現在Frank Lloyd Wright Revival Initiative フランク・ロイド・ライト建物再生促進機構による再建が進行中)。

2 パナマ3件、イタリア、メキシコ各2件、エジプト、エルサルバドル、インド、イラン各1件。

3 カナダに建設されたものは、ピッキン邸(オンタリオ州サバー島/1900/現存)とバンフ国立公園パビリオン(アルバータ州/1911/1939取り壊し)。また米国外に現存するものとして、1937年にペンシルヴァニア州ピッツバーグに実現し、1950年代に解体され、1974年に英国ロンドン、ビクトリア・アンド・アルバート美術館に移築保存されているカウフマン事務所(インテリア)がある。

4 第1案を眺めてみると、平面的な配置構成は実施されたものとほぼ同じであるが、断面構成、とりわけ中央長軸方向のそれは大きく異なる。正面玄関に入ってからの奥行き方向の広がりと垂直方向の伸びやかな吹き抜けを持つ大空間は未だなく、最上階のホールも南北方向の広がりしかない。

5 谷川正己「Wrightのアメリカ大使館計画案について」『日本建築学会東海支部研究報告集』1980年、pp.69-72

6 再採用部分は1階をレセプションホール、2階を大使公邸とし、その両側に翼部を取り付け一方を外交業務対応諸室、もう一方を展示広報対応諸室として全体を構成している。当時すでにアメリカ大使館は霊南坂にあったが、その土地はもともと当時の帝国ホテル会長大倉喜八郎(1837–1928)率いる大倉財閥の所有地であった。デモンストレーションとしてアメリカ大使館が選択された理由について今後さらに調査が必要である。

7 林邸と明記されたアーカイヴズ所蔵図面の計画案は、具体的には、実現されたものと部分的にも一致しない。

8 自身の6人の子どもがのびのびと過ごせる場所として、シーソーやブランコ、登り棒などの遊具が備えられ、畳敷以外の室内床はリグノイドという樹脂系床材でおおって安全に配慮していた。林愛作「児童庭園と其設備」『庭園』2(9)、1920年11月、pp.4–7

9 「ライトは日比谷公園の向かいのホテル敷地の西側に自分用の平屋のオフィス(約60×24フィート)を建てた。ホテルと同じ黄褐色のレンガで、緩やかな傾斜のある寄棟屋根である。北西の角には玄関ポーチがあり、南西にはライトの事務所があった。東側の壁には暖炉、南側には製図台、北側の壁から西側の壁にかけてはソファが置かれていた。その先には、南壁に6〜7台の製図台が並ぶ広々とした製図室があった」とされている。Kirishiki Shinjiro, ‘The Story of the Imperial Hotel, Tokyo,’ *The Japan Architect* 138, 1968, p.134。帝国ホテル『帝国ホテル百年の歩み』1990年、p.24の写真「ライト館の基礎工事風景」にライトのデザインした窓をもつ平家建ての建物が確認される。

10 帝国ホテル『帝国ホテル 写真で見る歩み』2003年に掲載されている絵はがき「帝国ホテルを取り巻く日比谷界隈の俯瞰」において、ライト館南東角部に動力棟を見ることができる。また『帝国ホテル百年の歩み』152頁の旧本館および周辺図において、ライト館とライト設計の別館との間に動力棟の所在を確認できる。アーカイヴズにはそれぞれ2階建てのU字形平面と直線形平面の案があるが、実現したのは、U字形平面であることもわかる。

11 『帝国ホテル百年の歩み』25頁には、「新館」とは別の建物として「動力室」の建築概要が明記されている。なお、本稿では独立建築物としてpower houseの訳語を「動力棟」としている。

12 新館オープンの新聞広告には「料理をはじめとして、西洋洗濯、通風装置、昇降機はもちろん、室内掃除に至るまで全館悉く電化されたる世界無類の電気ホテル」のうたい文句があった。『帝国ホテル百年の歩み』p.159

13 木造2階建て漆喰仕上げ、中庭をロの字形に囲む建物で、客室85室と各階に暖炉付きロビーが配されていた。そのうち2階南東諸室はライトの住居となり、2階ロビーは新たな現場事務所にも供された。

14 『帝国ホテル百年の歩み』p.258

15 正方形の中庭をロの字形に囲み、西に玄関ホール、南に居間兼客間、東に洋室1室と畳敷床の間付きの和室3室、北に浴室、女中室、台所が配される。食堂から45度方向に守衛室が突き出る。中庭は中心に正方形の花壇があり、周囲を温泉池が囲む。居間兼客間は西側にダイニングテーブル、北側に暖炉があり南半分が吹き抜け、暖炉上部中2階のバルコニーから居間が見下ろせる。さらに南側には崖下を見晴らす外部テラスがある。暖炉や一部の柱、基礎部分には大谷石が用いられており、屋根は栗板葺であった。

16 帝国ホテルの取り壊し反対運動は日本における最初の建築保存運動でもあった。

17 谷川正己「Odawara HOTELの所在地がNagoyaであるとする記載の誤りを証す: Frank Lloyd Wright研究12」『日本建築学会東海支部研究報告集』1974年2月、pp.209–212、谷川正己「Odawara Hotelをprojectとして處理してよいか: Frank Lloyd Wright研究146」『日本建築学会中国・九州支部研究報告第8号』1990年3月、pp.353-356、谷川正己「計画案Odawara Hotel再考: Frank Lloyd Wright研究187」『日本建築学会大会学術講演梗概集(九州)』1998年7月、pp.451–452

18 『広報小田原』No.712、小田原市、1997年12月、pp.2–4、同No.719、1998年3月、pp.4–5、同No.743、1999年3月、pp.2–4

19 キャンパスの南沢移転に伴い、1934年より明日館として現存。

20 校舎設立について羽仁もと子は「ライトさんの叔母君が、かつてその広い邸宅の一部に、名もホームスクールという、家庭そのもののような学校を持っておいでになったということが、特に自由学園の建築に興味をお持ちになる動機になった」と記している。羽仁もと子「自由学園について」『婦人之友』1921年3月、p.9

21 フランク・ロイド・ライト「自由学園の建築」『婦人之友』1922年6月、pp.8–9

22 棟札には遠藤新建築創作所、施工女良工務店と記されていた。この棟札は現在所在不明となっている。

23 1922年8月20日の「東京朝日新聞」第5面で「日比谷三角地帯に新理想郷を描く…設計はライト氏が 独創の置きみやげ」の見出しで記事とスケッチが掲載されており、井上祐一(1951–)らの研究によってライト作品であることが明らかにされた。本稿執筆時点でアーカイヴズに記録されていない。井上祐一、内田青蔵「「日比谷三角ビルディング計画案」について:ライトの設計の可能性について」『日本建築学会大会学術講演梗概集(北海道)』1995年7月、pp.103–104。

24 ライトのスケッチは敷地形状に沿った七角形と三角形の組み合わされた平面であったが、七角形平面はライトの全キャリア中これのみであると思われる。遠藤新の設計では外周16角形、内周8角形の平面に変更されている。

25 『新建築』1967年12月、新建築社、p.250

26 フランク・ロイド・ライト著、武田五一選『建築図案集』積善館本店、1916

27 谷川正己「Wrightと井上匡四郎との往復書簡について: Frank Lloyd Wright研究·194」『日本建築学会関東支部研究報告集』2000年、pp.413-416

28 谷川正己「Miharaという人物の特定に資する一資料: Frank Lloyd Wright研究·197」『日本建築学会大会学術講演梗概集(関東)』2001、pp.317–318

29 アーカイヴズ資料(2105.004)には首相邸(Minister's House)の書き込みが見られるが、後藤新平邸の敷地である。後藤は当時東京市長(Mayor of Tokyo)であった。

30 アントニン・レーモンド著、三沢浩訳『自伝アントニン・レーモンド』鹿島研究所出版会、1970年、p.75(新装版、鹿島出版会、2007年)参照。レーモンド設計の後藤新平邸は1923年に建設された。

31 この年(1921年)ライトはほとんどの期間を日本で過ごしているが、図面に記載された日付(5月27日、28日)と場所(ロサンゼルス)はその短い在米期間に当たる。

32 フランク・ロイド・ライト著、樋口清訳『自伝——ある芸術の形成』中央公論美術出版, 2000年、p.300、F. L. Wright, *An Autobiography*, Horizon Press, 1977, p.236

Frank Lloyd Wright's Architecture in Japan

Yutaka Mizukami

The majority of Wright's work is in his homeland, the United States of America. In 2019, eight of his works in the US were inscribed on the World Heritage List as the 20th-Century Architecture of Frank Lloyd Wright. According to the application documents, of the more than 1,100 designs created in Wright's lifetime, about 530 were built, of which about 430 still exist today.[1] However, among his works, 48 projects were designed outside the United States, including 16 projects in Japan, 13 in Canada, 8 in Iraq, and 11 in other regions,[2] of which only five projects still exist, including 4 in Japan and 1 in Canada.[3] Despite the limited number of projects beyond the United States, distinguished among them is his endeavor in Japan. It ranks first in the total number of projects implemented and designed, those completed, and those existing. Although Japan was an entirely new cultural hemisphere in the East Asia for Wright, he managed to create an impressive catalog of works.

Behind this was Wright's fascination with Japanese culture (see Ken Tadashi Oshima's opening essay) and his visit to Japan for constructing the new Imperial Hotel. He visited Japan seven times, even though the means of transportation at the time was a month-long ship trip each way. He first visited Japan in 1905, with his wife, Catherine (1889–1922), and the owner couple of Ward W. Willits House (1902–03), and it was his first ever travel overseas. The second trip was in 1913, which not only was a private getaway with his new partner, Mamah Borthwick (Cheney/ 1869–1914), but also a chance for his ukiyo-e painting acquisitions, and above all, a major opportunity for him to meet Aisaku Hayashi, the General Manager of the Imperial Hotel, to discuss the new construction. At the time, Wright had to present a counter-proposal to that by Kikutaro Shimoda (1866–1931), the architect Hayashi had initially approached. The perspective sketch for the first draft of the new Imperial Hotel's main building (project, 1913, Tokyo) was drawn in 1913.[4] In addition, Wright must have needed a track record of designing general public buildings and large-scale projects, or to present his design competence. The American Embassy (project, Tokyo, 1914), designed without commission, is considered to have had the intention to demonstrate such competency.[5] It seems to have been a rather rush assignment, given how it reuses the floor plan from the project of Shaw House in 1906.[6]

His first built work in Japan was a home for Aisaku Hayashi, the General Manager of the Imperial Hotel and one of Wright's very good friends. Hayashi House (1917, Tokyo) [Fig. 1] still remains in Komazawa, Tokyo.[7] At the time of construction, the site was on open land with very few houses. However, the Komazawa Course of the Tokyo Golf Club was already there, which was the first golf club founded in Japan by Hayashi himself, and the h doubled as the clubhouse and had a tennis court. It was named Horaikyo (friends gathering house) to entertain international guests.[8] Although it was built with a wooden structure, Oya stone was used at the entrance porch, fireplace, and four corners of the living room, much like the Imperial Hotel, and gold paint adorns the joints of the interior stonework. The interior work has since been extensively remodeled, except for the foyer and the area around the living room. There has also been a storehouse-like building made of Oya stone found on the northwest part. The Prairie style approach that Wright took during this era unfolds, including the textural composition of stone and wood, and the eaves that emphasize the horizontality in an elegant low posture. The site also installs a windmill, which is reminiscent of Wright's base ground, Taliesin.

On March 17, 1916, Aisaku Hayashi visited Taliesin, and Wright was finally able to sign the design contract for the new main building of the Imperial Hotel (Wright Building) (1914, Tokyo, partially demolished and relocated) . This is one of the largest architecture not only in Japan but also in his entire career. Wright Archives regards each building attached to the new main building as a separate work. In 1918, Frank Lloyd Wright Office-Studio at Imperial Hotel (1918, Tokyo, demolished) was built at a site that would later become the pond in front of the entrance. It was not another temporary office but was something instantly recognizable as Wright's design.[9] Subsequently, in 1919, the Imperial Hotel Power House (1919, Tokyo, demolished) was built ahead of the new main building.[10, 11] The new main building adopted electricity as the energy source for the entire building and thus needed a large amount of power supply.[12]

The former annex was built in 1906, as the first main building (1890, designed by Yuzuru Watanabe) lacked the number of rooms to accommodate guests, which however was destroyed in a fire in December 1919. Thus, the Imperial Hotel Annex (1920, Tokyo, demolished) was designed by Wright out of necessity.[13] [cat. no. 4-34] The new main building suffered no major destruction during the Great Kanto Earthquake on September 1st, 1923, which gained fame as the symbol of reconstruction, although the new annex was demolished due to damage beyond recovery.[14] Another one of his architecture was hit by the catastrophe; Fukuhara House (1920, Kanagawa, demolished) [Fig. 2] built as a villa for Shiseido's founder in Gora, Hakone, was destroyed by the disaster.[15]

The Wright Building, the new main building of the Imperial Hotel, played a role as the flagship hotel of Japan for many years but was unfortunately demolished in 1968.[16] However, the main entrance hall was disassembled to be relocated and preserved at Meiji Mura in Inuyama, Aichi.

Wright had designed another hotel in Japan. With Hayashi, the Imperial Hotel's General Manager, the Odawara Hotel (1917, Kanagawa, not completed) [cat. no. 2-66] was designed to be Japan's first resort hotel.[17] There even are some notes dedicated to Hayashi on the perspective drawing [cat. nos. 2-60, 63]. Although it is certain that the construction had started and was underway, it was never opened.[18] The Archives only posses two items, a perspective drawing and a layout plan sketched on a site survey map, while details are unknown.

Between his third visit in January 1917 and his final departure in July 1922, Wright spent more than half of his time in Japan, leaving behind several masterpieces other than his works at the Imperial Hotel. One of the forces supporting his achievements was his Japanese apprentice, Arata Endo. Jiyu Gakuen (1921, Tokyo) was an all-girls school founded in 1921 as a place to practice their ideal education in a home-like atmosphere by Motoko and Yoshikazu Hani,[16] to whom Endo introduced Wright. Arata Endo is even credited as the co-designer in the drawings.[20] Wright once said, "The students indeed look like flowers blooming in the schoolhouse. Trees and flowers are essentially one. Thus, the schoolhouse and students will become one."[21] For him, how the school was managed and built were both realization of his philosophy considering nature as "from one to variety."

Endo was also involved in designing Yamamura House (1917, Ashiya, Hyogo, now Yodoko Guest House) [cat. nos. 2-60, 61], the villa of the eighth heir to a sake brewer in Nada, Yamamura Shuzo. Tazaemon's son-in-law, a House of Representatives member Niro Hoshishima was a close friend of Endo's, which led to Wright's commission. As Wright returned to the United States in 1922, leaving his disciples with some schematic design sketches, Arata Endo and Makoto Minami (1892–1951) took over the design development.[22] Although it is a four-story building, it does not feel like one, as the step-like architecture sits along the ridge that connects to the Mount Rokko range on the back.

Niro Hoshishima was also a businessman, who showed Wright a triangular lot he owned near the Imperial Hotel and asked him to design a ten-story apartment/office building.[23] Just before returning to the States, Wright gave him sketches of the Hibiya Triangle Building (unbuilt project, 1922, Tokyo) [Fig. 3], which was given from Hoshishima to Endo to be translated into architectural drawings.[24] The construction was scheduled to start in 1923, but the plan was aborted due to the catastrophic earthquake.[25]

Wright also formed a bond with the architect Goichi Takeda. He met Takeda on both occasions of his first visit to Japan (1905) and his second (1913). During the second visit, he gave him the Wasmuth Portfolio, from which Takeda excerpted 32 drawings to publish the first collection of Wright's works in Japan.[26] When Wright left, he also donated three plaster models: the Imperial Hotel, the Unity Temple (1905–08), and the Motion Picture Theater (project, 1918, Tokyo) [cat. nos. 1-50, 3-28, 4-29]. There is no material left apart from this model of the theater, but the stage and the audience seats on the inside are elaborately crafted. Although not only the exterior but also the interior strongly resemble the project of Aline Barnsdall Motion Picture Theater in Los Angeles in 1920, this theater was designed for Ginza. On the elevation drawing for the Viscount Tadashiro Inoue House (project, 1918, Tokyo) [Fig. 4], some notes dedicated to Takeda can also be found. It was a two-story reinforced concrete structure planned on a vast site, which adopted materials such as Oya stone, scratched bricks, and copper plate roofing, and the robust design resembled the Imperial Hotel. It was meant to be one of the largest-scale residential projects in Japan, and the design fee was indeed paid for the schematic design, but it was never built.[17]

For Mihara House (unbuilt project, 1918, Tokyo), not only is there just one drawing the Archives, the details were long considered a mystery. However, thanks to the investigation Masami Tanigawa's investigation, it was revealed that Wright connected with the client through ukiyo-e.[28] Shigekichi Mihara (1862–1945) was the first president of the Japan Ukiyo-e Association, for which Wright created a poster for an exhibition. The project consisted of a gate-like architecture and the residence, but only the former has two elevations supplementing the drawing, which strongly resembles the Arthur Richards Chinese Restaurant proposal designed in Milwaukee in 1913, including the layout of the drawing.

Another project in which the connection to the client is a mystery is Goto House (unbuilt project, 1921, Tokyo) [Fig. 5]. The project was more of a guesthouse annex to the residence of the client, Shimpei Goto (1857–1929) who was the Mayor of Tokyo then. The Archives also own another draft that is mislabeled as the Prime Minister's House.[29] Antonin Raymond, who left Wright during the construction of the Imperial Hotel, was commissioned through an acquaintance to design Goto House,[30] but it is unknown whether Wright was commissioned.[31]

What Wright left behind in Japan, especially the new Imperial Hotel, impacted Japanese architecture at the time, in which even the term "Wright-style" was coined. Conversely, what did Japan offer to Wright? The question is one of the greatest subjects, and this essay could merely point out a fraction of the answer. Found on the third floor of the Yamamura House is the "30-degree refraction on a floor plan [cat. no. 2-65]", which is considered to be the first time it appeared in Wright's body of work. The refraction was made in the course of following the terrain on the ridge. Wright was struck by and quotes several times in his autobiography the Japanese phrase *shikataganai* (it can't be helped).[32] He was shocked by the Japanese concept of resignation towards catastrophes beyond human will, such as earthquakes and fires. The 30-degree refraction that was first introduced in Yamamura House to surrender to the natural landscape, would frequently appear in Wright's architectural designs thereafter. The Japanese philosophy of resigning oneself to nature gave Wright a breakthrough in his artistic expression.

1 "The 20th Century Architecture of Frank Lloyd Wright, Nomination to the World Heritage List by the United States of America (2016) Revised 2019," 248.
After completing the application, the Lockridge Medical Clinic was dismantled in January 2018. That November, the Woolsey Fire in Southern California destroyed the Arch Oboler Gatehouse Complex (1940) (for which a reconstruction project is underway by the Frank Lloyd Wright Revival Initiative).

2 3 in Panama, 2 each in Italy and Mexico, and 1 each in Egypt, El Salvador, India, and Iran.

3 Built in Canada were Pitkin House (Sapper Island, Ontario, 1900, existing) and Banff National Park Pavilion (Alberta, 1911, demolished in 1939). Moreover, in terms of projects that exist outside of the United States, Kaufmann Office (interior) which was constructed in Pittsburgh, Pennsylvania in 1937 and dismantled in the 1950s, was moved in 1974 to the Victoria and Albert Museum in London, United Kingdom.

4 Looking at the first draft, the layout plan is almost the same as that constructed, but the cross sections, especially the long central one, are very different. The expanding depth from the entrance and the generous space with a vertical atrium are nowhere to be found, and the top floor hall has only the expansion to the north-south direction.

5 Masami Tanigawa, 'On Wright's American Embassy Proposal,' *AIJ Tokai Chapter Architectural Research Meeting* (Tokyo: AIJ, 1980), pp.69–72.

6 In the reused version, the first floor was the reception hall, the second was the ambassador's residence, and two wings were attached to both sides with one serving as a diplomatic service room and the other as a public relations room. The U.S. Embassy Building already existed in Reinanzaka, but the land originally belonged to the Okura Zaibatsu (company syndicate) led by Kihachiro Okura (1837–1928), who then was the chairman of the Imperial Hotel. Further research is required as to why the U.S. Embassy Building was selected as the subject of the demonstration.

7 To be specific, the draft plan owned by the Archives labeled Hayashi House does not even partially match the constructed building.

8 Playground equipment, including seesaws, swings, and climbing poles, was installed to provide a place where his six children could play freely, while interior flooring was either tatami or covered with a resin-based material called lignoid to ensure safety.
Aisaku Hayashi, 'Jido teien to sono setsubi (Children's Garden and Its Equipment),' *Gardens* (Nov. 1920): pp.4–7.

9 "Wright had a one-story office (about 60 by 24 ft) built for himself on the west side of the hotel site across from Hibiya Park on the spot where he was finally to put the pool. No humble on-the-site-office this. It was of the same yellow-brown brick used in the hotel and had a gently sloping hipped roof. A single glance was enough to tell anyone that Wright had done the design. The entrance porch was in the northwest corner, and Wright's own office in the southwest. He had a fireplace on the east wall, a drafting desk on the south, and a sofa running from the north wall to the west wall. Beyond this room was a spacious drafting room with six or seven drafting desks lined up the south wall." Shinjiro Kirishiki, 'The Story of the Imperial Hotel, Tokyo,' *The Japan Architect*, no. 138, (Tokyo: Shinkenchiku-sha, 1968), p.134.
A one-story building with windows designed by Wright can be seen in the photo on p.24 titled "Foundation Work for Wright Building" from *100 Years of the Imperial Hotel History* published by the Imperial Hotel, 1990.

10 In "Imperial Hotel-a legend in pictures" (The Imperial Hotel, 2003, page unnoted) is a postcard titled "Overview of the Hibiya Neighborhood Around the Imperial Hotel," where the power house can be found on the southeast corner of the Wright Building. And on the plan of the original building and the neighborhood on p.152 of *100 Years of the Imperial Hotel History*, the power house can be confirmed between the Wright Building and the annex designed by Wright. The Archives own drafts with a two-storied U-shaped plan and a linear plan, but it is also apparent that it was the U-shaped plan that was constructed.

11 In *100 Years of the Imperial Hotel History*, the architectural outline of the "power house" is specified as a separate building from the "new building."
100 Years of the Imperial Hotel History (The Imperial Hotel, 1990), 25.
Here in this essay, it is specified as an individual architecture, therefore calling it the "power house."

12 The newspaper advertisement for the opening of the new building included a headline, "An unprecedented electric hotel, where everything from cooking to Western laundry, ventilation, elevators, and even room cleaning is fully electric." *100 Years of the Imperial Hotel History* (The Imperial Hotel, 1990), 159.

13 It was a two-story wooden structure with a stucco finish surrounding a courtyard in a square shape, which had 85 guest rooms and a lobby with a fireplace on each floor. The southeast room on the second floor became Wright's residence, and the lobby on the second floor was also used as the new construction office.

14 *100 Years of the Imperial Hotel History*, p.258.

15 The architecture surrounds the square courtyard, with an entrance hall on the west, a living room/guest room on the south, a western-style room and three tatami-floored Japanese-style rooms with tokonoma alcove on the east, and the bathroom, maid's room, and kitchen on the north. The janitor's room protrudes from the dining room at a 45-degree angle. The courtyard has a square flowerbed in the center, surrounded by a hot spring pond. The living room/guest room has a dining table on the west side, a fireplace on the

north with the south half being the atrium, and the second-floor balcony above the fireplace has a top-down view of the living room. In addition, there is an external terrace on the south side overlooking the cliffs below. Oya stone was used for the fireplace, some parts of the pillars, and the foundation, whereas the roof was thatched with chestnut boards.

16 The protest against the demolition of the Imperial Hotel was the first architectural preservation movement in Japan.

17 Masami Tanigawa, 'Proofing that Odawara Hotel's location was mislabeled Nagoya: Frank Lloyd Wright Studies 12,' *AIJ Tokai Chapter Architectural Research Meeting* (Tokyo, 1974): 209–212.
Masami Tanigawa, 'Should Odawara Hotel be treated as a project?: Frank Lloyd Wright Studies 146,' *AIJ Kyushu/Chugoku Chapter Architectural Research* (vol. 8, 1990): 353–356.
Masami Tanigawa, 'Reconsidering the Odawara Hotel Proposal: Frank Lloyd Wright Studies 187,' *AIJ Summaries of technical papers of annual meeting* (Kyushu, 1998): 451–452.

18 *Koho Odawara* (no.712, Dec 1,1997): pp.2–4.
Koho Odawara (no. 719, Mar 15, 1998): pp.4–5.
Koho Odawara (no. 743, Mar 15, 1999): pp.2–4.

19 As the campus relocated to Minamisawa, the building exists now as Myonichikan since 1934.

20 Regarding founding the school building, Motoko Hani wrote, "Mr. Wright's aunt having had a corner in her spacious mansion called the Home School, which was a home-like environment of a school, was one of the greatest incentives for him to take interest in the architecture for Jiyu Gakuen."
Motoko Hani, 'On Jiyu Gakuen,' *Fujin-no-tomo* (Mar 1921): p.9.

21 Frank Lloyd Wright, 'The Architecture of Jiyu Gakuen,' *Fujin-no-tomo* (Jun 1922): pp.8–9.

22 On the munafuda tag, Endo Shinkenchiku Sosakusho and Mera Komuten were credited. However, the whereabouts of this munafuda are currently unknown.

23 On page 5 of *Tokyo Asahi Shimbun* on August 20, 1922, an article and sketches were published under the headline, 'Drawing a New Utopia in the Hibiya Triangle—Designed by Mr. Wright as a Parting Gift of Creativity." It was revealed as Wright's work through the research by Yuichi Inoue (1951–). This is not yet recorded in the Archives as of today at the time of writing this.
Yuichi Inoue, Seizo Uchida, 'On the Hibiya Triangle Building Plan: The Possibilities in Wright's Design,' *AIJ Summaries of technical papers of annual meeting* (Hokkaido, 1995): pp.103–104.

24 Wright originally sketched a plan that combines heptagons and triangles to follow the shape of the terrain, and this is the only time in his entire career where he used heptagons. In Arata Endo's design, it was changed into hexadecagons on the outer perimeter and octagons on the inner.

25 *Shinkenchiku* (Dec 1967): p.250.

26 Frank Lloyd Wright, selection by Goichi Takeda, *Architectural Plans of Frank Lloyd Wright* (Osaka: Sekizenkan-honten, 1916).

27 Masami Tanigawa, 'On the correspondence between Wright and Tadashiro Inoue: Frank Lloyd Wright Studies 194', *AIJ Kanto Chapter Architectural Research Meeting* (2000): pp.413–416.

28 Masami Tanigawa, 'Materials Contributing to Identifying Mihara: Frank Lloyd Wright Studies 197,' *AIJ Summaries of technical papers of annual meeting* (Kanto, 2001): pp.317–318.

29 In the material preserved in the Archives (2105.004), there is a note reading "Prime Minister's House," although the site is that of Shinpei Goto's residence. However, Goto was the Mayor of Tokyo at the time.

30 Antonin Raymond, trans. Hiroshi Misawa, *Antonin Raymond: Autobiography* (Tokyo: Kajima Institute Publishing, 1970), p.75.
Raymond's design for Goto House was built in 1923.

31 Although Wright had spent most of this year (1921) in Japan, the date (May 27, 28) and location (Los Angeles) noted on the drawing was during his brief stay in the United States.

32 Frank Lloyd Wright, *An Autobiography* (Horizon Press, 1977), p.236.

SECTION 3

進歩主義教育の環境をつくる

Designing Progressive Educational Environments

ライトは、教育こそ民主主義の基本であると考え、その理想の提示として自ら一種の学校でもあるタリアセン・フェローシップ[cat. nos. 3-46, 47]を設立した。彼の心に深く植え付けられていたのは、当時の最も進歩的な教育理論であり、母方の一族ロイド・ジョーンズ家由来の信念であり、そして幼少期と青年建築家時代を過ごした19世紀の経験であった。1886年、ライトの叔母であるジェーンおよびエレン・ロイド・ジョーンズは、ウィスコンシン州スプリンググリーンにヒルサイド・ホームスクールという先駆的教育機関を設立した[cat. no. 3-1]。そこは後に1911年になってライトが自宅兼アトリエであるタリアセンを建設することになる、まさにその地であった。新興の児童発達理論に基づき、ヒルサイド・ホームスクールでは、ラテン語やギリシャ語といった古典的な学習分野の暗記、暗唱を中心とした従来型の教育方法を否定し、体験や実験による直接的な学びを優先した、子ども中心の新しいタイプの学習を推進した。ヒルサイド・ホームスクールで、生徒たちは数学、文学、歴史などの授業はもちろん、美術や体育と同様に製本、金属加工、ステンシル、デザインなどの実技科目も履修した。カリキュラムの核となるのは自然学習であった。ヒルサイド・ホームスクールは、庭園、耕作地、動物、田園など周囲の環境を生かして、動物学、農学、地質学、気候学、植物学の直接的な科学学習を行った[1][cat. nos. 3-3, 4]。

ヒルサイド・ホームスクールは、おそらく20世紀初頭における最も有名な実験的学校であり、ジョン・デューイ(1859–1952)が1896年にシカゴ大学に開設したラボラトリー・スクールに先駆けるものであった。デューイの実験学校では、彼が生活の基本となる社会的・経済的な活動であるとする料理、食物の栽培、道具を使った作業、織物の製作といった実社会の「仕事」を中心とした実践的なカリキュラムが提供された。学校で子どもたちは、トウモロコシを植えたり、卵のゆで方を教わったり、納屋の模型をつくったりと、積極的にこの「仕事」に参加した。このような実践的な活動は、具体的であり、遊びや想像力といった子どもたちの本能を刺激するものであったため、子どもたちをひきつけた[2]。

ライトの施主、同僚、友人はたいていは女性であったが、彼女らはシカゴにおけるこの「新たな教育」の参加者であり、教育と女性の権利が密接に関わっていることを実証する活動的なフェミニストや専門家であった。1895年から1909年まで、ライトのオークパークのスタジオでシニアデザイナーを務めたマリオン・マホニー[cat. no. 3-11]は、1894年にマサチューセッツ工科大学で建築の学位を取得した2人目の女性であり、イリノイ州で建築士免許を取得した最初の女性であった。彼女が深く関わっていたシカゴの活動家サークルは、ジェンダー平等運動の推進や、ジョン・デューイとエラ・フラッグ・ヤング(1845–1918)が主導した幼稚園や進歩主義教育の学校などの教育運動の推進を掲げていた。[3] マホニーの従兄弟で、ライトの仕事仲間であったドワイト・パーキンス(1867–1941)は、1905年から1910年にかけてシカゴ教育委員会の主任建築家を務め、新しい体験型教育に対応するための実験室、体育館、そしてアートスタジオを備えた学校を40件以上設計した[4]。

最も誠実なクライアントの一人であったクィーン・フェリー・クーンリー[cat. no. 3-25]は、イリノイ州リバーサイドに進歩主義教育「コテージ学校」を設立し、自ら教鞭を執った。そこでは美術や演劇や「実践による学び」を基本にして、子どもたちが自ら学習プログラムを計画していた。1906年、自宅の設計をライトに依頼した際には、彼女は伝統的な家庭的空間に、「ホームスクール」や「子どもたちの社会」として利用可能な別の空間を結びつける計画を求めた。当時の写真には、リビングルームでの学校の歴史劇、プー

1 ヒルサイド・ホームスクール(ウィスコンシン州ヒルサイド、1891–1915)の年次学校案内パンフレット[cat. no. 3-2]ウィスコンシン州歴史博物館)を参照のこと。

2 John Dewey, “The School and Social Progress,” in *The School and Society* (Chicago: 1900; rev. ed. 1915, 1943); reprinted with introduction by Leonard Carmichael (Chicago: University of Chicago Press, 1956), pp. 10–11; Dewey, “The School and Society,” in *The School and Society*, pp. 15–23.

ルサイドに立つローマの剣闘士、ギリシャの若き雄弁家の演説の様子などが写っている。「幼稚園運動」のリーダーとして知られ、自らジョン・デューイの信奉者であることを認めていたクィーン・フェリー・クーンリーは、シカゴ近郊にいくつかの幼稚園を設立している。ライト設計の有名なクーンリー・プレイハウス幼稚園(イリノイ州リバーサイド、1911年)はその一つであり、それは遊び心溢れるステンドグラス、演劇用のステージ、そして子どもたちが自然と触れ合う屋外教育庭園を備えていた[5][cat.nos.3-18, 3-22~24]。ライトのクライアントの一人で、ライトの叔母たちが運営していたヒルサイド・ホームスクールの長年の支援者であったスーザン・ローレンス・ダナ(1862-1942)も同様に、住宅の私的な機能と、地元であるイリノイ州スプリングフィールドの子どもたちのための教育・慈善活動に捧げられる半公共的空間とを結びつけるような住宅をライトに依頼した[6]。このような教育への関与は、イリノイ州オークパークにあるライトの自邸とスタジオにも示されている。1895年、ライトはこの自邸に大きなプレイルームを増築し[cat.no.3-12]、最初の妻キャサリン・トビンはそこで近所の子どもたちのための幼稚園のクラスを開いた[cat.nos.3-12, 13]。この部屋にはピアノが置かれ、子どもたちがつくった劇やミュージカルの舞台として、あるいは客席として利用できる段差のある座席が設けられた[7]。当時の写真には、ドイツの教育者で幼稚園の創始者であるフリードリヒ・フレーベルが推奨し、ライトの母親が幼少期の息子に実践的な探究を促すために取り入れたことがよく知られる教育法である、フレーベル教育の実践が写し出されている[8]。ライトは、個人的にもメイマー・ボートン・ボスウィック(1869-1914)という進歩的なフェミニストと深い関わりをもった。彼女はミシガン大学で修士号を取得した女性で元々はライトの施主であった。ボースウィックとライトは、スウェーデンの女性運動家エレン・ケイの思想と著作をアメリカの聴衆に伝える上で大きな役割を果たしたが、彼女は思いがけず夭逝した[cat.nos.3-14~17]。

ライトの進歩主義教育への関与は、彼の生涯と仕事を通して示されている。1920年代にはイリノイ州オークパークの子どもたちのためにオークパーク協会への設計競技案「キンダーシンフォニーズ」(1926年)と呼ばれる一連のプレイハウス[cat.nos.3-19~21]を設計した他、アフリカ系アメリカ人のためのローゼンワルド財団の学校計画案(1928年)[cat.no.3-45]、そして、カリフォルニア州ロサンゼルスのフェミニスト、アリーン・バーンズドールの自邸「立葵の家」を取り囲む[cat.nos.3-29, 30]、彼女の大規模な教育・演劇複合施設の一部を構成するリトル・ディッパー幼稚園およびコミュニティ・プレイハウス計画案(1923年)[cat.nos.3-26, 27]などを設計した。これらはいずれも、アクティブ・ラーニングや演劇制作のためのスペース、体育やレクリエーションのためのプールを取り入れた設計であった。このような教育改革は、教育を通じて社会の平等とよりよい生活を実現しようとする活動家たちの世界的な現象であり、日本においてもライトは1921年、東京に進歩的な自由学園[cat.nos.3-31~33]を設計している。羽仁もと子・吉一夫妻[cat.no.3-36]が女学校として設立した自由学園の教授法に彼は心から共鳴していた。自由学園の校舎は、同時期に設計していたローゼンワルド財団の学校計画案の校舎と非常によく似ている。1932年、タリアセン・フェローシップを設立した際、ライトはこれらの考え方を統合することになる。ウィスコンシン州スプリンググリーンの一族の根拠地であり、数十年前にヒルサイド・ホームスクールのあった同じ敷地で、同様に農業、ガーデニング、料理、建設作業など「実践によって学ぶ」活動が中心に据えられた[cat.nos.3-46~49]。このように、ライトの自然や風景への関心は、彼の教育論と密接な関係にあったことがわかるのである。

3 Alice T. Friedman, “Girl Talk: Feminism and Domestic Architecture at Frank Lloyd Wright's Oak Park Studio,” in *Marion Mahony Reconsidered*, ed. David Van Zanten (Chicago: University of Chicago Press, 2011), pp. 25-26

4 Jennifer Gray, Ready for Experiment: Dwight Perkins and Progressive Architectures in Chicago, 1893-1918, PhD Dissertation (Columbia University, 2011), p. 252.

5 前掲書 註3 pp. 45-47.

6 前掲書 註3 pp. 43-44.

7 前掲書 註3 p. 37.

8 Lisa D. Schrenk, *The Oak Park Studio of Frank Lloyd Wright* (Chicago: University of Chicago Press, 2021), pp. 11-12.

Wright considered education fundamental to democracy and even founded his own school of sorts, the Taliesin Fellowship, to advance that ideal. He was deeply embedded with the most progressive educational theories of his day, a preoccupation that stretched back to his mother's family, the Lloyd Joneses, and his formative years as a child and young architect in the nineteenth century. In 1886, Wright's aunts, Jane and Ellen Lloyd Jones, founded a pioneering education center called Hillside Home School in Spring Green, Wisconsin [cat. no. 3-1]. Wright would later build Taliesin, his own home and studio, on the same grounds in 1911. Informed by emerging child-development theories, Hillside advanced a new type of child-centered learning that rejected conventional teaching methods based on memorization and recitation of classical fields of study, such as Latin and Greek, in favor of direct learning through hands-on study and experimentation. At Hillside, while taking courses in mathematics, literature, and history, students also took manual training courses, such as bookbinding, metalworking, stenciling, and design, as well as art and physical education. Nature study was at the core of the curriculum. Hillside leveraged its surrounding environment—the gardens, cultivated plots, animals, and surrounding countryside—to support direct scientific study in zoology, agriculture, geology, climate, and botany [cat. nos. 3-3, 4].[1]

Hillside prefigured what was probably the most renowned experimental school at the turn of the twentieth century, the Laboratory School founded by John Dewey (1859–1952) in 1896 at the University of Chicago. The Lab School offered a hands-on curriculum organized around real-world "occupations," as Dewey called the basic social and economic activities of life, such as cooking, growing food, working with tools, making textiles, and so forth. Children actively participated in the occupations at school when they planted corn, learned to boil an egg, or built a model barn together. Such practical activities appealed to children because they were concrete and tapped their instincts for play and imagination.[2]

Many of Wright's clients, colleagues, and friends, mostly women, were part of this "new education" in Chicago and were active feminists and professionals, demonstrating the intersection of education and women's rights. Marion Mahony [cat. no. 3-11], Wright's senior designer in his Oak Park studio between 1895–1909, was only the second woman to graduate with an architecture degree from the Massachusetts Institute of Technology in 1894 and the first woman licensed to practice architecture in the state of Illinois. She also was deeply involved in activist circles in Chicago that advanced gender equality and education, including the kindergarten and progressive school movements led by John Dewey and Ella Flagg Young (1845–1918).[3] Her cousin and colleague of Wright's, Dwight Perkins (1867–1941), was the head architect of the Chicago School Board between 1905–1910 and designed over forty schools that included laboratories, gymnasiums, and art studios to accommodate the new hands-on education.[4]

One of Wright's most loyal clients, Queene Ferry Coonley [cat. no. 3-25], founded and taught at the progressive Cottage School in Riverside, Illinois, where children planned their own program of study based on the arts, theater, and learning by doing. When she commissioned Wright to design her house in 1906, she insisted that the program combine traditional domestic spaces with others that allowed her to create a "homeschool" and "children's community." Historic photographs depict school pageants in the living room, Roman gladiators on the terrace by the pool, and young Greek orators giving speeches. A leader in what was known as the

1 See annual prospectuses for Hillside Home School (Hillside, Wisconsin, 1891–1915), Wisconsin State Historical Society. [cat.no.3-2]

2 John Dewey, "The School and Social Progress," in *The School and Society* (Chicago: 1900; rev. ed. 1915, 1943); reprinted with introduction by Leonard Carmichael (Chicago: University of Chicago Press, 1956), pp. 10–11; Dewey, "The School and Society," in *The School and Society*, pp. 15–23.

3 Alice T. Friedman, "Girl Talk: Feminism and Domestic Architecture at Frank Lloyd Wright's Oak Park Studio," in *Marion Mahony Reconsidered*, ed. David Van Zanten (Chicago: University of Chicago Press, 2011), pp. 25–26.

"kindergarten movement" and self-described follower of John Dewey, Queene Coonley built several other kindergartens in the suburbs of Chicago, including Wright's well-known Coonley Playhouse (1911) [cat. nos. 3-18~24], which included playful stained glass, a stage for theatrical performances, and outdoor teaching gardens where children engaged with nature.[5] Susan Lawrence Dana, another client of Wright's and longtime supporter of his aunts' Hillside Home School, likewise commissioned a house in 1902 that combined the private functions of home with semi-public spaces devoted to educational and charitable activities for the children of Springfield, Illinois.[6] Such commitment to education manifested in Wright's own home and studio in Oak Park, Illinois. In 1895, Wright added a large playroom to the house [cat. no. 3-12], where his first wife, Catherine Tobin [cat. no. 3-13], offered kindergarten classes to neighborhood children. The space included a piano and tiered seating that could be used either as a stage or seating for the plays and musical productions the children created.[7] Historic photographs reveal evidence of Froebel group exercises on the floor, which Wright's mother famously introduced to her son when he was a child to encourage the hands-on exploration promoted by the German pedagogue, Friedrich Froebel, the inventor of kindergarten [cat. no. 3-7~12].[8] Even on a deeply personal level, Wright engaged with progressive and feminist directions, as evidenced by his relationship with Martha "Mamah" Borthwick (1869–1914), a client turned paramour who had earned a master's degree from the University of Michigan. Borthwick and Wright were instrumental in bringing the ideas and writing of Swedish feminist Ellen Key to American audiences before her untimely death [cat. no. 3-14~17].

Wright's engagement with progressive education would manifest throughout his life and career. In the 1920s, he designed a series of playhouses that he called Kindersymphonies (unbuilt project, 1926) [cat. nos. 3-19~21] for the children of Oak Park, Illinois; a Rosenwald School for African Americans in Virginia called the Hampton Normal and Agricultural Institute (unbuilt project, 1928) [cat. no. 3-45]; and the Little Dipper School and Community Playhouse (project, 1923) [cat. no. 3-26, 27] for the feminist Aline Barnsdall, which was intended to be part of Barnsdall's larger educational and theatrical complex surrounding Hollyhock House (1918–21) in Los Angeles, California [cat. no. 3-29, 30]. All of these designs incorporated spaces for active learning and theater production, as well as swimming pools for physical education and recreation. Such pedagogical reform was a global phenomenon as activists sought to advance social equality and better living through education, including in Japan, where Wright designed the progressive Jiyu Gakuen Girls' School in Tokyo in 1921 [cat. nos. 3-31~33]. Established by Yoshikazu and Motoko Hani [cat. no. 3-36], the pedagogy of the "Freedom School" dedicated to the education of girls fundamentally resonated with Wright. The building bears a striking resemblance to the Rosenwald School that Wright was designing around the same time. Wright would ultimately synthesize these ideas when he founded the Taliesin Fellowship in 1932, which likewise centered around farming, gardening, cooking, construction work, and other "learn by doing" activities that took place on his family compound in Spring Green, Wisconsin, on the same site that Hillside Home School had occupied decades earlier [cat. nos. 3-46~49]. In this way, we can see that Wright's interest in nature and landscape was inextricably related to his theories on education.

[Jennifer Gray]

4 Jennifer Gray, "Ready for Experiment: Dwight Perkins and Progressive Architectures in Chicago, 1893–1918," (PhD Diss., Columbia University, 2011), p. 252.

5 Friedman, "Girl Talk," pp. 45–47.

6 Ibid., pp. 43–44.

7 Ibid., p. 37.

8 Lisa D. Schrenk, *The Oak Park Studio of Frank Lloyd Wright* (Chicago: University of Chicago Press, 2021), pp. 11-12

14 ヒルサイド・ホームスクールの実験的教育

Experimental Pedagogy of Hillside Home School

● ヒルサイド・ホームスクール第一 | Hillside Home School I | ウィスコンシン州スプリンググリーン、1887年、教育施設 | Spring Green, Wisconsin, 1887, educational

3-1

3-3
3-4
3-5

● **ヒルサイド・ホームスクール第二** | Hillside Home School II | ウィスコンシン州スプリンググリーン、1902年、教育施設 | Spring Green, Wisconsin, 1902, educational

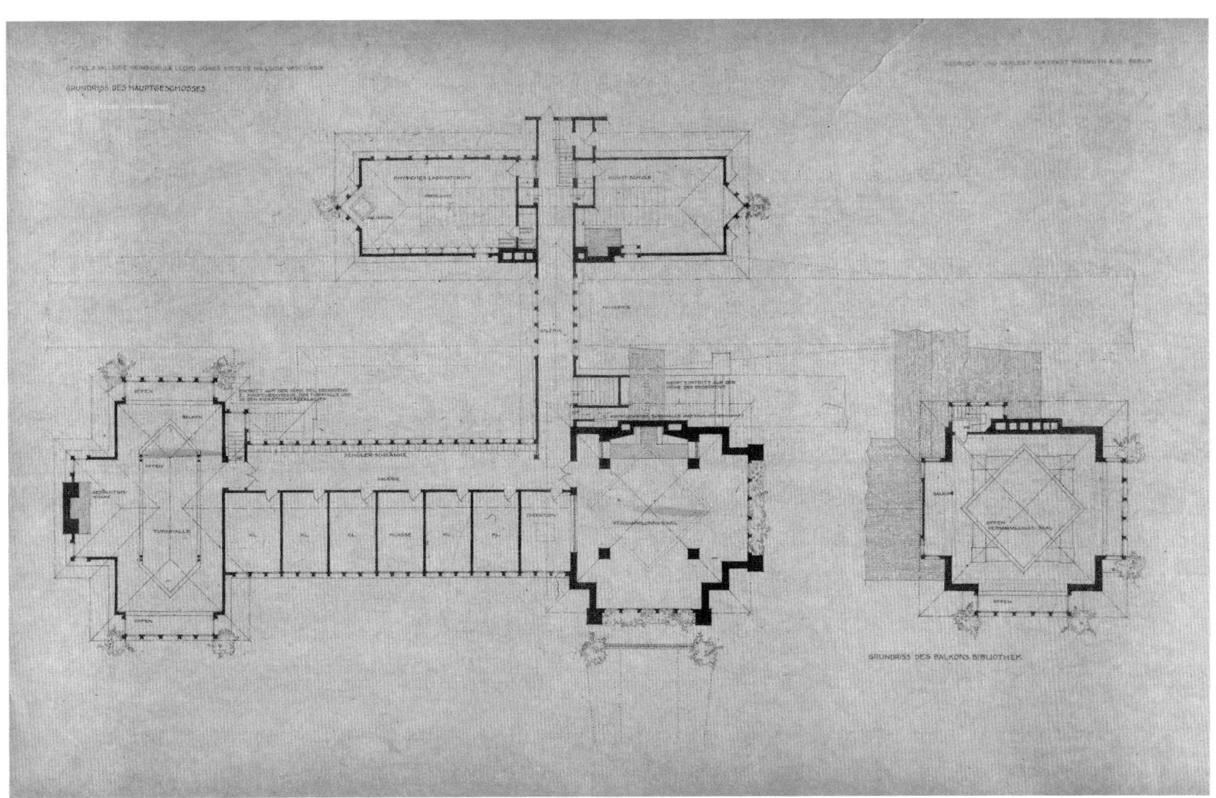

3-6

3-1 ヒルサイド・ホームスクール第一(ウィスコンシン州スプリンググリーン)1887年 旧校舎 | 建築、撮影:フランク・ロイド・ライト | 撮影:1892年
3-3 ヒルサイド・ホームスクールの女子体育授業 | 撮影:フランク・ロイド・ライト | 1900年頃
3-4 ヒルサイド・ホームスクールの化学授業 | 撮影:フランク・ロイド・ライト | 1915年
3-5 エレン・ロイド・ジョーンズ(左)とジェーン・ロイド・ジョーンズ姉妹(ヒルサイド・ホームスクール創設者、ライト叔母) | 撮影者、撮影年不詳
3-6 第10葉 ヒルサイド・ホームスクール第二、平面図『フランク・ロイド・ライトの建築と設計』| フランク・ロイド・ライト、出版:エルンスト・ヴァスムート社 | 1910年

3-1 Hillside Home School I, Spring Green, Wisconsin. Project, 1887. Exterior.
Frank Lloyd Wright, architect and photographer. Photo: 1892. Wisconsin Historical Society
3-3 Girls' Gym Class at Hillside Home School. Frank Lloyd Wright, photographer. Photo: c. 1900. Wisconsin Historical Society
3-4 Chemistry class at Hillside Home School. Frank Lloyd Wright, photographer. Photo: 1898. Wisconsin Historical Society
3-5 Ellen and Jane Lloyd Jones. Founders of the Hillside Home School and the aunts of Frank Lloyd Wright.
Photographer unidentified. undated. Wisconsin Historical Society
3-6 Plate X, Ground plan of the Hillside Home School II. Frank Lloyd Wright. Ernst Wasmuth, publisher,
Ausgeführte Bauten und Entwürfe von Frank Lloyd Wright, 1910. Toyota Municipal Museum of Art

15 シカゴ郊外の仕事場

Workplace in suburban Chicago

● **フランク・ロイド・ライト自邸とスタジオ** | Frank Lloyd Wright House and Studio

イリノイ州オークパーク、1889–1911年、住宅、事務所 | Oak Park, Illinois, 1889–1911, residential/office

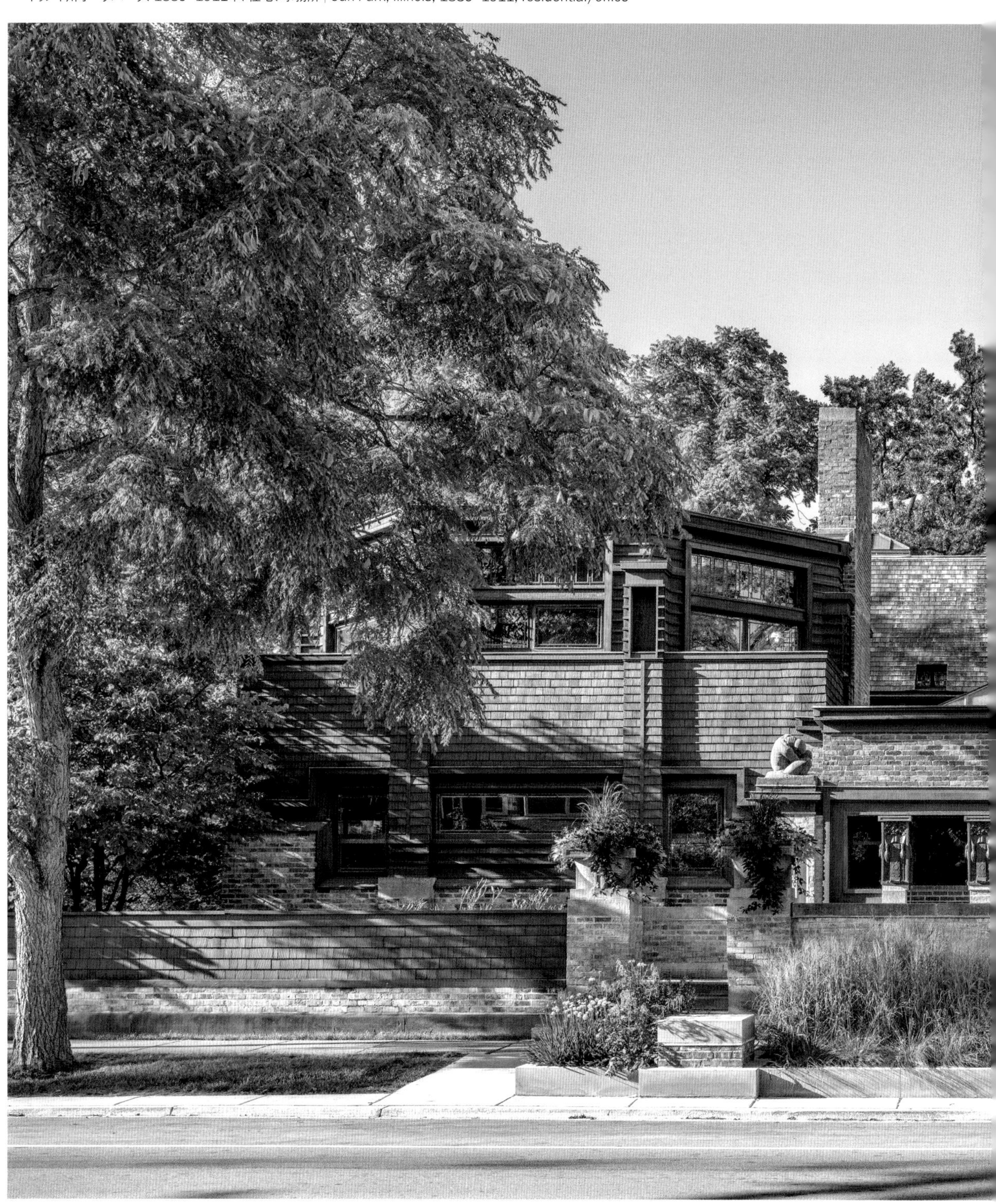

3-8 フランク・ロイド・ライト自邸とスタジオ(イリノイ州オークパーク)1889–1911年 スタジオの玄関テラス | 建築:フランク・ロイド・ライト、撮影:ジェームズ・コールフィールド | 2018年

3-8 Frank Lloyd Wright House and Studio, Oak Park, Illinois. Project, 1889–1911. Exterior view of the studio entrance terrace.
Frank Lloyd Wright, architect. James Caulfield, photographer. Photo: 2018

3-9

15 シカゴ郊外の仕事場

Workplace in suburban Chicago

キャサリン・トビン・ライトの幼稚園

Catherine Tobin Wright's kindergarten

女性建築家マリオン・マホニー

Marion Mahony: The first female architect in the state of Illinois

● **フランク・ロイド・ライト自邸 プレイルーム増築** | Frank Lloyd Wright House, Playroom Addition

イリノイ州オークパーク、1895年、住宅、教育施設 | Oak Park, Illinois, 1895, residential/educational

3-12
3-11

3-13

3-9 フランク・ロイド・ライト自邸とスタジオ(イリノイ州オークパーク) スタジオの設計室 | 建築:フランク・ロイド・ライト、撮影:ジェームズ・コールフィールド | 2013年
3-11 マリオン・マホニー(1871-1961) | 撮影:1894年
3-12 フランク・ロイド・ライト自邸とスタジオ(イリノイ州オークパーク) 子ども用プレイルーム | 建築:フランク・ロイド・ライト、撮影:ジェームズ・コールフィールド | 2013年
3-13 妻キャサリン・トビン・ライト(1871-1959) 夫がデザインしたドレスを着用している | 撮影:アーノルド | 撮影年不詳

3-9 Frank Lloyd Wright House and Studio, Oak Park, Illinois. Project, Drafting room. Frank Lloyd Wright, architect. James Caulfield, photographer. Photo: 2013
3-11 Marion Mahony Griffin (1871-1961), portrait. Photo: 1894. Massachusetts Institute of Technology, Cambridge, MA. Walter Burley and Marion Mahony Griffin Collection, Ryerson and Burnham Art and Architecture Archives, Art Institute of Chicago
3-12 Frank Lloyd Wright House and Studio, Oak Park, Illinois. Project, Playroom. Frank Lloyd Wright, architect. James Caulfield, photographer. Photo: 2013
3-13 Catherine Tobin Wright (1871 -1959), portrait. Arnold, photographer. undated. Courtesy of Frank Lloyd Wright Trust, Chicago

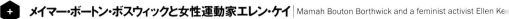

15 シカゴ郊外の仕事場

Workplace in suburban Chicago

メイマー・ボートン・ボスウィックと女性運動家エレン・ケイ | Mamah Bouton Borthwick and a feminist activist Ellen Key

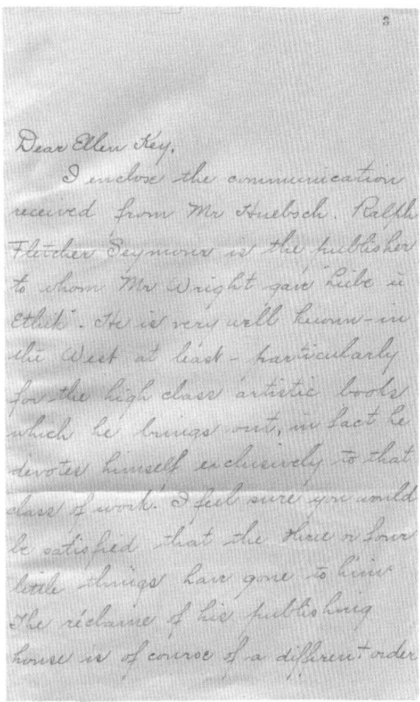

Dear Ellen Key,
I enclose the communication received from Mr Huebsch. Ralph Fletcher Seymour is the publisher to whom Mr Wright gave "Liebe u Ethik". He is very well known—in the West at least—particularly for the high class artistic books which he brings out, in fact he devotes himself exclusively to that class of work. I feel sure you would be satisfied that the three or four little things have gone to him. The réclame of his publishing house is of course of a different order

2

from that of Putnam's—so it is not a bad thing to have both?
Mr Putnam wrote asking me to suggest a title under which the Essays you mentioned could be gathered. I answered him suggesting "Personal Freedom". That might possibly necessitate some few changes in the selection, but I think it a subject upon which we Americans especially need your message, and it would reach the readers whom you would desire to influence. What do you think of it? I have had no answer to my letter yet. I am sending a couple of Essays, as you ask me to do, to the Ameri-

3

can Magazine and will send the others right along as they may wish. I am getting deep in your work again and expect to accomplish much in the next few months.
Fletcher Seymour is publishing "Love and Ethics" as the "only authorized translation". A copy will reach you shortly—It has been delayed.
With reverent love,
Mamah Bouton Borthwick

Taliesin
Spring Green
Wisconsin, U.S.A.

3-15

3-17

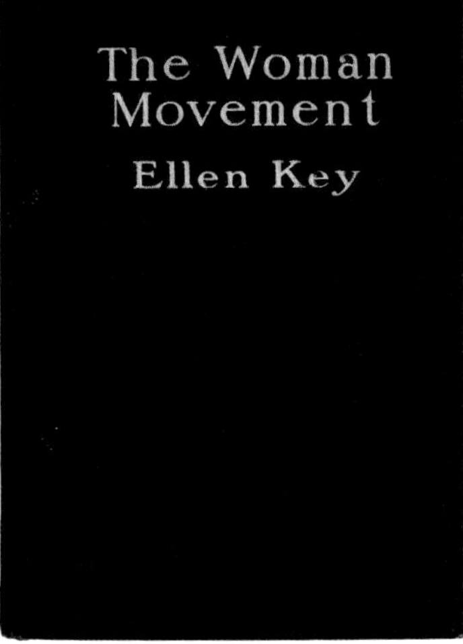

3-14

親愛なるエレン・ケイ

ヒブシュ氏(訳注:出版人)から受けとった通信を同封します。ラルフ・フレッチャー・シーモアは、ライト氏があなたの『恋愛と道徳』を託している出版社です。彼は、少なくとも欧米では、特に一流の芸術書の出版で定評があります。実際、彼はその種の仕事しか手がけません。あなたの小品を3、4点彼が受けとってくれれば、あなたはきっと満足する結果を得られるでしょう。彼の出版社の宣伝力は、もちろんパトナムス社のそれとは異なります。ですから両方と仕事することは、けして悪いことではないでしょう。

パトナム氏は、あなたがおっしゃっていたエッセイ集の題名を私に提案してほしいと書いてきました。私は彼に「個人の自由」という題名を提案しました。この題名ですと、ひょっとするとエッセイのセレクションを少し変更することが必要になるかもしれません。しかし、これは私たちアメリカ人が特にあなたのメッセージを必要としている主題であり、あなたが影響を与えたいと望んでいる読者に届くものだと思います。あなたのお考えをお聞かせください。私の手紙に対する返事はまだ来ていません。あなたに頼まれたように『アメリカン・マガジン』誌にあなたの2点のエッセイを送っており、先方が望めば他のエッセイも送るつもりです。私はまた、あなたの仕事に没頭しており、今後数か月で多くのことを成し遂げられると思っています。

フレッチャー・シーモアは『恋愛と道徳』を「唯一の公認翻訳本」として出版します。遅くなりましたが、まもなく完成された本があなたのお手元に届くでしょう。

敬虔な愛をこめて
メイマー・ボートン・ボスウィック

タリアセン
スプリンググリーン
ウィスコンシン州、アメリカ

3-14 『ウーマン・ムーヴメント』| 著:エレン・ケイ、訳:メイマー・ボートン・ボスウィック、出版:G.P.パトナムス社 | 1912年頃
3-15 メイマー・ボートン・ボスウィックからエレン・ケイにあてた手紙 | メイマー・ボートン・ボスウィック | 年記なし、1912年頃
3-17 メイマー・ボートン・ボスウィック(1869-1914) | シカゴ・トリビューン社 | 撮影年不詳

3-14 *The Woman Movement*. Ellen Key, author. Mamah Borthwick, translator. G.P. Putnams, publisher. c. 1912. Panasonic Shiodome Museum of Art
3-15 Mamah Borthwick, letter to Ellen Kay, undated (c. 1912). Mamah Bouton Borthwick. National Library of Sweden
3-17 Martha (Mamah) Bouton Borthwick Cheney (1869-1914), portrait. The Chicago Tribune, publisher. undated. Wisconsin Historical Society

16 クーンリー・プレイハウス幼稚園：風船と紙吹雪のモチーフの展開

Coonley Playhouse: Balloon and confetti motifs

● **クーンリー・プレイハウス幼稚園** | Coonley Playhouse | イリノイ州リバーサイド、1911年、教育施設 | Riverside, Illinois, 1911, educational

3-23

3-24

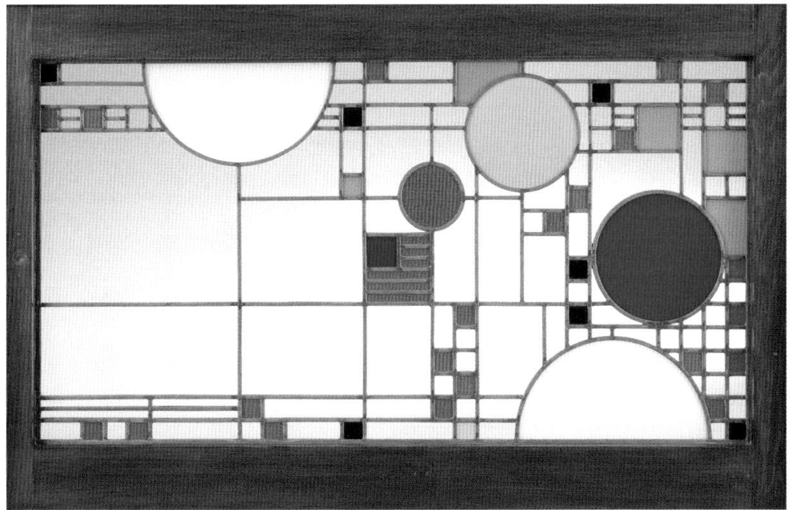

3-22

3-25

3-22 クーンリー・プレイハウス幼稚園 窓ガラス | デザイン：フランク・ロイド・ライト | 1912年頃
3-23 クーンリー・プレイハウス幼稚園（イリノイ州リバーサイド）1911年 | 建築：フランク・ロイド・ライト | 撮影：1912年頃
3-24 クーンリー・プレイハウス幼稚園（イリノイ州リバーサイド）1911年 室内 | 建築：フランク・ロイド・ライト | 撮影：1912年頃
3-25 クィーン・フェリー・クーンリー（1874-1958） | 撮影：1950年頃

3-22 Clerestory window from the Avery Coonley Playhouse, Riverside, Illinois. Frank Lloyd Wright, designer. c. 1912. Toyota Art Museum of Art
3-23 Coonley Playhouse, Riverside, Illinois. Project, 1911. Exterior view. Frank Lloyd Wright, architect.
Photo: c. 1912. Edgar Tafel architectural records and papers, 1919-2005, Avery Architectural & Fine Arts Library, Columbia University
3-24 Coonley Playhouse, Riverside, Illinois. Project, 1911. Interior view. Frank Lloyd Wright, architect.
Photo: c. 1912. Edgar Tafel architectural records and papers, 1919-2005, Avery Architectural & Fine Arts Library, Columbia University
3-25 Queene Ferry Coonley (1874-1958), portrait. Photo: c. 1950. The Avery Coonley School

3-18 クーンリー・プレイハウス幼稚園(イリノイ州リバーサイド)1911年 初期案 プレイハウスとステンドグラスが見える透視図 | フランク・ロイド・ライト | 1911年

3-18 Coonley Playhouse, Riverside, Illinois. Project, 1911. Perspective. Preliminary drawing showing playhouse and stained glass. Frank Lloyd Wright. 1911. Library of Congress, Architecture, Design and Engineering Drawings. LC-DIG-ppmsca-05582

● オークパーク公園協会への設計競技案「キンダーシンフォニーズ」| Playhouses for the Oak Park Playground Association (Kindersymphonies), unbuilt project | イリノイ州オークパーク、1926年、教育施設 | Oak Park, Illinois, 1926, educational

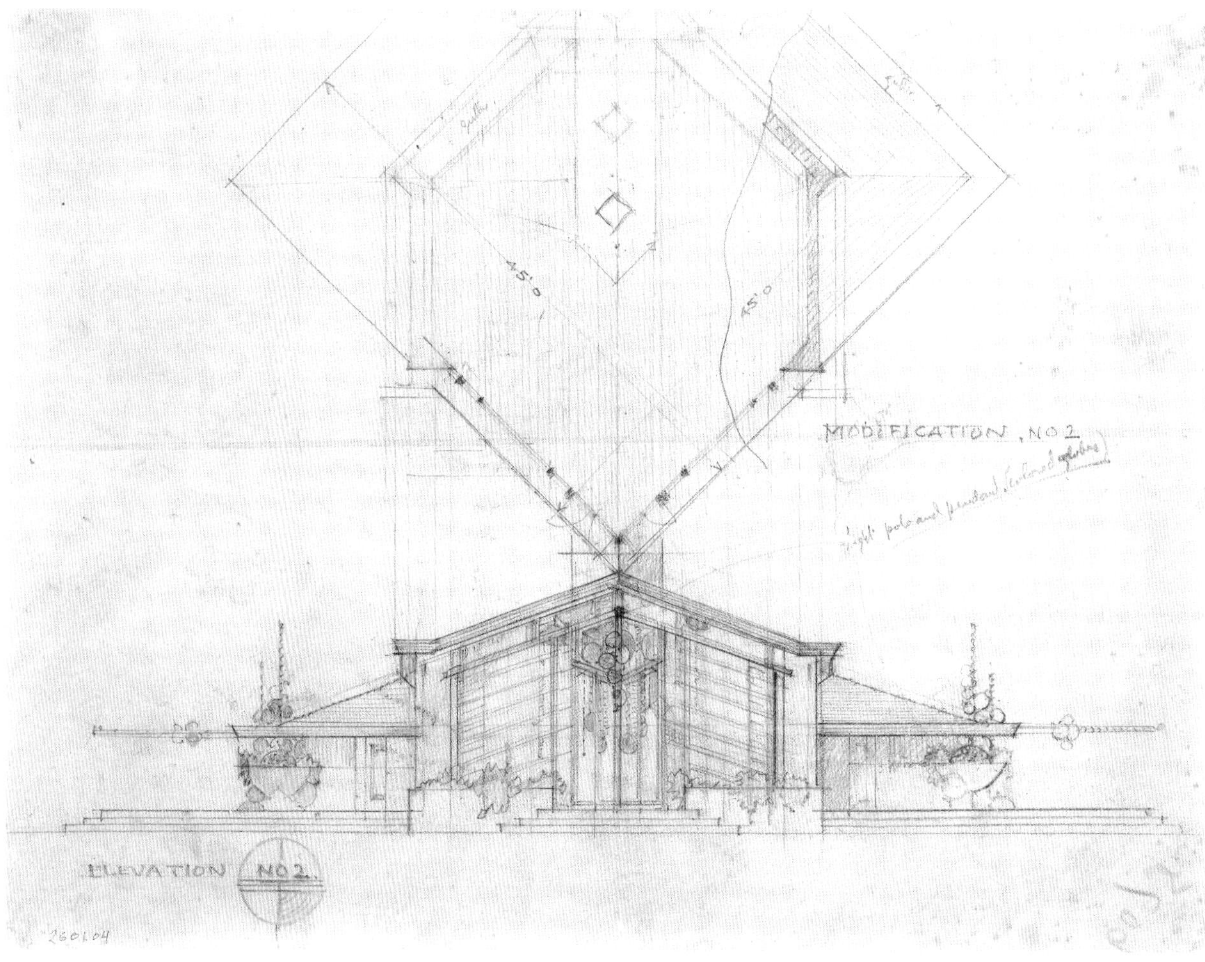

3-19

3-19 オークパーク公園協会への設計競技案「キンダーシンフォニーズ」(イリノイ州オークパーク) 1926年 (No. 2) | フランク・ロイド・ライト | 1926年
3-20 オークパーク公園協会への設計競技案「キンダーシンフォニーズ」(イリノイ州オークパーク) 1926年 (No. 3) | フランク・ロイド・ライト | 1926年
3-21 オークパーク公園協会への設計競技案「キンダーシンフォニーズ」(イリノイ州オークパーク) 1926年 (No. 4) | フランク・ロイド・ライト | 1926年

3-19 Playhouses for the Oak Park Playground Association (Kindersymphonies),
Oak Park, Illinois, Project, 1926. No. 2. Frank Lloyd Wright. 1926. Toyota Municipal Museum of Art
3-20 Playhouses for the Oak Park Playground Association (Kindersymphonies),
Oak Park, Illinois, Project, 1926. No. 3. Frank Lloyd Wright. 1926. Toyota Municipal Museum of Art
3-21 Playhouses for the Oak Park Playground Association (Kindersymphonies),
Oak Park, Illinois, Project, 1926. No. 4. Frank Lloyd Wright. 1926. Toyota Municipal Museum of Art

OAK PARK

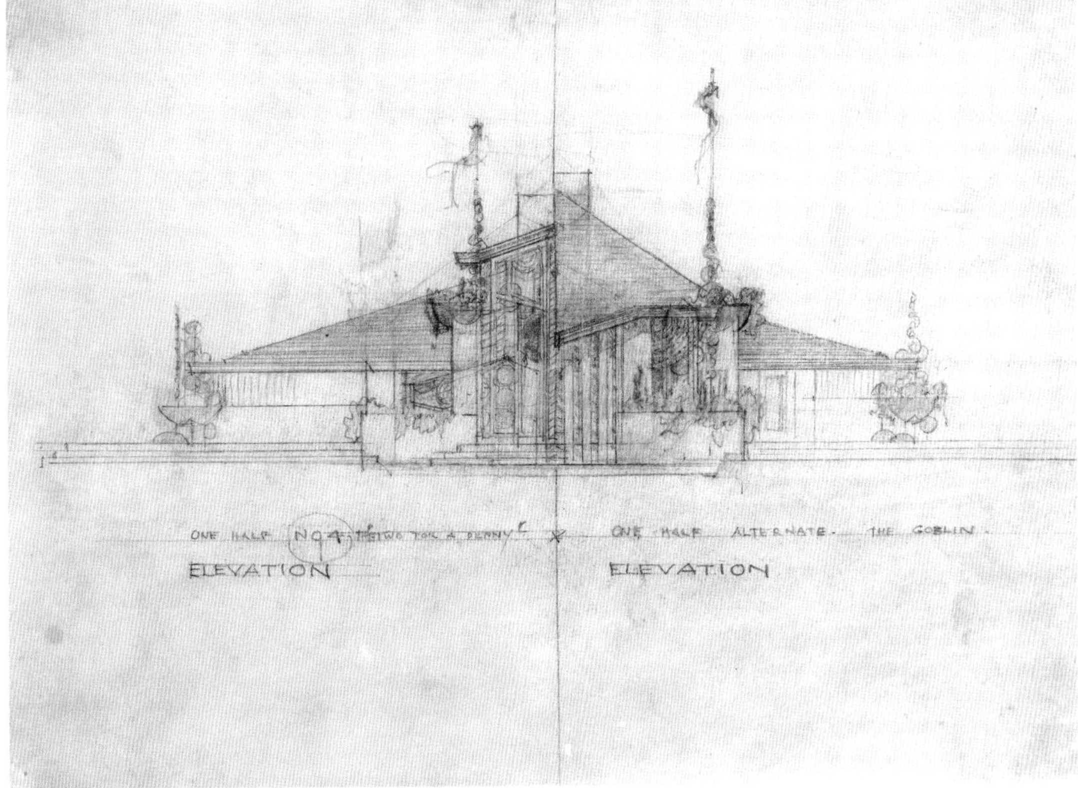
ONE HALF
ELEVATION
ONE HALF ALTERNATE - THE GOBLIN
ELEVATION

3-21
3-20

17 リトル・ディッパー・スクールと舞台

Little Dipper School and Stage

● リトル・ディッパー幼稚園とコミュニティ・プレイハウス計画案 | Little Dipper School and Community Playhouse for Aline Barnsdall, unbuilt project

カリフォルニア州ロサンゼルス、1923年、教育施設 | Los Angeles, California, 1923, educational

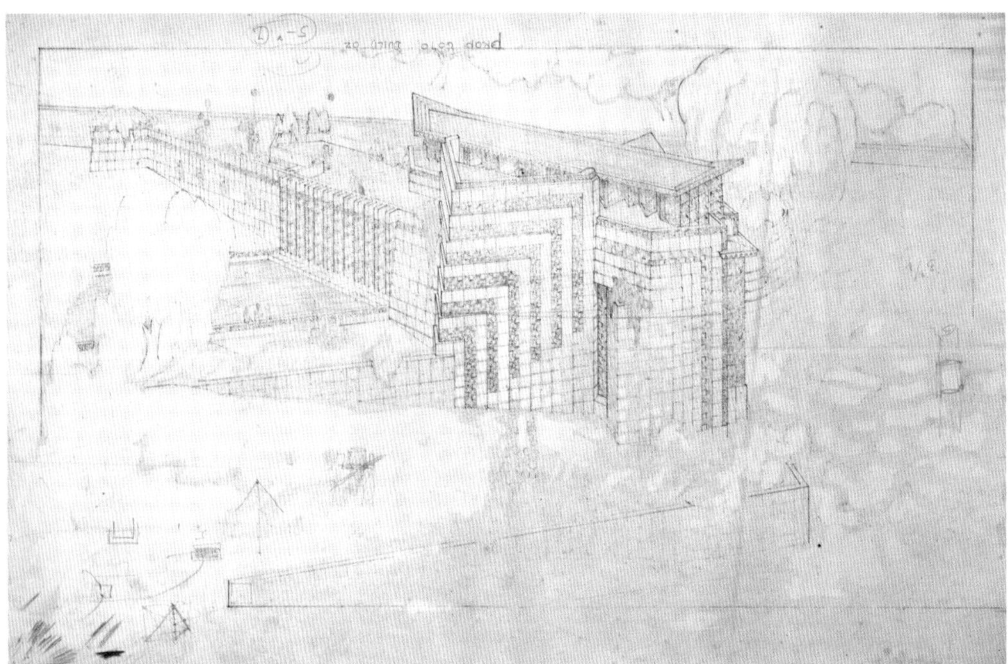

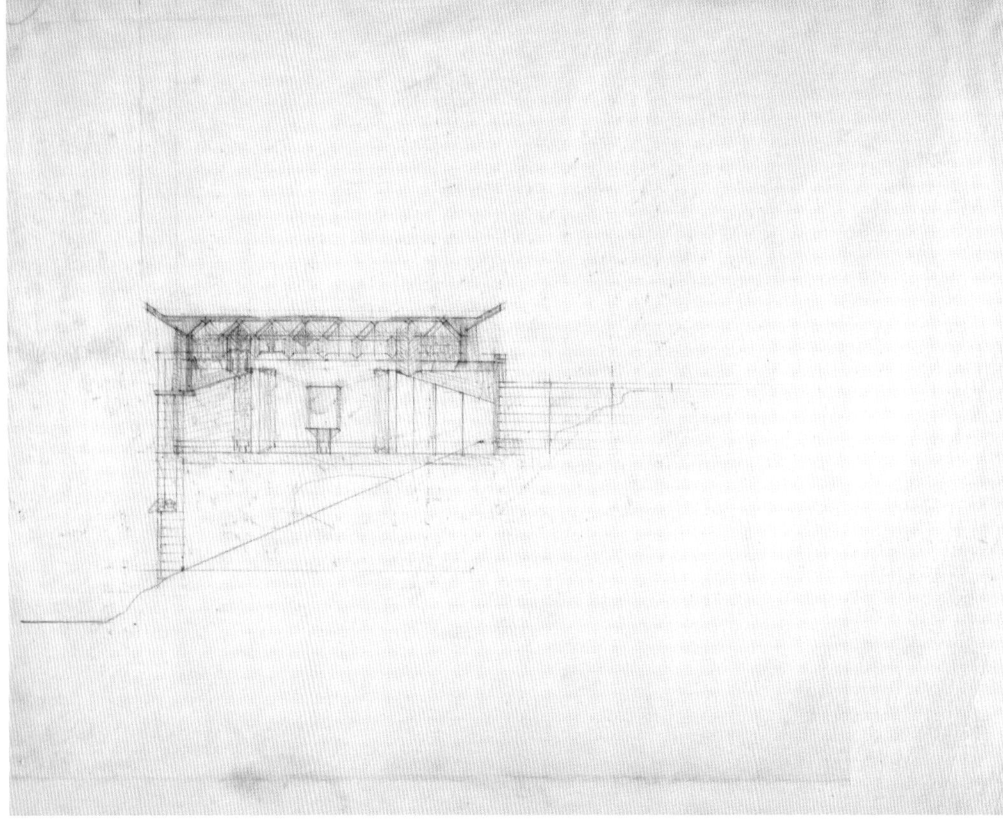

3-26
3-27

● **バーンズドール邸「立葵の家」** | Barnsdall House (Hollyhock House) | カリフォルニア州ロサンゼルス、1918–21年、住宅 | Los Angeles, California, 1917, residential

3-29

3-30

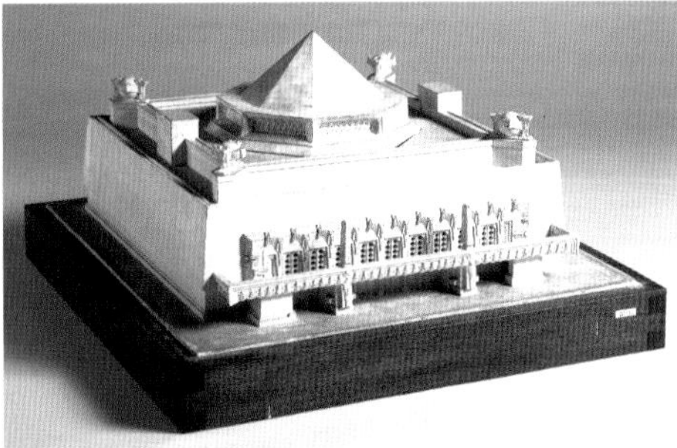

3-28

3-26 リトル・ディッパー幼稚園とコミュニティ・プレイハウス計画案（カリフォルニア州ロサンゼルス）1923年
ランドスケープ、テキスタイル・ブロック、基礎、ステンドグラスが描かれた外観図 | フランク・ロイド・ライト | 1923年
3-27 リトル・ディッパー幼稚園とコミュニティ・プレイハウス計画案（カリフォルニア州ロサンゼルス）1923年
ステンドグラス、テキスタイル・ブロックの基礎、バタフライ屋根が描かれた立面図 | フランク・ロイド・ライト | 1923年
3-28 模型 劇場計画案（または銀座活動写真館） | フランク・ロイド・ライト | 1918年頃
3-29 バーンズドール邸「立葵の家」（カリフォルニア州ロサンゼルス）1918–21年 外観、ハリウッドを遠方にのぞむ | 建築：フランク・ロイド・ライト | 撮影：1920年
3-30 アリーン・バーンズドール（1882–1946） | 撮影：1916年

3-26 Little Dipper School and Community Playhouse for Aline Barnsdall, Los Angeles, California. Project, 1923.
Exterior showing landscaping, textile block, construction and stained glass.Frank Lloyd Wright. 1923.
Prints and Photographs Division, Library of Congress, Washington, D.C. LC-DIG-ppmsca-85260 DLC
3-27 Little Dipper School and Community Playhouse for Aline Barnsdall, Los Angeles, California. Project, 1923.
Exterior showing stained glass, textile block construction, and butterfly roof. Frank Lloyd Wright. 1923.
Prints and Photographs Division, Library of Congress, Washington, D.C. LC-DIG-ppmsca-84875
3-28 Model. Tokyo Theater (also known as Ginza Movie Theater). Frank Lloyd Wright. c. 1918. Kyoto University
3-29 Barnsdall House (Hollyhock House), Los Angeles, California. Project, 1918–21. Exterior view, with Hollywood in the distance.
Frank Lloyd Wright, architect. Photo: 1920. Project photographs, circa 1887–2008, The Frank Lloyd Wright Foundation Archives
(The Museum of Modern Art | Avery Architectural & Fine Arts Library, Columbia University, New York)
3-30 Aline Barnsdall (1882–1946), portrait. Photo: 1916. Collection of David Devine and Michael Devine.
Courtesy of the City of Los Angeles Department of Cultural Affairs and Hollyhock House

18 木も花も本来ひとつ:自由学園とローゼンヴァルド学校計画

Jiyu Gakuen and the Rosenwald School Project: flowers belong to the tree, and tree belongs to its flowers.

● **自由学園** | Jiyu Gakuen School | 東京都、池袋、1921年、教育施設 | Tokyo, Japan, 1921, educational

3-33

3-36

3-34

3-31

3-32

3-37

3-31 自由学園(東京都、池袋)1921年 立面図 | フランク・ロイド・ライト | 1921年
3-32 自由学園明日館(東京都、池袋)1921年 正面ファサード | 建築:フランク・ロイド・ライト、遠藤新 | 撮影:2021年
3-33 自由学園明日館(東京都、池袋)1921年 食堂内観 | 建築:フランク・ロイド・ライト、遠藤新 | 撮影:2023年
3-34 フランク・ロイド・ライト氏送別会の日 | 撮影:1922年7月
3-36 自由学園開校を前に相談 左から:植村環(文学科長)、斎藤その子(実際科)、羽仁吉一、羽仁もと子、松岡久子(家庭科長) | 撮影:1921年1月頃
3-37 自由学園 食堂用椅子 | デザイン:遠藤新 | 1922年

3-31 Jiyu Gakuen School, Tokyo, Japan. Project, 1921. Elevation. Frank Lloyd Wright. 1921. The Frank Lloyd Wright Foundation Archives (The Museum of Modern Art | Avery Architectural & Fine Arts Library, Columbia University, New York)
3-32 Jiyu Gakuen School, Tokyo, Japan. Project, 1921. Exterior view to the façade. Frank Lloyd Wright and Arata Endo, architects. Photo: 2021. Jiyu Gakuen Myonichikan
3-33 Jiyu Gakuen School, Tokyo, Japan. Project, 1921. Interior view of the Dining hall. Frank Lloyd Wright and Arata Endo, architects. Photo: 2023. Jiyu Gakuen Myonichikan
3-34 Farewell with Frank Lloyd Wright at Jiyu Gakuen School. Photo: July 1922. Jiyu Gakuen Archives
3-36 Motoko (1873–1957) and Yoshikazu Hani at the table discussing the pedagogy with their colleagues. Photo: c. January 1921. Jiyu Gakuen Archives
3-37 Dining Chair from the Jiyu Gakuen School. Arata Endo, designer for Frank Lloyd Wright. 1922. Jiyu Gakuen Myonichikan

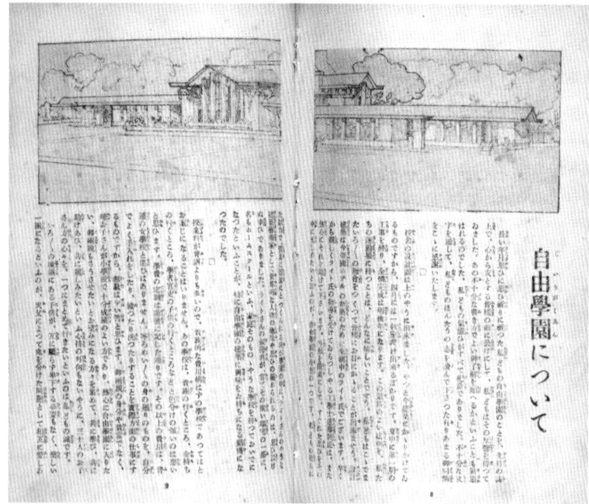

自由學園について

3-40

竣工したる自由學園
フランク ロイド ライト氏設計

3-41

3-43

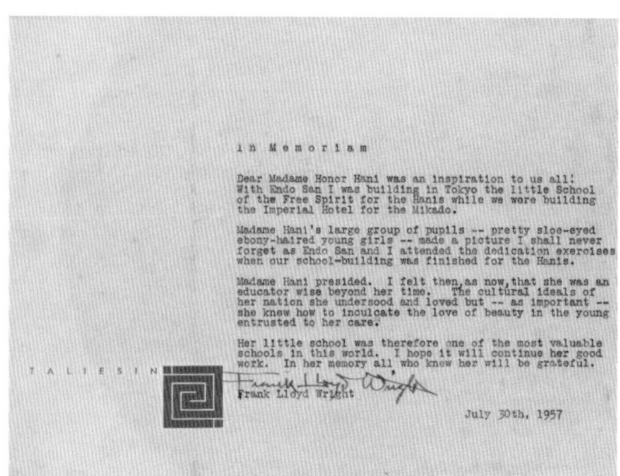

in Memoriam

Dear Madame Honor Hani was an inspiration to us all!
With Endo San I was building in Tokyo the little School of the Free Spirit for the Hanis while we were building the Imperial Hotel for the Mikado.

Madame Hani's large group of pupils -- pretty sloe-eyed ebony-haired young girls -- made a picture I shall never forget as Endo San and I attended the dedication exercises when our school-building was finished for the Hanis.

Madame Hani presided. I felt then,as now,that she was an educator wise beyond her time. The cultural ideals of her nation she undersood and loved but -- as important -- she knew how to inculcate the love of beauty in the young entrusted to her care.

Her little school was therefore one of the most valuable schools in this world. I hope it will continue her good work. In her memory all who knew her will be grateful.

TALIESIN

Frank Lloyd Wright

July 30th, 1957

3-44

追悼
1957年7月30日

敬愛する貴き羽仁夫人はわれわれ全てにとって一つの霊感であった。
私は東京で遠藤さんとともに羽仁さん方のために自由の精神の小さな学校を建築していた。一方でミカドのために帝国ホテルを建てながら。

建物が出来上がって落成式に遠藤さんとともに列したときに羽仁夫人の多勢の生徒たち——りんぼくの実のような目をした、黒檀の髪を持った若い少女たちは、私の決して忘れることのできない一幅の絵を作り出していた。

羽仁夫人がその式を司っていた。その時、今もそう思うと同じように、私は彼女を時代に先駆する賢い教育者であると感得した。彼女はその祖国の文化的思想を悟り、愛し——一層重要なこととして——彼女の手に委ねられた若き人々のうちに美を愛する心をどうして植えつけるかを知っていた。

それ故に彼女の小さな学校はこの広い世界の中でも最も価値の高い学校の一つであった。どうか彼女のよき仕事の続けられていくようにと切望する。

彼女を知るすべてのものは、彼女を思いおこして感謝の気持ちを持つことだろう。

フランク・ロイド・ライト　（訳：遠藤 楽『婦人之友』1957年10月号、婦人之友社）

● **ローゼンワルド財団の学校計画案** | Rosenwald School, unbuilt project | ヴァージニア州ハンプトン、1928年、教育施設 | Hampton, Virginia, 1928, educational

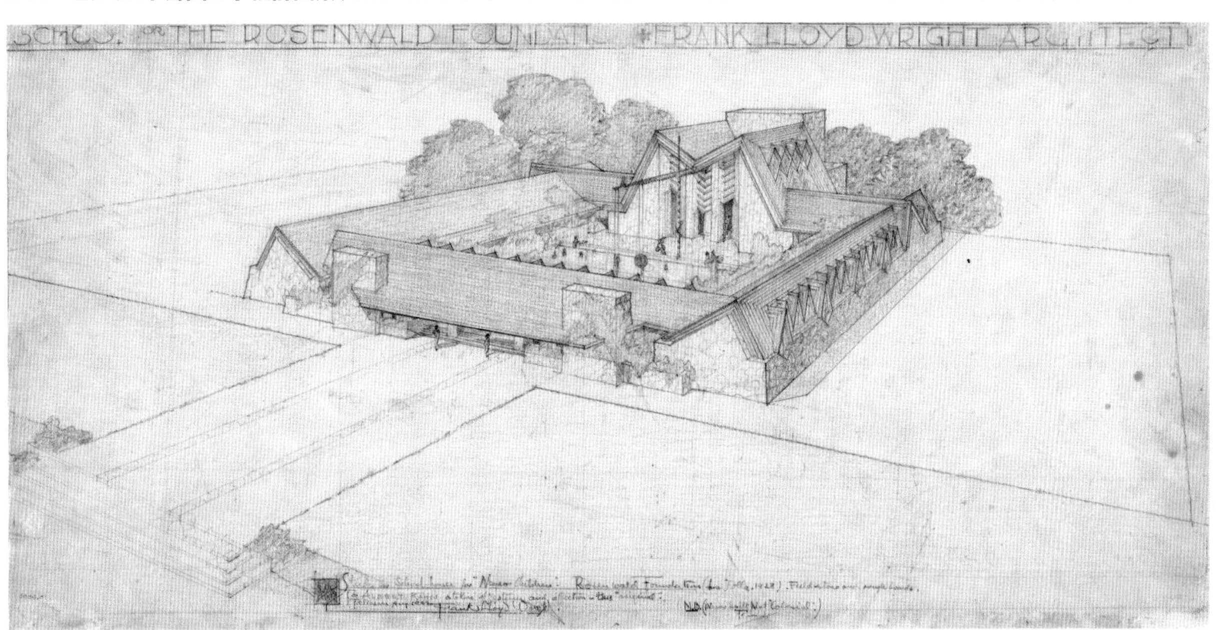

3-45

3-40　『婦人之友』1921年3月号 | 出版：婦人之友社
3-41　『婦人之友』1922年6月号 | 出版：婦人之友社
3-43　関東大震災救護活動絵巻4点 | 自由学園本科3年生有志(6回生) | 1923年
3-44　お悔やみ書簡(1957年7月30日、羽仁もと子追悼) | フランク・ロイド・ライト
3-45　ローゼンワルド財団の学校計画案(ヴァージニア州ハンプトン)1928年　透視図 | フランク・ロイド・ライト

3-40　*Fujin no Tomo* (*Ladies Friend Journal*), March 1921 issue. Fujin no Tomo-sha, publisher. Aomori Museum of Art
3-41　*Fujin no Tomo* (*Ladies Friend Journal*), June 1922 issue. Fujin no Tomo-sha, publisher. Jiyu Gakuen Archives
3-43　Record of the rescue mission carried out by the students of Jiyu Gakuen School at the Great Kanto Earthquake. Students from the Regular Course Third Grade of Jiyu Gakuen, creator. 1923. Jiyu Gakuen Archives
3-44　Frank Lloyd Wright, Memorial letter, July 30, 1957 upon death of Motoko Hani. Frank Lloyd Wright. July 30, 1957. Jiyu Gakuen Archives
3-45　Rosenwald School, Hampton, Virginia. Unbuilt Project, 1928. Perspective. Frank Lloyd Wright. The Frank Lloyd Wright Foundation Archives (The Museum of Modern Art | Avery Architectural & Fine Arts Library, Columbia University, New York)

⑲ 建築教育の場としてのタリアセン・フェローシップ

Taliesin Fellowship: A place for architectural education

● **タリアセン・フェローシップ建築群「ヒルサイド・シアター」** | Taliesin Fellowship Complex, Hillside Theater

ウィスコンシン州スプリンググリーン、1952年、教育施設 | Spring Green, Wisconsin, 1952, educational

3-47

3-46

3-49

3-46 映像「タリアセン・フェローシップ」| ダウ・フィルム社 | 撮影:1933年

3-47 タリアセン・フェローシップ建築群「ヒルサイド・シアター」(ウィスコンシン州スプリンググリーン)1952年 | 建築:フランク・ロイド・ライト、撮影:アンドリュー・ピラージ | 2016年

3-49 妻オルギヴァナ・ライト(1898-1985) | 撮影:ブラックストーン | 撮影年不詳

3-46 Film. Taliesin Fellowship. Dow Film 1933. The Frank Lloyd Wright Foundation Archives (The Museum of Modern Art | Avery Architectural & Fine Arts Library, Columbia University, New York)

3-47 Taliesin Fellowship Complex. Spring Green, Wisconsin. Project, 1952. Hillside Theater. Frank Lloyd Wright, architect. © Andrew Pielage, photographer. Photo: 2016. Courtesy of the Frank Lloyd Wright Foundation

3-49 Olgivanna Wright (1898-1985), third wife of architect Frank Lloyd Wright. Blackstone, photographer. undated. Wiscconsin Historical Society

SECTION 4

交差する世界に建つ帝国ホテル

Imperial Hotel at the Global Crossroads

4

東洋と西洋を往来するライトの旅は、言語的、視覚的、文化的なさまざまなかたちでの翻訳経験を彼に与え、10年に及ぶ帝国ホテルの設計を段階的に形づくった。1913年初めにライトは東京に戻り、およそ4か月間、候補地の調査や建物に使用するための材料の検討を行い、鹿鳴館の北側で初代帝国ホテルの西隣、日比谷公園に面した敷地で新ホテルの初期案に着手した[1]。彼が取り組んだのは、1912年7月30日の明治天皇崩御に伴って改元された大正時代の、国際化の進む日本にふさわしいデザインであった。ライトはこの間、敷地の不安定な土壌の調査を行った。東京湾の日比谷入江の一部であったこの場所は、封建時代の首都、江戸の建設に伴って埋め立てられた土地であった。初代および二代目帝国ホテルの敷地は、江戸城外堀に面していたが、外堀は1903年の日比谷公園の開園に向けて埋め立てられた。この場所にはもともと内務大臣官舎があったが、計画的に解体されることになり、現実の完成形をはるかに凌駕する素晴らしく変化に富んだ光景を提供した。

鳥瞰透視図によって示される1914年の初期案には、公的な中庭を囲み、左右対称の棟によって構成される複合施設が描かれている[2][cat. no. 4-8]。この左右対称で構成された建物は、ライトが1905年の旅で目にした東本願寺名古屋別院など、日本の寺院構成と響き合うところがあるが、厳密な左右対称性は側面から描かれており、皇居の方向から見た場合の左右非対称のパースペクティブが強調されている。

初期案にうかがえるのは、中央にある階段ピラミッド状の屋根による東洋と西洋の象徴的なイメージの統合である[cat. no. 4-7]。中央屋根の正確なプロポーションと細部の抽象化された幾何学構成は、さまざまな形で反復され、その象徴的な重要性と解釈の多様性を強調している。1905年の写真アルバムにある東本願寺名古屋別院経蔵のような日本の宝形屋根のほか[3]、メソアメリカ(メキシコのチチェン・イッツァのあるエル・カスティーヨ遺跡)からインドネシアまで、ライトの写真コレクションには階段ピラミッド形態のさまざまな先行例が含まれていた[4][cat. nos. 4-2~6]。ロビーやメインダイニングルームを備え、低く広がる中庭の構成は確かにこれらの先行例とは異なるが、明らかにライトはさまざまな文化に由来するグローバルな建築に学んでいた。

ライトは1913年にシカゴに戻ると、帝国ホテル初期案を練りながら、帝国ホテルとミッドウェイ・ガーデンズ[cat. no. 4-9]の両方の計画をさらに進めた。2つの建築は、左右対称な平面と断面の構成といった基本的な点で共通している。さらにいえば、シカゴと東京を往来するなかで生まれた建築デザインはどちらも同様にハイブリッドなものとみなせるだろう。それは、ライト自身が後にミッドウェイ・ガーデンズについて「多くの人にとって、それは総じてエジプト的であり、ある人たちにとってはマヤ文明的であり、他の人々にとっては完全に日本的であった。ただしそれらは、見る人皆にとって見慣れないものであり、神秘とロマンを掻き立てた」と回想したとおりである[5]。この時点で、旅と仕事の実体験は、東洋と西洋の厳密な区分を解消し、ライトに自由で多様な引用を可能とし、シカゴから東京、東京からシカゴという翻訳のなかに新しい意味を見いだしていった。

この地震大国の素材の性格を表現するために、ライトは煉瓦と石に代わる新たな可能性に目を向けた。明治時代の建物で失敗した無補強での煉瓦使用の代わりに、ライ

1 Kathryn Smith, "Frank Lloyd Wright and the Imperial Hotel: A Postscript," *Art Bulletin* (June 1, 1985), p. 298.

2 ライトの「公的中庭空間」の類型について、詳しくは、Robert McCarter, *Frank Lloyd Wright, Critical Lives* (London: Reaktion, 2006), pp. 136–59.を参照のこと。

3 Melanie Birk and Frank Lloyd Wright Home and Studio Foundation, *Frank Lloyd Wright's Fifty Views of Japan: The 1905 Photo Album* (San Francisco: Pomegranate, 1996), pp. 22–28.

4 前掲書 p. 36.

トは地元の生産者と共にすだれレンガ[cat. nos. 4-64, 5-6]という、鉄筋コンクリートの上に張る煉瓦のような質感をもつ中空のタイルを開発した[6]。そして、これらのタイルを大谷石で補強することにしたのである[cat. no. 5-7]。ライトは、この変幻自在の石に、イタリアの偉大な作品に使用されてきたトラバーチンに似た性質を認め、装飾的な柱や笠石、基壇や壺の構成に多孔性の質感を加えた。大谷石は、歩道や一般的な建物の外装などに日常的に使用される材料であったが、ライトは帝国ホテルのためにこの素材の際立った使用を主張し、その量は立方体にして10,200 m³にもなった[7]。彼はさらにテラコッタのテキスタイル・ブロックである装飾ブロック[cat. no. 4-63]も開発した。その四角いフレームの構成はホテル全体の形を想起させるものであった。

帝国ホテル以外にも、ライトは日本においてスケールもタイプも異なるさまざまな仕事に携わった。東京の自由学園(1921)[cat. no. 3-31]は、帝国ホテルと同じ左右対称の中庭の構成を使いながらも、児童に合わせてスケールは小さくし、木造で建てられた。帝国ホテル支配人林愛作をはじめとする個人の住宅は、遠藤新などライトの周辺にいた日本の建築家たちによって完成されることになった。一方、ライトが野心的に取り組んだ小田原ホテル計画(1917)[cat. no. 2-66]——片手で支えた盆を滝に差し架けるような構造をもつ——は完成をみなかったものの、デザインの基本となる構想は、ペンシルベニア州ミルランにあるライトの代表作、エドガー・カウフマン邸「落水荘」(1934-37)[cat. nos. 2-67, 68]のような後年のプロジェクトに引き継がれることになった。その後の日本国内において、ライトによる帝国ホテルのデザインは、国会議事堂(1936)のような有名建築の階段ピラミッド状屋根や、帝国ホテルのような連続した高窓を設け、伝統的な日本屋根を新古典主義建築の上に載せた、いわゆる「帝冠様式」と呼ばれる1930年代のデザインと共鳴しているのがわかるだろう。

しかしながら、帝国ホテルは、ライトの日本への強い関心を体現した最も英雄的な傑作としてあり続けている。残念なことに、完成したばかりのホテルは関東大震災に襲われて倒壊は免れたものの即刻被害を受け、さらに第二次世界大戦時には焼夷弾を受けて最上階孔雀の間と南翼のかなりの部分が失われることになった。進駐軍による接収時には、不幸にも大谷石がペンキで白く塗られるなど、ライトの当初の構想に対する冷淡な改変が加えられた。1940年の東京オリンピックは幻に終わったが、その準備期間であった1930年代には、さらなる近代化と増床を意図して早くもホテル取り壊しの動きが起こり、それは1964年のオリンピックに向けた建物高層化の検討において繰り返された。ホテルを残そうという努力により当初は解体が阻止されたが、1970年の大阪万博を機に東京を訪れる旅行者の急増を見越して、新しい高層の帝国ホテルをつくるために、1967年、解体の鉄球の一撃が加えられた。この時にはすでにホテルは老朽化し、ライトの当初のデザインに外付けのエアコンや他の装備が加えられていた。帝国ホテルの保存に向けた努力により、地方山間部という全く異なる環境ではあるが、博物館明治村に正面ロビー部分が移築(1976)されることになった。今や象徴的な建物となったこの正面ロビー部分と共に、そのドローイングや残された遺品の数々は、過去と未来、東と西を融合させたライトのダイナミックなビジョンの革新性を照らし出している。

Frank Lloyd Wright, *An Autobiography* (New York, Horizon Press, 1977), p. 214.(樋口清訳『ライト自伝——ある芸術の形成』中央公論美術出版、1988年、樋口清訳『ライト自伝——ある芸術の展開』中央公論美術出版、2000年)

6 帝国ホテル編『帝国ホテル100年のあゆみ』帝国ホテル、1990年、p. 98.

7 前掲書 p. 99.

Wright's journeys between East and West, experienced through various linguistic, visual, and cultural modes of translation, shaped his decade-long design phase for the Imperial Hotel. Wright returned to Tokyo in early 1913 for four months to study the proposed site, consider appropriate building materials, and work on a preliminary scheme for the new hotel. It was to be located just west of the first Imperial Hotel, which faced Hibiya Park, and north of the Rokumeikan.[1]

Wright was now designing for an increasingly internationalized Japan in the Taisho period, which had begun on July 30, 1912, upon the death of the Meiji Emperor. During this time, he examined the unstable soil conditions for the site, which was originally part of the Hibiya inlet of Tokyo Bay before being filled in with excess soil from the construction of the feudal capital of Edo. Both the first and second Imperial Hotel sites had faced the outer moats of Edo Castle before they were filled in, with the completion of Hibiya Park in 1903. Although the residence of the Minister of Home Affairs was located on the site, its planned demolition would provide an open stage for the wide range of fantastic, varied visions beyond the realized form.

Wright's preliminary 1914 scheme, drawn in an aerial perspective, depicts a complex defined by symmetrical wings enclosing public courtyards [cat. no. 4-8].[2] While this symmetrically composed building parti resonated with Japanese temple schemes, such as the Higashi-Honganji Temple in Nagoya that Wright had seen on his 1905 trip,[3] the strict symmetry is depicted from the side, emphasizing an asymmetrical perspective that would have been seen from the direction of the Imperial Palace.

This preliminary design could be seen to bring symbolic imagery of East and West together through its central stepped pyramidal roof [cat. no. 4-7]. The precise proportions and details of the abstracted geometric scheme of the Imperial's main roof would undergo many different iterations, underscoring its symbolic importance and multiplicity of interpretations. Wright's own photographic collection included diverse precedents of stepped pyramidal forms from Mesoamerica (El Castillo, Chichen Itza, Mexico) and Indonesia, as well as Japanese pyramidal roof forms. His 1905 photo album featured such examples from Japan, including the Sutra Library at Higashi-Honganji Temple (Nagoya-Betsuin) [cat. nos. 4-2~6].[4] Though the Imperial's lower courtyard composition, with its lobby and dining room, certainly differed from these precedents, Wright was clearly informed by global architecture from many cultures.

Wright developed both the Imperial Hotel and Midway Gardens [cat. no. 4-9] following his return to Chicago in 1913. Elaborating on the initial Imperial scheme, Wright approached the Midway project using similar basic symmetrical plan and section strategies. Moreover, both designs could be seen to be equally hybrid, with Wright traveling back and forth between Chicago and Tokyo. He later recalled of Midway Gardens: "To many it was all Egyptian, Mayan to some, very Japanese to others. But strange to all, it awakened a sense of mystery and romance in the beholder."[5] By this point, Wright's travels and direct work experiences had dissolved a strict Oriental-Occidental divide, enabling him to freely draw from multiple sources, with new meanings found in his translations from Chicago to Tokyo and back.

To express the material character of this seismically prone nation, Wright looked to new possibilities in place of brick and stone. Rather than using unreinforced brick that had failed in Meiji-period

1 Kathryn Smith, "Frank Lloyd Wright and the Imperial Hotel: A Postscript," *Art Bulletin* (June 1, 1985), p. 298.

2 For a further discussion of Wright's "Courtyard Public Space" typology, see Robert McCarter, *Frank Lloyd Wright*, Critical Lives (London: Reaktion, 2006), pp. 136–59.

3 Melanie Birk and Frank Lloyd Wright Home and Studio Foundation, *Frank Lloyd Wright's Fifty Views of Japan: The 1905 Photo Album* (San Francisco: Pomegranate, 1996), pp. 22–28.

buildings, Wright developed, along with a local producer, "scratch tiles": hollow tiles textured to appear like brick that would face reinforced concrete [cat. nos. 4-64, 5-6].[6] He then sought to complement these tiles with Oya stone [cat. no. 5-7]. He viewed this volcanic stone as akin to travertine, used for great works in Italy, which added porous texture to his composition of ornamented columns, capstones, bases, and urns. While Oya stone was used for everyday needs, such as sidewalk paving and common building faces, Wright advocated the prominent use of some 360,000 cubic feet (10,200 cubic meters) of this material for the Imperial Hotel.[7] He further developed terra-cotta textile blocks, whose square frame composition evoked the overall form of the hotel [cat. no. 4-63].

Beyond the Imperial, Wright worked in Japan on multiple scales and typologies. The Jiyu Gakuen School (1921) [cat. no. 3-22] in Tokyo employed the Imperial's symmetrical courtyard organization, but on a smaller scale appropriate to young children and constructed using a wood frame. Houses, including those for the Imperial Hotel's manager, Aisaku Hayashi (1917), would be completed by the circle of architects around Wright in Japan, including Arata Endo and others. While Wright's ambitious Odawara Hotel (project, 1917) [cat. no. 2-66]—which would have bridged a waterfall with cantilevered trays—would not be completed, the design's fundamental conceptual ideas would take form later in projects, such as Wright's masterwork Edgar J. Kaufmann House (Fallingwater) in Mill Run, Pennsylvania (1934–37) [cat. nos. 2-67, 68]. Within Japan, Wright's designs for the Imperial Hotel could be seen to find resonance in prominent buildings: the early stepped pyramid form appearing in the realized National Diet Building (1936) and the so-called "Imperial Crown Style" designs of the 1930s, in which traditional Japanese roofs on top of neoclassical structures were embraced with bands of clerestory windows akin to the Imperial Hotel design.

The Imperial, however, would remain Wright's most heroic major work embodying his intense interest in Japan. Sadly, the completed hotel was compromised almost instantly through damage sustained in the Great Kanto Earthquake and then again during fire bombings in World War II that would destroy the Peacock Room and much of the south wing. After the war, it was taken over by the Allied Occupation administration and underwent unfortunate transformations unsympathetic to Wright's original vision, such as painting the Oya stone white. A move to tear down the hotel for further modernization and more floors began as early as the 1930s. The first came in preparation for the unrealized 1940 Tokyo Olympics, only to be repeated by a push to build higher for the 1964 Olympics. While efforts to save the hotel initially forestalled demolition, the wrecking ball struck in 1967 to make way for a new high-rise Imperial Hotel in anticipation of additional visitors from the Osaka Expo 1970. By this time, the hotel had fallen into decay, with the unsightly addition of air conditioners and other compromises to Wright's original design. Preservation efforts for the Imperial Hotel resulted in the reconstruction of its lobby (1976) at the Meiji Mura architectural park, though within a very different, rural setting. The drawings and remaining artifacts related to this now iconic structure illuminate the evolution of Wright's dynamic vision fusing East and West, past and future.

[Ken Tadashi Oshima]

Ibid., 36.
Frank Lloyd Wright, *An Autobiography* (New York: Horizon Press, 1977), p. 214.

6 Imperial Hotel, *The Imperial: The First 100 Years* (Tokyo: Toppan Printing Company, 1990), p. 98.

7 Ibid., p. 99.

20 写真コレクションにみるデザイン・ソース
Design inspirations in the image collection

4-2

4-4

4-3

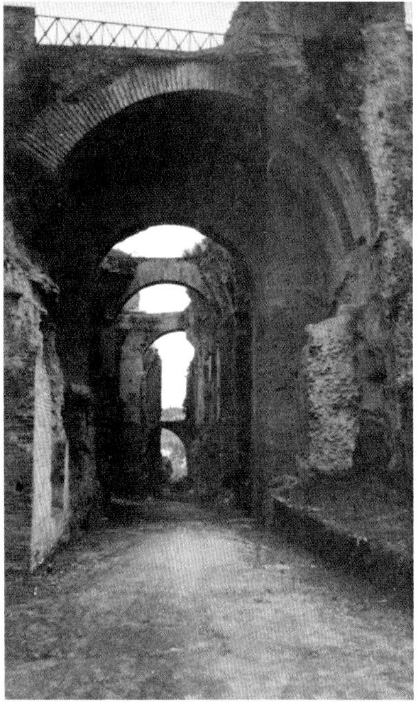
4-6

4-2 チェチェンイッツア遺跡ククルカンの神殿 | 撮影：ローラ・ギルピン | 1930年頃
4-3 チェチェンイッツア遺跡戦士の神殿 外観装飾の詳細 | 撮影：ローラ・ギルピン | 1930年頃
4-4 ボロブドゥール遺跡(インドネシア、ジャワ島中部) | 撮影：ヘルミグ社、ジャワ島 | 撮影年不詳
4-5 帝国ホテル二代目本館 外観の装飾。ライト自身によるトリミング | 撮影：フランク・ロイド・ライト | 撮影：1922年
4-6 古代ローマ円形劇場コロッセウム | 撮影：テイラー・A.ウーレイ | 1910年

4-2 Chichen-itza, Temple of Kukulcán, exterior view. Laura Gilpin, photographer. Photo: c. 1930.◆
4-3 Chichen-itza, Temple of Warriors, exterior view, details of ornament. Laura Gilpin, photographer. Photo c. 1930.◆
4-4 Borobudur, Central Java, Indonesia, exterior detail. Helmig & Co., Java, Indonesia., photographer. undated.◆
4-5 Imperial Hotel, Tokyo 1913-23. Exterior view, detail of decoration. Frank Lloyd Wright, photographer. Photo: 1922.◆
4-6 Roman amphitheatre, Colosseum. Taylor A. Woolley, photographer. Photo: 1910.◆

—

◆ Personal and Taliesin Fellowship photographs, 1870s-2004, The Frank Lloyd Wright Foundation Archives (The Museum of Modern Art | Avery Architectural & Fine Arts Library, Columbia University, New York)

4-5

21 共鳴するミッドウェイ・ガーデンズ
Resonance of Midway Gardens

● ミッドウェイ・ガーデンズ | Midway Gardens | イリノイ州シカゴ、1913–14年、娯楽施設 | Chicago, Illinois, 1913–14, recreational

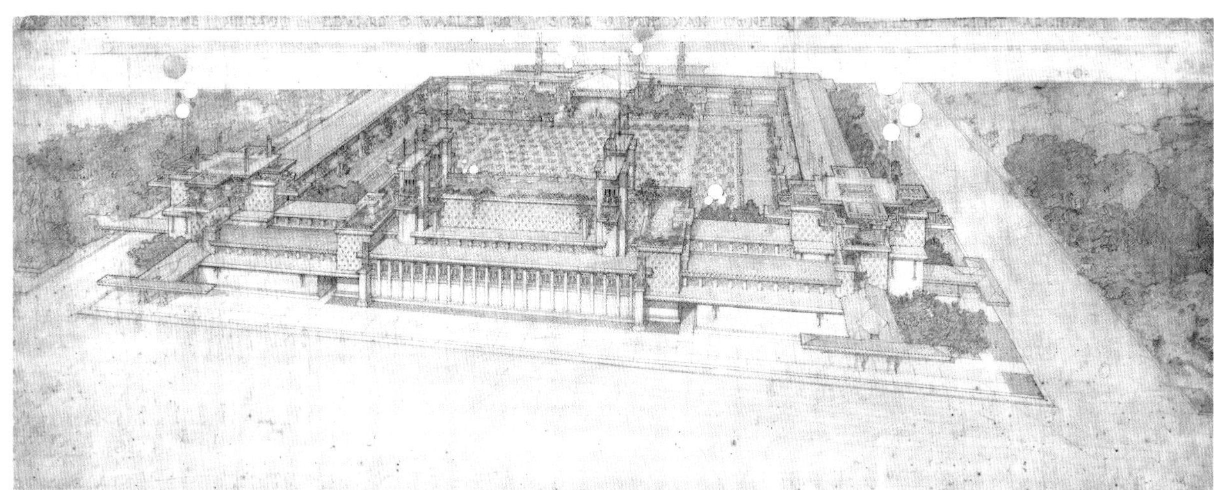

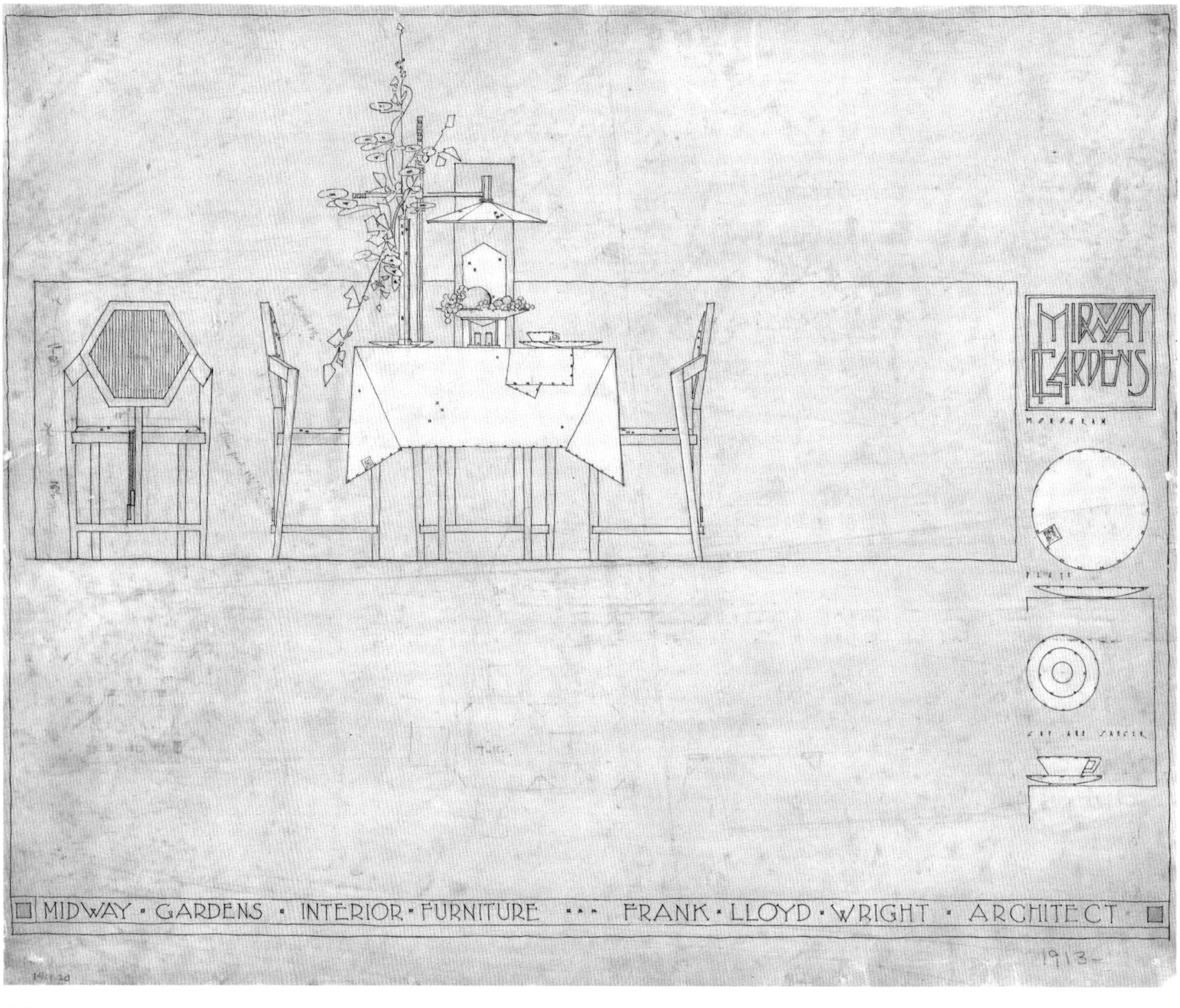

MIDWAY GARDENS

MIDWAY · GARDENS · INTERIOR · FURNITURE ··· FRANK · LLOYD · WRIGHT · ARCHITECT

1913–

4–9
4–10

4-11

4-12

4-14

4-13

4-9 ミッドウェイ・ガーデンズ(イリノイ州シカゴ)1913-14年 初期の構想図 | フランク・ロイド・ライト | 1913年
4-10 ミッドウェイ・ガーデンズ(イリノイ州シカゴ)1913-14年 家具と室内調度品のデザイン | フランク・ロイド・ライト | 1913年
4-11 ミッドウェイ・ガーデンズ(イリノイ州シカゴ)1913-14年 正面ファサード | 建築:フランク・ロイド・ライト、撮影:ヘンリー・ファーマン | 1914年
4-12 ミッドウェイ・ガーデンズ(イリノイ州シカゴ)1913-14年 中庭 | 建築:フランク・ロイド・ライト、撮影:ヘンリー・ファーマン | 1914年
4-13 ミッドウェイ・ガーデンズ(イリノイ州シカゴ)1913-14年 食堂内観 | 建築:フランク・ロイド・ライト、撮影:ヘンリー・ファーマン | 1914年
4-14 ミッドウェイ・ガーデンズ(イリノイ州シカゴ)1913-14年 彫刻と外壁タイル | 建築:フランク・ロイド・ライト、撮影:ヘンリー=ラッセル・ヒッチコック | 1914年

4-9 Midway Gardens, Chicago, Illinois. Project, 1913-14. First sketch. Frank Lloyd Wright. 1913.◆
4-10 Midway Gardens, Chicago, Illinois. Project, 1913-14. Interior furniture. Frank Lloyd Wright. 1913.◆
4-11 Midway Gardens, Chicago, Illinois. Project, 1913-14. Exterior view, front façade. Frank Lloyd Wright, architect. Henry Feuermann, photographer. Photo: 1914. Project photographs, circa 1887-2008.◆
4-12 Midway Gardens, Chicago, Illinois. Project, 1913-14. View of Court Yard. Frank Lloyd Wright, architect. Henry Feuermann, photographer. Photo: 1914. Project photographs, circa 1887-2008.◆
4-13 Midway Gardens, Chicago, Illinois. Project, 1913-14. Interior view of the dining room. Frank Lloyd Wright, architect. Henry Feuermann, photographer. Photo: 1914. Project photographs, circa 1887-2008.◆
4-14 Midway Gardens, Chicago, Illinois. Project, 1913-14. Exterior view, detail of decoration. Frank Lloyd Wright, architect. Hitchcock, Henry-Russell, photographer. Photo: 1914. Project photographs, circa 1887-2008.◆

◆ The Frank Lloyd Wright Foundation Archives (The Museum of Modern Art | Avery Architectural & Fine Arts Library, Columbia University, New York)

● 帝国ホテル二代目本館 | Imperial Hotel

東京都、日比谷、1913-23年、1976年に一部移築、宿泊施設 | Tokyo, Japan, 1913-23. partial reconstruction in 1968, hospitality

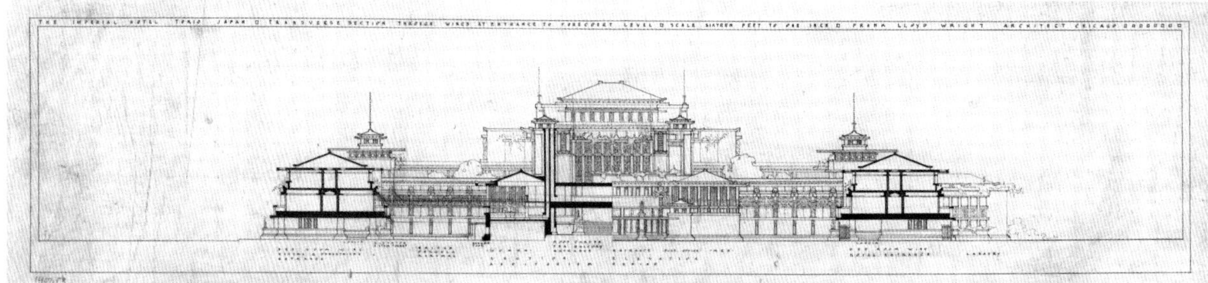

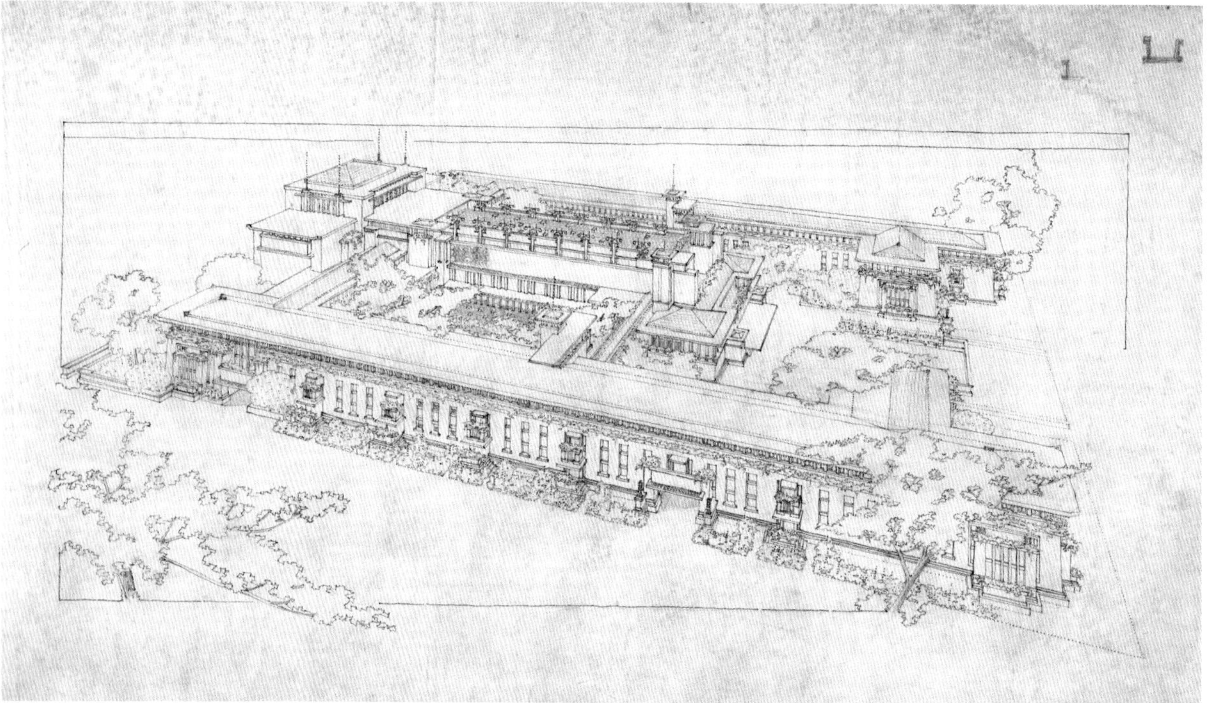

4-7
4-8

4-7 帝国ホテル二代目本館(東京、日比谷)1913-23年 第1案、地階横断面図 | フランク・ロイド・ライト | 1914年
4-8 帝国ホテル二代目本館(東京、日比谷)1913-23年 第1案、鳥瞰透視図 | フランク・ロイド・ライト | 1914年
4-15 帝国ホテル二代目本館(東京、日比谷)1913-23年 | 建築:フランク・ロイド・ライト、撮影:ジャネット・ラム・クラークソン | 1939年
4-16 帝国ホテル二代目本館(東京、日比谷)1913-23年 演芸場 | 建築:フランク・ロイド・ライト | 撮影者不詳
4-17 帝国ホテル二代目本館(東京、日比谷)1913-23年 池と北翼、玄関回り | 建築:フランク・ロイド・ライト | 撮影者不詳

4-7 Imperial Hotel, Tokyo, Japan. Project, 1913-23. Scheme 1, Transverse section. Frank Lloyd Wright. 1914.
The Frank Lloyd Wright Foundation Archives (The Museum of Modern Art | Avery Architectural & Fine Arts Library, Columbia University, New York)
4-8 Imperial Hotel, Tokyo, Japan. Project, 1913-23. Scheme 1, Aerial perspective. Frank Lloyd Wright. 1914.
The Frank Lloyd Wright Foundation Archives (The Museum of Modern Art | Avery Architectural & Fine Arts Library, Columbia University, New York)
4-15 Imperial Hotel, Tokyo, Japan. Project, 1913-23. Frank Lloyd Wright, architect. Janet Lamb Clarkson, photographer. Photo:1939. Imperial Hotel
4-16 Imperial Hotel, Tokyo, Japan. Project, 1913-23. Theatre. Frank Lloyd Wright, architect. Photographer unidentified. Imperial Hotel
4-17 Imperial Hotel, Tokyo, Japan. Project, 1913-23. Sculpture at the pond. Frank Lloyd Wright, architect. Photographer unidentified. Imperial Hotel

4-16

4-17

4-15

22 帝国ホテル二代目本館クロニクル

Chronicle of Wright's Imperial Hotel

西暦	和暦	月	日	出来事
1886	明治19年	2		内閣直属の臨時建築局設置(総裁 井上馨)。官庁集中計画にホテル建設が含まれる
1887	明治20年	7		基礎工事着工(メンツおよびチーツェに設計依頼)
		10		渋沢栄一、大倉喜八郎、横山孫一郎の3名、選挙により理事に就任、渋沢栄一を理事長に選任。仮事務所を日本土木会社内に置く
1888	明治21年	1		建設工事着工
		9		建築工事中止。建築設計・監理を渡辺譲に委嘱しなおす。翌月工事再着工
1890	明治23年	11	3	初代帝国ホテル開業
1906	明治39年	1	10	本館裏手に、別館新築工事着工
		3		日露戦争の終結により外来客増加、外国人宿泊客1日90人を突破
		9	4	四大ホテル同盟結成(帝国ホテル、富士屋ホテル、金谷ホテル、都ホテル)
1909	明治42年	8	18	林愛作、支配人として着任(10月5日、常務取締役に就任)
1910	明治43年	1	25	宮内省御用に指定される
1911	明治44年			シカゴの銀行家グーキンが建築家候補にライトを推す手紙を林愛作に送る
1912	明治45年			ライトと帝国ホテルの交信開始する
1913	大正2年			ライト来日(1905年の来日について2回目)。林と打ち合わせ、敷地を見学する。滞在中初期案を描く
1915	大正4年	7	26	宮内省より新館建設用敷地の使用許可下りる
		12	11	林支配人渡米、タリアセン滞在(1916年4月14日帰国)
1916	大正5年	3	17	林支配人、米国でライトと契約覚書を取り交わす
		11	22	臨時株主総会で新ホテル建設を決議(内務大臣官邸敷地跡、延建坪約6,000坪。費用130万円)
1917	大正6年	1		ライト3度目の来日(翌年4月まで)
				遠藤新参画。ライト、新ホテル設計をほぼ完成
1918	大正7年	11		ライト4度目の来日(翌年8月まで)
1919	大正8年	9		新ホテル建設工事起工(動力室から着工)
		12		ライト5度目の来日(翌年6月まで)。アントニン&ノエミ・レーモンド夫妻を伴う
1920	大正9年	3		病床に伏すライトの看病のため母と女医ルフ来日
		5		ライトの設計による別館新築工事、一部落成(上半期中に2階建ての新別館竣工)。専用室にライト入居。[cat. no. 4-34]
		12		ライト6度目の来日(翌年5月まで)
1921	大正10年	8		ライト7度目の来日(翌年7月まで)
1922	大正11年	4	16	本館地下室から出火、初代本館全焼
		7	1	二代目本館(ライト館)一部開業
		7		ライト帰国
		10	7	中央部の宴会場・演芸場完成
		11		グリル食堂および館内売店(アーケード)営業開始
1923	大正12年	4	19	副支配人犬丸徹三、支配人に就任
		8		8月末、二代目本館全館落成(鉄筋コンクリートおよび煉瓦コンクリート構造、地上5階・地下1階、延床面積1万535坪、客室数270室)
		9	1	二代目本館の落成披露準備中に関東大震災発生(別館は復旧困難となり取り壊し)
1940	昭和15年	3		隣の鹿鳴館の取り壊し始まる
1945	昭和20年	5	24	空襲により本館中央部から南館・別棟にかけて被爆(-25日)、 南館客室の2階以上全部と宴会場の大部分を焼失(焼失面積5,686坪、被害額約170万円)、一時営業を中止
		6	7	焼失を免れた残存部分で営業再開
		9	17	連合国軍の将官およびGHQ高官用宿舎として接収される
		11	22	自由営業を続けていた「グリル」「プルニエ」、完全接収となり一般への開放を禁止
1952	昭和27年	1	24	GHQ、接収施設の返還方針を発表
		3	15	帝国ホテルを宿舎としていた連合国軍高級将校ら山王ホテルへ移動(100人余の従業員も同時に移籍)、 3月16日、接収解除
		4	1	自由営業再開

1916 | 4-18a

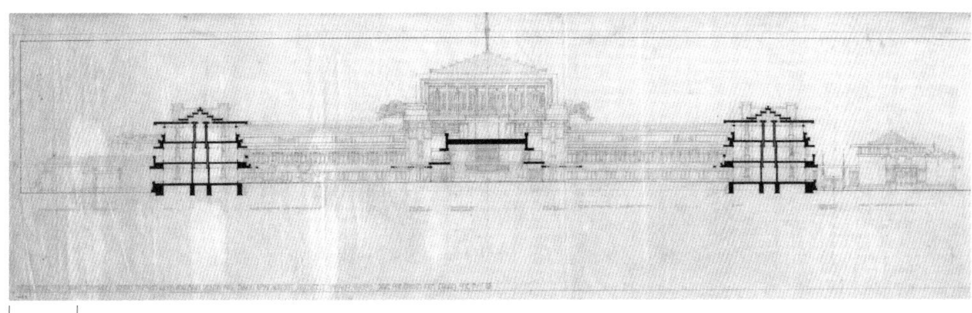
1914 | 4-18b

1917 | 4-18c

4-18d

4-18e

c.1935 | 4-18f

c.1922 | 4-1

1922 | 4-18g

1923 | 5-8

4-18h

c.1965 | 4-18j

1967	昭和42年	3	13	帝国ホテル新本館に対する構造設計審査会開催(東京ステーションホテルにて)
		7	31	早稲田大学明石研究室のライト館実測調査受け入れを承認
		11	8	メインダイニングルームで「帝国ホテルを守る会」、建築学会、文化財保護委員会、当社の4者会談開催
		11	15	二代目本館客室全面閉鎖
		11	21	佐藤栄作首相、二代目本館の一部を博物館明治村に移築を表明
		12	1	二代目本館取り壊し工事開始
		12	28	明治村、帝国ホテル二代目本館ロビーおよび前庭部分の移築を受け入れ決定
		12	28	二代目本館宴会場「孔雀の間」(ピーコックルーム)取り壊し開始
1968	昭和43年	2	15	二代目本館玄関ロビー部分を明治村へ移送開始
		2	25	二代目本館取り壊し工事完了
1970	昭和45年	3	6	三代目本館竣工。オールドインペリアルバーなどに、二代目本館で使用されていた壁画などを移築
1983	昭和58年	3	13	インペリアルタワー開業
1985	昭和60年			二代目本館玄関ロビー部分展示公開(博物館明治村)
2007	平成29年	6		ライト生誕150周年を機に「インペリアル タイムズ」(歴史を紹介する常設の展示スペース)をホテル内に新設
2021	令和3年	10	27	四代目本館のデザインアーキテクトとして田根剛氏を選ばれたことが発表される(2036年完成予定)

参考:『帝国ホテル120年史』および Kathryn Smith, "Frank Lloyd Wright and the Imperial Hotel: A Postscript", *The Art Bulletin*, 1985. vol. 67, no. 2

4-1 フランク・ロイド・ライト、帝国ホテルにて | 撮影者不詳 | 1922年頃
4-18a 林愛作と妻、タリアセンにて | 撮影者不詳 | 1916年
4-18b 帝国ホテル二代目本館(東京、日比谷) 第1案、宿泊棟とメイン・ダイニングを通る横断面図 | フランク・ロイド・ライト | 1914年
4-18c 帝国ホテル建築設計事務所にて。左から:ジョン・ロイド・ライト、遠藤新、フランク・ロイド・ライト、伊藤文四郎 | 撮影者不詳 | 1917年
4-18d 帝国ホテル二代目本館(東京、日比谷) 建設現場。鹿鳴館が背景に見える | 建築:フランク・ロイド・ライト
4-18e 帝国ホテル二代目本館(東京、日比谷) 建設現場。宴会場「孔雀の間(ピーコック・ルーム)」の装飾を建てている | 建築:フランク・ロイド・ライト
4-18f 絵葉書 帝国ホテル二代目本館(東京、日比谷) | 建築:フランク・ロイド・ライト | 撮影:1935年頃
4-18g 帝国ホテル二代目本館(東京、日比谷) 集合写真。左から:遠藤新、フランク・ロイド・ライト、林愛作、ポール・ミュラー | 建築:フランク・ロイド・ライト | 撮影:1922年
4-18h 日比谷公園から見た帝国ホテル二代目本館全景 | 建築:フランク・ロイド・ライト | 撮影年不詳
4-18j 絵葉書 1965年頃の帝国ホテル二代目本館(東京、日比谷) 全景 | 建築:フランク・ロイド・ライト | 1965年頃
4-18k 移築された帝国ホテル二代目本館の玄関部分 | 建築:フランク・ロイド・ライト、撮影:ToLoLo Studio、撮影協力:博物館明治村 | 2023年
4-18l ロジャース・レイシー・ホテル計画案(テキサス州ダラス)1946-47年 透視図 | フランク・ロイド・ライト
4-18m ロジャース・レイシー・ホテル計画案(テキサス州ダラス)1946-47年 吹き抜けより中庭を見下ろす | フランク・ロイド・ライト
4-18n 田根剛氏による帝国ホテル 東京 新本館イメージパース | ATTA- Atelier Tsuyoshi Tane Architects | 2022年
5-8 映像「関東大震災記録」| ブラック・ホーク映像 | 1923年

4-1 Frank Lloyd Wright at the Imperial Hotel. Photographer unidentified. Photo: c. 1922. Imperial Hotel
4-18a Aisaku and Takako Hayashi at Taliesin. Photographer unidentified. Photo: 1916. Personal and Taliesin Fellowship photographs, 1870s-2004, The Frank Lloyd Wright Foundation Archives (The Museum of Modern Art | Avery Architectural & Fine Arts Library, Columbia University, New York)
4-18b Imperial Hotel, Tokyo, Japan. Scheme 1, 1914. Transverse section through wings and main dining hall. Frank Lloyd Wright. 1914. The Frank Lloyd Wright Foundation Archives (The Museum of Modern Art | Avery Architectural & Fine Arts Library, Columbia University, New York)
4-18c At the construction office of the Imperial Hotel. From left: John Lloyd Wright, Endo Arata, Frank Lloyd Wright and Bunshiro Ito. Photographer unidentified. Photo: 1917. Gen Endo Collection
4-18d Imperial Hotel, Tokyo, Japan. Construction site. Rokumeikan can be seen in the back. Frank Lloyd Wright, architect. Imperial Hotel
4-18e Imperial Hotel, Tokyo, Japan. Construction site. Decoration of the Banquet hall (Peacock Room) can be seen lifted. Frank Lloyd Wright, architect. Imperial Hotel
4-18f Postcard. Imperial Hotel, Tokyo, Japan. Frank Lloyd Wright, architect. Photo: 1935. Imperial Hotel
4-18g Imperial Hotel, Tokyo, Japan. From left: Arata Endo, Frank Lloyd Wright, Aisaku Hayashi, Paul Muller. Photo: 1922. Imperial Hotel. Photo courtesy of Kanaya Hotel
4-18h Imperial Hotel, Tokyo, Japan. Exterior view from the Hibiya Park. Frank Lloyd Wright, architect. Undated. Imperial Hotel
4-18j Postcard. Imperial Hotel around 1965. Frank Lloyd Wright, architect. c. 1965. Imperial Hotel
4-18k Wright's Imperial Hotel Lobby and reflecting pool reconstructed at the Museum Meiji-Mura. Frank Lloyd Wright, architect. ToLoLo Studio, photographer. Photo: 2023. Courtesy of Museum Meiji-Mura
4-18l Rogers Lacey Hotel, Dallas, Texas. Unbuilt Project, 1946-47. Exterior perspective. Frank Lloyd Wright. The Frank Lloyd Wright Foundation Archives (The Museum of Modern Art | Avery Architectural & Fine Arts Library, Columbia University, New York)
4-18m Rogers Lacey Hotel, Dallas, Texas. Unbuilt Project, 1946-47. View of court. Frank Lloyd Wright. The Frank Lloyd Wright Foundation Archives (The Museum of Modern Art | Avery Architectural & Fine Arts Library, Columbia University, New York)
4-18n Imperial Hotel Tokyo New Main Building Image Perspective by Tsuyoshi Tane. ATTA- Atelier Tsuyoshi Tane Architects. 2022. Imperial Hotel
5-8 Film. The Japanese Earthquake of September 1, 1923. Blackhawk Films. The Frank Lloyd Wright Foundation Archives (The Museum of Modern Art | Avery Architectural & Fine Arts Library, Columbia University, New York)

2023 | 4-18k

2022 | 4-18n

● **ロジャース・レイシー・ホテル計画案** | Rogers Lacy Hotel, unbuilt project | テキサス州ダラス、1946-47年、宿泊施設 | Dallas, Texas, 1946-47, hospitality

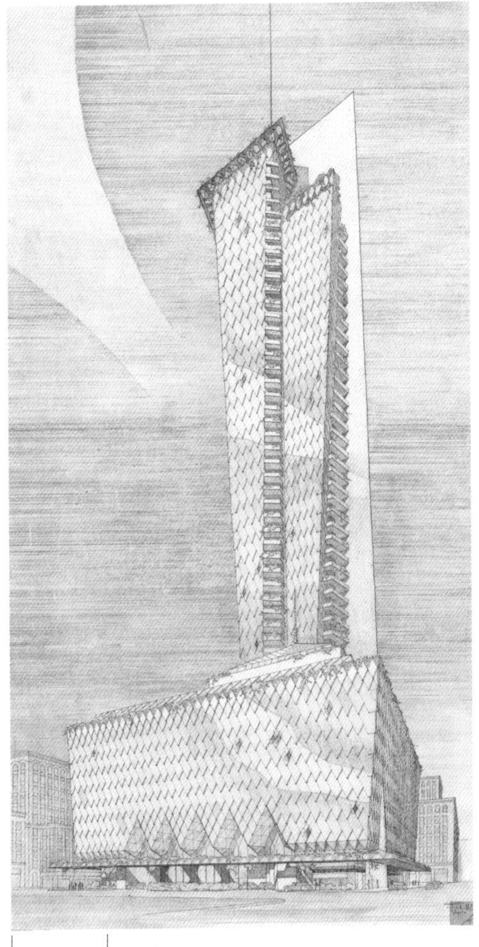

1946-47 | 4-18l

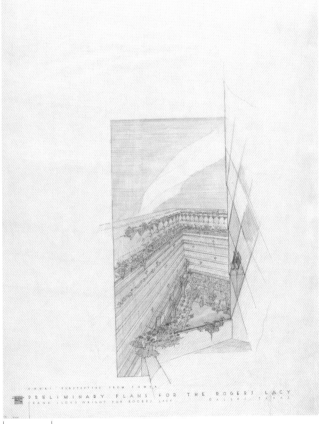

1946-47 | 4-18m

23 メガ・プロジェクトのはじまり

Start of a mega project

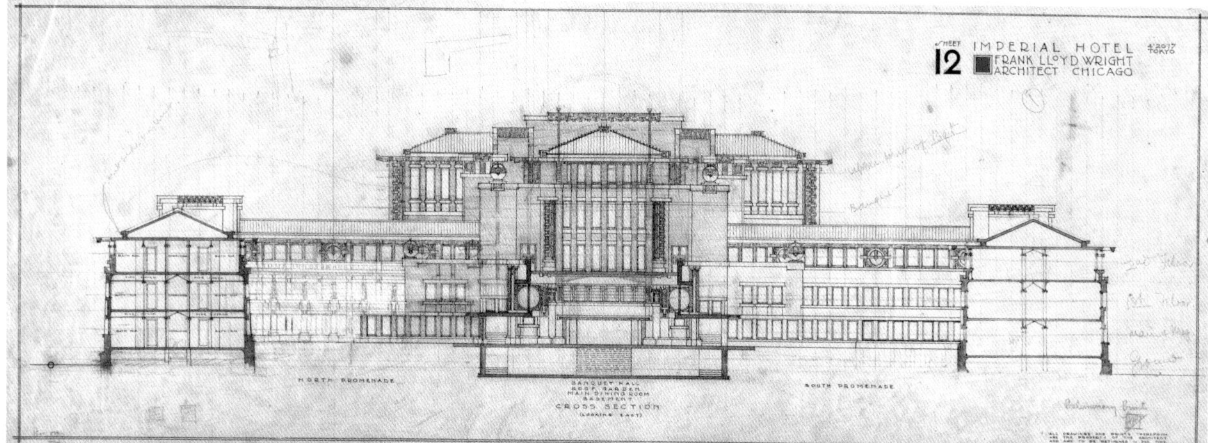

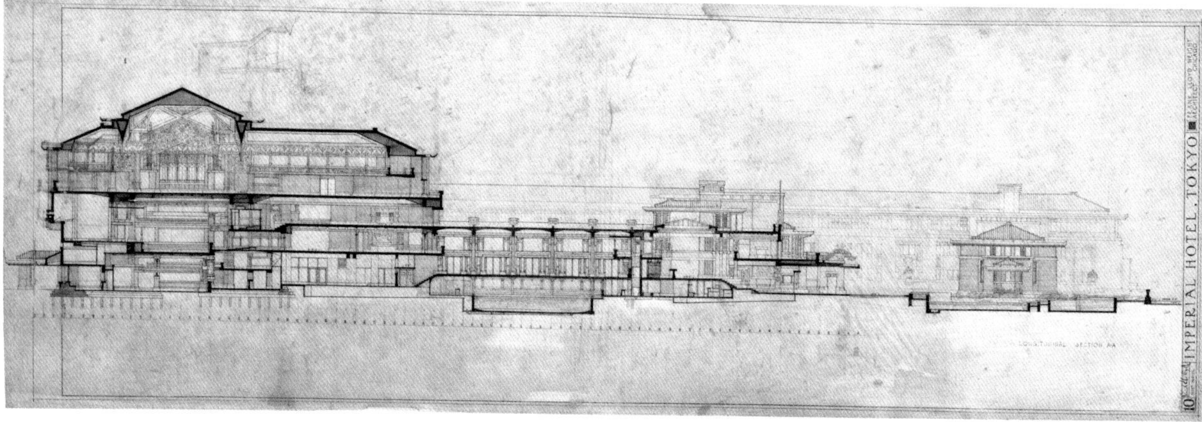

4-19

4-20

4-19 帝国ホテル二代目本館(東京、日比谷)1913–23年 第2案、横断面図 | フランク・ロイド・ライト | 1915年

4-20 帝国ホテル二代目本館(東京、日比谷)1913–23年 第2案、縦断面図 | フランク・ロイド・ライト | 1915年

4-21 帝国ホテル二代目本館(東京、日比谷)1913–23年 第2案、キャバレー・レストラン、演芸場、宴会場「孔雀の間(ピーコック・ルーム)」の断面図 | フランク・ロイド・ライト | 1915年

4-19 Imperial Hotel, Tokyo, Japan. Project, 1913–23. Scheme 2, 1915. Cross section. Frank Lloyd Wright.
The Frank Lloyd Wright Foundation Archives (The Museum of Modern Art | Avery Architectural & Fine Arts Library, Columbia University, New York)

4-20 Imperial Hotel, Tokyo, Japan. Project, 1913–23. Scheme 2, 1915. Longitudinal section. Frank Lloyd Wright.
The Frank Lloyd Wright Foundation Archives (The Museum of Modern Art | Avery Architectural & Fine Arts Library, Columbia University, New York)

4-21 Imperial Hotel, Tokyo, Japan. Project, 1913–23. Scheme 2, 1915. Section through Cabaret, auditorium, and banquet hall. Frank Lloyd Wright.
The Frank Lloyd Wright Foundation Archives (The Museum of Modern Art | Avery Architectural & Fine Arts Library, Columbia University, New York)

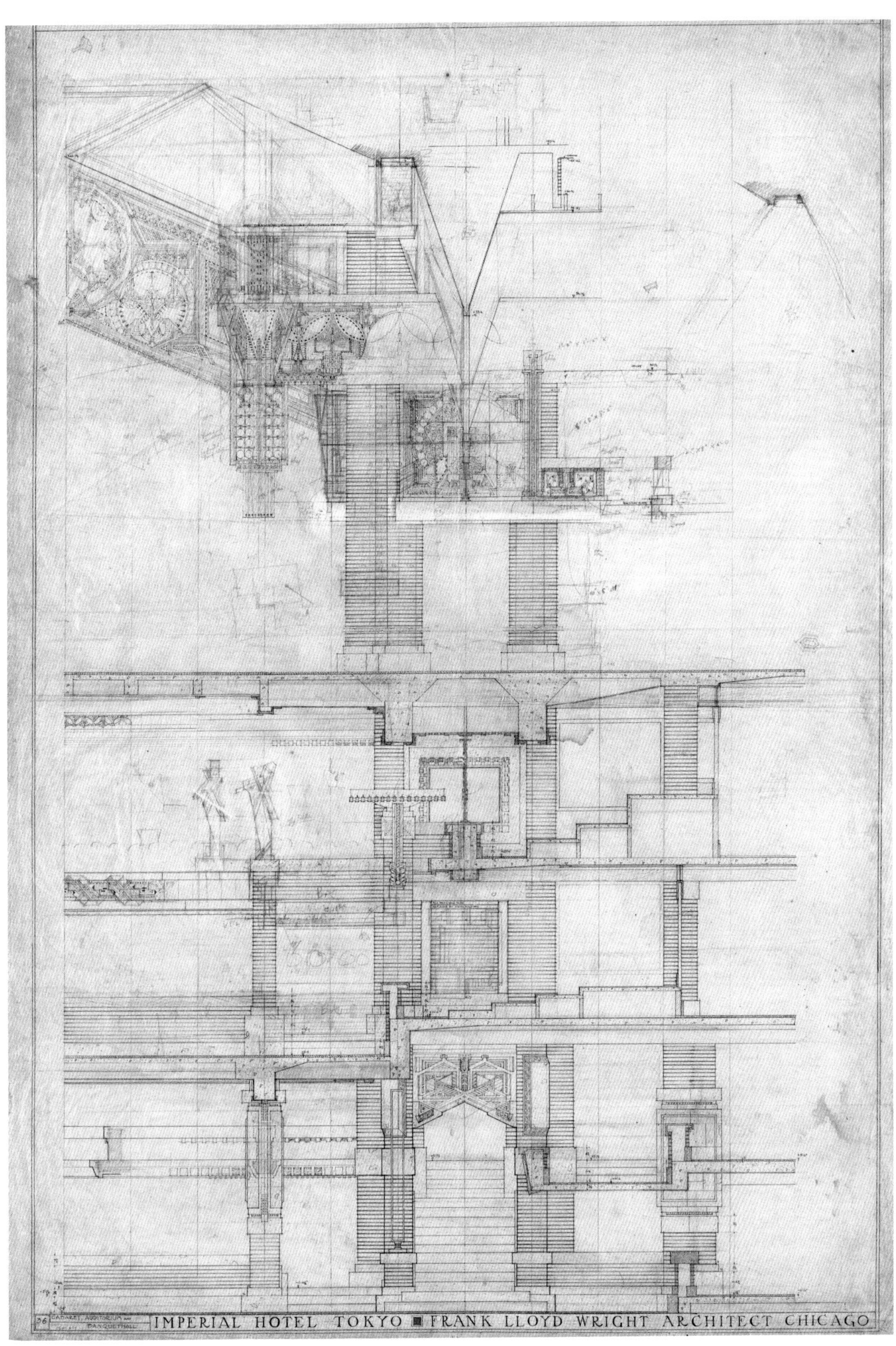
36
CABARET, AUDITORIUM AND BANQUET HALL
IMPERIAL HOTEL TOKYO ■ FRANK LLOYD WRIGHT ARCHITECT CHICAGO

4-21

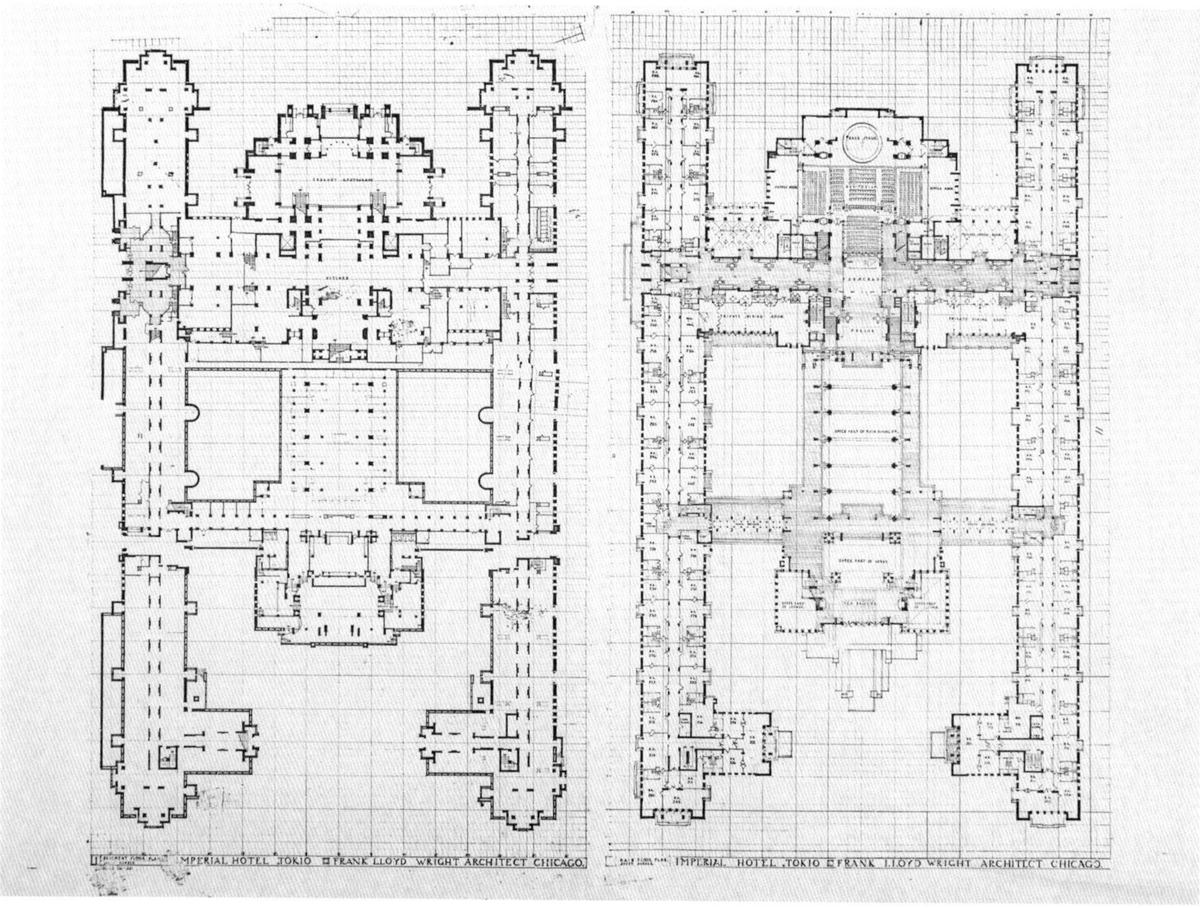

4-22

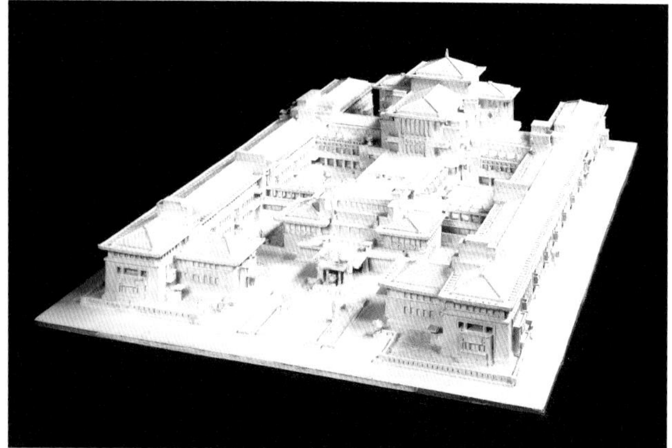

4-29

4-22 帝国ホテル二代目本館(東京、日比谷)1913-23年 地下1階平面図、メイン階(2階)平面図 | フランク・ロイド・ライト

4-29 模型(3Dスキャン&3Dプリンタによる) 帝国ホテル二代目本館 | 建築:フランク・ロイド・ライト、制作:京都工芸繊維大学 KYOTO Design Lab | 制作:2023年
(3D計測データを用いた3Dプリントレプリカを作成展示)

4-22 Imperial Hotel, Tokyo, Japan. Project, 1913-23. Basement floor plan, Main floor plan. Gen Endo Collection

4-29 Imperial Hotel Model (replica made by 3D scanning and 3D printing). Frank Lloyd Wright, architect.
KYOTO Design Lab, Kyoto Institute of Technology, fabricator of the replica. 2023

4-25

4-28

4-26

4-25 帝国ホテル二代目本館(東京、日比谷)1913-23年 宴会場「孔雀の間(ピーコック・ルーム)」へのプロムナード | 建築:フランク・ロイド・ライト | 撮影:1925年頃
4-26 帝国ホテル二代目本館(東京、日比谷)1913-23年 外観 南東方面を見る | 建築:フランク・ロイド・ライト | 撮影年不詳
4-28 絵葉書 帝国ホテル二代目本館(東京、日比谷)1913-23年 ロビー内観 | 建築:フランク・ロイド・ライト | 1965年頃

4-25 Imperial Hotel, Tokyo, Japan. Project, 1913-23. Interior view of the promenade to the banquet hall (Peacock Room)
4-26 Imperial Hotel, Tokyo, Japan. Project, 1913-23. View towards the direction of south west
4-28 Postcard. Imperial Hotel, Tokyo, Japan. Project, 1913-23. Entrance lobby

24 宿泊とエンターテインメント
Lodging and entertainment

4-34

4-31

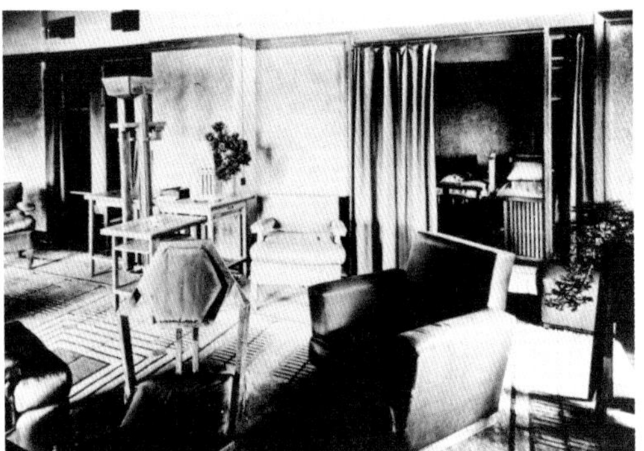
4-33

4-30

4-36

4-37

4-39

4-38

4-30 帝国ホテル二代目本館 客室のサイド・テーブル | デザイン：フランク・ロイド・ライト
4-31 帝国ホテル二代目本館（東京、日比谷）1913–23年 客室 | 建築：フランク・ロイド・ライト
4-33 帝国ホテル二代目本館（東京、日比谷）1913–23年 客室 | 建築：フランク・ロイド・ライト
4-34 帝国ホテル別館（東京、日比谷）1920年 ライトの居室内観 | 撮影者不詳 | 1920年
4-36 帝国ホテル二代目本館 ルーフ・ガーデンでの映画会プログラム（表紙） | 1937年
4-37 帝国ホテル二代目本館（東京、日比谷）1913–23年 ルーフ・ガーデンでの映画会 | 建築：フランク・ロイド・ライト
4-38 帝国ホテル二代目本館 パンフレット | デザイン：繁岡鑒一 | 1925–30年頃
4-39 帝国ホテル二代目本館 英語パンフレット | デザイン：繁岡鑒一 | 1925年

4-30 Side table from the guest room of the Imperial Hotel, Tokyo, Japan. Frank Lloyd Wright, designer. Imperial Hotel
4-31 Imperial Hotel, Tokyo, Japan. Project, 1913–23. Guest room. Frank Lloyd Wright, architect
4-33 Imperial Hotel, Tokyo, Japan. Project, 1913–23. Guest room. Frank Lloyd Wright, architect
4-34 Imperial Hotel Annex, Tokyo, Japan. Project, 1920. Interior of the living room in Wright's apartment. Photographer unidentified. Photo: 1920. Project photographs, circa 1887–2008, The Frank Lloyd Wright Foundation Archives (The Museum of Modern Art | Avery Architectural & Fine Arts Library, Columbia University, New York)
4-36 Imperial Hotel. Program cover of a film screening at the Roof Garden. 1937. Imperial Hotel
4-37 Imperial Hotel, Tokyo, Japan. Project, 1913–23. Film screening at the Roof Garden. Frank Lloyd Wright, architect. Imperial Hotel
4-38 Brochure from the Imperial Hotel. Kenichi Shigeoka, designer. c. 1925–30s. Imperial Hotel
4-39 Brochure from the Imperial Hotel. Kenichi Shigeoka, designer. 1925. Imperial Hotel

25 総合芸術としての帝国ホテル

Imperial Hotel as a total work of art

4-47

4-49

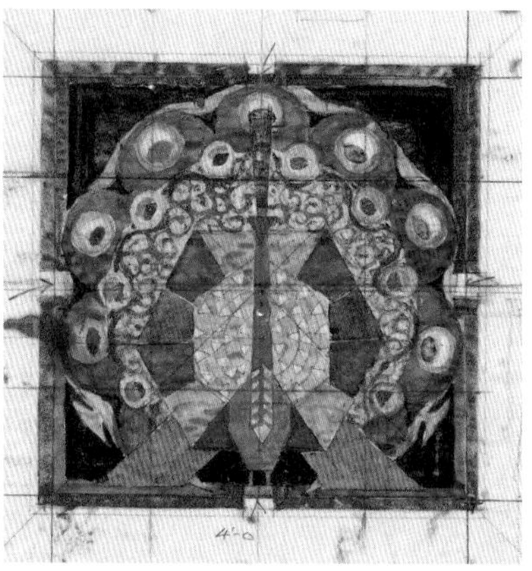

4-55

4-43

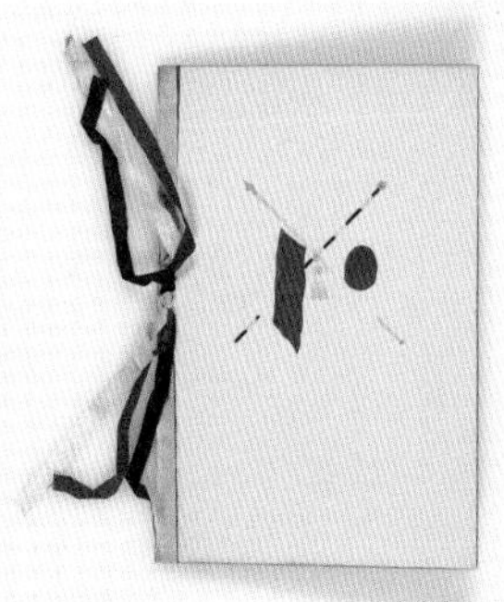

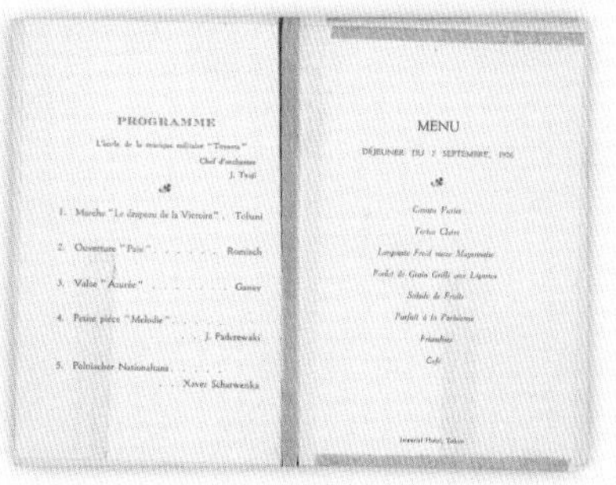

4-46

4-50

4-51

4-43 帝国ホテル二代目本館 キャバレー・レストランで用いられたディナー・ウェア | デザイン:フランク・ロイド・ライト、再製作:(株)ノリタケカンパニー | デザイン:1916-22年頃、再製作:1962-68年
4-46 帝国ホテル二代目本館で用いられていたメニュー | 1926年
4-47 帝国ホテル二代目本館 椅子「ピーコック・チェア」| デザイン:フランク・ロイド・ライト | デザイン:1913年頃、製作:1930年頃
4-49 帝国ホテル二代目本館 テーブル | デザイン:フランク・ロイド・ライト | デザイン:1913年頃、製作年不詳
4-50 帝国ホテル二代目本館 椅子 | デザイン:フランク・ロイド・ライト、修復:渡邊謙一郎(スタンダードトレード) | デザイン:1920年頃、修復:2023年
4-51 帝国ホテル二代目本館 2階ラウンジの椅子 | デザイン:フランク・ロイド・ライト | デザイン:1913年頃、再製作:1985年
4-55 帝国ホテル二代目本館 宴会場「孔雀の間(ピーコック・ルーム)」装飾スタディ | ノエミ・レーモンド | 1920年

4-43 Imperial Hotel. Cabaret Dinnerware. Frank Lloyd Wright, designer. Noritake, manufacturer. Design: 1916–1922. Reproduction 1962–68. Toyota Municipal Museum of Art
4-46 Imperial Hotel. Menu card. 1926. Imperial Hotel
4-47 Imperial Hotel. Chair from the Ballroom (Peacock Room) (in beige). Frank Lloyd Wright, designer. Design: c. 1913 Manufactured 1930. Toyota Municipal Museum of Art
4-49 Imperial Hotel, Tokyo, Japan. Table from the Ball Room (Peacock Room). Frank Lloyd Wright, designer. Design: c. 1913. Toyota Municipal Museum of Art
4-50 Imperial Hotel. Chair. Frank Lloyd Wright, designer. Kenichiro Watanabe, Design: c. 1920. Restoration: 2023
4-51 Imperial Hotel. Chair from the Second floor lounge. Frank Lloyd Wright, designer. Design: c. 1913 Manufactured 1985. Museum Meiji-Mura
4-55 Study of the mural in the Peacock Room of the Imperial Hotel. Noémi Raymond, designer for Frank Lloyd Wright. 1920. Koichi Kitazawa Collection

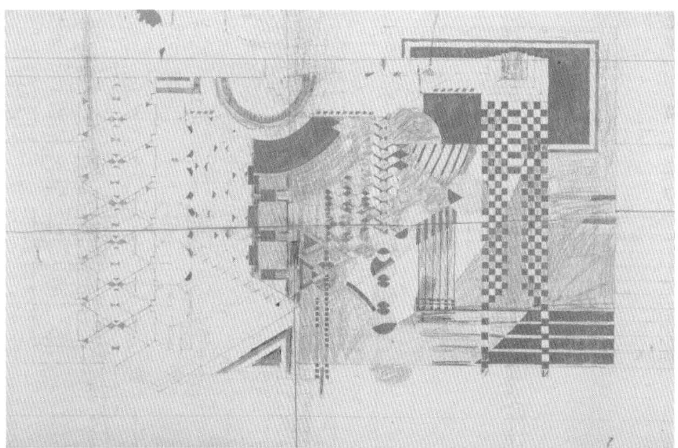

4-53

4-60

4-57

4-61

4-53 帝国ホテル二代目本館 プロムナード中央パーラー(宝の間)北側暖炉の上の着彩レリーフ | フランク・ロイド・ライト | 1921年
4-54 帝国ホテル二代目本館 演芸場の壁面装飾 原寸詳細図 | フランク・ロイド・ライト | 1915年頃
4-57 絵葉書 帝国ホテル二代目本館 宴会場「孔雀の間(ピーコック・ルーム)」| 1925-30年頃(昭和初期)
4-60 帝国ホテル二代目本館(東京、日比谷)1913-23年 プロムナード中央パーラー(宝の間)北側暖炉の上の大谷石の着彩レリーフ | 撮影年不詳
4-61 帝国ホテル二代目本館(東京、日比谷)1913-23年 メインダイニングの柱の装飾 | 撮影年不詳

4-53 Imperial Hotel. Carved stone and polychrome mural for the parlor northern fireplace.
Frank Lloyd Wright. 1921. Prints and Photographs Division, Library of Congress, Washington, D.C. LC-DIG-ppmsca-85262
4-54 Imperial Hotel. Full-size detailed drawing of wall decorations in the theater. Frank Lloyd Wright. c. 1915. Toyota Municipal Museum of Art
4-57 Postcard. Imperial Hotel. Banquet hall (Peacock Room). Frank Lloyd Wright.
4-60 Imperial Hotel, Tokyo, Japan. Project, 1913-23. Carved oya stone and polychrome mural from the parlor “Takara no Ma” northern fireplace.
Frank Lloyd Wright. undated. Imperial Hotel
4-61 Imperial Hotel, Tokyo, Japan. Project, 1913-23. Decoration of the pillar at the main dining room. Frank Lloyd Wright. undated. Imperial Hotel

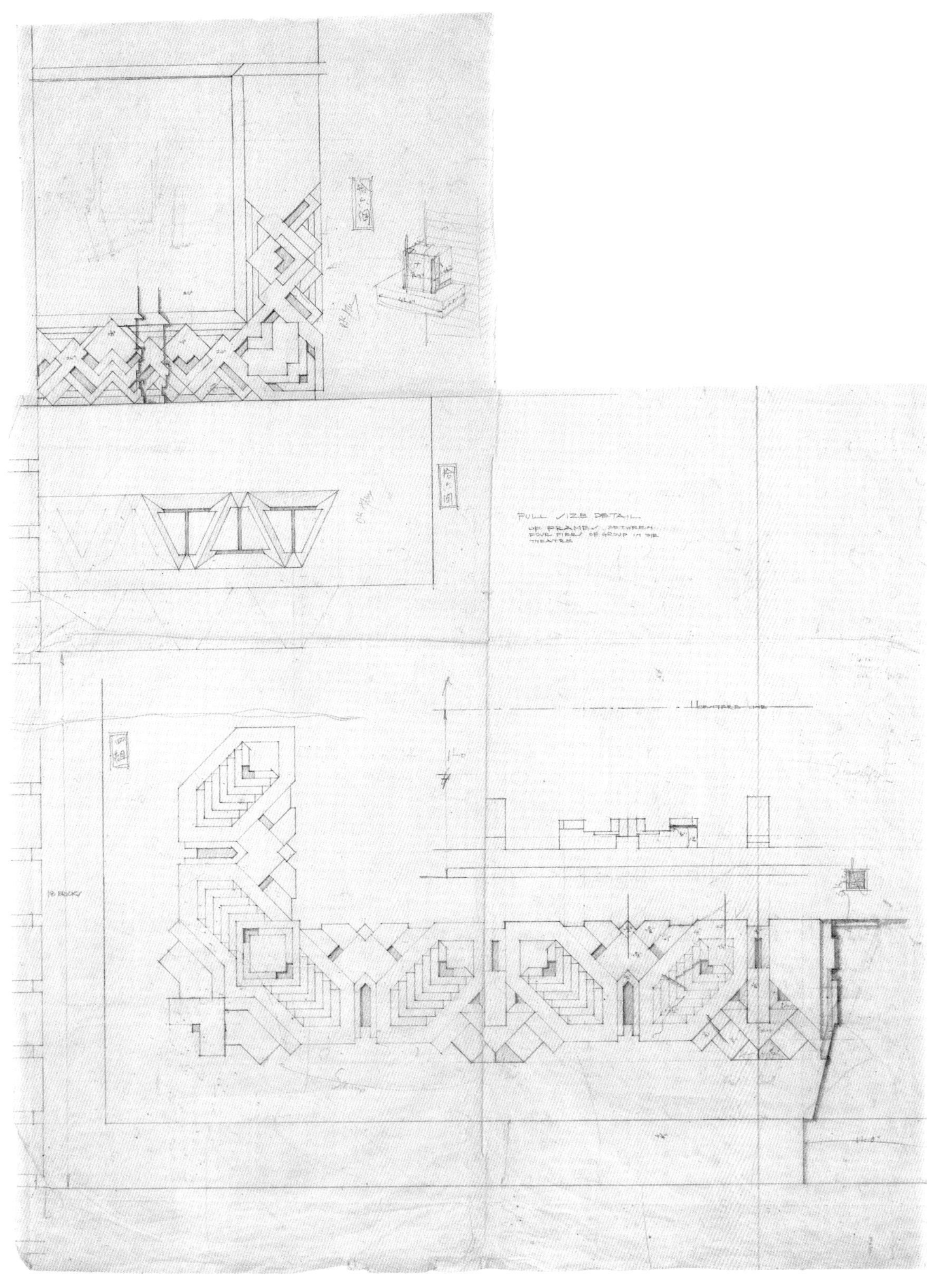
FULL SIZE DETAIL
OF FRAMES BETWEEN
FOUR PIERS OF GROUP IN THE
THEATRE

4-54

26 素材の探求：大谷石とすだれレンガ

Material exploration: Oya stone and Architectural Blocks

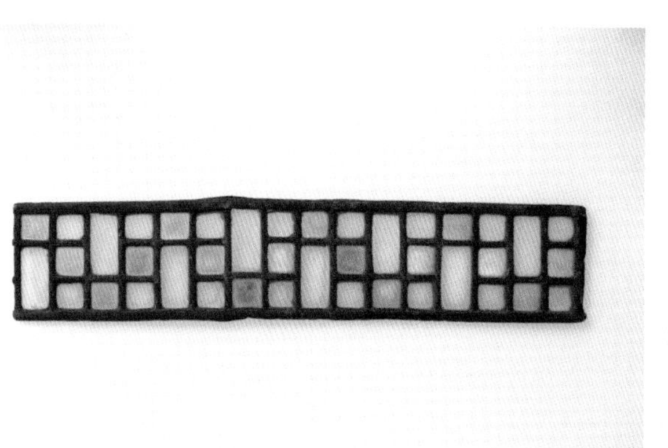

4-62

4-63

4-64

4-65

4-62 帝国ホテル二代目本館 金箔入りガラス | デザイン：フランク・ロイド・ライト | 1919-23年頃
4-63 帝国ホテル二代目本館 テラコッタの装飾ブロック | デザイン：フランク・ロイド・ライト | 1919-23年頃
4-64 帝国ホテル二代目本館 千鳥模様のすだれレンガ | デザイン：フランク・ロイド・ライト | 1919-23年頃
4-65 帝国ホテル二代目本館 照明・換気用に用いられるテラコッタの装飾ブロック(復刻版) | デザイン：フランク・ロイド・ライト
4-66 帝国ホテルの建設現場で働く日本の職人たちの空想的スケッチ | アントニン・レーモンド
4-70 帝国ホテル二代目本館(東京、日比谷)1913-23年 建設現場 | 撮影年不詳
4-71 フランク・ロイド・ライトから遠藤新、福原氏、羽仁もと子にあてた手紙 | 1928年4月12日
4-72 ライトを囲む宴会。前列左から3人目アントニン・レーモンド、4人目遠藤新、5人目ポール・ミュラー、7人目フランク・ロイド・ライト、8人目林愛作 | 1922年頃

4-62 Imperial Hotel. Fragment of window with square pattern decorated with gold leaf. Frank Lloyd Wright, designer. c. 1919-23. Imperial Hotel
4-63 Imperial Hotel. Architectural block / Terracotta textile block. Frank Lloyd Wright, designer. c. 1919-23. Imperial Hotel
4-64 Imperial Hotel. Architectural block / Scratch tile block. Frank Lloyd Wright, designer. c. 1919-23. Imperial Hotel
4-65 Imperial Hotel. Architectural block / Terracotta textile block (replica). Frank Lloyd Wright, designer. Imperial Hotel
4-66 Imaginative sketch, labourers working at the Imperial Hotel. Antonin Raymond. Koichi Kitazawa Collection
4-70 Imperial Hotel, Tokyo, Japan. Project, 1913-23. construction site. Photographer unidentified. undated. Imperial Hotel
4-71 Frank Lloyd Wright, letter to Arata Endo, Fukuhara and Hani, April 12, 1928. Frank Lloyd Wright, author. Gen Endo Collection
4-72 Dinner Party with Frank Lloyd Wright. Third from left Antonin Raymond, fourth Endo Arata, fifth Paul Muller, seventh Frank Lloyd Wright and eighth Aisaku Hayashi. c. 1922. Gen Endo Collection

27 ライト精神の継承

Passing down Wright's spirit

4-72

4-66

4-70

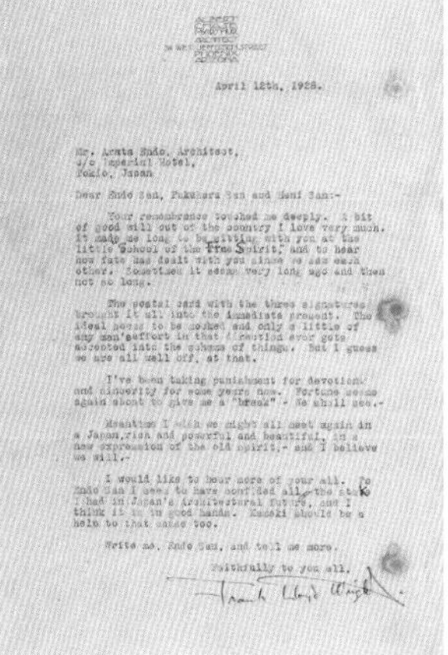

April 12th, 1928.

Mr. Arata Endo, Architect,
c/o Imperial Hotel,
Tokio, Japan

Dear Endo San, Fukuhara San and Hani San:-

Your remembrance touched me deeply. A bit of good will out of the country I love very much. It made me long to be sitting with you at the little School of the Free Spirit, and to hear how fate has dealt with you since we saw each other. Sometimes it seems very long ago and then not so long.

The postal card with the three signatures brought it all into the immediate present. The ideal seems to be mocked and only a little of any man's effort in that direction ever gets accepted into the scheme of things. But I guess we are all well off, at that.

I've been taking punishment for devotion and sincerity for some years now. Fortune seems again about to give me a "break" - We shall see.-

Meantime I wish we might all meet again in a Japan, rich and powerful and beautiful, in a new expression of the old spirit,- and I believe we will.-

I would like to hear more of you all. To Endo San I seem to have confided all the stake I had in Japan's Architectural future, and I think it is in good hands. Kameki should be a help to that cause too.

Write me, Endo San, and tell me more.

Faithfully to you all.

Frank Lloyd Wright

4-71

1928年4月12日

日本国、東京、帝国ホテル気付
建築家、遠藤新様

遠藤さん、福原さん、羽仁さん

あなた方との思い出に深く心を動かされました。私が大好きな国からの素敵な友好の証です。最後にわれわれが顔を合わせてから後、あなた方がどのような運命を辿ったかを、自由学園の小さな校舎で一緒に腰を下ろしながら聞いてみたいと切に願いました。あれはずいぶん昔の出来事のように思える時もあれば、そうでもなく感じることもあります。

三人のお名前が書かれた葉書が全てを今現在へと運んできてくれました。理想は徒労に終わったようで、そうした方向への人間の努力は、体制の中ではほんの僅かしか受け入れてもらえません。でも我々は皆、そのことは十分に経験しましたね。

私はここ数年の間、献身と誠意に対する罰を受けてきました。運命の女神は再び私にチャンスを与えてくれようとしていますが、さてどうなりますか。

そんな中で、私は豊かで力強く美しい、古くからの精神を新たに表現する日本で、再び皆さんと会えることを願い、それが叶うと信じています。

もっと私に皆さんの事を知らせてください。遠藤さんには私が日本の建築の未来のためにつぎ込んだ全てを託したつもりであり、良き手に委ねることができたと考えています。亀城もその目的のための助けとなってくれるでしょう。

手紙をください、遠藤さん。もっと話を聞かせてください。

敬愛する皆様へ、フランク・ロイド・ライト

4-73

4-75

4-76

4-73 甲子園ホテル(兵庫県西宮)現・武庫川女子大学会館、1930年 中庭の池からの全景 | 建築:遠藤新
4-75 土浦亀城邸(東京、品川)1935年 | 建築:土浦亀城
4-76 ニューホープの農場、1939-40年 前列左にアントニンとノエミ・レーモンド夫妻 | 建築:アントニン・レーモンド | 撮影:1940年

4-73 Koushien Hotel, Nishinomiya, Hyogo. Project, 1930. Exterior view, from across the pond. Arata Endo, architect. Gen Endo Collection
4-75 Kameki and Nobuko Tsuchiura House, Shinagawa, Tokyo. Project, 1935. Kameki Tsuchiura, architect. TSUCHIURA Kameki Archives
4-76 Raymond Farm, New Hope, Philadelphia, Project, 1939-40 (original house built 1726). Front row from left: Antonin, Noémi and son Claude. Antonin Raymond, architect. Photo: 1940. Raymond Collections, the Architectural Archives of the University of Pennsylvania

ライトの日本の弟子たち

田中厚子

初来日の1905年から1922年までにライトは7回来日した。帝国ホテルの建設に取り組んだ1916年からの5回の滞在期間を合わせると3年を超える[1]。その期間から戦後にかけて、ライトを尊敬する日本の若い建築家が、東京の帝国ホテル建築事務所やウィスコンシン州スプリンググリーンのタリアセンのライトの下で働き、ライトから直接学んだ。

タリアセンは、ライトの住まい兼仕事場である。ライトが妻のオルギヴァナ(1898–1985)と共にタリアセン・フェローシップという教育の場をつくるのは1932年のことで、それ以前は設計事務所しかなかった。つまり遠藤新[2](1917年4月–18年10月滞在)、藤倉憲二郎[3](1917年7月ごろ–18年10月滞在)、土浦亀城・信子夫妻[4](1924年1月–25年10月滞在)は、ライトの事務所の所員としてタリアセンに滞在し、ライトと共に暮らして仕事をしたのである[表1]。

1928年、ライトとオルギヴァナはフェローシップの準備を開始し、1932年に最初の学生が集まった。その数年後に、タリアセン・ウエスト(1938)の建設が始まり、夏を過ごすウィスコンシンと冬を過ごすアリゾナを往復するかたちになった。1929年から1959年までのフェローシップのリストを見ると、準備期に滞在した岡見健彦[5](1929年8月–31年ごろ滞在)、第二次大戦後に滞在した天野太郎[6](1952)以下、ハヤシ・シンイチロウ(1952)、ハヤシ・ヒデオ(1952)、星島光平(1954)、遠藤楽(1957)の名が見られる[7]。遠藤新や土浦夫妻が経験した環境とは異なるが、彼らもまた直接ライトに師事し、ライトの思想を受け継いだ弟子だといえる。

遠藤新と帝国ホテル、そしてレーモンド

ライトの日本の弟子としてまず挙げられるのは、ライトが「48番目のサムライ」「マイ・サン」と呼んで信頼した遠藤新である。1916年、帝国ホテル支配人の林愛作からのホテル設計依頼を受けて、翌年1月にライトが来日した時、林は既知の遠藤に声をかけ、ライトに紹介した。遠藤はすぐに帝国ホテルの製図にとりかかり、4月にライトとともに渡米、引き続きタリアセンで図面を準備した[8]。その後、藤倉憲二郎が、1918年2月にはルドルフ・シンドラー[9]が加わった[図1]。1918年10月、ライトが日本に発つと同時に、遠藤と藤倉はシカゴやニューヨークなどを視察し、12月末に帰国する[10]。以後遠藤は、1923年に帝国ホテルが完成するまで、ライトの右腕として帝国ホテルの建設に携わり、さらに自由学園(1921)[cat. no. 3-32]や山邑邸(現・ヨドコウ迎賓館、1918–24)[cat. nos. 2-60, 61]をライトと共同設計した。

ホテルが着工する直前、1919年の8月にライトはアメリカに戻り、12月末にアントニン・レーモンド夫妻を伴って来日した。レーモンドは、1916年5月から12月までタリアセンで帝国ホテルの初期段階の設計に携わっていたが、その後従軍し、スイスのジュネーブで諜報部員として活動した[11]。除隊後の1919年9月、ニューヨークに戻ったレーモンドはライトから帝国ホテルの仕事に誘われ、その年末にライトと共に来日した。

しかしレーモンドにとって帝国ホテルの仕事はマンネリズムにしか思えず、1年余りのうちに帝国ホテルに見切りをつけ、1921年の初めに米国建築合資会社を設立した[12]。ライトはその直後に、独立に向けて動いたレーモンドへの感情をあらわにした手紙を送っている[13]。おそらくレーモンドは日本におけるアメリカの建築家の需要を実感していたのであろう。すぐに多くの仕事を得て、日本の近代建築を語る上で欠かせない存在になった。

レーモンドがいた頃の帝国ホテル建築設計事務所のスタッフは、遠藤新、河野傳[14]、田上義也[15]、山崎、藤倉憲二郎、内山隈三[16]、渡辺己午蔵である[17]。およそ2年後の林愛作による建築関係給与支払い名簿(1922年2月10日付け)の22名のリストには、当時学生だった「ツチウラ」の名はあるが、レーモンドと藤倉はいない[18]。すでにレーモンドは独立しており、まもなく内山もレーモンドの事務所の所員となった。最終的に帝国ホテル建築事務所から、杉山雅則(1904–99)、内山、小茂田半次郎、富永譲吉、藤倉の5名が移籍したという[19]。

よく知られているように帝国ホテルの工事は遅れ、費用は倍増し、ライトは1922年7月に解雇されて離日した。そのあと遠藤は残された南側客室棟の工事だけでなく、ライトとの共同設計の自由学園や山邑

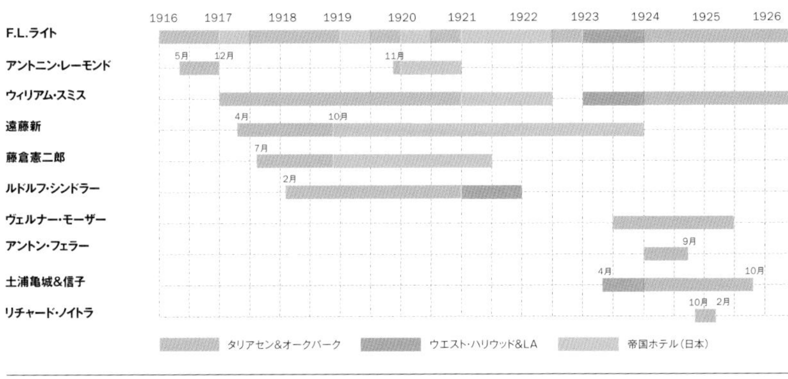

表1　ライト事務所滞在期間と場所(1916–26)　*開始・終了月はわかる範囲で記入した。

Table.1 Time and Place at Wright's Office (1916–26)

邸を完成させた。遠藤は生涯にわたり、ライトの思想に基づいた住宅や建築を数多く設計し、また遠藤の事務所からは、共同で事務所をもった南信、北海道で独自の北方建築を追求した田上義也、富士見高原療養所の設計で知られる柴田太郎、タリアセンに行った岡見健彦などの建築家を輩出した[20]。彼らの初期の住宅作品には「深い軒の出」「水平線の強調」「三面開口の部屋」など、ライトの住宅に似た特徴が見られるが、後にそれぞれの表現になったことが指摘されている[21]。

また1920～30年代にかけて、帝国ホテルに見られる形態、材料、装飾が流行し、住宅や商業施設などに用いられ、「ライト式」「ライト風」などの言葉も生まれた[22]。

図1　タリアセン。スミス、シンドラー、遠藤、藤倉、フロート。1918年(出典：Kathryn Smith, *Schindler House*, 2001、©Hans W.Winkel)

Fig.1　Taliesin. Smith, Schindler, Endo, Fujikura, and Floto. 1918. (©Hans W.Winkel)

図2　ロサンゼルスのスタジオでの信子、亀城、スミス｜土浦亀城アーカイブズ

Fig. 2　In the studio in Los Angeles. Nobuko, Kameki, and Smith, TSUCHIURA Kameki Archives

土浦亀城、ノイトラ、モーザーのモダニズム

東京帝国大学在学中にライトに憧れた土浦亀城は、遠藤を介して帝国ホテルの現場でアルバイトした。卒業後、すでにアメリカに戻っていたライトからの連絡を受けて、1923年4月に妻信子と共に渡米する。ロサンゼルス近郊ウェスト・ハリウッドのライト事務所はシングル張りの2階建てで、天井の高いスタジオが仕事場兼食堂だった[23][図2]。ウィリアム・スミス[24]と土浦夫妻はここに住み、ミラード夫人邸「ミニアトゥーラ」(1923-24)[cat.no.5-20]、ストーラー邸(1923-24)[cat.nos.5-25,26]、サミュエル・フリーマン邸などコンクリートブロックの住宅の現場管理と製図を担当した。

1924年の早春、夫妻はスミスと共に、ウィスコンシン州のタリアセンに移り、さらに1年半余りを過ごした。しかし、帝国ホテルという大プロジェクトがあった遠藤の頃とは違い、当時のライト事務所には、上記の住宅以外に実現した作品はなく、ナショナル生命保険会社ビル、ゴードン・ストロング自動車体験娯楽施設とプラネタリウム、ドヘニー・ランチ宅地開発、レイクタホなどの計画案が繰り返されていた。土浦がアントン・フェラーに宛てた手紙には、「実際の仕事がしたい」「ヨーロッパに行きたい」ことが何度も綴られている[25]。

ヨーロッパではすでに近代建築運動が勃興していた。土浦がタリアセンでヴェルナー・モーザー[26]やリチャード・ノイトラ[27]と数か月過ごしたことは、ライトに師事したと同様に、あるいはそれ以上の意味をもった。

スイスのモーザーは、1923年から25年までタリアセンに滞在、1925年にシカゴの建築事務所で働いた後、1926年にスイスに戻った。その後、シュトゥットガルトのドイツ工作連盟展(1927)やCIAM創設(1928)に関わり、スイスの新しい建築運動の中心的建築家として活躍した。ウィーン出身のリチャード・ノイトラは、1924年10月から翌年1月まで滞在し、その後ロサンゼルスを拠点にアメリカの近代建築をリードした。

ノイトラの妻、ディオーネ(1901-90)は、タリアセンの最初の印象をこう記している。「夕食後に若い日本の建築家の夫婦に紹介されました。妻も建築家で、小柄で痩せていて10歳の少女のようでした。(中略)実際彼らは、丘と森と空とライトだけの孤立した場所にいます。ライトへの尊敬が彼らを結びつけています」[28][図3]。

人里離れた牧歌的なタリアセンには、英国/カナダのスミス、オーストリアのフェラーとノイトラ夫妻、スイスのモーザー夫妻、日本の土浦夫妻が住むグローバルな顔ぶれが集まっていた。土浦にとって何より楽しかったのは、ノイトラやモーザーとのディスカッションだった[29]。彼らはライトを尊敬しつつも、作品の装飾性には懐疑的で、モーザーがル・コルビュジエ(1887-1965)の『建築をめざして』をライトに見せた時、「めったに感心した事のないライトがコルの作品を見ながら"This is something"と言った後で、如何なる内的進展が起こるだらうか、決して固有したことのない彼の設計に如何なる影響が現はれるだらうか、此れは僕等が非常に興味を持て注目してゐた問題であった」と土浦は記している[30]。

おそらくその頃のハイライトは、1924年秋にドイツのエーリヒ・メンデルゾーンがタリアセンを訪問した時であろう[図4]。土浦は後にこう記している。

「夕食後は、ライトの居間に集って、音楽談笑又音楽と夜の更けるまで興じた。メ氏はバッハを聴くと設計がしたくなると言って、蓄音機をかけながら紙を延べて、例の6Bの太い鉛筆を取出して、当時考案中だと言う工場のスケッチを、一筆書きの

ような迅速な勢で、書いては棄て、書いては棄て、忽ちに三十枚許り構図を作って、さあどれが良いだらうと言って吾々の顔を見た。翌日ライトは自動車でマヂソンまでメ氏を送って行った帰りに、6Bの鉛筆を一打程買って来たが、夫つきりライトは使はなかった」[31]。

土浦夫妻は1925年4月タリアセンの火災に臨場し、その後の再建に携わった。10月にタリアセンを辞し、車でシカゴを発ちニューヨークからアメリカ大陸を横断して、翌年1月に帰国した。大倉土木に勤め、期待されたようにライトのスタイルを踏襲した期間を経て、1930年前後から装飾のない工業的、合理的なモダニズム建築を目指すようになった。

彼らの合理的な形態の作品は、ライトの批判の対象になった。しかし、土浦自邸(1935)の流れるような空間構成のように、土浦の根底にはライトの影響が色濃くみられる。ノイトラ、モーザー、そしてレーモンドも「自然と建築の関係」や「人間的なスケール」を重視した。レーモンドがペンシルベニア州ニューホープにつくったレーモンド・ファームは、小さなタリアセンのように農場や家畜小屋があった。さらに、「F・L・ライトは食器棚や物入など最も重い家具は、構造の一部として造りつけるべきだと教え、移動家具は動きを助けるために軽くすべきだと教えた。(中略)私たちは常にその考え方を家具のデザインに活かし続けてきた」[32]と具体的に記している。

時代や地域によって、その度合いは異なるが、ライトの弟子たちはそれぞれ、自然や土地と建築との「あるべき姿」を模索した。それは遠藤新がいう有機的完一性(インテグリティ)と言い換えることもできる。

> まづ地所を見る/地所が建築を教えて呉れる/いかに建築が許されるか/いかに生活が許されるか/そしていかに生活が展びられるか/其をそこの自然から学ぶ。/其所に土も石も草も木もある/そこから建築がのびて来る。/其を逆の方から云う、自然から材料を貰う。/自然に合わせて物をつくる。そしてその作品を/提げて人間諸共、母なるまたは父なる自然に帰る[33]。

自然と建築の調和、箱からの解放、有機的な一体性。さらに遠藤は言う。

> 一番大切なのは、あの人の遺した形ではなしにあの人の考え方にあるのです[34]

戦後ライトに学んだ天野太郎がいうように、「彼ほど自然を愛し、自然を学んだ人も少ないだろう。自然は我々と共にあって自然は我々をはぐくむ。我々は自然に従って生活するように出来ていることを彼は恒に語る」[35]のである。

図3　7-7｜タリアセンの居間 左から:ライト、リチャード・ノイトラ、シルバ・モーザー、土浦亀城、信子、ヴェルナー・モーザー、ディオーネ・ノイトラ
撮影者不詳｜撮影:1924年頃

Fig. 3　7-7｜Livingroom at Taliesin. From left: Wright, Richard Neutra, Silva Moser (wife of Verner Moser), Kameki Tsuchiura, Nobuko Tsuchiura, Verner Moser, Dione Neutra.
Photographer unidentified, Photo: c.1924, TSUCHIURA Kameki Archives

図4　7-8｜E.メンデルゾーンのタリアセン訪問 左上より時計回りに:土浦亀城、土浦信子、シルバ・モーザー、ウィリアム・スミス、エーリヒ・メンデルゾーン、フランク・ロイド・ライト、リチャード・ノイトラ｜土浦亀城、信子夫妻のアルバム「Taliesin Life (1)」撮影:1924年｜土浦亀城アーカイブズ

Fig. 4　7-8｜Visit of Erich Mendelsohn to Taliesin. From top left clockwise: Kameki Tsuchiura, Nobuko Tsuchiura, Silva Moser, William Smith, Erich Mendelsohn, Frank Lloyd Wright, Richard Neutra. Tsuchiura album "Taliesin Life" (1), Photo: 1924, TSUCHIURA Kameki Archives

1 Kathryn Smith, Material and Structure in Frank Lloyd Wright's Imperial Hotel: Failure and Success, *Journal of Organic Architecture and Design*, Vol. 6, No. 3, 2018. p. 9（以下［Smith2018］）

2 遠藤新（1889–1951）福島県に生まれ、1914年東京帝国大学建築学科卒業。代表作に甲子園ホテル、加地邸、一連の自由学園校舎など。

3 藤倉憲二郎（1889–1959）東京に生まれ、学習院初等科・中等科卒。1910年に渡米し、1917年にコーネル大学建築学部を卒業。タリアセンから1918年12月、遠藤と共に帰国。1919年帝国ホテル建築事務所、21年から米国建築合資会社に勤務した。（堀勇良『日本近代建築人名総覧』中央公論新社、以下『総覧』、井上祐一『日本における大正・昭和前期の住宅にみるフランク・ロイド・ライトの影響に関する研究』学位論文、2004年、p.7、以下［井上2004］）

4 土浦亀城（1897–1996）東京帝国大学卒業後、妻の土浦信子（1900–98）と共にタリアセンへ。帰国後大倉土木に勤め、1935年に独立。主な作品に土浦自邸（1935）、野々宮アパート（1936）、強羅ホテル（1938）、国際観光会館（1954）など。信子はタリアセンで建築を学び、1937年ごろまで住宅などを設計した。

5 岡見健彦（1898–1972）東京に生まれ、1925年東京美術学校建築科卒業。遠藤新建築創作所に入所。1929年からタリアセンに滞在。帰国後の1932年に岡見健彦設計事務所設立。代表作に高輪教会（1932）、頌栄高等女学校記念堂（1937）など。

6 天野太郎（1918–90）広島県に生まれ、1945年早稲田大学理工学部建築学科卒業。鹿島建設入社。1952年渡米し、タリアセンで学ぶ。工学院大学を経て1962年から東京藝術大学で教える。代表作に音羽の家、新花屋敷ゴルフクラブ、武蔵嵐山カントリークラブ、東京藝術大学図書館など。

7 A Directory of Frank Lloyd Wright Associates: Apprentices 1929–1959。ちなみに同リストには625名が掲載されている。Hayashi Shinichiro：林七郎（林愛作の子息）の可能性がある。星島光平：星島建築設計事務所。遠藤楽（1927–2003）遠藤新の長男で建築創作所を引き継ぐ。

8 遠藤陶『帝国ホテル ライト館の幻影——孤高の建築家遠藤新の生涯』廣済堂出版、1997年

9 R. M. Schindler（1887–1953）オーストリア出身の建築家。ウィーン工科大学および芸術アカデミー卒業。1914年渡米、シカゴの設計事務所勤務の後、1918年2月タリアセンとオークパークのライト事務所に勤務。1920年ライトのバーンズドール邸「立葵の家」担当のためロサンゼルスに移り、独立後多くの住宅作品を残した。

10 前掲書8、pp.49–54

11 William Whitaker, Chronology of the Raymonds' Lives and Careers, *Crafting a Modern World, The Architecture and Design of Antonin and Noemi Raymond*, Princeton Architecture Press, 2006, p. 267.

12 ヴォーリズ事務所のL.W.スラック（1887–1970）と共同で設立。『自伝アントニン・レーモンド』三沢浩訳、鹿島研究所出版会、1970、pp.69–70（新装版、2007年、鹿島出版会）

13 ライトからレーモンド宛て、2021年2月8日付けの書簡。

14 河野傳（1886–1963）宮崎県出身。京都高等工芸学校図案科第一部卒業。1920–21年、帝国ホテル建築事務所勤務。1923–24年、箱根土地（株）建築部勤務。1927–31年、創作会建築事務所主催。箱根土地嘱託。1930–43年、東京滝野川コーノトン映画録音研究所主宰。

15 田上義也（1899–1991）栃木県出身。1916年早稲田工手学校建築科卒業。1919–22年、帝国ホテル建築事務所勤務。1924年、札幌市にて田上建築事務所主宰。代表作に網走郷土資料館、坂牛邸など。

16 内山隈三（1895–1927）神奈川県出身。中央工学校建築高等科卒業。1920–21年、帝国ホテル建築事務所勤務。1921–27年、米国建築合資会社（レーモンド建築事務所）に勤務し、東京女子大学（1921）、後藤新平邸（1922）、霊南坂の自邸（1923）などを担当した。

17 「Wright Family」のスケッチ『自伝アントニン・レーモンド』。遠藤新夫人のメモ書きのある遠藤楽建築創作所所蔵の「ライト館建設関係者の集まりの写真」には、剣持、藤倉、林、高橋、南、パパ、河野の名がある。前掲書 註3［井上2004］、pp.5–6

18 『帝国ホテル百年史1890—1990』帝国ホテル、1990年、p. 200

19 小室加津彦、速水清孝「草創期のレーモンド事務所の設計スタッフに付いて」『日本建築学会東北支部研究報告集計画系』第76号、2013年6月

20 南信（1892–1951）仙台に生まれ、仙台第二中学校・第二高等学校を経て、1917年に東京帝国大学工科大学建築学科を卒業、19年から日本トラスコン鋼材に勤務。同社から帝国ホテル建築事務所に派遣された。1922年10月遠藤南建築創作所を共同主宰、山邑邸の実施設計に従事。1925年大阪に南建築事務所を開設。1933年渡満、遠藤と共に新京に事務所設立、1943年帰国した。
柴田太郎（1901–84）長野県諏訪郡に生まれ、東京高等工業学校敷設工業教員養成所建築科卒業、帝国ホテル現場でアルバイト。1925年から遠藤新建築創作所勤務。1928年柴田太郎建築事務所設立。正木邸（1930）、富士見高原療養所（1937、1952）などの作品がある。前掲書 註3［井上2004］

21 前掲書 註3［井上2004］、pp.170–174

22 井上祐一、小野吉彦『ライト式建築』柏書房、2017年、p.12

23 1284 Harper Avenue, West Hollywood CA. Robert L.Sweeney, *Wright in Hollywood: Visions of A New Architecture*, MIT Press,1994, p.6.
キャサリン・スミス氏によれば、1980年代に取り壊されたが、同氏撮影の写真が残っている。

24 William Edward Sotherton-Smith（1891–after 1942）英国人。カナダを経て1916年頃にアメリカに渡り1917年から26年までタリアセン、オークパーク、東京およびロサンゼルスのライト事務所に勤めた。Smith、2018 p.10.

25 Anton Martin Feller（1892–1973）ウィーン工業高等学校、ETH Zurichで学ぶ。1915年、水力発電技師として赴任先のロシアで捕虜となりシベリアに送られる。中国経由で逃亡、1919–21年中村與資平事務所、22年米国建築合資会社、23年渡米し、ロサンゼルスの事務所に勤める。1923–24年、タリアセン、その後シカゴやニューヨークで設計に携わる。西澤泰彦『海を渡った日本人建築家——20世紀前半の中国東北地方における建築活動』彰国社、1996年、及びWilliam Blair Scott氏のご教示による。

26 Werner Max Moser（1896–1970）1921年ETH Zurichを卒業、ロッテルダムの設計事務所に勤め、1923年からタリアセン、25年にシカゴの複数の設計事務所で働き、26年にスイスに戻る。1927年のシュトゥットガルトのドイツ工作連盟展で、ミース・ファン・デル・ローエ（1886–1969）のアパート建築の家具造作を担当。1928年にはラサラでのCIAM設立メンバーとなる。主な作品にモーザーチェア（1931）、チューリッヒ会議センター（1938–39）、カラグプルのインド工科大学キャンパス（1952）など。

27 Richard J. Neutra（1892–1970）ウィーン工科大学卒業後、第一次世界大戦に従軍。1923年に渡米し、シカゴの事務所を経てタリアセンに滞在、25年よりロサンゼルスで設計活動を行った。主な作品にロヴェル健康住宅（1929）、カウフマン邸（1946）など。

28 Thomas S. Hines, *Richard Neutra and the Search for Modern Architecture*, Oxford University Press, 1982, p. 53.

29 1924年12月、土浦亀城からルドルフ・シンドラーに宛てた書簡。

30 土浦亀城「ライトを訪れたメンデルゾーン」『国際建築』1929年9月

31 同上

32 前掲書 註12、p.296

33 遠藤新「住宅小品十五種」はしがき『婦人之友』1924年5月、『建築家遠藤新作品集』中央公論美術出版、1991年、p.37

34 前掲書 註8、p.212

35 天野太郎「ライト追悼」『国際建築』1959年5月、吉原正編『有機的建築の発想——天野太郎の建築』建築資料研究社、2001年、pp.67–69

Frank Lloyd Wright and his Japanese Apprentices

Atsuko Tanaka

From his initial visit in 1905 through 1922, Frank Lloyd Wright made seven trips to Japan. This period, which included his five trips as the architect of the Imperial Hotel from 1916–1922, amounted to a total stay of over three years.[1] Throughout these years and extending into the post-war era, many young aspiring Japanese architects who admired Wright, worked and studied under him at the Imperial Hotel Architectural Design Office in Tokyo and at Taliesin in Spring Green, Wisconsin.

Taliesin served both as Wright's residence and workspace. Until 1932, when Wright and his wife, Olgivanna (1898–1985), established the Taliesin Fellowship as an additional educational platform, it primarily functioned as a design studio. Arata Endo[2] stayed at Taliesin from Apr 1917 to Oct 1918, Kenjiro Fujikura[3] from around Jul 1917 to Oct 1918, and the couple Kameki and Nobuko Tsuchiura[4] from Jan 1924 to Oct 1925, all as members of Wright's studio, living and working directly with Wright himself.

In 1928, the Wrights began to conceptualize the idea of the Fellowship, and by 1932, they had assembled its first apprentices. A few years later, construction of Taliesin West (1938) began, leading to the Fellowship alternating between spending summers in Wisconsin and winters at Taliesin West in Arizona. The list of Fellows between 1929 and 1959 includes Takehiko Okami,[5] who stayed during the preparation phase (Aug 1929 to around 1931), and others who stayed post World War II, Taro Amano[6] (1952), Shinichiro Hayashi (1952), Hideo Hayashi (1952), Kohei Hoshijima (1954), and Raku Endo (1957).[7] Although their environment differed from what Arata Endo and the Tsuchiuras had experienced, they too studied directly under Wright, carrying forward Wright's philosophy to the next generation.

Arata Endo, the Imperial Hotel, and Antonin Raymond

Arata Endo is the first to be mentioned as Wright's apprentice from Japan, a figure whom Wright deeply trusted and referred to as the "48th Samurai" and "My Son." Aisaku Hayashi, the General Manager of the Imperial Hotel, had already approached Endo before Wright arrived in Japan, in response to a hotel design request from Hayashi. He introduced Endo to Wright in January 1917. Endo immediately embarked on drafting the Imperial Hotel's designs, and in April, he traveled with Wright to the United States to continue the design work at Taliesin.[8] Kenjiro Fujikura then joined the project, followed by Rudolf Schindler[9] in February 1918. [Fig. 1] In October 1918, as Wright set off for Japan, Endo and Fujikura toured Chicago and New York, returning home at the end of December.[10] From then on, Endo continued to be involved in the construction of the Imperial Hotel as Wright's right-hand man until its completion in 1923. Furthermore, he codesigned other projects with Wright, such as the Jiyu Gakuen Girls' School (1921) [cat. no. 3-32] and the Yamamura House (1918–24) [cat. nos. 2-60, 61].

Just before the hotel construction commenced, Wright returned to the US in August 1919. He came back to Japan at the end of December, accompanied by Antonin Raymond and his wife Noèmi. Raymond had been involved in the preliminary design phase of the Imperial Hotel at Taliesin from May to December 1916 before enlisting in the army and serving as an intelligence officer based in Geneva, Switzerland.[11] Upon his discharge from the army and his return to New York in September 1919, Raymond was invited by Wright to work on the Imperial Hotel project, and they traveled to Japan together by the end of the year.

However, Raymond found the work on the Imperial Hotel to be monotonous and repetitive, and within a year, he decided to leave the project. He established the firm American Architectural and Engineering Company in early 1921.[12] Wright, shortly afterward, sent a letter to Raymond expressing his anger about Raymond's decision to set up his own architectural firm.[13] It is likely that Raymond had perceived a demand for American architects in Japan. He quickly obtained numerous commissions and became an indispensable figure in the field of modern Japanese architecture.

During Raymond's tenure on the Imperial Hotel project, the design office staff included Arata Endo, Tsutou Kono,[14] Yoshiya Tanoue,[15] Yamazaki, Kenjiro Fujikura, Kumazou Uchiyama,[16] and Mikozo Watanabe.[17] Nearly two years later, in the architecture-related payroll created by Aisaku Hayashi (dated February 10, 1922), twenty-two names are listed, one of which is "Tsuchiura," a student at the time. However, the names of Raymond and Fujikura are absent.[18] By this time, Raymond had already embarked on his independent career, and Uchiyama soon joined his firm. Ultimately, five members—Masanori Sugiyama (1904–99), Uchiyama, Hanjiro Komoda, Jyokichi Tominaga, and Fujikura—transferred from the Imperial Hotel architectural design office to Raymond's office.[19]

As is widely known, the construction of the Imperial Hotel was delayed, and costs doubled from the original budget, leading to Wright's dismissal and departure from Japan in July 1922. Following this, Endo not only oversaw the completion of the remaining construction on the southern guest rooms of the hotel but also finalized the collaborative projects with Wright, such as the Jiyu Gakuen Girls' School and the Yamamura House. Throughout his life, Endo designed numerous residences and buildings adhering to Wright's architectural philosophies.

Furthermore, Endo's architectural firm produced several notable architects, including Makoto Minami, with whom he shared a partnership, Yoshiya Tanoue, who explored his unique northern-style architecture in Hokkaido, Taro Shibata, recognized for his design of the Fujimi Kogen Sanatorium, and Takehiko Okami, who had spent time at Taliesin.[20] In their earlier residential works, characteristics similar to Wright's homes, such as "deep eaves," "emphasis on horizontal lines," and "rooms with openings on three sides" can be observed. However, it has been noted that they later evolved to create their own unique expressions in their designs.[21]

During the 1920s and 1930s, the form, materials, and decorations seen in the Imperial Hotel became fashionable and applied in residential and commercial buildings, leading to the creation of terms like "Wright-style (Wright-shiki)" or "Wrightian (Wright-fu)."[22]

The Modernism of Kameki Tsuchiura, Neutra, and Moser

Kameki Tsuchiura, who admired Wright during his time at Tokyo Imperial University, started working part-time at the Imperial Hotel site through Endo's introduction. After graduation, upon receiving a message from Wright, who had already returned to the US, he traveled to America with his wife Nobu in April 1923. Wright's West Hollywood studio was a two-storey residence covered by schingles, with a high-ceiling studio serving as a combined workspace and a dining area.[23] [Fig. 2] William E. Smith[24] and the Tsuchiuras resided here and managed the site and drafting for concrete block houses such as the Mrs. Millard House, La Miniatura (1923–24) [cat. no. 5-20], Storer House (1923–24) [cat. no. 5-25, 26], and Samuel Freeman House.

In the early spring of 1924, the Tsuchiuras and Smith relocated to Taliesin in Wisconsin, where they spent another year and a half. Unlike during Endo's time, when there were significant ongoing projects like the Imperial Hotel, the only realized works at Wright's studio at that time were the previously mentioned residential projects. Wright proposed plans for projects such as the National Life Insurance Company Building, the Gordon Strong Automobile Objective, Doheny Ranch Development, and the Lake Tahoe Project were repeatedly proposed. In his letters to Anton Feller, Tsuchiura often expressed his desire "to do real work" and "to go to Europe."[25]

In Europe, the modern architectural movement was already under way. The months Tsuchiura spent at Taliesin with Werner Moser[26] (1896–1970) and Richard Neutra (1892–1970)[27] held significance equal to or perhaps even greater than his mentorship under Wright.

Swiss architect Moser resided at Taliesin from 1923 to 1925. After working at an architectural firm in Chicago in 1925, he returned to Switzerland in 1926. He was then involved in the Werkbund Exhibition in Stuttgart (1927) and the founding of the International Congresses of Modern Architecture (CIAM) (1928), making significant contributions as a leading architect of the new architectural movement in Switzerland. Richard Neutra, a native of Vienna, stayed at Taliesin from October 1924 to January of the following year, after which he based himself in Los Angeles and lead modern architecture in the US.

Neutra's wife, Dione (1901–90), described her first impressions of Taliesin as follows:

> *After dinner, we were introduced to the young Japanese architect and his wife, who is also an architect and is as small and thin as a ten-year-old girl ... In reality, they are alone in this world because there are no neighbors, only meadows, forest, sky, and Wright. They have bonded through their respect for Wright.*[28] [Fig. 3]

The pastoral retreat of Taliesin was home to an international assembly, including the British-Canadian Smith, Austrians Feller and the Neutras, the Swiss Mosers, and the Japanese Tsuchiuras. What Tsuchiura enjoyed most were the discussions he had with Neutra and Moser.[29] While they had high regard for Wright, they held scepticism toward the ornamentation in his works. Tsuchiura noted the moment when Moser showed Le Corbusier's *Towards a New Architecture* to Wright as follows:

> *Wright, who rarely admires anything, commented 'This is something' while looking at Corbusier's work. We were greatly intrigued and attentive to what internal progress this might trigger and what influence might manifest on his intrinsic designs.*[30]

Perhaps a notable highlight from that time was in the autumn of 1924, when German architect Erich Mendelsohn visited Taliesin. [Fig. 4] Tsuchiura later chronicled the experience as follows:

> *After dinner, we would all gather in Wright's living room and engage in discussions about music, or listen to music until late at night. Mendelsohn would claim that listening to Bach inspired him to design, so he would set up his phonograph and, as the music played, he would spread out his papers, pull out his reliable thick 6B pencil, and start sketching rapidly. He was designing a factory at the time, and he would sketch quickly, discard, sketch again, discard again, until he made about thirty sketches. Then he would look at us and ask, 'Which one*

do you think is the best?' The next day, Wright bought about a dozen 6B pencils on his way back from driving Mendelsohn to Madison, but he never used them himself.[31]

The Tsuchiuras were present during the fire at Taliesin in April 1925, and took part in the subsequent reconstruction. They left Taliesin in October and drove from Chicago to New York before crossing the continental US and returning to Japan in January of the following year. Tsuchiura then started working at Okura Doboku, initially adhering to Wright's style as expected, but he began to shift towards a decoration-free, industrial, and rational modernist architecture around 1930.

Their rationalistic works became a target of criticism from Wright. However, Wright's deep influence can still be seen in Tsuchiura's work, such as the flowing spatial composition of the Tsuchiura House (1935). Neutra, Moser, and Raymond also emphasized the "relationship between nature and architecture" and the "human scale." Raymond Farm, built by Raymond in New Hope, Pennsylvania, was akin to a smaller version of Taliesin, complete with a farm and livestock pens. Raymond explicitly wrote,

F.L. Wright taught us that the heaviest pieces of furniture, such as cupboards and wardrobes, should be built as a part of the structure, and movable furniture should be light for easier movement. ...We have continually applied this concept to our furniture designs.[32]

While it varied by era and region, each of Wright's disciples pursued the "ideal form" of the interplay between nature, land, and architecture. This can also be termed as the "organic integrity" as Arata Endo would say.

First, observe the site. The site teaches you its architecture, how architecture is permitted, how life is permitted, and how life can develop. This is what we learn from nature. There is earth, stone, grass, and wood, from which architecture grows. To put it the other way, we receive materials from nature. We create in harmony with nature. And with that creation, we, along with humanity, return to Mother or Father Nature.[33]

The harmony between nature and architecture, liberation from the box, and organic wholeness. Endo goes on to say,

What is most important is not the forms that he left behind, but his way of thinking.[34]

As Taro Amano, who studied under Wright after the war, noted, "Few people have loved and learned from nature as much as Wright did. Nature exists alongside us and nurtures us. He consistently spoke of how we are made to live in accordance with nature."[35]

1 Kathryn Smith, "Material and Structure in Frank Lloyd Wright's Imperial Hotel: Failure and Success" in *Journal of Organic Architecture and Design*, Vol. 6 (No. 3, 2018): 9 (hereinafter referred to as "Smith 2018").

2 Arata Endo (1889-1951) was born in Fukushima. He studied at Soma Junior High School, Sendai Daini High School of Technology, and graduated from the Architecture Department of Tokyo Imperial University in 1914. His representative works include the Koshien Hotel, Kachi Villa, and a series of Jiyu Gakuen buildings.

3 Kenjiro Fujikura (1889–1959) was born in Tokyo. He graduated from Gakushuin Primary School and Boys' Junior High School. In 1910, he went to the United States and graduated from the Architecture Department of Cornell University in 1917. He returned home with Endo from Taliesin in December 1918. He worked in the Imperial Hotel Architectural Design Office in 1919, and then for the American Architectural and Engineering Company from 1921 (Takeyoshi Hori, *Comprehensive List of Modern Japanese Architects* (referred to as *Comprehensive List* hereafter), Yuichi Inoue, *Research on the influences of Frank Lloyd Wright on residential houses in Japan during the Taisho and early Showa periods*, doctoral dissertation, 2004, p.7. (hereinafter referred to as "Inoue 2004").

4 Kameki Tsuchiura (1897–1996) graduated from Tokyo Imperial University, then traveled to Taliesin with his wife Nobuko Tsuchiura (1900–1998). After returning to Japan, he worked at Okura Doboku, establishing his own practice in 1935. His notable works include Tsuchiura Residence (1935), Nonomiya Apartments (1936), Hotel Gora (1938), and International Tourism Hall (1954). Nobuko studied architecture at Taliesin, designing residential homes until around 1937.

5 Takehiko Okami (1898–1972) was born in Tokyo and graduated from the Architecture Department of Tokyo Fine Arts School in 1925. He joined Endo Arata's Architectural Studio. He stayed in Taliesin from 1929. After returning to Japan in 1932, he established the Okami Takehiko Architectural Design Office. His representative works include the Takanawa Church (1932), Shoei Girls' Senior High School Memorial Hall (1937).

6 Taro Amano (1918-1990) was born in Hiroshima. He graduated from the Architecture Department of Waseda University's Creative Science and Engineering in 1945. He joined Kajima Corporation. In 1952, he went to the United States to study at Taliesin. He taught at Kogakuin University and then from 1962 at Tokyo National University of Fine Arts and Music. His representative works include the House of Otowa, Shin-Hanayashiki Golf Club, Musashi Ranzan Country Club, and the Tokyo National University of Fine Arts and Music Library.

7 "A Directory of Frank Lloyd Wright Associates: Apprentices 1929-1959." The list includes 625 names. Hayashi Shinichiro: son of Aisaku Hayashi.

Kohei Hoshijima: Hoshijima architect and associates. Raku Endo (1927–2003): Eldest son of Arata Endo and succeeded the Architectural Office.

8 Tou Endo, "*Imperial Hotel: The Phantom of the Wright Building - The Life of the Isolated Architect Arata Endo*" (Tokyo: Kosaido Publishing, 1997) (hereinafter referred to as "Endo 1997").

9 R. M. Schindler (1887–1953) was an architect from Austrian. He graduated from Vienna University of Technology and the Academy of Fine Arts Vienna. In 1914, he migrated to the United States, working in an architectural firm in Chicago before joining Wright's offices in Taliesin and Oak Park in February 1918. He moved to Los Angeles in 1920 to take charge of Wright's Barnsdall House, and after establishing his own practice, he left behind a multitude of residential works.

10 Endo 1997, pp. 49–54.

11 William Whitaker, "Chronology of the Raymonds' Lives and Careers," *Crafting a Modern World, The Architecture and Design of Antonin and Noemi Raymond* (New York: Princeton Architecture Press, 2006), p. 267.

12 Founded with L.W.Slack (1887–1970) from W.M.Vories & Company Architects. "*Antonin Raymond An Autobiography*", translated by Hiroshi Misawa (Tokyo: Kajima Publishing, 1970), pp. 69–70.

13 Letter from Wright to Raymond dated February 8, 2021.

14 Tsutau Kawano (1886–1963) was born in Miyazaki. He graduated from the first part of the Design Department at Kyoto High School of Arts and Crafts. He worked at the Imperial Hotel Architectural Design Office from 1920–21. He was employed in the Architectural Department of Hakone Tochi Co. from 1923-24. He hosted the Sosakukai Architectural Office from 1927–31, while being commissioned by Hakone Tochi. He was the head of the Tokyo Takinogawa Kohnoton Film Recording Laboratory from 1930–43.

15 Yoshiya Tanoue (1899-1991) was born in Tochigi. He graduated from the Architecture Department of Waseda Technical High School in 1916. He worked at the Imperial Hotel Architectural Design Office from 1919–22. He established Tanoue Architectural Office in Sapporo City in 1924. His representative works include the Abashiri Museum and the Sakaushi Residence.

16 Kumazo Uchiyama (1895–1927) was born in Kanagawa. He graduated from the Advanced Architecture Course at Chuo Kogakko School. He worked at the Imperial Hotel Architectural Design Office from 1920–21. He worked at the American Architectural and Engineering Company (Raymond Architectural Design Office) from 1921–27 and was in charge of projects such as the Tokyo Women's Christian University (1921), Shimpei Goto Residence (1922), and Raymond Residence (1923).

17 "Wright Family" sketch in *Antonin Raymond An Autobiography*. Notes by Arata Endo's wife on the photo of the gathering of those involved in the construction of the Wright building, owned by Raku Endo Architectural Design Studio, includes names like Kenmochi, Fujikura, Hayashi, Takahashi, Minami, Papa, and Kohno. [Inoue 2004] pp. 5–6.

18 *The 100-Year History of the Imperial Hotel 1890–1990* (The Imperial Hotel, 1990), p. 200.

19 Katsuhiko Komuro and Kiyotaka Hayami, "On the Design Staffs of Antonin Raymond's Office in the Beginning," Architectural Research Reports of the Japan Architectural Society Tohoku Branch, Planning System No.76 (June 2013).

20 Makoto Minami (1892–1951) was born in Sendai and attended Sendai Second Junior High School and Second High School. Graduated from the Architecture Department of Tokyo Imperial University in 1917. Worked at Nihon Truscon Steel Co. from 1919. He was dispatched to the Imperial Hotel Architectural Design Office from the company. Co-founder of the Endo Minami Architectural Creative Office in 1922, working on the detailed design phase for the Yamamura Residence. Opened Minami Architecture Office in Osaka in 1925. He moved to Manchuria in 1933, along with Endo, opened an office in Beijing. Returned to Japan in 1943.
Taro Shibata (1901–1984) was born in Suwa region, Nagano. Graduated from the Architecture Department of Tokyo Higher Technical School for Teachers of Construction. He worked part-time at the Imperial Hotel site. Employed at Endo Arata Architectural Studio from 1925. Established Taro Shibata Architectural Office in 1928. His works include Masaki Residence (1930) and Fujimi Kogen Sanatorium (1937, 1952). [Inoue 2004]

21 Inoue 2004, pp. 170–174.

22 Yuichi Inoue, *Wright-style Architecture* (Tokyo: Kashiwa Shobo, 2017), p. 12.

23 Address is 1284 Harper Avenue, West Hollywood, CA. Robert L. Sweeney, *Wright in Hollywood: Visions of A New Architecture* (MIT Press,1994), p. 6. As reported by Kathryn Smith, the building was demolished in the 1980s but her photographed documentation of it remains.

24 William Edward Sotherton-Smith (1891–after 1942), a British national. Traveled to the United States via Canada around 1916 and served in Wright's studio in Taliesin, Oak Park, Tokyo, and Los Angeles from 1917–26. Referenced in Smith 2018, p. 10.

25 Anton Martin Feller (1892–1973). He studied at Vienna Technical High School and ETH Zurich. Captured and sent to Siberia while working as a hydroelectric engineer in Russia in 1915. Escaped via China. Worked at Yoshihei Nakamura Design Office (1919–21), the American Architectural and Engineering Company (1922), before moving to the US to work at Wright's Los Angeles studio in 1923. Spent time at Taliesin from 1923–24, later designing in Chicago and New York. Information derived from Yasuhiko Nishizawa's *Japanese Architects who crossed the sea* (Tokyo: Shokokusha, 1966), and from William Blair Scott.

26 Werner Max Moser (1896–1970). He graduated from ETH Zurich in 1921, served at an architectural firm in Rotterdam, and later at Taliesin from 1923. Worked at various design firms in Chicago in 1925 before returning to Switzerland in 1926. In 1927, he handled the furniture design for Mies van der Rohe's residential buildings at the Werkbund Exhibition in Stuttgart. He became a founding member of CIAM in La Sarraz in 1928. Notable works include Moser 1-256 chair (1931), the Conference Center in Zurich (1938–39), and the campus of the Indian Institute of Technology Kharagpur (1952).

27 Richard J. Neutra (1892–1970). He served in World War I after graduating from the Vienna University of Technology. Migrated to the US in 1923, working in a Chicago-based design firm before joining Taliesin. Operated in Los Angeles from 1925, executing design projects. Main works include Lovell Residence (1929) and Kaufmann Residence (1946).

28 Thomas S. Hines, *Richard Neutra and the Search for Modern Architecture*, Oxford University Press, 1982,p.53.

29 Letter from Kameki Tsuchiura to Rudolf Schindler, dated December 1924.

30 Kameki Tsuchiura, "Mendelsohn visiting Wright," *International Architecture* (September 1929).

31 Kameki Tsuchiura, "Mendelsohn visiting Wright," *International Architecture* (July 1930).

32 *Antonin Raymond An Autobiography*, p. 296.

33 Arata Endo, "15 Works of Houses," Foreword in *Fujin no Tomo* (May 1924) in A Collection of Arata Endo (Tokyo: Chuo Kouron Bijutsu Shuppan,1991), p. 37.

34 Endo 1997, p. 212.

35 Taro Amano, "A Tribute to Wright," *International Architecture* (May 1959) in *The Philosophy of Organic Architecture – Architecture of Taro Amano*, ed. Tadashi Yoshiwara (Tokyo: Kenchiku Shiryo Kenkyusha, 2001), pp. 67–69.

SECTION 5

ミクロ／マクロのダイナミックな振幅

Micro/Macro Dynamics of Wright's Building Blocks

5

ライトは生涯を通じて、「全体が部分のためにあること」と「部分が全体のためにあること――そこでは素材の本性、目的の本性、行為の全体の本性が必要性として明らかになる」ことを有機的に結びつける手段として、建築ブロックを取り入れた[1]。彼は『自伝』の中で、立方体、球、三角の基本的な形がそろったフレーベルの積み木「恩物」[cat. no. 5-1]が、幼少期、彼の指の感覚と「形態が感情になる」ということを常に結びつけたと述べている[2]。フレーベルの積み木は、生涯にわたって繰り返し検討される全体と部分の統合的でダイナミックな関係を維持するような空間体系を、新進の建築家にもたらしたのである。この包括的な手法の探求の一環として、ライトはアメリカ式システム工法住宅[cat. nos. 5-2~4]から、ウィスコンシン州マディソンのジェイコブズ第一邸(1936-37)をはじめとするユーソニアン住宅の設計[cat. nos. 5-34~37]に至るまで、あらゆるプレファブ工法に注目した。帝国ホテルでは、地元の素材である大谷石やテキスタイル・ブロックである中空レンガ[cat. no. 4-63]を使い、スケール感や構成要素と全体との関係を探る実験が行われた。当時、大谷石は歩道の舗装や建物外壁などに日常的に使われていたが、これはひとつの素材がさまざまな規模で有効となることを物語っていた。そしてライトは帝国ホテルではこの素材を率先して用い、その量は10,200m^3にものぼった。また、初期の建築手法となるテラコッタによるテキスタイル・ブロックである装飾ブロックを、その四角いフレームがホテル全体の平面を想起させるようにデザインした[3]。

普遍的な建築構法に対するライトの探求は、大火のあった環太平洋域の対岸から、ロサンゼルスとアリゾナにおける1920年代のコンクリート・ブロックのプロジェクトにおいて再浮上した。これらのプロジェクトは建築とインフラの両方を含んでいた。ライトのブロック・システムは、個別のブロックから橋、ダム、灌漑、道路、敷地造成などを含む地域計画全体にまで拡張可能なため、これらの計画案は建築とインフラストラクチャーの両方を兼ね備えていた。例えば、ドヘニー・ランチ宅地開発計画案(1923)[cat. nos. 5-27~30]は、リゾート施設、住宅、囲われた庭、緑化された屋上テラスが、橋と道路の定着システムによって一体となり――全て同じコンクリート・ブロックでつくられ――ロサンゼルス盆地の尾根と渓谷の地形に対応した、巨大人工構造物である[4]。

アリゾナ州チャンドラーに計画された高級ホテル、サン・マルコス砂漠リゾート・ホテル計画案(1928-29)[cat. nos. 5-32, 33]の設計は、ライトの最も野心的なブロック・システムといってよいだろう。敷地は数千エーカーの「純然たる山岳砂漠」で、利便性、居住性、快適性を確保する必要があった。ライトは壁だけでなく、内外装の仕上げ、構造床、天井に至るまで、ホテルをほぼ全面的に装飾のあるコンクリート・ブロックで建てる意向だった。暴風雨の際に水が流れる涸れ川アロヨを跨ぐコンクリート・ブロックの構造物にテラスや中庭、小さいプール、噴水などを組み入れた設計であった。つまりこの建物は、モンスーンの豪雨を

1 「フランク・ロイド・ライトとの対話」(ヒュー・ダウンズ インタビュー映像 1958年)、[cat. no. 5-48]も参照のこと。

2 Frank Lloyd Wright, "In the Cause of Architecture: In the Wake of the Quake-Concerning the Imperial Hotel, Tokyo," *The Western Architect*, February 1924, 17.

3 前掲書 註2

4 チャールズ・E.アグアー、バーデアナ・アグアー著、大木順子訳『フランク・ロイド・ライトのランドスケープデザイン』(丸善株式会社、2004年) p. 185.

せき止めてプールをつくり、ホテル内の水利施設に水を供給する、まさにダムの役割を兼ねていたのである[5]。

ライトはコンクリート・ブロックに敷地内の石を骨材として使うことが多く、ゆえに敷地計画やブロックパターンだけでなく、分子レベルでの自然との結びつきがある。カリフォルニア州パサデナにあるミラード夫人邸「ミニアトゥーラ」(1923–24)[cat. nos. 5-20~22]では、ライトは敷地内の砂、小石、土を使い、敷地内の2本のユーカリの成木から差し込む木漏れ日をイメージしたコンクリートブロックを成型している[6]。ライトは渓谷に邸宅を配することによってそこに巨大な水鏡を取り込んだ。敷地、植生、湿度、風向き、自然循環など、さまざまな要素を組み合わせ、南カリフォルニアの自然条件に最適な微気候を生み出した。ライトのアーカイヴには、ライトのロサンゼルスのスタジオで働き、タリアセンにも行った土浦亀城・信子の2人がアメリカ南西部の国立公園やランドスケープを旅した様子を捉えた写真[cat. no. 5-23]も多数あり、これによってコンクリート・ブロック建築とそのランドスケープを包括的かつグローバルに読み解くことができる。

メリーランド州シュガーローフ・マウンテンにあるゴードン・ストロング自動車体験娯楽施設とプラネタリウム計画案(1924–25)[cat. nos. 5-42, 43]の設計で初めて実証されたように、ライトのコンクリートへの関心は、その一体的な特質を受容するように展開していった。ライトのテキスタイルブロックの計画案の多くが、ランドスケープから成長しているように見えるとすれば、この自動車体験娯楽施設は、新しい現代的な風景の見方を提案するものだった。山頂を覆うように設けられた堂々たるコンクリートのスロープは、車に座ったまま宇宙へ昇っていくような体験ができる構造になっている。風景が途切れることなく車の周囲を回るため、フロントガラスは映画のスクリーンのような役割を果たした[7]。建物の中心にはプラネタリウムが併設され、頂上から周囲の景色を眺めることもできる。このように自動車体験娯楽施設は地上の自然も、その先の宇宙をも見渡すことができた。

1940年代から1950年代にかけて、ライトは簡易な組み立て式の建築技術を駆使して実現した、手頃な価格のユーソニアン・オートマチック住宅(1947)[cat. nos. 5-38~41]にみられるコンクリート・ブロック構造の一方で、ニューヨークにある最高傑作、グッゲンハイム美術館(1943–59)[cat. nos. 5-44~47]のような大規模プロジェクトにおける巨大で曲線的なコンクリートの形状を同時に実験していた。これらの計画案は、現代のコンクリートの柔軟性と拡張性、そして普遍的な素材と建築システムとしての可能性を示している。

5　前掲書 註4 p. 208.
6　前掲書 註4 p. 191.
7　Juliet Kinchin, "Driving Into the Future," in *Unbuilt Frank Lloyd Wright: Broadacre City, Everywhere or Nowhere*, *Frank Lloyd Wright Quarterly*, v. 32, n. 4 (Fall 2021), p. 36.

Throughout his life, Wright embraced building blocks as a means to organically connect "the whole to the part" and "part to the whole...where the nature of the materials, the nature of the purpose, the nature of the entire performance becomes a necessity.[1] He acknowledged in his *Autobiography* that his childhood "gifts" of Froebel wooden blocks [cat. no. 5-1] in the basic forms of the cube, sphere and triangular shapes never left the touch of his fingers with "form becoming *feeling*."[2] The Froebel blocks introduced the burgeoning architect to spatial systems that maintained an integral, dynamic relationship between the whole and its parts, which resurfaced throughout Wright's career. As part of this search for overarching methods, Wright looked to methods of prefabrication from his American System-Built Houses for the Richards company project (1915–17) [cat. nos. 5-2~4] to Usonian house designs [cat. nos. 5-34~37] including the Jacobs House in Madison, Wisconsin (1936–37). At the Imperial Hotel, Wright had experimented with local materials, the Oya stone, as well as with terracotta textile blocks, both of which allowed him to explore ideas about scale and parts to whole. At the time, Oya stone was commonly used for everyday needs, such as sidewalk paving and common building faces, which provided examples of how one material could operate at various scales. Wright advocated the prominent use of some 360,000 cubic feet (10,200 cubic meters) of this material for the Imperial Hotel, and he designed the building's terra cotta textile blocks, an early building system, such that their square frame composition evoked the overall plan of the hotel itself.[3]

Wright's search for universal building systems resurfaced on the other side of the Pacific Rim of Fire in his 1920s concrete block projects in Los Angeles and Arizona. These projects were both building and infrastructure, as Wright's block system was capable of scaling from an individual block to an entire community and encompass bridges, dams, irrigation, roadways, terracing, and more. Wright's unbuilt design for Doheny Ranch Development (1923) [cat. nos. 5-27~30], for example, is a megastructure that incorporates resort facilities, houses, walled gardens, and landscaped roof terraces linked together by a stabilizing system of bridges and roadways—all made from the same concrete block—capable of negotiating the ridge-ravine topography of the Los Angeles Basin.[4]

The design of San Marcos-in-the-Desert Hotel (unbuilt project, 1928–29) [cat. nos. 5-32,33], a luxury hotel planned for Chandler, Arizona, is arguably Wright's most ambitious block system. The site consisted of several thousand acres of "pure mountain desert" that had to be made accessible, habitable, and comfortable. Wright intended to build the hotel almost entirely of patterned concrete blocks, not only walls but also interior and exterior finishes, structural floors, and ceilings. The design integrated terraces, courts, plunge pools, and fountains into a concrete-block structure straddling

1 Hugh Downs 1958 interview with Frank Lloyd Wright, *The Master Architect: Conversations with Frank Lloyd Wright*, edited by Patrick J Meehan, Wiley-Interscience.

2 Frank Lloyd Wright, "In the Cause of Architecture: In the Wake of the Quake-Concerning the Imperial Hotel, Tokyo," *The Western Architect*, February 1924, 17.

3 Ibid., pp. 216–217.

4 Charles E. Aguar and Berdana Aguar, *Wrightscapes: Frank Lloyd Wright's Landscape Designs* (New York: McGraw-Hill, 2002), p. 185

an *arroyo*, a channel carved out by water during violent storms. Thus, the building doubled as a veritable dam, holding back the torrential rains of the monsoon season to create swimming pools that also fed the water features inside the hotel.[5]

Wright often used aggregate from the site to make his concrete blocks, and so the connection to nature is at the molecular level as well as in site planning and block patterns. This was the case at the Millard House (*La Miniatura*) (1923–24) [cat. nos. 5-20~22] in Pasadena, California, where Wright used onsite sand, pebbles, and soil to cast concrete blocks whose patterning evoked the dappling sunlight streaming through two mature eucalyptus trees on the property. Wright located the house in a ravine and incorporated a large reflecting pool. The result of this particular combination of site, vegetation, moisture content, wind direction, and natural circulation was a microclimate perfectly suited to the climate of southern California.[6] Photographs in Wright's archive support a global reading of his concrete-block architecture and their landscapes, with numerous snapshots [cat. no. 5-23] depicting apprentices Kameki and Nobuko Tsuchiura traveling through the national parks and landscapes of the American Southwest while working for Wright on textile-block house in Los Angeles and also visiting Taliesin in Wisconsin.

Wright's interest in concrete evolved to embrace its plastic qualities, as first demonstrated in his design for the Gordon Strong Automobile Objective and Planetarium (unbuilt project, 1924–25) [cat. nos. 5-42, 43] at Sugarloaf Mountain in Maryland. If most of Wright's textile-block projects appear to grow from their landscapes, the automobile objective afforded new, modern ways of viewing the landscape. An imposing concrete ramp straddling the summit, the structure provided drivers the experience of ascending into space while comfortably seated in their cars. With the landscape continuously revolving around them, the car's windshield functioned as a cinematic screen.[7] From the top, one could take in views of the surrounding countryside, while embedded in the heart of the building was a planetarium. The automobile objective thus provided views of both terrestrial nature and the cosmos beyond.

By the 1940s and 50s, Wright was simultaneously experimenting with concrete-block construction techniques—such as in the Usonian Automatic Houses [cat. nos. 5-38~41] that used simple, do-it-yourself building techniques to provide affordable housing—and with monumental, curved concrete forms, such as his masterpiece in New York, the Solomon R. Guggenheim Museum (1943–59) [cat. nos. 5-44~47]. Taken together, these projects demonstrate the flexibility and scalar qualities of modern concrete and its potential as a universal material and building system.

[Ken Tadashi Oshima and Jennifer Gray]

5 Ibid., p. 210.
6 Ibid., p. 192.

7 Juliet Kinchin, "Driving Into the Future," in *Unbuilt Frank Lloyd Wright: Broadacre City, Everywhere or Nowhere, Frank Lloyd Wright Quarterly*, v. 32, n. 4 (Fall 2021): p. 36.

28 フレーベル恩物:ユニット・システムの原点

Fröbel Gifts: The origin of the unit system

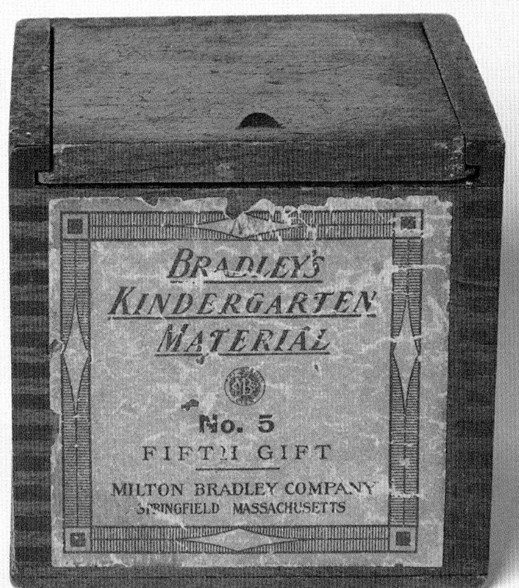

5-1

5-1 フレーベル恩物 第5恩物 | 考案:フリードリヒ・フレーベル、製作:ミルトン・ブラッドレー | 製作年不詳
5-2 アメリカ式システム工法住宅、リチャーズ社との共作。1915-17年 C3モデル平面図 | フランク・ロイド・ライト
5-3 アメリカ式システム工法住宅、リチャーズ社との共作。1915-17年 C3モデル外観透視図 | フランク・ロイド・ライト
5-4 アメリカ式システム工法住宅、リチャーズ社との共作。1915-17年 C3モデル内観透視図 | フランク・ロイド・ライト

5-1 Milton Bradley's Kindergarten Materials: Gift No. 3, No. 4 and No. 5. Friedrich Fröbel, designer.
Milton Bradley Company, manufacturer. undated. Aomori Museum of Art
5-2 American System-Built Houses for The Richards Company, Project, 1915-17. Plan oblique of model C3. Frank Lloyd Wright.
The Museum of Modern Art, New York. Gift of David Rockefeller, Jr. Fund, Ira Howard Levy Fund, and Jeffrey P. Klein Purchase Fund, 1993
DIGITAL IMAGE©2023, The Museum of Modern Art/Scala, Florence
5-3 American System-Built Houses for The Richards Company, Project, 1915-17. Exterior perspective of model C3. Frank Lloyd Wright.
The Museum of Modern Art, New York. Gift of David Rockefeller, Jr. Fund, Ira Howard Levy Fund, and Jeffrey P. Klein Purchase Fund, 1993
DIGITAL IMAGE©2023, The Museum of Modern Art/Scala, Florence
5-4 American System-Built Houses for The Richards Company, Project, 1915-17. Interior perspective of model C3. Frank Lloyd Wright.
The Museum of Modern Art, New York. Gift of David Rockefeller, Jr. Fund, Ira Howard Levy Fund, and Jeffrey P. Klein Purchase Fund, 1993
DIGITAL IMAGE©2023, The Museum of Modern Art/Scala, Florence

29 リチャーズ社の通販式プレファブ住宅

American System-Built Houses for the Richards Company

● **アメリカ式システム工法住宅** | American System-Built Houses | 1915-17年、住宅 | 1915-17, residential

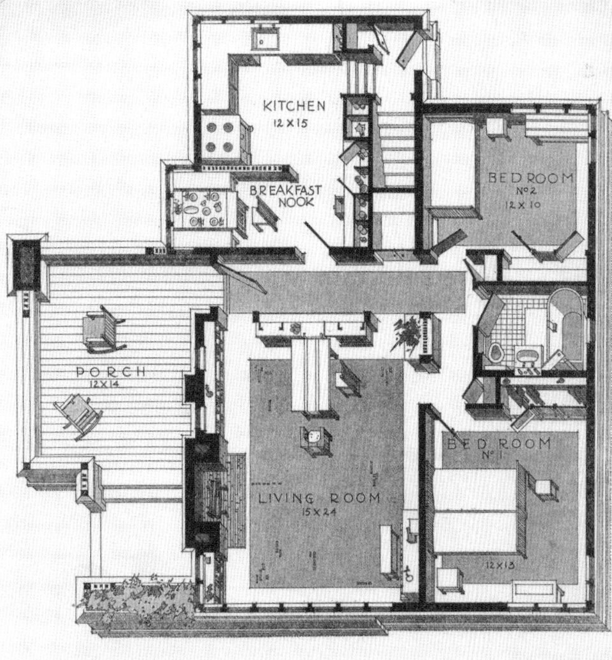

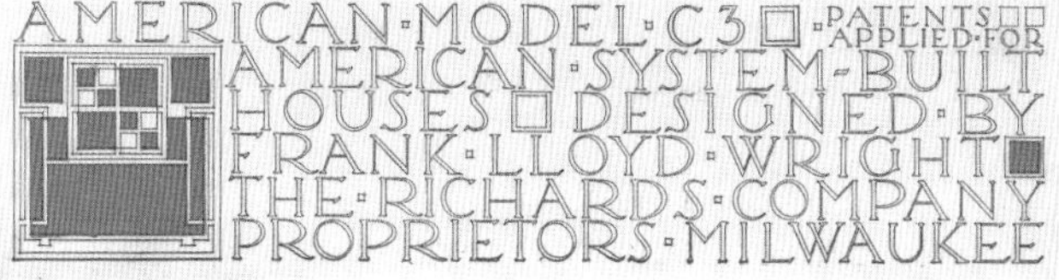

5-2

5-3
5-4

30 関東大震災に耐えた構造

Structure that survived the Great Kanto Earthquake

5-6
5-7

5-6 帝国ホテル二代目本館 すだれレンガ | デザイン:フランク・ロイド・ライト | 1919-23年頃
5-7 帝国ホテル二代目本館 大谷石のブロック | フランク・ロイド・ライト | 1919-23年頃
5-9 絵葉書 米国水兵の食料運搬 帝国ホテルにて 大正十二年九月一日大震災 | 1923年
5-10 絵葉書 帝劇付近 大正十二年九月一日大震災 | 1923年
5-11 絵葉書 大東京大惨害実況 宮城前の避難者 | 1923年
5-12 絵葉書 大正12.9.1 東京大震災実況 日比谷音楽堂倒壊実況 | 1923年
5-15 絵葉書 丸の内内外ビルヂング建築中の震災 | 1923年
5-16 絵葉書 大正12.9.1 東京大震災実況 惨憺たる丸の内内外ビルヂングの全壊 | 1923年
5-17 絵葉書 大正12.9.1 東京大震災実況 丸の内の亀裂 | 1923年
5-18 絵葉書 大正12.9.1 東京駅前震災猛火襲来避難実況 | 1923年

5-6 Scratch tileblock from the Imperial Hotel. Frank Lloyd Wright, designer. c. 1919-23. Imperial Hotel
5-7 Architectural block of Oya stone from the Imperial Hotel. Frank Lloyd Wright, designer. c. 1919-23. Museum Meiji-Mura
5-9 U.S. Navy carrying Supplies into the Imperial Hotel, Great Kanto Earthquake, 1 September 1923. Hideki Watanabe Collection
5-10 Vicinity of the Imperial Theater, Great Kanto Earthquake, 1 September 1923. Hideki Watanabe Collection
5-11 Refugees at the Imperial Palace Plaza, Great Kanto Earthquake, 1 September 1923. Hideki Watanabe Collection
5-12 The Destruction of the Music Hall at the Hibiya Park, Great Kanto Earthquake, 1 September 1923. Hideki Watanabe Collection
5-15 The Destruction at the construction site of the Marunouchi Naigai Building, Great Kanto Earthquake, 1 September 1923. Hideki Watanabe Collection
5-16 The Destruction of the Marunouchi Naigai Building, Great Kanto Earthquake, 1 September 1923. Hideki Watanabe Collection
5-17 Roads Cracked at Marunouchi, Great Kanto Earthquake, 1 September 1923. Hideki Watanabe Collection
5-18 Refugees at the Tokyo Station in Fire, Great Kanto Earthquake, 1 September 1923. Hideki Watanabe Collection

5-9
5-10
5-11
5-12

5-15
5-16
5-17
5-18

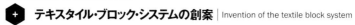

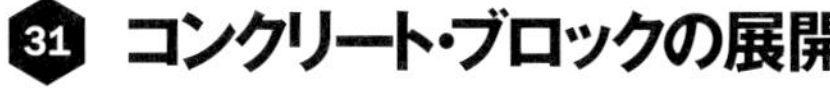

31 コンクリート・ブロックの展開

Development of concrete block

＋ テキスタイル・ブロック・システムの創案 | Invention of the textile block system

● ミラード夫人邸「ミニアトゥーラ」 | Millard House (La Miniatura) | カリフォルニア州パサデナ、1923-24年、住宅 | Pasadena, California, 1923-24, residential

5-20

5-21

5-22

5-23

● ストーラー邸 | Storer House | カリフォルニア州ロサンゼルス、1923–24年、住宅 | Los Angeles, California, 1923–24, residential

5-25

5-26

5-20　ミラード夫人邸「ミニアトゥーラ」(カリフォルニア州パサデナ)1923–24年 庭園側から見た透視図 | フランク・ロイド・ライト
5-21　ミラード夫人邸「ミニアトゥーラ」(カリフォルニア州パサデナ)1923–24年 庭からの外観 | 建築：フランク・ロイド・ライト | 撮影：1923年
5-22　ミラード夫人邸「ミニアトゥーラ」(カリフォルニア州パサデナ)1923–24年 居間内観 | 建築：フランク・ロイド・ライト | 撮影：1923年
5-23　ミラード夫人邸「ミニアトゥーラ」の建設現場にたたずむ土浦信子 | 撮影：土浦亀城 | 1923–24年頃
5-25　ストーラー邸(カリフォルニア州ロサンゼルス)1923–24年 外観、正面ファサード | フランク・ロイド・ライト | 1923年
5-26　ストーラー邸(カリフォルニア州ロサンゼルス)1923–24年 | 建築：フランク・ロイド・ライト | 撮影：水上優 | 2019年

5-20　Millard House (La Miniatura), Pasadena, California. Project, 1923–24. Exterior perspective from the garden. Frank Lloyd Wright. The Museum of Modern Art, New York. Gift of Mr. and Mrs. Walter Hochschild, 1981. DIGITAL IMAGE©2023, The Museum of Modern Art/Scala, Florence

5-21　Millard House (La Miniatura), Pasadena, California. Project, 1923–24. Exterior view from garden. Frank Lloyd Wright, architect. Photo: 1923. Project photographs, circa 1887–2008, The Frank Lloyd Wright Foundation Archives (The Museum of Modern Art | Avery Architectural & Fine Arts Library, Columbia University, New York)

5-22　Millard House (La Miniatura), Pasadena, California. Project, 1923–24. Interior view of the living room. Frank Lloyd Wright, architect. Pasadena Hiller, photographer. Photo: 1923. Project photographs, circa 1887–2008, The Frank Lloyd Wright Foundation Archives (The Museum of Modern Art | Avery Architectural & Fine Arts Library, Columbia University, New York)

5-23　Millard House (La Miniatura), Pasadena, California. Nobuko Tsuchiura at the Millard House under construction. Kameki Tsuchiura, photographer. c. 1923–24. Personal and Taliesin Fellowship photographs, 1870s–2004, The Frank Lloyd Wright Foundation Archives (The Museum of Modern Art | Avery Architectural & Fine Arts Library, Columbia University, New York)

5-25　Storer House, Los Angeles, California. Project, 1923–24. Exterior of the Façade. Frank Lloyd Wright. 1923. Prints and Photographs Division, Library of Congress, Washington, D.C. LC-DIG-ppmsca-09575

5-26　Storer House, Los Angeles, California. Project, 1923–24. Frank Lloyd Wright, architect. Yutaka Mizukami, photographer. Photo: 2019

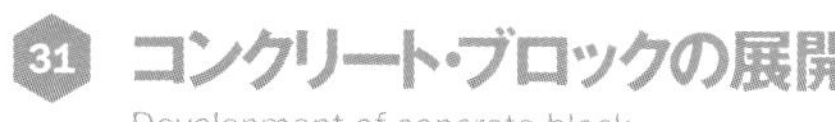

31 コンクリート・ブロックの展開

Development of concrete block

+ コンクリート・ブロックの拡張 | Expanding concrete block applications

● ドヘニー・ランチ宅地開発計画案 | Doheny Ranch development, unbuilt project

カリフォルニア州ロサンゼルス、1923年、都市計画 | Los Angeles, California, 1923, urban planning

5-27

5-28
5-31

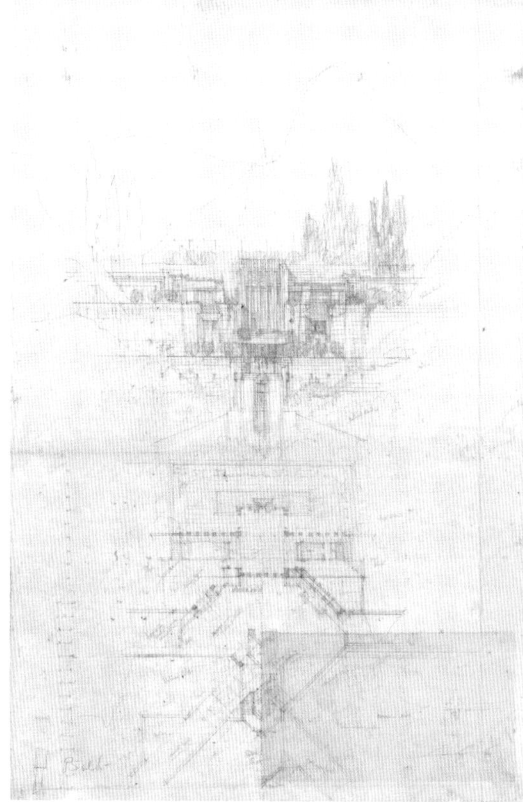

5-30

● サン・マルコス砂漠リゾート・ホテル計画案 | San Marcos-in-the-Desert Hotel, unbuilt project

アリゾナ州チャンドラー、1928–29年、宿泊施設 | Chandler, Arizona, 1928–29, hospitality

5-32

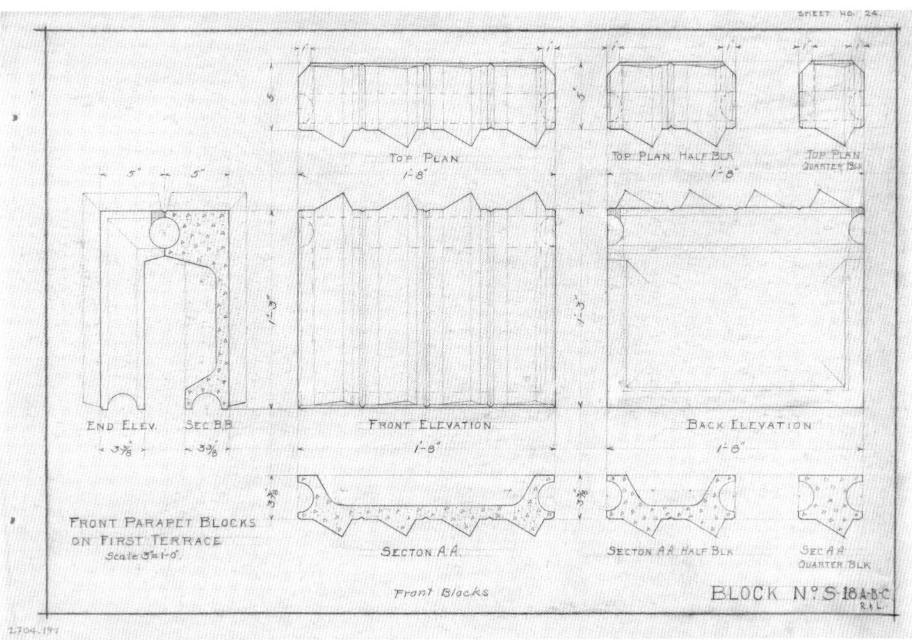

5-33

5-27　ドヘニー・ランチ宅地開発計画案(カリフォルニア州ロサンゼルス)1923年頃 透視図 | フランク・ロイド・ライト
5-28　ドヘニー・ランチ宅地開発計画案(カリフォルニア州ロサンゼルス)1923年頃 透視図 | フランク・ロイド・ライト
5-30　ドヘニー・ランチ宅地開発計画案(カリフォルニア州ロサンゼルス)1923年頃 Cタイプ住宅の外観図 | フランク・ロイド・ライト
5-31　ドヘニー・ランチ宅地開発計画地(現・トルースデール地所) | 撮影:2018年
5-32　サン・マルコス砂漠リゾート・ホテル計画案(アリゾナ州チャンドラー)1928–29年 透視図 | フランク・ロイド・ライト
5-33　サン・マルコス砂漠リゾート・ホテル計画案(アリゾナ州チャンドラー)1928–29年 コンクリート・ブロック詳細図 | フランク・ロイド・ライト

5-27　Doheny Ranch development, Los Angeles, California. Unbuilt Project, c. 1923. Perspective. Frank Lloyd Wright.
The Frank Lloyd Wright Foundation Archives (The Museum of Modern Art | Avery Architectural & Fine Arts Library, Columbia University, New York)
5-28　Doheny Ranch development, Los Angeles, California. Unbuilt Project, c. 1923. Perspective. Frank Lloyd Wright.
The Frank Lloyd Wright Foundation Archives (The Museum of Modern Art | Avery Architectural & Fine Arts Library, Columbia University, New York)
5-30　Doheny Ranch development, Los Angeles, California. Unbuilt Project, c. 1923. Exterior of House C. Frank Lloyd Wright.
Library of Congress Prints and Photographs Division Washington, D.C. LC-DIG-ppmsca-84878
5-31　Trousdale Estates in Beverly Hills, CA. Formerly known as Doheny Ranch. Wikimedia commons photo. 2018
5-32　San Marcos-in-the-Desert Hotel for Alexander Chandler, Chandler, Arizona. Unbuilt Project, 1928–29. Perspective. Frank Lloyd Wright.
The Frank Lloyd Wright Foundation Archives (The Museum of Modern Art | Avery Architectural & Fine Arts Library, Columbia University, New York)
5-33　San Marcos-in-the-Desert Hotel for Alexander Chandler, Chandler, Arizona. Unbuilt Project, 1928–29.
Detail of the concrete block. Frank Lloyd Wright. The Frank Lloyd Wright Foundation Archives
(The Museum of Modern Art | Avery Architectural & Fine Arts Library, Columbia University, New York)

32 ユーソニアン住宅──成長する建築
Usonian Houses: Architecture that grows up

- **ジェイコブズ第一邸** | Jacobs House | ウィスコンシン州マディソン、1936–37年、住宅 | Madison, Wisconsin, 1936-37, residential
- **ハナ邸「ハニカムハウス」** | Hanna House (Honeycomb House) | カリフォルニア州パロアルト、1936–37年、住宅 | Palo Alto, California, 1936–37, residential

5-34

5-36

5-37

5-34　ジェイコブズ第一邸(ウィスコンシン州マディソン)1936-37年 居間内観 | 建築:フランク・ロイド・ライト | 撮影:1938年
5-36　ハナ邸「ハニカムハウス」(カリフォルニア州パロアルト)1936-37年 鳥瞰 | 建築:フランク・ロイド・ライト
5-37　ハナ邸「ハニカムハウス」(カリフォルニア州パロアルト)1936-37年 居間内観 | 建築:フランク・ロイド・ライト
5-38　ユーソニアン・オートマチック住宅ビムソン邸計画案(アリゾナ州フェニックス)1949年 アクソメ詳細図 | フランク・ロイド・ライト
5-40　トレイシー邸(ワシントン州ノルマンディーパーク)1955年 居間側外観 | 建築:フランク・ロイド・ライト、撮影:アンドリュー・ヴァン・レウエン | 2012年
5-41　トレイシー邸(ワシントン州ノルマンディーパーク)1955年 ワークスペースとバスルーム側外観 | 建築:フランク・ロイド・ライト、撮影:アンドリュー・ヴァン・レウエン | 2012年

5-34　Jacobs House, Madison, Wisconsin. Project, 1936–37. Interior view, living room. Frank Lloyd Wright, architect.
Photo: 1938. Project photographs, circa 1887–2008,
The Frank Lloyd Wright Foundation Archives (The Museum of Modern Art | Avery Architectural & Fine Arts Library, Columbia University, New York)
5-36　Hanna House (Honeycomb House), Project 1936–37, Palo Alto, California. Aerial view. Frank Lloyd Wright, architect.
Courtesy of the Department of Special Collections, Stanford University Libraries
5-37　Hanna House (Honeycomb House), Project 1936–37, Palo Alto, California. Interior view to the living room. Frank Lloyd Wright, architect.
Courtesy of the Department of Special Collections, Stanford University Libraries
5-38　Usonian Automatic Housing for Walter Bimson, Phoenix, Arizona. Unbuilt Project, 1949. Axonometric of construction detail. Frank Lloyd Wright.
The Frank Lloyd Wright Foundation Archives (The Museum of Modern Art | Avery Architectural & Fine Arts Library, Columbia University, New York)
5-40　Tracy House. Normandy Park, Washington. Project, 1955. Exterior with a view to living room.
Frank Lloyd Wright, architect. © Andrew van Leeuwen, photographer. Photo: 2012
5-41　Tracy House. Normandy Park, Washington. Project, 1955. Exterior with a view to kitchen and workspace.
Frank Lloyd Wright, architect. © Andrew van Leeuwen, photographer. Photo: 2012

● **トレイシー邸** | Tracy House | シアトル州ノルマンディーパーク、1955年、住宅 | Normandy Park, Seattle, 1955, residential

5-40

5-41

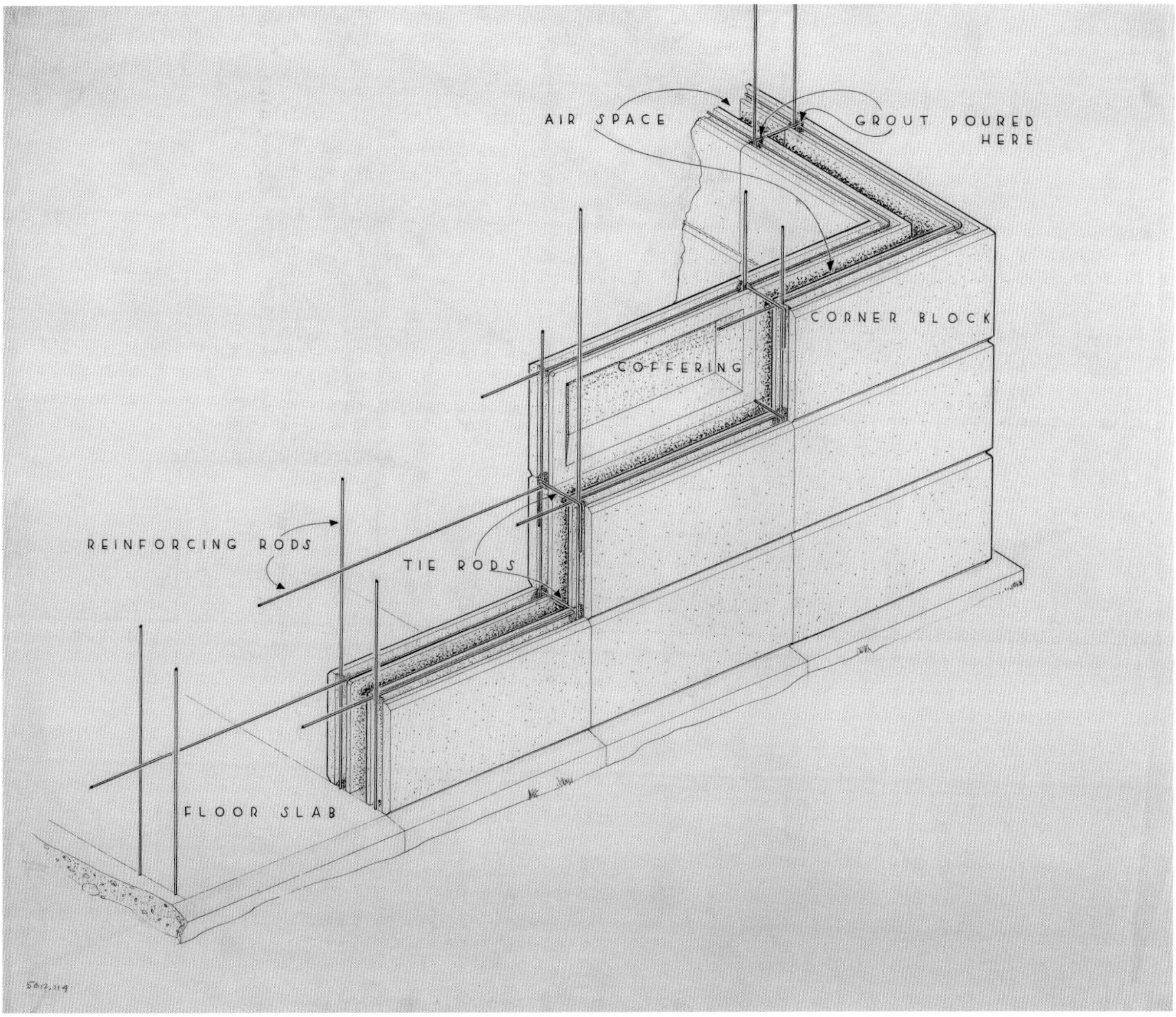

5-38

33 らせん状建築

Architetural design based on the helical spiral

● **グッゲンハイム美術館** | Solomon R. Guggenheim Museum | ニューヨーク、1943-59年、美術館 | New York, 1943-59, institutional civic

5-45

5-47

5-46

5-44

● ゴードン・ストロング自動車体験娯楽施設とプラネタリウム計画案 | Gordon Strong Automobile Objective and Planetarium, unbuilt project

メリーランド州シュガーローフマウンテン、1924–25年、娯楽施設 | Sugarloaf Mountain, Maryland, 1924–25, recreational

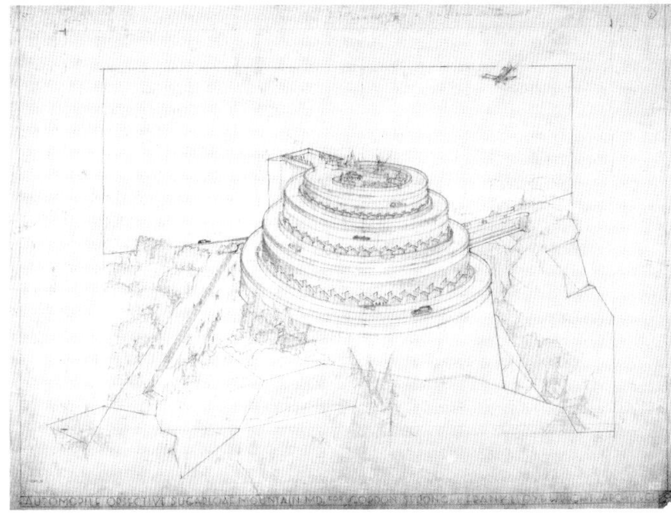

5-43
5-42

5-48

5-42 ゴードン・ストロング自動車体験娯楽施設とプラネタリウム計画案(メリーランド州シュガーローフマウンテン)1924–25年 鳥瞰透視図 | フランク・ロイド・ライト
5-43 ゴードン・ストロング自動車体験娯楽施設とプラネタリウム計画案(メリーランド州シュガーローフマウンテン)1924–25年 透視図 | フランク・ロイド・ライト | 1925年
5-44 グッゲンハイム美術館(ニューヨーク)1943–59年 透視図(複写) | フランク・ロイド・ライト
5-45 グッゲンハイム美術館(ニューヨーク)1943–59年 内観、吹き抜けから天井を見上げる | 建築:フランク・ロイド・ライト、撮影:ディヴィッド・ヒールド
5-46 グッゲンハイム美術館(ニューヨーク)1943–59年 | 建築:フランク・ロイド・ライト、撮影:ディヴィッド・ヒールド
5-47 グッゲンハイム美術館(ニューヨーク)1943–59年 内観、螺旋状スロープの展示ギャラリー | 建築:フランク・ロイド・ライト、撮影:ディヴィッド・ヒールド
5-48 有機的建築を説明するフランク・ロイド・ライトの手「ハンズ・シリーズ」| 撮影:ペドロ・ゲレロ | 1953年

5-42 Gordon Strong Automobile Objective and Planetarium, Sugarloaf Mountain, Maryland. Unbuilt Project, 1924–25. Aerial perspective. Frank Lloyd Wright. The Frank Lloyd Wright Foundation Archives (The Museum of Modern Art | Avery Architectural & Fine Arts Library, Columbia University, New York)
5-43 Gordon Strong Automobile Objective and Planetarium, Sugarloaf Mountain, Maryland. Unbuilt Project, 1924–25. Perspective. Frank Lloyd Wright. 1925. Prints and Photographs Division, Library of Congress, Washington, D.C. LC-DIG-ds-10423
5-44 The Solomon R. Guggenheim Museum, New York. Project, 1943–59. Exterior perspective. Frank Lloyd Wright. The Frank Lloyd Wright Foundation Archives (The Museum of Modern Art | Avery Architectural & Fine Arts Library, Columbia University, New York)
5-45 Interior of the Solomon R. Guggenheim Museum, New York. Frank Lloyd Wright, architect. Photo: David Heald © Solomon R. Guggenheim Foundation
5-46 The Solomon R. Guggenheim Museum, New York. Frank Lloyd Wright, architect. Photo: David Heald © Solomon R. Guggenheim Foundation
5-47 Interior of the Solomon R. Guggenheim Museum, New York. Frank Lloyd Wright, architect. Photo: David Heald © Solomon R. Guggenheim Foundation
5-48 Wright's Hands #10. Hands series. Pedro Guerrero, photographer. Photo: 1953 © The Estate of Pedro E. Guerrero

ユーソニアン・オートマチック・システム 個人の主権から公共デザインまで

マシュー・スコンスバーグ

1950年代初頭に生まれたユーソニアン・オートマチック建設システムによって、フランク・ロイド・ライトはユーソニア(文化先進的な北米地域を指し示すライトの造語)の市民に、個人や共同体の家を建設する手段を提供した。ライトは長年、低価格住宅の大規模な供給手法を模索しており、数多くの建設システム開発につなげてきた。しかし、ユーソニアン・オートマチックがそれらと異なるのは、オープンソースに近い考え方を持っており、誰もが自分の土地に、その土壌を使って、自分の建物を建てられることを明確に示すものであったことだ。

1954年の著書『自然の家』に初めて掲載されたアクソメ図[cat.no.5-38]が、ユーソニアン・オートマチック・システムの仕組みを的確に表している[1]。アイデアとしては簡単であり、機織りで布を織るように、縦横の接合部に鉄筋を通してコンクリート・ブロックを補強したものである。制約が少ないことから、小さな住宅から大きな公共施設まで、さらには擁壁や造成地、道路といったインフラまでをつくり出せる拡張性を持っていた。最も重要なことは、「織るように施工する」という基本理念が技能労働者や高度な専門技術、先進技術をほとんど要しないため、誰でも使えるシステムである、とライトが考えていたことである。しかも、材料は簡単に手に入るものであった。ライトは、このシステムの利用者がその地所から採れる土砂を骨材に使って、必要なコンクリート・ブロックを自ら打設することを想定していた。システムは完全に標準化されており、わずか12種類のコンクリート・ブロックで構成されていた。個人が小規模に利用することも、大人数で協力してより大規模な構造物をつくることもできた。このように、ユーソニアン・オートマチック・システムは、自立と共同、単独行為と協業との間の民主的な関係を象徴するような仕組みであった。

建物ではなくシステムを設計することに、どのような意味があるのだろうか。設計図は最終形を決定するものであるのに対して、システムには際限がなく、発展が望めるオープンエンドなものである。ライトは、ユーソニアン・オートマチック・システムが時とともに発展し、物質的にも社会的にも、より民主的な市民の連帯を生み出すことを思い描いていた。彼は、建築へのこうしたアプローチの政治的な可能性を、「完全に標準化されていながら、民主的な多様性の理想、つまり個人の主権を確立していることが自由な社会にふさわしい。このシステムは、真の建築に発展するはずだ」と説明した[2]。ユーソニアン・オートマチック・システムの意義は、社会的公正のための手段にほかならなかったのである。

先行事例

ライトによる低価格住宅のための設計は、20世紀はじめの『レディース・ホーム・ジャーナル』誌[cat.no.2-20]に初めて登場する。それは、当時一般的だった通信販売の手法を利用して、ライトの設計した住宅を大衆の手の届くものにする試みであった。その後の、アメリカ式システム工法住宅(1915-17)では、住宅の工場生産方式を実験的に導入した[cat.nos.5-2~4]。このシステムは、建物部材を工場でプレファブ生産することでコストを削減するものであり、完成品の品質を保証する認証を受けた施工業者によって施工された。アメリカ式システム工法住宅は、ライトにとって工業や機械化の効率性を利用しつつ、高品質で美しい製品をつくり出す初期の試みであった。

ライトが、民主主義の原動力としての工業と関わりを持ったのは、画期的な論考である「機械の美術工芸」を、シカゴで多面的に活動していた市民団体ハルハウスの聴衆に対して発表した1901年ごろからだと考えられる。この講演で彼は、機械とは「民主主義の大いなる先駆者」であると説いた。また彼は、ヴィクトル・ユゴー(1802-85)の『ノートル=ダム・ド・パリ』(1831)から、「印刷機は、知識を複写可能な印刷物の形で解放したことで、それまで建築が担っていた象徴的かつ公共的な役割を担うようになった。つまり書が建物にとってかわったのだ」という主張を引用した。建築が適切であり続けるためには、「偉大な都市の後に現れた、最初の偉大な機械」である印刷機から学ぶべきであるとライトは考えていた[3]。この目的のために、ライトは機械を建築生産の省力化の道具として利用し、文明にさらなる美しさ、多様性、威厳をもたらそうとした[4]。『シカゴ・トリビューン』紙はライトの主張を以下のようにまとめている。「隷属的な製品も、隷属的に見える製品も、どちらも存在すべきではない。むしろ機械生産は、真に芸術的であるべきだ」[5]。

ライトは、アメリカ式システム工法住宅によって建築と工業生産の融合に一定の成果を挙げた後、1920年代にはカリフォルニアでの活動のかたわら、周辺の砂漠気候に適した新たな材料であるコンクリートを用いた別の建設システムの実験を始めた。当時の住宅建設にコンクリートを用いることはほとんどなく、ライト自身もコンクリートを「建設業界の卑しき嫌われ者」[6]と呼んでいたが、その柔軟な性質に可能性を見いだし始めていたのだ。「コンクリートは一体的な材料であり、想像力に形を与えることができる。私はそこからなにかが編み出されるような気がした。建築が編み出されるのではないか。鉄を縦糸に、コンクリート・ブロックを横糸にして織り上げればよいのではないか。私は再びコンクリートに興味を抱き始めている」[7]。

コンクリート・ブロックを用いた初期の建築事例はロサンゼルスにおける一連の住宅であったが、絶え間なく降り注ぐ日差しを防ぐには、木材よりもコンクリートのほうが優れており、耐火性も期待できた。ミラード夫人邸「ミニアトゥーラ」(1923–24)[cat.nos.5–20~22]やストーラー邸(1923)[cat.nos.5–25,26]に始まり、ドヘニー・ランチ宅地開発計画案(1923–24)[cat.nos.5–27~30]へと続いた。ライトはこれらのプロジェクトにおいて、敷地から採取した土砂を混ぜながら豊かなパターンを有するブロックを成形することで、不定形でありながら可塑的な性質を持つコンクリートのテクトニック(構法的)な課題に取り組んだ[8]。この加工は、コンクリートに周囲の風景が持つ自然の風合いや色を加え、「木のような質感を持つ美しいもの」へと変化させたのである[9]。ブロックを使うことで、際限なく続けて施工が可能であり、どこまでも拡張できる。これをライトは、テキスタイル・ブロック・システムと名づけた。

1920年代のロサンゼルスで行われた初期のコンクリート・ブロックについての実験は、どこにでもあるありふれた材料を、美しく拡張性のある建設システムへ変容させることに成功した。しかし、このシステムには、ある程度の熟練した施工技術が必要とされたため、民主主義や参加型プロセスという観点からは応用可能性が限られていた。ライトはこの難問を、1930年代から50年代のユーソニアン住宅のプロジェクト群において認識していた。ユーソニアン住宅は、合板の芯を板材と目板で挟んだプレファブ式の「サンドイッチパネル」によって、低価格の住宅を生産する試みであった[cat.no.5–34]。ボード&バテン(幅の異なる木材を交互に用いた壁)によってユーソニアン住宅のコストは下がったものの、その設計と施工は複雑かつ精密なものであり、実習生が標準ディテールを習得したのち、施工を監督するため現場に赴く必要があった。後年にライト自身は「このような家は建築家の作品であって、施工業者や素人の力量でできるものではない。この仕組みを開示することには、偽造や模倣を生む大きなリスクが伴う」[10]と記している。

1930年代の社会的・経済的な危機の広がりは、民主主義を推進させる建築を目指したライトの志を一層高めたが、世界大恐慌により、建築と機械化の関係は再構築を迫られた。1929年にフェニックスで開業したアリゾナ・ビルトモア・ホテルの建設において、ライトはテキスタイル・ブロックを全面的に採用することに成功した。しかし一方で、チャンドラー近郊のサン・マルコス砂漠リゾート・ホテル計画案(1928–29)は、同じシステムを採用する最も野心的なプロジェクトであったものの、同年10月に起こった株式市場の暴落によって計画が頓挫している[cat.no.5–32]。1930年、ライトはプリンストン大学での一連の講義において、機械の力と、それがもたらす標準化によって、建築と人間生活の質を高めるどころか、むしろ低下の脅威にさらされるとの懸念を表明した[11][cat.no.7–28]。機械化と建築に関する不安は、住宅や不動産にも及んだ。後年にライトは、第2次世界大戦後に多数の退役軍人が帰還したことで急激に進んだ住宅不足に対処するため出現した郊外のプレファブ式宅地開発や、都市における高密高層住宅といった大規模住宅開発を批判している。

> 動物は柵や小屋につながれるが、人間は「収容される」というのか！ われらアメリカ人は、「個人の主権」という人間精神の普遍的な主張を、この地に植えつけた。今、重要なのは、工場を家にすることだ。全ての人には、自身の良心に忠実に、自由に思い描き、建てる権利がある。機械とは、人のために使うのに適した素晴らしい工場生産の道具であって、人に対して使うものではない[12]。

工場生産の行き着いた先は、1901年の講演「機械の美術工芸」でライトが警告した「隷属的に見える」状況や製品をもたらした。こうしてライトは、印刷機の成功例を建築で実現し、それにより社会の民主主義を進める新たな方法を模索することとなったのだ。ライトは20世紀初頭に初めて大量生産に取り組んで以来、複雑な工程を工場や熟練工に委託することで、最高のデザイン水準を維持しながらコスト削減を追求していたが、ユーソニアン・オートマチック・システムにおいては、機械生産に代わって「工場を家にする」選択肢を提示した。

ユーソニアン・オートマチック

1938年、ライトはワシントンD.C.の連邦建築家協会で講義を行い、「私は家を建てるにあたっては、現在の社会秩序の行き先を必ず予測する」と力強く主張した[13]。ライトはそれからわずか10年の間に、機械や熟練した職人に頼らず、単純で自由度が高く、素人でも利用できる新たな建設システム、セルフビルドを考案した。1949年には、ライトはテキスタイル・ブロック・システムを「ユーソニアン・オートマチック」として再考案し、わずか12種類の標準ブロック形状だけで、さまざまな規模の幅広い種類の建造物を建設できるまでにシステムを効率化した。「オートマチック」とは、施主が自ら家を建設できるようになることだとライトは説明している。これは、少なくともある程度の実現を果たした。

シアトルのエリザベスとウィリアム・トレイシー夫妻（1955）や、セント・ルイスのベットとセオドア・パッパス夫妻（1955）のように、自分たちでブロックを積んで家を建設した人もいた。シンシナティのビバリーとジェラルド・トンキンズ夫妻（1954）は、ライトの孫でタリアセンの実習生だったエリック・ロイド・ライト

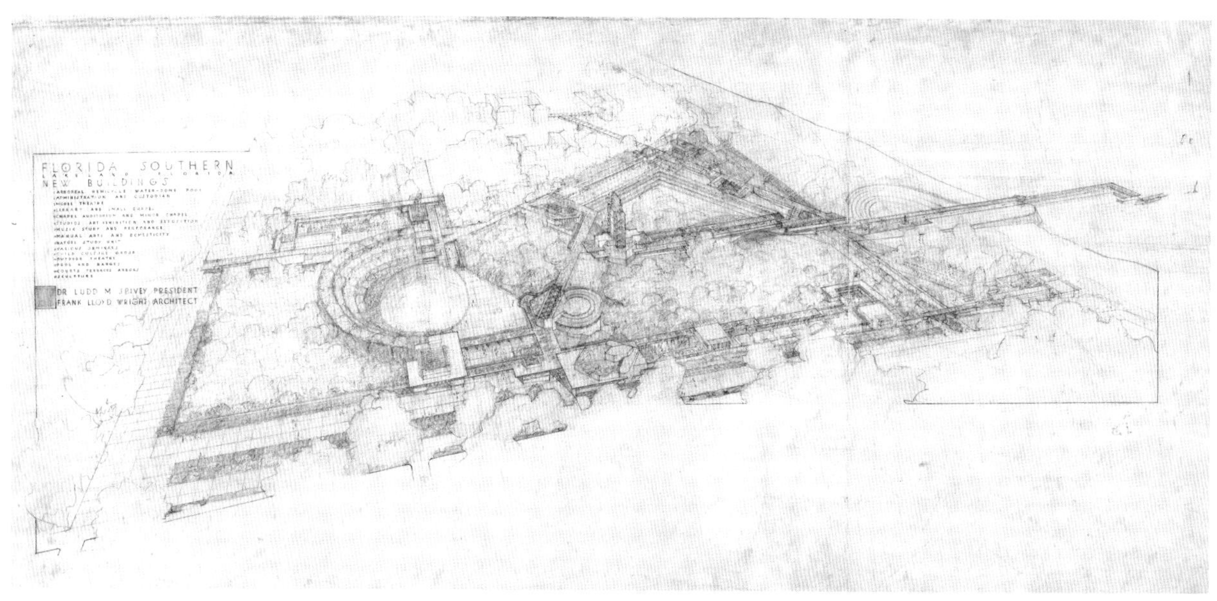

図1　フロリダ・サザン・カレッジ（フロリダ州レイクランド）1938年 鳥瞰透視図｜建築：フランク・ロイド・ライト

Fig.1　Florida Southern College, Lakeland, Florida, Project, 1938. Aerial perspective, Frank Lloyd Wright, architect.
The Frank Lloyd Wright Foundation Archives（The Museum of Modern Art | Avery Architectural & Fine Arts Library, Columbia University, New York）| FLWFA 3805.002

図2　タリアセン・ウェスト（アリゾナ州スコッツデール）1938年－
ロバート・ベハーカ「コンクリート・ブロックを用いた砂漠シェルター」
撮影：ロバート・ベハーカ｜1954年｜写真提供：ジェイニン・フェリス・ベハーカ・コレクション

Fig.2　Taliesin West, Scottsdale, Arizona. Begun 1938. Desert shelter using concrete blocks, 1954. Photograph by Robert Beharka. Collection Jeanine Ferris Beharka

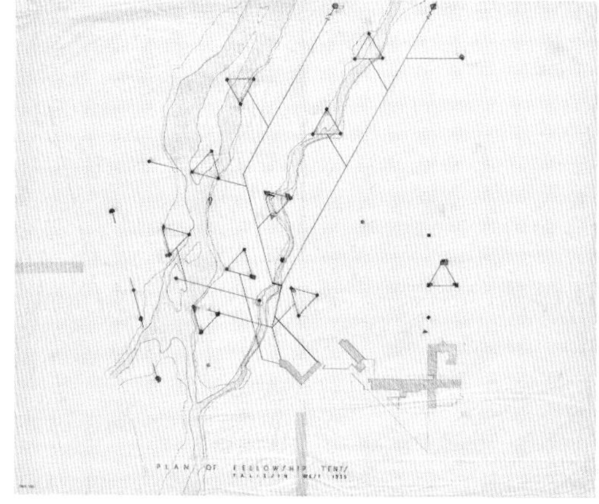

図3　タリアセン・フェローシップのテント平面図

Fig.3　Plan of Fellowship Tents, The Frank Lloyd Wright Foundation Archives（The Museum of Modern Art | Avery Architectural & Fine Arts Library, Columbia University, New York）| FLWFA 3803.230

(1929–2023)に、地元の施工者による自宅建設の監理を依頼し、家族や子どもにも軽度な作業を手伝わせている。いずれの家にも壁用、屋根用、軒端用といった12種類の標準ブロックが使用されており、ガラスがはめ込まれた非常に美しい穴あきコーナーブロックも組み込まれていた[cat. nos. 5-40, 41]。

ユーソニアン・オートマチックは、工場の生産方式というより、機械の生産技術を利用したものであった。ライトはそれ以前にも、1938年にフロリダ・サザン・カレッジのキャンパス設計を依頼された際に、セルフビルドでのコンクリート・ブロックの限界を小さなコミュニティのスケールで試している。そこでライトは、1920年代のテキスタイル・ブロック・システムのバリエーションを展開し、タリアセンの実習生を派遣して、フロリダの学生たちにこのシステムを使った建設を指導した。教育と参加型労働の民主的な統合を果たした結果、学生たちは市民規模のキャンパス建設でも一翼を担ったのである[図1]。ここでライトは、セルフビルドによって民主的な社会関係を進展させるという野望を一歩実現させている。フロリダ・サザン・カレッジの建設プロセスは参加型であったものの、学生たちは熟練した実習生やライト自身の監督と指導という恩恵を得ることができた。

1954年、ライトはタリアセンの全ての実習生に、著書『自然の家』に掲載されたユーソニアン・オートマチックのアクソメ図を用いた設計を行うように提案した。その年の12月に提出されたグループ設計課題は、現在もフランク・ロイド・ライト財団アーカイヴズに所蔵されている。実習生のひとりは、ユーソニアン・オートマチックを使った建物を、タリアセン・ウエスト周辺の砂漠のキャンパスに設けられたテントサイトに建設した[図2]。1955年には実習生のデイヴィッド・ダッジが、すべてのテントサイトの調査を行い、そこで小さな共同体を形成している生態的・建築的要素の組み合わせを精細に記録した[図3]。出版用のアクソメ図だけでなく、ほとんど知られていない、実習生たちのテントの平面図までもダッジが描いたことは特筆に値する。そこでは、個人主権の主張と公共デザインへの展望との関係が累積し、多様であり、入り組んでいることが示唆されている。

ライトは、個人と社会全体が調和した生きた共同体のたとえとして、森を引き合いに出しながら、テキスタイル・ブロックの家を「他の木々の間に佇む樹木そのもの」と表現した[14]。近年の森林生態学の研究によれば、多くの樹種が、土壌中の菌根ネットワークに助けられながら、根を通して情報を交換するだけでなく物質もやり取りしていることが明らかになった。こうした木の内部にある炭素量の約半分が、共同体中の別の木から供給されているのだという[15]。社会生態学という新たな学問分野が示しているのは、単なる類推にとどまらず、植物の共同体と同じことが人間にも当てはまるということである。強靭な共同体は、繊細に編みめぐらされた根によって成立するのだ。われわれの生活が、個人と公共、庭園と公園、小規模と大規模の間に編み出されるように、ユーソニアン・オートマチックは個人の主権と協力的な行動の両方に呼びかけるものである。

1 フランク・ロイド・ライト著、富岡義人訳『自然の家』(筑摩書房 2010年)
2 前掲書、p.256
3 Frank Lloyd Wright, "The Art and Craft of the Machine" (1901), reprinted in *The Essential Frank Lloyd Wright: Critical Writings on Architecture*, ed. Bruce Brooks Pfeiffer (Princeton: Princeton University Press, 2008), p. 24.
4 Ibid., pp. 28-29.
5 Art and the Machine (March 4, 1901)," accessed January 26, 2016, http://archives.chicagotribune.com/1901/03/04/page/6/article/among-the-new-books.
6 Frank Lloyd Wright, *An Autobiography*, 2nd edition. (New York: Duell, Sloan and Pearce, 1943), p. 241.
7 Ibid., p. 235.
8 Kenneth Frampton, "The Text-Tile Tectonic: The Origin and Evolution of Wright's Woven Architecture," in *On and By Frank Lloyd Wright: A Primer of Architectural Principles*, ed. Robert McCarter (New York: Phaidon 2011), pp. 181–183. ロバート・スウィーニーは、ライトのコンクリートブロックによる建築実験は、息子のロイド・ライトが1922年に設計したボールマン邸が最初であり、ライト初のコンクリートブロック住宅であるミラード邸は厳密にはテキスタイル・ブロック・ハウスではなかったと論じている。See Robert L. Sweeney and David G. DeLong, *Wright in Hollywood: Visions of a New Architecture*, annotated edition (Cambridge: MIT Press, 1994), 20, pp. 204–205.
9 Wright, *An Autobiography*, p. 242.
10 Wright, *The Natural House*, p. 89.
11 フランク・ロイド・ライト著、山形浩生訳『フランク・ロイド・ライトの現代建築講義』(白水社 2010年)
12 Frank Lloyd Wright, "Away with the Realtor," *Esquire*, October 1958.
13 Frank Lloyd Wright, *Washington Post*, sec. 2, October 26, 1938. Quoted in Robert Twombly, *Frank Lloyd Wright: His Life and His Architecture* (New York: John Wiley & Sons, 1979), p. 261.
14 Wright, *An Autobiography*, p. 242.
15 Tamir Klein, Rolf Siegwolf, and Christian Körner, "Belowground Carbon Trade among Tall Trees in a Temperate Forest," *Science* 352, no. 6283 (April 15, 2016): pp. 342–344.

Usonian Automatic System From Individual Sovereignty to Civic Design

Matthew Skjonsberg

With the Usonian Automatic construction system from the early 1950s, Frank Lloyd Wright provided citizens of Usonia—Wright's preferred term for a culturally advanced North America—with the means of building their own homes and communities. Though designing ways to provide moderate-cost housing on a large scale had preoccupied Wright for years—and resulted in his invention of numerous construction systems—the Usonian Automatic would be different: almost open source in its sensibility, it was explicitly intended to allow anyone to build their own buildings, of their own earth, on their own ground.

An axonometric drawing, first published in 1954 in *The Natural House*, demonstrates how the Usonian Automatic system worked.[1] The idea was simple: concrete blocks reinforced with steel rods running through vertical and horizontal joints, similar to a textile woven on a loom. Its open-ended nature meant that it was also scalable, capable of creating small houses, larger civic centers, as well as infrastructure, such as retaining walls, terraces, and roadways [cat. no. 5-38]. Most importantly, Wright intended that anyone could use the system, as its basic principle—weaving—required little in the way of skilled labor, expertise, or advanced technology. Moreover, the materials were easy to obtain. Wright intended that users of the system would themselves cast the concrete blocks using soil from their own property as the aggregate. The system was entirely standardized, consisting of just 12 variants of cast-concrete blocks. Individuals could use the system on a small scale or cooperate with others to build larger structures. In this way, the Usonian Automatic system approximated democratic relationships between self-reliance and community, as well as individual initiative and cooperative action.

What does it mean to draw a system rather than a building? A system is open-ended, capable of evolving and changing, whereas a blueprint prescribes a final product. Wright envisioned that the Usonian Automatic system would develop over time, yielding a more democratic civic fabric both materially and socially. He explained its political potential, describing such an approach to building as "becoming to a free society because, though standardized fully, it yet establishes the democratic ideal of variety—the sovereignty of the individual. A true architecture may evolve."[2] The Usonian Automatic system was to be nothing less than an instrument for social equity.

Precedents

Wright's first designs for moderate-cost housing appeared in the *Ladies' Home Journal* [cat. no. 2-20] at the turn of the twentieth century, attempting to democratize access to his house designs using mail-order strategies common at the time. He subsequently experimented with factory-produced housing in his American System-Built designs (1915–17) [cat. nos. 5-2~4]. This system reduced costs by prefabricating building components in a factory, which were then constructed by licensed contractors to ensure the quality of the results. The American System-Built Houses were an early attempt by Wright to harness the efficiencies of industry and mechanization, while still producing a high-quality and beautiful product.

Wright had, at least theoretically, engaged with industry as an agent of democracy as early as 1901, when he read his seminal essay "The Art and Craft of the Machine" to an audience at Hull House, a multifaceted civic organization in Chicago. In his speech, Wright argued that the machine was the "great forerunner of democracy." He cited Victor Hugo's argument in *Notre-Dame de Paris* (1831) that the printing press had superseded the symbolic and civic functions previously ascribed to architecture by emancipating knowledge in the form of reproducible type, and that the book had replaced the building. According to Wright, for architecture to remain relevant, it must learn the lesson of the printing press, "the first great machine, after the great city."[3] To this end, Wright sought to instrumentalize architectural production, utilizing the machine as a labor-saving tool to bring greater beauty, variety, and dignity to civilization.[4] The *Chicago Tribune* summarized Wright's argument as such: "This idea. . . says that there should be neither slave nor slave-like products. It asserts instead that machine production, at least in important subjects, can be and should be genuinely artistic."[5]

Wright achieved moderate success interfacing architecture and industrial production with the American System-Built Houses, and by the 1920s, while working in California, he began to experiment with another construction system that embraced a new material better suited to the desert climate of his environs: concrete. Residential construction at this time rarely used concrete. Wright once described it as "that despised outcast of the building industry."[6] However, he began to see possibilities in its malleability: "Concrete is a plastic material—susceptible to the impress of imagination. I saw a kind of weaving coming out of it. Why not weave a kind of building?... steel for warp and masonry units for woof in the weaving... I was getting interested again."[7]

The first new experimental projects built with concrete, a fire-resistant material, were a series of houses in Los Angeles, where concrete responds better than wood to the incessant sun. First at the Millard House (*La Miniatura*)

(1923–24) [cat. nos. 5-20~22] and Storer House (1923) [cat. nos. 5-25, 26], and then in subsequent projects like the Doheny Ranch development (project, 1923) [cat. nos. 5-27~30], Wright grappled with the tectonic challenges of concrete, namely its amorphous, plastic quality, by casting the concrete into richly patterned blocks made with earth taken from the building site.[8] This process imbued the concrete with the texture and natural color of the surrounding landscape, thus transforming the material into "a thing of beauty—textured like the trees."[9] Each of these projects capitalized on the open-ended weaving process and scalability of this system, which Wright described as his textile-block system, to build rambling complexes. The houses and retaining walls are nearly indistinguishable, stitched across the hilly sites and serving multiple functions, such as roadways for access and water catchment and terraced gardens for soil conservation and to create a cooling microclimate.

These early concrete-block experiments in Los Angeles during the 1920s succeeded in transforming a banal, ubiquitous material into a beautiful and scalable system of construction. However, the system had limited applicability with regard to democracy and participatory processes because it still required, at least to some degree, skilled labor. Wright acknowledged this conundrum in the context of his Usonian house projects of the 1930s–50s, another attempt to produce moderate-cost housing that relied on prefabricated "sandwich panels" made by sheathing a core of plywood in board and batten. [cat. no. 5-34] Sandwich panels lowered the cost of Usonian houses, but their design and construction were complex and precise, requiring apprentices to master the standard details and then travel to supervise construction. As Wright himself later wrote, "A home like this is an architect's creation. It is not a builder's nor an amateur's effort. There is considerable risk in exposing the scheme to imitation or emulation."[10]

The widespread social and economic crises of the 1930s reinvigorated Wright's ambitions for architecture to advance democracy; however, the Great Depression also forced him to reconfigure the relationship between architecture and mechanization. He successfully employed the textile-block system in the construction of the Arizona Biltmore Hotel in Phoenix, which opened in February 1929, but his most ambitious project employing the system, the San Marcos-in-the-Desert Hotel (project, 1928–29) in nearby Chandler, was derailed by the stock market crash that October. [cat. no. 5-32] In 1930, Wright gave a series of lectures at Princeton University, in which he expressed concern that machine power and the standardization it brings threatened to diminish rather than increase the quality of architecture and human life [cat. no. 7-28].[11] His trepidation about mechanization and architecture extended to housing and real estate. Wright later criticized mass housing developments—prefabricated tract housing in the suburbs and high-density, high-rise housing in cities—that were emerging to address widespread housing shortages precipitated by large numbers of veterans returning home after World War II:

> *Animals are penned or stabled. Humans are "housed!"... We Americans planted here on earth a sweeping assertion of man's spirit—the "sovereignty of the individual"... it is important now to take the factory to the house... the right of every man [is] to be true to his better self as himself, free to dream and build... Recognize the machine as the appropriate magnificent tool of pre-fabrication to be used for man, not on him.*[12]

Factory production, it seemed, had resulted in the very "slave-like" conditions and products that Wright had forewarned against in his 1901 speech "The Art and Craft of the Machine," leading him to explore new ways for architecture to realize the lessons of the printing press and, in so doing, advance social democracy. Since his first engagements with mass production in the early twentieth century, Wright had sought to reduce costs while maintaining the highest design standards by outsourcing complex processes to factories or his own highly trained associates. With the Usonian Automatic system, Wright advanced an alternative to machine production that would "take the factory to the house."

Usonian Automatic

In 1938, Wright gave a lecture to the Federal Architects' Association in Washington, D.C., where he boldly claimed, "I don't build a house without predicting the end of the present social order."[13] In just over a decade, Wright invented a new construction system that did not rely on machines or trained craftsmen but was simplified, open-ended, and accessible to non-experts: self-build. In 1949, Wright reinvented his textile-block system as the Usonian Automatic, streamlining the system until it consisted of just twelve standard block shapes, from which a wide variety of structures at different scales could be constructed. Wright explained that "automatic" meant that now homeowners could build these houses themselves. And they did—at least to some extent.

Some homeowners, such as Elizabeth and William Tracy in Seattle (1955) and Bette and Theodore Pappas in St. Louis (1955), cast their own blocks and effectively built their own houses. Beverly and Gerald Tonkens in Cincinnati (1954) engaged Wright's grandson and Taliesin apprentice, Eric Lloyd Wright (1929–2023), to supervise the construction of their house by a local contractor while still allowing the family and the children to participate, if less strenuously. In each case, the houses were built using the twelve standard blocks—including those for walls, roof, and fascia, and the particularly beautiful perforated corner blocks with glass inserts [cat. nos. 5–40, 41].

The Usonian Automatics harnessed the spirit of the machine rather than factory modes of production. Wright had earlier tested the limits of self-build concrete blocks at the scale of a small community when he was commissioned to design the campus of Florida Southern College in 1938. There Wright had deployed a variation of the textile-block system of the 1920s, sending Taliesin apprentices to instruct the Florida students in building with the system, and in a democratic synthesis of education and participatory labor—at a civic scale—the students helped to build their own campus [Fig. 1]. Here, Wright was able to further realize his ambitions for do-it-yourself construction to advance democratic social relations. However participatory the construction process of Florida Southern College was, the students still benefited from the considerable oversight and guidance of skilled apprentices and Wright himself.

In 1954, notably, the same year that the Usonian Automatic axonometric drawing was published in *The Natural House*, Wright suggested that all the Taliesin apprentices should create designs using the system. These design assignments were submitted collectively in December of that year and can still be found in the Frank Lloyd Wright Foundation Archives. One of the apprentices built a variation of the Usonian Automatic on one of the existing tent sites at Taliesin West [Fig. 2]. In 1955, apprentice David Dodge conducted a survey of all the tent sites, delineating in precise detail the combination of ecological and architectural factors that informed these micro-communities [Fig. 3]. It is noteworthy that Dodge drew both the published axonometric drawing and the little-known plan of Fellowship tents, suggesting something of the cumulative, varied, and non-linear character of the relationships between assertions of individual sovereignty and aspirations for civic design.

Invoking the forest as a metaphor for living communities that balanced the individual with the social whole, Wright described the textile-block house as a "tree itself standing there at home among the other trees."[14] Current research in forest ecology shows that diverse species of trees not only exchange information through their roots, assisted by mycorrhizal networks in the soil, but materials as well. The research indicates that about half of the carbon in these trees was supplied by other trees in their community.[15] Beyond mere analogy, the emerging discipline of sociobiology suggests that what is true for plant communities is also true for humans; resilient communities are established by the delicate weaving of roots. The Usonian Automatic is thus a call to both individual initiative and cooperative action, acknowledging that from the tapestry of our lives, a civic fabric is also woven—between private and public, garden and park, small scale and large.

1 Frank Lloyd Wright, *The Natural House*, (New York: Horizon Press, 1954).
2 Ibid., p. 205.
3 Frank Lloyd Wright, "The Art and Craft of the Machine" (1901), reprinted in *The Essential Frank Lloyd Wright: Critical Writings on Architecture*, ed. Bruce Brooks Pfeiffer (Princeton: Princeton University Press, 2008), p. 24.
4 Ibid., pp. 28–29.
5 Frank Lloyd Wright, "Art and the Machine (March 4, 1901)," accessed January 26, 2016, http://archives.chi-cagotribune.com/1901/03/04/page/6/article/among-the-new-books.
6 Frank Lloyd Wright, *An Autobiography*, 3rd edition. (New York: Duell, Sloan and Pearce, 1943), p. 241.
7 Ibid., p. 235.
8 Kenneth Frampton, "The Text-Tile Tectonic: The Origin and Evolution of Wright's Woven Architecture," in *On and By Frank Lloyd Wright: A Primer of Architectural Principles*, ed. Robert McCarter (New York: Phaidon 2011), pp. 181–183. Robert Sweeney has argued that Wright's experiments in concrete block construction followed the Bollman Residence, designed by his son Lloyd Wright in 1922, and that Wright's first concrete-block house, the Millard Residence, was not, by definition, a textile-block house. See Robert L. Sweeney and David G. DeLong, *Wright in Hollywood: Visions of a New Architecture*, annotated edition (Cambridge: MIT Press, 1994), pp. 204–205.
9 Wright, *An Autobiography*, p. 242.
10 Wright, *The Natural House*, p. 89.
11 Frank Lloyd Wright, *Modern Architecture, Being the Kahn Lectures for 1930* (Princeton: Princeton University Press, 1931). Reprinted in Pfeiffer, ed., *The Essential Frank Lloyd Wright*, pp. 159-216.
12 Frank Lloyd Wright, "Away with the Realtor," *Esquire*, October, 1958.
13 Frank Lloyd Wright, *Washington Post*, sec. 2, October 26, 1938. Quoted in Robert Twombly, *Frank Lloyd Wright: His Life and His Architecture* (New York: John Wiley & Sons, 1979), p. 261.
14 Wright, *An Autobiography*, p. 242.
15 Tamir Klein, Rolf Siegwolf, and Christian Körner, "Below Ground Carbon Trade among Tall Trees in a Temperate Forest," *Science* 352, no. 6283 (April 15, 2016): pp. 342–344.

SECTION 6

上昇する建築と環境の向上

Elevating Environments

帝国ホテルでライトは、1890年代にシカゴで編み出された湿地の上に高層ビルを建てる浮き筏基礎に着想を得て、東京の砂地や地震に対応するための独創的な構造方法を考案した。彼は、ダンクマール・アドラーとルイス・サリヴァンの事務所で働いていた頃からこの技法に親しんでおり、生涯にわたって数々の高層ビルの設計に斬新な工法や構造技術を導入してきた。

ニューヨーク州バッファローのリライアンス・ビル(1890–95)[cat.no.1-7]、アドラー&サリヴァン事務所のギャランティ・ビル(1890–95)に倣って、ライトはラーキン・ビル(1902–06)[cat.nos.6-1~8]を、天窓のある高さ23mの吹き抜けを持つ垂直型オフィスとして設計した。わずか6階建てではあるが、巨大な動線コアを備えた四隅の量塊が垂直性を強調している。帝国ホテルでも用いられた片持ちコンクリート構造に続いて、彼は、内部の柱から片持ちで差し出された床スラブを持つ25階建てガラス張りの建築、シカゴのナショナル生命保険会社ビル計画案(1923–25)の設計を提案した。この建物は、1つの堅固な量塊となることを避け、4つの翼棟で構成されることによってオフィス内に十分な光を提供した。また1926年、摩天楼規制に関する彼の区画整理研究における高層開発の密度に対する批判を予見させるものであった。

ニューヨークのセント・マークス教区のアパートメントタワー計画案(1927–29)[cat.no.6-21]の設計では、樹木の基本構造に倣うタップルート〔主根〕構造という有機的概念を採用した。この15階建て高層マンションは、大都市の中で互いにひしめき合って密集しているのではなく、自然に囲まれて個々に独立して建っており、彼の考える建築とランドスケープを融合させたアメリカ文化、ユーソニアを表現している。タップルート構造は構造壁としての内部間仕切りをなくし、カーテンウォールの採用によって自然光を十分に取り込むことを可能とした。このタップルート構造は、ジョンソン・ワックス社の15階建て研究タワー(1943)[cat.nos.6-18,19]において実現した。エレベーター、階段、水まわりを含む構造コアは地中に16.5m伸び、木の根のような安定をもたらしている。セント・マークス教区のアパートメントタワー計画のビジョンを彼が最終的に実現したのは、オクラホマ州バートルズヴィルにある19階建てのプライス・タワー(1956)[cat.nos.6-22~24]においてであった。ライトはこのタワーを「密林から抜け出た樹」という愛称で呼んだ。

ライトのタワーはますます高さを増していった。帝国ホテルはプレイリー・ハウスが水平方向に延び広がったものと見ることもできるが、設計過程を示すドローイングには彼の垂直志向の高まりが表れている。ライトの帝国ホテルは1967年に解体され、三代目は東京の高層化を反映した高層ホテル建築となった。この動向は現在も引き継がれ、2036年には四代目となる新たな帝国ホテルの完成が予定されている。日本の若手建築家である田根剛のデザイン[cat.no.4-18n]は、ロジャース・レイシー・ホテル計画案[cat.nos.4-18l,18m]をはじめとするライトの高層建築を想起させる。テキサス州ダラスに計画された47階建てのロジャース・レイシー・ホテル計画案(1946-47)は、開放的なアトリウムからそびえ立つ輝くダイヤモンド・ガラス・パネルで覆われたタワーが特徴的であった。ライトはシカゴに戻り、タップルート構造を用いた50階建てのオフィスと住宅の複合ビル、ゴールデン・ビーコン・アパートメント・タワー計画案(1956–57)[cat.no.6-29]を発表した。ライトの高層建築への探求の頂点は、シカゴに建設されたダイヤモンド形の底面をもつマイル・ハイ・イリノイ計画案(1956)[cat.no.6-28]であった。528階建てとなるこのビルの高さは、エンパイアステートビル(102階建て)の4倍以上になり、エジプトのピラミッドやパリのエッフェル塔など、世界の名だたる巨大建造物を圧倒していたはずだ。マイル・ハイ・イリノイは、都市の中心部を外に向かって押し出すのではなく、上方に押し上げようとするものであり、また周辺に他の大型高層ビルを建てる必要性を減じるものであった。実際には実現しなかったが、ライトはユーソニアと未来のリビング・シティの象徴として、ユートピア・プロジェクトであるブロードエーカー・シティ構想[cat.nos.7-53~55]の緑豊かなランドスケープの中にこの建物を配したのである。

At the Imperial Hotel, Wright devised an ingenious structural solution to deal with the sandy soil and seismic nature of Tokyo that was inspired by the floating raft foundations invented in Chicago to construct skyscrapers atop marshy soil in the 1890s. Wright would have been familiar with this technique from his time working in the offices of Dankmar Adler and Louis Sullivan, and he pioneered novel engineering and structural techniques in numerous skyscraper designs throughout his career.

In counterpoint to the precedents of the Reliance Building (1890–95) [cat. no. 1-7] and Sullivan and Adler's Guaranty Building in Buffalo, NY (1890–95), Wright designed the Larkin Company Administration Building (1902–06) [cat. nos. 6-1~8] as a vertical office with soaring 23-meter-high skylit courtyard. While only six stories tall, its massing with monumental circulation cores at the four corners intensified its verticality. Following the use of a cantilevered concrete structure in the Imperial Hotel, Wright proposed the design of the National Life Insurance Company Building (project, 1925) in Chicago, a 25-story glazed volume with floor slabs cantilevered from internal columns. In eschewing a solid mass, the building's four wings facilitated ample light to penetrate offices and foreshadowed Wright's criticism of density in high-rise development in his zoning study of skyscraper regulation in 1926.

His design for St. Mark's Towers (project, 1927–29) [cat. no. 6-21] in New York City embraced the organic concept of the tap root, after the basic structure of a tree. This design for 15-story apartment towers expressed Wright's conception of Usonia, his vision of American culture that synthesized architecture and landscape, because Wright envisioned these towers would be freestanding and surrounded by nature rather than crowded together as in large cities. The tap root structure freed the building of load-bearing interior partitions with its curtain wall facilitating ample natural illumination. Wright finally realized his tap root structure in the 15-story SC Johnson Research Tower (1943) [cat. nos. 6-18, 19]. The structural core containing the building's elevator, stairs, and restrooms extended 16.5 meters into the ground to provide stability like the roots of a tree. Wright finally realized his vision for the Saint Mark's Tower project in the 19-story Price Tower [cat. nos. 6-22~24] in Bartlesville, Oklahoma (1956), which Wright nicknamed "the tree that escaped the crowded forest."

The height of Wright's towers grew increasingly taller. While the Imperial Hotel could be seen to extend the horizontal reach of the prairie house, the design process drawings illustrate the rise of Wright's vertical aspirations. When the Imperial Hotel was demolished in 1967, it was replaced with a high-rise hotel reflecting the increasingly vertical development of Tokyo. This trend continues today, with the construction of a fourth New Imperial Hotel slated to be completed by 2036. Designed by young Japanese architect Tsuyoshi Tane, his design [cat. no. 4-18n] recalls some of Wright's own skyscrapers, notably the Roger Lacy Hotel. Wright's 47-story Rogers Lacy Hotel (project, 1946–47) [cat. no. 4-18l, 18m] for Dallas, Texas, featured a glistening diamond glass panel clad tower rising out of an open atrium. Wright returned to Chicago to propose his 50-story Golden Beacon Apartment tower (project, 1956–57) [cat. no. 6-29], a mixed-use office and residential apartment building based on the tap root structure. The apex of Wright's pursuit of the skyscraper was his unbuilt Mile-High Illinois [cat. no. 6-28] diamond spire for Chicago (project, 1956). With 528 stories, it would have been more than four times the height of the Empire State Building (102 stories) and would have towered over the world's great monuments, such as the Pyramids of Egypt and the Eiffel Tower in Paris, France. The Mile-High Illinois sought to push the urban core upwards rather than outwards, alleviating the need for other large skyscrapers in the vicinity. Though never physically realized, Wright included it nestled in the verdant landscape of his utopian project, Broadacre City (project, 1929–35) [cat. nos. 7-53~55], as a symbol of Usonia and the future of the Living City.

[Ken Tadashi Oshima]

34 快適さと機能の追求

Pursuit of comfort and functionality in high-rise buildings

● ラーキン・ビル | Larkin Company Administration Building | ニューヨーク州バッファロー、1902-06年、オフィスビル | Buffalo, New York, 1902-06, office building

6-1
6-1

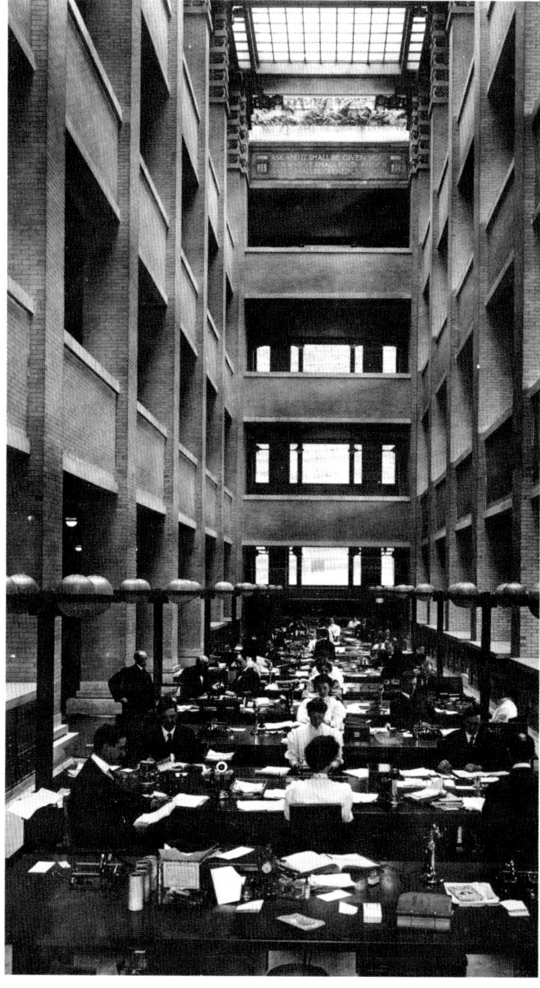

6-6

6-1 ライトのデザインによる椅子と机で執務するラーキン社社員『フランク・ロイド・ライト 竣工した建築』(ソフト・カバー版) | 著:フランク・ロイド・ライト、出版:エルンスト・ヴァスムート社 | 1911年
6-2 ラーキン・ビル(ニューヨーク州バッファロー)1902-06年 透視図 | フランク・ロイド・ライト | 1903年
6-4 第33葉a ラーキン・ビル、地階平面図および透視図『フランク・ロイド・ライトの建築と設計』| フランク・ロイド・ライト、出版:エルンスト・ヴァスムート社 | 1910年
6-6 ラーキン・ビル(ニューヨーク州バッファロー)1902-06年 内観、吹き抜け | 建築:フランク・ロイド・ライト | 撮影:1905年
6-7 ラーキン・ビル 椅子付き事務机 | デザイン:フランク・ロイド・ライト、製造:ヴァン・ドーン・アイアン・ワークス・カンパニー | 1904年頃
6-8 ラーキン・ビル 折りたたみ式サイドチェア | デザイン:フランク・ロイド・ライト、製造:ヴァン・ドーン・アイアン・ワークス・カンパニー | 1904年頃

6-1 View of Larkin Company clerks working at Frank Lloyd Wright-designed desk and chair. *Ausgeführte Bauten* (Executed Buildings). Frank Lloyd Wright, author. Ernst Wasmuth, publisher. 1911. Yutaka Mizukami Collection
6-2 Larkin Company Administration Building: Buffalo, New York. Project 1902-06. Perspective. Frank Lloyd Wright. 1903. Toyota Municipal Museum of Art
6-4 Plate XXXIIIa. Ground plan and Perspective of the Administration Building for the Larkin Company. *Ausgeführte Bauten und Entwürfe von Frank Lloyd Wright*. Frank Lloyd Wright. Ernst Wasmuth, publisher. 1910. Toyota Municipal Museum of Art
6-6 Larkin Company Administration Building, Buffalo, New York. Project, 1902-06. Interior view, atrium. Frank Lloyd Wright, architect. Photo: 1905. Project photographs, circa 1887-2008, The Frank Lloyd Wright Foundation Archives (The Museum of Modern Art | Avery Architectural & Fine Arts Library, Columbia University, New York)
6-7 Desk and Attached Chair from Larkin Company Administration Building. Frank Lloyd Wright, designer. Van Dorn Iron Works Company, manufacturer. c. 1904. Toyota Municipal Museum of Art
6-8 Folding Side Chair from Larkin Company Administration Building. Frank Lloyd Wright, designer. Van Dorn Iron Works Company, manufacturer. c. 1904. Toyota Municipal Museum of Art

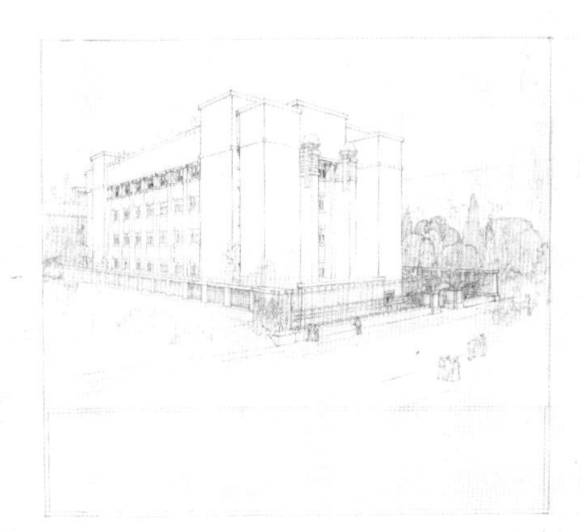

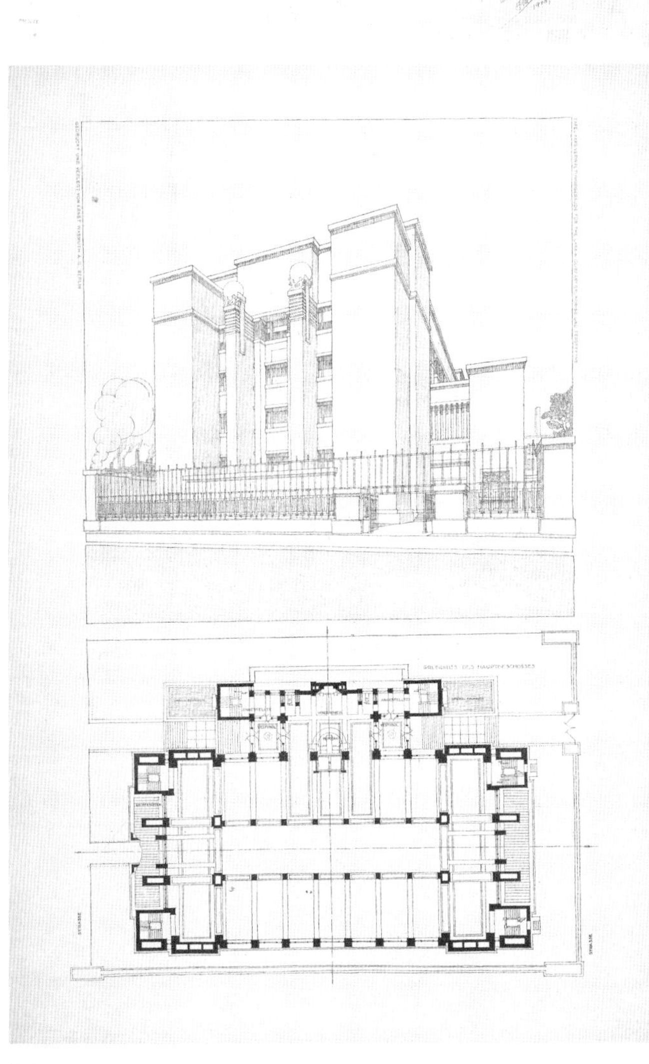

6-2
6-4

6-7

6-8

35 高層建築——樹状構造

Skyscraper with a structural core and cantilevered floors

● ジョンソン・ワックス・ビル | SC Johnson Administration Building

ウィスコンシン州ラシーン、1936–39年、1943–50年、オフィスビル | Racine, Wisconsin, 1936–39, 1943–50, office building

6-10

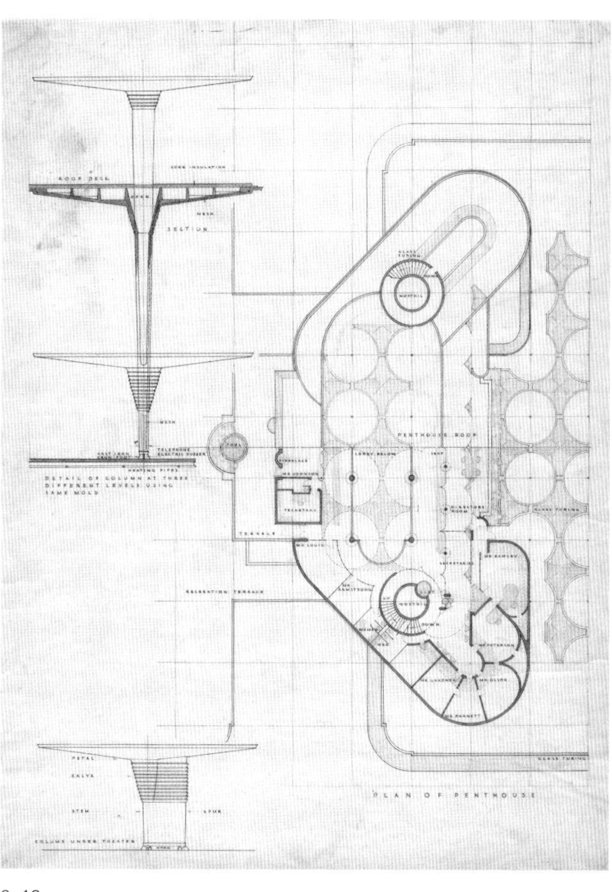

6-13

6-10　ジョンソン・ワックス・ビル（ウィスコンシン州ラシーン）1936–39年 樹状柱の耐荷重試験 | 建築：フランク・ロイド・ライト | 撮影：1937年
6-13　ジョンソン・ワックス・ビル（ウィスコンシン州ラシーン）1936–39年 柱詳細図および最上階平面 | フランク・ロイド・ライト
6-14　ジョンソン・ワックス・ビル（ウィスコンシン州ラシーン）1936–39年 本部棟 北西から中央執務室を見る | 建築：フランク・ロイド・ライト | 撮影：1954年頃
6-15　ジョンソン・ワックス・ビル（ウィスコンシン州ラシーン）1936–39年 本部棟 中央執務室 南を見る | 建築：フランク・ロイド・ライト | 撮影：2015年
6-16　ジョンソン・ワックス・ビル 本部棟 中央執務室の椅子 | デザイン：フランク・ロイド・ライト、製作：スチールケース・コーポレーション | 製作：1936年頃
6-17　ジョンソン・ワックス・ビル（ウィスコンシン州ラシーン）1936–39年 本部棟 中央執務室 ライトのデザインによる椅子と机で執務する社員 | 撮影：1939年

6-10 SC Johnson Administration Building, Racine, Wisconsin. Project, 1936–39. Stress test for columns. Frank Lloyd Wright, architect. Photo: 1937. Project photographs, circa 1887–2008, The Frank Lloyd Wright Foundation Archives (The Museum of Modern Art | Avery Architectural & Fine Arts Library, Columbia University, New York)

6-13 SC Johnson Administration Building, Racine, Wisconsin. Project, 1936–39. Detail of Column and Penthouse plan. Frank Lloyd Wright. The Frank Lloyd Wright Foundation Archives (The Museum of Modern Art | Avery Architectural & Fine Arts Library, Columbia University, New York)

6-14 View from the northwest of the Great Workroom in the SC Johnson Administration Building. Frank Lloyd Wright, architect. Photo: c. 1954. Courtesy of SC Johnson

6-15 View looking south into the Great Workroom of the SC Johnson Administration Building. Frank Lloyd Wright, architect. Photo: 2015. Courtesy of SC Johnson

6-16 Chair from the Great Workroom of the SC Johnson Administration Building. Frank Lloyd Wright, designer. Steelcase Corporation, manufacturer. c. 1936. Toyota Municipal Museum of Art

6-17 View of an SC Johnson clerk working at a Frank Lloyd Wright–designed desk and chair in the Great Workroom of the SC Johnson Administration Building. Photo: 1939. Courtesy of SC Johnson

6-16

6-14
6-17

6-15

● **ジョンソン・ワックス・研究タワー** | SC Johnson Research Tower | ウィスコンシン州ラシーン、1943年、研究施設 | Racine, Wisconsin, 1943, research facility

6-18

6-19

6-18 ジョンソン・ワックス・研究タワー(ウィスコンシン州ラシーン)1943年 | 建築:フランク・ロイド・ライト | 撮影:1954年頃
6-19 ジョンソン・ワックス・研究タワーで働く研究員 | 建築:フランク・ロイド・ライト | 撮影:1950年
6-21 セント・マークス教区のアパートメント・タワー計画案(ニューヨーク)1927–29年 鳥瞰透視図 | フランク・ロイド・ライト

6-18 SC Johnson Research Tower. Racine, Wisconsin. Project, 1943. Exterior view.
Frank Lloyd Wright, architect. Photo: c. 1954. Courtesy of SC Johnson
6-19 An SC Johnson scientist is shown working in the Frank Lloyd Wright-designed SC Johnson Research Tower.
Frank Lloyd Wright, architect. Photo: 1950. Courtesy of SC Johnson
6-21 St. Mark's Tower, New York. Unbuilt Project, 1927–29. Aerial perspective. Frank Lloyd Wright.
The Museum of Modern Art, New York. Jeffrey P. Klein Purchase Fund, Barbara Pine Purchase Fund, and Frederieke Taylor Purchase Fund, 1999

● セント・マークス教区のアパートメント・タワー計画案 | St. Mark's Tower, unbuilt project

ニューヨーク、1927–29年、集合住宅 | New York, 1927–29, residential

6-21

● **プライス・タワー** | Price Tower | オクラホマ州バートルズヴィル、1956年、オフィスビル、住宅 | Bartlesville, Oklahoma, 1956, office building/residential

6-23

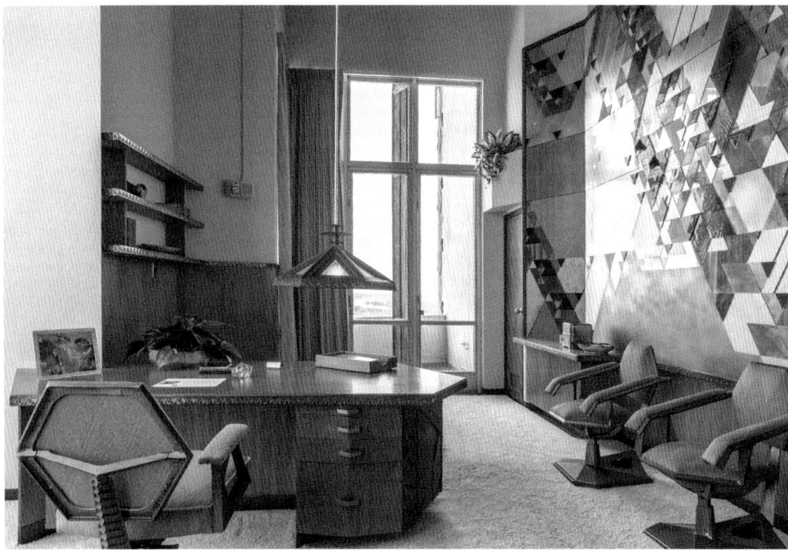

6-22
6-24

6-22 プライス・タワー(オクラホマ州バートルズヴィル)1956年 | 建築:フランク・ロイド・ライト、撮影:ダン・オドネル | 2008年
6-23 プライス・タワー(オクラホマ州バートルズヴィル)1956年 オフィス内観 | 建築:フランク・ロイド・ライト、撮影:ジョー・プライス | 1956年
6-24 プライス・タワー(オクラホマ州バートルズヴィル)1956年 19階エグゼクティブ・フロアのオフィスと居室内観 | 建築:フランク・ロイド・ライト、撮影:マーサ・アンブラー | 2017年

6-22 Price Company Tower, Bartlesville, Oklahoma. Project, 1956. Exterior. Frank Lloyd Wright, architect. Dan O'Donnell, photographer. Photo: 2008. Photo courtesy of Price Tower Art Center
6-23 Price Company Tower, Bartlesville, Oklahoma. Project, 1956. Interior view of the office. Frank Lloyd Wright, architect. Joe Price, photographer. Photo: 1956. Photo courtesy of Price Tower Art Center Joe Price PT collection
6-24 Price Company Tower, Bartlesville, Oklahoma. Project, 1956. Interior view of the 19th-floor executive office of H.C. Price and H.C. Price Company Corporate Apartment. Frank Lloyd Wright, architect. Martha Ambler, photographer. Photo: 2017. Photo courtesy of Price Tower Art Center

36 開けた大地に建つ高層建築——超高層ザ・マイル・ハイ・イリノイ

The Illinois: A mile-high skyscraper in a verdant landscape

● マイル・ハイ・イリノイ計画案 | The Mile-High Illinois, unbuilt project | イリノイ州シカゴ、1956年、オフィスビル | Chicago, Illinois, 1956, office building

6-28

6-30

6-31

● ゴールデン・ビーコン・アパートメント・タワー計画案 | Golden Beacon Apartment tower, unbuilt project

イリノイ州シカゴ、1956-57年、集合住宅 | Chicago, Illinois, 1956-57, residential

6-29

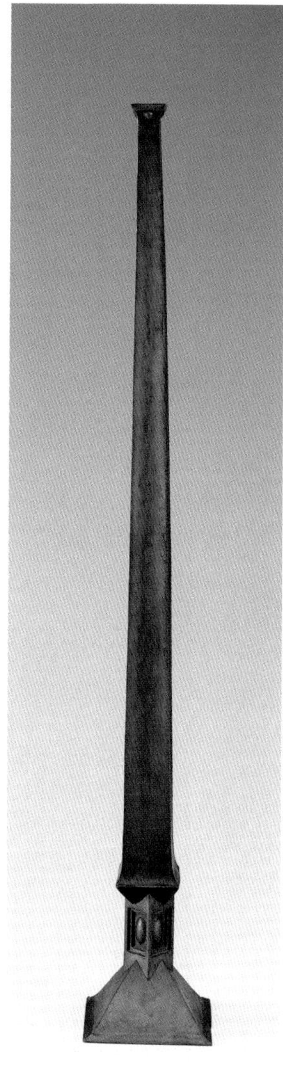

6-26

6-26 花入れ | デザイン：フランク・ロイド・ライト、製作：ジェームズ・A. ミラー＆ブラザー工房 | 1900年頃
6-28 マイル・ハイ・イリノイ計画案（イリノイ州シカゴ）1956年 透視図 | フランク・ロイド・ライト
6-29 ゴールデン・ビーコン・アパートメント・タワー計画案（イリノイ州シカゴ）1956-57年 透視図 | フランク・ロイド・ライト
6-30 マイル・ハイ・イリノイ計画案（イリノイ州シカゴ） フランク・ロイド・ライト記念日の記者発表会で公開されたプレゼンテーション | 撮影者不詳 | 1956年10月16日
6-31 マイル・ハイ・イリノイ計画案の図面を描くライト、タリアセンの設計室にて | 撮影：エドガー・オブマ | 1956年

6-26 Weed Holder. Frank Lloyd Wright, designer. Workshop of James A. Miller and Brother, maunfacturer. c. 1900. Toyota Municipal Museum of Art
6-28 The Mile-High Illinois, Chicago, Illinois. Unbuilt Project, 1956. Exterior perspective. Frank Lloyd Wright. The Frank Lloyd Wright Foundation Archives (The Museum of Modern Art | Avery Architectural & Fine Arts Library, Columbia University, New York)
6-29 Golden Beacon apartment tower for Charles Glore, Chicago, Illinois. Unbuilt Project, 1956-57. Exterior perspective. Frank Lloyd Wright. The Frank Lloyd Wright Foundation Archives (The Museum of Modern Art | Avery Architectural & Fine Arts Library, Columbia University, New York)
6-30 Exhibition Space for Frank Lloyd Wright Day at Sherman Hotel (Chicago, Illinois). Unveiling design for the Mile-High Illinois skyscraper at the October 16, 1956 Press Conference in Chicago. Photographer unidentified. Project photographs, circa 1887-2008, The Frank Lloyd Wright Foundation Archives (The Museum of Modern Art | Avery Architectural & Fine Arts Library, Columbia University, New York)
6-31 Frank Lloyd Wright at drafting table at Hillside, drawing the Mile-High Illinois. Edgar Obma, photographer. Photo: 1956. Personal and Taliesin Fellowship photographs, 1870s-2004, The Frank Lloyd Wright Foundation Archives (The Museum of Modern Art | Avery Architectural & Fine Arts Library, Columbia University, New York)

SECTION 7

多様な文化との邂逅

Wright and Global Cultures

7

自らの活動の範囲をアジア、ヨーロッパからラテンアメリカへとグローバルに広げていくなかで、ライトはさまざまな文化的要素を取り入れながら普遍的な構法、素材、装飾を追求していった。

帝国ホテルの仕事では、東洋と西洋の伝統を取り入れつつ両者の境界を「有機的に」解消し、その手法を他のプロジェクトでも実践していった。ライトが主宰するタリアセンの設計事務所はコスモポリタンな異文化の交流の場となり、建築家の土浦亀城・信子夫妻、リチャード・ノイトラ、エーリヒ・メンデルゾーンらがここで出会った[cat. nos. 7-6~8｜7-7と7-8は139頁に掲載]。

彼らはタリアセンのランドスケープのなかで共に暮らし働き、製図室で仕事上の交流にとどまらず、それぞれの国際的な文化背景や彼らを取り囲む美術やデザインの蒐集物に触発され、会話や音楽、食事を通じて社交した。美術や音楽といった互いの文化やそれぞれの個性を尊重することによって、個人的な絆が結ばれ言葉の壁を越えることができた。こうした多元的なつながりは、ノイトラが担当したゴードン・ストロング自動車体験娯楽施設とプラネタリウム計画案（メリーランド州シュガーローフ・マウンテン、1924–25）[cat. nos. 5-42, 43]のためのドローイングや、オランダの雑誌『ヴェンディンゲン』（1925）のライト特集号[cat. nos. 7-14~24]のための出版用ドローイングにも見てとることができる。さらにはアムステルダム会場を起点とするヨーロッパで最初のライトの作品展（1931）へと展開した[cat. nos. 7-29, 30]。

多様な文化へ向けられたライトの拡張する視野は、さらにネイティブ・アメリカンやメソ・アメリカンの文化、アフリカン・アメリカンの伝統に対する継続的な関心へと敷衍し、こうした文化的採用の根底にあるアメリカの社会と政治が抱える課題を幾分浮かび上がらせている。ナコマ・カントリー・クラブ計画案（ウィスコンシン州マディソン、1923–24）[cat. no. 7-47]は、ゴルフ文化と先住民の建築の実践を融合させたものである。一方でライトが南カリフォルニアに構えた設計スタジオ[cat. nos. 7-1, 2]では、その文化的風土のなかで、メソ・アメリカから太平洋対岸の日本から得たインスピレーションまでをも融合させた多様な地域的表現が形成された。

ライトが経験した世界への旅は、船や鉄道を用いたゆるやかな思索の時間を伴うものから始まったが、自動車や飛行機の利用は旅の時間を加速した。1937年に第1回全ソ連建築家会議への参加を目的としたライトのモスクワ訪問[cat. no. 7-51]は、ブロードエーカー・シティ構想[cat. no. 7-55]で表明された脱都市主義的な感情と、ソビエト連邦の反資本主義的信条との出合いとなった。1950年代にはライトは世界各地から学術栄誉賞を授与されたため、イギリス、ブラジル、メキシコを訪問し、地理上の到達範囲を広げた。

ライトのデザイン・モチーフがグローバルに展開されたその他の例として、遊び心ある円形のモチーフがある。これは帝国ホテルの食器デザイン[cat. no. 4-43]から、ゴード

1 この展覧会の名前はイタリア語では「フランク・ロイド・ライト作品展」であったが、ライトは「イタリア展」（The Italian Exhibition）と呼んでいた。その後「フランク・ロイド・ライト：生ける建築の60年」のタイトルで、1951–54年の3年間、ヨーロッパ各国と北アメリカを巡回した。Kathryn Smith, *Wright on Exhibit: Frank Lloyd Wright's Architectural Exhibitions*, (Princeton: Princeton University Press, 2017), pp. 237–238を参照のこと。

2 Maristella Casciato, "Wright and Italy: The Promise of Organic Architecture," *Frank Lloyd Wright: Europe and Beyond*, ed. Anthony Alofsin (Berkeley: University of California Press, 1999), pp. 93–95.

ン・ストロング自動車体験娯楽施設とプラネタリウム計画案やニューヨークのグッゲンハイム美術館(1943–59)[cat.no.5–45]、大バグダッド計画案(1957)[cat.no.7–52]まで各地で、そしてその後のデザインにも共鳴していった。

ライトのキュレーターとしての到達点は、1951年、イタリアのフィレンツェにある15世紀からのストロッツィ宮殿を利用した展示空間ラ・ストロッツィーナで開催された「生ける建築の60年」展[cat.no.7–44]であろう[1]。ブロードエーカー・シティ構想の巨大な模型が出品されたこの展覧会は、建築家の個展としては過去最大のものとなり、その後5年間にわたってヨーロッパと北米の会場を巡回した。ついでライトはイタリア建築の将来についての議論に深く関わることとなり、評論家のブルーノ・ゼヴィや建築家のカルロ・スカルパをはじめとする、イタリアの建築家や歴史家との関係を構築した[cat.no.7–45]。このことがきっかけとなり、ライトはヴェネチアのカナル・グランデに面したマシエリ記念学生会館計画(1951/52–55)[cat.no.7–36]の設計依頼を受けることとなった。スカルパが手がけたヴェネチア・ビエンナーレのジャルディーニ公園の「芸術の書館」(1950)と「ヴェネズエラ館」(1954–56)は、イタリアにおけるライト解釈の決定打となった。後にスカルパは第12回ミラノ・トリエンナーレのフランク・ロイド・ライト展(1960)の会場構成を担当する[2][cat.nos.7–41~43]。

ライトはアメリカの田園地帯に広がる生活とそこでの労働のラディカルな再構築として、1932年にブロードエーカー・シティ構想を提示した(1929–35)[cat.no.7–55]。この計画案は、世界的なパンデミックを経験し距離と分散の課題に取り組んだ現代世界にも共鳴する。テレコミュニケーション、自動車、飛行機といった近代技術は、1930年代に空間と時間の関係を再構築したが、今日の世界ではインターネットやドローンが「リビング・シティ」(いまを生きる社会)とは何かという根本的な問いを投げかける。ライトの計画案に鮮やかな色彩とディテールで生命を吹き込んだデイヴィッド・ロメロによるコンピューター・グラフィックス[cat.no.7–56]は、ブロードエーカー・シティ構想に内在する同時代性を示唆する。マイル・ハイ・イリノイ(1956)[cat.no.6–28]をはじめとする彼の画期的なランドマークは、小スケールのユーソニアン住宅とともに、あらゆる規模でユートピア社会を広げたいという理想を表す。ライトは自ら「永遠の変化の法則」を受け入れ、「私たちが望んでやまない成長とは、人類の過去の文明が築いて私たちに残してくれた叡智を、最終的に理解することにある。その間に、真理に沿ったとしても逆らったとしても、等しく真理に貢献することに慰められるのだ」と語っている[3]。リビング・シティ構想[cat.no.7–54]のビジョンの継続にライトが期待していたことは、創造的な魂をもつ社会であり、また自身の複層的なデザインがローカルとグローバルの両文脈のはざまで理解され続けることの重要性であった。

3 フランク・ロイド・ライト著、樋口清訳『テスタメント』(中央公論美術出版、2010)

Through the course of an increasingly global career spanning Asia, Europe, and Latin America, Wright embraced elements of multiple cultures in pursuing common construction methods, materials, and ornament. At the Imperial Hotel, Wright drew from eastern and western traditions, *organically* dissolving the boundaries between the two, a practice he would continue in other projects. Wright's own Taliesin studio served as a site of cross-cultural cosmopolitan encounters, including those between architects Kameki and Nobuko Tsuchiura, Richard Neutra, and Erich Mendelsohn. Living and working together in the Taliesin landscape, they experienced this interchange professionally in the drafting room as well as socially through conversations, music, and meals inspired by their respective international backgrounds and the surrounding collection of art and design [cat. nos. 7-6~8. For 7-7 and 7-8 see page 139]. Beyond any limitations of language, cultures of art, music, and individual character transcended barriers through personal bonds. These multi-dimensional links included the delineated drawings that Neutra made for the Gordon Strong Automotive Objective and Planetarium (project, Sugarloaf Mountain, Maryland, 1924–25) [cat. nos. 5-42, 43] and publication drawings for Wright's feature issues in the Dutch journal *Wendingen* (1925) [cat. nos. 7-14~24], followed by Wright's first European exhibition (1931) [cat. nos. 7-29, 30] in Amsterdam.

The breadth of this multi-cultural purview spanned Wright's ongoing interest in Native American and Mesoamerican cultures, as well as African American traditions, suggesting some of the social and political challenges in the United States underlying these cultural appropriations. The Nakoma Country Club (project, Madison, Wisconsin, 1923–24) [cat. no. 7-47] brought together the culture of golf with various indigenous building practices. By contrast, Wright's studio in the cultural climate of Southern California [cat. nos. 7-1, 2] shaped the wide range of regional expressions that fused inspirations from Mesoamerica and Japan on the Pacific Rim. While Wright's international travels were shaped by the contemplative pace of travel by ship and rail, their pace would be intensified by the automobile and airplane. Wright's trip to Soviet Russia to participate in the 1937 Conference of Architects in Moscow proved to be an encounter between Wright's anti-urban sentiments expressed in his Broadacre City vision [cat. no. 7-55] and Soviet anti-capitalist beliefs. Wright expanded his geographical reach in the 1950s with travel to the United Kingdom, Brazil, and Mexico, gaining academic honors worldwide. Other trajectories in global culture include the play of circular forms, found in Wright's design for the Imperial Hotel dinnerware [cat. no. 4-43], that would resonate with subsequent circular designs, from the Gordon Strong Automobile Objective [cat. no. 5-42], the Guggenheim Museum in New York (1943–59)

1 While the Italian title was "Mostra dell'Opera di Frank Lloyd Wright," Wright himself referred to it as "The Italian Exhibition." It subsequently became known as "Frank Lloyd Wright: 60 Years of Living Architecture" as it traveled for three years from 1951–54 around Europe and North America. Kathryn Smith, *Wright on Exhibit: Frank Lloyd Wright's Architectural Exhibitions*, (Princeton: Princeton University Press, 2017), 237–238.

2 Maristella Casciato, "Wright and Italy: The Promise of Organic Architecture," *Frank Lloyd Wright: Europe and Beyond*, ed. Anthony Alofsin (Berkeley: University of California Press, 1999), 93–95.

[cat. no. 5-45] and his Plan for Greater Baghdad (project, 1957) [cat. no. 7-52].

The apex of Wright's curatorial pursuits could be seen in his "Sixty Years of Living Architecture" exhibition [cat. no. 7-44] held in Florence, Italy, in 1951 at La Strozzina, a gallery housed in the fifteenth-century Palazzo Strozzi.[1] As the largest one-person show ever realized for an architect and featuring the massive model of Broadacre City, it traveled to venues throughout Europe and North America for the next five years. Wright was subsequently at the center of discussions of the future of Italian architecture and concretized relationships with architects and historians, including Bruno Zevi and Carlo Scarpa [cat. no. 7-45]. This also led to the commission for Wright to design Masieri Memorial student library and residence on the Grand Canal in Venice (project, 1951/52–55) [cat. no. 7-36]. Scarpa exercised the greatest influence on Wright's interpretation in Italy in his Pavilion of the Book of Art (1950) and the Venezuelan Pavilion (1954–56) at the Giardini di Castello at the Venice Biennale. Moreover, he would later design the 1960 Frank Lloyd Wright exhibition at the 12th Triennale di Milano [cat. nos. 7-41~43].[2]

While Wright first presented the concept of Broadacre City [cat. no. 7-55] in 1932 as a radical reimagining of living and working across the American countryside, it continues to have resonance in the contemporary world, addressing challenges of distancing and dispersal in the era of global pandemics. Modern technologies of telecommunications, automobiles, and airplanes had reshaped relationships of space and time in the 1930s, and today the world of the internet and drones continue to raise fundamental questions of what constitutes a "Living City." One can see the contemporaneity of Wright's Broadacre City in David Romero's renderings (2023) [cat. no. 7-56] brought to life in vivid color and detail. Wright's landmark projects, including the Mile-High Illinois (project, 1956) [cat. no. 6-28], are brought together with smaller-scale Usonian homes to bring Wright's ideal to the broader utopian society on all scales. Wright himself embraced an "eternal law of change," noting, "Growth, our best hope, consists in understanding at last what other civilizations have only known about and left to us, ourselves comforted meantime by the realization that all one does either for or against Truth serves it equally well."[3] Wright fundamentally looked to his continuing vision of the Living City [cat. no. 7-54] to advocate for a society with a creative soul and continued importance in understanding the complexity of his designs between local and global contexts.

[Ken Tadashi Oshima]

3 Frank Lloyd Wright, "A Testament" in Frank Lloyd Wright: Writings and Buildings: Selected by Edgar Kaufmann and Ben Raeburn (New York: Meridian Books, 1960), p. 439.

ライトへ注がれた同時代の目

Wright's reputation among his contemporaries

+ 土浦亀城・信子 帝国ホテルでの協力を経て

Kameki and Nobuko Tsuchiura: After cooperating at the Imperial Hotel

7-1

7-2

7-10

7-6

7-5

7-1 ハーパー・アヴェニュー(カリフォルニア州、西ハリウッド)のライトの事務所にて 左から:ウィル・スミス、土浦信子、ハリー・ウルフ「幸せな日々」| 撮影者不詳 | 1923-24年
7-2 ハーパー・アヴェニュー(カリフォルニア州、西ハリウッド)のライトの事務所での食事 左から:ハリー・ウルフ、土浦信子、ウィル・スミス | 撮影:土浦亀城 | 1923-24年
7-5 土浦亀城、信子夫妻とウィル・スミス ミッション・サンファン・カピストラーノにて | 撮影者不詳 | 1923-24年
7-6 タリアセンのスタジオ(左から:ライト、土浦亀城、リチャード・ノイトラ、ヴェルナー・モーザー、土浦信子) 土浦亀城、信子夫妻のアルバム「Taliesin Life(1)」| 撮影:1924年頃
7-10 フランク・ロイド・ライトとエーリヒ・メンデルゾーン 土浦亀城、信子夫妻のアルバム「Taliesin Life(1)」| 撮影:1924年

7-1 William E. Smith, Nobuko Tsuchiura and Harry Wolfe at the Harper Avenue Studio, West Hollywood: "Happy Days." Photographer unidentified. Photo: c. 1923-24. Personal and Taliesin Fellowship photographs, 1870s-2004, The Frank Lloyd Wright Foundation Archives (The Museum of Modern Art | Avery Architectural & Fine Arts Library, Columbia University, New York)
7-2 Harry Wolfe, Nobuko Tsuchiura, and William E. Smith dining at Harper Avenue studio, West Hollywood. Kameki Tsuchiura, photographer. Photo: c. 1923-24. Personal and Taliesin Fellowship photographs, 1870s-2004, The Frank Lloyd Wright Foundation Archives (The Museum of Modern Art | Avery Architectural & Fine Arts Library, Columbia University, New York)
7-5 Nobuko Tsuchiura, Kameki Tsuchiura, and William E. Smith at San Juan Capistrano Mission. Photographer unidentified. Photo: c. 1923-24. Personal and Taliesin Fellowship photographs, 1870s-2004, The Frank Lloyd Wright Foundation Archives (The Museum of Modern Art | Avery Architectural & Fine Arts Library, Columbia University, New York)
7-6 Frank Lloyd Wright and staff at Taliesin studio. From left: Wright, Kameki Tsuchiura, Richard Neutra, Werner Moser and Nobuko Tsuchiura. Photo: c. 1924. Imperial Hotel
7-10 Frank Lloyd Wright and Erich Mendelsohn. Tsuchiura album "Taliesin Life"(1). Photo: 1924. TSUCHIURA Kameki Archives

37 ライトへ注がれた同時代の目

Wright's reputation among his contemporaries

オランダ前衛との交流 | Relationship with the Dutch avant-garde

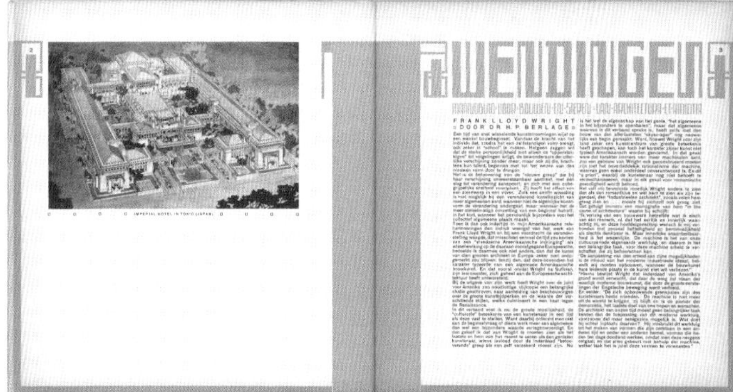

7-14

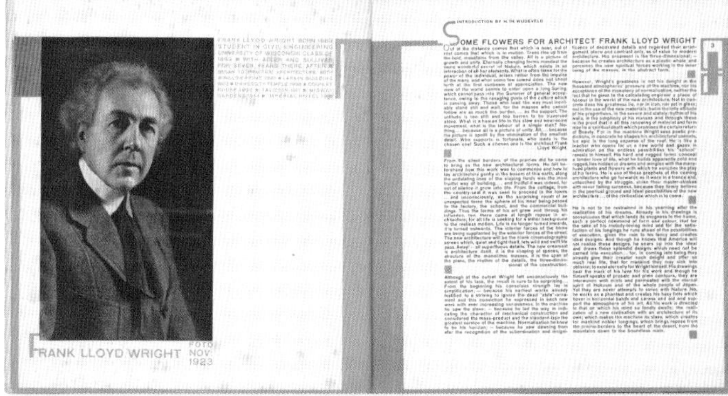

7-15

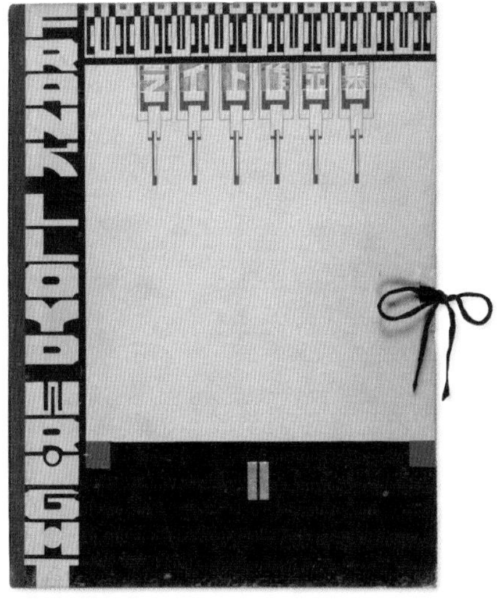

7-24

7-17

7-14 『ヴェンディンゲン』1921年4巻11号(表紙デザイン:エル・リシツキー) | 著:フランク・ロイド・ライト、ヘンドリクス・ベルラーヘ、出版:ホーヘ・ブリュッヘ&C.A. ミース社 | 1922年
7-15 『ヴェンディンゲン』1925年7巻3号 | 著:フランク・ロイド・ライト、H. ヴェイデフェルト、出版:ホーヘ・ブリュッヘ&C.A. ミース社 | 1925年
7-17 『ヴェンディンゲン』1925年7巻5号 | 著:フランク・ロイド・ライト、ルイス・マンフォード、出版:ホーヘ・ブリュッヘ&C.A. ミース社 | 1926年
7-24 『フランク・ロイド・ライト作品集II』| 著:フランク・ロイド・ライト、ヤーコブ・アウト、出版:洪洋社 | 1926年

7-14 *Wendingen*, vol. 4-11, 1921. Frank Lloyd Wright and H.P. Bergale, authors.
Hooge Brug and C.A. Mees, publisher. 1922. Nakanoshima Museum of Art Osaka
7-15 *Wendingen*, vol. 7-3, 1925. Frank Lloyd Wright and H. Wijdeveld, authors.
Hooge Brug and C.A. Mees, publisher. 1925. Nakanoshima Museum of Art Osaka
7-17 *Wendingen*, vol. 7-5, 1925. Frank Lloyd Wright and Louis Mumford, authors.
Hooge Brug and C.A. Mees, publisher. 1926. Nakanoshima Museum of Art Osaka
7-24 *Frank Lloyd Wright Sakuhin-shu (Works of Frank Lloyd Wright) volume 2.* Frank Lloyd Wright and J.J.P. Oud, authors. Koyo-sha, publisher. 1926

37 ライトへ注がれた同時代の目

Wright's reputation among his contemporaries

+ 各国で開かれたライト作品展 | European touring show

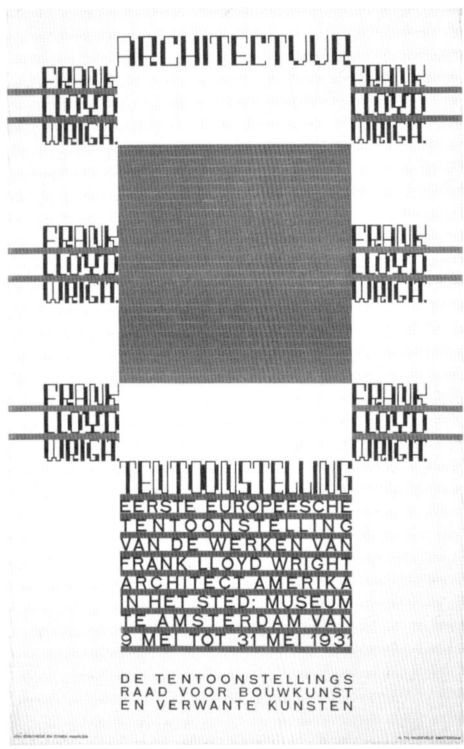

7-29
7-30

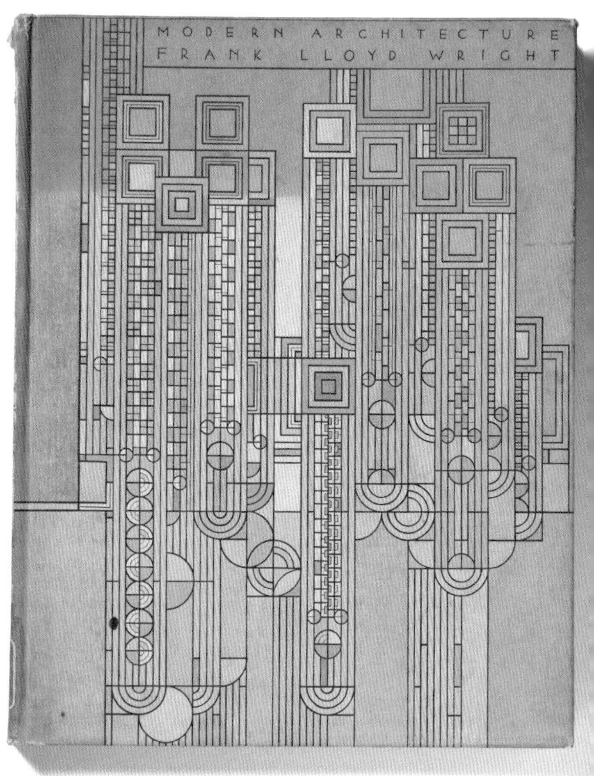

7-28

7-28 『近代建築』プリンストン大学におけるライトの連続講座の記録 | 著:フランク・ロイド・ライト、出版:オックスフォード大学出版(プリンストン大学出版) | 1931年
7-29 ポスター「フランク・ロイド・ライトの建築1893-1931年」展 | デザイン:ヘンドリクス・ヴェイデフェルト | 1931年
7-30 「フランク・ロイド・ライトの建築1893-1931年」展、アムステルダム市立美術館にて エントランスの装飾 | 撮影者不詳 | 1931年

7-28 *Modern Architecture. Being The Kahn Lectures For 1930*. Frank Lloyd Wright, author. Princeton university press, publisher. 1931. Tokyo City University, The KURATA Chikatada Archive
7-29 Poster. Architecture of Frank Lloyd Wright exhibition. Hendricus Theodorus Wijdeveld, designer. 1931. Toyota Municipal Museum of Art
7-30 The Work of Frank Lloyd Wright, 1893-1931 Exhibition at the Stedelijk Museum, Amsterdam. Photographer unidentified. Photo: 1931. Project photographs, circa 1887-2008, The Frank Lloyd Wright Foundation Archives
(The Museum of Modern Art | Avery Architectural & Fine Arts Library, Columbia University, New York)

ライトへ注がれた同時代の目

Wright's reputation among his contemporaries

アルヴァ・アアルト　北欧モダニズムとの交流 | Alvar Aalto: Relationship with Scandinavian Modernism

7-31
7-32

MASSACHUSETTS INSTITUTE OF TECHNOLOGY
SCHOOL OF ARCHITECTURE AND PLANNING
CAMBRIDGE 39, MASSACHUSETTS

December 13, 1945

Mr. Frank Lloyd Wright
Talieson
Green Spring, Wisconsin

Dear Frank:

Words cannot express how very much the visit to Talieson has meant to me -- both in head and heart reactions.

But I will say this -- if it is acceptable to you, I shall immediately make arrangements to take my boy out of the Technical University in Helsinki where he is taking the combined studies of Civil Engineering and Architecture and will send him to you by next summer or the following autumn. Will you please let me know if this will be acceptable to you.

I am so sorry that I had to dash for the train at Minneapolis and had no opportunity to bid you farewell.

My best regards to Madam Wright.

With best wishes of the Holiday Season for you and yours,

Sincerely,

Aalvar Aalto/dp

7-33　1945.12.13
ウィスコンシン州スプリンググリーン
タリアセン
フランク・ロイド・ライト様

親愛なるフランク

タリアセンへの訪問が私にとってどれほど大きな意味を持ったものであったか、言葉では言い表せません。頭にも心にも刺激を受けました。

しかし、これだけは申し上げておきたいのです。もしあなたが受け入れてくださるのなら、ヘルシンキ工科大学で土木工学と建築学の両方を学んでいる私の息子を直ちに引き取り、タリアセンで学ばせるため、来年の夏か、秋までにはあなたのもとに送り届けるよう手配したいと存じますが、よろしいでしょうか。

ミネアポリスでは、駆け足で列車に乗らなければならず、あなたにお別れを言う機会がなかったこと、本当に残念でした。

マダム・ライトにどうぞよろしくお伝えください。

良い休暇をおすごしください。

心より
アルヴァ・アアルト

7-31　アルヴァ・アアルト、長女ヨハナと長男ハミルカル「落水荘」のゲストハウスにて | 撮影：アイノ・アアルト | 1939年
7-32　アルヴァ・アアルトの長女ヨハナと長男ハミルカル「落水荘」のゲストハウスにて | 撮影：アイノ・アアルト | 1939年
7-33　アルヴァ・アアルトからフランク・ロイド・ライトに宛てた手紙 | アルヴァ・アアルト | 1945年12月13日

7-31　Alvar Aalto and his children, Johanna and Hamilkar at the Fallingwater (Edgar J. Kaufmann House) Guesthouse, Mill Run, Pennsylvania. Aino Aalto, photographer. Photo: 1939. Courtesy of Alvar Aalto Museum
7-32　Alvar Aalto's children, Johanna and Hamilkar at the Fallingwater (Edgar J. Kaufmann House) Guesthouse, Mill Run, Pennsylvania. Aino Aalto, photographer. Photo: 1939. Courtesy of Alvar Aalto Museum
7-33　Alvar Aalto, letter to Frank Lloyd Wright, 13 Dec 1945. Alvar Aalto. Courtesy of Alvar Aalto Museum

38 ライトとイタリア
Wright and Italy

+ 1910年のイタリア体験 | Experiences from the 1910 trip to Italy

7-34

7-35

7-34 ヴェルデ通りの眺望 | 撮影:テイラー・A. ウーレイ | 1910年
7-35 ヴェネツィアの運河沿いの館 | 撮影:テイラー・A. ウーレイ | 1910年

7-34 Viale Verde, street scene. Taylor A. Woolley, photographer. Photo: 1910. Personal and Taliesin Fellowship photographs, 1870s–2004, The Frank Lloyd Wright Foundation Archives (The Museum of Modern Art | Avery Architectural & Fine Arts Library, Columbia University, New York)
7-35 View of Venetian palazzo from canal. Taylor A. Woolley, photographer. Photo: 1910. Personal and Taliesin Fellowship photographs, 1870s–2004, The Frank Lloyd Wright Foundation Archives (The Museum of Modern Art | Avery Architectural & Fine Arts Library, Columbia University, New York)

38 ライトとイタリア
Wright and Italy

+ マシエリ記念学生会館とカルロ・スカルパ | Masieri Memorial and Carlo Scarpa

● **マシエリ記念学生会館計画案** | Masieri Memorial students' library and residence, unbuilt project
イタリア、ヴェネツィア、1951/1952-55年、教育施設 | Venice, Italy, 1951/1952-55, educational

7-36

7-36 マシエリ記念学生会館計画案(イタリア、ヴェネツィア)1951/1952-55年 透視図 | フランク・ロイド・ライト

7-36 Masieri Memorial students' library and residence, Venice, Italy. Unbuilt Project, 1951/1952-55. Exterior perspective. Frank Lloyd Wright. The Frank Lloyd Wright Foundation Archives (The Museum of Modern Art | Avery Architectural & Fine Arts Library, Columbia University, New York)

7-44
7-45

7-38
7-39
7-40

7-38 カルロ・スカルパによるマシエリ記念館(イタリア、ヴェネツィア)1952-83年 カナル・グランデからの全景(左の建物)
建築:カルロ・スカルパ、フランカ・セミ、撮影:ジョン・ヴォルパト | 2016年

7-39 カルロ・スカルパによるマシエリ記念館(イタリア、ヴェネツィア)1952-83年 内観、カナル・グランデを見る
建築:カルロ・スカルパ、フランカ・セミ、撮影:ジョン・ヴォルパト | 2016年

7-40 カルロ・スカルパによるマシエリ記念館(イタリア、ヴェネツィア)1952-83年 2階ラウンジ内観
建築:カルロ・スカルパ、フランカ・セミ、撮影:ジョン・ヴォルパト | 2016年

7-44 「生ける建築の60年」展 ストロッツィ宮(フィレンツェ)にて 左から:カルロ・スカルパ、アンジェロ・マシエリ、フランク・ロイド・ライト | 撮影:フォト・レヴィ | 1951年

7-45 フランク・ロイド・ライトとカルロ・スカルパ他、ヴェネツィア、サン・マルコ広場ドゥカーレ宮殿前にて | 撮影者不詳 | 1951年

7-38 Fondazione Angelo Masieri, Project 1952-83. Exterior view from the Grand Canal. Carlo Scarpa and Franca Semi, architects. John Volpato, photographer. Photo: 2016. Courtesy of Fondazione Angelo Masieri, Heritage Asset Management, Galerie Negropontes

7-39 Fondazione Angelo Masieri, Project 1952-83. Ground floor, Interior view to the Grand Canal. Carlo Scarpa and Franca Semi, architects. John Volpato, photographer. Photo: 2016. Courtesy of Fondazione Angelo Masieri, Heritage Asset Management, Galerie Negropontes

7-40 Fondazione Angelo Masieri, Project 1952-84. Interior view to the second floor lounge area. Carlo Scarpa and Franca Semi, architects. John Volpato, photographer. Photo: 2016. Courtesy of Fondazione Angelo Masieri, Heritage Asset Management, Galerie Negropontes

7-44 Frank Lloyd Wright with Carlo Scarpa and Angelo Masieri at Palazzo Strozzi, Florence. Foto Levi, photographer. Photo: 1951.
Personal and Taliesin Fellowship photographs, 1870s-2004, The Frank Lloyd Wright Foundation Archives
(The Museum of Modern Art | Avery Architectural & Fine Arts Library, Columbia University, New York)

7-45 Frank Lloyd Wright with Carlo Scarpa and others outside Doge's Palace, Venice. Photographer unidentified. Photo: 1951.
Personal and Taliesin Fellowship photographs, 1870s-2004, The Frank Lloyd Wright Foundation Archives
(The Museum of Modern Art | Avery Architectural & Fine Arts Library, Columbia University, New York)

7-42

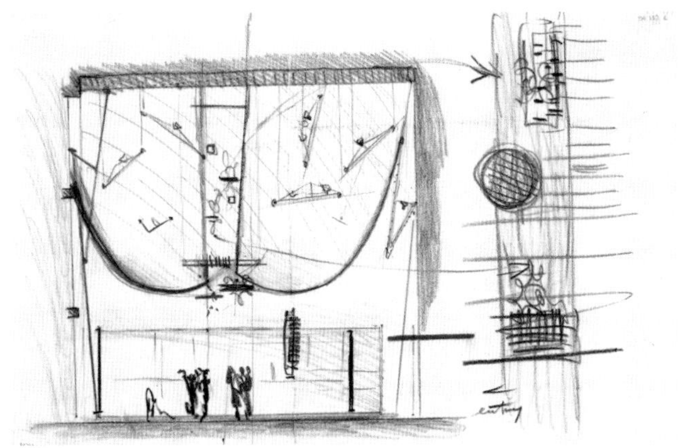

7-41

7-43

7-41 第12回ミラノ・トリエンナーレにおけるフランク・ロイド・ライト回顧展、会場構成カルロ・スカルパ 断面図 | カルロ・スカルパ | 1960年
7-42 第12回ミラノ・トリエンナーレにおけるフランク・ロイド・ライト回顧展、会場構成カルロ・スカルパ | 撮影:1960年
7-43 第12回ミラノ・トリエンナーレにおけるフランク・ロイド・ライト回顧展、会場構成カルロ・スカルパ | 撮影:1960年

7-41 Frank Lloyd Wright exhibition at the XII Milan Triennial. Project, 1960. Section. Carlo Scarpa, designer. 1960. MAXXI Museo nazionale delle arti del XXI secolo, Rome. MAXXI Architettura Collection, Carlo Scarpa Archive
7-42 Frank Lloyd Wright exhibition at the XII Milan Triennial. Project, 1960. Interior view. Carlo Scarpa, architect. Photo: 1960. MAXXI Museo nazionale delle arti del XXI secolo, Rome. MAXXI Architettura Collection, Carlo Scarpa Archive
7-43 Frank Lloyd Wright exhibition at the XII Milan Triennale, Project 1960. Interior view. Carlo Scarpa, architect. Photo: 1960. MAXXI Museo nazionale delle arti del XXI secolo, Rome. MAXXI Architettura Collection, Carlo Scarpa Archive

世界に向けたライトの目

Wright's gaze on the world

アメリカ先住民文化への関心 | Interest in Native American cultures

● ナコマ・カントリー・クラブ計画案 | Nakoma Country Club, unbuilt project

ウィスコンシン州マディソン、1923-24年、娯楽施設 | Madison, Wisconsin, 1923-24, recreational

7-47

7-46

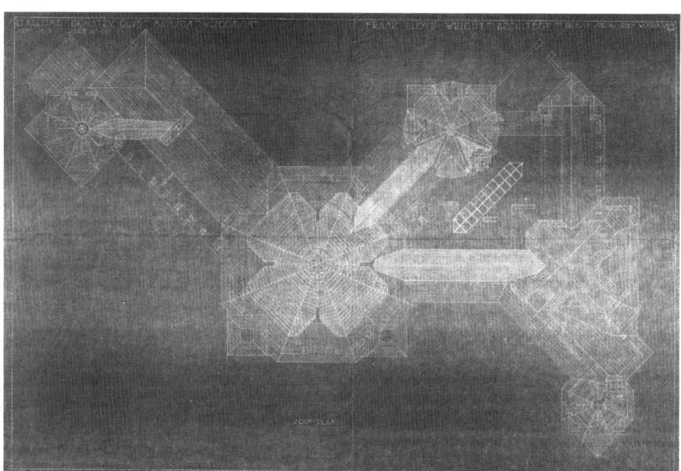

7-48

7-46 フランク・ロイド・ライト自邸とスタジオ(イリノイ州オークパーク)1889–1911年 主寝室内観 北側壁面にオルランド・ジャンニーニによる壁画が見える
建築:フランク・ロイド・ライト、撮影:ジェームズ・コールフィールド | 2013年

7-47 ナコマ・カントリー・クラブ計画案(ウィスコンシン州マディソン)1923–24年 北東から見た外観 | フランク・ロイド・ライト

7-48 ナコマ・カントリー・クラブ計画案(ウィスコンシン州マディソン)1923–24年 屋根伏図 | フランク・ロイド・ライト | 1924年

7-46 Frank Lloyd Wright House and Studio, Oak Park, Illinois. Project, 1889–1911. Bedroom with a northern view of the wall mural by Orlando Giannini. Frank Lloyd Wright, architect. James Caulfield, photographer. Photo: 2013

7-47 Nakoma Country Club, Madison, Wisconsin. Unbuilt Project, 1923–24. View from Northeast. Frank Lloyd Wright. The Frank Lloyd Wright Foundation Archives (The Museum of Modern Art | Avery Architectural & Fine Arts Library, Columbia University, New York)

7-48 Nakoma Country Club, Madison, Wisconsin. Unbuilt Project, 1923–24. Roof Plan. Frank Lloyd Wright. 1924. TSUCHIURA Kameki Archives

39 世界に向けたライトの目

Wright's gaze on the world

旅するライト | Wright on the move

7-49

7-50

7-51

7-49 飛行機の前のフランク・ロイド・ライト | 撮影者、撮影年不詳
7-50 ポートメイリオンの創設者、建築家クラフ・ウィリアムズ・エリスと歩くフランク・ロイド・ライト | 撮影：ニュース・クロニクル社マンチェスター | 1956年
7-51 アルキン夫妻とフランク・ロイド・ライト、ロシアにて | 撮影者不詳 | 1937年

7-49 Frank Lloyd Wright with airplane. Photographer unidentified. undated. Edgar Tafel architectural records and papers, 1919-2005, Avery Architectural & Fine Arts Library, Columbia University

7-50 Frank Lloyd Wright and Clough Williams-Ellis walking through Portmeirion village in Wales. News Chronicle, Manchester, photographer. Photo: 1956. Personal and Taliesin Fellowship photographs, 1870s-2004, The Frank Lloyd Wright Foundation Archives (The Museum of Modern Art | Avery Architectural & Fine Arts Library, Columbia University, New York)

7-51 Frank Lloyd Wright with Mr. and Mrs. Arkin in Russia. Photographer unidentified. Photo: 1937. Personal and Taliesin Fellowship photographs, 1870s-2004, The Frank Lloyd Wright Foundation Archives (The Museum of Modern Art | Avery Architectural & Fine Arts Library, Columbia University, New York)

39 世界に向けたライトの目

Wright's gaze on the world

イスラム文化圏への提案 | Proposals for Islamic Culture

● **大バグダッド計画案** | Plan for Greater Baghdad, unbuilt project | イラク、バグダッド、1957年、都市計画 | Baghdad, Iraq, 1957, urban planning

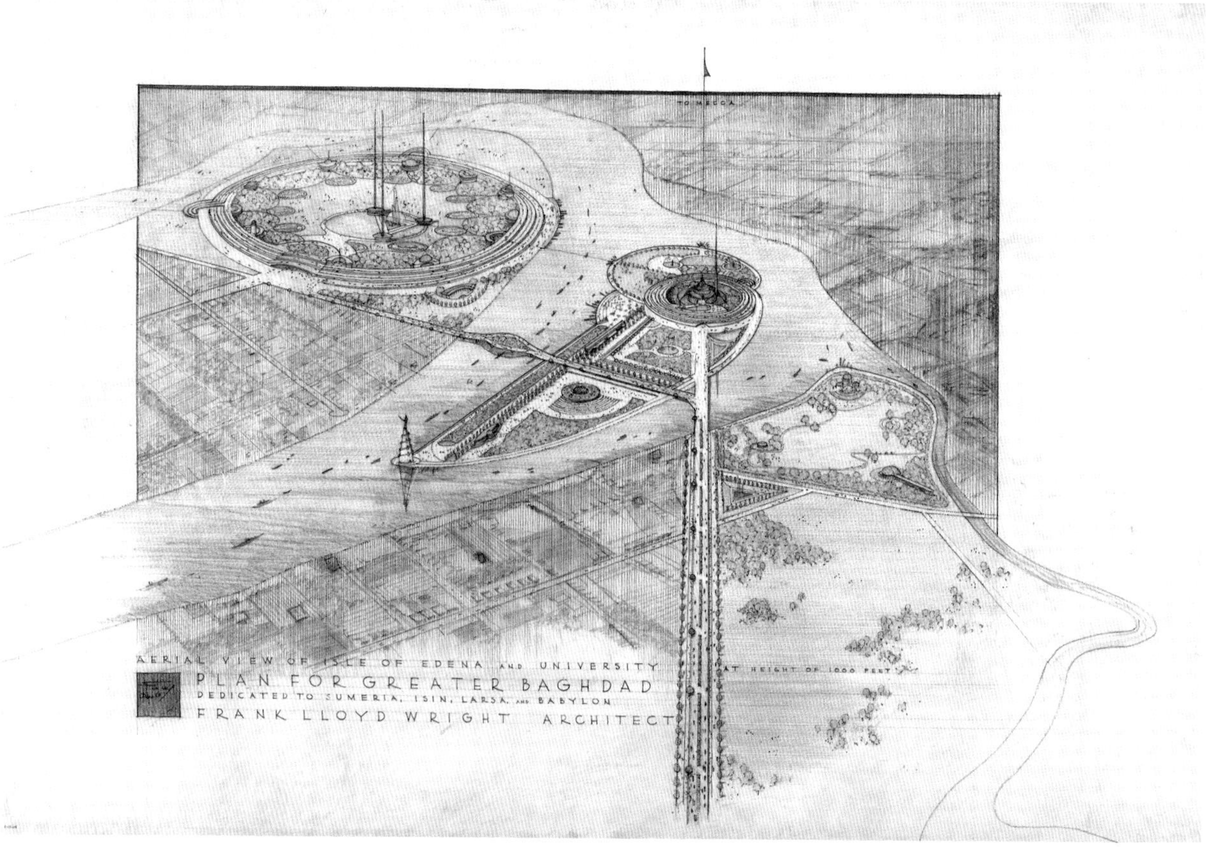

7-52

7-52　大バグダッド計画案（イラク、バグダッド）1957年 鳥瞰透視図 北から文化センターと大学をのぞむ | フランク・ロイド・ライト
7-53　『消えゆく都市』| 著：フランク・ロイド・ライト、出版：W.F. ペイソン社 | 1932年
7-54　リヴィング・シティ構想、1958年 鳥瞰透視図 | フランク・ロイド・ライト
7-55　展覧会に出品されたブロードエーカー・シティ構想の模型 | 構想：フランク・ロイド・ライト、撮影：ロイ・ピーターソン | 1934年

7-52　Plan for Greater Baghdad, Baghdad, Iraq. Unbuilt Project, 1957. Aerial perspective of the cultural center and university from the north. Frank Lloyd Wright. The Frank Lloyd Wright Foundation Archives (The Museum of Modern Art | Avery Architectural & Fine Arts Library, Columbia University, New York)
7-53　*The Disappearing City*. Frank Lloyd Wright, author. W. F. Payson, publisher. 1932. Gen Endo Collection
7-54　Living City. Unbuilt Project, 1958. Aerial perspective. Frank Lloyd Wright. The Frank Lloyd Wright Foundation Archives (The Museum of Modern Art | Avery Architectural & Fine Arts Library, Columbia University, New York)
7-55　Broadacre City. Master Plan, Unbuilt Project. View of model. Frank Lloyd Wright, architect. Roy Petersen, photographer. Photo: 1934. Project photographs, circa 1887–2008, The Frank Lloyd Wright Foundation Archives (The Museum of Modern Art | Avery Architectural & Fine Arts Library, Columbia University, New York)

40 未来へ向けた目：ブロードエーカー・シティ構想

Visions for the future: Broadacre City plan

- **リヴィング・シティ構想** | Living City, unbuilt project | 1958年、都市計画 | 1958, urban planning
- **ブロードエーカー・シティ構想** | Broadacre City, unbuilt project | 1929–35年、都市計画 | 1929–35, urban planning

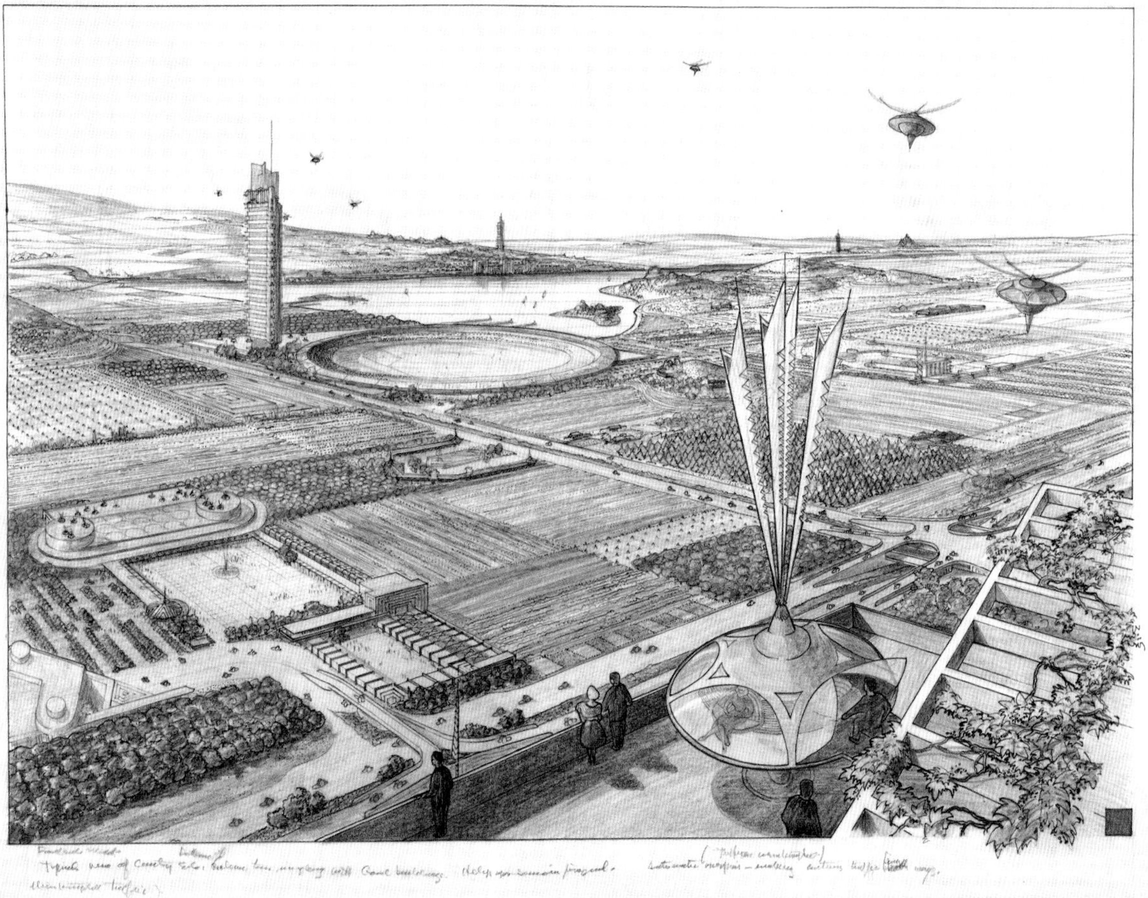

7-54

7-53

7-55

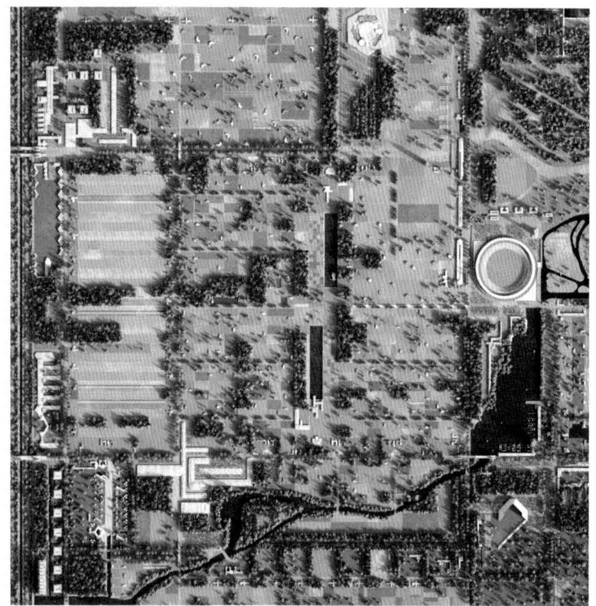

7-56

41 フランク・ロイド・ライトとの対話
Conversation with Frank Lloyd Wright

7-58

7-56 映像インスタレーション フランク・ロイド・ライトのブロードエーカー・シティ構想に基づくCGアニメーション
建築、構想：フランク・ロイド・ライト、制作：ディヴィッド・ロメロ、映像投影システム・インスタレーション設計：八嶋有司 | 2023年
7-58 フランク・ロイド・ライト、タリアセン・ウェストにて | 撮影者不詳 | 1954年

7-56 CG Animation based on Frank Lloyd Wright Broadacre City. Frank Lloyd Wright, architect.
David Romero, creator. Yushi Yashima for projection and installation. 2023
7-58 Frank Lloyd Wright at Taliesin West. Photographer unidentified. Photo: 1954. Personal and Taliesin Fellowship photographs, 1870s–2004, The Frank Lloyd Wright Foundation Archives (The Museum of Modern Art | Avery Architectural & Fine Arts Library, Columbia University, New York)

帝国ホテル・ライト館から新本館へ

田根 剛

遠い東の果ての島国。エジソンが白熱球を発明してまだ間もない頃、広大な大陸から広い大洋を渡り、幾日もの漆黒の闇夜を越え、陽が沈んでいく遠い海の水平線の果てを眺めながら、未知なる島国に向かって、建築家フランク・ロイド・ライトは1905年に日本を初めて訪れた。そして再び、1913年に帝国ホテルの建築家として再訪した。

建築家フランク・ロイド・ライト

ひとりの建築家を語るとき、その建築家を信じ、何と向き合い、何に葛藤をして、何か得て、何を失い、そこから何を学び、そして人生を終えたのか、それは誰にも知る由はない。F.L.ライトはアメリカの大らかな田園風景の大地、ウィスコンシンを原風景として生まれ育った建築家だ。建築家として拠点を幾度となく変え、失墜のどん底から何度も返り咲き、そしてひとりの人生に与えられた時間を超越した劇的な人生を送った。生涯1000以上のプロジェクトを手がけ、532の建物を実現した。歴史家はライトを近代建築の巨匠のひとりに祭り上げ、批評家はライトのスキャンダルを逆手に時代遅れの建築家として引き摺り下ろそうとしてきた。その記念碑的な建築や人生のスキャンダルの連続が、ライトをヒロイスティックに神格化する。

2023年7月、私は初めてシカゴを訪れ、ライトの建築を見てまわった。1905–08年のユニティ・テンプルはコンクリート造による地域コミュニティ施設、1905年のルッカリー・ビル改装はイタリア・カララ大理石を施した商業施設、1908–10年のロビー邸は極端に引き延ばされたプレイリー・スタイルを代表する邸宅。それらが数年の間のほぼ同時期の設計でありながら、異なる用途、異なる規模、異なる構造、素材、ディテールで構成される。またオークパーク近郊の自邸とスタジオ。その周辺には、約30件近い初期の住宅群が点在し、それぞれの住宅は特徴的で、それでいてひとつとして同じ建物がない。そしてその後のライトの生活と創作の場であり、フェローシップの学生と共に過ごしたタリアセンは、ウィスコンシンの穏やかな丘陵地に建つタリアセンの建築群、丘の上に建物をつくらず、それぞれはどれも独創的でありながら、その土地と深く呼応した建築であることに驚嘆する。ライトはスタイルをもたない。建築家のスタイルを押し付けるのではなく、それぞれの土地に建築がスタイルを発揮する。それがライトの建築だった。

帝国ホテル・ライト館

明治村でライトの帝国ホテルのロビーを見た衝撃はいまでも忘れられない［cat. no.4–18k］。明治期の木造技術を駆使した洋館や教会、郵便局や病院などを眺め、その先へと進んでいくと、終着地として帝国ホテルへと辿り着く。理想郷のように池に浮かぶような建築の姿を見たとき、それまで見てきた明治期の建物とは別格の圧倒的な存在感だった。大谷石の巨石が重なる濃密な外観は、それまでの明治期の建物に施された技巧を遥かに超越していた。建築の芸術性と創造性に溢れるライトのインスピレーションは圧倒的だった。そして尋常ではなかったであろう現場の緊張感、ドラフトマンとクラフトマンの共同作業、精魂を尽くした職人による物質の力、それらが時代を超えて建築の記憶として迫ってくる。

館内へ進むと、低く抑えられた庇を潜り、薄暗いレセプションの先へと歩むと、そこには三層吹き抜けのロビーがあり、再び息を呑む。そこは輝かしく、光に溢れ、華やかな劇場のように人が行き交う情景が目に浮かぶ。柱の芸術装飾であるオーナメントを間近に触れたときに衝撃が走った。そこには永遠の美を宿し、マヤ文明の遺跡のように石とテラコッタによる幾何学紋様のオーナメントが積み上がる。しかし、その芸術性に目を奪われていると、その背後を見落とす。それは発明だった。背後に照明が仕込まれ、空調の換気を組み込み、仕上げ材はコンクリートの型枠として打設され構造が一体となって建築を支えている。近代化にとってエンジニアリングは必要不可欠な存在だった。むしろ、エンジニアリングこそが近代化=モダンの象徴であった。今は当然に思える電気、水道、熱源は19世紀に発明されたばかりの設備であり、ライトはそれら構造・照明・暖房を即座に装飾や窓、家具、建具に融合した。そして、その土地の素材や自然の光や風と調和させるオーガニック・アーキテクチャーを発明したのだ。

ライトの建築はドローイングも含め視覚的に優れた印象を与えるが、その本質は音楽性にある。ライトの建築を体験すると、そこから音楽が聞こえてくる。それはベートーベンの音楽のように、強烈で劇的な抑揚、叙情性に溢れる深い旋律、革新的な発想と創造性、建築から一体となって溢れる交響曲のような光と造形と装飾による空間体験。しかし、その衝撃が落ち着き出すと、そこから穏やかな時間へと転調する。椅子にゆっくりと腰を下ろし、静かで心地よいピアノソナタを聴くように、優しく柔らかな時間が共存し、そこは約束された場所となる。

帝国ホテル・ライト館（二代目本館）は「東洋の宝石」と称され、世界の賓客を魅了し続けた。その建築は、過去のことや歴史ではない、今もまだその一部が存在する。その建築は饒舌にその精神を物語り、壮麗でありながら荘厳な、時代を超越した、奇跡のような建築であった。

図1　四代目帝国ホテル 東京 新本館イメージパース｜ATTA-Atelier Tsuyoshi Tane Architects｜2022年

Fig.1　Imperial Hotel Tokyo New Main Building Image Perspective by Tsuyoshi Tane | ATTA-Atelier Tsuyoshi Tane Architects | 2022 | Imperial Hotel

帝国ホテル・新本館

私は今、四代目となる帝国ホテル・新本館をデザインしている［cat. no. 4-18n］。帝国ホテルはライト館への期待を背負いながら、考古学的なアプローチによって、場所の記憶を掘り下げ、これからの新本館が目指す未来を構想している。

長きにわたる江戸時代が終わり、開国とともに世界へと扉を開き、日本は近代化を目指した。西洋文明の技術や文化が入り込んだ明治期、世界の賓客をもてなす迎賓館として、本格的西洋式の「帝国ホテル」は始まった。江戸城から皇居の建設とともに、内幸町周辺が上流階級社会と政治の中心の場所となった時代、初代帝国ホテルは、1890年に渡辺譲（1855-1930）設計によりヴィクトリアン調の迎賓館として建設された。そして1923年のF.L.ライト設計による二代目帝国ホテルは「東洋の宝石」と世界から称賛を受けた。都市が成長を目指し国際化が進む中で、グランドホテルとして1970年に高橋貞太郎（1892-1970）設計による三代目帝国ホテル・現本館が建つ。帝国ホテルは130年以上続くこの場所で「歴史の継承」と「未来への挑戦」を掲げる。世界からの賓客を迎え入れ、時代を彩る基壇部としての「迎賓館」と、人類が高さを求め天空を目指した象徴としての「塔」が、ひとつの建築として融合する。そこでは新規性より永続性を、表層より奥深さを、無機質より重厚感を、均質さよりも多様さによって未来を構築する。そのひとつひとつの時代の歩み、各世代の志、先人たちの偉業を継承しながら、四代目となる帝国ホテル新本館を構想している。

21世紀、世界はさらにグローバル化が進み、多様化し、大きく動き続けるであろう。また東京も次なる時代へと向かう未来がくるであろう。未来は確実に時代を変えていく。その度重なる時代の波がきたとき、建築における真価が問われる。

建築の創造とは、世代から世代へと受け継がれてきた人類の記憶の結晶である。場所に精神を宿し、物質を記憶に変え、未来は建築によって約束される。帝国ホテル・新本館は2036年の完成に向けて動き出している。

From the Imperial Hotel Wright Building to the New Main Building

Tsuyoshi Tane

To the islands in the Far East, shortly after Thomas Edison invented the incandescent light bulb, architect Frank Lloyd Wright traveled across the continent and ocean. He went to Japan for the first time in 1905, spending countless coal-black nights and watching innumerable suns set on the horizon. And in 1913, he returned as the architect for the Imperial Hotel.

Architect Frank Lloyd Wright

When telling the story of an architect, we would never know what the architect believed, what they faced, what they struggled with, what they won, what they lost, what they learned from the experience, nor how they spent the end of their life. F. L. Wright was an architect who was born and raised in Wisconsin, in a bucolic landscape of America. He relocated his base as an architect many times, came back from the bottom not once or twice, and lived a life full of drama during his time on earth. He worked on more than 1,000 projects and completed 532 buildings in his lifetime. Historians may put Wright on the pedestal as one of the greatest masters of modern architecture whereas critics have used Wright's scandals to dismiss him as an outdated architect. His monumental architecture and life filled with scandals have mythologized him as a heroic figure.

In July 2023, I visited Chicago for the first time to tour Wright's architecture. The Unity Temple (1905–08) is a public facility for the local community built with a concrete structure, the Rookery Building Remodeling in 1905 is a commercial facility adorned with Carara marble from Italy, and the Robie Residence (1908–10) represents the exaggeratedly elongated Prairie style. Although they were designed over a few years different timing, they consist of different programs, scales, structures, materials, and details. His Oak Park Home & Studio is surrounded by almost 30 of his early housing projects, each with its characteristics yet no two buildings are the same. In Taliesin, where Wright later lived and created spending time with his Fellowship apprentices, the Taliesen East buildings sit on the tranquil hill zone in Wisconsin. Although he never built any structure on the hill and gave each a unique design, it is astounding how the architecture connects deeply with the land. F. L. Wright did not have any specific style. He never imposed his style as an architect, but rather architecture should have a style. That was F. L. Wright's architecture.

Imperial Hotel Wright Building

I still remember the shock I experienced seeing Wright's Imperial Hotel lobby in Meiji Mura [cat. no. 4-18k]. Walking through the open-air museum with Western-style houses, a church, a post office, and a hospital constructed with cutting-edge techniques from the Meiji period, you will reach the Imperial Hotel as the final destination. When I saw how the building was as if it were floating on a pond in utopia, it had an overwhelming presence that stood out from any other Meiji-era architecture. The intense exterior constructed of giant Oya stones far surpassed any technique used in buildings from the Meiji period. Wright, who was filled with architectural artistry and creativity, also had devastatingly great inspirations. The tension on the site, the collaboration of draftsman and craftsmen, and the materiality brought about by the artisans who put their heart and soul all must have been extraordinary, which speak to us today as the memory architecture holds.

As I entered the building, I passed under the low eaves and walked past the dimly lit reception to arrive at the three-story atrium lobby, which once again took my breath away. I could imagine how it must have been filled with light and people coming and going like a glamorous theater. As I touched the ornaments of the decorative pillars, I was totally impressed. There I found eternal beauty, in the geometric ornaments made of stone and terracotta stacked like the ruins of the Mayan civilization. However, fascinated by the artistry, you would overlook what is behind the beauty. It was a pure invention. Lighting was installed behind the ornaments, while ventilation was incorporated, and finishing materials are cast as concrete forms and the structure is an integral part of the construction. Engineering was the essence of modernization or rather, engineering was the symbol of modernism. Electricity, water, and heat sources, which we today take for granted, were utilities that had been invented in the 19th century, and Wright immediately integrated through his ornamentation into the structure, lighting, heating, ventilation, and framings, furniture, and fittings through his ornamentation. That is how he invented 'organic architecture' that harmonizes with local materials, natural light, and wind.

F.L. Wright's architecture, including his drawings, gives an excellent visual impression, but its essence lies in its musicality. When you experience Wright's architecture, you seem to hear a sense of music. Like Beethoven's pieces, they offer a spatial experience filled with intense and dramatic cadence, deep melody full of lyricism, innovative ideas and creativity, and light, form, and decoration that overflows from a symphony in architecture. However, as soon as the initial impact starts to settle down, it modulates to a calmer experience. Just like sitting back in a chair listening to a quiet and comfortable piano sonata, the space becomes a promised place.

The Imperial Hotel Wright Building has been known as “the Jewel of the Orient,” which continued to attract distinguished guests from across all over the world. This architecture is not a thing of the past or history, as a part of it exists today. It still speaks to us of its spirit and was a magnificent yet majestic, timeless, and miraculous architecture.

Imperial Hotel New Main Building

Today, I am designing the new main building of the Imperial Hotel, the fourth generation of the hotel [cat. no. 4-18n]. It carries with it the expectations of the Imperial Hotel by the Wright Building. We take an archaeological approach to delve into the memory of the site and envision the future of the next new main building.

After the long Edo period, Japan opened its door to the world and strived for modernization. In the following Meiji era, when Western culture and technology were introduced, the Imperial Hotel opened as an authentic Western-style guest house to entertain guests from around the world. As the Edo Castle was reconstructed into the Imperial Palace and Uchisaiwaicho became the center of the upper social class and politics, the first Imperial Hotel was designed by Yuzuru Watanabe (1855–1930) in 1890 as a Victorian-style guest house. The second Imperial Hotel in 1923 designed by F. L. Wright received international praise as the Jewel of the Orient. Then in 1970, the current main building of the third-generation Imperial Hotel was designed by Teitaro Takahashi (1892–1970) as the grand hotel for urbanization and globalization. The Imperial Hotel aims to “carry on history” as well as “challenge to the future” from where it has been for 130 years. The Guest House, which welcomes guests from all over the world and serves as the foundation that illustrates the era, and the Tower, which symbolizes humankind’s pursuit to reach the sky, merge as one work of architecture. We aim to build the future with permanence rather than novelty, depth rather than superficiality, gravity rather than inorganicity, and diversity rather than homogeneity. We design the fourth-generation of the Imperial Hotel - new main building by inheriting the progress of each era, the aspiration of each generation, and the achievements of our predecessors.

In the 21st century, the world will continue to be more globalized, diversified, and move dynamically. Tokyo will also have to move on to the next era in the future. The future will certainly change the time. The true value of architecture will be tested when the waves of the times come again and again.

The creation of architecture is the crystallization of human memories, passed down across generation to generation. The future is promised by architecture, which gives spirit to places and transforms materials into memories. The Imperial Hotel - new main building is now in progress moving towards completion in 2036.

FRANK

LLOYD

WRIGHT

フランク・ロイド・ライト年表

Chronology

作成：水上優

	年齢	経歴	作品［竣工年］｜■＝計画案
1867年		6月8日、ウィスコンシン州リッチランド・センターに、バプテスト派説教者で音楽家でもあり先妻を亡くしていた父ウィリアム・ラッセル・キャリー・ライト（1825–1904）と、教師である母アンナ・ロイド・ジョーンズ・ライト（1838?–1923）の間の長子として、フランク・ロイド・ライト（出生時にはフランク・リンカーン・ライト）誕生。	
1869年	2歳	アイオワ州マクレガーに一家転居。	
1874年	7歳	マサチューセッツ州ウェイマウスに一家転居。	
1876年	9歳	フレデリック・フレーベルの「恩物」を母より与えられる。	
1877年	10歳	ウィスコンシン州マディソンに一家転居。	
		この夏ウィスコンシン州スプリンググリーン近郊のヘレナ渓谷にあるジェームズ・ロイド・ジョーンズ伯父（1850–1907）の農場で農作業を手伝いながら過ごす。	
1883年	16歳	両親別居始まる。	
1885年	18歳	両親離婚。父親ウィリアムが家族を去る。	
		このときライトは「フランク・リンカーン・ライト」から「フランク・ロイド・ライト」に改名。マディソン高校を出て、マディソンにあるウィスコンシン大学土木学科の学部長アラン・D. コノバー教授の下でドラフトマンとしてアルバイト。	
1886年	19歳	3月初旬、ウィスコンシン大学の土木コースに通うが、履修期間は2セメスター（学期）のみ。	● ユニティ・チャペル
		ライトの叔母ジェーン・ロイド・ジョーンズとエレン・ロイド・ジョーンズが、進歩主義教育の寄宿の学校としてヒルサイド・ホームスクール開設。	
		ライトの叔父ジェンキン・ロイド・ジョーンズの友人、ジョセフ・ライマン・シルスビー（1848–1913）と共同でロイド・ジョーンズ家のチャペル（ユニティ・チャペル）設計。	
1887年	20歳	1月、マディソンを離れシカゴに赴く。ジョセフ・ライマン・シルスビーの事務所に就職。 いったん辞めてビアーズ・クレイ・ダットン事務所に移るが、再度シルスビー事務所に戻る。	● ヒルサイド・ホームスクール第一
1888年	21歳	シルスビー事務所を辞め、アドラー＆サリヴァン事務所にドラフトマンとして就職。	
1889年	22歳	6月1日、裕福なビジネスマンの娘であるキャサリン・リー・トビン（1871–1959）と結婚。	● フランク・ロイド・ライト自邸
		サリヴァンから給料5,000ドルを前借りして、イリノイ州オークパークに自邸建設。	
1890年	23歳	アドラー＆サリヴァン事務所における住宅デザインの全てを任されるようになる。	
1891年	24歳	3月1日、長男フランク・ロイド・ライト・ジュニア（ロイド・ライト）誕生（–1975）。	● チャーンリー邸
1892年	25歳	アドラー＆サリヴァン事務所の就業時間外に、個人的に引き受けた数件の住宅を設計。これが後にサリヴァンに知れ、両者の確執を生むことになる。	
		12月12日、次男ジョン・ロイド・ライト誕生（–1972）。	
1893年	26歳	アドラー＆サリヴァン事務所より解雇。セシル・コーウィンと共にイリノイ州シカゴにあるシラー・ビル（サリヴァン設計、1891）の1501号室に事務所開設。	
		シカゴ万国博覧会開催。ライトは日本館「鳳凰殿」の建築現場をしばしば訪れたといわれる。	
1894年	27歳	イリノイ州エヴァンストンのユニバーシティ・ギルドで「建築と機械」と題して講演。	● ウィンズロー邸
		1月12日、長女キャサリン・ドロシー・ライト誕生（–1979）。	
		シカゴ美術館のシカゴ建築クラブで初めてのライト展。	
		イリノイ州リヴァーフォレストにウィンズロー邸竣工（ライトはウィンズロー邸を独立後最初の作品としている）。	
1895年	28歳	9月26日、三男デヴィッド・サミュエル・ライト誕生（–1997）。	● 自邸にプレイルーム増築
		オークパークの自邸にプレイルーム増築。	

主要参考文献

- Langmead, D., *Frank Lloyd Wright: A Bio-Bibliography*, Praeger Publishers, 2003.
- Pfeiffer B. B., 'A Selected Chronology of Frank Lloyd Wright's Life and Work, 1867-1959,' in David De Long, Ed. *Frank Lloyd Wright and The Living City*, Skira, 1998.
- Richard Cleary, et al., *Frank Lloyd Wright: From Within Outward*, Skira Rizzoli Publications, 2009.
- フランク・ロイド・ライト回顧展実行委員会『フランク・ロイド・ライト回顧展』毎日新聞社、1991

年	年齢	出来事	作品
1896年	29歳	ユニバーシティ・ギルドで「建築、建築家、クライアント」と題して講演。	
		セシル・コーウィンが事務所を辞める。	
1897年	30歳	ロバート・スペンサー、ドワイト・パーキンス、マイロン・ハントと共にシカゴのスタインウェイ・ホール1107号室に事務所移転。	
1898年	31歳	9月3日、次女フランシス・ライト誕生(-1959)。	● ライト自邸のスタジオ
		シカゴ・ルッカリー・ビル(設計バナーム&ルート(1886))内に事務所開設。	
1900年	33歳	シカゴ美術館の建築連盟で「美術の哲学」と題して講演。	● ブラッドリー邸「グレンロイド」 ● ヒコックス邸
		建築連盟の第2回年次総会で「建築家」と題して講演。	
		『アーキテクチュラル・レヴュー』誌6月号が「フランク・ロイド・ライトの作品」と題された特集記事を掲載。	
		シカゴ建築クラブでライト展。	
		12月、イギリスのアーツ・アンド・クラフツ運動の主唱者チャールズ・ロバート・アシュビー(1863-1942)に会う。	
1901年	34歳	3月6日、シカゴのハルハウスにて「機械によるアーツ・アンド・クラフツ」と題する講演(ハルハウス講演)を行う(アーツ・アンド・クラフツ運動を懐古的として批判し、機械が芸術家の手となることを積極的に評価)。	● ウィリッツ邸
		シカゴ建築クラブでライト展。	
		ジェームズ・ガンブル・ロジャーズと共に「ヨーロッパ首都のアメリカ大使館」コンペを審査。	
		ヘンリー・ウェブスター・トムリンソンとパートナーシップを組む(-1902)。計画案「プレイリー・タウンの住宅」(『レディース・ホーム・ジャーナル』誌、1901年2月号)と「たくさんの部屋のある小さな住宅」(同誌、1901年7月号)を発表(後者は、外観はブラッドリー邸、内部の空間構成はウィリッツ邸に酷似する)。	
		「地区銀行」計画案を『ブリックビルダー』誌8月号に発表(鉄筋コンクリート建築への関心がうかがえる)。	
		イリノイ州ハイランドパークにウォード・ウィリッツ邸竣工(プレイリー・ハウスの代表作。後の『ヴァスムート・ポートフォリオ』掲載のウィリッツ邸の透視図は、建物の手前に樹木を配することで奥行を表現する構図で知られ、日本の浮世絵を参照したことがうかがえる)。	
1902年	35歳	後に施主、後援者となるウィリアム・E. マーティンとダーウィン・D. マーティンに出会う。	● ピッキン邸 ● ヒルサイド・ホームスクール第二
		シカゴ建築クラブでライト展、併せて「芸術の哲学」講演。	
		ニューヨーク州バッファローにラーキン・ビル設計開始(ラーキン社の社長はダーウィン・D. マーティン)。	
1903年	36歳	11月15日、四男ロバート・レウェリン・ライト誕生(-1986)。	● ウィリアム・E. マーティン邸 ● チェイニー邸
		イリノイ州オークパークにエドウィン・チェイニー邸竣工(ライトは後に施主の妻メイマー・チェイニーと共に渡欧)。	
1904年	37歳	セントルイスで開催されたルイジアナ・パーチェス・エキスポジションに出席。	● ダナ邸
		父親ウィリアム死去。	
1905年	38歳	施主のウォード・ウィリッツ夫妻と共にライト夫妻初来日。ライトにとっては初の外国旅行。浮世絵蒐集を行う。	● ダーウィン・D. マーティン邸 ● ハーディ邸 ● ルッカリー・ビル改装
		京都において京都高等工芸学校教授であった武田五一に会った可能性が強い。	
		ウィスコンシン州ラシーンにトーマス・ハーディ邸竣工(後の『ヴァスムート・ポートフォリオ』掲載のハーディ邸の透視図は余白を大きくとった大胆な構図で知られ、日本の浮世絵を参照したことがうかがえる)。	
1906年	39歳	3月、シカゴ美術館において、ライト所有の広重の浮世絵コレクションを展示。作品リストと併せて、ライトの浮世絵に関する初のテクストとなる解説文「Hiroshige」を発表。	● ラーキン・ビル ● デローズ邸 ● ショー邸改造
1907年	40歳	シカゴ建築クラブでライト展。	

年	年齢	出来事	作品
1908年	41歳	『アーキテクチュラル・レコード』誌3月号がライト特集号を組む。これまで印刷されることのなかった数多くのライトの作品を87葉のイラストレーションによって紹介。併せて、初の書き下ろし論文「建築の大義のために」も掲載。この出版によって多くの読者にライトのアイデアが広まり始める。	● ユニティ・テンプル
		ハーバード大学のドイツ文化史教授クーノ・フランケがオークパークを訪れ、ライトに会う。後のエルンスト・ヴァスムート社によるライト作品集『フランク・ロイド・ライトの建築と設計』出版のきっかけをつくる。	
		シカゴ美術館での浮世絵展において、ライト・コレクションの浮世絵がフレデリック・グーキン、クラレンス・バッキンガム等のコレクションと共に展示される。	
1909年	42歳	家族を置いて、施主エドウィン・チェイニーの妻、メイマー・ボートン・ボスウィック・チェイニーと共に渡欧。	● クーンリー邸
		ミネアポリス建築クラブでライト展。	
1910年	43歳	ベルリン入りした後フィレンツェ北東の町フィエゾレに逗留。オークパークのスタジオから作品の図面と写真が送られ、息子ロイド・ライト、ドラフトマンのテイラー・ウーレイと共に羽根ペンとインディアン・インクでそれらをトレース。最終稿はベルリンに送られ、リトグラフに製版され、『フランク・ロイド・ライトの建築と設計』として出版。	● ロビー邸
		イリノイ州シカゴにフレデリック・ロビー邸竣工（プレイリー・ハウスの代表作）。	
		メイマー・チェイニーとバヴァリア、ヴェネチア、パリ、ロンドンを旅行。	
		エドウィン・チェイニーがメイマーと離婚。	
1911年	44歳	ヨーロッパから戻り、母方一族の根拠地ウィスコンシン州スプリンググリーン近くに新しい住宅兼仕事場となる複合施設、タリアセン（タリアセン第一）を建設（「タリアセン」とはウェールズ語で「輝ける眉」を意味する）。	● タリアセン第一 ● ブース邸計画案——■ ● クーンリー・プレイハウス幼稚園 ● バンフ国立公園パビリオン
		オランダの建築家H.P. ベルラーヘ（1856-1934）がアメリカを訪れ、ライトの作品を訪問し、翌1912年のチューリッヒでの講演のなかでラーキン・ビルを激賞。	
1912年	45歳	シカゴのオーケストラ・ホールに事務所開設。	
		日本の浮世絵についてのライトの理解を提示する著書『日本の浮世絵：或る解釈』出版。	
1913年	46歳	2度目の訪日。メイマーと共に1月12日出航。	● アーサー・リチャーズ中華レストラン案——■
		武田五一と再会し『フランク・ロイド・ライトの建築と設計』を贈呈。林愛作と会う。スポールディング兄弟のために100枚以上の浮世絵を購入。	
		6月18日帰国。	
		シカゴ建築クラブでライト展。	
		エドワード・C. ウォラーの依頼により、イリノイ州シカゴにミッドウェイ・ガーデン設計開始（ライトの高弟・遠藤新の代表作「甲子園ホテル」はミッドウェイ・ガーデンのデザインを参照していることがうかがえる）。	
1914年	47歳	4月から5月にかけて、シカゴ美術館でライト展「1911年以降の作品展」開催。これに併せて書き下ろし論文「建築の大義のために・その2」を『アーキテクチュラル・レコード』誌に掲載。	● ミッドウェイ・ガーデンズ ● モリ東洋美術ギャラリー ● タリアセン第二 ● アメリカ大使館——■ ● ウィリアム・スポールディングのための浮世絵ギャラリー——■
		ロバート・ファント・ホッフ（1887-1979）がタリアセンのライト訪問。	
		7月28日、第一次世界大戦勃発。	
		8月15日、精神不安定の使用人ジュリアン・カールトンがメイマー本人と彼女の先夫との子2人を含む6人を殺害し、タリアセン（タリアセン第一）に放火。	
		12月12日、彫刻家ミリアム・ノエル（1869-1930）と出会う。	
		焼け跡を再建し、タリアセン再建（タリアセン第二）。アンナ・ロイド・ライト、タリアセンに居を移す。	
1915年	48歳	ヒルサイド・ホームスクール閉鎖。	● ブース邸 ● アメリカ式システム工法住宅（-1917）——■
		プレファブリケーションの手法で建てられる一連の住宅（アメリカ式システム工法住宅）をデザイン。	

年	歳	事項	作品
1916年	49歳	3月17日、林愛作夫妻がタリアセンを訪問し帝国ホテル設計の契約覚書取り交わし。 帝国ホテルの仕事の傍ら、何度かアメリカに戻り、ロサンゼルスの事務所で進行中のバーンズドール邸「立葵の家」の仕事を指図。 3度目の訪日。ミリアム・ノエルおよび息子ジョンと共に12月28日出航。	
1917年	50歳	5月17日帰国、タリアセンに戻る。 シカゴ美術館主催によるファインアーツ・ビルでの「フランク・ロイド・ライトの浮世絵コレクション展」開催。それに併せてテクスト執筆(実名をあげて具体的に浮世絵の評価をし、蒐集についての歴史的経緯を説明)。 プレファブリケーション住宅「アメリカ式システム工法住宅」を発表。	• 林邸 • 小田原ホテル計画案――■ • 福原邸
1918年	51歳	ウィスコンシンのライトのもとへのサリヴァンからの電話により、サリヴァンと和解。 4度目の訪日。10月30日出航。日光、箱根を訪問。 帝国ホテルの絨毯の買い付けに中国訪問。思想家辜鴻銘(1857–1928)と会う。 11月11日、第一次世界大戦終結。	• 帝国ホテル 現場事務所
1919年	52歳	アメリカ合衆国で禁酒法公布(米国憲法修正第18条、1933年に廃止)。このためミッドウェイ・ガーデンズ閉鎖、建物は1929年に取り壊し。 帝国ホテル着工。動力棟から建設始まる。 9月25日帰国、タリアセンに戻る。 5度目の訪日。12月16日出航。	• 帝国ホテル 動力棟
1920年	53歳	ライトが病気になったため、81歳の母アンナが東京にライトを訪ねる。 7月10日帰国、タリアセンに戻る。 6度目の訪日。12月16日出航。	• バーンズドール邸劇場案――■ • 帝国ホテル 別館 • 劇場計画案(活動写真館)――■
1921年	54歳	5月帰国しロサンゼルスに戻り、7月20日タリアセンに戻る。 7度目の訪日。7月30日出航。	• バーンズドール邸「立葵の家」 • 自由学園
1922年	55歳	初代帝国ホテル失火。林愛作が支配人を辞す。これに起因して、ライトは完成を待たず7月22日に離日。 11月22日、キャサリンと離婚成立。	
1923年	56歳	2月9日、母アンナ死去。オークパークのユニティ・チャペルの墓地に葬られる。 ロサンゼルス、オリーヴ・ヒルに事務所開設。 7月、帝国ホテル全館完成。 9月1日、帝国ホテル竣工披露式典当日に関東大震災発生、東京の大半が壊滅的に被災。帝国ホテルは倒壊せずに残るが、福原邸は倒壊。 11月、ミリアム・ノエルと結婚。	• 帝国ホテル二代目本館 • ドヘニー・ランチ宅地開発計画案――■ • レイクタホ(–1924)――■ • リトルディッパー幼稚園とコミュニティ・プレイハウス――■ • ナコマ・カントリー・クラブ計画案(–1924)――■ • ナショナル生命保険会社ビル計画案(–1925)――■
1924年	57歳	4月、ミリアム・ノエルと別居。 4月11日、ルイス・H. サリヴァンのもとを訪れたライトが自伝『イデアの自伝』初版本を贈られる。その3日後の14日、サリヴァン死去。 11月30日、モンテネグロの裁判長イアン・バドヴィッチの娘オルギヴァナ・ミラノフ・ラゾヴィッチ・ヒンツェンブルク(1897–1985)とシカゴで出会う。 ドイツの建築家エーリヒ・メンデルゾーンがタリアセン(タリアセン第二)にライトを訪問。 ミラード夫人邸「ミニアトゥーラ」など、ロサンゼルス周辺で4件のテキスタイル・ブロック住宅建設。	• 山邑邸 • ミラード夫人邸「ミニアトゥーラ」 • ストーラー邸 • サミュエル・フリーマン邸 • ゴードン・ストロング自動車体験娯楽施設とプラネタリウム計画案(–1925)――■

年	歳	事項	作品
1925年	58歳	オルギヴァナと彼女の先夫との子スヴェトラーナ(1917-1946)がタリアセンに移る。	● エニス邸 ● タリアセン第三
		オランダの雑誌『ヴェンディンゲン』第7号がライト特集を組む。編者H. Th. ヴェイデフェルトに加え、V. スカリー、H. P. ベルラーヘ、J. J. P. アウト、E. メンデルゾーン、R. マレ=ステヴァンスらがエッセイを寄稿。L. H. サリヴァンのエッセイも収録。ライト自身も、「帝国ホテルに関する事柄」「ヨーロッパの我が共同者達へ」「建築の大義のために:第3の次元」の3つのエッセイを寄稿。「建築の大義のために」「建築の大義のために・その2」も再録。	
		4月20日、火災でタリアセンの住居部分全焼したが、隣接するスタジオ、保管庫、仕事場は免れた。すぐに再建。	
		ミリアム・ノエルが離婚申請。	
		12月3日、オルギヴァナとの間に娘ヨヴァンナ誕生。	
1926年	59歳	ウィスコンシン銀行が、ライトの負債に対してタリアセンを差し押さえ。	● キンダーシンフォニーズ設計競技案――■
		ミリアム・ノエルの嫌がらせからライト家族はミネソタに逃避。	
		ライトとオルギヴァナ、マン法違反によりミネアポリス近くで拘引。10月22日に釈放。	
		オルギヴァナの勧めで『自伝』執筆開始。	
		ライトの仕事とその使命に共感していた『アーキテクチュラル・レコード』誌編集者M. A. ミッケルセンが「建築の大義のために」というタイトルでライトに連続論文を依頼。5月に連載を始め、5本の論文にそれぞれ500ドルを払う。	
1927年	60歳	マン法違反の罪が取り下げられる。	● セント・マークス教区のアパートメント・タワー計画案(-1929)――■
		1月6日と7日、ライトの浮世絵コレクションの一部がニューヨークのアンダーソン・ギャラリーで展示およびオークション。ライトは販売カタログ用に紹介文を執筆。ウィスコンシン銀行が買い取ってタリアセン再建の費用が賄われた。	
		2月22日、タリアセンのスタジオで火災があったが最小限の被害でとどまる。図面や文書は無事。	
		8月25日、ミリアム・ノエルと離婚成立。	
		オルギヴァナとプエルトリコに旅行。	
		ベルギー王室美術協会の名誉会員に迎えられる。	
		ミッケルセンが『アーキテクチュラル・レコード』誌上にさらに9本の論文からなる「建築の大義のために」と題する連続論文を依頼(一連の連載では「素材の本性」が主題化されている)。とりわけ経済的に逼迫していたこの時期のライトに、一連の依頼は総額7,000ドルに上る収入をもたらした。	
		アリゾナ州フェニックスでオルギヴァナと共に冬を過ごす。	
1928年	61歳	アリゾナ・ビルトモア・ホテルのデザインのコンサルティング・アーキテクトとして呼ばれ、家族でアリゾナを訪れる。	● アリゾナ・ビルトモア・ホテル ● サン・マルコス砂漠リゾート・ホテル計画案(-1929)――■ ● ローゼンワルド財団の学校計画案――■
		カリフォルニア州ラ・ホヤに移り、アレクサンダー・チャンドラー博士のためのサン・マルコス砂漠リゾート・ホテル設計開始。	
		8月25日、カリフォルニア州ランチョ・サンタ・フェでオルギヴァナと結婚。スヴェトラーナと養子縁組。	
		ル・コルビュジエの『建築をめざして』の書評を執筆(基本的に批判的論調)。	

年	歳	事項	作品
1929年	62歳	A. チャンドラー博士の依頼によるサン・マルコス砂漠リゾート・ホテルおよびサン・マルコス・ウォーター・ガーデンを計画。その建設中の仕事場兼住居として、アリゾナ州チャンドラーで1月、「オカティラ」キャンプの建設が始まり、6週間で完成。5月までにホテル施工図完了。アリゾナの酷暑を避けて秋に着工する予定であったが、10月29日のニューヨーク株式大暴落によって全計画中止。	● オカティラ砂漠キャンプ ● ブロードエーカー・シティ構想（-1935）——■
		5月24日、アリゾナからウィスコンシンに帰り、その後ニューヨークへ行く。ニューヨークで長年の友人である牧師、ウィリアム・ノーマン・ガスリーの依頼による「セント・マークス教区のアパートメントタワー計画案」についての検討を重ねる（この計画は実現しなかったが、以後30年の間にキャンティレバーによる高層建築の案が次々と生み出され、後のジョンソン・ワックス・タワー研究棟やプライス・タワーの実現をみる）。	
		ベルリンの美術アカデミーの特別名誉会員の称号を政府より授与される。	
1930年	63歳	ミリアム・ノエルがミネソタ州ミネアポリスで死去。	
		5月、プリンストン大学において、学生に対して6回の講演（カーン講演）を行う（翌年、『近代建築』と題して講演録出版、訳書邦題『フランク・ロイド・ライトの現代建築講義』）。	
		10月1日と2日、国内巡回中のライトの作品展に関連して、シカゴ美術館において講演（翌年、『建築についての2つの講演』と題して講演録出版）。	
		カーン講演に付随するライトの作品展が、ニューヨークからウィスコンシン州マディソン、ミルウォーキーを巡回。	
1931年	64歳	同展が、オレゴン州ユージン巡回後、ヴェイデフェルト主導により、海外のアムステルダム、ベルリン、シュツットガルト、フランクフルト、ブリュッセル、アントワープを巡回。	
		ライト夫妻、パン・アメリカン・ユニオンのゲストとしてクリストファー・コロンブス記念灯台競技設計審査のためにブラジルのリオデジャネイロ訪問。	
		ブラジル中央建築家協会名誉会員。	
1932年	65歳	『自伝』出版。都市を主題とした著作『消えゆく都市』出版。	
		ライト夫妻、タリアセン・フェローシップを設立。ウィスコンシン州ヒルサイドにあるヒルサイド・ホームスクールの建物を改装してその用に充て、翌1933年からタリアセン・フェローシップ複合施設として増築を加える。	
		ニューヨーク近代美術館においてヘンリー・ラッセル・ヒッチコックとフィリップ・ジョンソンらが企画した「近代建築：インターナショナル・スタイル展」にライトの作品が加えられる。	
1933年	66歳	シカゴ世界博覧会開催。	● タリアセン・フェローシップ建築群「ヒルサイド」
		10月21日、タリアセン・フェローシップのメンバーでヒルサイド・ホームスクールの建物をタリアセン・フェローシップの総合施設に改修。	
		11月、ウィスコンシンのタリアセンからアリゾナへ向けて、フェローシップの大陸横断の初めての旅。始めの数年は、アリゾナ州チャンドラーにあるA. チャンドラーのハシエンダ・インに滞在。	
1934年	67歳	アリゾナ州チャンドラーのハシエンダ・インにて、ブロードエーカー・シティ構想模型制作開始。	
		後の施主となるエドガー・カウフマンと出会う。	
1935年	68歳	ブロードエーカー・シティ構想の完成模型がニューヨーク、ロックフェラー・センターの産業技術展での展示後、ウィスコンシン州マディソン、ペンシルベニア州ピッツバーグ、ワシントンD.C.、ウィスコンシン州ダッジビルのアイオワ・カウンティーフェア、ミシガン州マーケットを巡回。	● カウフマン事務所
1936年	69歳	12月、ひどい肺炎に罹る。砂漠の暖かい日差しの下で力を付けるために医者ミッチェル・モタノビッチから提案されたオルギヴァナの計らいで、アリゾナ州フェニックスを訪問。	

年	歳	出来事	作品
1937年	70歳	6月、ライト夫妻、ソビエト連邦に招かれて国際建築家会議に出席。セルゲイ・M. エイゼンシュテインに会い、長編ノーカット、未検閲の『イワン雷帝』を贈られる。	• エドガー・カウフマン邸「落水荘」 • ハナ邸「ハニカムハウス」 • ジェイコブズ第一邸
		ベイカー・ブロウネルとの共著『建築と近代生活』出版。	
		アリゾナ州スコッツデールに政府所有地800エーカーを購入。	
		ウィスコンシン州マディソンに、最初のユーソニアン住宅、ジェイコブズ第一邸竣工。以降1941年までに46件のユーソニアン住宅を設計。うち25件建設（"ユーソニア"はライトの理想とするジェファーソン的民主主義社会としてのアメリカを指し、"ユーソニアン"は民主主義の構成員としての自立した中産階級アメリカ市民を指す）。	
1938年	71歳	アリゾナ州スコッツデールにタリアセン・ウェストの建設開始。	• タリアセン・ウェスト • フロリダ・サザン・カレッジ
		『アーキテクチュラル・フォーラム』誌1月号がライト特集号を企画。編集長ハワード・マイヤーズの計らいでライト自ら特集号全体を監修。ライトの敬愛するヘンリー・デビット・ソローとウォルト・ホイットマンの詩句が引用され、ライトの作品とともに配される。	
		ライトの肖像が『タイム』誌の表紙を飾る。	
1939年	72歳	5月、RIBAからの招きでロンドンを訪れ、サルグレーブ・マナー・ボードで4夜にわたる講演（『有機的建築：民主主義の建築』と題してロンドンのルンド・ハンプトン社から講演録出版）。	• ジョンソン・ワックス・ビル
		コネティカット州ミドルタウンのウェズレーヤン大学から名誉教授として迎えられる。	
		9月1日、第二次世界大戦勃発。	
1940年	73歳	ニューヨーク近代美術館でライトの回顧展「フランク・ロイド・ライトの作品」展開催。	• オボーラー・ゲートハウス建築群
		フランク・ロイド・ライト財団を創立。	
1941年	74歳	英国王立建築家協会の名誉会員の栄誉、並びにロイヤル・ゴールド・メダルをジョージVI世より授与される。また、英国王立建築家協会のサー・ジョージ・ワトソンの講座の席を与えられる。サルグレーブ・マナー・ボードから学術賞を授与される。	
		フレデリック・A. グートハイムの編纂で著述集『建築について』出版。	
1942年	75歳	ウルグアイ国立建築家協会の名誉会員として迎えられる。	
1943年	76歳	大幅に増補改訂された『自伝』第2版出版。	• ジョンソン・ワックス・研究タワー
		メキシコ国立協会の名誉会員の称号を政府から授与される。	
		グッゲンハイム美術館の設計開始。	
1945年	78歳	8月15日、第二次世界大戦終結。	
		『消えゆく都市』を大幅に増補改訂した『民主主義が建設するとき』（訳書邦題『デモクラシイの眞髄』）出版。	
1946年	79歳	フィンランド王立アカデミーの名誉会員の称号を政府から授与される。	• ロジャース・レイシー・ホテル計画案（–1947）——■
		9月30日、自動車事故でオルギヴァナの娘スヴェトラーナ死去。	
1947年	80歳	プリンストン大学より芸術博士の名誉学位を受ける。	
		エーリヒ・メンデルゾーンが、タリアセン・ウェストにライトを再訪。	
1948年	81歳	『アーキテクチュラル・フォーラム』誌1月号が2度目のライト特集号。	
1949年	82歳	サリヴァンについて語った著書『天才と衆愚社会』出版。	
		アメリカン・ナショナル・インスティテュート・オブ・アンド・レターズより名誉会員として迎えられる。	
		アメリカ建築家協会（AIA）よりゴールド・メダル授与（AIAは建築の質を高めるよりも専門家のメンバーを守るために設立されたと批判して、ライトはアメリカ建築家協会に入っていなかった）。	
		AIAのフィラデルフィア支部よりゴールド・メダル授与。	
		ピーター・クーパー芸術振興賞授与。	
1950年	83歳	レイクランドのフロリダ・サザン・カレッジより名誉博士号授与。	
		ポピュラー・メカニック・マガジン社より百周年記念賞授与。	

年	年齢	事項	作品
1951年	84歳	『アーキテクチュラル・フォーラム』誌1月号が3度目のライト特集号。	● マシエリ記念学生会館計画案（1951/52-55年）――■
		模型や写真、オリジナル・ドローイングから成る「生ける建築の60年」と題したライトの作品展を、1月、フィラデルフィアのギンベル百貨店で開催。その後、フィレンツェのストロッツィ宮を皮切りにヨーロッパ巡回開始。	
		フィレンツェのメディチ・メダルをパラッツォ・ヴェッキオにおいて授与される。またヴェネツィアのパラッツォ・ドゥカーレ（元総督邸）においてザ・スター・オブ・ソリダリティの栄誉が贈られる。	
		アーロン・グリーンと共同で、サンフランシスコに西海岸事務所開設。	
1952年	85歳	「生ける建築の60年」展がフィレンツェからチューリッヒ、パリ、ミュンヘン、ロッテルダムを巡回。	● タリアセン・フェローシップ建築群「ヒルサイド・シアター」
		ウィスコンシン州スプリンググリーンにあるヒルサイド・ホームスクールが火事で一部延焼。	
1953年	86歳	「生ける建築の60年」展がメキシコ・シティ、ニューヨークを巡回。	
		ストックホルムの王立アカデミーの名誉会員の称号を政府から授与。また、フィンランド国立アカデミーの名誉会員の称号を政府から授与。	
		テレビのナショナル放送で、インタビュー放映。インタビュアーはヒュー・ダウンズ。	
		ホライゾン・プレス社より著書『建築の未来』出版。出版者ベン・レブハーンの計らいで以降、同社より毎年、ライトの著作・著述集が出版される。	
1954年	87歳	「生ける建築の60年」展、ロサンゼルスのバーンズドール邸「立葵の家」で閉幕。	● プラザ・ホテル内事務所兼住宅 ● トレイシー邸
		フィラデルフィアのフランクリン協会から表彰され、ブラウン・メダルを受賞。	
		イエール大学より美術博士号の名誉学位を贈られる。	
		ホライゾン・プレス社より住宅を主題とした著書『ナチュラル・ハウス』（訳書邦題『ライトの住宅』『自然の家』）出版。	
1955年	88歳	ウィスコンシン大学から芸術学名誉学位を贈られる。	
		ドイツのダルムシュタット技術協会から名誉博士号を贈られる。またスイスのチューリッヒ技術協会から名誉博士号を贈られる。	
		ニューヨーク、プラザ・ホテル内に事務所兼住宅を開設。	
		ホライゾン・プレス社より、エドガー・カウフマン編纂のライト著述集『アメリカの建築』出版。	
1956年	89歳	オルギヴァナとウェールズに旅行。	● プライス・タワー ● ゴールデン・ビーコン・アパートメント・タワー計画案（-1957）――■ ● マイル・ハイ・イリノイ計画案――■
		バンゴーのウェールズ大学より哲学博士号の名誉学位を贈られる。	
		10月17日、シカゴのリチャード・デイリー市長がこの1日を「フランク・ロイド・ライト・デー」にすることを宣言。	
		ホテル・シャーマンにおける展覧会で、「マイル・ハイ・イリノイ計画案」を発表。	
		ニューヨークで、グッゲンハイム美術館の建設開始（1959年、ライト没後に完成）。	
		ホライゾン・プレス社より同年竣工のプライス・タワーの建設記録『タワーの物語』出版。	
1957年	90歳	イラクのバグダッドに招待され、オペラ・ハウス、2つの博物館、郵便通信ビルの設計を委託される。	● 大バグダッド計画案――■
		オルギヴァナとロンドン、パリ、カイロを訪問。	
		マイク・ウォレスのインタビュー放映。	
		ホライゾン・プレス社より著書『テスタメント』（訳書邦題『ライトの遺言』『テスタメント』）出版。	
1958年	91歳	国立コンクリート・メイソンリー協会によりゴールド・メダルが贈られる。	● ロックリッジ診療所 ● リヴィング・シティ構想――■
		ホライゾン・プレス社により、前著『民主主義が建設するとき』の大幅な増補改訂版にして最後の著書『リヴィング・シティ』（訳書邦題『ライトの都市論』）出版。	
1959年		10代の若者のための建築の歴史についての執筆（イギリスのラスボーン・プレス社の『ワンダフル・ワールド・オブ・アーキテクチュア』企画）開始。	● グッゲンハイム美術館
		4月9日、アリゾナ州フェニックスで死去。享年91歳。	

一般公開作品リスト

Public Wright Site

作品名	州・県名	都市名	住所
The Rosenbaum House	Alabama	Florence	601 Riverview Dr, Florence, AL 35630
Arizona Biltmore Hotel	Arizona	Phoenix	24th St and Missouri, Phoenix, AZ 85016
First Christian Church	Arizona	Phoenix	6750 N 7th Ave, Phoenix, AZ 85013
Grady Gammage Memorial Auditorium	Arizona	Tempe	Arizona State University Campus, Gammage Pkwy and Apache Blvd, Tempe, AZ 85287
Taliesin West	Arizona	Scottsdale	12621 North Frank Lloyd Wright Blvd, Scottsdale, AZ 85259
Bachman-Wilson House	Arkansas	Bentonville	600 Museum Way, Bentonville, AR 72712
Ablin House	California	Bakersfield	4272 Country Club Dr, Bakersfield, CA 93306
Bazett House	California	Hillsborough	101 Reservoir Road, Hillsborough, CA 94010
The Hanna House	California	Stanford	Stanford University, Stanford, CA 94305-6115
Hollyhock House	California	Los Angeles	4800 Hollywood Blvd, Los Angeles, CA 90027
Marin County Civic Center	California	San Rafael	3501 Civic Center Dr, San Rafael, CA 94903
Nakoma Golf Resort	California	Clio	348 Bear Run Rr, Clio, CA, 96106
Pearce House	California	Bradbury	106 Bradbury Hills Ln, Bradbury, CA 91008
Florida Southern College	Florida	Lakeland	111 Lake Hollingsworth Dr, Lakeland, FL 33801
Lewis House	Florida	Tallahassee	3131 Okeeheepkee Rd, Tallahassee, FL 32303
Emil Bach House	Illinois	Chicago	7415 N. Sheridan Rd, Chicago, IL 60626
B. Harley Bradley House	Illinois	Kankakee	701 S. Harrison Ave, Kankakee, IL 60901
Charnley-Persky House	Illinois	Chicago	1365 N. Astor St, Chicago, IL 60610
Dana-Thomas House	Illinois	Springfield	301 E. Lawrence Ave, Springfield, IL 62703
Fabyan Villa	Illinois	Geneva	1925 S Batavia Ave, Geneva, IL 60134
Frank Lloyd Wright Home and Studio	Illinois	Oak Park	951 Chicago Ave, Oak Park, IL 60302
Laurent House	Illinois	Rockford	4646 Spring Brook Road | Rockford, IL 61114
Muirhead Farmhouse	Illinois	Hampshire	42W814 Rohrsen Rd, Hampshire, IL 60140
Pettit Chapel	Illinois	Belvidere	Belvidere Cemetery Office, 1121 N. Main St, Belvidere, IL 61008
Frederick C. Robie House	Illinois	Chicago	5757 S. Woodlawn Ave, Chicago, IL 60637
The Rookery	Illinois	Chicago	209 S. LaSalle St, Chicago, IL 60604
Unity Temple	Illinois	Oak Park	875 Lake St, Oak Park, IL 60301
John Christian House (Samara)	Indiana	West Lafayette	1301 Woodland Ave, West Lafayette, IN 47906
Cedar Rock	Iowa	Independence	2611 Quasqueton Diagonal Blvd, Independence, IA 52326
Park Inn Hotel	Iowa	Mason City	7 West State St, Mason City, IA 50401
Stockman House	Iowa	Mason City	530 1st St NE, Mason City, IA 50401
Frank Lloyd Wright's Allen House Museum	Kansas	Wichita	255 N. Roosevelt, Wichita, KS 67208
Affleck House	Michigan	Bloomfield Hills	925 Bloomfield Woods Court, Bloomfield Hills, MI
Melvyn Maxwell Smith House	Michigan	Bloomfield Township	5045 Ponvalley Rd, Bloomfield Twp, MI 48302
Meyer May House	Michigan	Grand Rapids	450 Madison Ave SE, Grand Rapids, MI 49503
Elam House	Minnesota	Austin	309 21st St SW, Austin, MN 55912
Francis Little House - Hallway	Minnesota	Minneapolis	Minneapolis Institute of Arts, 2400 Third Avenue South, Minneapolis, MN 55404
Willey House	Minnesota	Minneapolis	255 Bedford St SE, Minneapolis, MN 55414
Bott House	Missouri	Kansas City	3640 N. Briarcliff Rd. Kansas City MO 55912

作品名	州・県名	都市名	住所
Community Christian Church	Missouri	Kansas City	4601 Main St, Kansas City, MO 64112
The Kraus House	Missouri	St. Louis	120 N. Ballas Rd, St. Louis, MO 63122
Alpine Meadows Ranch	Montana	Montana	469 Bunkhouse Rd, Darby, Montana 59829
Zimmerman House and Kalil House	New Hampshire	Manchester	Currier Museum of Art, 201 Myrtle Way, Manchester, NH 03104
Blue Sky Mausoleum	New York	Buffalo	Forest Lawn Cemetery, 1411 Delaware Ave, Buffalo, NY 14209
Fontana Boathouse	New York	Buffalo	One Rotary Row, Buffalo, NY 14201
Francis Little House, Living Room	New York	New York	Metropolitan Museum of Art, New York, NY 10028
Graycliff	New York	Derby	6472 Old Lake Shore Rd, Derby, NY 14047
Solomon R. Guggenheim Museum	New York	New York	1071 5th Ave, New York, NY 10128
Darwin Martin House and Barton House	New York	Buffalo	125 Jewett Pkwy, Buffalo, NY 14214
Penfield House	Ohio	Willoughby Hills	2203 River Rd #9685, Willoughby Hills, OH 44094
Weltzheimer-Johnson House	Ohio	Oberlin	534 Morgan St, Oberlin, OH 44074
Westcott House	Ohio	Springfield	1340 East High St, Springfield, OH 45503
Price Tower	Oklahoma	Bartlesville	510 Dewey Ave, Bartlesville, OK 74003
The Gordon House	Oregon	Silverton	The Oregon Garden, 869 W. Main St, Silverton, OR 97381
Beth Sholom Synagogue	Pennsylvania	Elkins Park	8231 Old York Rd, Elkins Park, PA 19027
Duncan House and Lindholm House	Pennsylvania	Acme	Polymath Park, 187 Evergreen Lane, Acme, PA 15610
Fallingwater	Pennsylvania	Mill Run	PO Box R, Mill Run, PA 15464
Frank Lloyd Wright's Original San Francisco Office	Pennsylvania	Erie	Hagen History Center, 356 West 6th Street, Erie, PA 16507
Kentuck Knob	Pennsylvania	Chalk Hill	723 Kentuck Rd, Chalk Hill, PA 15421
Kalita Humphreys Theater	Texas	Dallas	Dallas Theater Center, 3636 Turtle Creek Blvd, Dallas, TX 75219
Pope-Leighey House	Virginia	Alexandria	9000 Richmond Hwy, Alexandria, VA 22309
American System-Built Homes, Model B1	Wisconsin	Milwaukee	2714 W. Burnham St, Milwaukee, WI 53215
Annunciation Greek Orthodox Church	Wisconsin	Milwaukee	9400 W. Congress, Milwaukee, WI 53225
Bernard Schwartz House	Wisconsin	Two Rivers	3425 Adams St, Two Rivers, Wisconsin 54241
A.D. German Warehouse	Wisconsin	Richland Center	300 S. Church St, Richland Center, WI 53581
Johnson Administration Building	Wisconsin	Racine	1525 Howe St, Racine, WI 53403
Monona Terrace	Wisconsin	Madison	1 John Nolen Dr, Madison, WI 53703
Seth Peterson Cottage	Wisconsin	Lake Delton	E9982 Fern Dell Rd, Lake Delton, WI 53940
Taliesin & Hillside	Wisconsin	Spring Green	Hwy 23 and County Hwy C, Spring Green, WI 53588
Unitarian Meeting House	Wisconsin	Madison	900 University Bay Drive, Madison, WI 53705
Wingspread	Wisconsin	Racine	33 East Four Mile Rd, Racine, WI 53402
Wyoming Valley School Cultural Arts Center	Wisconsin	Spring Green	PO Box 508, 6306 State Rd, Spring Green, WI 53588
帝国ホテル二代目本館 Imperial Hotel Entrance Hall and Lobby Reconstruction	愛知県 Aichi	犬山市 Inuyama-shi	博物館明治村 Museum Meiji-Mura
自由学園 Jiyu Gakuen School（Myonichikan）	東京都 Tokyo	豊島区 Toshima-ku	西池袋2-31-3 2-31-3, Nishi Ikebukuro, Toshima-ku
山邑邸 Yamamura House（Yodoko Guest House）	兵庫県 Hyogo	芦屋市 Ashiya-shi	山手町3-10 ヨドコウ迎賓館 3-10, Yamate-cho, Ashiya-shi

参考文献
Bibliography

ライトの著作

Wright, Frank Lloyd, *Ausgefürte Bauten und Entwürfe von Frank Lloyd Wright*, Ernst Wasmuth, Berlin, 1910.

Wright, Frank Lloyd, *Frank Lloyd Wright: Ausgeführte Bauten*, edited by C. R. Ashbee, Ernst Wasmuth, Berlin, 1911.

Wright, Frank Lloyd, *Frank Lloyd Wright: Eine Studie zu seiner Würdigung*, edited by C. R. Ashbee, Ernst Wasmuth, Berlin, 1911.

Wright, Frank Lloyd, *Frank Lloyd Wright*, Ernst Wasmuth, Berlin, 1911.

Wright, Frank Lloyd, *The Japanese Print: An Interpretation*, Ralph Fletcher Seymour, Chicago, 1912.

Wright, Frank Lloyd, *Experimenting with Human Lives*, Ralph Fletcher Seymour, Chicago, 1923.

Wright, Frank Lloyd, *Modern Architecture: Being the Kahn Lectures for 1930*, Princeton University Press, Princeton NJ, 1931.
(山形浩生訳『フランク・ロイド・ライトの現代建築講義』白水社、2009)

Wright, Frank Lloyd, *Two Lectures on Architecture, Chicago Art Institute*, Chicago, 1931.

Wright, Frank Lloyd, *An Autobiography*, Longmans, Green and Company, New York, 1932.

Wright, Frank Lloyd, *The Disappearing City*, William Farquhar Payson, New York, 1932.

Wright, Frank Lloyd and Baker Brownell, *Architecture and Modern Life*, Harper & Brothers Publishers, New York, 1937.

Wright, Frank Lloyd, *An Organic Architecture: The Architecture of Democracy*, Lund Humphries Publishers Ltd., London, 1939.

Wright, Frank Lloyd, *An Autobiography*, Duell, Sloan and Pearce, New York, 1943.

Wright, Frank Lloyd, *When Democracy Builds*, University of Chicago Press, Chicago, 1945.

Wright, Frank Lloyd, *When Democracy Builds*, Second Edition, University of Chicago Press, Chicago, 1945.
(二見甚郷訳『デモクラシイの眞髄』永晃社、1949)

Wright, Frank Lloyd, *Genius and the Mobocracy*, Duell, Sloan and Pearce, New York, 1949.

Wright, Frank Lloyd, and Edgar Kaufmann Jr., *Taliesin Drawings: Recent Architecture of Frank Lloyd Wright, Selected from His Drawings*, (Problems of Contemporary Art), Wittenborn Schultz Inc., New York, 1952.

Wright, Frank Lloyd, *The Future of Architecture*, Horizon Press, New York, 1953.

Wright, Frank Lloyd, *The Natural House*, Horizon Press, New York, 1954.
(遠藤楽訳『ライトの住宅:自然・人間・建築』彰国社、1967、富岡義人訳『自然の家』ちくま学芸文庫、2010)

Wright, Frank Lloyd, *The Story of the Tower*, Horizon Press, New York, 1956.

Wright, Frank Lloyd, *A Testament*, Horizon Press, New York, 1957.
(谷川正己・谷川睦子共訳『ライトの遺言』彰国社、1966、樋口清訳『テスタメント』中央公論美術出版、2010)

Wright, Frank Lloyd, *The Living City*, Horizon Press, New York, 1958.
(谷川正己・谷川睦子共訳『ライトの都市論』彰国社、1968)

没後出版

Wright, Frank Lloyd, Arthur Drexler, and Museum of Modern Art (New York), *The Drawings of Frank Lloyd Wright*, Horizon Press, New York, 1962.

Wright, Frank Lloyd, *Buildings Plans and Designs by Frank Lloyd Wright*, forwarded by William Wesley Peters, Horizon Press, New York, 1963.
(横山正訳『フランク・ロイド・ライト建築図面集』A.D.A. EDITA Tokyo、1976)

Wright, Frank Lloyd, *The Industrial Revolutions Runs Away*, Horizon Press, New York, 1969.

Wright, Frank Lloyd, and Hendricus Th. Wijdeveld, *The Work of Frank Lloyd Wright. The Life-Work of the American Architect Frank Lloyd Wright*, 1965 ed., Bramhall House, New York, 1971.

Wright, Frank Lloyd, *An Autobiography*, Horizon Press, New York, 1977.
(樋口清訳『ライト自伝──ある芸術の形成』中央公論美術出版、1988、樋口清訳『ライト自伝──ある芸術の展開』中央公論美術出版、2000)

Wright, Frank Lloyd, *Drawings and Plans of Frank Lloyd Wright: The Early Period (1893-1909)*, Dover Publications, New York, 1983.

Wright, Frank Lloyd, Terence Riley, Peter Reed, Anthony Alofsin, Museum of Modern Art (New York), and Frank Lloyd Wright Foundation, *Frank Lloyd Wright, Architect*, Harry N. Abrams, New York, 1994.
(テレンス・ライリー、ピーター・リード編著、京都大学工学部建築学教室内井研究室監訳『建築家 フランク・ロイド・ライト』デルファイ研究所、1995)

Wright, Frank Lloyd, Mike Wallace, Archetype Associates, and Frank Lloyd Wright Foundation, *Frank Lloyd Wright the Mike Wallace Interviews*, Archetype Associates, New York, 1994. videorecording, 1 videocassette (53 min.) : sd., col., b&w ; 1/2 in.

Wright, Frank Lloyd, *Frank Lloyd Wright the Mike Wallace Interviews*, Archetype Associates, New York, 1994. videorecording, 1 videocassette (53 min.) : sd., col., b&w ; 1/2 in.

Wright, Frank Lloyd, R. Nicholas Olsberg, Frank Lloyd Wright Archives, and Luna Imaging, *Frank Lloyd Wright Presentation and Conceptual Drawings*, Oxford University Press, Oxford, 1995.

Wright, Frank Lloyd, and Robert McCarter, *On and by Frank Lloyd Wright: A Primer of Architectural Principles*, Phaidon Press, London, 2005.

Wright, Frank Lloyd, ed., *The Essential Frank Lloyd Wright: Critical Writings on Architecture*, edited by Bruce Brooks Pfeiffer, Princeton University Press, Princeton, 2008.

Wright, Frank Lloyd, *The Florence Sketchbook of Frank Lloyd Wright, 1910*, Wittenborn Art Books, San Francisco, 2010.

Wright, Frank Lloyd, Kenneth Frampton, Carole Ann Fabian, and Barry Bergdoll, *Wright's Writings: Reflections on Culture and Politics 1894-1959*, Columbia University Press, New York, 2017.

ライトの言葉を集めたもの

Gutheim, Frederick ed., *Frank Lloyd Wright, On Architecture: selected writings*, Duell, Sloan and Pearce, New York, 1941.
(谷川睦子・谷川正己共訳『建築について(上)(下)』鹿島出版会、1980)

Gutheim, Frederick ed., *In the Cause of Architecture, Frank Lloyd Wright*, McGraw-Hill Publication, Pennsylvania, 1975.

Heywood, Robert B. ed., *The Works of the Mind*, University of Chicago Press, Chicago, 1947.

Kaufmann, Edgar, ed., *Frank Lloyd Wright, An American Architecture*, Horizon Press, New York, 1955.
（谷川正己・谷川睦子共訳『ライトの建築論』彰国社、1970）

Kaufmann, Edgar, and Ben Raeburn, ed., *Frank Lloyd Wright, Writings and Buildings*, Horizon Press, New York, 1960.
（谷川正己・谷川睦子訳『フランク・ロイド・ライト：建築の理念』A.D.A.EDITA Tokyo、1976）

Meehan, Patrick J., ed., *The Master Architect: Conversations with Frank Lloyd Wright*, John Wiley & Sons Inc., New Jersey, 1984.

Meehan, Patrick J., ed., *Truth Against the World: Frank Lloyd Wright Speaks for an Organic Architecture*, Preservation Press, Lafayette, 1992.

Peter, John, *The Oral History of Modern Architecture*, Harry N. Abrams, New York, 1994.
（小川次郎・小山光・繁昌朗共訳『近代建築の証言』TOTO出版、2001）

Pfeiffer, Bruce Brooks, ed., *The Collected Writings of Frank Lloyd Wright*, volume 1, Rizzoli, New York, 1992.

Pfeiffer, Bruce Brooks, ed., *The Collected Writings of Frank Lloyd Wright, volume 2*, Including *An Autobiography*, Rizzoli, New York, 1992.

Pfeiffer, Bruce Brooks, ed., *The Collected Writings of Frank Lloyd Wright, volume 3*, Rizzoli, New York, 1993.

Pfeiffer, Bruce Brooks, ed., *The Collected Writings of Frank Lloyd Wright, volume 4*, Rizzoli, New York, 1994.

Pfeiffer, Bruce Brooks, ed., *The Collected Writings of Frank Lloyd Wright, volume 5*, Rizzoli, New York, 1995.

Pfeiffer, Bruce Brooks, ed., *Frank Lloyd Wright, Letters to Apprentices*, The Press at California State University, Fresno, 1982.
（内井昭蔵・小林陽子共訳『フランク・ロイド・ライト 弟子達への手紙』丸善、1987）

Pfeiffer, Bruce Brooks, ed., *Frank Lloyd Wright, Letters to Architects*, The Press at California State University, Fresno, 1984.
（内井昭蔵訳『フランク・ロイド・ライト 建築家への手紙』丸善、1986）

Pfeiffer, Bruce Brooks, ed., *Frank Lloyd Wright, Letters to Clients*, The Press at California State University, Fresno, 1986.

Pfeiffer, Bruce Brooks, ed., *Frank Lloyd Wright: The Guggenheim Correspondence*, Southern Illinois University Press, Carbondale, 1986.

Pfeiffer, Bruce Brooks, ed., *Frank Lloyd Wright, His Living Voice*, The Press at California State University, Fresno, 1987.

Pfeiffer, Bruce Brooks, and Robert Wojtowicz, ed., *Frank Lloyd Wright & Lewis Mumford, Thirty Years of Correspondence*, Princeton Architectural Press, Princeton, 2001.
（富岡義人訳『ライト＝マンフォード往復書簡集1926-1959』鹿島出版会,2005）

Pfeiffer, Bruce Brooks, ed., *The Essential Frank Lloyd Wright: Critical Writings on Architecture*, Princeton University Press, Princeton, 2008.
（三輪直美訳『有機的建築——オーガニックアーキテクチャー』筑摩書房、2009）

ライト研究・作品集

Aguar, Charles E. and Berdeanne Aguar, *Wrightscapes: Frank Lloyd Wright's Landscape Designs*, McGraw-Hill, Pennsylvania, 2002.
（大木順子訳『フランク・ロイド・ライトのランドスケープデザイン』丸善、2004）

Alofsin, Anthony, *Frank Lloyd Wright, The Lost Years, 1910-1922*, The University of Chicago Press, Chicago, 1993.

Alofsin, Anthony, ed. *Frank Lloyd Wright: Europe and Beyond*, University of California Press, Berkeley, 1999.

Bergdoll, Barry, and Jennifer Gray, Museum of Modern Art (New York), and Avery Library, *Frank Lloyd Wright: Unpacking the Archive*, The Museum of Modern Art, New York, 2017.

Birk, Melanie, and Frank Lloyd Wright Home and Studio Foundation, *Frank Lloyd Wright and the Prairie*, Universe, New York, 1998.

Blake, Peter, *Frank Lloyd Wright: Architecture and Space*, Penguin Books, 1963.

Bolon, Carol R., Robert S. Nelson, and Linda Seidel, ed., *The Nature of Frank Lloyd Wright*, The University of Chicago Press, Chicago, 1988.

Brooks, Harold Allen ed., *Writings on Wright, selected comments on Frank Lloyd Wright*, The MIT Press, Cambridge, Massachusetts, 1991.

Casciato, Maristella, "Wright and Italy: The Promise of Organic Architecture", in *Frank Lloyd Wright: Europe and Beyond*, edited by Anthony Alofsin, University of California Press, Berkeley, 1999.

The Caxon Club ed., *Chicago by the Book: 1010 Publications That Shaped the City and Its Image*, featuring "Ausgeführte Bauten Und Entwürfe Von Frank Lloyd Wright [Completed Buildings and Designs by Frank Lloyd Wright]", University of Chicago Press, Chicago, 2018.

Cleary, Richard Louis, *Frank Lloyd Wright: From Within Outward*, Skira Rizzoli, New York, 2009.

De Long, David Gilson, ed., *Frank Lloyd Wright, Designs for an American Landscape 1922-1932*, Harry N. Abrams, New York, 1996.

Wright, Frank Lloyd, David Gilson De Long, Vitra Design Museum, Exhibitions International, and Frank Lloyd Wright Foundation, *Frank Lloyd Wright and the Living City*, (A travelling exhibition held at Vitra Design Museum, Weilam Rhein, Germany et al.) Skira, Milan, 1998.

Fell, Derek, *The Gardens of Frank Lloyd Wright*, Frances Lincoln Publushers, London, 2009.

Fishman, Robert, *Urban Utopias in the Twentieth Century, Ebenezer Howard, Frank Lloyd Wright, and Le Corbusier*, MIT Press, Massachusetts, 1977.

Gannett, William Channing, *The House Beautiful: A Book Designed by Frank Lloyd Wright*, Pomegranate, Communications, Inc. Petaluma, 1996.

Gill, Brendan, *Many Masks: A Life of Frank Lloyd Wright*, Putnam, G.P. Putnam's Sons, New York, 1987.
（ブレンダン・ギル著、塚口眞佐子訳『ライト 仮面の生涯』学芸出版社、2009）

Gray, Jennifer, ed., *Frank Lloyd Wright Tra America E Italia = Frank Lloyd Wright between USA and Italy*, Corraini Edizioni, Mantova, 2018.

Guerrero, Pedro E., *Picturing Wright: An Album from Frank Lloyd Wright's Photographer*, Pomegranate, Communications, Inc. Petaluma, 1993.

Guerrero, Pedro E., *Pedro E. Guerrero: A Photographer's Journey*, Princeton Architectural Press, Princeton, 2007.

Grant Hildebrand, *The Wright Space*, University of Washington Press, Seattle, 1991.

Hanks, David, *The Decorative Designs of Frank Lloyd Wright*, Dutton Books, New York, 1979.
（デヴィッド・D. ハンクス著、穂積信夫訳『ライトの装飾デザイン』彰国社、1981）

Henning, Randolph C., "At Taliesin", *Newspaper Columns by Frank Lloyd Wright and the Taliesin Fellowship, 1934-1937*, Southern Illinois University Press, Carbondale, 1992.

Hess, Alan, *Frank Lloyd Wright: Prairie Houses*, Rizzoli, New York, 2006.

Hess, Alan, *Frank Lloyd Wright: Mid-Century Modern*, Rizzoli, New York, 2007.

Hess, Alan, *Frank Lloyd Wright: The Buildings*, Rizzoli, New York, 2008.

Hitchcock, Henry-Russell, *In the Nature of Materials*, Hawthorn Books, Inc., New York, 1942.

Hoffmann, Donald, *Frank Lloyd Wright: Architecture and Nature*, Dover, New York, 1986.

Huxtable, Ada Louise, *Frank Lloyd Wright, A Life*,

Lipper/Viking Book, New York, 2004.
（エイダ・ルイーズ・ハクスタブル著、三輪直美訳『未完の建築家—フランク・ロイド・ライト』TOTO出版、2007）

Izzo, Alberto, and Camillo Gubitosi, Frank Lloyd Wright, Università di Napoli. Istituto di analisi architettonica., and Frank Lloyd Wright Foundation, *Frank Lloyd Wright, Three-Quarters of a Century of Drawings*, Horizon Press, New York, 1981.

James, Cary, *The Imperial Hotel; Frank Lloyd Wright and the Architecture of Unity*, C.E. Tuttle Co., Rutland, Vt., 1968.

Kaufmann, Jr. Edgar, *9 Commentaries on Frank Lloyd Wright*, the Architectural History Foundation, The MIT Press, Massachusetts, 1989.

Kaufmann, Jr. Edgar, Christopher Little, Thomas A. Heinz, and L.D. Astorino & Associates, *Fallingwater: A Frank Lloyd Wright Country House*, Abbeville Press, New York, 1986.

Kruty, Paul, *Prelude to the Prairie Style: Eight Models of Unbuilt Houses by Frank Lloyd Wright 1893-1901*, University of Illinois Press, Urbana, 2005.

Langmead, Donald, *Frank Lloyd Wright: A Bio-Bibliography*, Praeger Publishers, Westport, 2003.

Lampugnani, Vittorio Magnago, *Visionary Architecture of the 20th Century : Master Drawings from Frank Lloyd Wright to Aldo Rossi*, Thames and Hudson, London, 1983.

Laseau, Paul and James Tice, *Frank Lloyd Wright: Between Principle and Form*, Van Nostrand Reinhold, New York,1991.
（ポール・レイジュー、ジェームス・タイス著、倉島建美訳『ライト建築のタイポロジー 原理から形態へ』集文社、1998）

Levine, Neil, *The Architecture of Frank Lloyd Wright*, Princeton University Press, Princeton, 1996.

Levine, Neil, *The Urbanism of Frank Lloyd Wright*, Princeton University Press, Princeton, 2016.

Levy, Janey, *The Architecture of Frank Lloyd Wright: Understanding Concepts of Parallel And Perpendicular*, Powerkids Press, New York, 2005.

Malecki, Juan Sebastian "Frank Lloyd Wright's Argentinean Early Reception: The Case of Carlos Lange (1942-1953)." *Estudios del Hábitat* 17, no. 2, Universidad Nacional de La Plata, Buenos Aires, 2019.

Manson, Grant Carpenter, *Frank Lloyd Wright to 1910: The First Golden Age*, Reinhold Publishing Corporation, New York, 1958.

McCarter, Robert, ed., *Frank Lloyd Wright: A Primer on Architectural Principles*, Princeton Architectural Press, Princeton, 1991.

McCarter, Robert, *Unity Temple: Frank Lloyd Wright*, Architecture in Detail, Phaidon, London, 1997.

Meech, Julia, *Frank Lloyd Wright and the Art of Japan: The Architect's Other Passion*, Japan Society and Harry N. Abrams, New York, 2001.

Meehan, Patrick Joseph, *Frank Lloyd Wright: A Research Guide to Archival Sources*, Garland Bibliographies in Architecture and Planning, vol. 294, Taylor & Francis, New York, 1983.

Menocal, Narciso G., ed., *Wright Studies vol. 1: Taliesin 1911-1914*, Southern Illinois University Press, Carbondale, 1992.

Menocal, Narciso G., ed., *Wright Studies vol. 2: Fallingwater and Pittsburgh*, Southern Illinois University Press, Carbondale, 2000.

Nash, Eric Peter, *Frank Lloyd Wright, Force of Nature*, Todtri Productions Ltd., New York, 1996.

Nute, Kevin, *Frank Lloyd Wright and Japan: The Role of Traditional Japanese Art and Architecture in the Work of Frank Lloyd Wright*, Van Nostrand Reinhold, New York, 1993.
（ケヴィン・ニュート著、大木順子訳『フランク・ロイド・ライトと日本文化』鹿島出版会、1997）

O'Gorman, James F., *Three American Architects: Richardson, Sullivan, and Wright, 1865-1915*, University of Chicago Press, Chicago, 1991.

Patterson, Terry L., *Frank Lloyd Wright and the Meaning of Materials*, Van Nostrand Reinhold, Chicago, 1994.

Pfeiffer, Bruce Brooks, ed., *Frank Lloyd Wright: In the Realm of Ideas*, Southern Illinois University Press, Carbondale, 1988.

Pfeiffer, Bruce Brooks, *Frank Lloyd Wright, The Crowning Decade, 1949-1959*, Southern Illinois University Press, Carbondale, 1989.

Pfeiffer, Bruce Brooks, Frank Lloyd Wright, Frank Lloyd Wright Foundation., and Phoenix Art Museum, *Frank Lloyd Wright Drawings: Masterworks from the Frank Lloyd Wright Archives*, Harry N. Abrams, New York, 1990.
（ブルース・ブルックス・ファイファー著、吉富久美子訳『フランク・ロイド・ライトドローイング集』同朋舎出版、1991年）

Pfeiffer, Bruce Brooks, ed., *Frank Lloyd Wright: Master Builder*, Universe Publishing and The Frank Lloyd Wright Foundation, 1997.
（ブルース・ブルックス・ファイファー著、大木順子訳『巨匠フランク・ロイド・ライト』鹿島出版会、1999）

Pfeiffer, Bruce Brooks, Gössel P. ed., *Frank Lloyd Wright, Complete Works, Vol.3, 1943-1959*, Taschen, Köln, 2009.

Pfeiffer, Bruce Brooks, Gössel P. ed., *Frank Lloyd Wright, Complete Works, Vol.2, 1917-1942*, Taschen, Köln, 2010.

Pfeiffer, Bruce Brooks, Gössel P. ed., *Frank Lloyd Wright, Complete Works, Vol.1, 1885-1916*, Taschen, Köln, 2011.

Quinan, Jack, *Frank Lloyd Wright's Larkin Building: Myth and Fact*, Architectural History Foundation; MIT Press, Massachusetts, 1989.

Reed, Peter and Willian Kaizen ed., *The Show to End All Shows*, The Museum of Modern Art, New York, 2004.

Riley, Terence, *The International Style: Exhibition 15 and the Museum of Modern Art*, Rizzoli, New York, 1992.

Roberts, Ellen E. "Ukiyo-E in Chicago: Frank Lloyd Wright, Marion Mahony Griffin and the Prairie School." *Art in Print* 3, no. 2, 2013.

Rubin, Jeanne Spielman, *Intimate Triangle: Architecture of Crystals, Frank Lloyd Wright And The Froebel Kindergarten*, Polycrystal Book Service, Huntsville, 2002.

Sartori, Alberto, "Wright and South America," in *Frank Lloyd Wright: Europe and Beyond*, edited by Anthony Alofsin, University of California Press, Berkeley, 1999.

Satler, Gail, *Frank Lloyd Wright's Living Space: Architecture's Fourth Dimension*, Northern Illinois University Press, Dekalb, 1999.

Secrest, Meryle, *Frank Lloyd Wright: A Biography*, University of Chicago Press, Chicago, 1998.

Sergeant, John, *Frank Lloyd Wright's Usonian Houses: The Case for Organic Architecture*, Whitney Library of Design, New York, 1976.

Scully Jr., Vincent, *Frank Lloyd Wright*, George Braziller Inc., New York, 1960.

Siry, Joseph M. "Wright's Baghdad Opera House and Gammage Auditorium: In Search of Regional Modernity." *Art Bulletin* 87, no. 2, 2005.

Smith, Norris Kelly, *Frank Lloyd Wright: A study in architectural content*, American Life Foundation & Study Institute, Watkins Glen, New York, 1979.

Smith, Kathryn, *Frank Lloyd Wright, Hollyhock House and Olive Hill: Buildings and Projects for Aline Barnsdall*. Rizzoli, New York, 1992.

Smith, Kathryn, *Frank Lloyd Wright's Taliesin and Taliesin West*, Harry N. Abrams, New York, 1997.

Smith, Kathryn, *Frank Lloyd Wright: America's Master Architect*. 1st ed, Abbeville Press, New York, 1998.

Smith, Kathryn, *Wright on Exhibit: Frank Lloyd Wright's Architectural Exhibitions*, Princeton University Press, Princeton, 2017.

Storrer, Willian Allin, *The Frank Lloyd Wright Companion*, The University of Chicago Press, Chicago, 1993.
（岸田省吾監訳『フランク・ロイド・ライト全作品』丸善、2000）

Sullivan, Louis Henry, "Concerning the Imperial Hotel Tokyo, Japan by Louis H. Sullivan 1923", in

The Early Work of the Great Architect Frank Lloyd Wright, Gramercy Books, New York, 1994.

Sullivan, Louis Henry, Paul Edward Sprague, and Avery Library, *The Drawings of Louis Henry Sullivan: A Catalogue of the Frank Lloyd Wright Collection at the Avery Architectural Library*, Princeton University Press, Princeton, 1979.

Sweeny, Robert Lawrence, *Frank Lloyd Wright: An Annotated Bibliography*, Hennessey and Ingalls, Inc., Los Angeles, 1978.

Tafel, Edgar, *Years with Frank Lloyd Wright*, McGraw-Hill, New York, 1979.
(エドガー・ターフェル著、谷川正己・睦子共訳『知られざるフランク・ロイド・ライト』鹿島出版会、1992)

Turner, Paul Venable, and Frank Lloyd Wright, *Frank Lloyd Wright and San Francisco*, Yale University Press, New Haven and London, 2016.

Twombly, Robert C., *Frank Lloyd Wright: His Life and His Architecture*, John Wiley & Sons, Inc., New York, 1979.

Van Zanten, David, ed., *Marion Mahony Reconsidered*, University of Chicago Press, Chicago, 2011.

Ven, Cornelis Van de, *Space in Architecture*, Van Gorcum Ltd., Assen, 1980.
(佐々木宏訳『建築の空間』丸善、1981)

White, Morton Gabriel and Lucia White, *The Intellectual Versus the City: From Thomas Jefferson to Frank Lloyd Wright*, Harvard University Press and The MIT Press, Oxford and New York, 1962.

Wright, John Lloyd, *My Father Who is on Earth*, a new edition, Southern Illinois University Press, Carbondale, 1994.

Wright, Olgivanna Lloyd, *Frank Lloyd Wright: His Life, His Work, His Words*, Horizon Press, New York, 1966.
(オルギヴァンナ・L. ライト著、遠藤楽訳『ライトの生涯』彰国社、1977)

Zevi, Bruno, *Frank Lloyd Wright*, Birkhauser, Basel, 1998.

明石信道『旧帝国ホテルの実証的研究』東光堂書店、1972

天野太郎、樋口清、生田勉編『フランク・ロイド・ライト』彰国社、1954

浦辺鎮太郎・天野太郎『フランク・ロイド・ライト1』美術出版社、1967

「フランク・ロイド・ライトと現代」『a+u』1981年7月臨時増刊号、新建築社、1981

「フランク・ロイド・ライトのルーツ」『X-Knowledge Home』特別編集 no.4、エクスナレッジ、2005

岡野眞『フランク・ロイド・ライトの建築遺産』丸善、2005

大久保美春『フランク・ロイド・ライト：建築は自然への捧げ物』ミネルヴァ書房、2008

自由学園女子部卒業生会編『自由学園の歴史 I 雑司ヶ谷時代』婦人之友社、1985

『自由学園100年史』自由学園出版局、2021

谷川正己『フランク・ロイド・ライト』鹿島出版会、1967

谷川正己『ライトと日本』鹿島出版会、1977

谷川正己『the WRIGHTIANA・I』日本大学工学部建築学科谷川研究室、1994

谷川正己『the WRIGHTIANA・II』日本大学工学部建築学科谷川研究室、1994

谷川正己『the WRIGHTIANA・III』日本大学工学部建築学科谷川研究室、1994

谷川正己『the WRIGHTIANA・IV』日本大学工学部建築学科谷川研究室、1994

谷川正己『the WRIGHTIANA・V』日本大学工学部建築学科谷川研究室、1995

谷川正己編著『図面で見るF.L.ライト―日本での全業績』彰国社、1995

谷川正己『the WRIGHTIANA・VI』日本大学工学部建築学科谷川研究室、1997

谷川正己『the WRIGHTIANA・VII』日本大学工学部建築学科谷川研究室、1999

谷川正己『フランク・ロイド・ライトとはだれか』王国社、2001

谷川正己『フランク・ロイド・ライトの日本―浮世絵に魅せられた「もう1つの顔」』光文社、2004

『帝国ホテル百年の歩み』帝国ホテル、1990

『帝国ホテル百年史：1890-1990』帝国ホテル、1990

『帝国ホテル 写真で見る歩み』帝国ホテル、2003

『帝国ホテルの120年』帝国ホテル、2010

富岡義人『フランク・ロイド・ライト 大地に芽ばえた建築』丸善、2001

西尾雅敏『帝国ホテル中央玄関復原記』博物館明治村、2010

パルマー・J. A. 著、須藤自由児訳『環境の思想家たち 上―古代―近代編』みすず書房、2004

二川幸夫編『フランク・ロイド・ライト全集 第1巻〈モノグラフ 1887-1901〉』A.D.A.EDITA Tokyo、1986

二川幸夫編『フランク・ロイド・ライト全集 第2巻〈モノグラフ 1902-1906〉』A.D.A.EDITA Tokyo、1987

二川幸夫編『フランク・ロイド・ライト全集 第3巻〈モノグラフ 1907-1913〉』A.D.A.EDITA Tokyo、1987

二川幸夫編『フランク・ロイド・ライト全集 第4巻〈モノグラフ 1914-1923〉』A.D.A.EDITA Tokyo、1985

二川幸夫編『フランク・ロイド・ライト全集 第5巻〈モノグラフ 1924-1936〉』A.D.A.EDITA Tokyo、1985

二川幸夫編『フランク・ロイド・ライト全集 第6巻〈モノグラフ 1937-1941〉』A.D.A.EDITA Tokyo、1986

二川幸夫編『フランク・ロイド・ライト全集 第7巻〈モノグラフ 1942-1950〉』A.D.A.EDITA Tokyo、1988

二川幸夫編『フランク・ロイド・ライト全集 第8巻〈モノグラフ 1951-1959〉』A.D.A.EDITA Tokyo、1988

二川幸夫編『フランク・ロイド・ライト全集 第9巻〈プレリミナリー・スタディ 1889-1916〉』A.D.A.EDITA Tokyo、1985

二川幸夫編『フランク・ロイド・ライト全集 第10巻〈プレリミナリー・スタディ 1917-1932〉』A.D.A.EDITA Tokyo、1986

二川幸夫編『フランク・ロイド・ライト全集 第11巻〈プレリミナリー・スタディ 1933-1959〉』A.D.A.EDITA Tokyo、1987

二川幸夫編『フランク・ロイド・ライト全集 第12巻〈レンダリング 1887-1959〉』A.D.A.EDITA Tokyo、1984

二川幸夫編『フランク・ロイド・ライトの住宅 第1巻〈プレイリー・ハウス1889-1916〉』A.D.A.EDITA Tokyo、1991

二川幸夫編『フランク・ロイド・ライトの住宅 第2巻〈タリアセン〉』A.D.A.EDITA Tokyo、1990

二川幸夫編『フランク・ロイド・ライトの住宅 第3巻〈タリアセン・ウェスト〉』A.D.A.EDITA Tokyo、1989

二川幸夫編『フランク・ロイド・ライトの住宅 第4巻〈落水荘〉』A.D.A.EDITA Tokyo、1990

二川幸夫編『フランク・ロイド・ライトの住宅 第5巻〈1930, 40年代の名作〉』A.D.A.EDITA Tokyo、1990

二川幸夫編『フランク・ロイド・ライトの住宅 第6巻〈ユーソニアン・ハウスI〉』A.D.A.EDITA Tokyo、1991

二川幸夫編『フランク・ロイド・ライトの住宅 第7巻〈ユーソニアン・ハウスII〉』A.D.A.EDITA Tokyo、1991

二川幸夫編『フランク・ロイド・ライトの住宅 第8巻〈コンクリート及びコンクリート・ブロックの住宅〉』A.D.A.EDITA Tokyo、1991

三沢浩『フランク・ロイド・ライトのモダニズム』彰国社、2001

三沢浩『フランク・ロイド・ライト入門―その空間づくり四十八手』王国社、2008

水上優『フランク・ロイド・ライトの建築思想』中央公論美術出版、2013

アーリン・サンダーソン著、水上優訳『建築ガイドブック フランク・ロイド・ライト』丸善、2008

水上優『花美術館 vol.59 特集フランク・ロイド・ライト』蒼海出版、2018

有機的建築の会「第1回パネルディスカッション 有機的建築とは何か」有機的建築の会、1982

[出品作品一覧]

凡例

- 作品データは以下の順に記載した：作品資料番号、作品・資料名（所在地・建築期間）、作者名、製作・出版先、制作年・撮影年、寸法（高さ×幅、あるいは高さ×幅×奥行きcm）、技法／材質、所蔵先、クレジットの順に記載した。
- 汐留会場に不出品の作品は、作品資料番号の横に「*」を付した。
- その他、各会場で展示替えの都合により展示されていない場合もある。

SECTION 1
モダン誕生 シカゴ−東京、浮世絵的世界観

1-1
- フランク・ロイド・ライト、タリアセンにて
- 撮影者不詳
- 撮影：1924年
- 写真（複写）
- コロンビア大学 エイヴリー建築美術図書館 フランク・ロイド・ライト財団 アーカイヴズ

1-2
- リトル第二邸「北の家」窓ガラス
- デザイン：フランク・ロイド・ライト 製作：テンプル・アート・グラス・カンパニー
- 製作：1912年
- 149.0×54.8
- ガラス、鉛、木
- 豊田市美術館

1　モダン都市シカゴ

1-3
- 1871年のシカゴ大火後の空撮
- 撮影：ショー
- 撮影：1871年
- ステレオグラフ（複写）
- シカゴ歴史博物館

1-4
- 『シカゴ計画』（バーナム・プラン）
- 著：ダニエル・バーナム、エドワード・H. ベネット 図版：ジュール・ゲラン 出版：シカゴ商業クラブ
- 1909年
- 31.5×25.0×2.5
- 印刷、リトグラフ／紙、書籍
- 東京大学工学・情報理工学図書館 工1号館図書館A（社会基盤学）

1-5
- ルッカリー・ビル（イリノイ州シカゴ） エントランスホール
- 建築：バーナム＆ルート 改修：フランク・ロイド・ライト
- 撮影：1893年
- 写真（複写）
- シカゴ歴史博物館

1-6
- オーディトリアム・ビル（イリノイ州シカゴ）南西からの外観
- 建築：アドラー＆サリヴァン 撮影：J.W. テイラー
- 撮影：1897年
- 写真（複写）
- シカゴ歴史博物館

1-7
- リライアンス・ビル （イリノイ州シカゴ）
- 建築：チャールズ・アトウッド （バーナム設計事務所） 撮影：バーンズ・クロスビー社
- 撮影：1897−1904年
- 写真（ガラス乾板からの複写）
- シカゴ歴史博物館

+　シカゴ万国博覧会と鳳凰殿

1-8
- シカゴ万国博覧会 鳥瞰絵図
- 製作：ランド・マクナリー社
- 1893年
- オリジナル：74.9×101.6
- 印刷／紙（複写）
- シカゴ歴史博物館

1-9
- シカゴ万国博覧会 コート・オブ・オナーの大人工池の西端からの眺望
- 撮影者不詳
- 撮影：1893年
- 写真（複写）
- シカゴ歴史博物館

1-10
- シカゴ万国博覧会 交通館
- 撮影：C.P. ラムフォード
- 撮影：1893年
- 写真（複写）
- シカゴ歴史博物館

1-11
- シカゴ万国博覧会日本館 鳳凰殿
- 撮影：1893年
- オリジナル：11.0×25.5
- 写真（複写）
- 帝国ホテル

1-12 *
- 『閣龍世界博覧会 美術品画譜 第壱集』
- 画・著：久保田米僊
- 1893−94年
- 24.5×16.0×1.0
- 印刷／紙、書籍
- 公益財団法人 吉野石膏美術振興財団

1-13 *
- 『閣龍世界博覧会 美術品画譜 第弐集』
- 画・著：久保田米僊
- 1893−94年
- 24.5×16.0×1.0
- 印刷／紙、書籍
- 公益財団法人 吉野石膏美術振興財団

1-14
- 『閣龍世界博覧会 美術品画譜 第参集』
- 画・著：久保田米僊
- 1893−94年
- 24.5×16.0×1.0
- 印刷／紙、書籍
- 公益財団法人 吉野石膏美術振興財団

1-15
- 『閣龍世界博覧会 美術品画譜 第四集』
- 画・著：久保田米僊
- 1893−94年
- 24.5×16.0×1.0
- 印刷／紙、書籍
- 公益財団法人 吉野石膏美術振興財団

2　モダン都市東京

1-16
- 官庁集中計画 エンデ＆ベックマン 第一案
- 計画：ヘルマン・エンデ＆ ヴィルヘルム・ベックマン
- 1886年
- 45.0×31.0／53.0×41.0 （原図は縮尺1:5000）
- 写真／台紙
- 日本建築学会図書館

1-17
- 官庁集中計画 エンデ＆ベックマン 第二案
- 計画：ヘルマン・エンデ＆ ヴィルヘルム・ベックマン
- 1887年
- 49.0×35.0（原図は縮尺1:5000）
- インク、水彩／和紙、裏打ち
- 日本建築学会図書館

1-18
- 諸官庁新築眺望図『Arkitekten, Ende & Böckmann』
- ヘルマン・エンデ＆ ヴィルヘルム・ベックマン
- 1886年
- 34.0×46.5
- リトグラフ／紙
- 日本建築学会図書館

1-19
- 絵葉書 東京名所 東京駅（1914年）
- 9.0×14.0
- 印刷／紙、絵葉書
- 渡辺秀樹コレクション

1-20
- 絵葉書 東京名所 新築落成セル中央ステーション （1914年）
- 9.0×14.0
- 印刷／紙、絵葉書
- 渡辺秀樹コレクション

1-21
- 絵葉書 東京名所 馬場先門通り
- 9.0×14.0
- 印刷／紙、絵葉書
- 渡辺秀樹コレクション

1-22
- 絵葉書 東京名所第一輯 帝国劇場（1911年）
- 9.0×14.0
- 印刷／紙、絵葉書
- 渡辺秀樹コレクション

1-23
- 絵葉書 東京名所 海軍省（1894年）
- 9.0×14.0
- 印刷／紙、絵葉書
- 渡辺秀樹コレクション

1-24
- 絵葉書 東京名所第一輯 司法省（1895年）
- 9.0×14.0
- 印刷／紙、絵葉書
- 渡辺秀樹コレクション

1-25
- 絵葉書 東京名所 警視庁（1911年）
- 9.0×14.0
- 印刷／紙、絵葉書
- 渡辺秀樹コレクション

1-26
- 絵葉書 丸の内より俯瞰せる 日比谷公園扞に霞が関諸官庁
- 9.0×14.0
- 印刷／紙、絵葉書
- 渡辺秀樹コレクション

1-27
- 絵葉書 東京名所 帝国ホテル （一代目、1890年）
- 9.0×14.0
- 印刷／紙、絵葉書
- 渡辺秀樹コレクション

1-28
- 絵葉書 東京名所 日比谷公園正門（1903年）
- 9.0×14.0
- 印刷／紙、絵葉書
- 渡辺秀樹コレクション

1-29
- 絵葉書 東京名所 日比谷公園音楽堂（1905年）
- 9.0×14.0
- 印刷／紙、絵葉書
- 渡辺秀樹コレクション

1-30
- 絵葉書 大東京高架鉄道より据然たる帝国ホテル（1923年）を望む
- 9.0×14.0
- 印刷／紙、絵葉書
- 渡辺秀樹コレクション

1-31
- 絵葉書 東京 桜田門
- 9.0×14.0
- 印刷／紙、絵葉書
- 渡辺秀樹コレクション

1-32
- 絵葉書 第二次仮議事堂（1891年）
- 9.0×14.0
- 印刷／紙、絵葉書
- 渡辺秀樹コレクション

1-33
- 絵葉書 東京府庁舎と 東京市庁舎（1898年）
- 9.0×14.0
- 印刷／紙、絵葉書
- 渡辺秀樹コレクション

1-34
- 絵葉書 米国貴賓一行 新橋停車場着之光景
- 9.0×14.0
- 印刷／紙、絵葉書
- 渡辺秀樹コレクション

3　キャリアのはじまり

+　師サリヴァンと 自然モチーフの装飾

1-35
- シカゴで働き始めた頃の フランク・ロイド・ライト
- 撮影者不詳
- 撮影：1890年頃
- オリジナル：12.7×7.8
- 写真（複写）
- ウィスコンシン歴史博物館

1-36
- ベルフォンテーヌ墓地の ウェインライト家の墓 （ミズーリ州セントルイス）1892年 フランク・ロイド・ライトによる 門の装飾
- 建築：ルイス・サリヴァン レンダリング：フランク・ロイド・ライト
- 70.5×61.3
- インク、鉛筆／ドラフティング・クロス
- コロンビア大学 エイヴリー建築・美術図書館 ルイス・ヘンリー・サリヴァン・ コレクション

1-37
- ベルフォンテーヌ墓地の ウェインライト家の墓 （ミズーリ州セントルイス）1892年 装飾の詳細
- 建築：ルイス・サリヴァン
- 撮影：1996年
- 写真（複写）
- ヴァージニア大学リチャード・ ウィルソン建築アーカイヴ

1-38
- ベルフォンテーヌ墓地の ウェインライト家の墓 （ミズーリ州セントルイス）1892年
- 建築：ルイス・サリヴァン 撮影者不詳

[List of Works]

Notes

- The data of on each work is based on the information provided by the owner and is listed in the following order: catalogue number, title, place, project years, architect/artist's name, name of production company or publisher, date of production, technique and material, dimensions (H×W or H×W×D inch/cm), owner, credit, ID/accession number.
- The works which are not on display at Shiodome venue are indicated in the Japanese list with an asterisk mark put beside the catalogue numbers.
- Some works will be rotated due to the constraints of preservation.

SECTION 1 Modern Beginnings: Chicago – Tokyo and the Culture of Ukiyo-e

1-1
- Portrait of Frank Lloyd Wright at Taliesin, Spring Green, Wisconsin
- Photographer unidentified
- Photo: 1924
- Photograph (reproduction)
- Personal and Taliesin Fellowship photographs, 1870s–2004, The Frank Lloyd Wright Foundation Archives (The Museum of Modern Art | Avery Architectural & Fine Arts Library, Columbia University, New York)
- FLWFA 6004.001

1-2
- Art Glass Window from the Francis W. Little House (Northome)
- Frank Lloyd Wright, designer. Temple Art Glass Company, manufacturer
- 1912
- 149.0 x 54.8 cm
- Glass, lead, wood
- Toyota Municipal Museum of Art

1 Chicago, the modern metropolis

1-3
- Aerial view of ruins after the Chicago Fire of 1871
- Shaw, photographer
- Photo: 1871
- Stereographs (reproduction)
- Chicago History Museum
- ICHi-059803

1-4
- Plan of Chicago (Burnham Plan)
- Daniel Burnham and Edward H. Bennett, authors. Jules Guerin, lithographer. Commercial Club of Chicago, publisher
- 1909
- 31.5 x 25.0 x 2.5 cm
- Print, lithograph on paper / book
- Engineering Bldg. 1 Library A (Civil Engineering), Libraries for Engineering and Information Science & Technology, The University of Tokyo

1-5
- Interior view of the Rookery Building entrance hall, Chicago, Illinois
- Burnham & Root, architects. Frank Lloyd Wright, renovator. Photographer unidentified
- Photo: 1893
- Photograph (reproduction)
- Chicago History Museum
- ICHi-017281

1-6
- Auditorium Building, Chicago, Illinois. Exterior view from the southwest
- Adler & Sullivan, architects. J. W. Taylor, photographer
- Photo: 1897
- Photograph (reproduction)
- Chicago History Museum
- ICHi-018768

1-7
- Reliance Building, Chicago, Illinois
- Charles Atwood of D. H. Burnham & Company, architect. Barnes-Crosby Company, photographer
- Photo: 1897–1904
- Reproduction from glass negatives
- Chicago History Museum
- ICHi-001066

+ Chicago World's Fair and Ho-o-den

1-8
- Map of a bird's-eye view of the 1893 Chicago World's Fair, Chicago, Illinois
- Rand McNally & Co., creator
- 1893
- original: 29 1/2 x 49 in. (74.9 x 101.6 cm)
- Print on paper (reproduction)
- Chicago History Museum, ICHi-025161

1-9
- 1893 Chicago World's Fair, Chicago, Illinois. View across west end of Great Basin in the Court of Honor
- Photographer unidentified
- Photo: 1893
- Photograph (reproduction)
- Chicago History Museum, ICHi-025057

1-10
- 1893 Chicago World's Fair, Chicago, Illinois. Transportation Building
- C. P. Rumford, photographer
- Photo: 1893
- Photograph (reproduction)
- Chicago History Museum, ICHi-170223

1-11
- 1893 Chicago World's Fair, Chicago, Illinois. The Japanese Pavillion
- Photo: 1893
- Photograph (reproduction)
- Imperial Hotel
- 10001

1-12
- *Report on Chicago Columbian World Fair*. Volume 1
- Beisen Kubota, artist
- 1893–94
- 24.5 x 16.0 x 1.0 cm
- Print on paper / book
- Yoshino Gypsum Art Foundation

1-13
- *Report on Chicago Columbian World Fair*. Volume 2
- Beisen Kubota, artist
- 1893–94
- 24.5 x 16.0 x 1.0 cm
- Print on paper / book
- Yoshino Gypsum Art Foundation

1-14
- *Report on Chicago Columbian World Fair. Volume 3*
- Beisen Kubota, artist
- 1893–94
- 24.5 x 16.0 x 1.0 cm
- Print on paper / book
- Yoshino Gypsum Art Foundation

1-15
- *Report on Chicago Columbian World Fair. Volume 4*
- Beisen Kubota, artist
- 1893–94
- 24.5 x 16.0 x 1.0 cm
- Print on paper / book
- Yoshino Gypsum Art Foundation

2 Tokyo, the modern metropolis

1-16
- Ende & Böckmann Plan. Proposal for a new monumental center in Tokyo. (1)
- Hermann Ende and Wilhelm Böckmann, architects
- 1886
- 45.0 x 31.0 / 53.0 x 41.0 cm (original scale 1:5000)
- Photograph on card board
- Japan Architectural Institute

1-17
- Ende & Böckmann Plan. Proposal for a new monumental center in Tokyo. (2)
- Hermann Ende and Wilhelm Böckmann, architects
- 1887
- 49.0 x 35.0 cm (original scale 1:5000)
- Ink and watercolor on Japanese paper
- Japan Architectural Institute

1-18
- Ende Böckmann Plan. Proposal for a new monumental center for Tokyo. Aerial view. From the series *Arkitekten, Ende & Böckmann*
- Hermann Ende and Wilhelm Böckmann
- 1886
- 35 x 46.5 cm
- Lithograph
- Japan Architectural Institute

1-19
- Postcard, Tokyo Station, 1914. The Famous Views of Tokyo
- 9.0 x 14.0 cm
- Postcard
- Hideki Watanabe Collection

1-20
- Postcard, The Newly Built Tokyo Main Station, 1914. The Famous Views of Tokyo
- 9.0 x 14.0 cm
- Postcard
- Hideki Watanabe Collection

1-21
- Postcard, The Babasaki Gate Street. The Famous Views of Tokyo
- 9.0 x 14.0 cm
- Postcard
- Hideki Watanabe Collection

1-22
- Postcard, The Imperial Theater, 1911. The Famous Views of Tokyo, volume 1
- 9.0 x 14.0 cm
- Postcard
- Hideki Watanabe Collection

1-23
- Postcard, Ministry of the Navy, 1894. The Famous Views of Tokyo
- 9.0 x 14.0 cm
- Postcard
- Hideki Watanabe Collection

1-24
- Postcard, The Ministry of Justice, 1895. The Famous Views of Tokyo, volume 1
- 9.0 x 14.0 cm
- Postcard
- Hideki Watanabe Collection

1-25
- Postcard, The Metropolitan Police Office, 1911. The Famous Views of Tokyo
- 9.0 x 14.0 cm
- Postcard
- Hideki Watanabe Collection

1-26
- Postcard, Kasumigaseki Governmental Buildings and Hibiya Park Seen from Marunouchi
- 9.0 x 14.0 cm
- Postcard
- Hideki Watanabe Collection

1-27
- Postcard, Imperial Hotel (1st building), 1890. The Famous Views of Tokyo
- 9.0 x 14.0 cm
- Postcard
- Hideki Watanabe Collection

1-28
- Postcard, Main Gate of the Hibiya Park, 1903. The Famous Views of Tokyo
- 9.0 x 14.0 cm
- Postcard
- Hideki Watanabe Collection

1-29
- Postcard, Music Hall in Hibiya Park, 1905. The Famous Views of Tokyo
- 9.0 x 14.0 cm
- Postcard
- Hideki Watanabe Collection

1-30
- Postcard, View of the Magnificient Teikoku (Imperial) Hotel Building, 1923. Looking from the Elevated Railway
- 9.0 x 14.0 cm
- Postcard
- Hideki Watanabe Collection

1-31
- Postcard, The Sakurada Gate of the Imperial Palace
- 9.0 x 14.0 cm
- Postcard
- Hideki Watanabe Collection

1-32
- Postcard, Parliament (2nd temporary building), 1891
- 9.0 x 14.0 cm
- Postcard
- Hideki Watanabe Collection

1-33
- Postcard, Tokyo Prefectural Government Office and the Tokyo Metropolitan Government, 1898
- 9.0 x 14.0 cm
- Postcard
- Hideki Watanabe Collection

1-34
- Postcard, Arrival of a Group of US Distinguished Visitors at Shimbashi Station
- 9.0 x 14.0 cm
- Postcard
- Hideki Watanabe Collection

3 Early career

+ Louis Sullivan: A mentor, and his motifs of nature

1-35
- Portrait of Frank Lloyd Wright shortly after he arrived in Chicago
- Photographer unidentified
- c. 1890
- original: 5 x 7 in. (12.7 x 7.8 cm)
- Photograph (reproduction)
- Wisconsin Historical Society
- 26558

1-36
- Wainwright Tomb. Bellefontaine Cemetery, Saint Louis, Missouri. Project, 1892. Ornamental gate rendered by Frank Lloyd Wright
- Louis Sullivan, architect. Frank Lloyd Wright, renderer
- 27 3/4 x 24 1/8 in. (70.5 x 61.3 cm)
- Ink and pencil on drafting cloth
- Louis Henry Sullivan collection, 1873–1910, Avery Architectural & Fine Arts Library, Columbia University
- NYDA 1965.001.00035

1-37
- Wainwright Tomb. Bellefontaine Cemetery, Saint Louis, Missouri. Project, 1892. Exterior detail view
- Louis Sullivan, architect
- Photo: 1996
- Photograph (reproduction)
- Richard Guy Wilson Architecture Archive, University of Virginia

1-38
- Wainwright Tomb, Bellefontaine Cemetery, Saint Louis, Missouri. Exterior view
- Louis Sullivan, architect. Photographer unidentified
- Photo: c. 1920
- Photograph (reproduction)
- Personal and Taliesin Fellowship

1-1

1-2

1-3

1-4

1-5

1-6

1-7

1-8

1-9

1-10

1-11

1-12

1-13

1-14

1-15

1-16

1-17

1-18

1-19

1-20

1-21

1-22

1-23

1-24

1-25

1-26

1-27

1-28

1-29

1-30

1-31

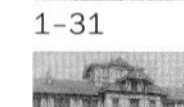

1-32

1-33

1-34

1-35

1-36

1-37

1-38

- 撮影：1920年頃
- 写真（複写）
- コロンビア大学
エイヴリー建築美術図書館
フランク・ロイド・ライト財団
アーカイヴズ

1-39
- 『建築装飾の体系
人間の力の原理に基づく』
- 著：ルイス・サリヴァン
出版：リツォーリ社（再版）
- 1924/1990年
- 44.2×36.0×2.3
- 印刷、紙／書籍
- 東京大学駒場図書館

1-40
- 『装飾の文法』
- 著・編：オーウェン・ジョーンズ
出版：デイ＆サン
- 1856年
- 34.0×24.0×5.0
- 印刷／紙、書籍
- 東京大学駒場博物館

+ 初期の実践

1-41
- 第1葉 ウィンズロー邸、透視図
『フランク・ロイド・ライトの建築と設計』
- フランク・ロイド・ライト
出版：エルンスト・ヴァスムート社
- 1910年
- 45.0×63.5
- リトグラフ／紙
- 豊田市美術館

1-42
- ウィンズロー邸
（イリノイ州リバーフォレスト）
1893–94年
- 建築：フランク・ロイド・ライト
撮影：ジェームズ・コールフィールド
- 撮影：2005年
- 写真（複写）

1-43
- ウィンズロー邸
（イリノイ州リバーフォレスト）
1893-94年 応接ホール内観
- 建築：フランク・ロイド・ライト
撮影：ジェームズ・コールフィールド
- 撮影：2014年
- 写真（複写）

1-44 *
- 第24葉 ヒコックス邸、
平面図および透視図
『フランク・ロイド・ライトの建築と設計』
- フランク・ロイド・ライト
出版：エルンスト・ヴァスムート社
- 1910年
- 63.5×45.0
- リトグラフ／紙
- 豊田市美術館

1-45 *
- ヒコックス邸 ハイバック・チェア
- デザイン：フランク・ロイド・ライト
- 1900年頃
- 129.6×46.9×50.3
- カシ
- 豊田市美術館

**4 ユニティ・テンプル：
鉄筋コンクリート造の神殿**

1-46
- 第64葉 ユニティ・テンプル、正面
『フランク・ロイド・ライトの建築と設計』
- フランク・ロイド・ライト
出版：エルンスト・ヴァスムート社
- 1910年
- 63.5×45.0
- リトグラフ／紙
- 豊田市美術館

1-47 *
- 第63葉 ユニティ・テンプル、透視図
『フランク・ロイド・ライトの建築と設計』
- フランク・ロイド・ライト
出版：エルンスト・ヴァスムート社
- 1910年
- 45.0×63.5
- リトグラフ／紙
- 豊田市美術館

1-48 *
- 第63葉 ユニティ・テンプル、立面図
『フランク・ロイド・ライトの建築と設計』
- フランク・ロイド・ライト
出版：エルンスト・ヴァスムート社
- 1910年
- 63.5×45.0
- リトグラフ／紙
- 豊田市美術館

1-49
- 第64葉 ユニティ・テンプル、平面図
『フランク・ロイド・ライトの建築と設計』
- フランク・ロイド・ライト
出版：エルンスト・ヴァスムート社
- 1910年
- 45.0×63.5
- リトグラフ／紙
- 豊田市美術館

1-50
- 模型 ユニティ・テンプル
- フランク・ロイド・ライト
- 1920年頃
- 29×102×65.5 縮尺1:100
- 石膏
- 京都大学

1-51
- ユニティ・テンプル
（イリノイ州オークパーク）1905–08年
外観、礼拝堂を左手に見る
- 建築：フランク・ロイド・ライト
撮影：ジェームズ・コールフィールド
- 撮影：2021年
- 写真（複写）

1-52
- ユニティ・テンプル
（イリノイ州オークパーク）1905–08年
礼拝堂内観、説教壇から見る
- 建築：フランク・ロイド・ライト
撮影：ジェームズ・コールフィールド
- 撮影：2019年
- 写真（複写）

1-53
- ユニティ・テンプル
（イリノイ州オークパーク）1905–08年
礼拝堂の照明器具
- 建築：フランク・ロイド・ライト
撮影：ジェームズ・コールフィールド
- 撮影：2018年
- 写真（複写）

1-54
- ユニティ・テンプル
（イリノイ州オークパーク）1905–08年
礼拝堂内観図
- フランク・ロイド・ライト
- 図面（複写）
- コロンビア大学
エイヴリー建築美術図書館
フランク・ロイド・ライト財団
アーカイヴズ

1-55
- 浮絵 歌舞妓芝居之図
- 歌川豊春
- 明和4（1767）年頃
- オリジナル：26.5×39.0
- 木版／紙（複写）
- 太田記念美術館

5 日本の発見

**+ 浮世絵的視覚と
建築ドローイング**

1-56
- デローズ邸
（インディアナ州サウスベンド）
1906年 透視図
- 建築：フランク・ロイド・ライト、
レンダリング：マリオン・マホニー
- オリジナル：47.0×65.4
- 原図：インク、鉛筆、
色鉛筆／紙（複写）
- コロンビア大学
エイヴリー建築美術図書館
フランク・ロイド・ライト財団
アーカイヴズ

1-57
- 第29葉 デローズ邸、
平面図および透視図
『フランク・ロイド・ライトの建築と設計』
- フランク・ロイド・ライト
出版：エルンスト・ヴァスムート社
- 1910年
- 63.5×45.0
- リトグラフ／紙
- 豊田市美術館

1-58
- 名所江戸百景
山下町日比谷外さくら田
- 歌川広重
- 安政4（1857）年
- 35.9×24.5
- 木版／紙

1-59 *
- 名所江戸百景 堀切の花菖蒲
- 歌川広重
- 安政4（1857）年
- 35.9×24.5
- 木版／紙

1-60 *
- 名所江戸百景
浅草川大川端宮戸川
- 歌川広重
- 安政4（1857）年
- 35.9×24.5
- 木版／紙

1-61 *
- 名所江戸百景 八ツ見のはし
- 歌川広重
- 安政3（1856）年
- 36.0×26.0
- 木版／紙
- 神奈川県立歴史博物館

1-62
- 名所江戸百景
真間の紅葉手古那の社継はし
- 歌川広重
- 安政4（1857）年
- 36.0×26.0
- 木版／紙
- 神奈川県立歴史博物館

1-63 *
- 名所江戸百景 霞かせき
- 歌川広重
- 安政4（1857）年
- 35.9×24.5
- 木版／紙

1-64 *
- 名所江戸百景
外桜田弁慶堀糀町
- 歌川広重
- 安政3（1856）年
- 35.9×24.5
- 木版／紙

1-65 *
- 名所江戸百景 芝愛宕山
- 歌川広重
- 安政4（1857）年
- 35.9×24.5
- 木版／紙

1-66
- 第15葉 ハーディ邸、透視図
『フランク・ロイド・ライトの建築と設計』
- フランク・ロイド・ライト
出版：エルンスト・ヴァスムート社
- 1910年
- 45.0×63.5
- リトグラフ／紙
- 豊田市美術館

1-67
- 東海道五拾三次 亀山 雪晴
- 歌川広重
- 天保4（1833）年頃
- 大判錦絵 24.6×37.2
- 木版／紙
- 神奈川県立歴史博物館

1-68
- フィエーゾレ、
ヴィリーノ・ベルヴェデーレの
ライトの住まいを見上げる、
前景に藪と塀
- 撮影：テイラー・A. ウーレイ
- 撮影：1910年
- 写真（複写）
- コロンビア大学
エイヴリー建築美術図書館
フランク・ロイド・ライト財団
アーカイヴズ

+ 日本初訪問

1-69 *
- 「ライトの来日旅行写真アルバム」
- 1905年
- 写真（複写）
- 写真提供：
フランク・ロイド・ライト・トラスト・
コレクション

1-70 *
- 東本願寺名古屋別院 本堂
「ライトの来日旅行写真アルバム」
- 撮影：フランク・ロイド・ライト
- 撮影：1905年
- 写真（複写）
- 写真提供：
フランク・ロイド・ライト・トラスト

1-71 *
- 岡山後楽園 延養亭と庭園
「ライトの来日旅行写真アルバム」
- 撮影：フランク・ロイド・ライト
- 撮影：1905年
- 写真（複写）
- コロンビア大学
エイヴリー建築美術図書館
フランク・ロイド・ライト財団
アーカイヴズ

1-72 *
- 京都平等院
「ライトの来日旅行写真アルバム」
- 撮影者不詳
- 写真（複写）
- コロンビア大学
エイヴリー建築美術図書館
フランク・ロイド・ライト財団
アーカイヴズ

1-73 *
- 長崎丸山遊郭の通り
- 撮影：アレキサンダー・ウールコット
- 撮影：1932年頃
- 写真（複写）
- コロンビア大学
エイヴリー建築美術図書館
フランク・ロイド・ライト財団
アーカイヴズ

**+ 日本美術愛好家、
アートディーラー、
展覧会プロデューサーとして**

1-74
- 『日本の浮世絵：或る解釈』
- 著：フランク・ロイド・ライト
出版：ラルフ・フレッチャー・シーモア
- 1912年
- 21.2×13.5
- 印刷／紙、書籍
- 成城大学図書館

1-75
- 『日本の浮世絵：或る解釈』
ライト自身による
書き込みのあるページ
- 著：フランク・ロイド・ライト
出版：ラルフ・フレッチャー・
シーモア

photographs, 1870s–2004, The Frank Lloyd Wright Foundation Archives (The Museum of Modern Art | Avery Architectural & Fine Arts Library, Columbia University, New York)
- FLWFA 7116.0044

1-39
- *A System of Architectural Ornament According with a Philosophy of Man's Powers*
- Louis H. Sullivan, author. Rizzoli, publisher (facsimile ed.)
- 1924/1990
- 44.2 x 36 x 2.3 cm
- Print on paper / book
- The Komaba Library, The University of Tokyo

1-40
- *The Grammar of Ornament*
- Owen Jones, author. London: Day & Son, publisher
- 1856
- 34.0 x 24.0 x 5.0 cm
- Print on paper / book
- Komaba Museum, The University of Tokyo

+ Early works

1-41
- Plate I. Perspective of Winslow House. *Ausgeführte Bauten und Entwürfe von Frank Lloyd Wright*
- Frank Lloyd Wright. Ernst Wasmuth, publisher
- 1910
- 45.0 x 63.5 cm
- Lithograph on paper
- Toyota Municipal Museum of Art

1-42
- Winslow House, River Forest, Illinois. Project, 1893–94. Exterior
- Frank Lloyd Wright, architect. James Caulfield, photographer
- Photo: 2005
- Photograph (reproduction)

1-43
- Winslow House, River Forest, Illinois. Project, 1893–94. Interior view of the reception hall
- Frank Lloyd Wright, architect. James Caulfield, photographer
- Photo: 2014
- Photograph (reproduction)

1-44
- Plate XXIV. Ground plan and perspective of the Hickox House. *Ausgeführte Bauten und Entwürfe von Frank Lloyd Wright*
- Frank Lloyd Wright. Ernst Wasmuth, publisher
- 1910
- 63.5 x 45.0 cm
- Lithograph on paper
- Toyota Municipal Museum of Art

1-45
- Tall-back Spindle Chair from the Hickox House
- Frank Lloyd Wright, designer
- c. 1900
- 129.6 x 46.9 x 50.3 cm
- oak
- Toyota Municipal Museum of Art

4 Unity Temple: A reinforced concrete sanctuary

1-46
- Plate LXIV. Facade of the Unity Temple. *Ausgeführte Bauten und Entwürfe von Frank Lloyd Wright*
- Frank Lloyd Wright. Ernst Wasmuth, publisher
- 1910
- 63.5 x 45.0 cm
- Lithograph on paper
- Toyota Municipal Museum of Art

1-47
- Plate LXIII. Perspective of the House and Temple for Unity Temple. *Ausgeführte Bauten und Entwürfe von Frank Lloyd Wright*
- Frank Lloyd Wright. Ernst Wasmuth, publisher
- 1910
- 45.0 x 63.5 cm
- Lithograph on paper
- Toyota Municipal Museum of Art

1-48
- Plate LXIII. Elevation of the House and Temple for Unity Church. *Ausgeführte Bauten und Entwürfe von Frank Lloyd Wright*
- Frank Lloyd Wright. Ernst Wasmuth, publisher
- 1910
- 63.5 x 45.0 cm
- Lithograph on paper
- Toyota Municipal Museum of Art

1-49
- Plate LXIV. Ground plan of Unity Temple Oak Park, Illinois. *Ausgeführte Bauten und Entwürfe von Frank Lloyd Wright*
- Frank Lloyd Wright. Ernst Wasmuth, publisher
- 1910
- 45.0 x 63.5 cm
- Lithograph on paper
- Toyota Municipal Museum of Art

1-50
- Model. Unity Temple, Oak Park, Illinois.
- Frank Lloyd Wright
- c.1920
- 29 x 102 x 65.5 cm (scale 1:100)
- Plaster
- Kyoto University

1-51
- Unity Temple, Oak Park, Illinois. Project, 1905–08. Exterior, sanctuary on the left side
- Frank Lloyd Wright, architect. James Caulfield, photographer
- Photo: 2021
- Photograph (reproduction)

1-52
- Unity Temple, Oak Park, Illinois. Project, 1905–08. Interior perspective, sanctuary, view from the pulpit
- Frank Lloyd Wright, architect. James Caulfield, photographer
- Photo: 2019
- Photograph (reproduction)

1-53
- Unity Temple, Oak Park, Illinois. Project, 1905–08. Lighting fixture in the sanctuary
- Frank Lloyd Wright, architect. James Caulfield, photographer
- Photo: 2018
- Photograph (reproduction)

1-54
- Unity Temple, Oak Park, Illinois. Project, 1905–08. Interior perspective, sanctuary
- Frank Lloyd Wright
- Drawing (reproduction)
- The Frank Lloyd Wright Foundation Archives (The Museum of Modern Art | Avery Architectural & Fine Arts Library, Columbia University, New York)
- FLW.DR.0611.021

1-55
- Kabuki Theater in Ukie Style
- Utagawa Toyoharu, artist
- c. 1767 (Meiwa 4)
- 26.0 x 39.0
- Woodblock print
- Ota Memorial Museum of Art

4 Discovery of Japan

+ Ukiyo-e through the lens of Wright and his architectural drawings

1-56
- DeRhodes House, South Bend, Indiana. Project, 1906. Exterior perspective
- Frank Lloyd Wright, architect. Marion Mahony Griffin, renderer
- 18 1/2 x 25 3/4 in. (47 x 65.4 cm)
- Ink, pencil and colored pencil on paper (reproduction)
- The Frank Lloyd Wright Foundation Archives (The Museum of Modern Art | Avery Architectural & Fine Arts Library, Columbia University, New York)
- FLW.DR.0602.001

1-57
- Plate XXIX. Ground plan and perspective of the DeRhodes House. *Ausgeführte Bauten und Entwürfe von Frank Lloyd Wright*
- Frank Lloyd Wright. Ernst Wasmuth, publisher
- 1910
- 63.5 x 45.0 cm
- Lithograph on paper
- Toyota Municipal Museum of Art

1-58
- *Yamashita-cho and Soto Sakurada in Hibiya*. From the series "One Hundred Famous Views of Edo"
- Utagawa Hiroshige, artist
- 1857 (Ansei 4)
- 35.9 x 24.5 cm
- Woodblock print

1-59
- *Irises at Horikiri*. From the series "One Hundred Famous Views of Edo"
- Utagawa Hiroshige, artist
- 1857 (Ansei 4)
- 35.9 x 24.5 cm
- Woodblock print

1-60
- *The Riverside of Sumida where the Asakusa and Miyato Rivers Branch*. From the series "One Hundred Famous Views of Edo"
- Utagawa Hiroshige, artist
- 1857 (Ansei 4)
- 35.9 x 24.5 cm
- Woodblock print

1-61
- *Yatsumi Bridge*. From the series "One Hundred Famous Views of Edo"
- Utagawa Hiroshige, artist
- 1856 (Ansei 3)
- 36.0 x 26.0 cm
- Woodblock print
- Kanagawa Prefectural Museum of Cultural History
- CW0005460

1-62
- *Maple Leaves and the Tekona Shrine and Tsugi Brdge at Mama*. From the series "One Hundred Famous Views of Edo"
- Utagawa Hiroshige, artist
- 1857 (Ansei 4)
- 36.0 x 26.0 cm
- Woodblock print
- Kanagawa Prefectural Museum of Cultural History
- CS0005546

1-63
- *Kasumigaseki*. From the series "One Hundred Famous Views of Edo"
- Utagawa Hiroshige, artist
- 1857 (Ansei 4)
- 35.9 x 24.5 cm
- Woodblock print

1-64
- *Benkei Moat and Kojimachi at Soto Sakurada*. From the series "One Hundred Famous Views of Edo"
- Utagawa Hiroshige, artist
- 1857 (Ansei 4)
- 35.9 x 24.5 cm
- Woodblock print

1-65
- *Atagoyama Hill in Shiba*. From the series "One Hundred Famous Views of Edo"
- Utagawa Hiroshige, artist
- 1857 (Ansei 4)
- 35.9 x 24.5 cm
- Woodblock print

1-66
- Plate XV. Perspective view of the Hardy House. *Ausgeführte Bauten und Entwürfe von Frank Lloyd Wright*
- Frank Lloyd Wright. Ernst Wasmuth, publisher
- 1910
- 63.5 x 45.0 cm
- Lithograph on paper
- Toyota Municipal Museum of Art

1-67
- Clear Weather After Snow at Kameyama. From the series "Fifty-three Stations on the Tokaido"
- Utagawa Hiroshige, artist
- c. 1834 (Tempo 4)
- Ōban; 24.6 x 37.2 cm
- Woodblock print
- Kanagawa Prefectural Museum of Cultural History
- CW0005009

1-68
- Villino Belvedere from below, garden and wall
- Taylor A. Woolley, photographer
- Photo: 1910
- Photograph (reproduction)
- Personal and Taliesin Fellowship photographs, 1870s–2004, The Frank Lloyd Wright Foundation Archives (The Museum of Modern Art | Avery Architectural & Fine Arts Library, Columbia University, New York)
- FLWFA 7109.0008

+ The first trip to Japan

1-69
- The Photo Album from the Wright's 1905 Trip to Japan
- 1905
- Photograph (reproduction)
- Collection of Frank Lloyd Wright Trust, Chicago

1-70
- Higashi-Honganji Temple, Nagoya-Betsuin, Nagoya. The 1905 Photo Album
- Frank Lloyd Wright, photographer
- Photo: 1905
- Photograph (reproduction)
- Courtesy of Frank Lloyd Wright Trust, Chicago

1-71
- Koraku-en, Okayama. Exterior of the main hall with gardens. The 1905 Photo Album
- Frank Lloyd Wright, photographer
- Photo: 1905
- Photograph (reproduction)
- Personal and Taliesin Fellowship photographs, 1870s–2004, The Frank Lloyd Wright Foundation Archives (The Museum of Modern Art | Avery Architectural & Fine Arts Library, Columbia University, New York)
- FLWFA 7121.0011

1-72
- Byōdō-in Temple, Kyoto, Japan
- Photographer unidentified
- Photograph (reproduction)
- Personal and Taliesin Fellowship photographs, 1870s–2004, The Frank Lloyd Wright Foundation Archives (The Museum of Modern Art | Avery Architectural & Fine Arts Library, Columbia University, New York)
- FLWFA 7007.0008

1-73
- Maruyama, Nagasaki, Japan. Street view
- Alexander Woollcott, photographer
- Photo: c. 1932
- Photograph (reproduction)
- Personal and Taliesin Fellowship photographs, 1870s–2004, The Frank Lloyd Wright Foundation Archives (The Museum of Modern Art | Avery Architectural & Fine Arts Library, Columbia University, New York)
- FLWFA 7203.0002

+ Wright as a collector of Japanese art, art dealer, and exhibition curator

1-74
- *The Japanese Print: An interpretation*
- Frank Lloyd Wright, author. The Ralph Fletcher Seymour, Chicago, publisher
- 1912
- 21.2 x 13.5 cm
- Print on paper / book
- Seijo University Library

1-75
- *The Japanese Print: An interpretation*. Page 3 showing annotations

1-39

1-59

1-60

1-61

1-62

1-63

1-64

1-65

1-66

1-67

1-68
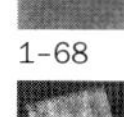
1-69

1-70
1-71

1-72

1-73
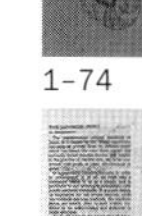
1-74

1-75

1-40 1-41 1-42 1-43 1-44 1-45 1-46 1-47 1-48 1-49 1-50 1-51 1-52 1-53 1-54 1-55 1-56 1-57 1-58

- 1912年
- 印刷、鉛筆/紙、書籍(複写)
- コロンビア大学
  エイヴリー建築美術図書館
  エイヴリー・クラシックス

1-76
- ウィリアム・スポールディングのための浮世絵ギャラリー計画案(マサチューセッツ州ボストン)
  1914年 縦展開図
- フランク・ロイド・ライト
- 51.4×82.9
- インク、鉛筆、色鉛筆/麻布
- コロンビア大学
  エイヴリー建築美術図書館
  フランク・ロイド・ライト財団
  アーカイヴズ

1-77
- シカゴ美術館における
  1908年の浮世絵展
- 撮影:1908年
- 写真(複写)
- シカゴ美術館

1-78
- 展示風景:シカゴ建築クラブの
  1907年の年次展
  シカゴ美術館にて
- 撮影:ファーマン・アンド・サンズ
- 撮影:1907年
- 写真(複写)
- コロンビア大学
  エイヴリー建築美術図書館
  フランク・ロイド・ライト財団
  アーカイヴズ

1-79
- 展示風景:シカゴ建築クラブの
  1914年の年次展、
  シカゴ美術館にて
- 撮影:ファーマン・アンド・サンズ
- 撮影:1914年
- 写真(複写)
- コロンビア大学
  エイヴリー建築美術図書館
  フランク・ロイド・ライト財団
  アーカイヴズ

1-80
- 名所江戸百景 亀戸天神境内
- 歌川広重
- 安政3(1856)年
- 35.9×24.5
- 木版/紙

1-81
- 東海道五拾三次 江尻 三保遠望
- 歌川広重
- 天保4(1833)年頃
- オリジナル:25.0×37.6
- 木版/紙(複写)
- 神奈川県立歴史博物館

1-82
- 二代目市川門之助の清十郎
  三代目瀬川菊之丞のおなつ
- 勝川春常
- 安永10/天明元(1781)年
- オリジナル:細判二枚続
  30.0×28.5
- 木版/紙(複写)
- ボストン美術館
  ビゲロー・コレクション

1-83
- 見立て浄瑠璃姫
- 礒田湖龍斎
- 江戸時代、1770年代初頭
- オリジナル:柱絵 69.5×12.0
- 木版/紙(複写)
- ボストン美術館スポールディング・コレクション

1-84
- 見立て浄瑠璃姫
- 礒田湖龍斎
- 江戸時代
- オリジナル:柱絵 63.8×12.0
- 木版/紙(複写)
- ボストン美術館スポールディング・コレクション

SECTION 2
「輝ける眉」からの眺望

6 アメリカ中西部 プレイリーの風土と気候

2-1
- 谷を下りる
- 撮影:フランク・ロイド・ライト
- 撮影:1898–1900年頃
- 7.6×23.5
- コロタイプ(複写)
- ウィスコンシン歴史博物館

2-2 *
- ヒルサイド・ホームスクール
  近くの風景
- 撮影:フランク・ロイド・ライト
- 撮影:1893–1900年頃
- 9.5×23.5
- コロタイプ(複写)
- ウィスコンシン歴史博物館

2-3
- 雪の積もったスケート池
- 撮影:フランク・ロイド・ライト
- 撮影:1895年頃
- 8.9×23.8
- コロタイプ(複写)
- ウィスコンシン歴史博物館

2-4
- タリアセン近くにたたずむ土浦信子
  土浦亀城、信子夫妻のアルバム
  「Taliesin Life (2)」
- 撮影:土浦亀城
- 撮影:1924–25年
- 写真(複写)
- 土浦亀城アーカイブズ

2-5
- タリアセンにつくられた水門
  土浦亀城、信子夫妻のアルバム
  「Taliesin Life (2)」
- 撮影:土浦亀城
- 撮影:1924–25年
- 写真(複写)
- 土浦亀城アーカイブズ

2-6
- タリアセンからの眺め
  土浦亀城、信子夫妻のアルバム
  「Taliesin Life (2)」
- 撮影:土浦亀城
- 撮影:1924–25年
- 写真(複写)
- 土浦亀城アーカイブズ

2-7
- タリアセンの丘の眺望、風車
  「ロメオとジュリエット」が見える。
  土浦亀城、信子夫妻のアルバム
  「Taliesin Life (2)」
- 撮影:土浦亀城
- 撮影:1924–25年
- 写真(複写)
- 土浦亀城アーカイブズ

2-8
- タリアセン鳥瞰写真
- 撮影年不詳
- 写真(複写)
- コロンビア大学
  エイヴリー建築美術図書館
  エドガー・ターフェル
  建築記録・資料

2-9
- 雪のタリアセン
  土浦亀城、信子夫妻のアルバム
  「Taliesin Life (2)」
- 建築:フランク・ロイド・ライト
  撮影:土浦亀城
- 撮影:1924–25年
- 写真(複写)
- 土浦亀城アーカイブズ

7 ルーツとしてのウェールズ

2-10
- 祖父リチャード・ロイド・ジョーンズとライトの一族
  後列左から:9番目ライトの両親
  ウィリアム・キャリー・ライト
  とアンナ・ロイド・ライト。
  前列左から:6番目妹のマジネルを抱いた少年フランク・ロイド・ライト。
- 撮影者不詳
- 撮影:1883年
- 写真(複写)
- ウィスコンシン歴史博物館

2-11
- フランク・ロイド・ライトと家族
  左から:叔父ジェンキン、
  ジェンキンの妻、ジェーン・ライト、
  息子ロイドを抱いた
  妻キャサリン・ライト、母アンナ、
  妹マジネル、ライト本人、
  ジェンキンの娘。
- 撮影者不詳
- 撮影:1890年頃
- 写真(複写)
- 写真提供:フランク・ロイド・ライト・トラスト

8 草原植物と『ハウス・ビューティフル』

2-12
- 『ハウス・ビューティフル』
- 著:ウィリアム・ガネット
  デザイン:フランク・ロイド・ライト
  出版:オーヴェルニュ・プレス、
  ハスブルック(ファクシミリ版)
- 1896–97/1963年
- 35.5×29.5×1.4
- 印刷/紙、書籍
- 東京大学駒場図書館

2-13 *
- 撫子に蝶
- 歌川広重
- 天保6–10(1836–40)年
- 34.0×8.0
- 木版/紙
- 神奈川県立歴史博物館

2-14 *
- 山茶花に雀
- 歌川広重
- 弘化年間(1845–48年)
- 33.0×9.0
- 木版/紙
- 神奈川県立歴史博物館

2-15
- 山茶花に雀(墨摺絵)
- 歌川広重
- 弘化年間(1845–48年)
- 35.7×9.3
- 木版/紙
- 神奈川県立歴史博物館

2-16
- 雀に秋海棠
- 歌川広重
- 弘化年間(1845–48年)
- 35.3×7.7
- 木版/紙
- 神奈川県立歴史博物館

2-17 *
- 梅に鶯
- 歌川広重
- 弘化年間(1845–48年)
- 33.3×7.7
- 木版/紙
- 神奈川県立歴史博物館

2-18 *
- 野菊に小鳥
- 歌川広重
- 弘化年間(1845–48年)
- 34.0×7.5
- 木版/紙
- 神奈川県立歴史博物館

2-19 *
- 第3葉 ウィンズロー邸の厩舎、
  平面図および透視図
  『フランク・ロイド・ライトの建築と設計』
- フランク・ロイド・ライト
  出版:エルンスト・ヴァスムート社
- 1910年
- 45.0×63.5
- リトグラフ/紙
- 豊田市美術館

9 住空間の革新

2-20 *
- 『レディース・ホーム・ジャーナル』
  1901年2月号
- 出版:カーチス社
- 42.5×29.0
- 印刷/紙、定期刊行物
- 水上優コレクション

2-21
- 『レディース・ホーム・ジャーナル』
  1901年7月号
- 出版:カーチス社
- 41.5×29.0
- 印刷/紙、定期刊行物
- 水上優コレクション

+ 花の環で世界をめぐる

2-22
- 第32葉 ダーヴィン・D.マーティン邸、
  鳥瞰図
  『フランク・ロイド・ライトの建築と設計』
- フランク・ロイド・ライト
  出版:エルンスト・ヴァスムート社
- 1910年
- 45.0×63.5
- リトグラフ/紙
- 豊田市美術館

2-23
- 第33葉 ダーヴィン・D.マーティン邸、
  平面図
  『フランク・ロイド・ライトの建築と設計』
- フランク・ロイド・ライト
  出版:エルンスト・ヴァスムート社
- 1910年
- 45.0×63.5
- リトグラフ/紙
- 豊田市美術館

2-24
- ダーヴィン・D.マーティン邸
  (ニューヨーク州バッファロー)
  1903–05年
- 建築:フランク・ロイド・ライト
  撮影:トーマス・ラッセル
- 撮影:1904年頃
- 写真(複写)
- コロンビア大学
  エイヴリー建築美術図書館
  フランク・ロイド・ライト財団
  アーカイヴズ

2-25
- ダーヴィン・D.マーティン邸
  (ニューヨーク州バッファロー)
  1903–05年 空撮
- 建築:フランク・ロイド・ライト
  撮影:マシュー・ディガティ
- 撮影:2022年
- 写真(複写)
- フランク・ロイド・ライト マーティン・ハウス

2-26
- ダーヴィン・D.マーティン邸
  (ニューヨーク州バッファロー)
  1903–05年
  庭園のフロリサイクル(花の環)
- 建築:フランク・ロイド・ライト
  撮影:マシュー・ディガティ
- 撮影:2021年
- 写真(複写)
- フランク・ロイド・ライト マーティン・ハウス

- Frank Lloyd Wright, author. The Ralph Fletcher Seymour, Chicago, publisher
- 1912
- Carbon typescript: Pencil corrections (Reproduction)
- Avery Classics, Avery Architectural & Fine Arts Library, Columbia University, New York
- AA685 W9 W9394 c.2

1-76
- Japanese Prints Gallery for William Spaulding, Boston, Massachusetts. Unbuilt Project, 1914. Longitudinal section
- Frank Lloyd Wright
- 20 1/4 x 32 5/8 in. (51.4 x 82.9 cm)
- Ink, pencil and colored pencil on linen
- The Frank Lloyd Wright Foundation Archives (The Museum of Modern Art | Avery Architectural & Fine Arts Library, Columbia University, New York)
- FLW.DR.1902.004

1-77
- Exhibition of Japanese Prints at the Art Institute of Chicago, 1908
- Photo: 1908
- Photograph (reproduction)
- The Art Institute of Chicago
- Photo © The Art Institute of Chicago / Art Resource, NY
- AR6180859

1-78
- Chicago Architectural Club Annual Exhibition at the Art Institute of Chicago, Chicago, Illinois
- Fuermann and Sons, photographer
- Photo: 1907
- Photograph (reproduction)
- Project photographs, circa 1887-2008, The Frank Lloyd Wright Foundation Archives (The Museum of Modern Art | Avery Architectural & Fine Arts Library, Columbia University)
- FLWFA 0700.0005

1-79
- Chicago Architectural Club Annual Exhibition at the Art Institute of Chicago, Chicago, Illinois.
- Fuermann and Sons, photographer
- Photo: 1914
- Photograph (reproduction)
- Project photographs, circa 1887-2008, The Frank Lloyd Wright Foundation Archives (The Museum of Modern Art | Avery Architectural & Fine Arts Library, Columbia University)
- FLWFA 1500.0008

1-80
- Precincts of the Kameido Tenjin Shrine. From the series "One Hundred Famous Views of Edo"
- Utagawa Hiroshige, artist
- 1856 (Ansei 3)
- 35.9 x 24.5 cm
- Woodblock print

1-81
- *Distant View of Miho at Ejiri*. From the series "The Fifty-three Stations of the Tokaido"
- Utagawa Hiroshige, artist
- c. 1833 (Tempo 4)
- original: Ōban; (26.0 x 36.0 cm)
- Woodblock print
- Kanagawa Prefectural Museum of Cultural History
- CW0001379

1-82
- *Actors Ichikawa Monnosuke II as Seijûrô (R) and Segawa Kikunojô III as Onatsu (L)*
- Katsukawa Shunjô, artist
- 1781 (An'ei 10/Tenmei 1)
- Hosoban diptych; 11 13/16 x 11 1/4 in. (30 x 28.5 cm)
- Woodblock print (reproduction)
- Museum of Fine Arts Boston. William Sturgis Bigelow Collection
- Photograph © 2023 Museum of Fine Arts, Boston
- 11.18460-1

1-83
- A Modern Version of the Story of *Ushiwakamaru* *Serenading Jôruri-hime*
- Isoda Koryûsai, artist
- about early 1770s
- Hashira-e; 27 3/8 x 4 3/4 in. (69.5 x 12 cm)
- Woodblock print (reproduction)
- Museum of Fine Arts Boston. William S. and John T. Spaulding Collection
- Photograph © 2023 Museum of Fine Arts, Boston
- 21.8348

1-84
- *A Modern Version of Ushiwakamaru (Yoshitsune)* Serenading Jôruri-hime
- Isoda Koryûsai, artist
- Edo period
- Hashira-e; 25 1/8 x 4 3/4 in. (63.8 x 12 cm)
- Woodblock print (reproduction)
- Museum of Fine Arts Boston. William S. and John T. Spaulding Collection
- Photograph © 2023 Museum of Fine Arts, Boston
- 21.8356

SECTION 2
Views from the Shining Brow

6 Prairies of the American Midwest: Landscape and climate

2-1
- Down the Valley
- Frank Lloyd Wright, photographer
- Photo: c. 1898-1900
- original: 3 x 9.25 in.
- collotype (reproduction)
- Wisconsin Historical Society
- 25568

2-2
- Landscape Near Hillside Home School
- Frank Lloyd Wright, photographer
- Photo: c. 1893-1900
- original: 3.75 x 9.25 in.
- collotype (reproduction)
- Wisconsin Historical Society
- 25569

2-3
- Snow-Covered Skating Pond
- Frank Lloyd Wright, photographer
- Photo: c. 1895
- original: 3.5 x 9.375 in.
- collotype (reproduction)
- Wisconsin Historical Society
- 25570

2-4
- Landscape near Taliesin with Nobuko Tsuchiura. Kameki and Nobuko Tsuchiura's photo album "Taliesin Life"(2)
- Kameki Tsuchiura, photographer
- Photo: 1924-25
- Photograph (reproduction)
- TSUCHIURA Kameki Archives

2-5
- Watergate at Taliesin. Kameki and Nobuko Tsuchiura's photo album "Taliesin Life"(2)
- Kameki Tsuchiura, photographer
- Photo: 1924-25
- Photograph (reproduction)
- TSUCHIURA Kameki Archives

2-6
- View from Taliesin. Kameki and Nobuko Tsuchiura's photo album "Taliesin Life"(2)
- Kameki Tsuchiura, photographer
- Photo: 1924-25
- Photograph (reproduction)
- TSUCHIURA Kameki Archives

2-7
- Landscape at Taliesin with a view of Romeo and Juliet Windmill. Kameki and Nobuko Tsuchiura's photo album "Taliesin Life"(2)
- Kameki Tsuchiura, photographer
- Photo: 1924-25
- Photograph (reproduction)
- TSUCHIURA Kameki Archives

2-8
- Taliesin. Aerial view
- undated
- Photograph (reproduction)
- Edgar Tafel architectural records and papers, 1919-2005, Avery Architectural & Fine Arts Library, Columbia University

2-9
- Taliesin in snow. Kameki and Nobuko Tsuchiura's photo album "Taliesin Life"(2)
- Frank Lloyd Wright, architect. Kameki Tsuchiura, photographer
- Photo: 1924-25
- Photograph (reproduction)
- TSUCHIURA Kameki Archives

7 Welsh heritage

2-10
- The Lloyd Jones Family. Back row from left: ninth is William Carey Wright and his wife Anna (Frank Lloyd Wright's parents). Front row from left: sixth is Frank Lloyd Wright holding his sister Maginel
- Photographer unidentified
- Photo: 1883
- original: 10 x 8 in.
- Photograph (reproduction)
- Wisconsin Historical Society
- PH 6046.1

2-11
- The Wright family on the front steps of the Oak Park Home, c. 1890. From left to right: Jenkin Lloyd-Jones, Jenkins' wife, Jane Wright, Catherine Wright (Frank Lloyd Wright Jr. in her arms), Anna Lloyd Wright, Maginel Wright, Frank Lloyd Wright, and Jenkin's daughter
- Photographer unidentified
- Photo: c. 1890
- Photograph (reproduction)
- Courtesy of Frank Lloyd Wright Trust, Chicago

8 Prairie plants and House Beautiful

2-12
- *The House Beautiful* (Facsimile edition)
- William C. Gannett, author. Frank Lloyd Wright, designer. Auvergne Press, publisher. Hasbrouck, publisher for Facsimile edition
- 1896-97/1963
- 35.5 x 29.5 x 1.4 cm
- Print on paper / book
- The Komaba Library, University of Tokyo

2-13
- *Nadeshiko (Pink) Butterfly and Poem*
- Utagawa Hiroshige, artist
- 1836-40 (Tempo 6-10)
- 34.0 x 8.0 cm
- Woodblock print
- Kanagawa Prefectural Museum of Cultural History
- CW0005156

2-14
- *Sparrow and Camellia sasanqua*
- Utagawa Hiroshige, artist
- 1845-48 (Kôka)
- 33.0 x 9.0cm
- Woodblock print
- Kanagawa Prefectural Museum of Cultural History
- CW0003270

2-15
- *Sparrow and Camellia sasanqua*
- Utagawa Hiroshige, artist
- 1845-48 (Kôka)
- 35.7 x 9.3 cm
- Woodblock print
- Kanagawa Prefectural Museum of Cultural History
- CW0003271

2-16
- *Sparrow and Begonia grandis*
- Utagawa Hiroshige, artist
- 1845-48 (Kôka)
- 35.3 x 7.7 cm
- Woodblock print
- Kanagawa Prefectural Museum of Cultural History
- CW0005157

2-17
- *Japanese nightingale and plum*
- Utagawa Hiroshige, artist
- 1845-48 (Kôka)
- 33.3 x 7.7 cm
- Woodblock print
- Kanagawa Prefectural Museum of Cultural History
- CW0005158

2-18
- *Dickybird and wild crysanthemum*
- Utagawa Hiroshige, artist
- 1845-48 (Kôka)
- 34.0 x 7.5 cm
- Woodblock print
- Kanagawa Prefectural Museum of Cultural History
- CW0005160

2-19
- Plate III. Ground plan and perspective of the stable for the Winslow House. *Ausgeführte Bauten und Entwürfe von Frank Lloyd Wright*
- Frank Lloyd Wright. Ernst Wasmuth, publisher
- 1910
- 63.5 x 45.0 cm
- Lithograph on paper
- Toyota Municipal Museum of Art

9 Innovation of dwelling space

2-20
- *Ladies Home Journal*, Feb 1901 issue
- The Curtis Publishing Company, Philadelphia, publisher
- 42.5x29 cm
- Print on paper / periodical
- Yutaka Mizukami Collection

2-21
- *Ladies Home Journal*, Jul 1901 issue
- The Curtis Publishing Company, Philadelphia, publisher
- 41.5x29 cm
- Print on paper / periodical
- Yutaka Mizukami Collection

+ Traversing the World through the Floricycle

2-22
- Plate XXXII, Bird-eye view of the dwelling for Darwin D. Martin House. *Ausgeführte Bauten und Entwürfe von Frank Lloyd Wright*
- Frank Lloyd Wright. Ernst Wasmuth, publisher
- 1910
- 45.0 x 63.5 cm
- Lithograph on paper
- Toyota Municipal Museum of Art

2-23
- Plate XXXII, Ground plan of the Darwin D. Martin House. *Ausgeführte Bauten und Entwürfe von Frank Lloyd Wright*
- Frank Lloyd Wright. Ernst Wasmuth, publisher
- 1910
- 45.0 x 63.5 cm
- Lithograph on paper
- Toyota Municipal Museum of Art

2-24
- Darwin D. Martin House, Buffalo, New York. Project 1903-05. Exterior view
- Frank Lloyd Wright, architect. Thomas Russell, photographer
- Photo: c. 1904
- Photograph (reproduction)
- Project photographs, circa 1887-2008, The Frank Lloyd Wright Foundation Archives (The Museum of Modern Art | Avery Architectural & Fine Arts Library, Columbia University, New York)
- FLWFA 0405.0024

2-25
- Darwin D. Martin House, Buffalo, New York. Project 1903-05. Aerial view
- Frank Lloyd Wright, architect. Matthew Digati, photographer
- Photo: 2022
- Photograph (reproduction)
- Courtesy of Frank Lloyd Wright's Martin House

1-76

1-77

1-78

1-79

1-80

1-81

1-82

1-83, 1-84

2-1

2-2

2-3

2-4

2-5

2-6

2-7

2-8

2-9

2-10

2-11

2-12

2-13, 2-14

2-15, 2-16

2-17, 2-18

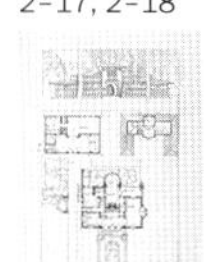
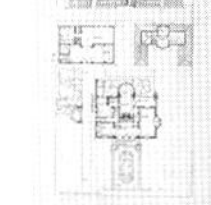

2-19

2-20

2-21

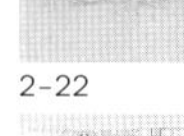

2-22

2-23

2-24

2-25

2-26

2-27
- ダーヴィン・D.マーティン邸（ニューヨーク州バッファロー）
1903–05年
バレル・チェアが並べられた
応接ホール
- 建築：フランク・ロイド・ライト
撮影：マシュー・ディガティ
- 撮影：2022年
- 写真（複写）
- フランク・ロイド・ライト マーティン・ハウス

+ 外と内をつなぐ庭

2-28
- クーンリー邸（イリノイ州リバーサイド）
1906–09年 初期案、外観とステンド・グラスが見える透視図
- フランク・ロイド・ライト
- 1907年
- 39.3×85.5
- 石墨／紙
- 米国議会図書館版画写真部

2-29
- クーンリー邸（イリノイ州リバーサイド）
1906–09年 テラスのスタディ
- フランク・ロイド・ライト、
レンダリング：ウィリアム・ドラモンド
- 1911年
- 55.9×76.2
- インク、色鉛筆／紙
- 豊田市美術館

2-30 ＊
- 第57葉 クーンリー邸、
透視図および窓ガラスのデザイン
『フランク・ロイド・ライトの建築と設計』
- フランク・ロイド・ライト
出版：エルンスト・ヴァスムート社
- 1910年
- 45.0×63.5
- リトグラフ／紙
- 豊田市美術館

2-31 ＊
- 第56葉 クーンリー邸、
平面図および内部空間
『フランク・ロイド・ライトの建築と設計』
- フランク・ロイド・ライト
出版：エルンスト・ヴァスムート社
- 1910年
- 45.0×63.5
- リトグラフ／紙
- 豊田市美術館

2-32 ＊
- 第57葉 クーンリー邸、平面図
『フランク・ロイド・ライトの建築と設計』
- フランク・ロイド・ライト
出版：エルンスト・ヴァスムート社
- 1910年
- 45.0×63.5
- リトグラフ／紙
- 豊田市美術館

2-33
- クーンリー邸 椅子
- デザイン：フランク・ロイド・ライト、
ジョージ・M.ニーデッケン（共同制作）
製作：ニーデッケン=ウォルブリッジ社
- 製造：1908年頃
- 100.2×37.5×46.8
- カシ
- 豊田市美術館

2-34
- クーンリー邸 壁面照明器具
- デザイン：フランク・ロイド・ライト
- 1908年頃
- 18.4×22.9×27.9
- ガラス、ブロンズ
- 豊田市美術館

2-35
- クーンリー邸（イリノイ州リバーサイド）
1906–09年 池越しに見た正面外観
- 建築：フランク・ロイド・ライト
- 撮影：1907年頃
- 写真（複写）
- コロンビア大学
エイヴリー建築美術図書館
エドガー・ターフェル
建築記録・資料

2-36 ＊
- クーンリー邸（イリノイ州リバーサイド）
1906–09年 車寄せから見た外観
- 建築：フランク・ロイド・ライト
- 撮影：1907年頃
- 写真（複写）
- コロンビア大学
エイヴリー建築美術図書館
エドガー・ターフェル
建築記録・資料

2-37 ＊
- クーンリー邸（イリノイ州リバーサイド）
1906–09年 庭
- 建築：フランク・ロイド・ライト
- 撮影：1907年頃
- 写真（複写）
- コロンビア大学
エイヴリー建築美術図書館
エドガー・ターフェル
建築記録・資料

2-38
- クーンリー邸（イリノイ州リバーサイド）
1906–09年 庭の格子垣
- 建築：フランク・ロイド・ライト
- 撮影：1907年頃
- 写真（複写）
- コロンビア大学
エイヴリー建築美術図書館
エドガー・ターフェル
建築記録・資料

2-39
- クーンリー邸（イリノイ州リバーサイド）
1906–09年 食堂内観、
ニーデッケンによる壁画を
正面に見る
- 建築：フランク・ロイド・ライト
撮影：ジェームズ・コールフィールド
- 撮影：2019年
- 写真（複写）

+ プレイリー・ハウスの到達点——有機的建築

2-40
- ロビー邸（イリノイ州シカゴ）
1908–10年
- 建築：フランク・ロイド・ライト
撮影：ファーマン＆サンズ
- 撮影：1908–10年頃
- 写真（複写）
- コロンビア大学
エイヴリー建築美術図書館
フランク・ロイド・ライト財団
アーカイヴズ

2-41
- ロビー邸（イリノイ州シカゴ）
1908–10年
- 建築：フランク・ロイド・ライト
撮影：ジェームズ・コールフィールド
- 撮影：2013年
- 写真（複写）

2-42
- 第37葉 ロビー邸、透視図
『フランク・ロイド・ライトの
建築と設計』
- フランク・ロイド・ライト
出版：エルンスト・ヴァスムート社
- 1910年
- 45.0×63.5
- リトグラフ／紙
- 豊田市美術館

2-43
- 第37葉 ロビー邸、平面図
『フランク・ロイド・ライトの
建築と設計』
- フランク・ロイド・ライト
出版：エルンスト・ヴァスムート社
- 1910年
- 45.0×63.5
- リトグラフ／紙
- 豊田市美術館

2-44
- ロビー邸（イリノイ州シカゴ）
1908–10年 居間から暖炉を見る
- 建築：フランク・ロイド・ライト、
撮影：ジェームズ・コールフィールド
- 撮影：2019年
- 写真（複写）

+ エコロジー住宅の発想

2-45
- ロビー邸（イリノイ州シカゴ）
1908–10年 南側窓
- 建築：フランク・ロイド・ライト
撮影：ジェームズ・コールフィールド
- 撮影：2014年
- 写真（複写）

10 在来と外来：ジェンス・ジェンセンの庭園思想

2-46
- ブース邸計画案
（イリノイ州グレンコー）1911年
第1案、透視図
- フランク・ロイド・ライト
- 1911年
- 54.6×81.0
- 鉛筆、色鉛筆／
イラストレーション・ボード
- ニューヨーク近代美術館
Christopher H. Browne
Purchase Fund, 2002

2-47
- ジェンス・ジェンセンによる
ブース邸計画案
第1案、植栽計画
- デザイン：ジェンス・ジェンセン
- 1911年
- オリジナル：94.9×80.0
- 原図：インク／麻（複写）
- ミシガン大学図書館
デジタル・コレクション

2-48
- ジェンス・ジェンセンによる
「集いの輪」
- デザイン：ジェンス・ジェンセン
- 撮影年不詳
- 写真（複写）
- モートン植物園
スターリング・モートン図書館

2-49 ＊
- 名所江戸百景
せき口上水端はせを庵椿やま
- 歌川広重
- 安政4（1857）年
- 35.9×24.5
- 木版／紙

11 タリアセン：最初の理想郷

2-50
- フィエーゾレ、
ヴィリーノ・ベルヴェデーレの
ライトの住まい。
壁面に図面が見える
- 撮影：テイラー・A.ウーレイ
- 撮影：1910年
- 写真（複写）
- コロンビア大学
エイヴリー建築美術図書館
フランク・ロイド・ライト財団
アーカイヴズ

2-51
- フィエーゾレ、
ヴィリーノ・ベルヴェデーレの
ライトの住まい。
バラのあずまやのある中庭
- 撮影：テイラー・A.ウーレイ
- 撮影：1910年
- 写真（複写）
- コロンビア大学
エイヴリー建築美術図書館
フランク・ロイド・ライト財団
アーカイヴズ

2-52
- ヴィリーノ・ベルヴェデーレからの
フィエーゾレ眺望
- 撮影：テイラー・A.ウーレイ
- 撮影：1910年
- 写真（複写）
- コロンビア大学
エイヴリー建築美術図書館
フランク・ロイド・ライト財団
アーカイヴズ

2-53
- タリアセン第一
（ウィスコンシン州スプリンググリーン）
中庭より西をのぞむ
- 建築：フランク・ロイド・ライト
撮影：ファーマン・アンド・サンズ
- 撮影：1912年頃
- 写真（複写）
- ウィスコンシン歴史博物館

2-54
- タリアセン第二
（ウィスコンシン州スプリンググリーン）
- 建築：フランク・ロイド・ライト
撮影：ヘンリー・ファーマン
- 撮影：1915年
- 写真（複写）
- コロンビア大学
エイヴリー建築美術図書館
フランク・ロイド・ライト財団
アーカイヴズ

2-55
- タリアセン第二
（ウィスコンシン州スプリンググリーン）
食堂
- 建築：フランク・ロイド・ライト
撮影：ファーマン・アンド・サンズ
- 撮影：1920年頃
- 写真（複写）
- ウィスコンシン歴史博物館

2-56
- タリアセン
（ウィスコンシン州スプリンググリーン）
ライトの書斎
- 建築：フランク・ロイド・ライト
- 撮影：1947年
- 写真（複写）
- コロンビア大学
エイヴリー建築美術図書館
エドガー・ターフェル
建築記録・資料

2-57
- タリアセン（ウィスコンシン州スプリンググリーン） 全景
- 建築：フランク・ロイド・ライト
撮影：アンドリュー・ピラージ
- 撮影：2015年
- 写真（複写）
- フランク・ロイド・ライト財団

2-58
- タリアセン（ウィスコンシン州スプリンググリーン） 居間
- 建築：フランク・ロイド・ライト
撮影：アンドリュー・ピラージ
- 撮影：2011年
- 写真（複写）
- フランク・ロイド・ライト財団

12 地形と建築

2-59
- 模型 山邑邸
- 制作：兵庫県立大学
環境人間学部水上研究室
- 制作：2023年
- 60.0×70.0×105.0 縮尺1:100
- ミクストメディア

2-60
- 山邑邸（現・ヨドコウ迎賓館）
（兵庫県芦屋市）1918–24年 遠景
- 建築：フランク・ロイド・ライト
撮影：山田新治郎
- 撮影：2021年

2-26
- Darwin D. Martin House, Buffalo, New York. Project 1903–05. View of the Floricycle
- Frank Lloyd Wright, architect. Matthew Digati, photographer
- Photo: 2021
- Photograph (reproduction)
- Courtesy of Frank Lloyd Wright's Martin House

2-27
- Darwin D. Martin House, Buffalo, New York. Project 1903–05. Interior of the reception room showing barrel chairs
- Frank Lloyd Wright, architect. Matthew Digati, photographer
- Photo: 2022
- Photograph (reproduction)
- Courtesy of Frank Lloyd Wright's Martin House

+ Connecting outside and inside via a garden

2-28
- Coonley House, Riverside, Illinois. Project 1906–09. Perspective. Preliminary drawing showing house and stained glass
- Frank Lloyd Wright
- 1907
- 15 1/2 x 33 11/16 in. (drwg) 39.3 x 85.5 cm (drwg)
- Graphite on paper
- Prints and Photographs Division, Library of Congress, Washington, D.C.
- LC-DIG-ppmsca-84876

2-29
- Coonley House, Riverside, Illinois. Project 1906–09. Study for the Terrace
- Frank Lloyd Wright. William Drummond, renderer
- 1911
- 55.9 x 76.2 cm
- Ink and colored pencil on paper
- Toyota Municipal Museum of Art

2-30
- Plate LVII. Coonley House. Perspective and the detail of the Window Art Glass. *Ausgeführte Bauten und Entwürfe von Frank Lloyd Wright*
- Frank Lloyd Wright. Ernst Wasmuth, publisher
- 1910
- 45.0 x 63.5 cm
- Lithograph on paper
- Toyota Municipal Museum of Art

2-31
- Plate LVI. Coonley House. Plan and Interior Perspective. *Ausgeführte Bauten und Entwürfe von Frank Lloyd Wright*
- Frank Lloyd Wright. Ernst Wasmuth, publisher
- 1910
- 45.0 x 63.5 cm
- Lithograph on paper
- Toyota Municipal Museum of Art

2-32
- Plate LVII. Coonley House. Plan. *Ausgeführte Bauten und Entwürfe von Frank Lloyd Wright*
- Frank Lloyd Wright. Ernst Wasmuth, publisher
- 1910
- 45.0 x 63.5 cm
- Lithograph on paper
- Toyota Municipal Museum of Art

2-33
- Chair from the Coonley House
- Frank Lloyd Wright in collaboration with George M. Niedecken, designers. Niedecken-Walbridge, manufacturer.
- c. 1908
- 100.2 x 37.5 x 46.8 cm
- oak
- Toyota Municipal Museum of Art

2-34
- Lighting fixture from the Coonley House
- Frank Lloyd Wright, designer
- c. 1908
- 18.4 x 22.9 x 27.9 cm
- Glass, bronze
- Toyota Art Museum of Art

2-35
- Coonley House, Riverside, Illinois Project, 1906–09. Exterior view from across reflecting pool
- Frank Lloyd Wright, architect
- Photo: c. 1907
- Photograph (reproduction)
- Edgar Tafel architectural records and papers, 1919–2005, Avery Architectural & Fine Arts Library, Columbia University

2-36
- Coonley House, Riverside, Illinois. Exterior view, from porte cochere
- Wright, Frank Lloyd, architect
- Photo: c. 1907
- Photograph (reproduction)
- Edgar Tafel architectural records and papers, 1919–2005, Avery Architectural & Fine Arts Library, Columbia University

2-37
- Coonley House, Riverside, Illinois. Exterior view, gardens
- Wright, Frank Lloyd, architect
- Photo: c. 1907
- Photograph (reproduction)
- Edgar Tafel architectural records and papers, 1919–2005, Avery Architectural & Fine Arts Library, Columbia University

2-38
- Coonley House, Riverside, Illinois. Exterior view, garden trellis
- Wright, Frank Lloyd, architect
- Photo: c. 1907
- Photograph (reproduction)
- Edgar Tafel architectural records and papers, 1919–2005, Avery Architectural & Fine Arts Library, Columbia University

2-39
- Coonley House, Riverside, Illinois. Project, 1906–09. Dining room interior. View towards the mural by George M. Niedecken
- Frank Lloyd Wright, architect. James Caulfield, photographer
- Photo: 2019
- Photograph (reproduction)

+ Organic Architecture: The achievement of prairie houses

2-40
- Robie House, Chicago, Illinois. Exterior view
- Frank Lloyd Wright, architect. Henry Fuermann, photographer
- Photo: c. 1908–10
- Photograph (reproduction)
- Project photographs, c. 1887–2008, The Frank Lloyd Wright Foundation Archives (The Museum of Modern Art | Avery Architectural & Fine Arts Library, Columbia University, New York, New York)
- FLWFA 0908.0024

2-41
- Robie House, Chicago, Illinois. Project 1908–10. Exterior view
- Frank Lloyd Wright, architect. James Caulfield, photographer
- Photo: 2013
- Photograph (reproduction)

2-42
- Plate XXXVII, Perspective of the city dwelling for Frederick C. Robie, Chicago, Illinois. *Ausgeführte Bauten und Entwürfe von Frank Lloyd Wright*
- Frank Lloyd Wright. Ernst Wasmuth, publisher
- 1910
- 45.0 x 63.5 cm
- Lithograph on paper
- Toyota Municipal Museum of Art

2-43
- Plate XXXVII, Ground plan of the city dwelling for Frederick C. Robie, Chicago, Illinois. *Ausgeführte Bauten und Entwürfe von Frank Lloyd Wright*
- Frank Lloyd Wright. Ernst Wasmuth, publisher
- 1910
- 45.0 x 63.5 cm
- Lithograph on paper
- Toyota Municipal Museum of Art

2-44
- Robie House, Chicago, Illinois. Project, 1908–10. Interior view of the living room
- Frank Lloyd Wright, architect. James Caulfield, photographer
- Photo: 2019
- Photograph (reproduction)

+ Ideas for ecological dwelling

2-45
- Robie House, Chicago, Illinois. Project, 1908–10. Interior view to the balcony
- Frank Lloyd Wright, architect. James Caulfield, photographer
- Photo: 2014
- Photograph (reproduction)

10 Native and exotic plants: Jens Jensen's concept of landscaping

2-46
- Booth House. Glencoe, Illinois, Unbuilt Project, 1911. Perspective of scheme 1
- Frank Lloyd Wright
- 1911
- 21 1/2 x 31 7/8 in. (54.6 x 81.0 cm)
- Pencil and colored pencil on illustration board
- The Museum of Modern Art, New York. Christopher H. Browne Purchase Fund, 2002
- DIGITAL IMAGE©2023, The Museum of Modern Art/Scala, Florence
- 247.2002

2-47
- Booth House, Glencoe, Illinois, Unbuilt Project, 1911. Planting plan by Jens Jensen, scheme 1
- Frank Lloyd Wright, architect. Jens Jensen, landscape designer
- 1911
- original: 37 3/8 x 31 1/2 in. (94.9 x 80.0 cm)
- Ink on linen. (reproduction)
- University of Michigan Library Digital Collections

2-48
- Council Ring designed by Jens Jensen
- Jens Jensen, landscape designer
- undated
- Photograph (reproduction)
- Courtesy of The Morton Arboretum, Lisle, Illinois, USA

2-49
- *Basho's Hut on Tsubakiyama Hill beside the Sekiguchi Canal*
- Utagawa Hiroshige, artist
- 1857 (Ansei 4)
- 35.9 x 24.5 cm
- Woodblock print
- Private Collection

11 Taliesin: The first utopia

2-50
- Interior with drawings at Villino Belvedere, Fiesole
- Taylor A. Woolley, photographer
- Photo: 1910
- Photograph (reproduction)
- Personal and Taliesin Fellowship photographs, 1870s–2004, The Frank Lloyd Wright Foundation Archives (The Museum of Modern Art | Avery Architectural & Fine Arts Library, Columbia University, New York)
- FLWFA 7109.0026

2-51
- Villino Belvedere rose arbor and outdoor dining table
- Taylor A. Woolley, photographer
- Photo: 1910
- Photograph (reproduction)
- Personal and Taliesin Fellowship photographs, 1870s–2004, The Frank Lloyd Wright Foundation Archives (The Museum of Modern Art | Avery Architectural & Fine Arts Library, Columbia University, New York)
- FLWFA7109.0003

2-52
- Fiesole, from Villino Belvedere
- Taylor A. Woolley, photographer
- Photo: 1910
- Photograph (reproduction)
- Personal and Taliesin Fellowship photographs, 1870s–2004, The Frank Lloyd Wright Foundation Archives (The Museum of Modern Art | Avery Architectural & Fine Arts Library, Columbia University, New York)
- FLWFA 7109.0012

2-53
- Taliesin I, Spring Green, Wisconsin. Courtyard looking west
- Frank Lloyd Wright, architect. Henry Fuermann and Sons, photographer
- Photo: c. 1912
- original: 8 x 10 in.
- Photograph (reproduction)
- Wisconsin Historical Society
- 83032

2-54
- Taliesin II, Spring Green, Wisconsin. Exterior view
- Frank Lloyd Wright, architect. Henry Fuermann, photographer
- Photo: 1915
- Photograph (reproduction)
- Project photographs, circa 1887–2008, The Frank Lloyd Wright Foundation Archives (The Museum of Modern Art | Avery Architectural & Fine Arts Library, Columbia University, New York)
- FLWFA 1403.0028

2-55
- Taliesin II, Spring Green, Wisconsin. Dining Room
- Frank Lloyd Wright, architect. Henry Fuermann and Sons, photographer
- Photo: c. 1920
- original: 8 x 10 in.
- Photograph (reproduction)
- Wisconsin Historical Society
- 83015

2-56
- Taliesin, Spring Green, Wisconsin. Interior view, Frank Lloyd Wright's study
- Frank Lloyd Wright, architect
- Photo: 1947
- Photograph (reproduction)
- Edgar Tafel architectural records and papers, 1919–2005, Avery Architectural & Fine Arts Library, Columbia University

2-57
- Taliesin, Spring Green, Wisconsin. Panoramic view
- Frank Lloyd Wright, architect. ©Andrew Pielage, photographer
- Photo: 2015
- Photograph (reproduction)
- Courtesy of the Frank Lloyd Wright Foundation

2-58
- Taliesin, Spring Green, Wisconsin. Interior view of the living room
- Frank Lloyd Wright, architect. ©Andrew Pielage, photographer
- Photo: 2011
- Photograph (reproduction)
- Courtesy of the Frank Lloyd Wright Foundation

12 Terrain and architecture

2-59
- Model. Yamamura House, Ashiya, Japan. Project, 1918–24.
- Frank Lloyd Wright, architect. Mizukami Laboratory, School of Human Science and Environment, University of Hyogo, fabricator
- 60.0×70.0×105.0 cm scale 1:100
- 2023
- mixed media

2-60
- Yamamura House (Yodoko Guest House), Ashiya, Japan. Project, 1918–24. Panoramic view
- Frank Lloyd Wright, architect. Shinjiro Yamada, photographer
- 2021

2-27

2-28

2-29

2-30

2-31

2-32

2-33

2-34

2-35

2-36

2-37

2-38

2-39

2-40

2-41

2-42

2-43

2-44

2-45

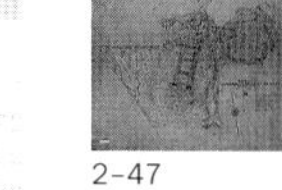
2-46

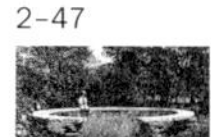
2-47

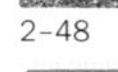

2-48

2-49

2-50

2-51

2-52

2-53

2-54

2-55

2-56

2-57

2-58

2-59

2-60

- 写真

2–61 ＊
- 山邑邸(現・ヨドコウ迎賓館)(兵庫県芦屋市)1918–24年 玄関
- 建築:フランク・ロイド・ライト 撮影:山田新治郎
- 撮影:2022年
- 写真

2–62 ＊
- 山邑邸(現・ヨドコウ迎賓館) 建築装飾
- デザイン:フランク・ロイド・ライト
- 24.5×24.5
- 銅

2–63 ＊
- 山邑邸(現・ヨドコウ迎賓館)(兵庫県芦屋市)1918–24年 窓の装飾から光が差し込んでいる
- 建築:フランク・ロイド・ライト 撮影:山田新治郎
- 撮影:2021年
- 写真(複写)

2–64
- 山邑邸(現・ヨドコウ迎賓館)(兵庫県芦屋市)1918–24年 実測立面図 西立面図、東立面図
- フランク・ロイド・ライト
- 1985年
- 54.7×79.0
- 白焼図/紙
- 遠藤現コレクション

2–65
- 山邑邸(現・ヨドコウ迎賓館)(兵庫県芦屋市)1918–24年 実測平面図 3、4階
- フランク・ロイド・ライト
- 1985年
- 54.5×79.3
- 白焼図/紙
- 遠藤現コレクション

2–66
- 小田原ホテル計画案(神奈川県小田原市)1917年 透視図
- フランク・ロイド・ライト
- 31.0×62.3
- 鉛筆/トレーシング・ペーパー
- コロンビア大学 エイヴリー建築美術図書館 フランク・ロイド・ライト財団 アーカイヴズ

2–67
- エドガー・カウフマン邸「落水荘」(ペンシルベニア州ミルラン) 1934–37年
- 建築:フランク・ロイド・ライト 撮影:アンドリュー・ピラージ
- 撮影:2018年
- 写真(複写)

2–68
- エドガー・カウフマン邸「落水荘」(ペンシルベニア州ミルラン) 1934–37年 居間内観
- 建築:フランク・ロイド・ライト 撮影:二川幸夫
- 撮影:1980年代
- 写真(複写)
- GA / A.D.A. EDITA Tokyo Co., Ltd.

2–69
- 映像「落水荘の建設現場」
- 撮影:1930年代後半
- 映像4分
- コロンビア大学 エイヴリー建築美術図書館 フランク・ロイド・ライト財団 アーカイヴズ

2–70
- 名所江戸百景 王子不動之瀧
- 歌川広重
- 安政4(1857)年
- 35.8×24.5
- 木版/紙

2–71
- 名所江戸百景 目黒千代か池
- 歌川広重
- 安政3(1856)年
- 35.8×24.5
- 木版/紙

2–72
- 日光 霧降の滝 「ライトの来日旅行写真アルバム」
- 撮影者不詳
- 写真(複写)
- 写真提供:フランク・ロイド・ライト・トラスト

2–73 ＊
- サルト・デル・アルバの滝、メキシコ
- 撮影者不詳
- 撮影年不詳
- 写真(複写)
- コロンビア大学 エイヴリー建築美術図書館 フランク・ロイド・ライト財団 アーカイヴズ

13 タリアセン・ウェスト:砂漠のなかのもうひとつの理想郷

2–74
- 『リバティ』誌のための表紙デザイン案 柱サボテンとサボテンの花
- デザイン:フランク・ロイド・ライト
- 1927–28年
- 33.2×52.6
- 色鉛筆、石墨/トレーシングペーパー
- 米国議会図書館版画写真部

2–75
- 『リバティ』誌のための表紙デザイン案 4月の雨
- デザイン:フランク・ロイド・ライト
- 1926–27年
- 33.0×52.3
- 色鉛筆、石墨/トレーシングペーパー
- 米国議会図書館版画写真部

2–76
- サボテンの横に立つ ジェンス・ジェンセン
- 撮影:コーネリア・ブライアリー
- 撮影年不詳
- 写真(複写)
- コロンビア大学 エイヴリー建築美術図書館 フランク・ロイド・ライト財団 アーカイヴズ

2–77
- パッカード社製の自家用車に乗ったライト、妻オルギヴァナと娘たち。オカティラ砂漠キャンプ(アリゾナ州チャンドラー近く)にて
- 撮影者不詳
- 撮影:1928年
- 写真(複写)
- コロンビア大学 エイヴリー建築美術図書館 フランク・ロイド・ライト財団 アーカイヴズ

2–78
- タリアセン・ウェスト(アリゾナ州スコッツデール)1938年– 外観 山を遠方にのぞむ
- 建築:フランク・ロイド・ライト 撮影:ペドロ・E. ゲレロ
- 撮影:1940年
- 写真(複写)
- コロンビア大学 エイヴリー建築美術図書館 フランク・ロイド・ライト財団 アーカイヴズ

2–79
- タリアセン・ウェスト(アリゾナ州スコッツデール) 1938年– サボテンの見える外観
- 建築:フランク・ロイド・ライト
- 撮影:1940年
- 写真(複写)
- コロンビア大学 エイヴリー建築美術図書館 フランク・ロイド・ライト財団 アーカイヴズ

2–80
- タリアセン・ウェスト(アリゾナ州スコッツデール) 1938年– 全景
- 建築:フランク・ロイド・ライト 撮影:フォスケット
- 撮影:2016年
- 写真(複写)
- フランク・ロイド・ライト財団

2–81
- タリアセン・ウェスト(アリゾナ州スコッツデール) 1938年– ガーデンルーム内観
- 建築:フランク・ロイド・ライト 撮影:アンドリュー・ピラージ
- 撮影:2020年
- 写真(複写)
- フランク・ロイド・ライト財団

2–82
- 映像「タリアセン・ウェストのフランク・ロイド・ライト」
- 1953年
- 5分
- 映像
- コロンビア大学 エイヴリー建築美術図書館 フランク・ロイド・ライト財団 アーカイヴズ

SECTION 3 進歩主義教育の環境をつくる

14 ヒルサイド・ホームスクールの実験的教育

3–1
- ヒルサイド・ホームスクール第一(ウィスコンシン州スプリンググリーン) 1887年 旧校舎
- 建築、撮影:フランク・ロイド・ライト
- 撮影:1892年
- オリジナル:22.2×12.1
- 写真(複写)
- ウィスコンシン歴史博物館

3–2
- ヒルサイド・ホームスクール第一 学校案内パンフレット 1891–92年
- エレン・C. ロイド・ジョーンズ、ジェーン・ロイド・ジョーンズ
- 発行:1891
- 印刷/紙、機関誌(複写)
- ウィスコンシン歴史博物館

3–3
- ヒルサイド・ホームスクールの女子体育授業
- 撮影:フランク・ロイド・ライト
- 撮影:1900年頃
- オリジナル:20.3×25.4
- 写真(複写)
- ウィスコンシン歴史博物館

3–4
- ヒルサイド・ホームスクールの化学授業
- 撮影:フランク・ロイド・ライト
- 撮影:1898年
- オリジナル:18.7×18.1
- 写真(複写)
- ウィスコンシン歴史博物館

3–5
- エレン・ロイド・ジョーンズ(左)とジェーン・ロイド・ジョーンズ姉妹(ヒルサイド・ホームスクール創設者、ライト叔母)
- 撮影者不詳
- 撮影年不詳
- オリジナル:10.8×14.0
- 写真(複写)
- ウィスコンシン歴史博物館

3–6
- 第10葉 ヒルサイド・ホームスクール第二、平面図『フランク・ロイド・ライトの建築と設計』
- フランク・ロイド・ライト 出版:エルンスト・ヴァスムート社
- 1910年
- 45.0×63.5
- リトグラフ/紙
- 豊田市美術館

15 シカゴ郊外の仕事場

3–7
- フランク・ロイド・ライト自邸とスタジオ(イリノイ州オークパーク) 1889–1911年 スタジオの待合室
- 建築:フランク・ロイド・ライト 撮影:ヘンリー=ラッセル・ヒッチコック
- 撮影:1897年
- 写真(複写)
- コロンビア大学 エイヴリー建築美術図書館 フランク・ロイド・ライト財団 アーカイヴズ

3–8
- フランク・ロイド・ライト自邸とスタジオ(イリノイ州オークパーク) 1889–1911年 スタジオの玄関テラス
- 建築:フランク・ロイド・ライト 撮影:ジェームズ・コールフィールド
- 撮影:2018年
- 写真(複写)

3–9
- フランク・ロイド・ライト自邸とスタジオ(イリノイ州オークパーク) 1889–1911年 スタジオの設計室
- 建築:フランク・ロイド・ライト 撮影:ジェームズ・コールフィールド
- 撮影:2013年
- 写真(複写)

3–10
- CG映像 フランク・ロイド・ライト自邸とスタジオ(増築の変遷)
- 制作:工学院大学建築学部 鈴木研究室
- 制作:2023年
- 3分20秒
- CGアニメーション
- 工学院大学建築学部 鈴木敏彦研究室

+ 女性建築家マリオン・マホニー

3–11
- マリオン・マホニー(1871–1961年)
- 撮影:1894年
- 写真(複写)
- マサチューセッツ工科大学/ウォルター・バーレイ&マリオン・マホニー・グリフィン・コレクション/シカゴ美術館レイアソン&バーナム美術建築アーカイブ

+ キャサリン・トビン・ライトの幼稚園

3–12
- フランク・ロイド・ライト自邸とスタジオ(イリノイ州オークパーク) 子ども用プレイルーム
- 建築:フランク・ロイド・ライト 撮影:ジェームズ・コールフィールド
- 撮影:2013年
- 写真(複写)

- Photograph (reproduction)

2-61
- Yamamura House (Yodoko Guest House), Ashiya, Japan. Project, 1918–24. Entrance
- Frank Lloyd Wright, architect. Shinjiro Yamada, photographer
- 2022
- Photograph (reproduction)

2-62
- Ornament from Yamamura House
- Frank Lloyd Wright, designer
- 2021
- 24.5 x 24.5 cm
- copper

2-63
- Yamamura House, Ashiya, Japan. Sunlight casting through the window ornament
- Frank Lloyd Wright, architect. Shinjiro Yamada, photographer
- Photo: 2021
- Photograph (reproduction)

2-64
- Yamamura House, Ashiya, Japan. West and East measured elevation
- Frank Lloyd Wright, architect
- 1985
- 54.7 x 79.0 cm
- Diazoprint
- Gen Endo Collection

2-65
- Yamamura House, Ashiya, Japan. Third and forth floor, measured plan
- Frank Lloyd Wright, architect
- 1985
- 54.5 x 79.3 cm
- Diazoprint
- Gen Endo Collection

2-66
- Odawara Hotel, Odawara, Japan. Unbuilt Project, 1917. Perspective
- 12 3/16 x 24 1/2 in. (31.0 x 62.3 cm)
- Pencil on tracing paper
- The Frank Lloyd Wright Foundation Archives (The Museum of Modern Art | Avery Architectural & Fine Arts Library, Columbia University, New York)
- FLW.DR.1706.003

2-67
- Edgar J. Kaufmann House (Fallingwater), Mill Run, Pennsylvania. Project, 1934–37. Exterior
- Frank Lloyd Wright, architect. ©Andrew Pielage, photographer. All Rights Reserved
- Photo: 2018
- Photograph (reproduction)
- Courtesy of the Western Pennsylvania Conservancy

2-68
- Edgar J. Kaufmann House (Fallingwater), Mill Run, Pennsylvania. Project, 1934–37. Interior view of the living room
- ©Yukio Futagawa, photographer
- Photo: 1980s
- Photograph (reproduction)
- Courtesy of GA / A.D.A. EDITA Tokyo Co., Ltd.

2-69
- Film. Edgar J. Kaufmann House (Fallingwater), under construction.
- late 1930s
- film 4 minutes
- The Frank Lloyd Wright Foundation Archives (The Museum of Modern Art | Avery Architectural & Fine Arts Library, Columbia University, New York)
- FLWFM 037 and 070

2-70
- *The Fudo Waterfall at Oji*. From the series "One Hundred Famous Views of Edo"
- Utagawa Hiroshige, artist
- 1857 (Ansei 4)
- Ōban; 35.8 x 24.5cm
- Woodblock print

2-71
- *Chiyogaike Pond of Meguro*. From the series "One Hundred Famous Views of Edo"
- Utagawa Hiroshige, artist
- 1856 (Ansei 3)
- Ōban; 35.8 x 24.5 cm
- Woodblock print

2-72
- Kirifuri Falls, Nikko. The 1905 Photo Album
- Photographer unidentified
- Photograph (reproduction)
- Courtesy of Frank Lloyd Wright Trust, Chicago

2-73
- El Salto Del Abra, Mexico
- Photographer unidentified
- undated
- Photograph (reproduction)
- Personal and Taliesin Fellowship photographs, 1870s–2004, The Frank Lloyd Wright Foundation Archives (The Museum of Modern Art | Avery Architectural & Fine Arts Library, Columbia University, New York)
- FLWFA 7999.0001

13 Taliesin West: Another utopia in the desert

2-74
- Cover design for *Liberty* Magazine. *Saguaro Forms and Cactus Flowers*
- Frank Lloyd Wright, designer
- 1927–28
- 13 1/16 x 20 3/4 in. (drwg) 33.2 x 52.6 cm. (drwg)
- Colored pencil and graphite on tracing paper
- Prints and Photographs Division, Library of Congress, Washington, D.C.
- LC-DIG-ppmsca-84873

2-75
- Cover design for *Liberty* Magazine. *April Showers*
- Frank Lloyd Wright, designer
- 1926–27
- 13 x 20 5/8 in. (drwg) 33.0 x 52.3 cm. (drwg)
- Colored pencil and graphite on tracing paper
- Prints and Photographs Division, Library of Congress, Washington, D.C.
- LC-DIG-ppmsca-84874

2-76
- Jens Jensen with cactus
- Cornelia Brierly, photographer
- undated
- Photograph (reproduction)
- Personal and Taliesin Fellowship photographs, 1870s–2004, The Frank Lloyd Wright Foundation Archives (The Museum of Modern Art | Avery Architectural & Fine Arts Library, Columbia University, New York)
- FLWFA6505.0034

2-77
- Frank Lloyd Wright desert compound and studio, near Chandler, Arizona. Frank Lloyd Wright, Olgivanna Lloyd Wright, and daughters in Packard at Ocatilla
- Photographer unidentified
- Photo: 1928
- Photograph (reproduction)
- Project photographs, circa 1887–2008, The Frank Lloyd Wright Foundation Archives (The Museum of Modern Art | Avery Architectural & Fine Arts Library, Columbia University, New York)
- FLWFA 2702.0037

2-78
- Taliesin West, Scottsdale, Arizona. Project begun 1938. Exterior view
- Frank Lloyd Wright, architect. Pedro E. Guerrero, photographer
- Photo: 1940
- Photograph (reproduction)
- Project photographs, circa 1887–2008, The Frank Lloyd Wright Foundation Archives (The Museum of Modern Art | Avery Architectural & Fine Arts Library, Columbia University, New York)
- FLWFA 3803.0198

2-79
- Taliesin West, Scottsdale, Arizona. Project begun 1938. Exterior view, with cactuses
- Frank Lloyd Wright, architect
- Photo: 1940
- Photograph (reproduction)
- Project photographs, circa 1887–2008, The Frank Lloyd Wright Foundation Archives (The Museum of Modern Art | Avery Architectural & Fine Arts Library, Columbia University, New York)
- FLWFA 3803.0066

2-80
- Taliesin West, Scottsdale, Arizona. Project begun 1938. Panoramic view
- Frank Lloyd Wright, architect. ©Foskett, photographer
- Photo: 2016
- Photograph (reproduction)
- Courtesy of the Frank Lloyd Wright Foundation

2-81
- Taliesin West, Scottsdale, Arizona. Project begun 1938. Interior view of the Garden Room
- Frank Lloyd Wright, architect. ©Andrew Pielage, photographer
- Photo: 2020
- Photograph (reproduction)
- Courtesy of the Frank Lloyd Wright Foundation

2-82
- Film. Frank Lloyd Wright at Taliesin West
- 1953
- film 5 minutes
- The Frank Lloyd Wright Foundation Archives (The Museum of Modern Art | Avery Architectural & Fine Arts Library, Columbia University, New York)
- FLWFM 131

SECTION 3
Designing Progressive Educational Environments

14 Experimental pedagogy of Hillside Home School

3-1
- Hillside Home School I, Spring Green, Wisconsin. Project, 1887. Exterior
- Frank Lloyd Wright, architect and photographer
- Photo: 1892
- original: 8.75 x 4.75 in.
- photograph (reproduction)
- Wisconsin Historical Society
- 25562

3-2
- Hillside Home School I. School Brochure 1891–92
- Ellen C. Lloyd Jones, Jane Lloyd Jones
- 1891
- Print on paper / periodical (reproduction)
- Wisconsin Historical Society

3-3
- Girls' Gym Class at Hillside Home School
- Frank Lloyd Wright, photographer
- Photo: c. 1900
- original: 8 x 10 in.
- photograph (reproduction)
- Wisconsin Historical Society
- 4008

3-4
- Chemistry class at Hillside Home School
- Frank Lloyd Wright, photographer
- Photo: 1898
- original: 7.375 x 7.125 in.
- photograph (reproduction)
- Wisconsin Historical Society
- 25556

3-5
- Ellen and Jane Lloyd Jones. Founders of the Hillside Home School and the aunts of Frank Lloyd Wright
- Photographer unidentified
- undated
- 4.25 x 5.5 in.
- photograph (reproduction)
- Wisconsin Historical Society
- 87747

3-6
- Plate X, Ground plan of the Hillside Home School II. *Ausgeführte Bauten und Entwürfe von Frank Lloyd Wright*
- Frank Lloyd Wright. Ernst Wasmuth, publisher
- 1910
- 45 x 63.5 cm
- Lithograph on paper
- Toyota Municipal Museum of Art

15 Workplace in Suburban Chicago

3-7
- Frank Lloyd Wright House and Studio, Oak Park, Illinois. Project, 1889–1911. Interior view, reception hall to the studio
- Frank Lloyd Wright, architect. Henry-Russell Hitchcock, photographer
- Photo: 1897
- Photograph (reproduction)
- The Frank Lloyd Wright Foundation Archives (The Museum of Modern Art | Avery Architectural & Fine Arts Library, Columbia University, New York)
- FLWFA 9506.0211

3-8
- Frank Lloyd Wright House and Studio, Oak Park, Illinois. Project, 1889–1911. Exterior view of the studio entrance terrace
- Frank Lloyd Wright, architect. James Caulfield, photographer
- Photo: 2018
- Photograph (reproduction)

3-9
- Frank Lloyd Wright House and Studio, Oak Park, Illinois. Project, 1889–1911. Drafting room
- Frank Lloyd Wright, architect. James Caulfield, photographer
- Photo: 2013
- Photograph (reproduction)

3-10
- CG Animation. Frank Lloyd Wright Home and Studio, 1889–1911. Extensions and Transitions
- Frank Lloyd Wright, architect. Toshihiro Suzuki Laboratory, School of Architecture at Kogakuin University, fabricator Courtesy of Frank Lloyd Wright Trust
- 2023
- 3 minutes 20 seconds
- computer graphics animation
- Suzuki Laboratory, School of Architecture at Kogakuin University

+ Marion Mahony: The first female architect in the state of Illinois

3-11
- Marion Mahony Griffin (1871–1961), portrait
- Photo: 1894
- Photograph (reproduction)
- Massachusetts Institute of Technology, Cambridge, MA. Walter Burley and Marion Mahony Griffin Collection, Ryerson and Burnham Art and Architecture Archives, Art Institute of Chicago
- Digital file #200104_230526-001.

+ Catherine Tobin Wright's kindergarten

3-12
- Frank Lloyd Wright House and Studio, Oak Park, Illinois. Project, 1889–1911. Playroom
- Frank Lloyd Wright, architect. James Caulfield, photographer
- Photo: 2013
- Photograph (reproduction)

3-13
- Catherine Tobin Wright (1871–1959), portrait

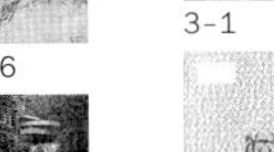

2-61 2-62 2-63 2-64 2-65 2-66 2-67 2-68 2-69 2-70 2-71 2-72 2-73 2-74 2-75 2-76 2-77 2-78 2-79

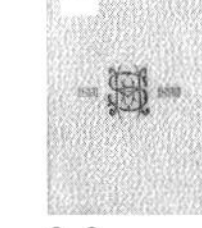

2-80 2-81 2-82 3-1 3-2 3-3 3-4 3-5 3-6 3-7 3-8 3-9 3-10 3-11 3-12 3-13

3-13
- 妻キャサリン・トビン・ライト（1871–1959）夫がデザインしたドレスを着用している
- 撮影：アーノルド
- 撮影年不詳
- 5.0×9.5
- 写真（複写）
- フランク・ロイド・ライト・トラスト

+　メイマー・ボートン・ボスウィックと女性運動家エレン・ケイ

3-14
- 『ウーマン・ムーヴメント』
- 著：エレン・ケイ
  訳：メイマー・ボートン・ボスウィック
  出版：G.P. パトナムス社
- 1912年頃
- 20.0×14.0×4.0
- 印刷／紙、書籍
- パナソニック汐留美術館

3-15
- メイマー・ボートン・ボスウィックからエレン・ケイにあてた手紙
- メイマー・ボートン・ボスウィック
- 年記なし、1912年頃
- インク／紙、手紙（複写）
- スウェーデン国立図書館

3-16　*
- フランク・ロイド・ライトからエレン・ケイにあてた手紙
- 1914年12月8日
- インク／紙、手紙（複写）
- スウェーデン国立図書館

3-17
- メイマー・ボートン・ボスウィック（1869–1914）
- シカゴ・トリビューン社
- 撮影年不詳
- 写真（複写）
- ウィスコンシン歴史博物館

16　クーンリー・プレイハウス幼稚園：風船と紙吹雪のモチーフの展開

3-18
- クーンリー・プレイハウス幼稚園（イリノイ州リバーサイド）1911年初期案 プレイハウスとステンドグラスが見える透視図
- フランク・ロイド・ライト
- 1911年
- 25.5×41.9
- 石墨、色鉛筆／紙
- 米国議会図書館版画写真部

3-19
- オークパーク公園協会への設計競技案「キンダーシンフォニーズ」（イリノイ州オークパーク）1926年（No. 2）
- フランク・ロイド・ライト
- 1926年
- 24.5×31.8
- 鉛筆、色鉛筆／トレーシング・ペーパー
- 豊田市美術館

3-20
- オークパーク公園協会への設計競技案「キンダーシンフォニーズ」（イリノイ州オークパーク）1926年（No. 3）
- フランク・ロイド・ライト
- 1926年
- 27.4×31.8
- 石墨、色鉛筆／トレーシング・ペーパー
- 豊田市美術館

3-21
- オークパーク公園協会への設計競技案「キンダーシンフォニーズ」（イリノイ州オークパーク）1926年（No. 4）
- フランク・ロイド・ライト
- 1926年
- 22.6×31.8
- 鉛筆、色鉛筆／トレーシング・ペーパー
- 豊田市美術館

3-22
- クーンリー・プレイハウス幼稚園窓ガラス
- デザイン：フランク・ロイド・ライト
- 1912年頃
- 61.0×97.5
- ガラス、鉛、木
- 豊田市美術館

3-23
- クーンリー・プレイハウス幼稚園（イリノイ州リバーサイド）1911年
- 建築：フランク・ロイド・ライト
- 撮影：1912年頃
- 写真（複写）
- コロンビア大学
  エイヴリー建築美術図書館
  エドガー・ターフェル
  建築記録・資料

3-24
- クーンリー・プレイハウス幼稚園（イリノイ州リバーサイド）1911年室内
- 建築：フランク・ロイド・ライト
- 撮影：1912年頃
- 写真（複写）
- コロンビア大学
  エイヴリー建築美術図書館
  エドガー・ターフェル
  建築記録・資料

3-25
- クィーン・フェリー・クーンリー（1874–1958）
- 撮影：1950年頃
- 写真（複写）
- エイヴリー・クーンリー・スクール

17　リトル・ディッパー・スクールと舞台

3-26　*
- リトル・ディッパー幼稚園とコミュニティ・プレイハウス計画案（カリフォルニア州ロサンゼルス）1923年 ランドスケープ、テキスタイル・ブロック、基礎、ステンドグラスが描かれた外観図
- フランク・ロイド・ライト
- 1923年
- 47.5×73.0
- 白焼図、色鉛筆／紙
- 米国議会図書館版画写真部

3-27
- リトル・ディッパー幼稚園とコミュニティ・プレイハウス計画案（カリフォルニア州ロサンゼルス）1923年 ランドスケープ、テキスタイル・ブロック、基礎、バタフライ屋根が描かれた立面図
- フランク・ロイド・ライト
- 1923年
- 43.2×53.0
- 石墨／トレーシング・ペーパー
- 米国議会図書館版画写真部

3-28
- 模型 劇場計画案（または銀座活動写真館）
- フランク・ロイド・ライト
- 1918年頃
- 71.5×81.4×34.5 縮尺1:100
- 石膏
- 京都大学

3-29
- バーンズドール邸「立葵の家」（カリフォルニア州ロサンゼルス）1918–21年 外観。ハリウッドを遠方にのぞむ
- 建築：フランク・ロイド・ライト
- 撮影：1920年
- 写真（複写）
- コロンビア大学
  エイヴリー建築美術図書館
  フランク・ロイド・ライト財団
  アーカイヴズ

3-30
- アリーン・バーンズドール（1882–1946）
- 撮影：1916年
- 写真（複写）
- ホリーホックハウス・デイヴィッド＆マイケル・デヴァイン・コレクション

18　木も花も本来ひとつ：自由学園とローゼンワルド学校計画

3-31
- 自由学園（東京、池袋）1921年立面図
- フランク・ロイド・ライト
- 1921年
- 27.5×81.1
- インク／トレーシング・ペーパー
- コロンビア大学
  エイヴリー建築美術図書館
  フランク・ロイド・ライト財団
  アーカイヴズ

3-32
- 自由学園明日館（東京、池袋）1921年 正面ファサード
- 建築：フランク・ロイド・ライト、遠藤新
- 撮影：2021年
- 写真（複写）
- 自由学園明日館

3-33
- 自由学園明日館（東京、池袋）1921年 食堂内観
- 建築：フランク・ロイド・ライト、遠藤新
- 撮影：2023年
- 写真（複写）
- 自由学園明日館

3-34
- フランク・ロイド・ライト氏送別会の日
- 撮影：1922年7月
- 写真（複写）
- 自由学園資料室

3-35
- 竣工当時の明日館食堂お食事時間
- 撮影：1922年4月頃
- 写真（複写）
- 自由学園資料室

3-36
- 自由学園開校を前に相談
  左から：植村環（文学科長）、斎藤その子（実際科）羽仁吉一、羽仁もと子、松岡久子（家庭科長）
- 撮影：1921年1月頃
- 写真（複写）
- 自由学園資料室

3-37
- 自由学園 食堂用椅子
- デザイン：遠藤新
- 1922年
- 78.4（SH37.3）×33.0×39.7
- 木
- 自由学園明日館

3-38　*
- 模型 自由学園
- 建築：フランク・ロイド・ライト
  制作：日本大学工学部建築学科
  谷川正己研究室
- 制作：1990年
- 32.0×85.0×62.0 縮尺1:100
- ミクストメディア
- 自由学園明日館

3-39　*
- 自由学園（東京、池袋）初期案平面図 部屋別概要の記載（フランク・ロイド・ライト財団から寄贈された複写）
- フランク・ロイド・ライト
- 1921年
- 61.5×73.5
- 白焼図／紙（複写）
- 自由学園明日館

3-40
- 『婦人之友』1921年3月号
- 出版：婦人之友社
- 1921年
- 21×13.5×1
- インク／紙、定期刊行物
- 青森県立美術館

3-41
- 『婦人之友』1922年6月号
- 出版：婦人之友社
- 1922年
- 21×13.5×1
- インク／紙、定期刊行物（複写）
- 自由学園資料室

3-42　*
- 第一回作品展覧会
  絵画・図案・手芸 パンフレット
- 出版：自由学園
- 1922年
- 18.7×13.2
- 印刷／紙、機関誌
- 自由学園資料室

3-43
- 関東大震災救護活動絵巻4点
- 自由学園本科3年生有志（6回生）
- 1923年
- ①29×79 cm ②29.3×75.5 cm ③29×79.6 cm ④ 29.5×79.2 cm
- インク、水彩／紙
- 自由学園資料室

3-44
- お悔やみ書簡（1957年7月30日、羽仁もと子追悼）
- フランク・ロイド・ライト
- 1957年7月30日
- 22×28
- インク／紙
- 自由学園資料室

3-45
- ローゼンワルド財団の学校計画案（ヴァージニア州ハンプトン）1928年透視図
- フランク・ロイド・ライト
- 31.4×65.9
- 鉛筆、色鉛筆／トレーシング・ペーパー
- コロンビア大学
  エイヴリー建築美術図書館
  フランク・ロイド・ライト財団
  アーカイヴズ

19　建築教育の場としてのタリアセン・フェローシップ

3-46
- 映像「タリアセン・フェローシップ」
- ダウ・フィルム社
- 撮影：1933年
- 5分
- 映像
- コロンビア大学
  エイヴリー建築美術図書館
  フランク・ロイド・ライト財団
  アーカイヴズ

3-47
- タリアセン・フェローシップ建築群「ヒルサイド・シアター」（ウィスコンシン州スプリンググリーン）1952年
- 建築：フランク・ロイド・ライト
  撮影：アンドリュー・ピラージ
- 撮影：2016年
- 写真（複写）
- フランク・ロイド・ライト財団

- Arnold, photographer
- undated
- 2 x 3.75 in.
- Photograph (reproduction)
- Courtesy of Frank Lloyd Wright Trust, Chicago

+ Mamah Bouton Borthwick and a feminist activist Ellen Key

3-14
- *The Woman Movement*
- Ellen Key, author. Mamah Borthwick, translator. G.P. Putnams, publisher
- c. 1912
- 20.0 x 14.0 x 4.0 cm
- Print on paper / book
- Panasonic Shiodome Museum of Art

3-15
- Mamah Borthwick, letter to Ellen Kay, undated (c. 1912)
- Mamah Bouton Borthwick
- Ink on paper/ letter (reproduction)
- National Library of Sweden
- L4la

3-16
- Frank Lloyd Wright, letter to Ellen Kay, undated
- Frank Lloyd Wright, author
- Ink on paper/ letter (reproduction)
- National Library of Sweden
- L4la

3-17
- Martha (Mamah) Bouton Borthwick Cheney (1869–1914), portrait
- The Chicago Tribune, publisher
- undated
- 8 x 10 in.
- Photograph (reproduction)
- Wisconsin Historical Society
- 3970

16 Coonley Playhouse: Balloon and confetti motifs

3-18
- Coonley Playhouse, Riverside, Illinois. Project, 1911. Perspective. Preliminary drawing showing playhouse and stained glass
- Frank Lloyd Wright
- 1911
- 10 x 161/2 in. (drwg) 25.5 x 41.9 cm (drwg)
- graphite and colored pencil on paper
- Library of Congress, Architecture, Design and Engineering Drawings
- LC-DIG-ppmsca-05582

3-19
- Playhouses for the Oak Park Playground Association (Kindersymphonies), Oak Park, Illinois. Unrealized Project, 1926. No. 2
- Frank Lloyd Wright
- 1926
- 24.5 x 31.8 cm
- pencil and colored pencil on tracing paper
- Toyota Municipal Museum of Art

3-20
- Playhouses for the Oak Park Playground Association (Kindersymphonies), Oak Park, Illinois. Project, 1926. No. 3
- Frank Lloyd Wright
- 1926
- 27.4 x 31.8 cm
- graphite and colored pencil on tracing paper
- Toyota Municipal Museum of Art

3-21
- Playhouses for the Oak Park Playground Association (Kindersymphonies), Oak Park, Illinois. Project, 1926. No. 4
- Frank Lloyd Wright
- 1926
- 22.6 x 31.8 cm
- pencil and colored pencil on paper
- Toyota Municipal Museum of Art

3-22
- Clerestory window from the Coonley Playhouse
- Frank Lloyd Wright, designer
- c. 1912
- 61.0 x 97.5 cm
- glass, lead, wood
- Toyota Municipal Museum of Art

3-23
- Coonley Playhouse, Riverside, Illinois. Project, 1911. Exterior view
- Frank Lloyd Wright, architect
- Photo: c. 1912
- Photograph (reproduction)
- Edgar Tafel architectural records and papers, 1919–2005, Avery Architectural & Fine Arts Library, Columbia University

3-24
- Coonley Playhouse, Riverside, Illinois. Project, 1911. Interior view
- Frank Lloyd Wright, architect
- Photo: c. 1912
- Photograph (reproduction)
- Edgar Tafel architectural records and papers, 1919–2005, Avery Architectural & Fine Arts Library, Columbia University

3-25
- Queene Ferry Coonley (1874–1958), portrait
- Photo: c. 1950
- original: 5.5 x 5 in.
- Photograph (reproduction)
- The Avery Coonley School

17 Little Dipper Community Playhouse

3-26
- Little Dipper School and Community Playhouse for Aline Barnsdall, Los Angeles, California. Project, 1923. Exterior showing landscaping, textile block, construction and stained glass
- Frank Lloyd Wright
- 1923
- 18 3/4 x 28 3/4 in. (drwg) 47.5 x 73.0 cm. (drwg)
- Diazo print and colored pencil on paper
- Prints and Photographs Division, Library of Congress, Washington, D.C.
- LC-DIG-ppmsca-85260 DLC

3-27
- Little Dipper School and Community Playhouse for Aline Barnsdall, Los Angeles, California. Project, 1923. Exterior showing stained glass, textile block construction, and butterfly roof
- Frank Lloyd Wright
- 1923
- 17 1/16 x 20 7/8 in. (drwg) 43.2 x 53.0 cm. (drwg)
- Graphite on tracing paper
- Prints and Photographs Division, Library of Congress, Washington, D.C.
- LC-DIG-ppmsca-84875

3-28
- Model. Tokyo Theater (also known as Ginza Movie Theater)
- Frank Lloyd Wright
- c. 1918
- 71.5 x 81.4 x 34.5 cm scale 1:100
- plaster
- Kyoto University

3-29
- Barnsdall House (Hollyhock House), Los Angeles, California. Project, 1918–21. Exterior view, with Hollywood in the distance
- Frank Lloyd Wright, architect
- Photo: 1920
- Photograph (reproduction)
- Project photographs, circa 1887–2008, The Frank Lloyd Wright Foundation Archives (The Museum of Modern Art | Avery Architectural & Fine Arts Library, Columbia University, New York)
- FLWFA 1705.0011

3-30
- Aline Barnsdall (1882–1946), portrait
- Photo: 1916
- Photograph (reproduction)
- Collection of David Devine and Michael Devine. Courtesy of the City of Los Angeles Department of Cultural Affairs and Hollyhock House

18 Jiyu Gakuen and Rosenwald School project: flowers belong to the tree, and tree belongs to its flowers

3-31
- Jiyu Gakuen School, Tokyo, Japan. Project, 1921. Elevation
- Frank Lloyd Wright
- 1921
- 10 13/16 x 31 15/16 in. (27.46 x 81.12 cm)
- Ink on tracing paper
- The Frank Lloyd Wright Foundation Archives (The Museum of Modern Art | Avery Architectural & Fine Arts Library, Columbia University, New York)
- FLW.DR.2101.012

3-32
- Jiyu Gakuen School, Tokyo, Japan. Project, 1921. Exterior view to the façade
- Frank Lloyd Wright and Arata Endo, architects
- Photo: 2021
- Photograph (reproduction)
- Jiyu Gakuen Myonichikan

3-33
- Jiyu Gakuen School, Tokyo, Japan. Project, 1921. Interior view of the Dining hall
- Frank Lloyd Wright and Arata Endo, architects
- Photo: 2023
- Photograph (reproduction)
- Jiyu Gakuen Myonichikan

3-34
- Farewell with Frank Lloyd Wright at Jiyu Gakuen School
- Photo: July 1922
- Photograph (reproduction)
- Jiyu Gakuen Archives
- 20180313001

3-35
- Students at the dining hall of Jiyu Gakuen School
- Photo: c. April 1922
- Photograph (reproduction)
- Jiyu Gakuen Archives
- 20180319001

3-36
- Motoko (1873–1957) and Yoshikazu Hani at the table discussing the pedagogy with their colleagues
- Photo: c. January 1921
- Photograph (reproduction)
- Jiyu Gakuen Archives
- 歴史 I 01-01

3-37
- Dining Chair from the Jiyu Gakuen School
- Arata Endo, designer for Frank Lloyd Wright
- 1922
- 78.4 (SH37.3) x 33.0 x 39.7 cm
- wood
- Jiyu Gakuen Myonichikan

3-38
- Model. Jiyu Gakuen School, Tokyo, Japan.
- Tanigawa Laboratory, Nihon University, fabricator
- Production: 1990
- 32.0 x 85.0 x 62.0 cm scale: 1:100
- Mixed media
- Jiyu Gakuen Myonichikan Archives

3-39
- Jiyu Gakuen School, Tokyo, Japan. Ground Floor Plan
- Frank Lloyd Wright
- 1921
- drawing 61.5 x 73.5 cm
- Ink on paper, A reproduction of FLWDR 2101.001 given from the Frank Lloyd Foundartion to Jiyu Gakuen School
- Jiyu Gakuen Myonichikan Archives

3-40
- *Fujin no Tomo* (Ladies Friend Journal), March 1921 issue
- Fujin no Tomo-sha, publisher
- 1921
- 21 x 13.5 x 1 cm
- Ink on paper
- Aomori Museum of Art

3-41
- *Fujin no Tomo* (Ladies Friend Journal), June 1922 issue
- Fujin no Tomo-sha, publisher
- 1922
- original: 21 x 13.5 x 1 cm
- Ink on paper (reproduction)
- Jiyu Gakuen Archives

3-42
- Pamphlet of the First Exhibition "Art, Design and Crafts" by Jiyu Gakuen School Students
- Jiyu Gakuen School, publisher
- 1922
- 18.7 x 13.2 cm
- Ink on paper
- Jiyu Gakuen Archives

3-43
- Record of the rescue mission carried out by the students of Jiyu Gakuen School at the Great Kanto Earthquake
- Students from the Regular Course Third Grade of Jiyu Gakuen, creator
- 1923
- ①29 x 79 cm ②29.3 x 75.5 cm ③29 x 79.6 cm ④29.5 x 79.2 cm
- Pen and watercolor on paper
- Jiyu Gakuen Archives

3-44
- Frank Lloyd Wright, Memorial letter, July 30, 1957 upon death of Motoko Hani
- Frank Lloyd Wright
- July 30, 1957
- 22 x 28 cm
- Pencil and ink on paper
- Jiyu Gakuen Archives

3-45
- Rosenwald School, Hampton, Virginia. Unbuilt Project, 1928. Perspective
- Frank Lloyd Wright
- 12 3/4 x 25 15/16 in. (31.43 x 65.88 cm)
- Pencil and colored pencil on tracing paper
- The Frank Lloyd Wright Foundation Archives (The Museum of Modern Art | Avery Architectural & Fine Arts Library, Columbia University, New York)
- FLW.DR.2904.001

19 Taliesin Fellowship: A place for architectural education

3-46
- Film. Taliesin Fellowship
- Dow Film
- 1933
- 5 minutes
- film
- The Frank Lloyd Wright Foundation Archives (The Museum of Modern Art | Avery Architectural & Fine Arts Library, Columbia University, New York)
- FLWFM 043

3-47
- Taliesin Fellowship Complex. Spring Green, Wisconsin. Project, 1952. Hillside Theater
- Frank Lloyd Wright, architect. © Andrew Pielage, photographer
- Photo: 2016
- Photograph (reproduction)
- Courtesy of the Frank Lloyd Wright Foundation

3-48
- Taliesin West. Scottsdale, Arizona. Project, begun 1938. Interior of the drafting room
- Frank Lloyd Wright, architect. Jill Richards, photographer.
- Photo: 2019
- Photograph (reproduction)
- Courtesy of the Frank Lloyd Wright Foundation

3-49
- Olgivanna Wright (1898–1985), third wife of architect Frank Lloyd Wright
- Blackstone, photographer
- undated

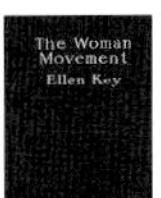

3-14

3-15

3-16

3-17

3-18

3-19

3-20

3-21

3-22

3-23

3-24

3-25

3-26

3-27

3-28

3-29

3-30

3-31

3-32

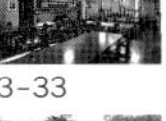
3-33

3-34

3-35

3-36

3-37

3-38

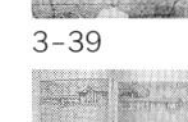
3-39

3-40

3-41

3-42

3-43

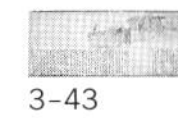
3-44

3-45

3-46

3-47

3-48

3-49

3-48
- タリアセン・ウェスト
（アリゾナ州スコッツデール）1938年－
設計室内観
- 撮影：2019年
- 写真（複写）
- フランク・ロイド・ライト財団

3-49
- 妻オルギヴァナ・ライト
（1898-1985）
- 撮影：ブラックストーン
- 撮影年不詳
- オリジナル：22.9×35.6
- 写真（複写）
- ウィスコンシン歴史博物館

SECTION 4
交差する世界に建つ帝国ホテル

4-1
- フランク・ロイド・ライト、
帝国ホテルにて
- 撮影者不詳
- 撮影：1922年頃
- 写真（複写）
- 帝国ホテル

20 写真コレクションにみるデザイン・ソース

4-2
- チチェエン・イッツア遺跡
ククルカンの神殿
- 撮影：ローラ・ギルピン
- 撮影：1930年頃
- 写真（複写）
- コロンビア大学
エイヴリー建築美術図書館
フランク・ロイド・ライト財団
アーカイヴズ

4-3
- チチェエン・イッツア遺跡戦士の
神殿 外観装飾の詳細
- 撮影：ローラ・ギルピン
- 撮影：1930年頃
- 写真（複写）
- コロンビア大学
エイヴリー建築美術図書館
フランク・ロイド・ライト財団
アーカイヴズ

4-4
- ボロブドゥール遺跡
（インドネシア、ジャワ島中部）
- 撮影：ヘルミグ社、ジャワ島
- 撮影年不詳
- 写真（複写）
- コロンビア大学
エイヴリー建築美術図書館
フランク・ロイド・ライト財団
アーカイヴズ

4-5
- 帝国ホテル二代目本館
外観の装飾。ライト自身による
トリミング
- 撮影：フランク・ロイド・ライト
- 撮影：1922年
- 写真（複写）
- コロンビア大学
エイヴリー建築美術図書館
フランク・ロイド・ライト財団
アーカイヴズ

4-6
- 古代ローマ円形劇場コロッセウム
- 撮影：テイラー・A. ウーレイ
- 撮影：1910年
- 写真（複写）
- コロンビア大学
エイヴリー建築美術図書館
フランク・ロイド・ライト財団
アーカイヴズ

21 共鳴するミッドウェイ・ガーデンズ

4-7
- 帝国ホテル二代目本館
（東京、日比谷）第1案、1914年
地階横断面図
- フランク・ロイド・ライト
- 24.5×87.6
- インク、鉛筆／ドラフティング・クロス
- コロンビア大学
エイヴリー建築美術図書館
フランク・ロイド・ライト財団
アーカイヴズ

4-8
- 帝国ホテル二代目本館
（東京、日比谷）第1案、1914年
鳥瞰透視図
- フランク・ロイド・ライト
- 38.4×89.2
- インク、鉛筆、色鉛筆／
ドラフティング・クロス
- コロンビア大学
エイヴリー建築美術図書館
フランク・ロイド・ライト財団
アーカイヴズ

4-9
- ミッドウェイ・ガーデンズ
（イリノイ州シカゴ）1913-14年
初期の構想図
- フランク・ロイド・ライト
- 1913年
- 41.3×101.6
- 鉛筆、色鉛筆／ドラフティング・クロス
- コロンビア大学
エイヴリー建築美術図書館
フランク・ロイド・ライト財団
アーカイヴズ

4-10
- ミッドウェイ・ガーデンズ
（イリノイ州シカゴ）1913-14年
家具と室内調度品のデザイン
- フランク・ロイド・ライト
- 1913年
- 41.2×51.4
- 鉛筆、色鉛筆／紙
- コロンビア大学
エイヴリー建築美術図書館
フランク・ロイド・ライト財団
アーカイヴズ

4-11
- ミッドウェイ・ガーデンズ
（イリノイ州シカゴ）1913-14年
正面ファサード
- 建築：フランク・ロイド・ライト
撮影：ヘンリー・ファーマン
- 撮影：1914年
- 写真（複写）
- コロンビア大学
エイヴリー建築美術図書館
フランク・ロイド・ライト財団
アーカイヴズ

4-12
- ミッドウェイ・ガーデンズ
（イリノイ州シカゴ）1913-14年
中庭
- 建築：フランク・ロイド・ライト
撮影：ヘンリー・ファーマン
- 撮影：1914年
- 写真（複写）
- コロンビア大学
エイヴリー建築美術図書館
フランク・ロイド・ライト財団
アーカイヴズ

4-13
- ミッドウェイ・ガーデンズ
（イリノイ州シカゴ）1913-14年
食堂内観
- 建築：フランク・ロイド・ライト
撮影：ヘンリー・ファーマン
- 撮影：1914年
- 写真（複写）
- コロンビア大学
エイヴリー建築美術図書館
フランク・ロイド・ライト財団
アーカイヴズ

4-14
- ミッドウェイ・ガーデンズ
（イリノイ州シカゴ）1913-14年
彫刻と外壁タイル
- 建築：フランク・ロイド・ライト
撮影：ヘンリー＝ラッセル・
ヒッチコック
- 撮影：1914年
- 写真（複写）
- コロンビア大学
エイヴリー建築美術図書館
フランク・ロイド・ライト財団
アーカイヴズ

4-15
- 帝国ホテル二代目本館
（東京、日比谷）1913-23年
- 建築：フランク・ロイド・ライト
撮影：ジャネット・ラム・クラークソン
- 撮影：1939年
- オリジナル：17.0×24.5
- 写真（複写）
- 帝国ホテル

4-16
- 帝国ホテル二代目本館
（東京、日比谷）1913-23年 演芸場
- 建築：フランク・ロイド・ライト
- 撮影者不詳
- オリジナル：10.5×18.0
- 写真（複写）
- 帝国ホテル

4-17
- 帝国ホテル二代目本館
（東京、日比谷）1913-23年
池と北翼、玄関回り
- 建築：フランク・ロイド・ライト
- 撮影者不詳
- オリジナル：17.5×12.0
- 写真（複写）
- 帝国ホテル

22 帝国ホテル二代目本館クロニクル

4-18a
- 林愛作と妻、タリアセンにて
- 撮影者不詳
- 撮影：1916年
- 写真（複写）
- コロンビア大学
エイヴリー建築美術図書館
フランク・ロイド・ライト財団
アーカイヴズ

4-18b
- 帝国ホテル二代目本館
（東京、日比谷）第1案 宿泊棟と
メイン・ダイニングを通る横断面図
- フランク・ロイド・ライト
- 1914年
- オリジナル：47.0×198.8
- インク、鉛筆／麻布（複写）
- コロンビア大学
エイヴリー建築美術図書館
フランク・ロイド・ライト財団
アーカイヴズ

4-18c
- 帝国ホテル建築設計事務所にて。
左から：ジョン・ロイド・ライト、
遠藤新、フランク・ロイド・ライト、
伊藤文四郎
- 撮影者不詳
- 撮影：1917年
- オリジナル：9.0×14.5
- 写真（複写）
- 遠藤現コレクション

4-18d
- 帝国ホテル二代目本館
（東京、日比谷）建設現場。
鹿鳴館が背景に見える
- 建築：フランク・ロイド・ライト
- オリジナル：11.0×15.5
- 写真（複写）
- 帝国ホテル

4-18e
- 帝国ホテル二代目本館
（東京、日比谷）建設現場。
宴会場「孔雀の間」の
装飾を建てている
- 建築：フランク・ロイド・ライト
- オリジナル：11.0×15.5
- 写真（複写）
- 帝国ホテル

4-18f
- 絵葉書 帝国ホテル二代目本館
（東京、日比谷）
- 建築：フランク・ロイド・ライト
- 撮影：1935年頃
- オリジナル：9.0×14.0
- 印刷／紙、絵葉書（複写）
- 帝国ホテル

4-18g
- 帝国ホテル二代目本館
（東京、日比谷） 集合写真。
左より：遠藤新、フランク・ロイド・ライト、
林愛作、ポール・ミュラー
- 建築：フランク・ロイド・ライト
- 撮影：1922年
- 22.0×28.0
- 写真（複写）
- 帝国ホテル 写真協力：金谷ホテル

4-18h
- 日比谷公園から見た帝国ホテル
二代目本館全景
- 建築：フランク・ロイド・ライト
- 撮影年不詳
- オリジナル：13.0×29.5
- 写真（複写）
- 帝国ホテル

4-18i
- 戦前の帝国ホテル二代目本館
中央に鹿鳴館、左に帝国ホテル
- 建築：フランク・ロイド・ライト
- 1941年以前
- オリジナル：9.5×14.5
- 写真（複写）
- 帝国ホテル

4-18j
- 絵葉書 1965年頃の帝国ホテル
二代目本館（東京、日比谷） 全景
- 建築：フランク・ロイド・ライト
- 1965年頃
- 写真（複写）
- 帝国ホテル

4-18k
- 移築された帝国ホテル二代目
本館の玄関部分
- 建築：フランク・ロイド・ライト
撮影：ToLoLo Studio
- 撮影：2023年
- 写真（複写）
- 撮影協力：博物館明治村

4-18l
- ロジャース・レイシー・ホテル計画案
（テキサス州ダラス）1946-47年
透視図
- フランク・ロイド・ライト
- オリジナル：85.7×76.8
- 原図：色鉛筆、インク／
トレーシング・ペーパー（複写）
- コロンビア大学
エイヴリー建築美術図書館
フランク・ロイド・ライト財団
アーカイヴズ

4-18m
- ロジャース・レイシー・ホテル計画案
（テキサス州ダラス）1946-47年
吹き抜けより中庭を見下ろす
- フランク・ロイド・ライト
- オリジナル：85.7×76.8
- 原図：色鉛筆、インク／
トレーシング・ペーパー（複写）
- コロンビア大学
エイヴリー建築美術図書館
フランク・ロイド・ライト財団
アーカイヴズ

4-18n
- 田根剛氏による帝国ホテル
東京 新本館イメージパース

- 9 x 14 in.
- photographic print b/w (reproduction)
- Wisconsin Historical Society
- 87748

SECTION 4
Imperial Hotel at the Global Crossroads

4-1
- Frank Lloyd Wright at the Imperial Hotel
- Photographer unidentified
- Photo: c. 1922
- Photograph (reproduction)
- Imperial Hotel
- T000011-10029

20 Design inspirations in the image collection

4-2
- Chichen-itza, Temple of Kukulcán, exterior view
- Laura Gilpin, photographer
- Photo: c. 1930
- Photograph (reproduction)
- Personal and Taliesin Fellowship photographs, 1870s-2004, The Frank Lloyd Wright Foundation Archives (The Museum of Modern Art | Avery Architectural & Fine Arts Library, Columbia University, New York)
- FLWFA 7006.0002

4-3
- Chichen-itza, Temple of Warriors, exterior view, details of ornament
- Laura Gilpin, photographer
- Photo c. 1930
- Photograph (reproduction)
- Personal and Taliesin Fellowship photographs, 1870s-2004, The Frank Lloyd Wright Foundation Archives (The Museum of Modern Art | Avery Architectural & Fine Arts Library, Columbia University, New York)
- FLWFA 7006.0011

4-4
- Borobudur, Central Java, Indonesia, exterior detail
- Helmig & Co., Java, Indonesia., photographer
- undated
- Photograph (reproduction)
- Personal and Taliesin Fellowship photographs, 1870s-2004, The Frank Lloyd Wright Foundation Archives (The Museum of Modern Art | Avery Architectural & Fine Arts Library, Columbia University, New York)
- FLWFA 7008.0003

4-5
- Imperial Hotel, Tokyo 1913-23. Exterior view, detail of decoration
- Frank Lloyd Wright, photographer
- Photo: 1922
- Photograph (reproduction)
- Personal and Taliesin Fellowship photographs, 1870s-2004, The Frank Lloyd Wright Foundation Archives (The Museum of Modern Art | Avery Architectural & Fine Arts Library, Columbia University, New York)
- FLWFA 1509.061 / FLWFA 1509.0000

4-6
- Roman amphitheater, Colosseum
- Taylor A. Woolley, photographer
- Photo: 1910
- Photograph (reproduction)
- Personal and Taliesin Fellowship photographs, 1870s-2004, The Frank Lloyd Wright Foundation Archives (The Museum of Modern Art | Avery Architectural & Fine Arts Library, Columbia University, New York)
- FLWFA 7109.0006

21 Resonance of Midway Gardens

4-7
- Imperial Hotel, Tokyo, Japan. Project, 1913-23. Scheme 1, 1914. Transverse section
- Frank Lloyd Wright
- 9 5/8 x 34 1/2 in. (24.5 x 87.6 cm)
- Ink and pencil on drafting cloth
- The Frank Lloyd Wright Foundation Archives (The Museum of Modern Art | Avery Architectural & Fine Arts Library, Columbia University, New York)
- FLW.DR.1409.053

4-8
- Imperial Hotel, Tokyo, Japan. Project, 1913-23. Scheme 1, 1914. Aerial perspective
- Frank Lloyd Wright
- 15 1/8 x 35 1/8 in. (38.4 x 89.2 cm)
- Ink, pencil, and colored pencil on drafting cloth
- The Frank Lloyd Wright Foundation Archives (The Museum of Modern Art | Avery Architectural & Fine Arts Library, Columbia University, New York)
- FLW.DR.1409.042

4-9
- Midway Gardens, Chicago, Illinois. Project, 1913-14. First sketch
- Frank Lloyd Wright
- 1913
- 16 1/4 x 40 in. (41.3 x 101.6 cm)
- Pencil and colored pencil on drafting cloth
- The Frank Lloyd Wright Foundation Archives (The Museum of Modern Art | Avery Architectural & Fine Arts Library, Columbia University, New York)
- FLW.DR.1401.007

4-10
- Midway Gardens, Chicago, Illinois. Project, 1913-14. Interior furniture
- Frank Lloyd Wright
- 1913
- 16 3/16 x 20 1/4 in. (41.2 x 51.4 cm)
- Pencil and colored pencil on paper
- The Frank Lloyd Wright Foundation Archives (The Museum of Modern Art | Avery Architectural & Fine Arts Library, Columbia University, New York)
- FLW.DR.1401.020

4-11
- Midway Gardens, Chicago, Illinois. Project, 1913-14. Exterior view, front façade
- Frank Lloyd Wright, architect. Henry Feuermann, photographer
- Photo: 1914
- Photograph (reproduction)
- Project photographs, circa 1887-2008, The Frank Lloyd Wright Foundation Archives (The Museum of Modern Art | Avery Architectural & Fine Arts Library, Columbia University, New York)
- FLWFA 1401.0028

4-12
- Midway Gardens, Chicago, Illinois. Project, 1913-14. View of Court Yard
- Frank Lloyd Wright, architect. Henry Feuermann, photographer
- Photo: 1914
- Photograph (reproduction)
- Project photographs, circa 1887-2008, The Frank Lloyd Wright Foundation Archives (The Museum of Modern Art | Avery Architectural & Fine Arts Library, Columbia University, New York)
- FLWFA 1401.0032

4-13
- Midway Gardens, Chicago, Illinois. Project, 1913-14. Interior view of the dining room
- Frank Lloyd Wright, architect. Henry Feuermann, photographer
- Photo: 1914
- Photograph (reproduction)
- Project photographs, circa 1887-2008, The Frank Lloyd Wright Foundation Archives (The Museum of Modern Art | Avery Architectural & Fine Arts Library, Columbia University, New York)
- FLWFA 1403.0039

4-14
- Midway Gardens, Chicago, Illinois. Project, 1913-14. Exterior view, detail of decoration
- Frank Lloyd Wright, architect. Hitchcock, Henry-Russell, photographer
- Photo: 1914
- Photograph (reproduction)
- Project photographs, circa 1887-2008, The Frank Lloyd Wright Foundation Archives (The Museum of Modern Art | Avery Architectural & Fine Arts Library, Columbia University, New York)
- FLWFA 1401.0148

4-15
- Imperial Hotel, Tokyo, Japan. Project, 1913-23
- Frank Lloyd Wright, architect. Janet Lamb Clarkson, photographer
- Photo: 1939
- original: 17 x 24.5 cm
- Photograph (reproduction)
- Imperial Hotel
- T000012-11002

4-16
- Imperial Hotel, Tokyo, Japan. Project, 1913-23. Theater
- Frank Lloyd Wright, architect. Photographer unidentified
- original: 10.5 x 18 cm
- Photograph (reproduction)
- Imperial Hotel
- 14076B

4-17
- Imperial Hotel, Tokyo, Japan. Project, 1913-23. Sculpture at the pond
- Frank Lloyd Wright, architect. Photographer unidentified
- original: 17.5 x 12.0 cm
- Photograph (reproduction)
- Imperial Hotel
- T000012-11013

22 Chronicle of Wright's Imperial Hotel

4-18a
- Aisaku and Takako Hayashi at Taliesin
- Photographer unidentified
- Photo: 1916
- Photograph (reproduction)
- Personal and Taliesin Fellowship photographs, 1870s-2004, The Frank Lloyd Wright Foundation Archives (The Museum of Modern Art | Avery Architectural & Fine Arts Library, Columbia University, New York)
- FLWFA 6702.0008

4-18b
- Imperial Hotel, Tokyo, Japan. Scheme 1, 1914. Transverse section through wings and main dining hall
- Frank Lloyd Wright
- 1914
- original: 18 1/2 x 78 1/4 in. (47 x 198.8 cm)
- Ink and pencil on linen. (reproduction)
- The Frank Lloyd Wright Foundation Archives (The Museum of Modern Art | Avery Architectural & Fine Arts Library, Columbia University, New York)
- FLW.DR.1409.031

4-18c
- At the construction office of the Imperial Hotel. From left: John Lloyd Wright, Endo Arata, Frank Lloyd Wright and Bunshiro Ito
- Photographer unidentified
- Photo: 1917
- original: 9.0 x 14.5 cm
- Photograph (reproduction)
- Gen Endo Collection

4-18d
- Imperial Hotel, Tokyo, Japan. Construction site. Rokumeikan can be seen in the back
- Frank Lloyd Wright, architect
- original: 11.5 x 15.5 cm
- Photograph (reproduction)
- Imperial Hotel
- 10079

4-18e
- Imperial Hotel, Tokyo, Japan. Construction site. Decoration of the Banquet hall (Peacock Room) can be seen lifted
- Frank Lloyd Wright, architect
- original: 11.0 x 15.5 cm
- Photograph (reproduction)
- Imperial Hotel
- 10069

4-18f
- Postcard. Imperial Hotel, Tokyo, Japan
- Frank Lloyd Wright, architect
- Photo: 1935
- original: 9.0 x 14.0 cm
- postcard (reproduction)
- Imperial Hotel
- 21080

4-18g
- Imperial Hotel, Tokyo, Japan. From left: Arata Endo, Frank Lloyd Wright, Aisaku Hayashi, Paul Muller
- Photo: 1922
- original: 22 x 28 cm
- Photograph (reproduction)
- Imperial Hotel
- Photo courtesy of Kanaya Hotel
- T000011-10094

4-18h
- Imperial Hotel, Tokyo, Japan. Exterior view from the Hibiya Park
- Frank Lloyd Wright, architect
- Undated
- original: 13.0 x 29.5 cm
- Photograph (reproduction)
- Imperial Hotel
- T000012-11073

4-18i
- Imperial Hotel, Tokyo, Japan. Rokumeikan in the center and the Imperial Hotel on the left
- Frank Lloyd Wright, architect
- before 1941
- original: 9.5 x 14.5
- Photograph (reproduction)
- Imperial Hotel
- T000012-11072

4-18j
- Postcard. Imperial Hotel around 1965
- Frank Lloyd Wright, architect
- c. 1965
- Photograph (reproduction)
- Imperial Hotel
- 11036

4-18k
- Wright's Imperial Hotel Lobby and reflecting pool reconstructed at the Museum Meiji-Mura
- Frank Lloyd Wright, architect. ToLoLo Studio, photographer
- Photo: 2023
- Photograph (reproduction)
- Courtesy of Museum Meiji-Mura

4-18l
- Rogers Lacey Hotel, Dallas, Texas. Unbuilt Project, 1946-47. Exterior perspective
- Frank Lloyd Wright
- 33 3/4 x 30 1/4 in. (85.7 x 76.8 cm)
- Colored pencil and ink on tracing paper (reproduction)
- The Frank Lloyd Wright Foundation Archives (The Museum of Modern Art | Avery Architectural & Fine Arts Library, Columbia University, New York)
- FLW.DR.4606.001

4-18m
- Rogers Lacey Hotel, Dallas, Texas. Unbuilt Project, 1946-47. View of court
- Frank Lloyd Wright
- 33 3/4 x 30 1/4 in. (85.7 x 76.8 cm)
- Colored pencil and ink on tracing paper (reproduction)
- The Frank Lloyd Wright Foundation Archives (The Museum of Modern Art | Avery Architectural & Fine Arts Library, Columbia University, New York)
- FLW.DR.4606.008

4-18n
- Imperial Hotel Tokyo New Main Building Image Perspective by Tsuyoshi Tane
- ATTA- Atelier Tsuyoshi Tane Architects
- 2022

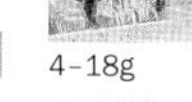
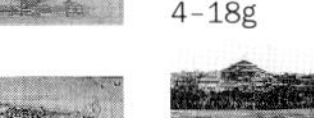

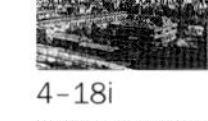
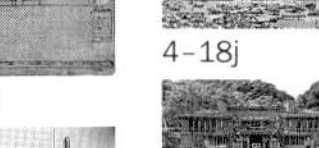

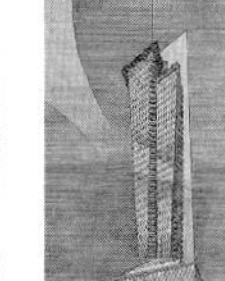
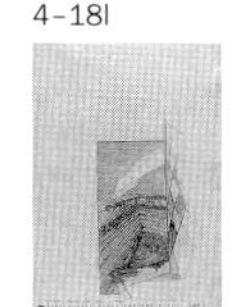

4-1 4-2 4-3 4-4 4-5 4-6 4-7 4-8 4-9 4-10 4-11 4-12 4-13 4-14 4-15

4-16 4-17 4-18a 4-18b 4-18c 4-18d 4-18e 4-18f 4-18g 4-18h 4-18i 4-18j 4-18k 4-18l 4-18m 4-18n

- ATTA– Atelier Tsuyoshi Tane Architects
- 2022年
- コンピューターグラフィックス
- 帝国ホテル
- 検討段階のものであり 今後行政協議等により変更となる 可能性があります

23　メガ・プロジェクトのはじまり

4–19
- 帝国ホテル二代目本館 (東京、日比谷)1913–23年 第2案、横断面図
- フランク・ロイド・ライト
- 1915年
- 37.9×102.1
- インク、鉛筆、色鉛筆/ドラフティング・クロス
- コロンビア大学 エイヴリー建築美術図書館 フランク・ロイド・ライト財団 アーカイヴズ

4–20
- 帝国ホテル二代目本館 (東京、日比谷)1913–23年 第2案、縦断面図
- フランク・ロイド・ライト
- 1915年
- 52.5×154.5
- インク、鉛筆/ドラフティング・クロス
- コロンビア大学 エイヴリー建築美術図書館 フランク・ロイド・ライト財団 アーカイヴズ

4–21
- 帝国ホテル二代目本館 (東京、日比谷)1913–23年 第2案、キャバレー・レストラン、演芸場、宴会場「孔雀の間(ピーコック・ルーム)」の断面図
- フランク・ロイド・ライト
- 1915年
- 147.3×103.5
- インク、鉛筆、色鉛筆/ドラフティング・クロス
- コロンビア大学 エイヴリー建築美術図書館 フランク・ロイド・ライト財団 アーカイヴズ

4–22
- 帝国ホテル二代目本館 (東都、日比谷)1913–23年 地下1階平面図、メイン階(2階)平面図
- フランク・ロイド・ライト
- 45.5×61.0 縮尺1:192
- 白焼図
- 遠藤現コレクション

4–23　＊
- 帝国ホテル二代目本館 (東京、日比谷) 地階(1階)平面図、宴会場(4階)平面図
- フランク・ロイド・ライト
- 45.5×61.0 縮尺1:192
- 白焼図
- 遠藤現コレクション

4–24　＊
- 帝国ホテル二代目本館 (東京、日比谷) ルーフ階(3階)平面図
- フランク・ロイド・ライト
- 61.0×45.5 縮尺1:192
- 白焼図
- 遠藤現コレクション

4–25　＊
- 帝国ホテル二代目本館 (東京、日比谷)1913–23年 宴会場「孔雀の間(ピーコック・ルーム)」へのプロムナード
- 建築:フランク・ロイド・ライト
- 撮影:1925年頃
- オリジナル:10.5×15.0
- 紙/印刷、絵葉書(複写)
- 帝国ホテル

4–26　＊
- 帝国ホテル二代目本館 (東京、日比谷)1913–23年 外観 南東方面を見る
- 建築:フランク・ロイド・ライト
- 撮影年不詳
- オリジナル:11.0×15.5
- 写真(複写)
- 帝国ホテル

4–27　＊
- 帝国ホテル二代目本館 (東京、日比谷) 1913–23年 外観 南西方面を見る
- 建築:フランク・ロイド・ライト
- 撮影年不詳
- オリジナル:10.5×15.5
- 写真(複写)
- 帝国ホテル

4–28　＊
- 絵葉書 帝国ホテル二代目本館 (東京、日比谷)1913–23年 ロビー内観
- 建築:フランク・ロイド・ライト
- 1965年頃
- オリジナル:12.0×17.0
- 絵葉書(複写)
- 帝国ホテル

4–29
- 模型 3D計測データを用いた3Dプリントレプリカ 帝国ホテル二代目本館模型
- 建築:フランク・ロイド・ライト 制作:京都工芸繊維大学 KYOTO Design Lab
- 制作:2023年
- 36.0×84.5×139.5(オリジナル:44.0×109.0×170.0 縮尺1:100)
- オリジナルは石膏。 レプリカ:塗装、ジェッソ/PLA樹脂
- 京都大学(原作模型所蔵)

24　宿泊とエンターテインメント

4–30
- 帝国ホテル二代目本館 客室のサイド・テーブル
- デザイン:フランク・ロイド・ライト
- 72.0×70.0×66.0
- 木

4–31
- 帝国ホテル二代目本館 (東京、日比谷)1913–23年 客室
- オリジナル:10.5×17.0
- 写真(複写)
- 帝国ホテル

4–32
- 帝国ホテル二代目本館 (東京、日比谷)1913–23年 客室
- オリジナル:11.5×17.5
- 写真(複写)
- 帝国ホテル

4–33
- 帝国ホテル二代目本館 (東京、日比谷)1913–23年 客室
- オリジナル:12.0×17.0
- 印刷/紙、絵葉書(複写)
- 帝国ホテル

4–34
- 帝国ホテル別館(東京、日比谷)、1920年 ライトの居室内観
- 撮影者不詳
- 撮影:1920年
- 写真(複写)
- コロンビア大学 エイヴリー建築美術図書館 フランク・ロイド・ライト財団 アーカイヴズ

4–35
- 帝国ホテル二代目本館 (東京、日比谷) アーケード入口
- オリジナル:12.0×165
- 写真(複写)
- 帝国ホテル

4–36
- 帝国ホテル二代目本館 ルーフ・ガーデンでの映画会 プログラム(表紙)
- 1937年
- オリジナル:11.5×16.0
- 印刷/紙(複写)
- 帝国ホテル

4–37
- 帝国ホテル二代目本館 (東京、日比谷)1913–23年 ルーフ・ガーデンでの映画会
- 建築:フランク・ロイド・ライト
- オリジナル:11.5×16.0
- 印刷/紙、絵葉書(複写)
- 帝国ホテル

4–38
- 帝国ホテル二代目本館 パンフレット
- デザイン:繁岡鑒一
- 1925–30年頃
- 15.5×18.5
- 印刷/紙、パンフレット
- 帝国ホテル

4–39
- 帝国ホテル二代目本館 英語パンフレット
- デザイン:繁岡鑒一
- 1925年
- 9.0×19.5
- 印刷/紙、パンフレット
- 帝国ホテル

4–40　＊
- 『帝国ホテル』
- 高梨由太郎編 出版:洪洋社
- 1925年
- 26.0×19.0×1.5
- 印刷/紙、書籍
- 遠藤現コレクション

4–41
- 帝国ホテル二代目本館 パンフレット
- デザイン:繁岡鑒一
- 1925–30年頃
- 9.0×19.5
- 印刷/紙、パンフレット
- 水上優コレクション

4–42
- 絵葉書 帝国ホテル二代目本館 宴会場「孔雀の間」
- 9.0×13.8
- 印刷/紙、絵葉書
- 水上優コレクション

25　総合芸術としての帝国ホテル

4–43
- 帝国ホテル二代目本館 キャバレー・レストランで用いられたディナー・ウェア
- デザイン:フランク・ロイド・ライト 再製作:(株)ノリタケカンパニー
- デザイン:1916–22年頃、再製作:1962–68年
- ディナープレート(2枚):各ϕ27.0 cm、サラダ・プレート(2枚):各ϕ19.4 cm、パン皿(2枚):各ϕ16.2 cm、フルーツ・ボウル(2枚):各ϕ14.5 cm、カップ(2個):各5.5×10.7 cm、ϕ8.6 cm、ソーサー(2枚):各ϕ13.5 cm
- 磁器
- 豊田市美術館

4–44
- 帝国ホテル二代目本館で用いられていたコーヒーポット
- デザイナー不詳
- 17.0×ϕ8.0
- 銀
- 帝国ホテル

4–45
- 帝国ホテル二代目本館で用いられていたクリーマー
- デザイナー不詳
- 7.5×ϕ7.5
- 銀
- 帝国ホテル

4–46
- 帝国ホテル二代目本館で用いられていたメニュー
- 1926年
- 16.0×10.5 閉じた状態
- 印刷/紙
- 帝国ホテル

4–47
- 帝国ホテル二代目本館 椅子「ピーコック・チェア」
- デザイン:フランク・ロイド・ライト
- デザイン:1913年頃 製作:1930年頃
- 椅子:96.0×38.8×41.5
- カシ、ニレ、モミジバフウ
- 豊田市美術館

4–48　＊
- 帝国ホテル二代目本館 椅子「ピーコック・チェア」
- デザイン:フランク・ロイド・ライト
- デザイン:1913年頃 製作:椅子1950年以降
- 98.5×39.5×45.9
- 木
- 豊田市美術館

4–49　＊
- 帝国ホテル二代目本館 テーブル
- デザイン:フランク・ロイド・ライト
- デザイン:1913年頃 製作年不詳
- 59.2×88.3×88.7
- 木
- 豊田市美術館

4–50
- 帝国ホテル二代目本館 椅子
- デザイン:フランク・ロイド・ライト 修復:渡邊謙一郎 (スタンダード トレード)
- デザイン:1920年頃 修復:2023年
- 95.5×39.5×43.5
- 木

4–51　＊
- 帝国ホテル二代目本館 2階ラウンジの椅子
- デザイン:フランク・ロイド・ライト
- デザイン:1913年頃 再製作:1985年
- 96.5(SH42.0)×40.5×44.5
- 木、籐、合成皮革
- 博物館明治村

4–52　＊
- 帝国ホテル二代目本館 プロムナード中央パーラー(宝の間) 南側暖炉の上の着彩レリーフ
- フランク・ロイド・ライト
- 1921年
- 56.7×88.9
- 色鉛筆、白焼図/紙
- 米国議会図書館版画写真部

4–53　＊
- 帝国ホテル二代目本館 プロムナード中央パーラー(宝の間) 北側暖炉の上の着彩レリーフ
- フランク・ロイド・ライト
- 1921年
- 56.5×87.6
- 色鉛筆、白焼図/紙
- 米国議会図書館版画写真部

4–54　＊
- 帝国ホテル二代目本館 演芸場の壁面装飾 原寸詳細図
- フランク・ロイド・ライト

- computer graphic
- Imperial Hotel
- This is in the preliminary stage and subject to change as developed

23 Start of a mega project

4-19
- Imperial Hotel, Tokyo, Japan. Project, 1913-23. Scheme 2, 1915. Cross section
- Frank Lloyd Wright
- 14 15/16 x 40 3/16 in. (37.9 x 102.1 cm)
- Ink, pencil, and colored pencil on drafting cloth
- The Frank Lloyd Wright Foundation Archives (The Museum of Modern Art | Avery Architectural & Fine Arts Library, Columbia University, New York)
- FLW.DR.1509.050

4-20
- Imperial Hotel, Tokyo, Japan. Project, 1913-23. Scheme 2, 1915. Longitudinal section
- Frank Lloyd Wright
- 20 11/16 x 60 13/16 in. (52.5 x 154.5 cm)
- Ink and pencil on drafting cloth
- The Frank Lloyd Wright Foundation Archives (The Museum of Modern Art | Avery Architectural & Fine Arts Library, Columbia University, New York)
- FLW.DR.1509.650

4-21
- Imperial Hotel, Tokyo, Japan. Project, 1913-23. Scheme 2, 1915. Section through Cabaret, auditorium, and banquet hall
- Frank Lloyd Wright
- 58 x 40 3/4 in. (147.3 x 103.5 cm)
- Ink, pencil, and colored pencil on drafting cloth
- The Frank Lloyd Wright Foundation Archives (The Museum of Modern Art | Avery Architectural & Fine Arts Library, Columbia University, New York)
- FLW.DR.1509.674

4-22
- Imperial Hotel, Tokyo, Japan. Basement floor plan. Main floor plan
- Frank Lloyd Wright
- 45.5 x 61.0 cm
- Diazo Print
- Gen Endo Collection

4-23
- Imperial Hotel, Tokyo, Japan. Ground floor plan. Banquet Hall Plan
- Frank Lloyd Wright
- 45.5 x 61.0 cm
- Diazo Print
- Gen Endo Collection

4-24
- Imperial Hotel, Tokyo, Japan. Roof floor plan
- Frank Lloyd Wright
- 61 x 45.5 cm
- Diazo Print
- Gen Endo Collection

4-25
- Imperial Hotel, Tokyo, Japan. Project, 1913-23. Interior view of the promenade to the banquet hall (Peacock Room)
- Frank Lloyd Wright, architect
- Photo: c. 1925
- original: 10.5 x 15.0 cm
- Postcard (reproduction)
- Imperial Hotel
- 15-04P 14066

4-26
- Imperial Hotel, Tokyo, Japan. Project, 1913-23. View towards the direction of south west
- Frank Lloyd Wright, architect
- undated
- original: 11.0 x 15.5 cm
- Photograph (reproduction)
- Imperial Hotel
- 12064

4-27
- Imperial Hotel, Tokyo, Japan. Project, 1913-23. View towards the direction of south east
- Frank Lloyd Wright, architect
- undated
- original: 10.5 x 15.5 cm
- Photograph (reproduction)
- Imperial Hotel
- 12067

4-28
- Postcard. Imperial Hotel, Tokyo, Japan. Project, 1913-23. Entrance lobby
- Frank Lloyd Wright, architect
- c. 1965
- original: 12.0 x 17.0 cm
- Print on paper / postcard (reproduction)
- Imperial Hotel
- 13016

4-29
- Imperial Hotel model (replica made by 3D scanning and 3D print)
- Frank Lloyd Wright, architect. KYOTO Design Lab, Kyoto Institute of Technology, fabricator of the replica
- Fabrication of the replica: 2023
- original: 44.0 x 109.0 x 170.0 cm scale 1:100
- Paint and gesso on PLA resin
- Kyoto University owner of original model

24 Lodging and entertainment

4-30
- Side table from the guest room of the Imperial Hotel
- Frank Lloyd Wright, designer
- 72 x 70 x 66 cm
- wood
- Imperial Hotel
- T002161

4-31
- Imperial Hotel, Tokyo, Japan. Project, 1913-23. Guest room
- Frank Lloyd Wright, architect
- Photograph (reproduction)
- Imperial Hotel
- 13057

4-32
- Imperial Hotel, Tokyo, Japan. Project, 1913-23. Guest room
- Frank Lloyd Wright, architect
- Photograph (reproduction)
- Imperial Hotel
- 13058

4-33
- Imperial Hotel Annex, Tokyo, Japan. Project, 1920. Guest room
- Frank Lloyd Wright, architect
- Print on paper / postcard (reproduction)
- Imperial Hotel
- T000014-13055

4-34
- Imperial Hotel Annex, Tokyo, Japan. Project, 1920. Interior of the living room in Wright's apartment
- Photographer unidentified
- Photo: 1920
- Photograph (reproduction)
- Project photographs, circa 1887-2008, The Frank Lloyd Wright Foundation Archives (The Museum of Modern Art | Avery Architectural & Fine Arts Library, Columbia University, New York)
- FLWFA 1604.0004

4-35
- Imperial Hotel, Tokyo, Japan. Project, 1913-23. Arcade (shopping mall) entrance
- Photograph (reproduction)
- Imperial Hotel
- T000017-16016

4-36
- Imperial Hotel. Program cover of a film screening at the Roof Garden
- 1937
- original: 11.5 x 16.0 cm
- Print on paper (reproduction)
- Imperial Hotel
- T000017-16027

4-37
- Imperial Hotel, Tokyo, Japan. Project, 1913-23. Film screen at the Roof Garden
- Frank Lloyd Wright, architect
- original: 11.5 x 16.0 cm
- Print on paper / postcard (reproduction)
- Imperial Hotel
- 16028

4-38
- Brochure from the Imperial Hotel
- Kenichi Shigeoka, designer
- 1925-30s
- 15.5 x 18.5 cm
- Print on paper / pamphlet
- Imperial Hotel
- 00317

4-39
- Brochure from the Imperial Hotel
- Kenichi Shigeoka, designer
- 1925
- 9.0 x 19.5 cm
- Print on paper / pamphlet
- Imperial Hotel
- 003318

4-40
- *Teikoku Hotel*
- Yutaro Takanashi, editor. Koyo-sha, publisher
- 1925
- 26.0 x 19.0 x 1.5 cm
- Print on paper / book
- Gen Endo Collection

4-41
- Brochure from the Imperial Hotel, Tokyo, Japan
- Kenichi Shigeoka, designer
- 1925-30s
- 15.5 x 18.5 cm
- Print on paper / pamphlet
- Yutaka Mizukami Collection

4-42
- Imperial Hotel, Tokyo, Japan. Postcard of the Banquet room (Peacock Room)
- Print on paper / postcard (reproduction)
- Yutaka Mizukami Collection

25 Imperial Hotel as a total work of art

4-43
- Imperial Hotel. Cabaret Dinnerware
- Frank Lloyd Wright, designer. Noritake, manufacturer
- Design: 1916-1922. Reproduction 1962-68
- Dinner plate (2pcs.): ϕ27.0 cm, Salad plate (2pcs.): ϕ19.4 cm, Bread plate (2pcs.): ϕ16.2 cm, Fruit bowl (2pcs.): ϕ14.5 cm, Cup (2pcs.): 5.5 x 10.7 cm, ϕ8.6 cm, Saucer (2pcs.): ϕ13.5 cm
- Ceramic
- Toyota Municipal Museum of Art

4-44
- Imperial Hotel, Tokyo, Japan. Coffee pot
- Designer unidentified
- 17.0 x ϕ8.0 cm
- Silver
- Imperial Hotel

4-45
- Imperial Hotel. Creamer
- Designer unidentified
- 7.5 x ϕ7.5 cm
- Silver
- Imperial Hotel

4-46
- Imperial Hotel. Menu card
- 1926
- 16.0 x 10.5 cm
- Print on paper
- Imperial Hotel

4-47
- Imperial Hotel. Chair from the Ballroom (Peacock Room) (in beige)
- Frank Lloyd Wright, designer
- Design: c. 1913 Manufactured 1930
- 96.0 x 38.8 x 45.5 cm
- Wood
- Toyota Municipal Museum of Art

4-48
- Imperial Hotel. Chair from the Ballroom (Peacock Room) (in yellow)
- Frank Lloyd Wright, designer
- Design: c. 1913 Manufactured after 1950
- 98.5 x 39.5 x 45.9 cm
- Wood
- Toyota Municipal Museum of Art

4-49
- Imperial Hotel. Table from the Ball Room (Peacock Room)
- Frank Lloyd Wright, designer
- Design: c. 1913
- 59.2 x 88.3 x 88.7 cm
- Wood
- Toyota Municipal Museum of Art

4-50
- Imperial Hotel. Chair
- Frank Lloyd Wright, designer. Kenichiro Watanabe
- Design: c. 1920 Restoration: 2023
- 95.5 x 39.5 x 43.5 cm
- Wood

4-51
- Imperial Hotel. Chair from the Second floor lounge
- Frank Lloyd Wright, designer
- Design: c. 1913 Manufactured 1985
- 96.5(SH42.0) x 40.5 x 44.5 cm
- wood, rattan, artificial leather
- Museum Meiji-Mura

4-52
- Imperial Hotel. Carved stone and polychrome mural for the parlor southern fireplace
- Frank Lloyd Wright
- 1921
- 22 3/8 x 34 15/16 in. (drwg) 56.7 x 88.9 cm (drwg)
- Diazo print and colored pencil on paper
- Prints and Photographs Division, Library of Congress, Washington, D.C.
- LC-DIG-ppmsca-85261

4-53
- Imperial Hotel. Carved stone and polychrome mural for the parlor northern fireplace
- Frank Lloyd Wright
- 1921
- 22 1/4 x 34 1/2 in. (drwg) 56.5 x 87.6 cm (drwg)
- Diazo print and colored pencil on paper
- Prints and Photographs Division, Library of Congress, Washington, D.C.
- LC-DIG-ppmsca-85262

4-54
- Imperial Hotel. Full-size detailed drawing of wall decorations in the theater
- Frank Lloyd Wright
- c. 1915
- 130.8 x 99.7 cm
- Pencil on tracing paper
- Toyota Municipal Museum of Art
- 5771

4-55
- Study of the mural in the Peacock Room of the Imperial Hotel
- Noémi Raymond, designer for Frank Lloyd Wright
- 1920
- original: L 19.0 x 16.0 cm R 21.0 x 20.5 cm
- Water color and pencil on tracing paper (reproduction)
- Koichi Kitazawa Collection

4-56
- Postcard. Imperial Hotel, Tokyo, Japan. Project, 1913-23. Postcard. Dining room
- Frank Lloyd Wright, architect
- original: 11.0 x 15.5 cm
- Photograph (reproduction)
- Imperial Hotel
- T000016-15029

4-57
- Postcard. Imperial Hotel. Banquet hall (Peacock Room)
- Frank Lloyd Wright, architect
- 1925-30s
- Postcard (reproduction)
- Imperial Hotel
- T000015-14001

4-40

4-41

4-42

4-43

4-44

4-45

4-46

4-47
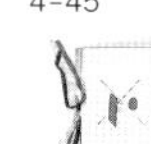
4-48

4-49

4-50

4-51

4-52

4-53
4-54

4-55
4-56

4-57
4-58

4-19 4-20 4-21 4-22 4-23 4-24 4-25 4-26 4-27 4-28 4-29 4-30 4-31 4-32 4-33 4-34 4-35 4-36 4-37 4-38 4-39

- 1915年頃
- 130.8×99.7
- 鉛筆/トレーシングペーパー
- 豊田市美術館

4-55
- 帝国ホテル二代目本館　宴会場「孔雀の間(ピーコック・ルーム)」装飾スタディ
- ノエミ・レーモンド
- 1920年
- オリジナル:L 19.0×16.0 R 21.0×20.5
- 水彩/トレーシング・ペーパー(複写)
- 北澤興一コレクション

4-56
- 絵葉書　帝国ホテル二代目本館(東京、日比谷)　大食堂
- オリジナル:11.0×15.5
- 写真(複写)
- 帝国ホテル

4-57
- 絵葉書　帝国ホテル二代目本館 宴会場「孔雀の間」
- 1925–30年頃(昭和初期)
- 写真(複写)
- 帝国ホテル

4-58　*
- 帝国ホテル二代目本館 2階ラウンジ
- 1925–30年頃(昭和初期)
- 写真(複写)
- 帝国ホテル

4-59　*
- 帝国ホテル二代目本館(東京、日比谷)　プロムナード中央パーラー(宝の間)　南側暖炉の上の大谷石の着彩レリーフ
- 撮影年不詳
- オリジナル:11.0×16.0
- 写真(複写)
- 帝国ホテル

4-60　*
- 帝国ホテル二代目本館(東京、日比谷)　プロムナード中央パーラー(宝の間)　北側暖炉の上の大谷石の着彩レリーフ
- フランク・ロイド・ライト
- 撮影年不詳
- オリジナル:11.0×16.0
- 写真(複写)
- 帝国ホテル

4-61
- 帝国ホテル二代目本館(東京、日比谷) メインダイニングの柱の装飾
- フランク・ロイド・ライト
- 撮影年不詳
- オリジナル:24.5×21.0
- 写真(複写)
- 帝国ホテル

26　素材の探求:大谷石とすだれレンガ

4-62
- 帝国ホテル二代目本館 金箔入りガラス
- デザイン:フランク・ロイド・ライト
- 1919–23年頃
- 6.0×29.0×0.5
- 金箔、ガラス、金属
- 帝国ホテル

4-63
- 帝国ホテル二代目本館 テラコッタの装飾ブロック
- デザイン:フランク・ロイド・ライト
- 1919–23年頃
- 22.0×21.5×6.5
- テラコッタ
- 帝国ホテル

4-64
- 帝国ホテル二代目本館 千鳥模様のすだれレンガ
- デザイン:フランク・ロイド・ライト
- 1919–23年頃
- 8.0×15.0×8.0
- レンガ
- 帝国ホテル

4-65
- 帝国ホテル二代目本館 照明・換気用に用いられるテラコッタの装飾ブロック(復刻版)
- デザイン:フランク・ロイド・ライト
- 10.0×13.0×13.0
- テラコッタ
- 帝国ホテル

27　ライト精神の継承

4-66
- 帝国ホテルの建設現場で働く日本の職人たちの空想的スケッチ
- アントニン・レーモンド
- 25×17.5
- 水彩/紙
- 北澤興一コレクション

4-67
- 帝国ホテルの建設現場で働く日本の職人たちの空想的スケッチ
- アントニン・レーモンド
- 53.5×50.0
- オリジナル:グワッシュ/紙(複製)
- 北澤興一コレクション

4-68
- 帝国ホテル二代目本館(東京、日比谷)　建設現場
- 撮影年不詳
- オリジナル:12.0×16.5
- 写真(複写)
- 帝国ホテル

4-69
- 帝国ホテル二代目本館(東京、日比谷)　建設現場
- 撮影年不詳
- オリジナル:11.0×15.0
- 写真(複写)
- 帝国ホテル

4-70
- 帝国ホテル二代目本館(東京、日比谷)1913–23年 建設現場
- 撮影年不詳
- オリジナル:12.0×16.5
- 写真(複写)
- 帝国ホテル

4-71
- フランク・ロイド・ライトから遠藤新、福原氏、羽仁もと子にあてた手紙
- 1928年4月12日
- 27.0×18.7
- インク/紙
- 遠藤現コレクション

4-72
- ライトを囲む宴会　前列左から3人目アントニン・レーモンド、4人目遠藤新、5人目ポール・ミュラー、7人目フランク・ロイド・ライト、8人目林愛作
- 1922年頃
- オリジナル:12.5×26.0
- 写真(複写)
- 写真提供:遠藤現

4-73
- 甲子園ホテル 現・武庫川女子大学甲子園会館(兵庫県西宮)1930年 中庭の池からの全景
- 建築:遠藤新
- オリジナル:11.5×15.5
- 写真(複写)
- 写真提供:遠藤現

4-74
- 甲子園ホテル 現・武庫川女子大学甲子園会館(兵庫県西宮)1930年 玄関側からの外観
- 撮影:ジョン(ジャック)・アーウィン・ヒグビー
- 撮影:2013年
- オリジナル:11.5×15.5
- 写真(複写)
- 写真提供:遠藤現

4-75
- 土浦亀城邸(東京、品川) 1935年
- 建築:土浦亀城
- 写真(複写)
- 土浦亀城アーカイブズ

4-76
- ニューホープの農場、1939–40年 前列左にアントニンとノエミ・レーモンド夫妻
- 建築:アントニン・レーモンド
- 撮影:1940年
- 写真(複写)
- ペンシルベニア大学建築アーカイヴズ・レーモンドコレクション

SECTION 5
ミクロ/マクロのダイナミックな振幅

28　フレーベル恩物:ユニット・システムの原点

5-1
- フレーベル恩物　第3恩物、第4恩物、第5恩物
- 考案:フリードリヒ・フレーベル 製作:ミルトン・ブラッドレー
- 製作年不詳
- 9.0×10.0×10.0, 6.5×7.0×7.0
- 木
- 青森県立美術館

29　リチャーズ社の通販式プレファブ住宅

5-2
- アメリカ式システム工法住宅、リチャーズ社との共作。1915–17年 C3モデル平面図
- フランク・ロイド・ライト
- 27.9×21.6
- リトグラフ/紙
- ニューヨーク近代美術館 Gift of David Rockefeller, Jr. Fund, Ira Howard Levy Fund, and Jeffrey P. Klein Purchase Fund, 1993

5-3
- アメリカ式システム工法住宅、リチャーズ社との共作。1915–17年 C3モデル外観透視図
- フランク・ロイド・ライト
- 27.9×21.6
- リトグラフ/紙
- ニューヨーク近代美術館 New York. Gift of David Rockefeller, Jr. Fund, Ira Howard Levy Fund, and Jeffrey P. Klein Purchase Fund, 1993

5-4
- アメリカ式システム工法住宅、リチャーズ社との共作。1915–17年 C3モデル内観透視図
- フランク・ロイド・ライト
- 27.9×21.6
- リトグラフ/紙
- ニューヨーク近代美術館 New York. Gift of David Rockefeller, Jr. Fund, Ira Howard Levy Fund, and Jeffrey P. Klein Purchase Fund, 1993

5-5　*
- 『レディース・ホーム・ジャーナル』1907年4月号
- 出版:カーチス社
- 41.5×29.0
- 印刷/紙、雑誌
- 水上優コレクション

30　関東大震災に耐えた構造

5-6
- 帝国ホテル二代目本館 すだれレンガ
- デザイン:フランク・ロイド・ライト
- 1919–23年頃
- 6.5×21.5×6.5
- レンガ
- 帝国ホテル

5-7
- 帝国ホテル二代目本館 大谷石のブロック
- フランク・ロイド・ライト
- 1919–23年頃
- 21×20.8×20.0
- 大谷石
- 博物館明治村

5-8　*
- 映像「関東大震災記録」
- ブラック・ホーク映像
- 1923年
- 3分
- 映像
- コロンビア大学 エイヴリー建築美術図書館 フランク・ロイド・ライト財団 アーカイヴズ

5-9
- 絵葉書　米国水兵の食料運搬 帝国ホテルにて 大正十二年九月一日　大震災
- 9.0×14.0
- 印刷/紙、絵葉書
- 渡辺秀樹コレクション

5-10
- 絵葉書　帝劇付近 大正十二年九月一日大震災
- 1923年
- 9.0×14.0
- 印刷/紙、絵葉書
- 渡辺秀樹コレクション

5-11
- 絵葉書　大東京大惨害実況 宮城前の避難者
- 1923年
- 9.0×14.0
- 印刷/紙、絵葉書
- 渡辺秀樹コレクション

5-12
- 絵葉書　大正12.9.1　東京大震災実況　日比谷音楽堂倒壊実況
- 1923年
- 9.0×14.0
- 印刷/紙、絵葉書
- 渡辺秀樹コレクション

5-13
- 絵葉書 丸の内郵船ビルヂングの震災
- 1923年
- 14.0×9.0
- 印刷/紙、絵葉書
- 渡辺秀樹コレクション

5-14
- 絵葉書　東京大地震の惨状 丸の内ビルヂング
- 1923年
- 14.0×9.0
- 印刷/紙、絵葉書
- 渡辺秀樹コレクション

5-15
- 絵葉書　丸の内内外ビルヂング 建築中の震災
- 1923年
- 9.0×14.0
- 印刷/紙、絵葉書
- 渡辺秀樹コレクション

5-16
- 絵葉書　大正12.9.1

4-58
- Imperial Hotel, Tokyo, Japan. Project, 1913-23. Second floor lounge
- Frank Lloyd Wright, architect
- 1930s
- Photograph (reproduction)
- Imperial Hotel
- T000014-13053

4-59
- Imperial Hotel, Tokyo, Japan. Carved oya stone and polychrome mural from the parlor "Takara no Ma" southern fireplace
- Frank Lloyd Wright
- undated
- original: 11 x 16 cm
- Photograph (reproduction)
- Imperial Hotel
- 13036

4-60
- Imperial Hotel, Tokyo, Japan. Carved oya stone and polychrome mural from the parlor "Takara no Ma" northern fireplace
- Frank Lloyd Wright
- undated
- original: 11 x 16 cm
- Photograph (reproduction)
- Imperial Hotel
- 13037

4-61
- Imperial Hotel, Tokyo, Japan. Decoration of the pillar at the main dining room
- Frank Lloyd Wright
- undated
- original: 24.5 x 21 cm
- Photograph (reproduction)
- Imperial Hotel
- 15052

26 Material exploration: Oya stone and architectural blocks

4-62
- Imperial Hotel. Fragment of window with square pattern decorated with gold leaf
- Frank Lloyd Wright, designer
- c. 1919-23
- 6.0 x 29.0 x 0.5 cm
- Gold, glass, metal
- Imperial Hotel
- 002172

4-63
- Imperial Hotel. Architectural block / Terracotta textile block
- Frank Lloyd Wright, designer
- c. 1919-23
- 22.0 x 21.5 x 6.5 cm
- Terra Cotta
- Imperial Hotel
- 002173

4-64
- Imperial Hotel. Architectural block / Scratch tile block
- Frank Lloyd Wright, designer
- c. 1919-23
- 8.0 x 15.0 x 8.0 cm
- Brick
- Imperial Hotel
- 003945

4-65
- Imperial Hotel. Architectural block / Terracotta textile block (replica)
- Frank Lloyd Wright, designer
- 10.0 x 13.0 x 13.0 cm
- Terra Cotta
- Imperial Hotel
- 002167

27 Passing down Wright's spirit

4-66
- Imaginative sketch, labourers working at the Imperial Hotel
- Antonin Raymond
- 10 3/4 x 7 3/4 in. (25 x 17.5 cm)
- Watercolor on paper
- Koichi Kitazawa Collection

4-67
- Imaginative sketch, labourers working at the Imperial Hotel
- Antonin Raymond
- 53.5 x 50.0 cm
- Gouache on paper (reproduction)
- Koichi Kitazawa Collection

4-68
- Imperial Hotel, Tokyo, Japan. construction site
- Photographer unidentified
- undated
- original: 12.0 x 16.5 cm
- Photograph (reproduction)
- Imperial Hotel
- 10039

4-69
- Imperial Hotel, Tokyo, Japan. construction site
- Photographer unidentified
- undated
- original: 11.0 x 15.0 cm
- Photograph (reproduction)
- Imperial Hotel
- 10054

4-70
- Imperial Hotel, Tokyo, Japan. Project, 1913-23. construction site
- Photographer unidentified
- undated
- original: 12.0 x 16.5 cm
- Photograph (reproduction)
- Imperial Hotel
- 10074

4-71
- Frank Lloyd Wright, letter to Arata Endo, Fukuhara and Hani
- Frank Lloyd Wright, author
- 12 April 1928
- 27.0 x 18.7 cm
- Ink on paper
- Gen Endo Collection

4-72
- Dinner Party with Frank Lloyd Wright. Third from left Antonin Raymond, fourth Endo Arata, fifth Paul Muller, seventh Frank Lloyd Wright and eighth Aisaku Hayashi
- c. 1922
- original: 12.5 x 26.0 cm
- Photograph (reproduction)
- Photo Courtesy of Gen Endo

4-73
- Koushien Hotel, Nishinomiya, Japan. Project, 1930. Exterior view from across the pond
- Arata Endo, architect
- Photo: 1930
- original: 11.5 x 15.5 cm
- Photograph (reproduction)
- Photo Courtesy of Gen Endo

4-74
- Koushien Hotel, Nishinomiya, Japan. Project, 1930. Exterior view from entrance
- John (Jack) Erwin Higbee, photographer
- Photo: 2013
- original: 11.5 x 15.5 cm
- Photograph (reproduction)
- Courtesy of Gen Endo
- Copyright © 2013 John (Jack) Erwin Higbee

4-75
- Kameki and Nobuko Tsuchiura House, Shinagawa, Tokyo. Project, 1935
- Kameki Tsuchiura, architect
- Photograph (reproduction)
- TSUCHIURA Kameki Archives

4-76
- Raymond Farm, New Hope, Philadelphia, Project, 1939-40 (original house built 1726). Front row from left: Antonin, Noémi and son Claude
- Antonin Raymond, architect
- Photo: 1940
- Photograph (reproduction)
- Raymond Collections, the Architectural Archives of the University of Pennsylvania

SECTION 5 Micro/Macro Dynamics of Wright's Building Blocks

28 Fröbel Gifts: The origin of the unit system

5-1
- Milton Bradley's Kindergarten Materials: Gift No.3, No.4 and No.5
- Friedrich Fröbel, designer. Milton Bradley Company, manufacturer
- undated
- 9.0 x 10.0 x 10.0 cm. 6.5 x 7.0 x 7.0 cm
- Wood
- Aomori Museum of Art

29 American System-Built Houses for the Richards Company

5-2
- American System-Built Houses for The Richards Company. Project, 1915-17. Plan oblique of model C3
- Frank Lloyd Wright
- 11 x 8 1/2 in. (27.9 x 21.6 cm)
- Lithograph on paper
- The Museum of Modern Art, New York. Gift of David Rockefeller, Jr. Fund, Ira Howard Levy Fund, and Jeffrey P. Klein Purchase Fund, 1993
- DIGITAL IMAGE©2023, The Museum of Modern Art/Scala, Florence
- 155.1993.7

5-3
- American System-Built Houses for The Richards Company. Project, 1915-17. Exterior perspective of model C3
- Frank Lloyd Wright
- 11 x 8 1/2 in. (27.9 x 21.6 cm)
- Lithograph on paper
- The Museum of Modern Art, New York. Gift of David Rockefeller, Jr. Fund, Ira Howard Levy Fund, and Jeffrey P. Klein Purchase Fund, 1993
- DIGITAL IMAGE©2023, The Museum of Modern Art/Scala, Florence
- 155.1993.8

5-4
- American System-Built Houses for The Richards Company. Project, 1915-17. Interior perspective of model C3
- Frank Lloyd Wright
- 11 x 8 1/2 in. (27.9 x 21.6 cm)
- Lithograph on paper
- The Museum of Modern Art, New York. Gift of David Rockefeller, Jr. Fund, Ira Howard Levy Fund, and Jeffrey P. Klein Purchase Fund, 1993
- DIGITAL IMAGE©2023, The Museum of Modern Art/Scala, Florence
- 155.1993.9

5-5
- *Ladies Home Journal*, April 1907 issue
- The Curtis Publishing Company, publisher
- 41.5 x 29 cm
- Print on paper / periodical
- Yutaka Mizukami Collection

30 Structure that survived the Great Kanto Earthquake

5-6
- Scratch tile block from the Imperial Hotel.
- Frank Lloyd Wright, designer
- c. 1919-23
- 6.5 x 21.5 x 6.5 cm
- brick
- Imperial Hotel
- 003946

5-7
- Architectural block of Oya stone from the Imperial Hotel, Tokyo, Japan
- Frank Lloyd Wright, designer
- c. 1919-23
- 21 x 20.8 x 20.0 cm
- Oya stone
- Museum Meiji-Mura

5-8
- Film. The Japanese Earthquake of September 1, 1923
- Blackhawk Films
- 1923
- 3 minutes
- film
- The Frank Lloyd Wright Foundation Archives (The Museum of Modern Art | Avery Architectural & Fine Arts Library, Columbia University, New York)
- FLWFM 132

5-9
- Postcard. U.S. Navy carrying Supplies into the Imperial Hotel, Great Kanto Earthquake, 1 September 1923
- 1923
- 9.0 x 14.0 cm
- Postcard
- Hideki Watanabe Collection

5-10
- Postcard. Vicinity of the Imperial Theater, Great Kanto Earthquake, 1 September 1923
- 1923
- 9.0 x 14.0 cm
- Postcard
- Hideki Watanabe Collection

5-11
- Postcard. Refugees at the Imperial Palace Plaza, Great Kanto Earthquake, 1 September 1923
- 1923
- 9.0 x 14.0 cm
- Postcard
- Hideki Watanabe Collection

5-12
- Postcard. The Destruction of the Music Hall at the Hibiya Park, Great Kanto Earthquake, 1 September 1923
- 1923
- 9.0 x 14.0 cm
- Postcard
- Hideki Watanabe Collection

5-13
- Postcard. The Destruction of the Marunouchi Yusen Building, Great Kanto Earthquake, 1 September 1923
- 1923
- 14.0 x 9.0 cm
- Postcard
- Hideki Watanabe Collection

5-14
- Postcard. The Destruction of the Marunouchi Building, Great Kanto Earthquake, 1 September 1923
- 1923
- 14.0 x 9.0 cm
- Postcard
- Hideki Watanabe Collection

5-15
- Postcard. The Destruction at the construction site of the Marunouchi Naigai Building, Great Kanto Earthquake, 1 September 1923
- 1923
- 9.0 x 14.0 cm
- Postcard
- Hideki Watanabe Collection

5-16
- Postcard. The Destruction of the Marunouchi Naigai Building, Great Kanto Earthquake, 1 September 1923
- 1923
- 9.0 x 14.0 cm
- Postcard
- Hideki Watanabe Collection

5-17
- Postcard. Roads Cracked at Marunouchi, Great Kanto Earthquake, 1 September 1923
- 1923
- 9.0 x 14.0 cm
- Postcard
- Hideki Watanabe Collection

5-18
- Postcard. Refugees at the Tokyo Station in Fire, Great Kanto Earthquake, 1 September 1923
- 1923
- 9.0 x 14.0 cm
- Postcard
- Hideki Watanabe Collection

5-19
- The Story of "The Imperial: an emotional experience in building."

4-59

4-60

4-61

4-62

4-63

4-64

4-65

4-66

4-67

4-68

4-69

4-70

4-71

4-72

4-73

4-74

4-75

4-76

5-1

5-2

5-3

5-4

5-5

5-6

5-7

5-8

5-9

5-10

5-11

5-12

5-13

5-14

5-15

5-16

5-17

5-18

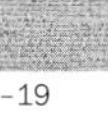

5-19

東京大震災実況 惨憺たる丸の内
内外ビルヂングの全壊
- 1923年
- 9.0×14.0
- 印刷／紙、絵葉書
- 渡辺秀樹コレクション

5-17
- 絵葉書 大正12.9.1
東京大震災実況 丸の内の亀裂
- 1923年
- 9.0×14.0
- 印刷／紙、絵葉書
- 渡辺秀樹コレクション

5-18
- 絵葉書 大正12.9.1
東京駅前震災猛火襲来避難実況
- 1923年
- 9.0×14.0
- 印刷／紙、絵葉書
- 渡辺秀樹コレクション

5-19
- 「帝国ホテルのはなし：建築叙情」
- 著：フランク・ロイド・ライト
- 1927年頃
- インク／紙（ホログラム複写）
- コロンビア大学
エイヴリー建築美術図書館
フランク・ロイド・ライト財団
アーカイヴズ

---

31 コンクリート・ブロックの展開

＋ テキスタイル・ブロック・システムの創案

5-20
- ミラード夫人邸「ミニアトゥーラ」
（カリフォルニア州パサデナ）
1923-24年
庭園側から見た透視図
- フランク・ロイド・ライト
- 52.7×49.8
- 色鉛筆、石墨／紙
- ニューヨーク近代美術館 Gift of Mr. and Mrs. Walter Hochschild, 1981

5-21
- ミラード夫人邸「ミニアトゥーラ」
（カリフォルニア州パサデナ）
1923-24年 庭からの外観
- 建築：フランク・ロイド・ライト
- 撮影：1923年
- 写真（複写）
- コロンビア大学
エイヴリー建築美術図書館
フランク・ロイド・ライト財団
アーカイヴズ

5-22
- ミラード夫人邸「ミニアトゥーラ」
（カリフォルニア州パサデナ）
居間内観
- 建築：フランク・ロイド・ライト
- 撮影：1923年
- 写真（複写）
- コロンビア大学
エイヴリー建築美術図書館
フランク・ロイド・ライト財団
アーカイヴズ

5-23
- ミラード夫人邸「ミニアトゥーラ」
（カリフォルニア州パサデナ）の
建設現場にたたずむ土浦信子
- 撮影：土浦亀城
- 1923-24年頃
- 写真（複写）
- コロンビア大学
エイヴリー建築美術図書館
フランク・ロイド・ライト財団
アーカイヴズ

5-24
- ミラード夫人邸「ミニアトゥーラ」
（カリフォルニア州パサデナ）の
建設現場
- 撮影：土浦亀城
- 1923-24年頃
- 写真（複写）
- 土浦亀城アーカイブズ

5-25
- ストーラー邸（カリフォルニア州ロサンゼルス）1923-24年
外観 正面ファサード
- フランク・ロイド・ライト
- 1923年
- 38.7×71.3
- 石墨、色鉛筆／和紙
- 米国議会図書館版画写真部

5-26 ＊
- ストーラー邸（カリフォルニア州ロサンゼルス）1923-24年
- 建築：フランク・ロイド・ライト
- 撮影：水上優
- 撮影：2019年
- 写真（複写）

＋ コンクリート・ブロックの拡張

5-27
- ドヘニー・ランチ宅地開発計画案
（カリフォルニア州ロサンゼルス）
1923年頃 透視図
- フランク・ロイド・ライト
- 31.9×73.8
- 鉛筆、色鉛筆／
トレーシング・ペーパー
- コロンビア大学
エイヴリー建築美術図書館
フランク・ロイド・ライト財団
アーカイヴズ

5-28
- ドヘニー・ランチ宅地開発計画案
（カリフォルニア州ロサンゼルス）
1923年頃 透視図
- フランク・ロイド・ライト
- 42.6×57.2
- 鉛筆、色鉛筆／
トレーシング・ペーパー
- コロンビア大学
エイヴリー建築美術図書館
フランク・ロイド・ライト財団
アーカイヴズ

5-29
- ドヘニー・ランチ宅地開発計画案
（カリフォルニア州ロサンゼルス）
1923年頃 ランドスケープとテキスタイル・ブロック住宅のある透視図
- フランク・ロイド・ライト
- 35.0×89.5
- 石墨／和紙
- 米国議会図書館版画写真部

5-30 ＊
- ドヘニー・ランチ宅地開発計画案
（カリフォルニア州ロサンゼルス）
1923年頃 Cタイプ住宅の外観図
- フランク・ロイド・ライト
- 50.7×78.1
- 石墨、色鉛筆／和紙
- 米国議会図書館版画写真部

5-31
- ドヘニー・ランチ宅地開発計画地
（現・トルースデール地所）
- 撮影：2018年
- 写真（複写）

5-32
- サン・マルコス砂漠リゾート・ホテル計画案（アリゾナ州チャンドラー）1928-29年 透視図
- フランク・ロイド・ライト
- 41.6×139.9
- 鉛筆／紙
- コロンビア大学
エイヴリー建築美術図書館
フランク・ロイド・ライト財団
アーカイヴズ

5-33
- サン・マルコス砂漠リゾート・ホテル計画案（アリゾナ州チャンドラー）1928-29年
コンクリート・ブロック詳細図
- フランク・ロイド・ライト
- 30.64×45.72
- 鉛筆／紙
- コロンビア大学
エイヴリー建築美術図書館
フランク・ロイド・ライト財団
アーカイヴズ

---

32 ユーソニアン住宅 成長する建築

5-34
- ジェイコブズ第一邸（ウィスコンシン州マディソン）1936-37年 居間内観
- フランク・ロイド・ライト
- 撮影：1938年
- 写真（複写）
- コロンビア大学
エイヴリー建築美術図書館
フランク・ロイド・ライト財団
アーカイヴズ

5-35
- ユーソニアン住宅の
原寸モデル展示
- 制作：有限責任事業組合
森の製材リソラ、磯矢建築事務所
- 2.685×8.9×4.5 m
- 杉赤身材、天神原（南伊豆町）産

5-36
- ハナ邸「ハニカムハウス」
（カリフォルニア州パロ・アルト）
1936-37年 鳥瞰
- 建築：フランク・ロイド・ライト
- 写真（複写）
- スタンフォード大学特別コレクション

5-37
- ハナ邸「ハニカムハウス」
（カリフォルニア州パロ・アルト）
1936-37年 居間内観
- 建築：フランク・ロイド・ライト
- 写真（複写）
- スタンフォード大学特別コレクション

5-38
- ユーソニアン・オートマチック住宅
ピムソン邸計画案
（アリゾナ州フェニックス）1949年
アクソメ詳細図
- フランク・ロイド・ライト
- オリジナル：52.1×63.5
- 鉛筆、紙（複写）
- コロンビア大学
エイヴリー建築美術図書館
フランク・ロイド・ライト財団
アーカイヴズ

5-39
- トレイシー邸
（ワシントン州ノルマンディーパーク）
1955年 玄関を見る
- 撮影：アンドリュー・ヴァン・レウエン
- 撮影：2012年
- 写真（複写）

5-40
- トレイシー邸
（ワシントン州ノルマンディーパーク）
1955年 居間側外観
- 建築：フランク・ロイド・ライト
撮影：アンドリュー・ヴァン・レウエン
- 撮影：2012年
- 写真（複写）

5-41
- トレイシー邸
（ワシントン州ノルマンディーパーク）
1955年 ワークスペースとバスルーム側外観
- 建築：フランク・ロイド・ライト
撮影：アンドリュー・ヴァン・レウエン
- 撮影：2012年
- 写真（複写）

---

33 らせん状建築

5-42
- ゴードン・ストロング自動車体験娯楽施設とプラネタリウム計画案
（メリーランド州シュガーローフマウンテン）
1924-25年 鳥瞰透視図
- フランク・ロイド・ライト
- 60.6×80.5
- 鉛筆／トレーシング・ペーパー
- コロンビア大学
エイヴリー建築美術図書館
フランク・ロイド・ライト財団
アーカイヴズ

5-43
- ゴードン・ストロング自動車体験娯楽施設とプラネタリウム計画案
（メリーランド州シュガーローフマウンテン）
1924-25年 透視図
- フランク・ロイド・ライト
- 1925年
- 55.0×82.6
- 石墨、色鉛筆／
トレーシング・ペーパー
- 米国議会図書館版画写真部

5-44 ＊
- グッゲンハイム美術館
（ニューヨーク）1943-59年
透視図（複写）
- フランク・ロイド・ライト
- オリジナル：66.0×101.0
- オリジナル：鉛筆、色鉛筆／
トレーシング・ペーパー（複写）
- コロンビア大学
エイヴリー建築美術図書館
フランク・ロイド・ライト財団
アーカイヴズ

5-45
- グッゲンハイム美術館
（ニューヨーク）1943-59年 内観
吹き抜けから天井を見上げる
- 建築：フランク・ロイド・ライト
撮影：ディヴィッド・ヒールド
- 写真（複写）
- 写真提供：グッゲンハイム美術館

5-46
- グッゲンハイム美術館
（ニューヨーク）1943-59年
- 建築：フランク・ロイド・ライト
撮影：ディヴィッド・ヒールド
- 写真（複写）
- 写真提供：グッゲンハイム美術館

5-47
- グッゲンハイム美術館
（ニューヨーク）1943-59年 内観
螺旋状スロープの展示ギャラリー
- 建築：フランク・ロイド・ライト
撮影：ディヴィッド・ヒールド
- 写真（複写）
- 写真提供：グッゲンハイム美術館

5-48
- 有機的建築を説明する
フランク・ロイド・ライトの手
「ハンズ・シリーズ」
- 撮影：ペドロ・ゲレロ
- 撮影：1953年
- 写真（複写）
- エステート・オブ・ペドロ・ゲレロ

SECTION 6
上昇する建築と環境の向上

---

34 快適さと機能の追求

6-1
- 『フランク・ロイド・ライト
竣工した建築』（ソフト・カバー版）
- 著：フランク・ロイド・ライト
出版：エルンスト・ヴァスムート社
- 1911年
- 30.5×22
- 印刷／紙、書籍
- 水上優コレクション

6-2
- ラーキン・ビル（ニューヨーク州バッファロー）1902-06年 透視図

Personal memoir of designing the Imperial Hotel in Tokyo
- Frank Lloyd Wright, author
- c. 1927
- Holograph manuscript (reproduction)
- The Frank Lloyd Wright Foundation Archives (The Museum of Modern Art | Avery Architectural & Fine Arts Library, Columbia University, New York)
- FLWFA 2401.032

31 Development of concrete block

+ Invention of the textile block system

5-20
- Millard House (La Miniatura), Pasadena, California. Project, 1923–24. Exterior perspective from the garden
- Frank Lloyd Wright
- 20 3/4 x 19 5/8 in. (52.7 x 49.8 cm)
- Colored pencil and graphite on paper
- The Museum of Modern Art, New York. Gift of Mr. and Mrs. Walter Hochschild, 1981
- DIGITAL IMAGE©2023, The Museum of Modern Art/Scala, Florence
- 240.1981

5-21
- Millard House (La Miniatura), Pasadena, California. Project, 1923–24. Exterior view from garden
- Frank Lloyd Wright, architect
- Photo: 1923
- Photograph (reproduction)
- Project photographs, circa 1887–2008, The Frank Lloyd Wright Foundation Archives (The Museum of Modern Art | Avery Architectural & Fine Arts Library, Columbia University, New York)
- FLWFA 2302.0066

5-22
- Millard House (La Miniatura), Pasadena, California. Interior view of the living room
- Frank Lloyd Wright, architect. Pasadena Hiller, photographer
- Photo: 1923
- Photograph (reproduction)
- Project photographs, circa 1887–2008, The Frank Lloyd Wright Foundation Archives (The Museum of Modern Art | Avery Architectural & Fine Arts Library, Columbia University, New York)
- FLWFA 2302.0004

5-23
- Millard House (La Miniatura), Pasadena, California. Nobuko Tsuchiura at the the Millard House under construction
- Kameki Tsuchiura, photographer
- c. 1923–24
- Photograph (reproduction)
- Personal and Taliesin Fellowship photographs, 1870s–2004, The Frank Lloyd Wright Foundation Archives (The Museum of Modern Art | Avery Architectural & Fine Arts Library, Columbia University, New York)
- FLWFA 6833.0041

5-24
- Millard House (La Miniatura), Pasadena, California. Construction site
- Kameki Tsuchiura, photographer
- c. 1923–24
- Photograph (reproduction)
- TSUCHIURA Kameki Archives

5-25
- Storer House, Los Angeles, California. Exterior of the Façade
- Frank Lloyd Wright
- 1923
- 15 3/16 x 28 1/8 in. (drwg) 38.7 x 71.3 cm (drwg)
- Graphite and colored pencil on Japanese paper
- Prints and Photographs Division, Library of Congress, Washington, D.C.
- LC-DIG-ppmsca-09575

5-26
- Storer House, Los Angeles, California. Project, 1923–24
- Frank Lloyd Wright, architect.
- Yutaka Mizukami, photographer
- Photo: 2019
- Photograph (reproduction)

+ Expanding concrete block applications

5-27
- Doheny Ranch development, Los Angeles, California. Unbuilt Project, c. 1923. Perspective
- Frank Lloyd Wright
- 12 9/16 x 29 1/16 in. (31.9 x 73.8 cm)
- Pencil, colored pencil on tracing paper
- The Frank Lloyd Wright Foundation Archives (The Museum of Modern Art | Avery Architectural & Fine Arts Library, Columbia University, New York)
- FLW.DR.2104.005

5-28
- Doheny Ranch development, Los Angeles, California. Unbuilt Project, c. 1923. Perspective
- Frank Lloyd Wright
- 16 3/4 x 22 1/2 in. (42.6 x 57.2 cm)
- Pencil, colored pencil on tracing paper
- The Frank Lloyd Wright Foundation Archives (The Museum of Modern Art | Avery Architectural & Fine Arts Library, Columbia University, New York)
- FLW.DR.2104.006

5-29
- Doheny Ranch development Los Angeles, California. Unbuilt Project, c. 1923. Perspective showing landscaping and textile block building
- Frank Lloyd Wright
- 1923
- 13 3/4 x 35 1/4 in. (drwg) 35.0 x 89.5 cm
- Graphite on Japanese paper
- Library of Congress Prints and Photographs Division Washington, D.C.
- LC-DIG-ppmsca-84877

5-30
- Doheny Ranch Development, Los Angeles, California. Unbuilt Project, c. 1923. Exterior of House C
- Frank Lloyd Wright
- 1923
- 20 x 30 13/16 in. (drwg) 50.7 x 78.1 cm
- Graphite and colored pencil on Japanese paper
- Library of Congress Prints and Photographs Division Washington, D.C.
- LC-DIG-ppmsca-84878

5-31
- Trousdale Estates in Beverly Hills, CA. Formerly known as Doheny Ranch
- Wikimedia commons photo
- 2018
- Photograph (reproduction)

5-32
- San Marcos-in-the-Desert Resort Hotel for Alexander Chandler, Chandler, Arizona. Unbuilt Project, 1928–29. Perspective
- Frank Lloyd Wright
- 16 7/16 x 54 7/8 in. (41.8 x 139.4 cm)
- Pencil on paper
- The Frank Lloyd Wright Foundation Archives (The Museum of Modern Art | Avery Architectural & Fine Arts Library, Columbia University, New York)
- FLW.DR.2704.047

5-33
- San Marcos-in-the-Desert Resort Hotel for Alexander Chandler, Chandler, Arizona. Unbuilt Project, 1928–29. Detail of the concrete block
- Frank Lloyd Wright
- 12 1/16 x 18 in. (30.64 x 45.72 cm)
- Pencil on paper
- The Frank Lloyd Wright Foundation Archives (The Museum of Modern Art | Avery Architectural & Fine Arts Library, Columbia University, New York)
- FLW.DR.2704.141

32 Usonian Houses: Architecture that grows up

5-34
- Jacobs house, Madison, Wisconsin. Interior view, living room
- Frank Lloyd Wright, architect
- Photo: 1938
- Photograph (reproduction)
- Project photographs, circa 1887–2008, The Frank Lloyd Wright Foundation Archives (The Museum of Modern Art | Avery Architectural & Fine Arts Library, Columbia University, New York)
- FLW.FA 3702.0003

5-35
- Life Sized Model of an Usonian House
- Forest Sawmill Risola Limited Liability Partnership, Isoya Architectural Office and creator
- 2023
- 2.685 x 8.9 x 4.5 m
- Japanese cedar from Tenjimbara, Minami-Izu, Japan

5-36
- Hanna House (Honeycomb House), project 1936–37, Palo Alto, California. Aerial view
- Frank Lloyd Wright, architect
- Photograph (reproduction)
- Courtesy of the Department of Special Collections, Stanford University Libraries
- zz359kv5866

5-37
- Hanna House (Honeycomb House), project 1936–37, Palo Alto, California. Interior view to the living room
- Frank Lloyd Wright, architect
- Photograph (reproduction)
- Courtesy of the Department of Special Collections, Stanford University Libraries
- ng833kg5782

5-38
- Usonian Automatic Housing for Walter Bimson, Phoenix, Arizona. Unbuilt Project, 1949. Axonometric of construction detail
- Frank Lloyd Wright
- original: 52.1 x 63.5 cm
- Pencil on paper (reproduction)
- The Frank Lloyd Wright Foundation Archives (The Museum of Modern Art | Avery Architectural & Fine Arts Library, Columbia University, New York)
- FLWFA 5612.114

5-39
- Tracy House. Normandy Park, Washington. Project, 1955. Exterior with a view to the entrance
- Frank Lloyd Wright, architect. ©Andrew van Leeuwen, photographer
- Photo: 2012
- Photograph (reproduction)

5-40
- Tracy House. Normandy Park, Washington. Project, 1955. Exterior with a view to living room
- Frank Lloyd Wright, architect. ©Andrew van Leeuwen, photographer
- Photo: 2012
- Photograph (reproduction)

5-41
- Tracy House. Normandy Park, Washington. Project, 1955. Exterior with a view to kitchen and workspace
- Frank Lloyd Wright, architect. ©Andrew van Leeuwen, photographer
- Photo: 2012
- Photograph (reproduction)

33 Architetural design based on the helical spiral

5-42
- Gordon Strong Automobile Objective and Planetarium, Sugarloaf Mountain, Maryland. Unbuilt Project, 1924–25. Aerial perspective
- Frank Lloyd Wright
- 23 7/8 x 31 11/16 in. (60.6 x 80.5 cm)
- Pencil on tracing paper
- The Frank Lloyd Wright Foundation Archives (The Museum of Modern Art | Avery Architectural & Fine Arts Library, Columbia University, New York)
- FLW.DR.2505.052

5-43
- Gordon Strong Automobile Objective and Planetarium, Sugerloaf Mountain, Maryland. Unbuilt Project, 1924–25. Perspective
- Frank Lloyd Wright
- 1925
- 21 5/8 x 32 1/2 in. (drwg) 55.0 x 82.6 cm
- Graphite and colored pencil on tracing paper
- Prints and Photographs Division, Library of Congress, Washington, D.C.
- LC-DIG-ds-10423

5-44
- The Solomon R. Guggenheim Museum, New York. Project, 1943–59. Exterior perspective
- Frank Lloyd Wright
- original: 66.0 x 101.0 cm
- Pencil, colored pencil and ink on tracing paper (reproduction)
- The Frank Lloyd Wright Foundation Archives (The Museum of Modern Art | Avery Architectural & Fine Arts Library, Columbia University, New York)
- FLW.DR.4305.017

5-45
- Interior of the Solomon R. Guggenheim Museum, New York
- Frank Lloyd Wright, architect. Photo: David Heald
- Photograph (reproduction)
- © Solomon R. Guggenheim Foundation
- SRGM2018_ph001

5-46
- The Solomon R. Guggenheim Museum, New York
- Frank Lloyd Wright, architect. Photo: David Heald
- Photograph (reproduction)
- © Solomon R. Guggenheim Foundation
- SRGM_ph002

5-47
- Interior of the Solomon R. Guggenheim Museum, New York
- Frank Lloyd Wright, architect. Photo: David Heald
- Photograph (reproduction)
- © Solomon R. Guggenheim Foundation
- SRGM2018_ph042

5-48
- Wright's Hands #10. Hands series
- Pedro Guerrero, photographer
- Photo: 1953
- Photograph (reproduction)
- © The Estate of Pedro E. Guerrero

SECTION 6
Elevating Environments

34 Pursuit of comfort and functionality in high-rise buildings

6-1
- View of Larkin Company clerks working at Frank Lloyd Wright-designed desk and chair. *Ausgeführte Bauten* (Executed Buildings)

5-20

5-21

5-22

5-23

5-24

5-25

5-26

5-27

5-28

5-29

5-30

5-31

5-32

5-33

5-34

5-35

5-36

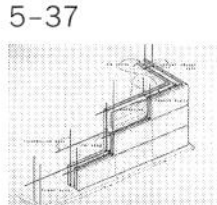
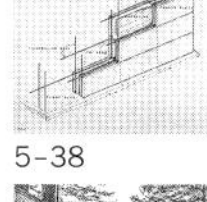
5-37

5-38

5-39

5-40

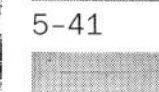
5-41

5-42

5-43

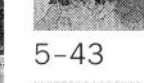

5-44

5-45

5-46

5-47

5-48

6-1

6-2

- フランク·ロイド·ライト
- 1903年
- 42.9×57.2
- 鉛筆/トレーシング·ペーパー
- 豊田市美術館

6-3 ＊
- 第33葉　ラーキン·ビル、
平面図および透視図
『フランク·ロイド·ライトの建築と設計』
- フランク·ロイド·ライト
出版:エルンスト·ヴァスムート社
- 1910年
- 63.5×45.0
- リトグラフ/紙
- 豊田市美術館

6-4 ＊
- 第33葉a　ラーキン·ビル、
地階平面図および透視図
『フランク·ロイド·ライトの建築と設計』
- フランク·ロイド·ライト
出版:エルンスト·ヴァスムート社
- 1910年
- 63.5×45.0
- リトグラフ/紙
- 豊田市美術館

6-5 ＊
- 第33葉　ラーキン·ビル、
内観透視図
『フランク·ロイド·ライトの建築と設計』
- フランク·ロイド·ライト
出版:エルンスト·ヴァスムート社
- 1910年
- 63.5×45.0
- リトグラフ/紙
- 豊田市美術館

6-6
- ラーキン·ビル(ニューヨーク州
バッファロー)1902-06年
内観　吹き抜け
- 撮影:1905年
- 写真(複写)
- コロンビア大学
エイヴリー建築美術図書館
フランク·ロイド·ライト財団
アーカイヴズ

6-7
- ラーキン·ビル　椅子付き事務机
- デザイン:フランク·ロイド·ライト
製造:ヴァン·ドーン·アイアン·
ワークス·カンパニー
- 1904年頃
- 61.0×122.0×109.0
- 木、スチール
- 豊田市美術館

6-8 ＊
- ラーキン·ビル
折りたたみ式サイドチェア
- デザイン:フランク·ロイド·ライト
製造:ヴァン·ドーン·アイアン·
ワークス·カンパニー
- 1904年頃
- 94.0×51.1×51.1
- 木、スチール
- 豊田市美術館

6-9
- 『フランク·ロイド·ライト
ある建築家の生涯より』
(ソフト·カバー版)
- 著:フランク·ロイド·ライト
編:H.ド·フリース
出版:エルンスト·ポラック社
- 1926年
- 30.5×22
- 印刷/紙、書籍
- 東京都市大学図書館
(蔵田周忠文庫)

35　高層建築——樹状構造

6-10
- ジョンソン·ワックス·ビル
(ウィスコンシン州ラシーン)
樹状柱の耐荷重試験
- 建築:フランク·ロイド·ライト
- 撮影:1937年
- 写真(複写)
- コロンビア大学
エイヴリー建築美術図書館
フランク·ロイド·ライト財団
アーカイヴズ

6-11
- ジョンソン·ワックス·ビル
(ウィスコンシン州ラシーン)
樹状柱の耐荷重試験
- 建築:フランク·ロイド·ライト
撮影:ジェームス·トムソン
- 撮影:1937年
- 写真(複写)
- コロンビア大学
エイヴリー建築美術図書館
フランク·ロイド·ライト財団
アーカイヴズ

6-12
- 映像　ジョンソン·ワックス·ビル
樹状柱の耐荷重試験
- 撮影:1937年
- 2分40秒
- 映像
- コロンビア大学
エイヴリー建築美術図書館
フランク·ロイド·ライト財団
アーカイヴズ

6-13
- ジョンソン·ワックス·ビル
(ウィスコンシン州ラシーン)1936-39年
柱詳細図および最上階平面
- フランク·ロイド·ライト
- オリジナル:89.5×65.7
- インク、水彩、鉛筆、色鉛筆/紙(複写)
- コロンビア大学
エイヴリー建築美術図書館
フランク·ロイド·ライト財団
アーカイヴズ

6-14
- ジョンソン·ワックス·ビル
(ウィスコンシン州ラシーン)　本部棟
北西から中央執務室を見る
- 撮影:1954年頃
- 写真(複写)
- 写真提供:SCジョンソン社

6-15
- ジョンソン·ワックス·ビル
(ウィスコンシン州ラシーン)　本部棟
中央執務室　南を見る
- 撮影:2015年
- 写真(複写)
- 写真提供:SCジョンソン社

6-16
- ジョンソン·ワックス·ビル 本部棟
中央執務室の椅子
- デザイン:フランク·ロイド·ライト
製作:スチールケース·
コーポレーション
- 製作:1936年頃
- 88.9×45.7×50.8
- スチール、布
- 豊田市美術館

6-17
- ジョンソン·ワックス·ビル
(ウィスコンシン州ラシーン)　本部棟
中央執務室
ライトのデザインによる
椅子と机で執務する社員
- 撮影:1939年
- 写真(複写)
- 写真提供:SCジョンソン社

6-18
- ジョンソン·ワックス·研究タワー
(ウィスコンシン州ラシーン)1943年
- 撮影:1954年頃
- 写真(複写)
- 写真提供:SCジョンソン社

6-19
- ジョンソン·ワックス·研究タワー
(ウィスコンシン州ラシーン)で
働く研究員
- 撮影:1950年
- 写真(複写)
- 写真提供:SCジョンソン社

6-20 ＊
- セント·マークス教区の
アパートメント·タワー計画案
(ニューヨーク)1927-29年　透視図
- フランク·ロイド·ライト
- オリジナル:68.6×33.2
- オリジナル:鉛筆、色鉛筆/
トレーシング·ペーパー(複写)
- コロンビア大学
エイヴリー建築美術図書館
フランク·ロイド·ライト財団
アーカイヴズ

6-21
- セント·マークス教区の
アパートメント·タワー計画案
(ニューヨーク)1927-29年
鳥瞰透視図
- フランク·ロイド·ライト
- 60.3×38.1
- 鉛筆、色鉛筆/
トレーシング·ペーパー
- ニューヨーク近代美術館Jeffrey
P. Klein Purchase Fund,
Barbara Pine Purchase Fund,
and Frederieke Taylor Purchase
Fund, 1999.

6-22
- プライス·タワー(オクラホマ州
バートルズヴィル)1956年
- 建築:フランク·ロイド·ライト
撮影:ダン·オドネル
- 撮影:2008年
- 写真(複写)
- 写真提供:プライス·タワー·
アート·センター

6-23
- プライス·タワー(オクラホマ州
バートルズヴィル)1956年
オフィス内観
- 建築:フランク·ロイド·ライト
撮影:ジョー·プライス
- 撮影:1956年
- 写真(複写)
- 写真提供:プライス·タワー·
アート·センター
ジョー·プライス·PT·コレクション

6-24
- プライス·タワー(オクラホマ州
バートルズヴィル)1956年
19階エグゼクティブフロアの
オフィスと居室内観
- 建築:フランク·ロイド·ライト
撮影:マーサ·アンブラー
- 撮影:2017年
- 写真(複写)
- 写真提供:プライス·タワー·
アート·センター

6-25
- 模型　プライス·タワー
- 制作:兵庫県立大学環境人間学
部水上研究室
- 制作:2023年
- 75.0×65.0×65.0 縮尺1:100
- ミクストメディア
- 75.0×65.0×65.0

**36　開けた大地に建つ
高層建築——
超高層ザ·マイル·ハイ·イリノイ**

6-26
- 花入れ
- デザイン:フランク·ロイド·ライト
製作:ジェームズ·A. ミラー&
ブラザー工房
- 1900年頃
- 74.0×10.5×10.5
- 銅
- 豊田市美術館

6-27 ＊
- ナショナル生命保険会社ビル
計画案(イリノイ州シカゴ)
1923-25年
ニューヨーク近代美術館で
2014年に開催された
「フランク·ロイド·ライト密度と過疎」
展で制作されたライトボックス
- 製作:2014年
- 106.5×66.7×6.4
- ライトボックスによる複製
- ニューヨーク近代美術館

6-28
- マイル·ハイ·イリノイ計画案
(イリノイ州シカゴ)1956年　透視図
- フランク·ロイド·ライト
- オリジナル:266.7×76.2
- 鉛筆、インク/麻布(複写)
- コロンビア大学
エイヴリー建築美術図書館
フランク·ロイド·ライト財団
アーカイヴズ

6-29 ＊
- ゴールデン·ビーコン·アパート
メント計画案(イリノイ州シカゴ)
1956-57年　透視図
- フランク·ロイド·ライト
- オリジナル:117.5×57.8
- オリジナル:色鉛筆、絵具/紙(複写)
- コロンビア大学
エイヴリー建築美術図書館
フランク·ロイド·ライト財団
アーカイヴズ

6-30
- マイル·ハイ·イリノイ計画案
(イリノイ州シカゴ)
フランク·ロイド·ライト記念日の
記者発表会で公開された
プレゼンテーション
- 撮影者不詳
- 撮影:1956年10月16日
- 写真(複写)
- コロンビア大学
エイヴリー建築美術図書館
フランク·ロイド·ライト財団
アーカイヴズ

6-31
- マイル·ハイ·イリノイ計画案
(イリノイ州シカゴ)の図面を描く
ライト、タリアセンの設計室にて
- 撮影:エドガー·オブマ
- 撮影:1956年
- 写真(複写)
- コロンビア大学
エイヴリー建築美術図書館
フランク·ロイド·ライト財団
アーカイヴズ

**SECTION 7
多様な文化との邂逅**

37　ライトへ注がれた同時代の目

**+　土浦亀城·信子
帝国ホテルでの協力を経て**

7-1
- ハーパー·アヴェニュー
(カリフォルニア州、西ハリウッド)の
ライトの事務所にて
左から:ウィル·スミス、土浦信子、
ハリー·ウルフ「幸せな日々」
- 撮影者不詳
- 1923-24年
- 写真(複写)
- コロンビア大学
エイヴリー建築美術図書館
フランク·ロイド·ライト財団
アーカイヴズ

7-2
- ハーパー·アヴェニュー
(カリフォルニア州、西ハリウッド)の
ライトの事務所での食事
左から:ハリー·ウルフ、土浦信子、
ウィル·スミス
- 撮影:土浦亀城
- 撮影:1923-24年頃

- Frank Lloyd Wright, author. Ernst Wasmuth, publisher
- 1911
- 30.5 x 22 cm
- Print on paper / book
- Yutaka Mizukami Collection

6-2
- Larkin Company Administration Building: Buffalo, New York. Project 1902-06. Perspective
- Frank Lloyd Wright
- 1903
- 42.9 x 57.2 cm
- Pencil on tracing paper
- Toyota Municipal Museum of Art

6-3
- Plate XXXIII. Ground Plan and Perspective of the Administration Building for the Larkin Company. *Ausgeführte Bauten und Entwürfe von Frank Lloyd Wright*
- Frank Lloyd Wright. Ernst Wasmuth, publisher
- 1910
- 63.5 x 45.0 cm
- Lithograph on paper
- Toyota Municipal Museum of Art

6-4
- Plate XXXIIIa. Ground plan and Perspective of the Administration Building for the Larkin Company. *Ausgeführte Bauten und Entwürfe von Frank Lloyd Wright*
- Frank Lloyd Wright. Ernst Wasmuth, publisher
- 1910
- 63.5 x 45.0 cm
- Lithograph on paper
- Toyota Municipal Museum of Art

6-5
- Plate XXXIII. Interior of the Administration Building for the Larkin Company. *Ausgeführte Bauten und Entwürfe von Frank Lloyd Wright*
- Frank Lloyd Wright. Ernst Wasmuth, publisher
- 1910
- 63.5 x 45.0 cm
- Lithograph on paper
- Toyota Municipal Museum of Art

6-6
- Larkin Building, Buffalo, New York. Interior view, atrium
- Frank Lloyd Wright, architect
- Photo: 1905
- Photograph (reproduction)
- Project photographs, circa 1887-2008, The Frank Lloyd Wright Foundation Archives (The Museum of Modern Art | Avery Architectural & Fine Arts Library, Columbia University, New York)
- FLWFA 0403.0063

6-7
- Desk and Attached Chair from Larkin Building
- Frank Lloyd Wright, designer. Van Dorn Iron Works Company, manufacturer
- c. 1904
- 61.0 x 122.0 x 109.0 cm
- Steel, wood
- Toyota Municipal Museum of Art

6-8
- Folding Side Chair from Larkin Building, Buffalo, New York
- Frank Lloyd Wright, designer. Van Dorn Iron Works Company, manufacturer
- c. 1904
- 94.0 x 51.1 x 51.1 cm
- Steel, wood
- Toyota Municipal Museum of Art

6-9
- *Frank Lloyd Wright, Aus dem Lebenswerke eines Architekten*
- Frank Lloyd Wright, author, H. De Fries, editor. Verlag Ernst Pollak, Berlin, publisher
- 1926
- 29 x 23 x 1 cm
- Print on paper / book
- Tokyo City University, The KURATA Chikatada Archive

35 Skyscraper with a structural core and cantilevered floors

6-10
- SC Johnson Administration Building, Racine, Wisconsin. Stress test for columns
- Frank Lloyd Wright, architect
- Photo: 1937
- Photograph (reproduction)
- Project photographs, circa 1887-2008, The Frank Lloyd Wright Foundation Archives (The Museum of Modern Art | Avery Architectural & Fine Arts Library, Columbia University, New York)
- FLWFA 3601.0022

6-11
- SC Johnson Administration Building, Racine, Wisconsin. Stress test for columns
- Frank Lloyd Wright, architect. James Thomson, photographer
- Photo: 1937
- Photograph (reproduction)
- Project photographs, circa 1887-2008, The Frank Lloyd Wright Foundation Archives (The Museum of Modern Art | Avery Architectural & Fine Arts Library, Columbia University, New York)
- FLWFA 3601.0132

6-12
- Film. Testing the Column: SC Johnson
- 1937
- 2 minutes 40 seconds
- film
- The Frank Lloyd Wright Foundation Archives (The Museum of Modern Art | Avery Architectural & Fine Arts Library, Columbia University, New York)
- Avery 10226981 30-1

6-13
- SC Johnson Administration Building, Racine, Wisconsin. Project, 1936-39. Detail of Column and Penthouse plan
- Frank Lloyd Wright
- Original: 35 1/4 x 25 7/8 in. (89.54 x 65.72 cm)
- Black ink and wash with pencil and colored pencil on paper (reproduction)
- The Frank Lloyd Wright Foundation Archives (The Museum of Modern Art | Avery Architectural & Fine Arts Library, Columbia University, New York)
- FLW.DR.3601.007

6-14
- View from the northwest of the Great Workroom in the SC Johnson Administration Building
- Frank Lloyd Wright, architect
- Photo: c. 1954
- Photograph (reproduction)
- Courtesy of SC Johnson
- PD-10415-810

6-15
- View looking south into the Great Workroom of the SC Johnson Administration Building
- Frank Lloyd Wright, architect
- Photo: 2015
- Photograph (reproduction)
- Courtesy of SC Johnson
- 2015 -09

6-16
- Chair from the Great Workroom of the SC Johnson Administration Building
- Frank Lloyd Wright, designer. Steelcase Corporation, manufacturer
- c. 1936
- 88.9 x 45.7 x 50.8 cm
- Steel, fabric
- Toyota Municipal Museum of Art
- 485

6-17
- View of an SC Johnson clerk working at a Frank Lloyd Wright-designed desk and chair in the Great Workroom of the SC Johnson Administration Building
- Photo: 1939
- Photograph (reproduction)
- Courtesy of SC Johnson
- PD-3980-57

6-18
- SC Johnson Research Tower, Racine, Wisconsin. Project, 1943. Exterior view.
- Frank Lloyd Wright, architect
- Photo: c. 1954
- Photograph (reproduction)
- Courtesy of SC Johnson
- PD-10380-81001

6-19
- An SC Johnson scientist is shown working in the Frank Lloyd Wright-designed SC Johnson Research Tower
- Frank Lloyd Wright, architect
- Photo: 1950
- Photograph (reproduction)
- Courtesy of SC Johnson
- PD-14305-45.01

6-20
- St. Mark's Towers, New York. Unbuilt Project, 1927-29. Exterior perspective
- Frank Lloyd Wright
- original: 27 x 13 1/16 in. (68.6 x 33.2 cm)
- Pencil and colored pencil on tracing paper (reproduction)
- The Frank Lloyd Wright Foundation Archives (The Museum of Modern Art | Avery Architectural & Fine Arts Library, Columbia University, New York)
- FLW.DR.2905.041

6-21
- St. Mark's Towers, New York. Unbuilt Project, 1927-29. Aerial perspective
- Frank Lloyd Wright
- 23 3/4 x 15 in. (60.3 x 38.1 cm)
- Pencil and colored pencil on tracing paper
- The Museum of Modern Art, New York. Jeffrey P. Klein Purchase Fund, Barbara Pine Purchase Fund, and Frederieke Taylor Purchase Fund, 1999
- DIGITAL IMAGE©2023, The Museum of Modern Art/Scala, Florence
- 278.1999

6-22
- Price Company Tower, Bartlesville, Oklahoma. Project, 1956. Exterior
- Frank Lloyd Wright, architect. Dan O'Donnell, photographer
- Photo: 2008
- Photograph (reproduction)
- Photo courtesy of Price Tower Art Center

6-23
- Price Company Tower, Bartlesville, Oklahoma. Project, 1956. Interior view of the office
- Frank Lloyd Wright, architect. Joe Price, photographer
- Photo: 1956
- Photograph (reproduction)
- Photo courtesy of Price Tower Art Center Joe Price PT collection

6-24
- Price Company Tower, Bartlesville, Oklahoma. Project, 1956. Interior view of the 19th-floor executive office of H.C. Price and H.C. Price Company Corporate Apartment
- Frank Lloyd Wright, architect. Martha Ambler, photographer
- Photo: 2017
- Photograph (reproduction)
- Photo courtesy of Price Tower Art Center

6-25
- Model. Price Tower for Harold C. Price, Sr., Bartlesville, Oklahoma
- Frank Lloyd Wright, architect, Mizukami Laboratory, School of Human Science and Environment, University of Hyogo, fabricator
- Mixed media
- 75.0 x 65.0 x 65.0 cm scale 1:100

36 The Illinois: A mile-high skyscraper in a verdant landscape

6-26
- Weed Holder
- Frank Lloyd Wright, designer. Workshop of James A. Miller and Brother, maunfacturer
- c. 1900
- 74.0 x 10.5 x 10.5 cm
- Copper
- Toyota Municipal Museum of Art

6-27
- National Life Insurance Company Building, Chicago, Illinois. Unbuilt project, 1923-25. Lightbox reproduction shown at the exhibition "Frank Lloyd Wright and the City: Density vs. Dispersal". MoMA, NY, February 1-June 1, 2014
- reproduction fabricated in 2014
- 106.5 x 66.7 x 6.4 cm
- Drawing reproduced on a light box
- The Museum of Modern Art, New York. The Frank Lloyd Wright Foundation Archives (The Museum of Modern Art | Avery Architectural & Fine Arts Library, Columbia University, New York)
- DIGITAL IMAGE © 2023, The Museum of Modern Art / SCALA, Florence. Photographer: Thomas Griesel
- FLW.DR.2404.002

6-28
- The Mile-High Illinois, Chicago, Illinois. Unbuilt Project, 1956. Exterior perspective
- Frank Lloyd Wright
- 8 ft 9 in. x 30 in. (266.7 x 76.2 cm)
- Pencil, ink on linen. (reproduction)
- The Frank Lloyd Wright Foundation Archives (The Museum of Modern Art | Avery Architectural & Fine Arts Library, Columbia University, New York)
- FLW.DR.5617.002

6-29
- Golden Beacon apartment tower for Charles Glore, Chicago, Illinois. Unbuilt Project, 1956-57. Exterior perspective
- Frank Lloyd Wright
- 46 1/4 x 22 3/4 in.
- Colored pencil, paint on paper. (reproduction)
- The Frank Lloyd Wright Foundation Archives (The Museum of Modern Art | Avery Architectural & Fine Arts Library, Columbia University, New York)
- FLW.DR.5615.004

6-30
- Exhibition Space of Frank Lloyd Wright Day at Sherman Hotel (Chicago, Illinois). Unveiling design for the Mile High Illinois skyscraper at the October 16 1956 Press Conference in Chicago
- Photographer unidentified
- 1956
- Photograph (reproduction)
- Project photographs, circa 1887-2008, The Frank Lloyd Wright Foundation Archives (The Museum of Modern Art | Avery Architectural & Fine Arts Library, Columbia University, New York)
- FLWFA 5639.0001

6-31
- Frank Lloyd Wright at drafting table at Hillside, drawing the Mile-High Illinois
- Edgar Obma, photographer
- Photo: 1956
- Photograph (reproduction)
- Personal and Taliesin Fellowship photographs, 1870s-2004, The Frank Lloyd Wright Foundation Archives (The Museum of Modern Art | Avery Architectural & Fine Arts Library, Columbia University, New York)
- FLWFA 6007.0025

SECTION 7
Wright and Global Cultures

37 Wright's reputation among his contemporaries

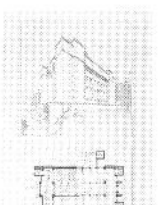
6-3

6-4

6-5

6-6

6-7

6-8

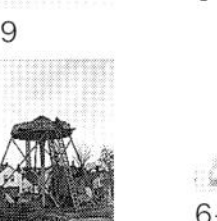
6-9

6-10

6-11

6-12

6-13

6-14

6-15

6-16

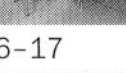
6-17

6-18

6-19

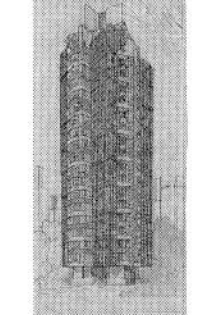
6-20

6-21

6-22

6-23

6-24

6-25

6-26

6-27

6-28, 6-29

6-30

6-31

7-1

- 写真(複写)
- コロンビア大学
  エイヴリー建築美術図書館
  フランク・ロイド・ライト財団
  アーカイヴズ

7-3
- 花咲くユッカの前の土浦亀城、
  信子夫妻 カリフォルニア州
  サン・ガブリエル山地にて
- 撮影:ウィリアム・スミス
- 撮影:1923–24年頃
- 写真(複写)
- コロンビア大学
  エイヴリー建築美術図書館
  フランク・ロイド・ライト財団
  アーカイヴズ

7-4
- 教会の鐘の前にたたずむ
  土浦亀城、信子夫妻 ミッション・
  サンファン・カピストラーノにて
- 撮影:ウィリアム・スミス
- 撮影:1923 24年頃
- 写真(複写)
- コロンビア大学
  エイヴリー建築美術図書館
  フランク・ロイド・ライト財団
  アーカイヴズ

7-5
- 土浦亀城、信子夫妻とウィル・スミス
  ミッション・サンファン・
  カピストラーノにて
- 撮影者不詳
- 1923–24年頃
- 写真(複写)
- コロンビア大学
  エイヴリー建築美術図書館
  フランク・ロイド・ライト財団
  アーカイヴズ

7-6
- タリアセンのスタジオ
  (左から:ライト、土浦亀城、
  リチャード・ノイトラ、
  ヴェルナー・モーザー、土浦信子)
  土浦亀城、信子夫妻のアルバム
  「Taliesin Life (1)」
- 撮影:1924年頃
- 12.0×17.0
- 写真(複写)
- 帝国ホテル

7-7
- タリアセンの居間
  左から:ライト、リチャード・ノイトラ、
  シルバ・モーザー夫人、土浦亀城、
  信子、ヴェルナー・モーザー、
  ディオーネ・ノイトラ夫人
- 撮影者不詳
- 撮影:1924年頃
- 写真(複写)
- 土浦亀城アーカイブズ

7-8
- エーリヒ・メンデルゾーンの
  タリアセン訪問
  左上より時計回りに:土浦亀城、
  土浦信子、シルバ・モーザー夫人、
  ウィリアム・スミス、
  エーリヒ・メンデルゾーン、
  フランク・ロイド・ライト、
  リチャード・ノイトラ
  土浦亀城、信子夫妻のアルバム
  「Taliesin Life (1)」
- 撮影:1924年
- 写真(複写)
- 土浦亀城アーカイブズ

7-9
- エーリヒ・メンデルゾーンの
  タリアセン訪問
  左から:メンデルゾーン、
  フランク・ロイド・ライト、
  リチャード・ノイトラ
  土浦亀城、信子夫妻のアルバム
  「Taliesin Life (1)」
- 撮影:1924年
- 写真(複写)
- 土浦亀城アーカイブズ

7-10
- フランク・ロイド・ライトと
  エーリヒ・メンデルゾーン
  土浦亀城、信子夫妻のアルバム
  「Taliesin Life (1)」
- 撮影:1924年
- 写真(複写)
- 土浦亀城アーカイブズ

7-11
- フランク・ロイド・ライトから
  土浦信子への手書きの献辞入り
  ヴァスムート "To big little Nobu,
  Frank Lloyd Wright, Taliesin,
  November 11 25."
  (小柄で偉大なノブへ、ライトより、
  1925年11月11日)
- 著:フランク・ロイド・ライト
  出版:エルンスト・ヴァスムート社
- 1910年
- 65.0×40.0
- 印刷/紙、書籍
- 土浦亀城アーカイブズ

7-12
- ライト『Autobiography(自伝)』
  増補改訂版(土浦亀城旧蔵)
- 著:フランク・ロイド・ライト
  出版:デュエル・スローン・ピアース社
- 1932/43年
- 22.0×21.8×4.0
- 印刷/紙、書籍
- 土浦亀城アーカイブズ

+ オランダ前衛との交流

7-13
- 『フランク・ロイド・ライト』
- 著:フランク・ロイド・ライト
  編:ヘンドリクス・ヴェイデフェルト
  出版:ホーヘ・ブリュッヘ&
  C.A. ミース社
- 1925年
- 34.0×33.0×2.5
- 印刷/紙、書籍
- 東京都市大学図書館
  (仲田定之助文庫)

7-14
- 『ヴェンディンゲン』1921年4巻11号
  (表紙デザイン:エル・リシツキー)
- 著:フランク・ロイド・ライト、
  ヘンドリクス・ベルラーへ
  出版:ホーヘ・ブリュッヘ&
  C.A. ミース社
- 1922年
- 34.0×34.0
- 印刷/紙、定期刊行物
- 大阪中之島美術館

7-15
- 『ヴェンディンゲン』1925年7巻3号
- 著:フランク・ロイド・ライト、
  H. ヴェイデフェルト
  出版:ホーヘ・ブリュッヘ&
  C.A. ミース社
- 1925年
- 34.0×34.0
- 印刷/紙、定期刊行物
- 大阪中之島美術館

7-16 *
- 『ウエンディンゲン』1925年7巻4号
- 著:フランク・ロイド・ライト
  出版:ホーヘ・ブリュッヘ&
  C.A. ミース社
- 1925年
- 34.0×34.0
- 印刷/紙、定期刊行物
- 大阪中之島美術館

7-17 *
- 『ウェンディンゲン』1925年7巻5号
- 著:フランク・ロイド・ライト、
  ルイス・マンフォード
  出版:ホーヘ・ブリュッヘ&
  C.A. ミース社
- 1926年
- 34.0×34.0
- 印刷/紙、定期刊行物
- 大阪中之島美術館

7-18 *
- 『ウェンディンゲン』1925年7巻6号
- 著:フランク・ロイド・ライト、
  ロベール・マレ=ステヴァンス
  出版:ホーヘ・ブリュッヘ&
  C.A. ミース社
- 1926年
- 34.0×34.0
- 印刷/紙、定期刊行物
- 大阪中之島美術館

7-19 *
- 『ウェンディンゲン』1925年7巻7号
- 著:フランク・ロイド・ライト、
  エーリヒ・メンデルゾーン
  出版:ホーヘ・ブリュッヘ&
  C.A. ミース社
- 1926年
- 34.0×34.0
- 印刷/紙、定期刊行物
- 大阪中之島美術館

7-20 *
- 『ウエンディンゲン』1925年7巻8号
- 著:フランク・ロイド・ライト、
  ルイス・サリヴァン
  出版:ホーヘ・ブリュッヘ&
  C.A. ミース社
- 1926年
- 34.0×34.0
- 印刷/紙、定期刊行物
- 大阪中之島美術館

7-21 *
- 『ウェンディンゲン』1925年7巻9号
- 著:フランク・ロイド・ライト
  出版:ホーヘ・ブリュッヘ&
  C.A. ミース社
- 1926年
- 34.0×34.0
- 印刷/紙、定期刊行物
- 大阪中之島美術館

7-22
- フランク・ロイド・ライトから
  ヴェイデフェルトにあてた書簡、
  1930年8月6日
- 著:フランク・ロイド・ライト
- 1930年8月6日
- インク/紙
- 写真提供:オランダ建築協会
  ヘット・ニュー・インスティテュート、
  ヘット・スヒップ

7-23
- 『フランク・ロイド・ライト作品集I』
- 著:フランク・ロイド・ライト、
  エーリヒ・メンデルゾーン
  出版:洪洋社
- 1926年
- 25.8×19.3
- 印刷/紙、書籍

7-24 *
- 『フランク・ロイド・ライト作品集II』
- 著:フランク・ロイド・ライト、
  ヤーコプ・アウト
  出版:洪洋社
- 1926年
- 25.8×19.3
- 印刷/紙、書籍

7-25 *
- 『フランク・ロイド・ライト作品集III』
- 著:フランク・ロイド・ライト、
  ヘンドリクス・ベルラーヘ
  出版:洪洋社
- 1927年
- 25.8×19.3
- 印刷/紙、書籍

7-26 *
- 『フランク・ロイド・ライト作品集IV』
- 著:フランク・ロイド・ライト、
  アドルフ・ベーネ
  出版:洪洋社
- 1928年
- 25.8×19.3
- 印刷/紙、書籍

7-27 *
- 『フランク・ロイド・ライト作品集V』
- 著:フランク・ロイド・ライト
  出版:洪洋社
- 1928年
- 25.8×19.3
- 印刷/紙、書籍

+ 各国で開かれたライト作品展

7-28
- 『近代建築』プリンストン大学に
  おけるライトの連続講座の記録
- 著:フランク・ロイド・ライト
  出版:オックスフォード大学出版
  (プリンストン大学出版)
- 1931年
- 27×21×1.5
- 印刷/紙、書籍
- 東京都市大学(蔵田文庫)

7-29
- ポスター「フランク・ロイド・ライトの
  建築1893–1931年」展
- デザイン:
  ヘンドリクス・ヴェイデフェルト
- 1931年
- 76.8×48.8
- リトグラフ/紙
- 豊田市美術館

7-30
- 「フランク・ロイド・ライトの建築
  1893–1931年」展、
  アムステルダム市立美術館にて
  エントランスの装飾
- 撮影者不詳
- 撮影:1931年
- 写真(複写)
- コロンビア大学
  エイヴリー建築美術図書館
  フランク・ロイド・ライト財団
  アーカイヴズ

**+ アルヴァ・アアルト
北欧モダニズムとの交流**

7-31
- アルヴァ・アアルト、
  長女ヨハナと長男ハミルカル
  「落水荘」のゲストハウスにて
- 撮影:アイノ・アアルト
- 撮影:1939年
- 写真(複写)
- アルヴァ・アアルト美術館

7-32
- アルヴァ・アアルトの
  長女ヨハナと長男ハミルカル
  「落水荘」のゲストハウスにて
- 撮影:アイノ・アアルト
- 撮影:1939年
- 写真(複写)
- アルヴァ・アアルト美術館

7-33
- アルヴァ・アアルトから
  フランク・ロイド・ライトに宛てた手紙
- アルヴァ・アアルト
- 1945年12月13日
- インク、紙(複製)
- アルヴァ・アアルト美術館

---

38 ライトとイタリア

+ 1910年のイタリア体験

7-34
- ヴェルデ通りの眺望
- 撮影:テイラー・A. ウーレイ
- 撮影:1910年
- 写真(複写)
- コロンビア大学
  エイヴリー建築美術図書館
  フランク・ロイド・ライト財団
  アーカイヴズ

7-35
- ヴェネツィアの運河沿いの館
- 撮影:テイラー・A. ウーレイ
- 撮影:1910年

+ Kameki and Nobuko Tsuchiura: After Cooperating at the Imperial Hotel

7-1
- William E. Smith, Nobuko Tsuchiura and Harry Wolfe at the Harper Avenue Studio, West Hollywood: "Happy Days."
- Photographer unidentified
- Photo: c. 1923-24
- Photograph (reproduction)
- Personal and Taliesin Fellowship photographs, 1870s-2004, The Frank Lloyd Wright Foundation Archives (The Museum of Modern Art | Avery Architectural & Fine Arts Library, Columbia University, New York)
- FLWFA 6833.0031

7-2
- Harry Wolfe, Nobuko Tsuchiura and William E. Smith dining at Harper Avenue studio, West Hollywood
- Kameki Tsuchiura, photographer
- Photo: c. 1923-24
- Photograph (reproduction)
- Personal and Taliesin Fellowship photographs, 1870s-2004, The Frank Lloyd Wright Foundation Archives (The Museum of Modern Art | Avery Architectural & Fine Arts Library, Columbia University, New York)
- FLWFA 6833.0030

7-3
- Nobuko Tsuchiura and Kameki Tsuchiura with yucca in bloom, San Gabriel Mountain
- William E. Smith, photographer
- Photo: c. 1923-24
- Photograph (reproduction)
- Personal and Taliesin Fellowship photographs, 1870s-2004, The Frank Lloyd Wright Foundation Archives (The Museum of Modern Art | Avery Architectural & Fine Arts Library, Columbia University, New York)
- FLWFA 6833.0033

7-4
- Nobuko Tsuchiura and Kameki Tsuchiura near the bell on roof of chapel in San Juan Capistrano
- William E. Smith, photographer
- Photo: c. 1923-24
- Photograph (reproduction)
- Personal and Taliesin Fellowship photographs, 1870s-2004, The Frank Lloyd Wright Foundation Archives (The Museum of Modern Art | Avery Architectural & Fine Arts Library, Columbia University, New York)
- FLWFA 6833.0035

7-5
- Nobuko Tsuchiura, Kameki Tsuchiura, and William E. Smith at San Juan Capistrano Mission
- Photographer unidentified
- Photo: c. 1923-24
- Photograph (reproduction)
- Personal and Taliesin Fellowship photographs, 1870s-2004, The Frank Lloyd Wright Foundation Archives (The Museum of Modern Art | Avery Architectural & Fine Arts Library, Columbia University, New York)
- FLWFA 6833.0037

7-6
- Frank Lloyd Wright and staff at Taliesin studio. From left: Wright, Kameki Tsuchiura, Richard Neutra, Werner Moser and Nobuko Tsuchiura
- Photo: c. 1924
- Photograph (reproduction)
- Imperial Hotel
- 10031

7-7
- Livingroom at Taliesin. From left: Wright, Richard Neutra, Silva Moser (wife of Verner Moser), Kameki Tsuchiura, Nobuko Tsuchiura, Verner Moser, Dione Neutra
- Photographer unidentified
- Photo: c. 1924
- Photograph (reproduction)
- TSUCHIURA Kameki Archives

7-8
- Visit of Erich Mendelsohn to Taliesin. From top left clockwise: Kameki Tsuchiura, Nobuko Tsuchiura, Silva Moser, William Smith, Erich Mendelsohn, Frank Lloyd Wright, Richard Neutra. Tsuchiura album "Taliesin Life"(1)
- Photo: 1924
- Photograph (reproduction)
- TSUCHIURA Kameki Archives

7-9
- Visit of Erich Mendelsohn to Taliesin. From left, Mendelsohn, FLWright, Richard Neutra. Tsuchiura album "Taliesin Life"(1)
- Photo: 1924
- Photograph (reproduction)
- TSUCHIURA Kameki Archives

7-10
- Frank Lloyd Wright and Erich Mendelsohn. Tsuchiura album "Taliesin Life"(1)
- Photo: 1924
- Photograph (reproduction)
- TSUCHIURA Kameki Archives

7-11
- *Ausgeführte Bauten und Entwürfe von Frank Lloyd Wright (Wasmuth portfolio)*. With a handwritten dedication from Wright to Nobuko Tsuchiura. "To big little Nobu, Frank Lloyd Wright, Taliesin, November 11 25."
- Frank Lloyd Wright, architect. Ernst Wasmuth, publisher
- 1910
- Print on paper / book
- TSUCHIURA Kameki Archives

7-12
- *Frank Lloyd Wright: An Autobiography*. Enlarged and revised version (owned by Kameki Tsuchiura)
- Frank Lloyd Wright, author. Duell, Sloan, and Pearce, publisher
- 1932/43
- Print on paper / book
- TSUCHIURA Kameki Archives

+ Relationship with the Dutch avant-garde

7-13
- *Frank Lloyd Wright*
- Frank Lloyd Wright, author. H. Wijdevelt, editor. Hooge Brug and C.A. Mees, publisher
- 1925
- 34 x 33 x 2.5 cm
- Print on paper / book
- Tokyo City University, The NAKADA Sadanosuke Archive

7-14
- *Wendingen*, vol. 4-11, 1921
- Frank Lloyd Wright and H.P. Bergale, authors. Hooge Brug and C.A. Mees, publisher
- 1922
- 34.0 x 34.0 cm
- Print on paper / book
- Nakanoshima Museum of Art, Osaka

7-15
- *Wendingen*, vol. 7-3, 1925
- Frank Lloyd Wright and H. Wijdeveld, authors. Hooge Brug and C.A. Mees, publisher
- 1925
- 34.0 x 34.0 cm
- Print on paper / book
- Nakanoshima Museum of Art, Osaka

7-16
- *Wendingen*, vol. 7-4, 1925
- Frank Lloyd Wright author. Hooge Brug and C.A. Mees, publisher
- 1925
- 34.0 x 34.0 cm
- Print on paper / book
- Nakanoshima Museum of Art, Osaka

7-17
- *Wendingen*, vol. 7-5, 1925
- Frank Lloyd Wright and Louis Mumford, authors. Hooge Brug and C.A. Mees, publisher
- 1926
- 34.0 x 34.0 cm
- Print on paper / book
- Nakanoshima Museum of Art, Osaka

7-18
- *Wendingen*, vol. 7-6, 1925
- Frank Lloyd Wright and Robert Mallet-Stevens, authors. Hooge Brug and C.A. Mees, publisher
- 1926
- 34.0 x 34.0 cm
- Print on paper / book
- Nakanoshima Museum of Art, Osaka

7-19
- *Wendingen*, vol. 7-7, 1925
- Frank Lloyd Wright and Erich Mendelsohn, authors. Hooge Brug and C.A. Mees, publisher
- 1926
- 34.0 x 34.0 cm
- Print on paper / book
- Nakanoshima Museum of Art, Osaka

7-20
- *Wendingen*, vol. 7-8, 1925
- Frank Lloyd Wright and Louis Sullivan, authors. Hooge Brug and C.A. Mees, publisher
- 1926
- 34.0 x 34.0 cm
- Print on paper / book
- Nakanoshima Museum of Art, Osaka

7-21
- *Wendingen*, vol. 9, 1925
- Frank Lloyd Wright, author. Hooge Brug and C.A. Mees, publisher
- 1926
- 34.0 x 34.0 cm
- Print on paper / book
- Nakanoshima Museum of Art, Osaka

7-22
- Frank Lloyd Wright, letter to Wijdeveld, August 6, 1930
- Frank Lloyd Wright, author
- August 6, 1930
- Ink on paper (reproduction)
- © Nieuwe Instituut, Rotterdam, cooperation partner of Amsterdam School Museum het Schip, Amsterdam

7-23
- *Frank Lloyd Wright Sakuhin-shu (Works of Frank Lloyd Wright) volume 1*
- Frank Lloyd Wright and Erich Mendelsohn, authors. Koyo-sha, publisher
- 1926
- 25.8 x 19.3 cm
- Print on paper / book

7-24
- *Frank Lloyd Wright Sakuhin-shu (Works of Frank Lloyd Wright) volume 2*
- Frank Lloyd Wright and J.J.P. Oud, authors. Koyo-sha, publisher
- 1926
- 25.8 x 19.3 cm
- Print on paper / book

7-25
- *Frank Lloyd Wright Sakuhin-shu (Works of Frank Lloyd Wright) volume 3*
- Frank Lloyd Wright and H.P. Bergale, authors. Koyo-sha, publisher
- 1927
- 25.8 x 19.3 cm
- Print on paper / book

7-26
- *Frank Lloyd Wright Sakuhin-shu (Works of Frank Lloyd Wright) volume 4*
- Frank Lloyd Wright and Adolf Behne, authors. Koyo-sha, publisher
- 1928
- 25.8 x 19.3 cm
- Print on paper / book

7-27
- *Frank Lloyd Wright Sakuhin-shu (Works of Frank Lloyd Wright) volume 5*
- Frank Lloyd Wright author. Koyo-sha, publisher
- 1928
- 25.8 x 19.3 cm
- Print on paper / book

+ European touring show

7-28
- *Modern Architecture. Being The Kahn Lectures For 1930*
- Frank Lloyd Wright, author. Princeton university press, publisher
- 1931
- 27 x 21 x 1.5 cm
- Print on paper / book
- Tokyo City University, The KURATA Chikatada Archive

7-29
- Poster. Architecture of Frank Lloyd Wright exhibition
- Hendricus Theodorus Wijdeveld, designer
- 1931
- 76.8 x 48.8 cm
- lithograph on paper
- Toyota Municipal Museum of Art
- 460

7-30
- The Work of Frank Lloyd Wright, 1893-1931 Exhibition at the Stedelijk Museum, Amsterdam.
- Photographer unidentified
- Photo: 1931
- Photograph (reproduction)
- Project photographs, circa 1887-2008, The Frank Lloyd Wright Foundation Archives (The Museum of Modern Art | Avery Architectural & Fine Arts Library, Columbia University, New York)
- FLWFA 3100.0002

+ Alvar Aalto: Relationship with Scandinavian Modernism

7-31
- Alvar Aalto and his children, Johanna and Hamilkar at the Fallingwater (Edgar J. Kaufmann House) Guesthouse, Mill Run, Pennsylvania
- Aino Aalto, photographer
- Photo: 1939
- Photograph (reproduction)
- Courtesy of Alvar Aalto Museum

7-32
- Alvar Aalto's children, Johanna and Hamilkar at the Fallingwater (Edgar J. Kaufmann House) Guesthouse, Mill Run, Pennsylvania
- Aino Aalto, photographer
- Photo: 1939
- Photograph (reproduction)
- Courtesy of Alvar Aalto Museum

7-33
- Alvar Aalto, letter to Frank Lloyd Wright, 13 Dec 1945
- Alvar Aalto
- Ink on typed paper / letter (reproduction)
- Courtesy of Alvar Aalto Museum

38 Wright and Italy

+ Experiences from the 1910 trip to Italy

7-34
- Viale Verde, street scene
- Taylor A. Woolley, photographer
- Photo: 1910
- Photograph (reproduction)
- Personal and Taliesin Fellowship photographs, 1870s-2004, The Frank Lloyd Wright Foundation Archives (The Museum of Modern Art | Avery Architectural & Fine Arts Library, Columbia University, New York)
- FLWFA 7109.0007

7-35
- View of Venetian palazzo from canal
- Taylor A. Woolley, photographer
- Photo: 1910
- Photograph (reproduction)
- Personal and Taliesin Fellowship photographs, 1870s-2004, The Frank Lloyd Wright Foundation Archives (The Museum of Modern Art | Avery Architectural & Fine Arts Library, Columbia University, New York)

7-2

7-3

7-4

7-5

7-6

7-7

7-8

7-9

7-10

7-11

7-12

7-13

7-14
7-15
7-16

7-17
7-18

7-19

7-20
7-21
7-22

7-23
7-24

7-25
7-26

7-27
7-28

7-29
7-30

7-31
7-32

7-33
7-34

7-35

7-36

- 写真（複写）
- コロンビア大学
  エイヴリー建築美術図書館
  フランク・ロイド・ライト財団
  アーカイヴズ

＋ マシエリ記念学生会館とカルロ・スカルパ

7-36
- マシエリ記念学生会館計画案
  （イタリア、ヴェネツィア）
  1951／1952–55年 透視図
- フランク・ロイド・ライト
- オリジナル：63.5×49.5
- 原図：色鉛筆、水彩／
  トレーシング・ペーパー（複写）
- コロンビア大学
  エイヴリー建築美術図書館
  フランク・ロイド・ライト財団
  アーカイヴズ

7-37
- カルロ・スカルパによる
  マシエリ記念館 地階排気口詳細
- カルロ・スカルパ、フランカ・セミ
- 撮影：ジョン・ヴォルパト
- 撮影：2016年
- 写真（複写）
- マシエリ財団ヘリテージ資産管理
  ギャラリー・ネグロポンテ

7-38
- カルロ・スカルパによる
  マシエリ記念館（イタリア、ヴェネツィア）
  1952–83年 カナル・グランデからの全景（左の建物）
- 建築：カルロ・スカルパ、
  フランカ・セミ
  撮影：ジョン・ヴォルパト
- 撮影：2016年
- 写真（複写）
- マシエリ財団ヘリテージ資産管理
  ギャラリー・ネグロポンテ

7-39
- カルロ・スカルパによる
  マシエリ記念館（イタリア、ヴェネツィア）
  1952–83年
  内観、カナル・グランデを見る
- 建築：カルロ・スカルパ、
  フランカ・セミ
  撮影：ジョン・ヴォルパト
- 撮影：2016年
- 写真（複写）
- マシエリ財団ヘリテージ資産管理
  ギャラリー・ネグロポンテ

7-40
- カルロ・スカルパによる
  マシエリ記念館（イタリア、ヴェネツィア）
  1952–83年 2階ラウンジ内観
- 建築：カルロ・スカルパ、
  フランカ・セミ
  撮影：ジョン・ヴォルパト
- 撮影：2016年
- 写真（複写）
- マシエリ財団ヘリテージ資産管理
  ギャラリー・ネグロポンテ

7-41
- 第12回ミラノ・トリエンナーレにおけるフランク・ロイド・ライト回顧展、
  会場構成カルロ・スカルパ
  断面図
- カルロ・スカルパ
- 1960年
- オリジナル：29.5×46.5
- 原図：鉛筆、色鉛筆／
  トレーシング・ペーパー（複写）
- イタリア国立21世紀美術館

7-42
- 第12回ミラノ・トリエンナーレにおけるフランク・ロイド・ライト回顧展、
  会場構成カルロ・スカルパ
- 会場構成：カルロ・スカルパ
- 撮影：1960年
- オリジナル：30.5×38.6
- 写真／金属で裏打ち（複写）
- イタリア国立21世紀美術館

7-43
- 第12回ミラノ・トリエンナーレにおけるフランク・ロイド・ライト回顧展、
  会場構成カルロ・スカルパ
- 会場構成：カルロ・スカルパ
- 撮影：1960年
- オリジナル：30.5×37.9
- 写真／金属で裏打ち（複写）
- イタリア国立21世紀美術館

7-44
- 「生ける建築の60年」展
  ストロッツィ宮（フィレンツェ）にて
  左より：カルロ・スカルパ、
  アンジェロ・マシエリ、
  フランク・ロイド・ライト
- 撮影：フォト・レヴィ
- 撮影：1951年
- 写真（複写）
- コロンビア大学
  エイヴリー建築美術図書館
  フランク・ロイド・ライト財団
  アーカイヴズ

7-45
- フランク・ロイド・ライトと
  カルロ・スカルパ他、ヴェネツィア、
  サン・マルコ広場
  ドゥカーレ宮殿前にて
- 撮影者不詳
- 撮影：1951年
- 写真（複写）
- コロンビア大学
  エイヴリー建築美術図書館
  フランク・ロイド・ライト財団
  アーカイヴズ

39 世界に向けたライトの目

＋ アメリカ先住民文化への関心

7-46
- フランク・ロイド・ライト自邸と
  スタジオ（イリノイ州オークパーク）
  主寝室内観 北側壁面に
  オルランド・ジャンニーニによる
  壁画が見える
- 建築：フランク・ロイド・ライト
  撮影：ジェームズ・コールフィールド
- 撮影：2013年
- 写真（複写）

7-47
- ナコマ・カントリー・クラブ計画案
  （ウィスコンシン州マディソン）
  1923–24年 北東から見た外観
- フランク・ロイド・ライト
- 65.1×91.8
- 鉛筆、色鉛筆／
  トレーシング・ペーパー、
  書き込みのある紙の上にマウント
- コロンビア大学
  エイヴリー建築美術図書館
  フランク・ロイド・ライト財団
  アーカイヴズ

7-48
- ナコマ・カントリー・クラブ計画案
  （ウィスコンシン州マディソン）
  1923–24年 屋根伏図
- フランク・ロイド・ライト
- 1924年
- 原図：92.0×144.0
- 青焼図／紙（複写）
- 土浦亀城アーカイブズ

＋ 旅するライト

7-49
- 飛行機の前のフランク・ロイド・ライト
- 撮影者不詳
- 撮影年不詳
- 写真（複写）
- コロンビア大学
  エイヴリー建築美術図書館
  エドガー・ターフェル
  建築記録・資料

7-50
- ポートメイリオンの創設者、
  建築家クラフ・ウィリアムズ・エリスと歩くフランク・ロイド・ライト
- 撮影：ニュース・クロニクル社
  マンチェスター
- 撮影：1956年
- 写真（複写）
- コロンビア大学
  エイヴリー建築美術図書館
  フランク・ロイド・ライト財団
  アーカイヴズ

7-51
- アルキン夫妻と
  フランク・ロイド・ライト、ロシアにて
- 撮影者不詳
- 撮影：1937年
- 写真（複写）
- コロンビア大学
  エイヴリー建築美術図書館
  フランク・ロイド・ライト財団
  アーカイヴズ

＋ イスラム文化圏への提案

7-52
- 大バグダッド計画案
  （イラク、バグダッド）1957年
  鳥瞰透視図
  北から文化センターと大学をのぞむ
- フランク・ロイド・ライト
- 88.9×131.9
- インク、鉛筆、色鉛筆／
  トレーシング・ペーパー
- コロンビア大学
  エイヴリー建築美術図書館
  フランク・ロイド・ライト財団
  アーカイヴズ

40 未来へ向けた目：ブロードエーカー・シティ構想

7-53
- 『消えゆく都市』
- 著：フランク・ロイド・ライト
  出版：W.F. ペイソン社
- 1932年
- 21.5×21.5×1.4
- 印刷／紙、書籍
- 遠藤現コレクション

7-54
- リヴィング・シティ構想、
  1958年 鳥瞰透視図
- フランク・ロイド・ライト
- 81.9×99.1
- インク、鉛筆、色鉛筆／
  トレーシング・ペーパー
- コロンビア大学
  エイヴリー建築美術図書館
  フランク・ロイド・ライト財団
  アーカイヴズ

7-55
- 展覧会に出品された
  ブロードエーカー・シティ構想の
  模型
- 構想：フランク・ロイド・ライト
  撮影：ロイ・ピーターソン
- 撮影：1934年
- 写真（複写）
- コロンビア大学
  エイヴリー建築美術図書館
  フランク・ロイド・ライト財団
  アーカイヴズ

7-56
- 映像インスタレーション
  フランク・ロイド・ライトの
  ブロードエーカー・シティ構想に
  基づくCGアニメーション
- 建築、構想：フランク・ロイド・ライト
  制作：ディヴィッド・ロメロ
  映像投影システム・
  インスタレーション設計：八嶋有司
- 2023年
- 2分30秒
- 映像

41 フランク・ロイド・ライトとの対話

7-57
- フランク・ロイド・ライトとの対話
- 制作：ナショナル・
  ブロードキャスティング・
  カンパニー他
- 1953年
- 10分
- 映像
- ナショナル・ブロードキャスティング・
  カンパニー／Getty Images
  コロンビア大学
  エイヴリー建築美術図書館
  フランク・ロイド・ライト財団
  アーカイヴズ

7-58
- フランク・ロイド・ライト、
  タリアセン・ウェストにて
- 撮影者不詳
- 撮影：1954年
- 写真（複写）
- コロンビア大学
  エイヴリー建築美術図書館
  フランク・ロイド・ライト財団
  アーカイヴズ

- FLWFA 7109.0028

+ **Masieri Memorial and Carlo Scarpa**

7-36
- Masieri Memorial students' library and residence, Venice, Italy. Unbuilt Project, 1951 / 1952-55. Exterior perspective
- Frank Lloyd Wright
- original: 63.5 x 49.5 cm
- Colored pencil and water color on tracing paper (reproduction)
- The Frank Lloyd Wright Foundation Archives (The Museum of Modern Art | Avery Architectural & Fine Arts Library, Columbia University, New York)
- FLW.DR.5306.002

7-37
- Fondazione Angelo Masieri. Project, 1952-83. Detail of the chimney on the ground floor
- Carlo Scarpa and Franca Semi, architects. John Volpato, photographer
- Photo: 1939
- Photograph (reproduction)
- Courtesy of: Fondazione Angelo Masieri, Heritage Asset Management, Galerie Negropontes

7-38
- Fondazione Angelo Masieri, Project 1952-83. Exterior view from the Grand Canal
- Carlo Scarpa and Franca Semi, architects. John Volpato, photographer
- Photo: 2016
- Photograph (reproduction)
- Courtesy of Fondazione Angelo Masieri, Heritage Asset Management, Galerie Negropontes

7-39
- Fondazione Angelo Masieri, Project 1952-83. Ground floor, Interior view to the Grand Canal
- Carlo Scarpa and Franca Semi, architects. John Volpato, photographer
- Photo: 2016
- Photograph (reproduction)
- Courtesy of Fondazione Angelo Masieri, Heritage Asset Management, Galerie Negropontes

7-40
- Fondazione Angelo Masieri, Project 1952-84. Interior view to the second floor lounge area
- Carlo Scarpa and Franca Semi, architects. John Volpato, photographer
- Photo: 2016
- Photograph (reproduction)
- Courtesy of Fondazione Angelo Masieri, Heritage Asset Management, Galerie Negropontes

7-41
- Frank Lloyd Wright exhibition at the XII Milan Triennial. Project, 1960. Section
- Carlo Scarpa
- 1960
- original: 29.5 x 46.5 cm
- Pencil and colored pencil on tracing paper (reproduction)
- MAXXI Museo nazionale delle arti del XXI secolo, Rome. MAXXI Architettura Collection, Carlo Scarpa Archive
- 53688

7-42
- Frank Lloyd Wright exhibition at the XII Milan Triennial. Project, 1960. Interior view
- Carlo Scarpa, architect
- Photo: 1960
- original: 30.5 x 38.6 cm
- B/W photo on metal support (reproduction)
- MAXXI Museo nazionale delle arti del XXI secolo, Rome. MAXXI Architettura Collection, Carlo Scarpa Archive
- F28804

7-43
- Frank Lloyd Wright exhibition at the XII Milan Triennale, Project 1960. Interior view
- Carlo Scarpa, architect
- Photo: 1960
- original: 30.5 x 37.9 cm
- B/W photo on metal support (reproduction)
- MAXXI Museo nazionale delle arti del XXI secolo, Rome. MAXXI Architettura Collection, Carlo Scarpa Archive
- F28810

7-44
- Frank Lloyd Wright with Carlo Scarpa and Angelo Masieri at Palazzo Strozzi, Florence
- Foto Levi, photographer
- Photo: 1951
- Photograph (reproduction)
- Personal and Taliesin Fellowship photographs, 1870s-2004, The Frank Lloyd Wright Foundation Archives (The Museum of Modern Art | Avery Architectural & Fine Arts Library, Columbia University, New York)
- FLWFA 6808.0008

7-45
- Frank Lloyd Wright with Carlo Scarpa and others outside Doge's Palace, Venice
- Photographer unidentified
- Photo: 1951
- Photograph (reproduction)
- Personal and Taliesin Fellowship photographs, 1870s-2004, The Frank Lloyd Wright Foundation Archives (The Museum of Modern Art | Avery Architectural & Fine Arts Library, Columbia University, New York)
- FLWFA 6808.0016

39 Wright's gaze on the world

+ **Interest in Native American cultures**

7-46
- Frank Lloyd Wright House and Studio, Oak Park, Illinois. Project, 1889-1911. Bedroom with a northern view of the wall mural by Orlando Giannini
- Frank Lloyd Wright, architect. James Caulfield, photographer
- Photo: 2013
- Photograph (reproduction)

7-47
- Nakoma Country Club, Madison, Wisconsin. Unbuilt Project, 1923-24. View from Northeast
- Frank Lloyd Wright
- 25 5/8 x 36 1/8 in. (65.1 x 91.8 cm)
- pencil and colored pencil on tracing paper mounted on sheet with annotations
- The Frank Lloyd Wright Foundation Archives (The Museum of Modern Art | Avery Architectural & Fine Arts Library, Columbia University, New York)
- FLW.DR.2403.037

7-48
- Nakoma Country Club, Madison, Wisconsin. Unbuilt Project, 1923-24. Roof Plan
- Frank Lloyd Wright
- 1924
- original: 97.0 x 144.0 cm
- Blue print (reproduction)
- TSUCHIURA Kameki Archives

+ **Wright on the move**

7-49
- Frank Lloyd Wright with airplane
- Photographer unidentified
- undated
- Photograph (reproduction)
- Edgar Tafel architectural records and papers, 1919-2005, Avery Architectural & Fine Arts Library, Columbia University

7-50
- Frank Lloyd Wright and Clough Williams-Ellis walking through Portmeirion village in Wales
- News Chronicle, Manchester, photographer
- Photo: 1956
- Photograph (reproduction)
- Personal and Taliesin Fellowship photographs, 1870s-2004, The Frank Lloyd Wright Foundation Archives (The Museum of Modern Art | Avery Architectural & Fine Arts Library, Columbia University, New York)
- FLWFA 6806.0002

7-51
- Frank Lloyd Wright with Mr. and Mrs. Arkin in Russia
- Photographer unidentified
- Photo: 1937
- Photograph (reproduction)
- Personal and Taliesin Fellowship photographs, 1870s-2004, The Frank Lloyd Wright Foundation Archives (The Museum of Modern Art | Avery Architectural & Fine Arts Library, Columbia University, New York)
- FLWFA 6827.0001

+ **Proposals for Islamic Culture**

7-52
- Plan for Greater Baghdad, Baghdad, Iraq. Unbuilt Project, 1957. Aerial perspective of the cultural center and university from the north
- Frank Lloyd Wright
- 35 x 51 15/16 in. (88.9 x 131.9 cm)
- Ink, pencil, and colored pencil on tracing paper
- The Frank Lloyd Wright Foundation Archives (The Museum of Modern Art | Avery Architectural & Fine Arts Library, Columbia University, New York)
- FLW.DR.5733.008

40 Visions for the future: Broadacre City plan

7-53
- *The Disappearing City*
- Frank Lloyd Wright, author. W. F. Payson, publisher
- 1932
- 21.5 x 21.5 x 1.4 cm
- Print on paper / book
- Gen Endo Collection

7-54
- Living City. Unbuilt Project, 1958. Aerial perspective
- Frank Lloyd Wright
- 32 1/4 x 39" (81.9 x 99.1 cm)
- Ink, pencil and colored pencil on tracing paper
- The Frank Lloyd Wright Foundation Archives (The Museum of Modern Art | Avery Architectural & Fine Arts Library, Columbia University, New York)
- FLW.DR.5825.002

7-55
- Broadacre City. Master Plan, Unbuilt Project. View of model
- Frank Lloyd Wright, architect. Roy Petersen, photographer
- Photo: 1934
- Photograph (reproduction)
- Project photographs, circa 1887-2008, The Frank Lloyd Wright Foundation Archives (The Museum of Modern Art | Avery Architectural & Fine Arts Library, Columbia University, New York)
- FLWFA 3402.0017

7-56
- CG Animation based on Frank Lloyd Wright Broadacre City
- Frank Lloyd Wright, architect. David Romero, creator. Yushi Yashima for projection and installation
- 2023
- 2 minutes 30 seconds
- Computer graphics animation

41 Conversation with Frank Lloyd Wright

7-57
- Video. A Conversation with Frank Lloyd Wright / FLLW#12 Architect from Wisconsin
- National Broadcasting Company et al
- 1953
- 10 minutes
- video / film
- National Broadcasting Company / Getty Images. The Frank Lloyd Wright Foundation Archives (The Museum of Modern Art | Avery Architectural & Fine Arts Library, Columbia University, New York) and FLWFM 164

7-58
- Frank Lloyd Wright at Taliesin West
- Photographer unidentified
- Photo: 1954
- Photograph (reproduction)
- Personal and Taliesin Fellowship photographs, 1870s-2004, The Frank Lloyd Wright Foundation Archives (The Museum of Modern Art | Avery Architectural & Fine Arts Library, Columbia University, New York)
- FLWFA 6007.0406

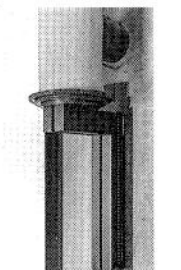
7-37

7-38

7-39

7-40

7-41

7-42

7-43

7-44

7-45

7-46

7-47

7-48

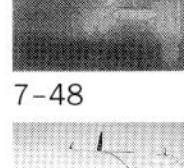
7-49

7-50

7-51

7-52

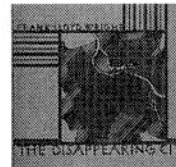

7-53

7-54

7-55

7-56

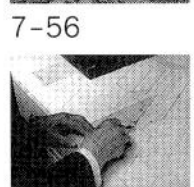
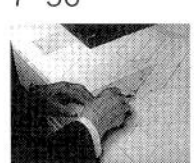
7-57

7-58

[写真クレジット一覧 | IMAGE CREDITS]

カッコ内は作品番号に対応する。
各作品資料の所蔵先における目録番号は、
222～247頁に記載した
巻末の作品資料リストに記載した。

Numbers in parentheses refer to the catalogue number, preceded by page numbers. The accession numbers of each material are shown in the exhibition list on pages through 222 to 247.

コロンビア大学エイヴリー建築美術図書館
フランク・ロイド・ライト財団アーカイヴズ
The Frank Lloyd Wright Foundation Archives (The Museum of Modern Art | Avery Architectural & Fine Arts Library, Columbia University, New York)
042頁[1-1]、013頁[4-53]、052頁[1-54]、053頁[1-56, 1-68]、054頁[1-71, 1-73]、055頁[1-79]、056頁[1-76]、066頁[2-24]、071頁[2-50, 2-52, 2-54]、073頁[2-66]、074頁[2-69]、075頁[2-76, 2-79, 2-82]、103頁[3-29]、105頁[3-31]、107頁[3-45]、108頁[3-46]、116頁[4-9, 4-10]、117頁[4-11, 4-12, 4-13, 4-14]、118頁[4-7, 4-8]、121頁[4-18a, 4-18b]、123頁[4-18l, 4-18m]、124頁[4-19, 4-20]、125頁[4-21]、128頁[4-34]、154頁[5-21, 5-22, 5-23]、156頁[5-27, 5-28]、157頁[5-32, 5-33]、158頁[5-34]、159頁[5-38]、160頁[5-44]、161頁[5-42]、164頁[fig.1, fig.3]、172頁[6-6]、174頁[6-10, 6-13]、181頁[6-28, 6-30, 6-31]、182頁[6-29]、188頁[7-1, 7-2, 7-5]、190頁[7-30]、192頁[7-35]、193頁[7-36]、194頁[7-44, 7-45]、196頁[7-47]、197頁[7-49, 7-50, 7-51]、198頁[7-52]、199頁[7-54, 7-55]、201頁[7-58]、Back cover

[**映像** | **for films**]
The Frank Lloyd Wright Foundation Archives (The Museum of Modern Art | Avery Architectural & Fine Arts Library, Columbia University, New York)
074頁[2-69]、075頁[2-82]、108頁[3-46]、121頁[5-8]

Personal and Taliesin Fellowship photographs, 1870s-2004, The Frank Lloyd Wright Foundation Archives (The Museum of Modern Art | Avery Architectural & Fine Arts Library, Columbia University, New York)
114頁[4-2, 4-3, 4-4, 4-6]、115頁[4-5]、192頁[7-34, 7-35]

Edger Tafel architectural records and paper, 1919-2005, Avery Architectural & Fine Arts Library, Columbia University
062頁[2-8]、067頁[2-35]、097頁[3-23, 3-24]、197頁[7-49]

Louis Henry Sullivan collection, 1873-1910, Avery Architectural & Fine Arts Library, Columbia University
048頁[1-36]

ニューヨーク近代美術館
DIGITAL IMAGE©2023, The Museum of Modern Art/SCALA, Florence
070頁[2-46]、151頁[5-2, 5-3, 5-4]、154頁[5-20]、179頁[6-21]、Front cover

米国議会図書館版画写真部
Prints and Photographs Division, Library of Congress, Washington, D.C.
067頁[2-28]、075頁[2-74]、102頁[3-26, 3-27]、132頁[4-52]、155頁[5-25]、156頁[5-30]、161頁[5-43]

アルヴァ・アアルト美術館
Courtesy of Alvar Aalto Museum
191頁[7-31, 7-32]

イタリア国立21世紀美術館
MAXXI Museo nazionale delle arti del XXI secolo, Rome. MAXXI Architettura Collection, Carlo Scarpa Archive
195頁[7-41, 7-42, 7-43]

ウィスコンシン歴史博物館
Wisconsin Historical Society
048頁[1-35]、062頁[2-1, 2-2]、063頁[2-10]、071頁[2-53]、090頁[3-1, 3-3, 3-4, 3-5]、096頁[3-17]、108頁[3-49]

エイヴリー・クーンリー・スクール
The Avery Coonley School
097頁[3-25]

遠藤現コレクション
Gen Endo Collection
121頁[4-18c]、135頁[4-72]、136頁[4-73]

Courtesy OMA
018頁[fig. 3]

大阪中之島美術館
Osaka Nakanoshima Museum of Art, Osaka
189頁[7-14, 7-17]

太田記念美術館
Ota Memorial Museum of Art
052頁[1-55]

神奈川県立歴史博物館
Kanagawa Prefectural Museum of Cultural History
053頁[1-61, 1-62, 1-67]、064頁[2-13, 2-14, 2-16, 2-18]

北澤興一コレクション
Koichi Kitazawa Collection
130頁[4-55]、135頁[4-66]
写真協力：工学院大学建築学部鈴木敏彦研究室

京都大学
Kyoto University
051頁[1-50]、103頁[3-28]、126頁[4-29]
写真協力：ふくやま美術館

グッゲンハイム美術館
© Solomon R. Guggenheim Foundation. Photo: David Heald.
160頁[5-45, 5-46, 5-47]

シカゴ美術館
Photo © The Art Institute of Chicago / Art Resource, NY
056頁[1-77]

シカゴ歴史博物館
Chicago History Museum
044頁[1-3, 1-5, 1-6, 1-7]、045頁[1-8, 1-9, 1-10]

自由学園資料室
Jiyu Gakuen Archives
104頁[3-34, 3-36]、106頁[3-43, 3-44]

自由学園明日館
Jiyu Gakuen Archives
104頁[3-33]、105頁[3-32]

SCジョンソン社
Courtesy of SC Johnson
175頁[6-14, 6-17]、176-177頁[6-15]、
178頁[6-18, 6-19]

スウェーデン国立図書館
National Library of Sweden
096頁[3-15]

スタンフォード大学図書館特別コレクション
Courtesy of the Department of Special Collections, Stanford University Libraries
158頁[5-36, 5-37]

成城大学図書館
Seijo University Library
056頁[1-74]

土浦亀城アーカイブズ
TSUCHIURA Kameki Archives
062頁[2-5, 2-7]、136頁[4-75]、138頁[fig.1, fig.2]、
154頁[5-23]、188頁[7-10]、196頁[7-48]

帝国ホテル
Imperial Hotel
121頁[4-1]

帝国ホテル
- ATTA- Atelier Tsuyoshi Tane Architects
123頁[4-18n]、203頁[fig.1, fig.2]
[検討段階のものであり今後行政協議等により
変更となる可能性があります。]

帝国ホテル
Imperial Hotel
121[4-18g]
写真協力：金谷ホテル Courtesy of the Kanaya Hotel.

豊田市美術館
Toyota Municipal Museum of Art
043頁[1-2]、049頁[1-41]、050頁[1-44, 1-45]、
051頁[1-47, 1-49]、053頁[1-57, 1-66]、064頁[2-19]、
066頁[2-22, 2-23]、067頁[2-29, 2-33, 2-34]、
068頁[2-42]、091頁[3-6]、097頁[3-22]、100頁[3-19]、
101頁[3-20, 3-21]、130頁[4-43, 4-47, 4-49]、
133頁[4-54]、173頁[6-2, 6-4, 6-7, 6-8]、
175頁[6-16]、182頁[6-26]、190頁[7-29]

プライス・タワー・アート・センター
写真提供：プライス・タワー
Price Tower Art Center
Photo courtesy of Price Tower – Dan O'Donnell, photographer.
180頁[6-22]

Price Tower Art Center
Photo courtesy of Price Tower – Martha Ambler, photographer.
180頁[6-24]

プライス・タワー・アート・センター
ジョー・プライス・PT・コレクション
Price Tower Art Center – Joe Price PT collection
180頁[6-23]

フランク・ロイド・ライト財団
Courtesy of the Frank Lloyd Wright Foundation.
076頁[2-80] – © Foskett
072頁[2-58]、076頁[2-81] – © Andrew Pielage

フランク・ロイド・ライト・トラスト
Courtesy of Frank Lloyd Wright Trust, Chicago
054頁[1-70]、063頁[2-10]、095頁[3-13]

フランク・ロイド・ライト・トラスト・コレクション
Collection of Frank Lloyd Wright Trust, Chicago
054頁[1-69]

ボストン美術館
Photograph © 2023 Museum of Fine Arts, Boston
056頁[1-82, 1-83]

マサチューセッツ工科大学／
ウォルター・バーレイ＆
マリオン・マホニー・グリフィン・コレクション／
シカゴ美術館レイアソン＆バーナム
美術建築アーカイブ
Massachusetts Institute of Technology, Cambridge, MA. Walter Burley and Marion Mahony Griffin Collection, Ryerson and Burnham Art and Architecture Archives, Art Institute of Chicago.
095頁[3-11]

マシエリ財団ヘリテージ
資産管理ギャラリー・ネグロポンテ
Courtesy of Fondazione Angelo Masieri, Heritage Asset Management, Galerie Negropontes
194頁[7-38, 7-39, 7-40]

フランク・ロイド・ライト マーティン・ハウス
Courtesy of Frank Lloyd Wright's Martin House.
Matthew Digati, photographer.
066頁[2-25, 2-27]、068頁[2-41, 2-44]、069頁[2-45]

ミシガン大学図書館デジタル・コレクション
University of Michigan Library Digital Collection
070頁[2-47]

モートン植物園スターリング・モートン図書館
Courtesy of The Morton Arboretum, Lisle, Illinois, U.S.A.
070頁[2-48]

ペンシルベニア大学建築アーカイヴズ
レーモンドコレクション
Raymond Collection, The Architectural Archives of the University of Pennsylvania
136頁[4-76]

ロサンゼルス市役所文化課ホリーホックハウス
Courtesy of the City of Los Angeles Department of Cultural Affairs and Hollyhock House
103頁[3-30]

Robert Beharka
(Collection Jeanine Ferris Beharka)
164頁[fig.2]

James Caulfield
049頁[1-42, 1-43]、052頁[1-51, 1-52, 1-53]、
092-093頁[3-8]、094頁[3-9]、095頁[3-12]、
196頁[7-47]

©Yukio Futagawa
Courtesy of GA A.D.A. EDITA Tokyo Co. Ltd.
074頁[2-68]

© The Estate of Pedro E. Guerrero
161頁[5-48]

Yutaka Mizukami
078頁[fig.1]、155頁[5-26]

© Andrew Pielage
074頁[2-67]

David Romero
200頁[7-56]

Studio ToLoLo (谷川ヒロシ)
Hiroshi Tanigawa, photographer.
123頁[4-18k]、131頁[4-51]、152頁[5-6, 5-7]

© Andrew van Leeuwen
159頁[5-40, 5-41]

山田新治郎
Shinjiro Yamada
073頁[2-60, 2-63]

その他の図面、資料の撮影・複写は所蔵先の協力のもと、
株式会社インフォマージュ[048頁1-39]および
それ以外は株式会社千代田スタジオ(相馬徳之)がおこなった。

[監修・著者]

ケン・タダシ・オオシマ｜Ken Tadashi Oshima｜ワシントン大学教授。建築史協会(S.A.H.)の理事長(2016-18)。「フランク・ロイド・ライト生誕150周年：紐解かれるアーカイヴ」展(ニューヨーク近代美術館、2017年)のキュレーション、執筆に参画。主要著書・共書に『Kiyonori Kikutake Between Land and Sea』(Lars Müller, 2015)、『グローバル・エンズ：始まりに向けて』(TOTO出版,2012)、『International Architecture in Interwar Japan: Constructing Kokusai Kenchiku』(University of Washington Press、2009)、『Arata Isozaki』(Phaidon、2009)、『Visions of the Real 20世紀のモダン・ハウス：理想の実現 I・II』(a+u特別号、2000)。

ジェニファー・グレイ｜Jennifer Gray｜フランク・ロイド・ライト財団副代表、タリアセン・インスティテュート・ディレクター。研究テーマは近代建築と、20世紀初頭の社会変革における建築家と活動家による建築、都市、景観の活用。「フランク・ロイド・ライト生誕150周年：紐解かれるアーカイヴ」展(ニューヨーク近代美術館、2017年)などライトに関する二つの展覧会のキュレーションと図録制作に参画。フランク・ロイド・ライト・ビルディング・コンサーバンシーの理事。コロンビア大学大学院建築・計画・保存学部(GSAPP)、コーネル大学建築・芸術・都市計画学部(AAP)で教鞭をとった。ニューヨーク近代美術館(MoMA)およびコロンビア大学エイヴリー建築美術図書館でキュレーターを歴任。コロンビア大学で博士号を取得。

[著者]

水上 優｜Yutaka Mizukami｜兵庫県立大学環境人間学部教授。ドコモモ・ジャパン理事。日本建築学会歴史意匠委員会建築論・建築意匠小委員会委員。日本建築学会近畿支部建築論部会主査。ライトの建築思想と作品の関わりを研究。著書に『フランク・ロイド・ライトの建築思想』(中央公論美術出版、2013)、『花美術館』vol.59、(蒼海出版、2018)他。翻訳書に『建築ガイドブック/フランク・ロイド・ライト』(丸善、2008)他。日本建築学会編『建築論事典』(彰国社，2008)の「フランク・ロイド・ライト」項担当。ふくやま美術館における展覧会「フランク・ロイド・ライトと武田五一/日本趣味と近代建築」(2007)図録制作に参画し「フランク・ロイド・ライトと『茶の本』/「空間」概念をめぐって」寄稿。 2016年より重要文化財旧山邑家住宅(現ヨドコウ迎賓館)保存修理委員。「F.L.ライト設計旧山邑邸の世界遺産的価値を考える国際シンポジウム」(2022年11月)を主催。

田中厚子｜Atsuko Tanaka｜近代建築史研究者、神奈川大学非常勤講師。主な研究テーマは、日米建築交流史、建築のジャポニスム、建築と女性など。東京藝術大学建築科卒業、同大学修士課程修了。南カリフォルニア建築大学修士課程修了。博士(工学)。日本工業大学・東京電機大学・武蔵大学非常勤講師(2008-2017)、芝浦工業大学特任教授(2017-21)。主な著書に『土浦亀城と白い家』(鹿島出版会、2014)、『アメリカの名作住宅に暮らす』(建築資料研究社、2009)『ビッグ・リトル・ノブ ライトの弟子・女性建築家土浦信子』(共著・ドメス出版、2001)『アメリカの木造住宅の旅』(共著・丸善、1992)など。

マシュー・スコンスバーグ｜Matthew Skjonsberg｜スイス、サンティミエのプラクシス研究所所長。2018年から2022年まで未来都市研究所グローバル(FCLG)のアソシエイト・ディレクターおよび景観都市研究所(LUS)の博士課程コーディネーターを務め、スイス連邦工科大学チューリッヒ校(ETHZ)で「新しい市民景観と公衆衛生」を出講した。ウィスコンシン州出身であり、1997年から2001年までタリアセン・アプレンティスを経験し、その後2002年から12年までタリアセンで教鞭をとった。「フランク・ロイド・ライト生誕150周年：紐解かれるアーカイヴ」展(ニューヨーク近代美術館、2017年)のキュレーションと執筆、および国連アビタ3の「開かれた都市へ キト・ペーパーとニュー・アーバン・アジェンダ」(2017年)に参画した。最近の著書・展覧会に『The Living City: Park Systems from Lausanne to Los Angeles』(EPFL, 2019)。現在は書籍と展覧会シリーズ「Living Cities: Inventing Park Systems」をスイス、オランダ、カナダの国立公園博物館と共同で準備中(Park Books、2024年予定)。

田根 剛｜Tsuyoshi Tane｜建築家。1979年東京生まれ。ATTA - Atelier Tsuyoshi Tane Architectsを設立、フランス・パリを拠点に活動。場所の記憶から建築をつくる「Archaeology of the Future」をコンセプトに、現在ヨーロッパと日本を中心に世界各地で多数のプロジェクトが進行中。主な作品に『エストニア国立博物館』(2016)、『弘前れんが倉庫美術館』(2020)、『アルサーニ・コレクション財団・美術館』(2021)、『帝国ホテル 東京・新本館』(2036年完成予定)など多数。主な受賞に、シュヴァリエ芸術文化勲章、フランス国外建築賞グランプリ、フランス建築アカデミー新人賞、エストニア文化基金賞グランプリ、第67回芸術選奨文部科学大臣新人賞、毎日デザイン賞2021など多数受賞。著書に『TSUYOSHI TANE Archaeology of the Future』(TOTO出版、2018)など。

[**Supervisor/Author**]

Ken Tadashi Oshima is Professor of Architecture, University of Washington. Dr. Oshima was President of the Society of Architectural Historians from 2016-18. He was a co-curator and author for "Frank Lloyd Wright Unpacking the Archive (MoMA, 2017) and is author of *Kiyonori Kikutake Between Land and Sea* (2015), *Global Ends—Towards the Beginning* (2012), *International Architecture in Interwar Japan: Constructing Kokusai Kenchiku* (2009), *Arata Isozaki* (2009) and "Visions of the Real: Modern Houses in the 20th Century I, II" (*a+u* special issues, 2000).

Jennifer Gray is the Vice President and Director of the Taliesin Institute at the Frank Lloyd Wright Foundation. Her research focuses on modern architecture and how designers and activists used architecture, cities, and landscapes to advance social change at the turn of the 20th century. Dr. Gray has curated two exhibitions and produced two catalogues on Wright, including Frank Lloyd Wright at 150: Unpacking the Archive at the Museum of Modern Art in New York. She serves on the Board of Directors of the Frank Lloyd Wright Building Conservancy. She has taught at the Graduate School of Architecture, Planning and Preservation (GSAPP) at Columbia University; the school of Architecture, Art, and Planning (AAP) at Cornell University, and the Museum of Modern Art (MoMA) in New York, and she is the former Curator of Drawings and Archives at Avery Architectural & Fine Arts Library, Columbia University. Gray received her PhD from Columbia University.

[**Author**]

Yutaka Mizukami is Professor of School of Human Science and Environment, the University of Hyogo. Dr. Mizukami is an executive board member of DOCOMOMO Japan, a member of Subcommittee on the Architectural Theory and Design at the Architectural Institute of Japan and the chief of Subcommittee on the Architectural Theory at Kinki Branch of the Architectural Institute of Japan. His research focused on the relationship between Frank Lloyd Wright's architectural thought and works. He was author of *Frank Lloyd Wright's Architectural Thought* (Chuo Koron Bijutu Syuppan, 2013), *Hana Bijutukan*, vol. 59, special issue of Frank Lloyd Wright (Sokai Syuppan, 2018) and so on. He translated Architectural Guide Book of Frank Lloyd Wright (Maruzen, 2008) and was in charge of the chapter of "Frank Lloyd Wright" in the *Encyclopedia of Architectural Theory* edited by the Architectural Institute of Japan (Shokokusha, 2008). Mizukami participated to produce catalogue of the exhibition "Frank Lloyd Wright and Goichi Takeda: Japanese Tastes and Modern Architecture" at Fukuyama Museum of Art (2007) and contributed by "Frank Lloyd Wright and the Book of Tea: Around the Concept of Space." He was a member of Conservation and Restoration Committee of Yamamura House since 2016 and produced the International Symposium on the Outstanding Universal Value of Yamamura House by F. L. Wright (2022).

Atsuko Tanaka is an architectural historian and a part-time lecturer at Kanagawa University. She Graduated from Tokyo University of the Art (Tokyo Geijutsu Daigaku) with a B.A. and MA in Architecture, and received and M.Arch from the Southern California Institute of Architecture, Los Angeles. Her research focuses on intercultural exchange in architecture between Japan and the US, Japonisme in architecture and women in architectural design. She was a specially-appointed professor at Shibaura Institute of Technology (2017-21), part-time lecturer at Musashi University, Tokyo Denki University, Nippon Institute of Technology (2008-2017). Her Publications include *Tsuchiura Kameki to Shiroi Ie* (Within White Boxes: The Architecture of Kameki Tsuchiura,2014), *Amerika no Meisaku Jutaku ni Kurasu* (Living in Great American Houses, 2009), *Big Little Nobu: Raito no Deshi, Josei Kenchikuka Tsuchiura Nobuko* (Big Little Nobu: Apprentice to Frank Lloyd Wright, co-author, 2001).

Matthew Skjonsberg is Director of Praxis Institute in Saint Imier, Switzerland. Dr. Skjonsberg was Associate Director of Future Cities Laboratory Global (FCLG), Doctoral Program Coordinator for the Institute of Landscape and Urban Studies (LUS), and Lecturer on 'New Civic Landscapes and Public Health' at the Swiss Federal Institute of Technology in Zürich (ETHZ) from 2018-2022. Skjonsberg is a Wisconsin native, and was an apprentice at Taliesin, the Frank Lloyd Wright School of Architecture, from 1997-2001, subsequently teaching there from 2002-12. He was a co-curator and author for "Frank Lloyd Wright Unpacking the Archive" (MoMA, 2017), and was a contributing researcher to "Towards an Open City: The Quito Papers and the New Urban Agenda (2017) for the United Nations-Habitat III. Recent books and exhibitions include "The Living City: Park Systems from Lausanne to Los Angeles" (EPFL, 2019), and he is currently preparing the book and exhibition series "Living Cities: Inventing Park Systems" with the Swiss, Dutch, and Canadian National Park Museums (Park Books, 2024).

Tsuyoshi Tane is a Paris-based Japanese architect. He founded ATTA - Atelier Tsuyoshi Tane Architects in Paris France, after being co-founder of DGT. Tsuyoshi believes in the idea of architecture belongs to a memory of the place that creates architecture for the future as his concept - "Archaeology of the Future". His major works are the best known for the creation of "The Estonian National Museum"(2016), "Hirosaki Museum of Contemporary Art"(2020), "The Al Thani Collection"(2021) and currently working on the "Imperial Hotel Tokyo". (To be completed in 2036). In his career, he has received numerous awards and honors, including, Chevalier de l'ordre des Arts et des Lettres (appointed by the French ministry of Culture in 2022) , Grand Prix AFEX - French Architects Overseas 2021 and 2016, Estonian Cultural Endowment Grand Prix, the 67th Japanese Ministry new face Award of Minister of Education Award for Fine Arts, the 67th Mainichi Design Awards 2021 and many others. He published the monograph *TSUYOSHI TANE Archaeology of the Future* (TOTO Publishing).

［展示物制作］

模型

山邑邸模型、プライス・タワー模型
兵庫県立大学環境人間学部 水上研究室
– 井上陽香、奥村 奏、青木歌音、植田 陸、草野琴音、中原 伶、中村華菜栞、長岡秀馬、菱垣連海、藤木ひなた、増田里佳子

3Dスキャン計測データを用いた
3Dプリントレプリカ
帝国ホテル二代目本館模型
– 3D計測・制作：
井上智博［京都工芸繊維大学｜KYOTO Design Lab テクニカルスタッフ］
バルナ・ゲルゲイ・ペーター［同大学｜KYOTO Design Lab 特任研究員］
岩崎有希、中島由喜、森 湖音［同大学｜学生］
– 企画：前田尚武
– 監修：津田和俊［同大学｜未来デザイン・工学機構 講師］
– 計測・撮影協力：京都大学［原作模型所蔵］

ユーソニアン住宅の原寸モデル
– 制作：磯矢亮介、関口悌治［磯矢建築事務所］
– 原案：遠藤現
– 展示協力：有限責任事業組合 森の製材リソラ

映像

フランク・ロイド・ライト自邸とスタジオ
増築の変遷
工学院大学建築学部鈴木敏彦研究室
– 構成：桜井悠樹、内間アレクサンドラ
– モデリング：城谷栄一、稲岡敬士、植田梨生
– 動画編集：王思遠
– ディレクション：鈴木敏彦
– 監修：遠藤現、大村理恵子

コロンビア大学エイヴリー建築美術図書館
フランク・ロイド・ライト財団アーカイヴズ蔵
各映像の編集
– コロンビア大学エイヴリー建築美術図書館
フランク・ロイド・ライト財団アーカイヴズおよび
室谷心太郎

映像インスタレーション
フランク・ロイド・ライトの
ブロードエーカー・シティ構想に基づく
CGアニメーション
– 制作：デイヴィッド・ロメロ
– 映像投影システム・インスタレーション設計：
八嶋有司

- 敬称略
- 制作物は本展のために新たに制作したものを掲載した。

［展覧会］

企画・構成
– ケン・タダシ・オオシマ［本展監修者、ワシントン大学教授］
– ジェニファー・グレイ［本展特別アドヴァイザー、フランク・ロイド・ライト財団副代表、タリアセン・インスティテュート・ディレクター］
– 大村理恵子［パナソニック汐留美術館主任学芸員］

日本側アドヴァイザリー・ボード
– 遠藤 現［一級建築士事務所 U-HOUSE合同会社、NPO法人有機的建築アーカイブ代表理事］
– 日野原健司［太田記念美術館主席学芸員］
– 前田尚武［京都市京セラ美術館企画推進ディレクター、京都美術工芸大学特任教授］
– 水上 優［兵庫県立大学環境人間学部教授］

制作・運営［各館学芸担当］
– 豊田市美術館（千葉真智子、西﨑紀衣）
– パナソニック汐留美術館（大村理恵子）
– 青森県立美術館（板倉容子）

展覧会事務局
– 東京新聞（小山田有希、千代祥平）

展覧会ストーリーボード解説執筆・監修
– 板倉容子
– 遠藤 現
– ケン・タダシ・オオシマ
– 大村理恵子
– ジェニファー・グレイ
– 田中厚子
– 千葉真智子
– 西﨑紀衣
– 服部真吏［東京大学総括プロジェクト機構国際建築拠点総括寄付講座学術支援専門職員］
– 水上 優

会場グラフィック
– 刈谷悠三+角田奈央+久保海音［neucitora］

［図録］

監修・著
– ケン・タダシ・オオシマ
– ジェニファー・グレイ

著
– マシュー・スコンスバーグ［プラクシス研究所、サンティミエ］
– 田中厚子
– 田根 剛
– 水上 優

監訳
– 水上 優

英文翻訳
– フレーズ・クレーズ

編集
– 豊田市美術館+パナソニック汐留美術館+青森県立美術館

デザイン
– 刈谷悠三+角田奈央［neucitora］

制作
– 渡辺奈美+土屋沙希［鹿島出版会］

- 名前は五十音順に掲載した。敬称略。

[Exhibition]

Curators	- Ken Tadashi Oshima [Supervisor of the exhibition. Professor of Architecture, University of Washington] - Jennifer Gray [Special Advisor of the exhibition. Vice President and Director of the Taliesin Institute at the Frank Lloyd Wright Foundation] - Rieko Omura [Senior curator, Panasonic Shiodome Museum of Art]
Advisory board members	- Gen Endo [founder of U-HOUSE LLC and the representative of the board of directors of the Archives of Organic Architecture Japan] - Kenji Hinohara [Chief curator, Ota Memorial Museum of Art] - Naotake Maeda [Director of operations and exhibition design, Kyoto City KYOCERA Museum of Art and Specially appointed professor, Kyoto Arts And Crafts University] - Yutaka Mizukami [Professor, School of Human Science and Environment, University of Hyogo]
Organizers (curators)	- Toyota Municipal Museum of Art (Machiko Chiba and Norie Nishizaki) - Panasonic Shiodome Museum of Art (Rieko Omura) - Aomori Museum of Art (Yoko Itakura)
Administration office	- The Tokyo Shimbun (Yuuki Oyamada and Shohei Chishiro)
Authors of the exhibition storyboard texts	- Machiko Chiba - Gen Endo - Jennifer Gray - Mari Hattori [Project Academic Support Specialist, SEKISUI HOUSE-KUMA LAB, International Architectural Education Platform, THE UNIVERSITY OF TOKYO] - Yoko Itakura - Yutaka Mizukami - Norie Nishizaki - Ken Tadashi Oshima [supervisor] - Rieko Omura - Atsuko Tanaka
Exhibition Graphic Design	- Yuzo Kariya, Nao Kakuta, Kaito Kubo [neucitora]

[Catalogue]

Supervisors and Authors	- Jennifer Gray and Ken Tadashi Oshima
Authors	- Yutaka Mizukami - Atsuko Tanaka - Tsuyoshi Tane - Matthew Skjonsberg
Translation	- Fraze Craze Inc.
Supervisor of texts in Japanese	- Yutaka Mizukami
Editors	- Toyota Municipal Museum of Art, Panasonic Shiodome Museum of Art and Aomori Museum of Art
Design	- Yuzo Kariya, Nao Kakuta [neucitora]
Production	- Nami Watanabe, Saki Tsuchiya [Kajima Institute Publishing Co., Ltd.]

フランク・ロイド・ライト――世界を結ぶ建築

2023年11月10日 第1刷発行
2024年2月20日　第3刷発行

監修・著
ケン・タダシ・オオシマ+ジェニファー・グレイ

編者
豊田市美術館+パナソニック 汐留美術館+青森県立美術館

発行者
新妻 充

発行所
鹿島出版会
〒104-0061 東京都中央区銀座6-17-1
銀座6丁目-SQUARE 7階
電話 03-6264-2301
振替 00160-2-180883

印刷
三美印刷

製本
牧製本

ISBN 978-4-306-04706-8 C0070

本書の内容に関するご意見・ご感想は下記までお寄せ下さい。
URL: https://www.kajima-publishing.co.jp/
e-mail: info@kajima-publishing.co.jp